Automated Planning
Theory and Practice

About the Authors

Malik Ghallab is Directeur de Recherche at CNRS, the French national organization for scientific research. His main interests lay at the intersection of robotics and AI, in the robust integration of perception, action, and reasoning capabilities within autonomous robots. He contributed to topics such as object recognition, scene interpretation, heuristics search, pattern matching and unification algorithms, knowledge compiling for real-time synchronous systems, temporal planning, and supervision systems. His work on the latter topic has been focused on the development of the IxTeT system for planning and chronicle recognition. IxTeT has been applied to robotics as well as to other domains, example, scheduling and process supervision. Malik Ghallab is head of the French national robotics program *Robea* and director of the LAAS-CNRS institute in Toulouse.

Dana Nau is a professor at the University of Maryland in the Department of Computer Science and the Institute for Systems Research. His research interests include AI planning and searching as well as computer-integrated design and manufacturing. He received his Ph.D. from Duke University in 1979, where he was a National Science Foundation (NSF) graduate fellow. He has more than 250 technical publications. He has received an NSF Presidential Young Investigator award, an Outstanding Faculty award, several "best paper" awards, and several prizes for competition-level performance of his AI planning and game-playing programs. He is a Fellow of the American Association for Artificial Intelligence (AAAI).

Paolo Traverso is Head of Division at ITC-IRST in Trento, Italy. The Division is active in the fields of automated planning, model checking, case-based reasoning and machine learning, distributed systems, and agents. His main research interests include automated reasoning, planning under uncertainty, and the synthesis of controllers. He has contributed to research on mechanized metatheories, formal verification, knowledge management, embedded systems, and logics for the integration of planning, acting, and sensing. for a list of recent publications. He is a member of the Editorial Board of the Journal of Artificial Intelligence Research, a member of the Executive Council of the International Conference on Automated Planning and Scheduling, and a member of the Board of Directors of the Italian Association for Artificial Intelligence.

Automated Planning
Theory and Practice

Malik Ghallab

LAAS-CNRS, Toulouse, France

Dana Nau

University of Maryland, College Park, USA

Paolo Traverso

ITC-IRST, Trento, Italy

ELSEVIER

Amsterdam Boston Heidelberg
London New York Oxford
Paris San Diego San Francisco
Singapore Sydney Tokyo

MORGAN KAUFMANN PUBLISHERS

Morgan Kaufmann Publishers is an imprint of Elsevier

Senior Editor	Denise E. M. Penrose
Publishing Services Manager	Simon Crump
Editorial Coordinator	Emilia Thiuri
Editorial Assistant	Valerie Witte
Cover Design	Yvo Riezebos Design
Cover Image	Steam-boat, by Fernand Leger. Courtesy of Art Resource.
Text Design	Rebecca Evans & Associates
Composition	Cepha Imaging PVT India
Technical Illustration	Dartmouth Publishing, Inc.
Copyeditor	Chrysta Meadowbrooke
Proofreader	Daril Bentley
Indexer	Steve Rath

Morgan Kaufmann Publishers is an imprint of Elsevier.
500 Sansome Street, Suite 400, San Francisco, CA 94111

This book is printed on acid-free paper.

Library of Congress Cataloging-in-Publication Data
Application submitted

ISBN-13: 978-1-55860-856-6
ISBN-10: 1-55860-856-7

For information on all Morgan Kaufmann publications, visit our Web site at *www.mkp.com.*

Printed and bound by CPI Group (UK) Ltd, Croydon, CR0 4YY

Transferred to Digital Print 2011

To our parents,
some of whom did not live long enough
to see this book finished.

Contents

Foreword

I am very pleased to have this opportunity to write a foreword to *Automated Planning: Theory and Practice.* With this wonderful text, three established leaders in the field of automated planning have met a long-standing need for a detailed, comprehensive book that can be used both as a text for college classes—complete with student exercises—and as a reference book for researchers and practitioners. In recent years, comprehensive texts have been written for several of the other major areas of Artificial Intelligence (AI), including machine learning, natural-language processing, and constraint satisfaction processing, but until now, the field of planning has been devoid of such a resource, despite the considerable number of advances in and the significant maturation of planning research in the past decade. With *Automated Planning: Theory and Practice,* Dana Nau, Malik Ghallab, and Paolo Traverso have filled that void and have done so with a remarkably clear and well-written book.

The authors made an important decision about what to emphasize in the text. Although, as they point out in the Preface, "the bulk of research on automated planning focuses on ... classical planning," they decided not to devote a proportional amount of their text to this restrictive framework but instead to showcase and emphasize techniques that move beyond the classical strictures. They don't ignore classical techniques: indeed, they provide a comprehensive coverage of them. But they then go on to provide ample coverage of such topics as temporal planning and resource scheduling, planning under uncertainty, and the use of a wide range of modern techniques for plan generation, including propositional satisfiability, constraint satisfaction, and model checking.

Making good on its name, the book also includes a large section on the practice of AI planning, including several case studies both of application classes such as robot planning and of specific fielded applications such as the Deep Space 1 Remote Agent and the Bridge Baron game player. These case studies illustrate the process by which the relatively generic methods of automated planning are transformed into powerful domain-dependent tools and also show that, as a result of this transformation, automated planning can be made useful—that planning is good for much more than just stacking towers of blocks. (Now if only I could transform my own bridge-playing strategies so effectively!)

Automated Planning: Theory and Practice is a terrific contribution to the AI literature and will be widely used not only by those of us already active in the field of planning but also by our students and colleagues who want to know more this important area of research.

Martha E. Pollack
University of Michigan

Preface

One motivation for studying automated planning is very practical: the need for information processing tools that provide affordable and efficient planning resources. Such tools are needed for use in complex and changing tasks that involve demanding safety and/or efficiency requirements. They are needed for integrating more autonomy and intelligent control capabilities in complex artifacts. Automated planning technology is already capable enough to be useful in a variety of demanding applications, in areas ranging from controlling space vehicles and robots to deploying emergency operations and playing the game of bridge.

Another motivation for automated planning is more theoretical. Planning is an important component of rational behavior. If one purpose of Artificial Intelligence (AI) is to grasp the computational aspects of intelligence, then certainly planning, as the reasoning side of acting, is a key element in such a purpose.

These two motivations create the potential for synergy between theory and practice in automated planning. By observing what works well in practice, it is possible to develop better theories of planning. These better theories will in turn lead to better planning systems for practical applications.

The intent of this textbook is to give readers an understanding of automated planning theory and automated planning practice and how they relate to each other. The book contains a set of theoretical chapters to introduce the theory of automated planning and a set of case-study chapters to illustrate how to adapt and combine automated planning techniques in a variety of application domains.

Material Covered

The published literature related to automated planning is quite large, and it is not feasible in a single book to give detailed discussions of all of it. Our choice of what to cover was motivated by the following considerations.

The bulk of research on automated planning focuses on a restricted form called *classical planning*. We feel strongly that for the field of automated planning to realize its full potential, it needs to move beyond classical planning. For that reason, while covering classical planning as prerequisite introductory material, we have devoted large parts of the book to extended classes of automated planning that relax the various restrictions required by classical planning.

We also devoted a large part of the book to descriptions of application-oriented work. These chapters are mainly illustrative case studies. From the application point of view, the field of planning is still in an early stage. It has not yet developed a mature engineering methodology to enable us to present a comprehensive mapping from the features of an application domain to the planning techniques that best address these features. We do hope that this book can contribute to the development of such a mature technology.

Using This Book

This book may be used both as a graduate-level textbook and as an information source for professionals in the field. We assume that readers already know the basic concepts of search algorithms, data structures, computational complexity, and programming languages at the level that one might get in an undergraduate computer science curriculum. Prior knowledge of heuristic search and first-order logic would also be helpful but probably is not strictly necessary since Appendices A and B provide overviews of those topics.

The book is composed of twenty-four chapters, which are organized into seven parts, and three appendices. Parts I and II cover a restricted model of planning problems and algorithms for planning within that model. Part III deals with heuristics and control strategies for planning; and Parts III to V discuss several extended models and planning algorithms. Part VI is devoted to five case studies and applications. In Part VII, the last chapter discusses briefly other problems and techniques related to planning, example, planning and acting or planning and learning, to which it was not possible to devote a full chapter.

Figure 1 shows which chapters depend on which others. The required precedence relationship is indicated by solid lines. The figure shows that one may proceed along several possible paths when studying the book. In particular, several of the application-oriented chapters can be tackled quite early. The book contains more material than can fit into a single semester. The precedence relationship between chapters can help teachers decide which chapters to cover.[1]

Web Site

The publisher's Web site offers additional material related to this book. It contains links to related work; links to planning programs that may be downloaded at books.elsevier.com/mk/1558608567; copies of slides that have been used in lectures based on this book; and additional illustrations, examples, and exercises as may be appropriate.

1. As an example of what can be covered in a single semester, a recent course on planning at the University of Maryland covered the following chapters: 1, 2 (skipping set-theoretic representation), 3, 4, 5, 6, a quick overview of 7, most of 9, 10, 11, 14, 15, most of 16, most of 17, 20, 22, and 23. The course also included term projects in which the students, in groups of two or three people, proposed and carried out research projects on topics related to automated planning.

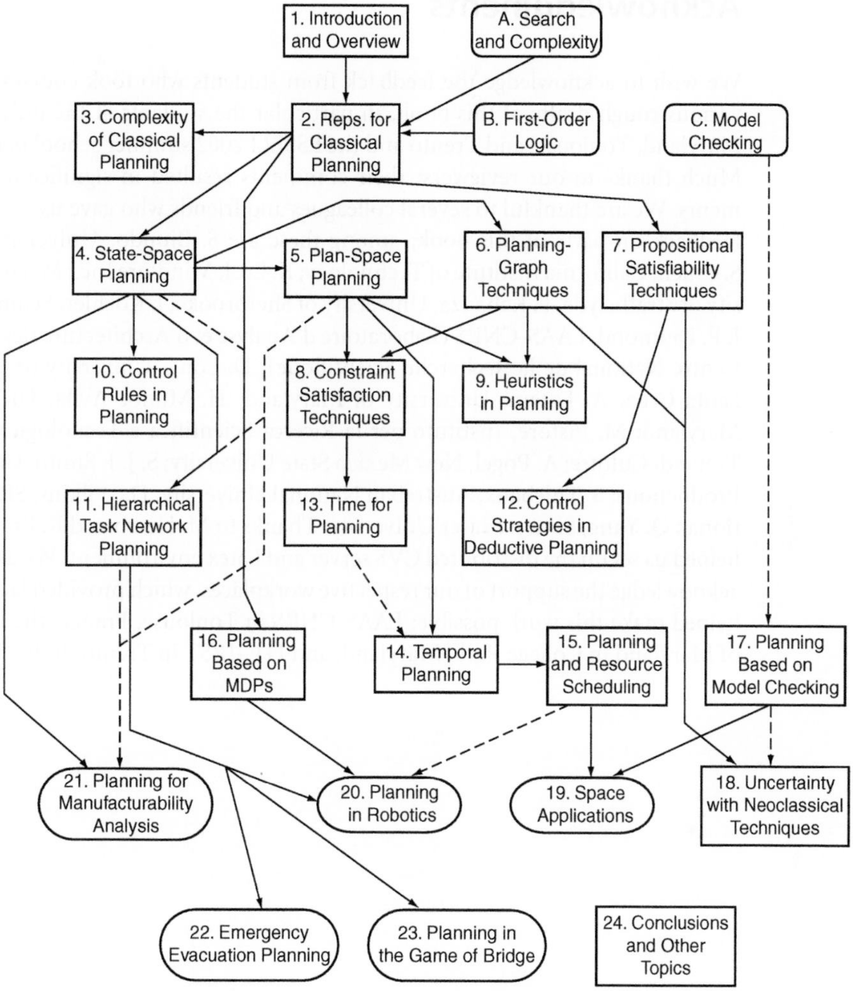

Figure 1: Dependencies among the chapters. Boxes with rounded corners represent appendices, boxes with square corners represent theoretical chapters, and ovals represent case-study chapters. A solid line means that one chapter is needed in order to understand another. A dashed line means that one chapter is not necessary for another but may help the reader understand it more deeply. The dependencies for Chapter 24 are not shown because each of its sections would need a different set of lines.

Acknowledgments

We wish to acknowledge the feedback from students who took courses based on various rough drafts of this book, in particular the students at the universities of Maryland, Toulouse, and Trento and the ESSLLI 2002 summer school participants. Much thanks to our reviewers; their comments resulted in significant improvements. We are thankful to several colleagues and friends who gave us very valuable feedback on parts of this book; among these are S. Biundo, University of Ulm; S. Chien, California Institute of Technology; K. Erol, Mindlore Inc.; M. Fox, University of Strathclyde; F. Kabanza, University of Sherbrooke; J. Koehler, Schindler Lifts; J. P. Laumond, LAAS-CNRS (Laboratoire d'Analyse et d'Architecture des Systémes, Centre National de la Recherche Scientifique); D. Long, University of California, Santa Cruz; A. Lotem, University of Maryland; H. Muñoz-Avila, University of Maryland; M. Pistore, Instituto per la Ricerca Scientifica e Tecnologica/Instituto Trend di Culture; A. Pogel, New Mexico State University; S. J. J. Smith, Great Game Productions; S. Thiebaux, Australian National University; D. Wilkins, SRI International; Q. Yang, Simon Fraser University. Thanks to M. Herrb and R. Prajoux, who helped us set up the distributed CVS server and Latex environment. We also wish to acknowledge the support of our respective workplaces, which provided facilities that helped make this work possible: LAAS-CNRS in Toulouse, France, the University of Maryland in College Park, Maryland, and ITC-IRST in Trento, Italy.

Table of Notation

Notation	*Meaning*
a, A	Action
A	Set of actions
c	Constraint
$C, \mathcal{C}$	Set of constraints
$\delta(u, m, \sigma)$	Task network produced from u by decomposing it with the method m under the substitution σ
$\delta(w, u, m, \sigma)$	Task network produced from w by decomposing u with the method m under the substitution σ
$\text{effects}(o)$	Effects of an operator or action
$\text{effects}^+(o)$	Positive effects of an operator or action
$\text{effects}^-(o)$	Negative effects of an operator or action
$\mathcal{F}$	Set of *tqe*s (temporally qualified expressions) or temporal constraints
g	Goal formula
g^+, g^-	Sets of positive and negative literals in g
$\gamma(s, a)$	Progression, i.e., the state or set of states produced by applying a to s
$\gamma^{-1}(s, a)$	Regression
$\Gamma(s)$	Set of all immediate successors of s
$\hat{\Gamma}(s)$	Transitive closure of $\Gamma(s)$
$\Gamma^{-1}(g)$	Set of all states whose immediate successors satisfy g
$\hat{\Gamma}^{-1}(g)$	Transitive closure of $\Gamma^{-1}(g)$
h	Heuristic function, history
m, M	HTN method, set of methods
$\text{name}(o)$	Name of an operator or action
$\text{network}(m)$	Network of subtasks of a method m
o, O	Operator, set of operators
$P = (O, s_0, g)$	Statement of a classical planning problem
$P_a(s' \mid s)$	Probability of s' if a is executed in s
$\mathcal{P}$	Planning problem
$\mathcal{P} = (\Sigma, s_0, S_g)$	Set-theoretic or classical planning problem
$\Phi = (\mathcal{F}, \mathcal{C})$	Chronicle or temporal database
π, Π	Plan, set of plans

(continued)

Notation	*Meaning*
precond(o)	Preconditions of an operator or action
precond$^+$(o)	Positive preconditions of an operator or action
precond$^-$(o)	Negative preconditions of an operator or action
s, S	State, set of states
s_0, S_0	Initial state, set of initial states
S_g	Set of goal states
σ	Substitution
$\Sigma = (S, A, \gamma)$	State-transition system, set-theoretic planning domain, or classical planning domain
subtasks(m)	Subtasks of a method m
t_u	Task associated with a task node u
τ	Decomposition tree
$\theta(e/\mathcal{F})$	Set of enabling conditions
u	Task node
w	Task network
.	Concatenation, e.g., $e.E$ or $E.e$ or $E.E'$, where e is an expression and E, E' are sequences
•	Composition of two relations, e.g., $r_1 \bullet r_2$
$(a_1, a_2, \ldots, a_k)$	k-tuple (where k is fixed)
$\langle a_1, a_2, \ldots, a_n \rangle$	Sequence (where n may vary)

CHAPTER 1

Introduction and Overview

1.1 First Intuitions on Planning

Planning is the reasoning side of acting. It is an abstract, explicit deliberation process that chooses and organizes actions by anticipating their expected outcomes. This deliberation aims at achieving as best as possible some prestated objectives. Automated planning is an area of Artificial Intelligence (AI) that studies this deliberation process computationally.

Some of our actions require planning, but many do not. In our everyday activities we are always acting, and we do anticipate the outcome of our actions, even if we are not fully aware of anticipating [64]. But we act much more frequently than we explicitly plan our actions: we are not often conscious of performing an explicit deliberation process prior to acting. When the purpose of an action is immediate given our knowledge of that action, or when we perform well-trained behaviors for which we have prestored plans, or when the course of an action can be freely adapted while acting, then we usually act and adapt our actions without explicitly planning them.

A purposeful activity requires deliberation when it addresses new situations or complex tasks and objectives or when it relies on less familiar actions. Planning is also needed when the adaptation of actions is constrained, for example, by a critical environment involving high risk or high cost, by a joint activity with someone else, or by an activity to be synchronized with a dynamic system. Since planning is a very complicated, time-consuming, and costly process, we resort to planning only when it is strictly needed or when the trade-off of its cost versus its benefit compels us to plan. Furthermore, we generally seek only good, feasible plans rather than optimal plans[480].

One motivation for automated planning is very practical: designing information processing tools that give access to affordable and efficient planning resources. Some professionals face complex and changing tasks that involve demanding safety and/or efficiency requirements. Imagine, as an example, a rescue operation after a natural disaster such as an earthquake or a flood. That operation may involve a large number of actors and require the deployment of a communication and transportation infrastructure. It relies on careful planning and the assessment of several alternate plans. But it is also time constrained and it demands immediate decisions that must be supported with a planning tool. The need for such a tool is also felt by organizers of simpler and more mundane tasks such as organizing a social meeting or professional travel for a group of persons. At the individual level, a planning resource that is seamlessly integrated with electronic organizers or web services could be of great benefit in handling constraints, offering alternate plans not yet considered, and pointing out critical actions and what may need to be relaxed [443, 445].

Another motivation for automated planning is more theoretical. Planning is an important component of rational behavior. If one purpose of AI is to grasp the computational aspects of intelligence, then certainly planning, as the reasoning side of acting, is a key element in such a purpose. The challenge here is to study planning not as an independent abstract process but as a fully integrated component of deliberative behavior.

An important combination of the practical and the theoretical motivations for automated planning is the study and design of autonomous intelligent machines. Such a study is of practical concern because some of our complex artifacts such as satellites and spacecraft require autonomy and deliberative behavior. These artifacts cannot always be teleoperated because of operational constraints or because of a demanding interaction with nonexpert humans that is more natural at the task level than at the low level of control signals. The study of autonomous intelligent machines is also of theoretical concern because planning as a fully integrated component of deliberative behavior requires embodiment into a machine that can sense and act as well as it reasons on its actions.

1.2 Forms of Planning

Because there are various types of actions, there are also various forms of planning. Examples include path and motion planning, perception planning and information gathering, navigation planning, manipulation planning, communication planning, and several other forms of social and economic planning.

Path and motion planning is concerned with the synthesis of a geometric path from a starting position in space to a goal and of a control trajectory along that path that specifies the state variables in the configuration space of a mobile system, such as a truck, a mechanical arm, a robot, or a virtual character. Motion planning takes into account the model of the environment and the kinematic and dynamic constraints of the mobile system. It is a well-advanced area that appears today to be quite mature and offers a wide range of efficient and reliable methods.

Motion planning can be seen as a particular case of the generic problem of planning control actions for dynamic systems. While motion planning seeks a trajectory in the configuration space of a mobile system, the generic planning problem is concerned with more abstract state spaces. Consider, as an example, the problem of controlling a ceramic plant or a blast furnace from its current state to a desired state. When these two states are close enough, a corrective control action can be computed from their difference. If the desired state is too far apart from the current one (e.g., for driving the furnace to a shutdown state), then a sequence of control actions that meets some constraints and criteria must be planned.

Perception planning is concerned with plans involving sensing actions for gathering information. It arises in tasks such as modeling environments or objects, identifying objects, localizing through sensing a mobile system, or more generally identifying the current state of the environment. An example of these tasks is the design of a precise virtual model of an urban scene from a set of images. Perception planning addresses questions such as which information is needed and when it is needed, where to look for it, which sensors are most adequate for this particular task, and how to use them. It requires models of available sensors and their capabilities and constraints. It relies on decision theory for problems of which and when information is needed, on mathematical programming and constraint satisfaction for the viewpoint selection and the sensor modalities.

Data gathering is a particular form of perception planning which is concerned not with sensing but instead with querying a system: e.g., testing a faulty device in diagnosis or searching databases distributed over a network. The issues are which queries to send where and in what order.

Navigation planning combines the two previous problems of motion and perception planning in order to reach a goal or to explore an area. The purpose of navigation planning is to synthesize a policy that combines localization primitives and sensor-based motion primitives, e.g., visually following a road until reaching some landmark, moving along some heading while avoiding obstacles, and so forth.

Manipulation planning is concerned with handling objects, e.g., to build assemblies. The actions include sensory-motor primitives that involve forces, touch, vision, range, and other sensory information. A plan might involve picking up an object from its marked sides, returning it if needed, inserting it into an assembly, and pushing lightly till it clips mechanically into position.

Communication planning arises in dialog and in cooperation problems between several agents, human or artificial. It addresses issues such as when and how to query needed information and which feedback should be provided.

There is a wide range of other kinds of planning problems, particularly in social and economic realms. As examples, urban planning involves the deployment and organization of an urban infrastructure (e.g., public transportation, schools, hospitals) in order to meet the needs of a community, family planning deals with demography, and financial planning focuses on narrow financial optimization.

1.3 Domain-Independent Planning

A natural approach for these diverse forms of planning is to address each problem with the specific representations and techniques adapted to the problem. One develops predictive models for the type of actions to be planned for and for the states of the system in which they take place. Computational tools for running these models, in order to predict and assess the effects of alternate actions and plans in various situations, exploit the specifics of the domain. For example, geometry, kinematics, and dynamics are the tools needed for motion or manipulation planning. Mathematical programming and optimization techniques are the tools widely used in various forms of economic planning.

These *domain-specific* approaches to specific forms of planning are certainly well justified. They are highly successful in most of the application areas mentioned earlier. However, they are frustrating for several reasons.

- Some commonalities to all these forms of planning are not addressed in the domain-specific approaches. The study of these commonalities is needed for understanding the process of planning; it may help improve the domain-specific approaches.
- It is more costly to address each planning problem anew instead of relying on and adapting some general tools.
- Domain-specific approaches are not satisfactory for studying and designing an autonomous intelligent machine. Its deliberative capabilities will be limited to areas for which it has domain-specific planners, unless it can develop by itself new domain-specific approaches from its interactions with its environment.

For all these reasons, automated planning is interested in *domain-independent* general approaches to planning. For solving a particular problem, a domain-independent planner takes as input the problem specifications and knowledge about its domain. Automated planning is not meant to be opposed to domain-specific planning techniques, just as automated reasoning is not intended to replace every arithmetic and floating-point calculus processor and other specialized reasoning techniques in a computer. Because planning is the reasoning side of acting, the purpose of automated planning is to develop general approaches to this particular form of reasoning that may build on and can be well integrated with domain-specific planning tools.

Domain-independent planning relies on abstract, general models of actions. These models range from very simple ones that allow only for limited forms of reasoning to models with richer prediction capabilities. There are in particular the following forms of models and planning capabilities.

- *Project planning*, in which models of actions are reduced mainly to temporal and precedence constraints, e.g., the earliest and latest start times of an action or its latency with respect to another action. Project planning is used for interactive plan edition and verification. A possible plan is given by the user as input to a project-planning tool that checks the feasibility of the constraints and computes several useful attributes of the given plan such as its critical paths. Here, the models of the actions in the plan (i.e., their effects and their interactions) remain mostly in the mind of the user.

- *Scheduling and resource allocation*, in which the action models include the above types of constraints plus constraints on the resources to be used by each action. A scheduling tool takes as input the actions to be carried out together with resource constraints and optimization criteria. The tool returns a temporal organization and resource allocation for the given actions in order to meet all the constraints and optimize the criteria.
- *Plan synthesis*, in which the action models enrich the precedent models with the conditions needed for the applicability of an action and the effects of the action on the state of the world. A plan synthesis tool takes as input the models of all known actions, a description of the state of the world, and some objective. The tool returns an organized collection of actions whose global effect, if they are carried out and if they perform as modeled, achieves the objective.

Automated planning is concerned with the general form of plan synthesis. Although it is still in its early stages theoretically, automated planning already is advanced enough to be useful in demanding applications, several of which are discussed in Part VI of this book.

Automated planning already has several success stories; one is the control of the spacecraft *Deep Space 1*. This spacecraft was launched from Cape Canaveral on October 24, 1998, and was retired on December 18, 2001, after it completed its mission successfully by encountering Comet Borrelly and returning the best images and other science data ever returned about a comet. The *Deep Space 1* mission successfully tested a number of advanced technologies. Among these was the Autonomous Remote Agent software system. The Autonomous Remote Agent, which was based on automated planning techniques, successfully operated *Deep Space 1* between May 17 and May 21, 1999. Chapter 19 discusses *Deep Space 1* in greater detail.

1.4 Conceptual Model for Planning

A conceptual model is a simple theoretical device for describing the main elements of a problem. It can depart significantly from the computational concerns and algorithmic approaches for solving that problem. However, it can be very useful for explaining basic concepts, for clarifying restrictive assumptions, for analyzing requirements on representations and trade-offs, and for proving semantic properties.

Since planning is concerned with choosing and organizing actions for changing the state of a system, a conceptual model for planning requires a general model for a dynamic system. Most of the planning approaches described in this book rely on a general model, which is common to other areas of computer science, the model of *state-transition systems* [146] (also called *discrete-event systems*).

Formally, a state-transition system is a 4-tuple $\Sigma = (S, A, E, \gamma)$, where:

- $S = \{s_1, s_2, \ldots\}$ is a finite or recursively enumerable set of states;

- $A = \{a_1, a_2, \ldots\}$ is a finite or recursively enumerable set of actions;
- $E = \{e_1, e_2, \ldots\}$ is a finite or recursively enumerable set of events; and
- $\gamma: S \times A \times E \rightarrow 2^S$ is a state-transition function.

A state-transition system may be represented by a directed graph whose nodes are the states in S. If $s' \in \gamma(s, u)$, where u is a pair (a, e), $a \in A$ and $e \in E$, then the graph contains an arc from s to s' that is labeled with u. Each such arc is called a *state transition*. It can be convenient to introduce a neutral event ϵ to account for transitions that are due only to actions and, symmetrically, a neutral action no-op for denoting transitions caused solely by an event. We write $\gamma(s, a, \epsilon)$ as $\gamma(s, a)$ and $\gamma(s, \text{no-op}, e)$ as $\gamma(s, e)$.

Example 1.1 Figure 1.1 shows a state-transition system involving a container in a pile, a crane that can pick up and put down the container, and a robot that can can carry the container and move it from one location to another. Here, the set of states is $\{s_0, s_1, s_2, s_3, s_4, s_5\}$, the set of actions is {take, put, load, unload, move1, move2}, and there are no events. The arc (s_0, s_1) is labeled with the action take, the arc (s_4, s_5) with the action move2, and so forth. Each state transition is *deterministic*, i.e., it leads to just one other state. ■

Both events and actions contribute to the evolution of the system. The difference lies in whether the planner has any control over them or not. *Actions* are transitions that are controlled by the plan executor. If a is an action and $\gamma(s, a)$ is not empty, then action a is *applicable* to state s; applying it to s will take the system to some state in $\gamma(s, a)$. *Events* are transitions that are *contingent*: instead of being controlled by the plan executor, they correspond to the internal dynamics of the system. They should be taken into account by planning, but they cannot be chosen or triggered. If e is an event and $\gamma(s, e)$ is not empty, then e may *possibly* occur when the system is in state s; its occurrence in s will bring the system to some state in $\gamma(s, e)$.

A precise specification of the semantics of the transition function, as defined by $\gamma : S \times A \times E \rightarrow 2^S$, requires a refinement of this conceptual model. One model, the Markov game model, supposes that no action takes place in states where events occur and vice versa. That is, S is partitioned into *action states* and *event states*. An alternative model is to suppose that actions can "compete" with events in the same states. That is, if we apply a to s and $\gamma(s, e)$ is not empty, then the next state can be any element of $\gamma(s, a, e)$.[1]

Given a state transition system Σ, the purpose of planning is to find which actions to apply to which states in order to achieve some objective when starting

---

1. We will refer in Chapter 14 to a model where an action with time-dependent effects makes a state transition and start a process that triggers, at some later state, an event that causes another state transition [194].

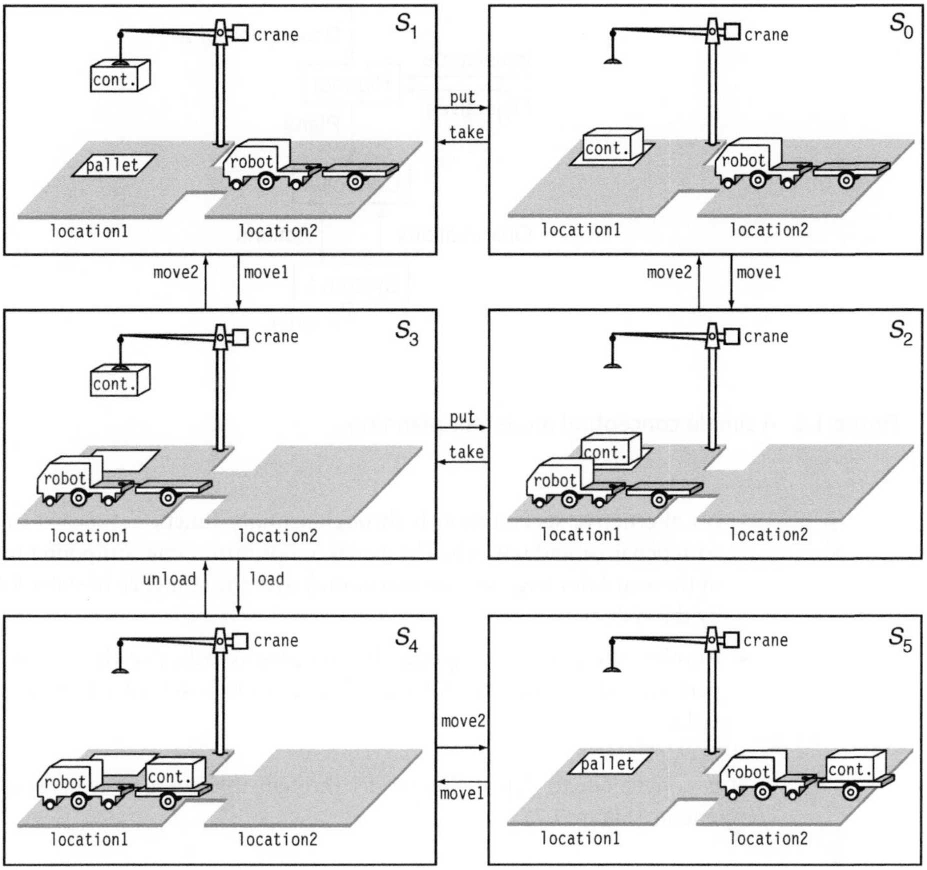

Figure 1.1 A state-transition system for a simple domain involving a crane and a robot for transporting containers.

from some given situation. A *plan* is a structure that gives the appropriate actions. The objective can be specified in several different ways.

- The simplest specification consists of a *goal state* s_g or a set of goal states S_g. In this case, the objective is achieved by any sequence of state transitions that ends at one of the goal states. For example, if the objective in Figure 1.1 is to have the container loaded onto the robot cart, then the set of goal states is $S_g = \{s_4, s_5\}$.
- More generally, the objective is to satisfy some condition over the sequence of states followed by the system. For example, one might want to require states to be avoided, states the system should reach at some point, and states in which it should stay.

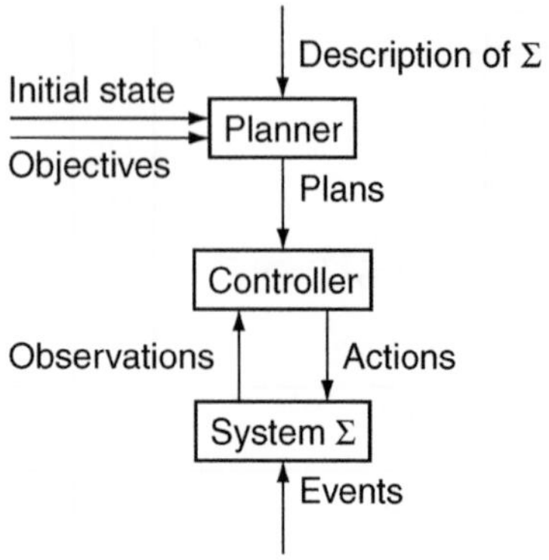

Figure 1.2 A simple conceptual model for planning.

- An alternative specification is through a utility function attached to states, with penalties and rewards. The goal is to optimize some compound function of these utilities (e.g., sum or maximum) over the sequence of states followed by the system.
- Another alternative is to specify the objective as tasks that the system should perform. These tasks can be defined recursively as sets of actions and other tasks.

It is convenient to depict this model through the interaction between three components (Figure 1.2).

1. A *state-transition system* Σ evolves as specified by its state-transition function γ, according to the events and actions that it receives.
2. A *controller*, given as input the state s of the system, provides as output an action a according to some plan.
3. A *planner*, given as input a description of the system Σ, an initial situation, and some objective, synthesizes a plan for the controller in order to achieve the objective.

An important element must be added to this model: the information that the controller has about the current state of the system. In general, this information is not complete. Partial knowledge about the state can be modeled as an observation function $\eta: S \rightarrow O$ that maps S into some discrete set $O = \{o_1, o_2, \ldots\}$ of possible observations. The input to the controller is then the observation $o = \eta(s)$ corresponding to current state.

Notice that the controller performs its task along with the dynamics of the state-transition system. It works *online* with Σ. On the other hand, the planner is not directly connected to Σ. It works *offline*. It relies on a formal description of the

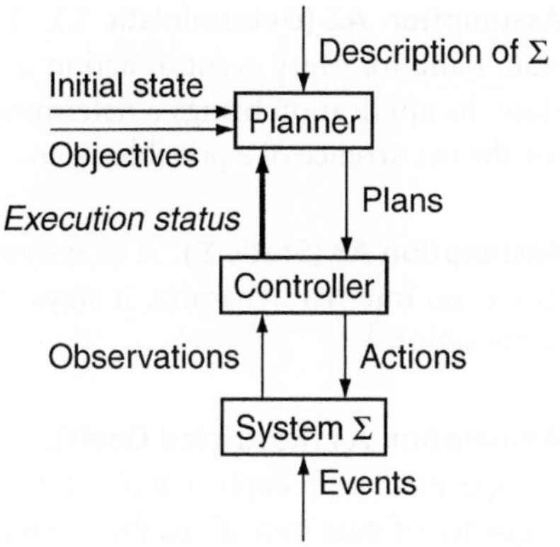

Figure 1.3 A conceptual model for dynamic planning.

system, together with an initial state for the planning problem and the required goal. It is concerned not with the actual state of the system at the time the planning occurs but instead with what states the system may be in when the plan is executing.

Most of the time, there are differences between the physical system to be controlled and its model, as described by Σ. In general, planning is restricted to the model formally represented by Σ. The controller is supposed to be robust enough to cope with the differences between Σ and the real world. Dealing with observations that depart from what is expected in the plan requires more complex control mechanisms than are needed for just observing the state and applying the corresponding action. Several enhancements to this conceptual model are required to address a deliberative goal-directed behavior. A more realistic model interleaves planning and acting, with plan supervision, plan revision, and replanning mechanisms. There is a need for a closed loop between the planner and the controller (Figure 1.3). The latter returns to the planner the *execution status* of the plan to enable dynamic planning.

1.5 Restricted Model

This conceptual model is not meant to be directly operational. Instead, it will be used throughout this book as a reference for our representations. Let us consider it as a starting point for assessing various restrictive assumptions, particularly the following ones.

Assumption A0 (Finite Σ). The system Σ has a finite set of states.

Assumption A1 (Fully Observable Σ). The system Σ is *fully observable*, i.e., one has complete knowledge about the state of Σ. In this case the observation function η is the identity function.

Assumption A2 (Deterministic Σ). The system Σ is *deterministic*, i.e., for every state s and for every event or action u, $|\gamma(s, u)| \leq 1$. If an action is applicable to a state, its application brings a deterministic system to a single other state; similarly for the occurrence of a possible event.

Assumption A3 (Static Σ). The system Σ is *static*, i.e., the set of events E is empty. Σ has no internal dynamics; it stays in the same state until the controller applies some action.[2]

Assumption A4 (Restricted Goals). The planner handles only *restricted goals* that are specified as an explicit goal state s_g or set of goal states S_g; the objective is any sequence of state transitions that ends at one of the goal states. Extended goals such as states to be avoided and constraints on state trajectories or utility functions are not handled under this restricted assumption.

Assumption A5 (Sequential Plans). A solution plan to a planning problem is a linearly ordered finite sequence of actions.

Assumption A6 (Implicit Time). Actions and events have no duration; they are instantaneous state transitions. This assumption is embedded in state-transition systems, a model that does not represent time explicitly.

Assumption A7 (Offline Planning). The planner is not concerned with any change that may occur in Σ *while* it is planning; it plans for the given initial and goal states regardless of the current dynamics, if any.

The simplest case, which we will call the *restricted model*, combines all eight restrictive assumptions: complete knowledge about a deterministic, static, finite system with restricted goals and implicit time. Here planning reduces to the following problem:

> Given $\Sigma = (S, A, \gamma)$, an initial state s_0 and a subset of goal states S_g, find a sequence of actions $\langle a_1, a_2, \ldots, a_k \rangle$ corresponding to a sequence of state transitions $(s_0, s_1, \ldots, s_k)$ such that $s_1 \in \gamma(s_0, a_1)$, $s_2 \in \gamma(s_1, a_2), \ldots, s_k \in \gamma(s_{k-1}, a_k)$, and $s_k \in S_g$.

Since the system is deterministic, if γ is applicable to s then $\gamma(s, a)$ contains one state s'. To simplify the notation, we will say $\gamma(s, a) = s'$ rather than $\gamma(s, a) = \{s'\}$. For this kind of system, a plan is a sequence $\langle a_1, a_2, \ldots, a_k \rangle$ such that $\gamma(\gamma(\ldots\gamma(\gamma(s_0, a_1), a_2), \ldots, a_{k-1}), a_k)$ is a goal state.

The assumption about complete knowledge (Assumption A0) is needed only at the initial state s_0 because the deterministic model allows all of the other states to

---

2. This assumption is not properly named because the plan is intended precisely to change the state of the system; what is meant here is that the system remains static *unless controlled transitions take place.*

be predicted with certainty. The plan is unconditional, and the controller executing the plan is an *open-loop controller*, i.e., it does not get any feedback about the state of the system.

This restricted case may appear trivial: planning is simply searching for a path in a graph, which is a well-known and well-solved problem. Indeed, if we are given the graph Σ explicitly then there is not much more to say about planning for this restricted case. However even for a very simple application domain, the graph Σ can be so large that specifying it explicitly is not feasible. In the simple example introduced earlier (Example 1.1), in which a robot has to move containers, suppose there are five locations, three piles of containers per location, three robots, and one hundred containers. Then Σ has about 10^{277} states, which is about 10^{190} times as many states as even the largest estimates [562] of the number of particles in the universe! Thus it is impossible in any practical sense to list all of Σ's states implicitly. Consequently, there is a need for powerful *implicit* representations that will enable us to describe useful subsets of S in a way that is compact and can easily be searched.

Classical and *neoclassical* approaches to planning will be covered in Parts I and II of the book, respectively. Most of these approaches rely on an implicit representation based on logic for describing states and on *ad hoc* state-transition operators for representing actions. Specific rules and assumptions are required for defining and easily computing the next state $\gamma(s, a)$.

Planning as theorem proving, within the restricted model of this section, relies entirely on a logic representation for describing both states and state-transition operators. The idea is to use a set of logical formulas to describe not just single states but instead the entire set of states and the relationships among them. This approach will be covered in Part II.

The remaining parts of the book consider other approaches in order to deal with less restricted models of planning.

1.6 Extended Models

Several interesting models are obtained by relaxing some of the restrictive assumptions. We now review briefly the models that will be covered later.

Relaxing Assumption A0 (Finite Σ). An enumerable, possibly infinite set of states may be needed, e.g., to describe actions that construct or bring new objects in the world or to handle numerical state variables. This raises issues about decidability and termination to planners that will be discussed in Parts I and III.

Relaxing Assumption A1 (Fully Observable Σ). If we allow a static, deterministic system to be partially observable, then the observations of Σ will not fully disambiguate which state Σ is in. For each observation o, there may be more than one state s such that $\eta(s) = o$. Without knowing which state in $\eta^{-1}(o)$ is the current state, it is no longer possible to predict with certainty what state Σ will be in after each action. This case will be covered in Part V.

Relaxing Assumption A2 (Deterministic Σ). In a static but nondeterministic system, each action can lead to different possible states, so the planner may have to consider alternatives. Usually nondeterminism requires relaxing assumption A5 as well. A plan must encode ways for dealing with alternatives, e.g., *conditional* constructs of the form "do a and, depending on its result, do either b or c" and *iterative* constructs like "do a until a given result is obtained." Notice that the controller has to observe the state s: here we are planning for *closed-loop control.*

If the complete knowledge assumption (assumption A1) is also relaxed, this leads to another difficulty: the controller does not know exactly the current state s of the system at run-time. A limiting case is *null observability*, where no observations at all can be done at run-time. This leads to a particular case of planning for open-loop control called *conformant planning.*

Part V describes different approaches for dealing with nondeterminism. Some of them extend techniques used in classical planning (like graph-based or satisfiability-based planning), while others are designed specifically to deal with nondeterminism, like planning based on Markov Decision Processes (MDPs) and planning as model checking.

Relaxing Assumption A3 (Static Σ). We can easily deal with a dynamic system Σ if it is deterministic and fully observable, and if we further assume that for every state s there is at most one contingent event e for which $\gamma(s, e)$ is not empty and that e will necessarily occur in s. Such a system can be mapped into the restricted model: one redefines the transition for an action a as $\gamma(\gamma(s, a), e)$, where e is the event that occurs in the state $\gamma(s, a)$.

In the general model of possible events that may or may not occur in a state and "compete" with actions, a dynamic system is nondeterministic from the viewpoint of the planner even if $|\gamma(s, u)| \leq 1$. Deciding to apply action a in s does not focus the planner's prediction to a single state transition. Here again, a conditional plan will be needed.

Relaxing Assumption A4 (Restricted Goals). Controlling a system may require more complex objectives than reaching a given state. One would like to be able to specify to the planner an *extended goal* with requirements not only on the final state but also on the states traversed, e.g., critical states to be avoided, states that the system should go through, states it should stay in, and other constraints on its trajectories. It may also be desirable to optimize utility functions, e.g., to model a system that must function continuously over an indefinite period of time. We will consider such extended goals in several places throughout the book.

Relaxing Assumption A5 (Sequential Plans). A plan may be a mathematical structure that can be richer than a simple sequence of actions. As examples, one may consider a plan to be a partially ordered set, a sequence of sets, a conditional plan that forces alternate routes depending on the outcome and current context of execution, a universal plan or policy that maps states to appropriate actions, or a deterministic or nondeterministic automaton that determines what action to execute depending on the previous history of execution. Relaxing assumption A5 is often required when other assumptions are relaxed, as we have seen in the case of nondeterministic systems (assumption A3) or when relaxing assumptions A1, A3, A4, and A6. Plans as partially ordered sets or as sequences of sets of actions, studied in Chapter 6 and in Part II, are more easily handled than conditional plans and policies that will be seen in Part V.

Relaxing Assumption A6 (Implicit Time). In many planning domains, action duration and concurrency have to be taken into account. Time may also be needed for expressing temporally constrained goals and occurrence of events with respect to an absolute time reference. However, time is abstracted away in the state-transition model.[3] This conceptual model considers actions or events as instantaneous transitions: at each clock tick, the controller synchronously reads the observation for the current state (if needed) and applies the planned action. To handle time explicitly will require an extension to our conceptual model; this will be considered in Part IV.

Relaxing Assumption A7 (Offline Planning). The control problem of driving a system toward some objectives has to be handled online with the dynamics of that system. While a planner may not have to worry about all the details of the actual dynamics, it cannot ignore completely how the system will evolve. At the least, it needs to check online whether a solution plan remains valid and, if needed, to revise it or replan. Other approaches consider planning as a process that modifies the controller online. Issues with online planning will be surveyed in Part VI.

These extensions cannot be handled directly within the restricted model. However, in some cases that we will illustrate later, they can be handled indirectly, possibly at the cost of a blowup of the domain description.

1.7 A Running Example: Dock-Worker Robots

Whenever possible, we will illustrate the planning procedures and techniques in this book on a simple yet nontrivial running example called the *Dock-Worker Robots* or *DWR* domain. Here we describe it only informally, but it will serve as an example for various planning formalisms throughout the book.

The environment is a generalization of Example 1.1 (see page 6). It represents a harbor with several locations corresponding to docks, docked ships, storage areas for containers, and parking areas for trucks and trains. This harbor is served by several robot carts and cranes that move containers in order to load and unload ships.

3. Other formalisms, such as *timed automata*, extend state-transition systems with explicit representation of time.

An abstract version of this domain can be defined by giving five finite sets of constant symbols plus one additional symbol.

- A set of *locations* {l1, l2,...}: A location can be a storage area, a dock, a docked ship, or a parking or passing area.
- A set of *robots* {r1, r2,...}: Each robot is a container carrier cart that can be loaded and can transport just *one* container at a time. When a robot is within some location it can move to any other adjacent location.
- A set of *cranes* {k1, k2,...}: A crane belongs to a single location; it can manipulate containers within that location, between piles and robots.
- A set of *piles* {p1, p2,...}: A pile is a fixed area attached to a single location. At the bottom of each pile is a *pallet*, on top of which are stacked zero or more containers.
- A set of *containers* {c1, c2,...}: A container can be stacked in some pile on top of the pallet or some other container, loaded on top of a robot, or held by a crane.
- A symbol pallet: This denotes the pallet that sits at the bottom of a pile. There is no need to have separate symbols for individual pallets because each pallet is uniquely identified by the pile it is in.

Locations do not necessarily have piles. A location without piles is a parking or passing area for robots. Any location that has piles also has one or more cranes. A crane can move a container from the top of a pile to an empty robot or to the top of another pile at the same location. We will assume that a location can be occupied by at most one robot at a time. The topology of the domain is denoted using instances of the following predicates.

- adjacent(l, l'): Location l is adjacent to location l'.
- attached(p, l): Pile p is attached to location l.
- belong(k, l): Crane k belongs to location l.

Those three predicates denote fixed relationships that do not change over time. The current configuration of the domain is denoted using instances of the following predicates, which represent relationships that change over time.

- occupied(l): Location l is already occupied by a robot.
- at(r, l): Robot r is currently at location l.
- loaded(r, c): Robot r is currently loaded with container c.
- unloaded(r): Robot r is not loaded with a container.
- holding(k, c): Crane k is currently holding container c.
- empty(k): Crane k is not holding a container.

- in(c, p): Container c is currently in pile p.
- on(c, c'): Container c is on some container c' or on a pallet within a pile.
- top(c, p): Container c sits on top of pile p. If pile p is empty, this will be denoted as top(pallet, p).

These nine predicates are not independent. For example, unloaded(r) holds if and only if there is no c such that loaded(r, c) holds. Similarly, empty(k) holds if and only if there is no c such that holding(k, c) holds, and top(c, p) holds if and only if there is no container c' such that on(c', c) holds. The reasons for these relationships and how they are maintained in the domain will be discussed in Chapter 2.

There are five possible actions in the DWR domain.

- *Move* a robot r from some location l to some adjacent and unoccupied location l'.
- *Take* a container c with an empty crane k from the top of a pile p colocated with k in the same location l.
- *Put* down a container c held by a crane k on top of a pile p colocated with k in the same location l.
- *Load* with a container c held by a crane k an unloaded robot r that is within the same location l.
- *Unload* a container c with empty crane k from a loaded robot r within the same location l.

More formal specifications of the DWR domain and several problem instances are given in the rest of this book.[4]

Variants of the DWR Domain. At certain points, in order to give detailed explanations of intricate data structures and algorithms, we will need a simpler version of the DWR domain. In the *Simplified DWR* domain, locations have no piles and no cranes, locations offer unlimited floor space for containers and robots, and every robot is equipped with an arm for loading and unloading a container. In this case, there are only three actions: moving, loading, and unloading.

At various points, we also will enrich the DWR domain in order to illustrate enhanced planning possibilities. Chapter 20 will even describe a realistic instance of the domain that has been deployed experimentally. Here are some examples of the kinds of extensions we will consider.

Space constraints are not taken into account in the basic domain. An explicit handling of space will require metric models. For example, one may slightly enrich the domain by stating that a location can hold at most a given number of robots

4. The web site at http://www.laas.fr/planning/ contains auxiliary material for this book. It includes the Planning Domain Description Language specification and a few problem instances of the DWR domain.

instead of just one. Another extension is to allow more than one action to occur concurrently because there are several independent robots and cranes. Resources will have to be made explicit in order to constrain the concurrency to nonconflicting actions. Realistically, explicit time is also needed because a feasible organization of actions and resources is a function of durations. Goals also have to be constrained in time (e.g., with respect to the arrival and departure of ships). Finally, partial information and uncertainty about the state of the world and about effects of actions needs to be modeled.

PART I

Classical Planning

A *restricted state-transition system* is one that meets all of the restrictive assumptions A0 through A7 given in Chapter 1. It is a deterministic, static, finite, and fully observable state-transition system with restricted goals and implicit time. Such a system is denoted $\Sigma = (S, A, \gamma)$ instead of (S, A, E, γ) because there are no contingent events. Here S, A, and γ are finite, and $\gamma(s, a)$ is a single state when a is applicable to s.

A planning problem for a restricted state-transition system $\Sigma = (S, A, \gamma)$ is defined as a triple $\mathcal{P} = (\Sigma, s_0, g)$, where s_0 is an initial state and g corresponds to a set of goal states. A solution to $\mathcal{P}$ is a sequence of actions $(a_1, a_2, \ldots, a_k)$ corresponding to a sequence of state transitions $(s_0, s_1, \ldots, s_k)$ such that $s_1 = \gamma(s_0, a_1), \ldots, s_k = \gamma(s_{k-1}, a_k)$, and s_k is a goal state. The planning problem is to synthesize such a sequence of actions.

Classical planning refers generically to planning for restricted state-transition systems.[1] There are several motivations for studying classical planning problems.

- As usual in science when one is facing a very complex problem, it is very useful to make restrictive assumptions in order to work out well-founded models and approaches. In planning, assumptions A0 through A7 led to this baseline class. Classical planning is now a well-formalized and well-characterized problem. It is important, at least for pedagogical reasons, to have a good understanding of its representations and properties.
- Classical planning opened the way to algorithms and techniques that scale up reasonably well (presented in Parts II and III).

1. This class of planning problems is also referred to in the literature as *STRIPS planning*, in reference to STRIPS, an early planner for restricted state-transition systems [189].

- As long as one keeps in mind that this is a restrictive and unrealistic model that is not to be studied only for its own sake, many extensions to more realistic planning models can be studied from this baseline (Parts III and IV).

The main issues in classical planning are the following:

- How to represent the states and the actions in a way that does not explicitly enumerate S, A, and γ. Without such a representation, it is not possible to develop domain-independent approaches to planning.
- How to perform the search for a solution efficiently: which search space, which algorithm, and what heuristics and control techniques to use for finding a solution.

This part of the book is devoted to classical planning in two particular types of search spaces: state spaces (Chapter 4) and plan spaces (Chapter 5). Chapter 2 describes the representations used in classical planning. To explain why planning is a problem even in this restricted model, Chapter 3 analyzes the complexity of classical planning.

CHAPTER 2

Representations for Classical Planning

2.1 Introduction

A necessary input to any planning algorithm is a description of the problem to be solved. In practice, it usually would be impossible for this problem description to include an explicit enumeration of all the possible states and state transitions: Such a problem description would be exceedingly large, and generating it would usually require more work than solving the planning problem. Instead, a problem representation is needed that does not explicitly enumerate the states and state transitions but makes it easy to compute them on-the-fly.

In this chapter, we discuss three different ways to represent classical planning problems. Each of them is equivalent in expressive power, in the sense that a planning domain represented in one of these representations can also be represented using either of the other representations.

1. In a *set-theoretic representation* (Section 2.2), each state of the world is a set of propositions, and each action is a syntactic expression specifying which propositions belong to the state in order for the action to be applicable and which propositions the action will add or remove in order to make a new state of the world.
2. In a *classical representation* (Section 2.3), the states and actions are like the ones described for set-theoretic representations except that first-order literals and logical connectives are used instead of propositions. This is the most popular choice for restricted state-transition systems.
3. In a *state-variable representation* (Section 2.5), each state is represented by a tuple of values of n state variables $\{x_1, \ldots, x_n\}$, and each action is represented by a partial function that maps this tuple into some other tuple of values of the n state variables. This approach is especially useful for representing domains in which a state is a set of attributes that range over finite domains and whose values change over time.

There are also various ways to extend these approaches. Examples include the use of logical axioms to infer things about states of the world and the use of more general logical formulas to describe the preconditions and effects of an action. Section 2.4 gives an overview of such approaches for classical representations.

2.2 Set-Theoretic Representation

In this section we discuss set-theoretic representations of classical planning problems. For brevity, we will usually call such problems *set-theoretic planning problems*, and we will refer to the representation scheme as *set-theoretic planning*.

2.2.1 Planning Domains, Problems, and Solutions

A set-theoretic representation relies on a finite set of proposition symbols that are intended to represent various propositions about the world.

Definition 2.1 Let $L = \{p_1, \ldots, p_n\}$ be a finite set of *proposition symbols*. A *set-theoretic planning domain* on L is a restricted state-transition system $\Sigma = (S, A, \gamma)$ such that:

- $S \subseteq 2^L$, i.e., each state s is a subset of L. Intuitively, s tells us which propositions currently hold. If $p \in s$, then p holds in the state of the world represented by s, and if $p \notin s$, then p does not hold in the state of the world represented by s.
- Each action $a \in A$ is a triple of subsets of L, which we will write as $a = (\text{precond}(a), \text{effects}^-(a), \text{effects}^+(a))$. The set precond$(a)$ is called the *preconditions* of a, and the sets effects$^+(a)$ and effects$^-(a)$ are called the *effects* of a. We require these two sets of effects to be disjoint, i.e., effects$^+(a) \cap$ effects$^-(a) = \emptyset$. The action a is *applicable* to a state s if precond$(a) \subseteq s$.
- S has the property that if $s \in S$, then, for every action a that is applicable to s, the set $(s - \text{effects}^-(a)) \cup \text{effects}^+(a) \in S$. In other words, whenever an action is applicable to a state, it produces another state. This is useful to us because once we know what A is, we can specify S by giving just a few of its states.
- The state-transition function is $\gamma(s, a) = (s - \text{effects}^-(a)) \cup \text{effects}^+(a)$ if $a \in A$ is applicable to $s \in S$, and $\gamma(s, a)$ is undefined otherwise.

■

Definition 2.2 A *set-theoretic planning problem*[1] is a triple $\mathcal{P} = (\Sigma, s_0, g)$, where:

- s_0, the *initial state*, is a member of S.

1. When the meaning is clear from context, we will drop the adjective *set-theoretic* and just say *planning domain* and *planning problem*.

- $g \subseteq L$ is a set of propositions called *goal propositions* that give the requirements that a state must satisfy in order to be a goal state. The set of goal states is $S_g = \{s \in S \mid g \subseteq s\}$.

■

Definition 2.2 specifies what a planning problem is semantically, but it is not the syntactic specification we would use to describe a planning problem to a computer program. The latter will be discussed in Section 2.2.3.

Example 2.1 Here is one possible set-theoretic representation of the domain described in Example 1.1.

$L = \{$ongground, onrobot, holding, at1, at2$\}$, where:

ongground means that the container is on the ground;
onrobot means that the container is on the robot;
holding means that the crane is holding the container;
at1 means that the robot is at location 1; and
at2 means that the robot is at location 2.

$S = \{s_0, \ldots, s_5\}$, where:

$s_0 = \{$onground, at2$\}$; $s_1 = \{$holding, at2$\}$;
$s_2 = \{$onground, at1$\}$; $s_3 = \{$holding, at1$\}$; and
$s_4 = \{$onrobot, at1$\}$; $s_5 = \{$onrobot, at2$\}$.

$A = \{$take, put, load, unload, move1, move2$\}$ where:

take	=	({onground},	{onground},	{holding});
put	=	({holding},	{holding},	{onground});
load	=	({holding, at1},	{holding},	{onrobot});
unload	=	({onrobot, at1},	{onrobot},	{holding});
move1	=	({at2},	{at2},	{at1}); and
move2	=	({at1},	{at1},	{at2}).

■

Definition 2.3 A *plan* is any sequence of actions $\pi = \langle a_1, \ldots, a_k \rangle$, where $k \geq 0$. The *length* of the plan is $|\pi| = k$, the number of actions. If $\pi_1 = \langle a_1, \ldots, a_k \rangle$ and $\pi_2 = \langle a'_1, \ldots, a'_j \rangle$ are plans, then their *concatenation* is the plan $\pi_1 \cdot \pi_2 = \langle a_1, \ldots, a_k, a'_1, \ldots, a'_j \rangle$.

■

The state produced by applying π to a state s is the state that is produced by applying the actions of π in the order given. We will denote this by extending the state-transition function γ as follows:

$$\gamma(s, \pi) = \begin{cases} s & \text{if } k = 0 \text{ (i.e., } \pi \text{ is empty)} \\ \gamma(\gamma(s, a_1), \langle a_2, \ldots, a_k \rangle) & \text{if } k > 0 \text{ and } a_1 \text{ is applicable to } s \\ \text{undefined} & \text{otherwise} \end{cases}$$

Definition 2.4 Let $\mathcal{P} = (\Sigma, s_0, g)$ be a planning problem. A plan π is a *solution* for $\mathcal{P}$ if $g \subseteq \gamma(s_0, \pi)$. A solution π is *redundant* if there is a proper subsequence of π that is also a solution for $\mathcal{P}$; π is *minimal* if no other solution plan for $\mathcal{P}$ contains fewer actions than π. ■

Note that a minimal solution cannot be redundant.

Example 2.2 In the planning domain described in Example 2.1, suppose the initial state is s_0 and g = {onrobot, at2}. Let:

π_1 = ⟨move2, move2⟩
π_2 = ⟨take, move1⟩
π_3 = ⟨take, move1, put, move2, take, move1, load, move2⟩
π_4 = ⟨take, move1, load, move2⟩
π_5 = ⟨move1, take, load, move2⟩

Then π_1 is not a solution because it is not applicable to s_0; π_2 is not a solution because although it is applicable to s_0, the resulting state is not a goal state; π_3 is a redundant solution; and π_4 and π_5 are the only minimal solutions. ■

2.2.2 State Reachability

If s is a state, then the set of all *successors* of s is

$$\Gamma(s) = \{\gamma(s, a) \mid a \in A \text{ and } a \text{ is applicable to } s\}.$$

If we let $\Gamma^2(s) = \Gamma(\Gamma(s)) = \bigcup\{\Gamma(s') \mid s' \in \Gamma(s)\}$, and similarly for $\Gamma^3, \ldots, \Gamma^n$, then the set of states *reachable* from s is the *transitive closure*:

$$\hat{\Gamma}(s) = \Gamma(s) \cup \Gamma^2(s) \cup \ldots.$$

An action a is said to be *relevant* for a goal g iff $g \cap \text{effects}^+(a) \neq \emptyset$ and $g \cap \text{effects}^-(a) = \emptyset$. Intuitively, these conditions state that a can contribute toward producing a state in $S_g = \{s \in S \mid g \subseteq s\}$. Let us define the *regression set* of a goal g, for an action a that is relevant for g, to be the minimal set of propositions required in a state s in order to apply a to s and to get g:

$$\gamma^{-1}(g, a) = (g - \text{effects}^+(a)) \cup \text{precond}(a).$$

Thus for any state s, $\gamma(s, a) \in S_g$ iff $\gamma^{-1}(g, a) \subseteq s$, i.e., s is a superset of the regression set.

The set of the regression sets over all actions relevant for a goal g is:

$$\Gamma^{-1}(g) = \{\gamma^{-1}(g, a) \mid a \in A \text{ is relevant for } g\}.$$

A goal state is reachable in a single step from a state s iff s is a superset of an element of $\Gamma^{-1}(g)$, i.e., there is $s' \in \Gamma^{-1}(g)$: $s' \subseteq s$. Similarly, the set of all regression sets of g in two steps is $\Gamma^{-2}(g) = \Gamma^{-1}(\Gamma^{-1}(g))$, etc., and the set of all regression sets of g, whose supersets are states from which g is *reachable*, is the transitive closure:

$$\hat{\Gamma}^{-1}(g) = \Gamma^{-1}(g) \cup \Gamma^{-2}(g) \cup \ldots.$$

Proposition 2.1 *A planning problem $\mathcal{P} = (\Sigma, s_0, g)$ has a solution iff $S_g \cap \hat{\Gamma}(s_0) \neq \emptyset$.*

Proposition 2.2 *A planning problem $\mathcal{P} = (\Sigma, s_0, g)$ has a solution iff s_0 is a superset of some element in $\hat{\Gamma}^{-1}(g)$.*

2.2.3 Stating a Planning Problem

For set-theoretic planning, we have defined the planning domain $\Sigma = (S, A, \gamma)$, which is independent of any particular goal or initial state, and the planning problem $\mathcal{P} = (\Sigma, s_0, g)$, which includes a domain, an initial state, and a goal.

We began this chapter by mentioning the need for a way to specify $\mathcal{P}$ without giving all of the members of S and γ explicitly. To accomplish that, we will use the *statement* of $\mathcal{P}$, defined to be the triple $P = (A, s_0, g)$. $\mathcal{P}$ and P can be regarded as semantic and syntactic specifications, respectively (for more about this, see Section 2.3.4).

One difficulty is that the statement of a planning problem is ambiguous because it does not specify the set of states S (see Example 2.3).

Example 2.3 Let $P = (\{\mathsf{a1}\}, s_0, \mathsf{g})$, where:

$$\mathsf{a1} = (\{\mathsf{p1}\}, \{\mathsf{p1}\}, \{\mathsf{p2}\})$$
$$s_0 = \{\mathsf{p1}\}$$
$$g = \{\mathsf{p2}\}$$

Then P is the statement of the planning problem $\mathcal{P}$, in which:

$$L = \{\mathsf{p1}, \mathsf{p2}\}$$
$$S = \{\{\mathsf{p1}\}, \{\mathsf{p2}\}\}$$
$$\gamma(\{\mathsf{p1}\}, \mathsf{a1}) = \{\mathsf{p2}\}$$

However, P is also the statement of the planning problem $\mathcal{P}'$, in which:

$$\begin{aligned} L &= \{\mathtt{p1}, \mathtt{p2}, \mathtt{p3}\} \\ S &= \{\{\mathtt{p1}\}, \{\mathtt{p2}\}, \{\mathtt{p1}, \mathtt{p3}\}, \{\mathtt{p2}, \mathtt{p3}\}\} \\ \gamma(\{\mathtt{p1}\}, \mathtt{a1}) &= \{\mathtt{p2}\} \\ \gamma(\{\mathtt{p1}, \mathtt{p3}\}, \mathtt{a1}) &= \{\mathtt{p2}, \mathtt{p3}\} \end{aligned}$$

Note, however, that p3 plays no role in problem $\mathcal{P}'$: the set $\hat{\Gamma}^{-1}(g)$ of regression sets and the set $\hat{\Gamma}(s_0)$ of states reachable from s_0 are the same in both $\mathcal{P}$ and $\mathcal{P}'$:

$$\hat{\Gamma}^{-1}(g) = \{\{\mathtt{p1}\}, \{\mathtt{p2}\}\}; \quad \hat{\Gamma}(s_0) = \{\{\mathtt{p1}\}, \{\mathtt{p2}\}\}$$

■

The following proposition generalizes the final equation:

Proposition 2.3 *Let $\mathcal{P}$ and $\mathcal{P}'$ be two planning problems that have the same statement. Then both $\mathcal{P}$ and $\mathcal{P}'$ have the same set of reachable states $\hat{\Gamma}(s_0)$ and the same set of solutions.*

This proposition means that the statement of a planning problem is unambiguous enough to be acceptable as a specification of a planning problem.

2.2.4 Properties of the Set-Theoretic Representation

We now discuss some advantages and disadvantages of the set-theoretic representation scheme.

Readability. One advantage of the set-theoretic representation is that it provides a more concise and readable representation of the state-transition system than we would get by enumerating all of the states and transitions explicitly.

Example 2.4 Consider the DWR domain shown in Figure 2.1. The robot can be at either loc1 or loc2. The robot can be empty or can be holding any one of the containers, and likewise for the crane. The rest of the containers can be distributed in any order between pile1 and pile2. The total number of possible states is 2,580,480 (see Exercise 2.17). If we used a state-transition representation in which the states were named $s_1, s_2, \ldots, s_{2,580,480}$, it would be difficult to keep track of what each state meant.

In a set-theoretic representation, we can make each state's meaning more obvious by using propositions to represent the statuses of the containers, the

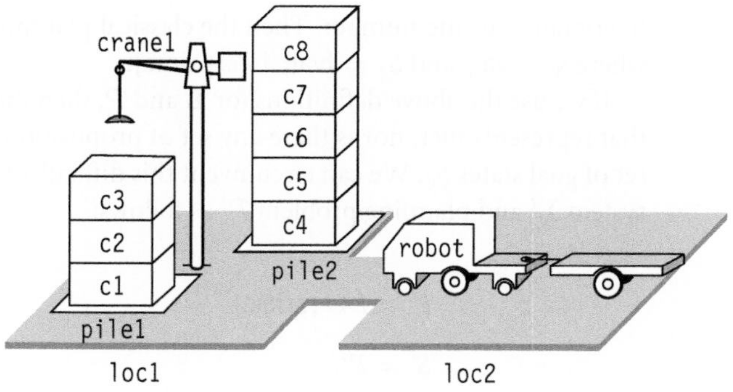

Figure 2.1 A DWR state for Example 2.4.

crane, and the robot. For example, the state shown in Figure 2.1 might be represented as:

{nothing-on-c3, c3-on-c2, c2-on-c1, c1-on-pile1,
nothing-on-c8, c8-on-c7, c7-on-c6, c6-on-c5,
c5-on-c4, c4-on-pile2, robot-at-loc2, crane-empty}

Furthermore, the set-theoretic representation lets us avoid specifying all 2,580,480 of the states (and their associated state transitions) explicitly because we can generate them as needed using techniques such as the ones described next. ■

Computation. A proposition in a state s is assumed to *persist* in $\gamma(s, a)$ unless explicitly mentioned in the effects of a. These effects are defined with two subsets: effects$^+(a)$, the propositions to *add* to s, and effects$^-(a)$, the propositions to *remove* from s in order to get the new state $\gamma(s, a)$. Hence, the transition function γ and the applicability conditions of actions rely on very easily computable *set operations*: if precond$(a) \subseteq s$, then $\gamma(s, a) = (s - \text{effects}^-(a)) \cup \text{effects}^+(a)$.

Expressivity. A significant problem is that not every state-transition system Σ has a set-theoretic representation. The work-around is to construct a state-transition system Σ' that is equivalent to Σ but does have a set-theoretic representation (see Example 2.5).

Example 2.5 Suppose a computer has an n-bit register r and a single operator incr that assigns $r \leftarrow r + 1 \bmod m$, where $m = 2^n$. Let $L = \{\text{val}_0, \ldots, \text{val}_{m-1}\}$, where each val$_i$ is the proposition "the register r contains the value i." Then we can represent the computer as a state-transition system $\Sigma = (S, A, \gamma)$, where each state is a member of L, $A = \{\text{incr}\}$, and $\gamma(\text{val}_i, \text{incr}) = \text{val}_{i+1} \bmod m$ for each i. Now, suppose that r contains some value c in the initial state and that the goal is for r

to contain a prime number. Then the classical planning problem is $\mathcal{P} = (\Sigma, s_0, g)$, where $s_0 = \mathsf{val}_c$ and $S_g = \{\mathsf{val}_i \mid i \text{ is prime}\}$.

If we use the above definitions for Σ and $\mathcal{P}$, then there is no set-theoretic action that represents incr, nor is there any set of propositions $g \subseteq 2^L$ that represents the set of goal states S_g. We can circumvent this difficulty by defining a state-transition system Σ' and planning problem $\mathcal{P}'$ as follows:

$$L' = L \cup \{\mathsf{prime}\}$$
$$S' = 2^{L'}$$
$$A' = \{\mathsf{incr}_0, \ldots, \mathsf{incr}_{m-1}\}$$
$$\gamma'(\mathsf{val}_i, \mathsf{incr}_i) = \begin{cases} \{\mathsf{prime}, \mathsf{val}_{i+1} \bmod m\} & \text{if } i+1 \bmod m \text{ is prime} \\ \{\mathsf{val}_{i+1} \bmod m\} & \text{otherwise} \end{cases}$$
$$\Sigma' = (S', A', \gamma')$$
$$S'_g = \{s \subset 2^{L'} \mid \mathsf{prime} \in s\}$$
$$\mathcal{P}' = (\Sigma', s_0, S_{g'})$$

$\mathcal{P}'$ has the following set-theoretic representation:

$$g' = \{\mathsf{prime}\};$$
$$\text{precond}(\mathsf{incr}_i) = \{\mathsf{val}_i\}, \quad i = 0, \ldots, n$$
$$\text{effects}^-(\mathsf{incr}_i) = \begin{cases} \{\mathsf{val}_i, \neg\, \mathsf{prime}\} & \text{if } i \text{ is prime} \\ \{\mathsf{val}_i\} & \text{otherwise} \end{cases}$$
$$\text{effects}^+(\mathsf{incr}_i) = \begin{cases} \{\mathsf{val}_{i+1} \bmod m, \mathsf{prime}\} & \text{if } i+1 \bmod m \text{ is prime} \\ \{\mathsf{val}_{i+1} \bmod m\} & \text{otherwise} \end{cases}$$

However, creating this set-theoretic representation incurs a large computational cost. There are 2^n different actions, and in order to write all of them, we must compute all of the prime numbers from 1 to 2^n. ■

Another expressivity issue with this representation scheme is that not every set of propositions in L corresponds to a meaningful state of a domain we are trying to represent.

Example 2.6 Consider the domain of Example 2.1 (see page 21). The state {holding} is ambiguous in our intended interpretation of the domain because it does not contain a proposition that gives the robot location. Furthermore, the state {holding, at2, onrobot} is not consistent with our intended interpretation because it says that the container is both on the crane and on the robot. ■

If the actions of a planning problem and s_0 are written correctly, then an ambiguous or inconsistent state s will never appear in any solution to the planning problem: either s will not be reachable from s_0 (i.e., $s \notin \hat{\Gamma}(s_0)$) or g will not be reachable from s (i.e., s is not a superset of an element of $\Gamma^{-1}(g)$). However, this puts all the burden of a good definition of a domain on the specification of the set of actions.

2.3 Classical Representation

The classical representation scheme generalizes the set-theoretic representation scheme using notation derived from first-order logic.[2] States are represented as sets of logical atoms that are true or false within some interpretation. Actions are represented by *planning operators* that change the truth values of these atoms.

2.3.1 States

To develop a language for classical planning, we will start with a first-order language $\mathcal{L}$ in which there are finitely many predicate symbols and constant symbols and *no* function symbols; thus every term of $\mathcal{L}$ is either a variable symbol or a constant symbol. We will augment $\mathcal{L}$ to include some additional symbols and expressions. For the predicate and constant symbols of $\mathcal{L}$, we will use alphanumeric strings that are at least two characters long (e.g., crane1 or r2) with a sans-serif font. For the variable symbols, we will use single characters, possibly with subscripts (e.g., x or y_{13}).

A *state* is a set of ground atoms of $\mathcal{L}$. Since $\mathcal{L}$ has no function symbols, the set S of all possible states is guaranteed to be finite. As in the set-theoretic representation scheme, an atom p holds in s iff $p \in s$. If g is a set of literals (i.e., atoms and negated atoms), we will say that s *satisfies* g (denoted $s \models g$) when there is a substitution σ such that every positive literal of $\sigma(g)$ is in s and no negated literal of $\sigma(g)$ is in s.

Example 2.7 Suppose we want to formulate a DWR planning domain in which there are two locations (loc1, loc2), one robot (r1), one crane (crane1), two piles (p1, p2), and three containers (c1, c2, c3). The set of constant symbols is {loc1, loc2, r1, crane1, p1, p2, c1, c2, c3, pallet}. Recall that pallet is a symbol that denotes the object that sits at the bottom of a pile; hence if a pile p3 is empty, then top(pallet, p3). One of the states is the state s_1 shown in Figure 2.2. ■

2. See Appendix B for an introduction and first-order logic.

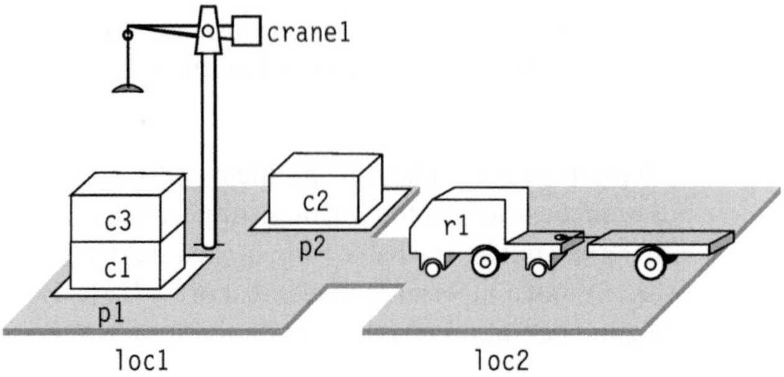

Figure 2.2 The DWR state s_1 = {attached(p1,loc1), attached(p2,loc1), in(c1,p1), in(c3,p1), top(c3,p1), on(c3,c1), on(c1,pallet), in(c2,p2), top(c2,p2), on(c2,pallet), belong(crane1,loc1), empty(crane1), adjacent(loc1,loc2), adjacent(loc2,loc1), at(r1,loc2), occupied(loc2), unloaded(r1)}.

Note that the truth value of an atom may vary from state to state. For example, at(r1,loc2) holds in the state depicted in Figure 2.2, but it does not hold in a state where robot r1 moves to location loc1. Hence, the predicate at can be considered as a function of the set of states; it will be called a *fluent* or *flexible relation*. However, not every predicate symbol in $\mathcal{L}$ is necessarily fluent. For example, the truth value of adjacent(loc1,loc2) is not intended to vary from state to state for a given DWR domain. A state-invariant predicate such as adjacent is called a *rigid relation*.

Note also that although $\mathcal{L}$ is a first-order language, a state is not a set of first-order formulas—it is just a set of ground atoms. Both here and in the set-theoretic representation scheme, we use the *closed-world assumption*: an atom that is not explicitly specified in a state does not hold in that state.

2.3.2 Operators and Actions

The transition function γ is specified generically through a set of planning operators that are instantiated into actions.

Definition 2.5 In classical planning, a *planning operator* is a triple o = (name(o), precond(o), effects(o)) whose elements are as follows:

- name(o), the *name* of the operator, is a syntactic expression of the form $n(x_1, \ldots, x_k)$, where n is a symbol called an *operator symbol*, $x_1, \ldots, x_k$ are all of the variable symbols that appear anywhere in o, and n is unique (i.e., no two operators in $\mathcal{L}$ have the same operator symbol).
- precond(o) and effects(o), the *preconditions* and *effects* of o, respectively, are generalizations of the preconditions and effects of a set-theoretic

action: instead of being sets of propositions, they are sets of literals (i.e., atoms and negations of atoms). ■

Rigid relations cannot appear in the effects of any operator o because they are invariant over all the states; they can be used only in precond(o). In other words, any predicate in effects(o) is a flexible relation.

Rather than writing $o = (\text{name}(o), \text{precond}(o), \text{effects}(o))$ to define a planning operator, we will usually write operator definitions as shown in Example 2.8.

Example 2.8 Here are the planning operators for the DWR domain.

move(r, l, m)
;; robot r moves from location l to an adjacent location m
precond: adjacent(l, m), at(r, l), $\neg$ occupied(m)
effects: at(r, m), occupied(m), $\neg$ occupied(l), $\neg$ at(r, l)

load(k, l, c, r)
;; crane k at location l loads container c onto robot r
precond: belong(k, l), holding(k, c), at(r, l), unloaded(r)
effects: empty(k), $\neg$ holding(k, c), loaded(r, c), $\neg$ unloaded(r)

unload(k, l, c, r)
;; crane k at location l takes container c from robot r
precond: belong(k, l), at(r, l), loaded(r, c), empty(k)
effects: $\neg$ empty(k), holding(k, c), unloaded(r), $\neg$ loaded(r, c)

put(k, l, c, d, p)
;; crane k at location l puts c onto d in pile p
precond: belong(k, l), attached(p, l), holding(k, c), top(d, p)
effects: $\neg$ holding(k, c), empty(k), in(c, p), top(c, p), on(c, d), $\neg$ top(d, p)

take(k, l, c, d, p)
;; crane k at location l takes c off of d in pile p
precond: belong(k, l), attached(p, l), empty(k), top(c, p), on(c, d)
effects: holding(k, c), $\neg$ empty(k), $\neg$ in(c, p), $\neg$ top(c, p), $\neg$ on(c, d), top(d, p)

■

The purpose of an operator's name is to provide an unambiguous way to refer to the operator or to substitution instances of the operator without having to write their preconditions and effects explicitly. If o is an operator or an *operator instance* (i.e., a substitution instance of an operator), then name(o) refers unambiguously to o. Thus, when it is clear from the context, we will write name(o) to refer to the entire operator o.

Example 2.9 take(k, l, c, d, p) is the last of the operators in Example 2.8, and take(crane1,loc1,c1,c2,p1) is the following operator instance:

```
take(crane1,loc1,c1,c2,p1)
   ;; crane crane1 at location loc1 takes c1 off of c2 in pile p1
   precond:  belong(crane1,loc1), attached(p1,loc1),
             empty(crane1), top(c1,p1), on(c1,c2)
   effects:  holding(crane1,c1), ¬empty(crane1), ¬in(c1,p1),
             ¬top(c1,p1), ¬on(c1,c2), top(c2,p1)
```

■

Definition 2.6 For any set of literals L, L^+ is the set of all atoms in L, and L^- is the set of all atoms whose negations are in L. In particular, if o is an operator or operator instance, then precond$^+(o)$ and precond$^-(o)$ are o's positive and negative preconditions, respectively, and effects$^+(o)$ and effects$^-(o)$ are o's positive and negative effects, respectively. ■

Definition 2.7 An *action* is any ground instance of a planning operator. If a is an action and s is a state such that precond$^+(a) \subseteq s$ and precond$^-(a) \cap s = \emptyset$, then a is *applicable* to s, and the result of applying a to s is the state:

$$\gamma(s, a) = (s - \text{effects}^-(a)) \cup \text{effects}^+(a).$$

■

Thus, like in set-theoretic planning, state transitions can easily be computed using set operations.

Example 2.10 take(crane1,loc1,c3,c1,p1) is applicable to the state s_1 of Figure 2.2. The result is the state $s_5 = \gamma(s_1, \text{take(crane1, loc1, c1, c2, p1)})$ shown in Figure 2.3. ■

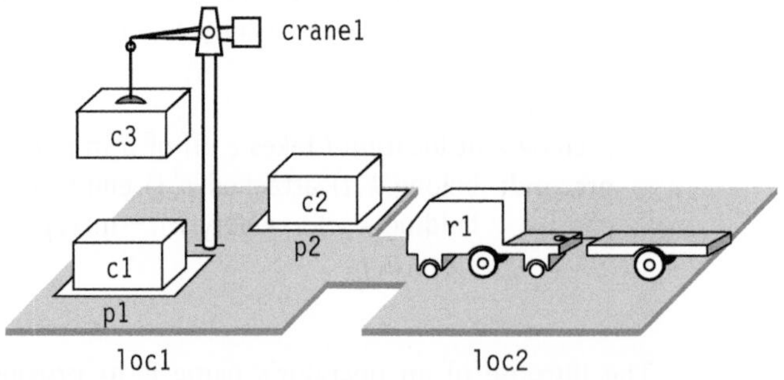

Figure 2.3 The DWR state s_5 = {attached(p1,loc1), in(c1,p1), top(c1,p1), on(c1,pallet), attached(p2,loc1), in(c2,p2), top(c2,p2), on(c2,pallet), belong(crane1,loc1), holding(crane1,c3), adjacent(loc1,loc2), adjacent(loc2,loc1), at(r1,loc2), occupied(loc2), unloaded(r1)}.

2.3.3 Plans, Problems, and Solutions

Here are the definitions of classical planning domains, problems, plans, and solutions.

Definition 2.8 Let $\mathcal{L}$ be a first-order language that has finitely many predicate symbols and constant symbols. A *classical planning domain*[3] in $\mathcal{L}$ is a restricted state-transition system $\Sigma = (S, A, \gamma)$ such that:

- $S \subseteq 2^{\{\text{all ground atoms of } \mathcal{L}\}}$;
- $A = \{$all ground instances of operators in $O\}$, where O is a set of operators as defined earlier;
- $\gamma(s, a) = (s - \text{effects}^-(a)) \cup \text{effects}^+(a)$ if $a \in A$ is applicable to $s \in S$, and otherwise $\gamma(s, a)$ is undefined; and
- S is closed under γ, i.e., if $s \in S$, then for every action a that is applicable to s, $\gamma(s, a) \in S$.

■

Definition 2.9 A *classical planning problem* is a triple $\mathcal{P} = (\Sigma, s_0, g)$, where:

- s_0, the initial state, is any state in set S;
- g, the goal, is any set of ground literals; and
- $S_g = \{s \in S \mid s \text{ satisfies } g\}$.

The *statement* of a planning problem $\mathcal{P} = (\Sigma, s_0, g)$ is $P = (O, s_0, g)$.

■

The statement of a planning problem is the syntactic specification that we would use, e.g., to describe $\mathcal{P}$ to a computer program. Its properties are like those for set-theoretic planning (Section 2.2.3): More than one classical planning problem may have the same statement, but if two classical problems have the same statement, then they will have the same set of reachable states and the same set of solutions.

Since g contains negated atoms, the definition of γ^{-1} differs from the one in Definition 2.1 (see page 20). An action a is *relevant* for g, i.e., a can produce a state that satisfies g, if:

- $g \cap \text{effects}(a) \neq \emptyset$, i.e., a's effects contribute to g; and
- $g^+ \cap \text{effects}^-(a) = \emptyset$ and $g^- \cap \text{effects}^+(a) = \emptyset$, i.e., a's effects do not conflict with g.

---

3. Our definition of a planning domain is more specific than the usual informal use of that expression. A domain is relative to a language $\mathcal{L}$; e.g., in the DWR example we would know from $\mathcal{L}$ all the constants, locations, piles, robots, cranes, and containers there are in the domain. The informal use is to say that a domain is a set of operators, i.e., that a domain includes all planning problems whose statements can be expressed with O and some initial state and goal.

If a is relevant for g, then:

$$\gamma^{-1}(g, a) = (g - \text{effects}(a)) \cup \text{precond}(a)$$

The set of all regression sets over all actions relevant for a goal g is as before:

$$\Gamma^{-1}(g) = \{\gamma^{-1}(g, a) \mid a \text{ is an operator instance relevant for } g\}$$

$\hat{\Gamma}(s_0)$ and $\hat{\Gamma}^{-1}(g)$ have the same properties as earlier.

The definitions of a plan and the result of applying it to a state are the same as they were in set-theoretic planning. A plan π is a solution for $\mathcal{P}$ if $\gamma(s_0, \pi)$ satisfies g. As before, a solution is redundant if a proper subsequence of it is a solution, and its length is shortest or minimal if no solution contains fewer actions.

Example 2.11 Consider the following plan:

$$\pi_1 = \langle \text{take(crane1, loc1, c3, c1, p1)}, \text{move(r1, loc2, loc1)}, \text{load(crane1, loc1, c3, r1)} \rangle$$

This plan is applicable to the state s_1 shown in Figure 2.2, producing the state s_6 shown in Figure 2.4. π_1 is a minimal solution to the DWR problem $\mathcal{P}_1$ whose initial state is s_1 and whose goal formula is:

$$g_1 = \{\text{loaded(r1, c3)}, \text{at(r1, l2)}\}$$

π_1 is also a solution to the DWR problem $\mathcal{P}_2$ whose initial state is s_1 and whose goal formula is $g_2 = \{\text{at(r1, loc1)}\}$, but in this case π_1 is redundant. ■

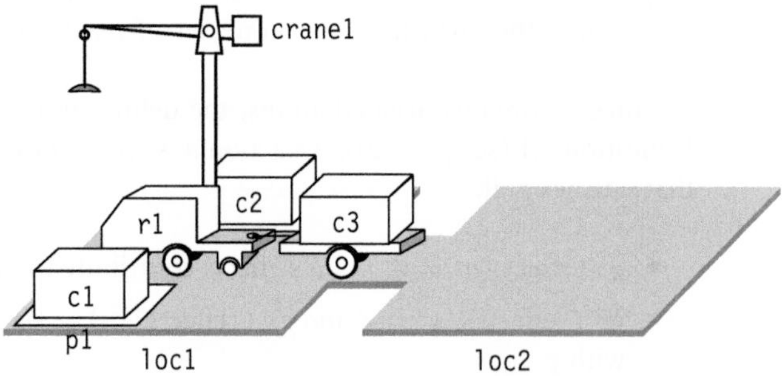

Figure 2.4 The state s_6 = {attached(p1,loc1), in(c1,p1), top(c1,p1), on(c1,pallet), attached(p2,loc1), in(c2,p2), top(c2,p2), on(c2,pallet), belong(crane1,loc1), empty(crane1), adjacent(loc1,loc2), adjacent(loc2,loc1), at(r1,loc1), occupied(loc1), loaded(r1,c3)}.

2.3.4 Semantics of Classical Representations

So far, we have deliberately blurred the distinction between the syntactic specification of a classical planning problem and what it means. The distinction is analogous to the distinction between a logical theory and its models (see Appendix B). Intuitively, the semantics is given by Σ and the syntax is specified by P.

Suppose $P = (O, s_0, g)$ is the statement of a classical planning problem $\mathcal{P}$. Let Σ be the restricted state-transition system for $\mathcal{P}$, and I is a function, called an *interpretation*, such that (see Figure 2.5):

- For every state t of P, $I(t)$ is a state of Σ.
- For every operator instance o of P, $I(o)$ is an action of Σ.

To specify the semantics of the representation, we define the pair (Σ, I) to be a *model* of P if for every state t of P and every operator instance o of P:

$$\gamma(I(s), I(o)) = I((s - \text{effects}^-(o)) \cup \text{effects}^+(o))$$

This distinction between P and Σ is needed in order to establish the soundness property[4] of a representation scheme.

In classical planning, we have used a first-order language $\mathcal{L}$ but have used none of the inferential capabilities of first-order logic. As a consequence, the question of whether Σ is a model of P is quite trivial. However, there are cases where we might like to extend the classical planning formalism to allow states, goals, and operators to contain nonatomic first-order formulas. With such an extension, the semantic considerations are more complicated (see Section 2.4.5).

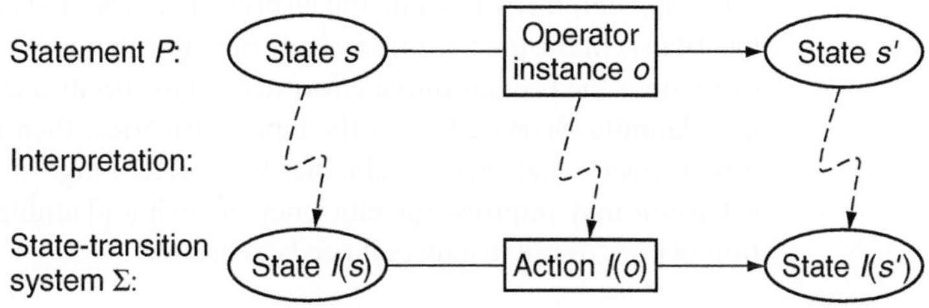

Figure 2.5 Interpretation of a planning domain as a state-transition system.

4. See Appendix B.

2.4 Extending the Classical Representation

Since the classical planning formalism is very restricted, extensions to it are needed in order to describe interesting domains. It is possible to extend the classical planning formalism, while staying within the same model of restricted state-transition systems, by allowing expressions that are more general than just collections of literals in the preconditions and effects of the operator, as well as in the descriptions of states. The following subsections discuss several examples.

2.4.1 Simple Syntactical Extensions

One of the simplest extensions is to allow the goal formula g to be any existentially closed conjunct of literals, such as $\exists x\ \exists y(\mathsf{on}(x, \mathsf{c1}) \wedge \mathsf{on}(y, \mathsf{c2}))$. This brings no increase in expressive power, for if g is an existentially closed conjunct, it can be replaced by a single ground atom p and a planning operator whose precondition is g with the quantifiers removed and whose effect is p. However, in some cases the extension may make the planning representation look more natural for human readers.

Another simple extension is to allow the use of *typed variables and relations*. The statement of a problem can involve not only the specification of O, s_0, and g but also the definition of sets of constants. For example, in the DWR domain, the set of constants is partitioned into classes such as locations, robots, cranes, piles, and containers.

A typed variable ranges over a particular set, e.g., l is in locations, r in robots. A type is a unary predicate whose truth value does not change from state to state. Figure 2.6 illustrates how to specify part of the DWR domain using typed variables; the notation is that of the PDDL planning language [387].

Like the previous extension, this one gives no increase in expressive power. If we want to say that a variable l must be of type location, we can do this within ordinary classical planning by introducing location as a new predicate symbol and including location(l) in the precondition of any operator that uses l. However, this extension can reduce the programming effort needed to specify a classical planning domain: if a planning system enforces the type restrictions, then the domain author has a way to ensure that each variable has the correct range of values. Furthermore, the extension may improve the efficiency of such a planning system by reducing the number of ground instances it needs to create.

2.4.2 Conditional Planning Operators

There are many situations in which we might want the effects of an action to depend on the input situation. One of the simplest examples would be to model the effects of a push button that turns a lamp off if the lamp is on and vice versa. One way to do this is to extend the classical operator formalism to include conditional operators as described below.

```
(define (domain dwr)
  (:requirements :strips :typing)
  (:types location pile robot crane container)
  (:predicates
    (adjacent ?l1 ?l2 - location) (attached ?p - pile ?l - location)
    (belong ?k - crane ?l - location)
    (at ?r - robot ?l - location) (occupied ?l - location)
    (loaded ?r - robot ?c - container) (unloaded ?r - robot)
    (holding ?k - crane ?c - container) (empty ?k - crane)
    (in ?c - container ?p - pile) (top ?c - container ?p - pile)
    (on ?k1 - container ?k2 - container))
  (:action move
    :parameters (?r - robot ?from ?to - location)
    :precondition (and (adjacent ?from ?to)
          (at ?r ?from) (not (occupied ?to)))
    :effect (and (at ?r ?to) (not (occupied ?from))
          (occupied ?to) (not (at ?r ?from))))
  (:action load
    :parameters (?k - crane ?c - container ?r - robot)
    :vars (?l - location)
    :precondition (and (at ?r ?l) (belong ?k ?l)
          (holding ?k ?c) (unloaded ?r))
    :effect (and (loaded ?r ?c) (not (unloaded ?r))
          (empty ?k) (not (holding ?k ?c))))
```

Figure 2.6 A partial PDDL specification of the DWR domain. adjacent is declared to be a binary predicate symbol whose arguments both are of type location, attached is declared to be a binary predicate symbol whose first arguments have type pile and location, and so forth.

A *conditional operator* o is an $(n+1)$-tuple,

$$n, t_1, t_2, \ldots, t_n,$$

where n is a syntactic expression $o(x_1, \ldots, x_k)$ as in the usual classical operator definition, and each t_i is a pair $(\text{precond}_i, \text{effects}_i)$ such that precond_i is a set of preconditions and each effects_i is a set of effects.

Let a be a ground instance of a conditional operator, s be a state, and $I = \{i : s \text{ satisfies } \text{precond}_i(a)\}$. If $I \neq \emptyset$, then we say that o is applicable to the state s and that the result is the state:

$$\gamma(s, a) = (s - \bigcup_{i \in I} \text{effects}_i^+(a)) \cup \bigcup_{i \in I} \text{effects}_i^-(a)$$

Instead of a set of pairs $(\text{precond}_i, \text{effects}_i)$, an operator with conditional effects is usually written in an equivalent but more compact expression, as illustrated in Example 2.12. The operator has the usual unconditional preconditions and effects followed by the conditional effects and their qualifying conditions. Syntactical facilities such as nested conditionals are also allowed by many planning languages.

Example 2.12 In Example 2.8 (see page 29), the location of a container loaded on a robot or held by a crane is not explicit. Suppose we need to keep this location explicit, e.g., with the at predicate. Since the location changes for a container loaded on a robot with a move operator, we can respecify a new move operator with a condition effect as follows:

move(r, l, m, c)
;; robot r with possibly a container c moves from location l to location m
precond: adjacent(l, m), at(r, l), $\neg$ occupied(m)
effects: at(r, m), occupied(m), $\neg$ occupied(l), $\neg$ at(r, l),
(*when* loaded(r, c) *then* at(c, m), $\neg$ at(c, l))

In the last line, the construct *when* is followed by an additional precondition; when loaded(r, c) is true in state s, then the additional effects at(c, m) and $\neg$ at(c, l) take place in state $\gamma(s, a)$. This operator is equivalent to two pairs $(\text{precond}_i, \text{effects}_i)$ corresponding to the two cases of a loaded and an unloaded robot. ■

2.4.3 Quantified Expressions

Suppose we have robots that can hold several containers, and suppose we want to keep track of the location of all containers, as discussed in Example 2.12. One way to express this is to extend the operator representation so that effects(o) is not just a set of literals but a logical formula in which some of the literals represent additional preconditions and other literals represent effects that will occur if those preconditions are satisfied. To represent this, we might use a notation such as the following:

move(r, l, m, x)
;; robot r moves from location l to m with possibly several containers
precond: at(r, l)
effects: $\neg$ at(r, l), at(r, m),
(*forall* x *when* loaded(r, x) *then* at(x, m), $\neg$ at(x, l))

In the final line of the operator, the literal loaded(r, x) is an additional precondition, and the literals at(x, m) and $\neg$ at(x, l) are effects that will occur for *every* container x such that the precondition is satisfied. For example, suppose we apply the action $a =$ move(r1, l1, l2) to this state:

$$s = \{\text{at(r1, l1), at(c1, l1), at(c2, l1), loaded(r1, c1), loaded(r1, c2)}\}$$

In this case, the positive and negative effects of a will be:

$$\text{effects}^+(a) = \{\text{at(r1, l2), at(c1, l2), at(c2, l2)}\}$$
$$\text{effects}^-(a) = \{\neg\,\text{at(r1, l1)}, \neg\,\text{at(c1, l1)}, \neg\,\text{at(c2, l1)}\}$$

These effects will produce this state:

$$\gamma(s, a) = \{\text{at(r1, l2), at(c1, l2), at(c2, l2), loaded(r1, c1), loaded(r1, c2)}\}$$

Because of our assumption of finite domains, the *forall* quantifier can be expanded into a finite expression. In the case of the previous move operator, this expression is a finite conjunction of conditional effects for all the containers of the problem.

Quantified expressions can also be convenient for specifying concisely the initial state or the goal of a planning problem, e.g., for saying that all the robots are initially unloaded or that the goal is to have all containers stacked into a destination pile. Typed variables and rigid predicates for testing the types are very useful for handling efficiently quantified expressions.

2.4.4 Disjunctive Preconditions

Continuing the previous example, suppose that we can move the robot cart from location l to location m under either of two conditions: either there must be a road from l to m, or the cart must have all-wheel drive. One way to represent this is to extend the operator representation so that precond(o) may be any logical formula composed of conjuncts and disjuncts of literals. Then we could create an operator such as the following:

move(r,l,m)
  ;; move robot cart r from location l to location m
  precond: at(r, l)
      $\wedge$(road(l, m) $\vee$ all-wheel-drive(r))
  effects: $\neg$ at(r, l), at(r, m),
      (*forall* x *when* loaded(r, x) *then* at(x, m), $\neg$ at(x, l))

Thus, the action move(r1,l1,l2) would be applicable to the state

$$\{\text{road(l1, l2), at(r1, l1), at(c1, l1), at(c1, l1), loaded(c1, r1), loaded(c2, r1)}\}$$

and to the state

$$\{\text{all-wheel-drive(r1), at(r1, l1), at(c1, l1), at(c1, l1), loaded(c1, r1), loaded(c2, r1)}\}$$

but would not be applicable to the state

$$\{\text{at(r1, l1), at(c1, l1), at(c1, l1), loaded(c1, r1), loaded(c2, r1)}\}$$

2.4.5 Axiomatic Inference

Sometimes we may want to infer conditions that are not stated explicitly in a state of the world. For example, it could be useful in the DWR domain to have two formulas saying that the adjacent property between locations is symmetric and that a crane is empty iff it is not holding anything:

$$\forall l\, \forall l'\ (\mathsf{adjacent}(l,l') \leftrightarrow \mathsf{adjacent}(l',l)) \tag{2.1}$$

$$\forall k\ (\forall x\ \neg\, \mathsf{holding}(k,x)) \leftrightarrow \mathsf{empty}(k) \tag{2.2}$$

Furthermore, we might also like to say that in the initial state s_0 of a particular DWR problem, all containers are in location loc1, i.e.:

$$\forall c\ (\mathsf{container}(c) \rightarrow \mathsf{in}(c, \mathsf{loc1})) \tag{2.3}$$

Formula 2.1 can easily be introduced into the classical planning formalism because adjacent is a predicate whose truth value does not change from state to state: it is a rigid relation. Recall that rigid relations do not appear in the *effects* of any operator because their truth values do not change; they may appear only in preconditions. Hence, whatever is deduced with a formula like Formula 2.1 remains true everywhere. However, special care needs to be taken with Formula 2.2 because holding and empty both are flexible relations.

To handle Formula 2.2 properly, we need to remove empty from the effects of all operators and to rewrite Formula 2.2 as two implications that give the truth value of empty from that of holding, for all cranes and containers being held:

$$\forall k\ (\neg\exists x\ \mathsf{holding}(k,x) \rightarrow \mathsf{empty}(k))$$

$$\forall k\ (\exists x\ \mathsf{holding}(k,x) \rightarrow \neg\mathsf{empty}(k))$$

This technique establishes a further distinction between two classes of flexible relations.

1. *Primary relations*, such as holding, can appear in the effects and preconditions of operators.
2. *Secondary relations*, such as empty, cannot appear in effects but only in preconditions; secondary relations are deduced from primary and secondary relations.

In a way, secondary relations are a "syntactical sugar" that simplifies the specification of operators. States and state transitions are entirely defined by primary relations.

What about Formula 2.3, which is intended to be true in just one particular state? If we rely solely on the machinery that we introduced so far for representing and computing state transitions, i.e., difference and union of sets, then clearly Formula 2.3 cannot be handled in a general way. We have to restrict the language so that the only nonatomic formulas allowed must be true everywhere. However, because we are restricting the language to finite domains, formulas such as Formula 2.3 can be dealt with using an *expansion* of the formula into its corresponding ground atoms. This technique is also applied to quantified formulas in effects of operators (see Section 2.4.3).

Although some of the original approaches to AI planning were based on axiomatic inference [249], many classical planners do not use it. This is mainly in order to avoid complications such as the ones described above. As a general rule, it is much easier to use axiomatic inference in planners that keep track of the current state, which is something that most classical planners do not do. Axiomatic inference plays an important role in several successful nonclassical planners (see Chapters 10 and 11) that keep track of the current state.

2.4.6 Function Symbols

The planning language $\mathcal{L}$ can be extended to include function symbols. However, function symbols must be used with care because their presence can make planning problems undecidable (see Chapter 3). Also, some classical planning procedures work by creating all possible ground instances of every atom, which is not possible with function symbols because there may be infinitely many ground atoms.

2.4.7 Attached Procedures

Attached procedures can sometimes be used to evaluate predicates and function symbols. For example, suppose we want to formulate a DWR domain such that each container c has a numeric weight weight(c), and we can load c onto a robot r only if the container's weight is less than the robot's weight limit maxweight(r). Then for the load operator, we might have a constraint less(weight(c),maxweight(r)), where less is a predicate evaluated by a procedure that returns true if weight(c) < maxweight(r)) and false otherwise.

The ability to perform computations with attached procedures can be crucial in real-world planning problems. However, attached procedures require other computational means than set difference and union for computing $\gamma(s, a)$. An attached procedure usually cannot be called unless all of its variables have been bound—a requirement that causes great difficulty for many classical planning procedures.

2.4.8 Extended Goals

Recall from Chapter 1 the notion of *extended goals*, which are requirements not only on the final state of the problem but also on the states traversed to get from the initial state to the final state. Part V of this book describes some formalisms that explicitly incorporate extended goals, but these are not classical planning formalisms.

Extended goals are not allowed in classical planning problems *per se*, but certain kinds of planning problems with extended goals can be mapped into equivalent classical planning problems.[5] Here are several examples.

- Consider a DWR domain in which there is some location bad-loc to which we never want our robots to move. We can express this by changing the move operator to include an additional precondition $\neg$ at(r, bad-loc).
- Consider a DWR problem in which we want r1 to go first to loc1 and later to loc2. We can express this by adding an additional effect visited(m) to the move operator and putting both visited(loc1) and at(loc2) into the problem's goal formula.
- Suppose we want to require every solution to contain five actions or fewer. Like the above problem, this one requires us to extend classical planning to include function symbols. Then we can put an atom count(f(f(f(f(f(0)))))) in the initial state, add a precondition count(f(y)) to every action, and add effects $\neg$count(f(y)) and count(y) to every action.
- Consider a DWR problem in which we want r1 to visit loc1 twice. This problem cannot be translated into a classical planning problem that has the same set of solutions as the original problem. We could keep track of whether we have visited loc1 twice by introducing two different move operators move_1 and move_2 that have slightly different preconditions and effects—but if we do this, then we no longer have the same set of solutions as in the original planning problem. We can ensure that r1 visits loc1 twice if we extend the classical formalism to include the predicate symbols, function symbols, and attached procedures needed to perform integer arithmetic. If we do this, then we can put into the initial state a set of atoms consisting of visited(l,0) for every location l. Next, we can modify the move(r, l, m) operator to have a precondition visited(m, i) and effects $\neg$visited(m, i) and visited($m, i + 1$). Finally, we can add an additional goal visited(loc1, 2).
- Suppose we want to require that the number of times r1 visits loc1 must be at least three times the number of times it visits loc2. This again requires us to extend classical planning by introducing integer arithmetic. In this case, we can modify the planning problem as follows. First, put atoms into the initial state of the form visited(r, l, 0) for every robot r and every location l. Next, modify the operator move(r, l, m) to have an additional precondition visited(r, m, i) and additional effects $\neg$visited(r, m, i) and visited($r, m, i + 1$). Finally, modify the goal to include the atoms visited(r1,loc1,i), visited(r1,loc2,j), and $i \geq 3j$.

In several of these examples, it was necessary to extend classical planning to accommodate function symbols and integer arithmetic. As we discussed in

5. Unlike the other subsections, this one does not discuss a way to extend the classical representation scheme. Instead, it discusses how to map certain kinds of nonclassical planning problems into classical planning problems.

Sections 2.4.6 and 2.4.7, not all classical planning algorithms can be extended to accommodate these things. Furthermore, even with these extensions, certain kinds of extended goals cannot be accommodated (e.g., see Example 10.6).

2.5 State-Variable Representation

The state-variable representation is a third representation for classical planning systems, equivalent in expressiveness to the two previous ones, set-theoretic representation and classical representation. The main motivation here is to rely on *functions* instead of flexible *relations.*

2.5.1 State Variables

For example, consider the atom at(r1, loc1) in the classical representation of the DWR domain: it represents an element of a relation between a robot r1 and a location loc1. The truth value of this relation varies from one state to another. However, because r1 cannot be at two places at once and it is necessarily somewhere, then, for any given state s, there is *one and only one* location l such that at(r1, l) holds in s. In our intended model of this domain, this relation is a *function* that maps the set of states into the set of locations.

It can be advantageous to represent this relation using an explicit functional notation, e.g., $\text{rloc}_{\text{r1}} : S \rightarrow \text{locations}$, such that the value of $\text{rloc}_{\text{r1}}(s)$ gives the unique location of robot r1 in state s. Here, the symbol rloc_{r1} is a *state-variable symbol* that denotes a *state-variable function* whose values are characteristic attributes of the current state.

Furthermore, if there are several robots in a domain, it is convenient to rely on a more general notation in order to refer to the location of any robot r. Hence, instead of defining one state-variable rloc_{r1} for each robot in the domain, we will use a function from the set of robots and the set of states into the set of locations, e.g., $\text{rloc}(\text{r1}, s) = \text{loc1}$.

Let D be the finite set of all constant symbols in a planning domain. For example, in the DWR domain, D might include containers, robots, locations, cranes, and so forth. It is convenient to partition D into various *classes* of constants, such as the classes of robots, locations, cranes, and containers. We will represent each constant by an *object symbol* such as r1, loc2, or crane1.

In order to write unground expressions (see upcoming discussions), we will use *object variables.* These are variable symbols that range over sets of constants.[6] Each object variable v will have a range D^v that is the union of one or more classes. A term is either a constant or an object variable.

6. These are the usual variables in a first-order language, qualified here as object variables to distinguish them from state variables.

A k-ary *state variable* is an expression of the form $x(v_1, \ldots, v_k)$, where x is a state-variable symbol, and each v_i is either an object symbol or an object variable. A state variable denotes an element of a state-variable function,

$$x : D_1^x \times \ldots \times D_k^x \times S \rightarrow D_{k+1}^x,$$

where each $D_i^x \subseteq D$ is the union of one or more classes.

Example 2.13 Consider a simplified DWR domain in which there are no piles and no cranes; robots can load and unload containers autonomously. As we said earlier, we can use rloc(r1, s) to designate the current location of the robot r1. In a state s we might have rloc(r1, s) = loc1; in another state s' we might have rloc(r1, s') = loc2; hence rloc: robots $\times S \rightarrow$ locations.

Similarly, cpos(c1, s) could designate the current position of the container c1, which is either a location or a robot if c1 is on a robot. Thus in a state s we might have cpos(c1, s) = loc1, and in another state we might have cpos(c1, s') = r1. Hence cpos: containers $\times S \rightarrow$ locations $\cup$ robots.

Finally, rload: robots $\times S \rightarrow$ containers $\cup$ {nil} can be used as a state variable to identify which container is loaded on a robot, if any. ■

Since all state variables depend on the current state, the $(k+1)$th argument of a k-ary state variable will be left implicit: $x(v_1, \ldots, v_k) = v_{k+1}$ refers implicitly to the value of this state variable in the current state s.

A state variable $x(c_1, \ldots, c_k)$ is *ground* if each c_i is a constant in D_i^x. A state variable $x(v_1, \ldots, v_k)$ is *unground* if one or more of $v_1, \ldots, v_k$ are object variables. For example, rloc(r) is an unground state variable, and rloc(r1) and cpos(c1) are ground state variables.

A state variable is intended to be a characteristic attribute of a state. Hence, in this representation a state s is specified by giving the values in s of all the ground state variables. More specifically, for every ground state variable $x(c_1, \ldots, c_k)$, a state s includes a syntactic expression of the form $x(c_1, \ldots, c_k) = c_{k+1}$ such that c_{k+1} is the value of $x(c_1, \ldots, c_k)$ in s, each c_i being a constant in the appropriate range.

Notice that the state variables are not necessarily independent, in the sense that they may not take any values within their respective domains independently of each other. In Example 2.13 we have rload (r) = c iff cpos (c) = r, e.g., we cannot have a meaningful state s with rload(r1) = c1 and cpos(c1) = loc2.

Example 2.14 Continuing the previous example, consider a planning problem that has one robot (r1), three containers (c1, c2, c3), and three locations (l1, l2, l3). Here are some examples of possible states for this problem:

$$s_0 = \{\text{rloc(r1)} = \text{l1}, \text{rload(r1)} = \text{nil}, \text{cpos(c1)} = \text{l1}, \text{cpos(c2)} = \text{l2}, \text{cpos(c3)} = \text{l2}\}$$

$$s_1 = \{\text{rloc(r1)} = \text{l1}, \text{rload(r1)} = \text{c1}, \text{cpos(c1)} = \text{r1}, \text{cpos(c2)} = \text{l2}, \text{cpos(c3)} = \text{l2}\}$$

■

Some properties, such as adjacent(loc1, loc2) in the DWR domain, do not vary from one state to another. We called these properties *rigid relations*. For a k-ary rigid relation $r(v_1, \ldots, v_k)$, there will be sets $D_1^r, \ldots, D_k^r$ such that each D_i^r is the union of one or more classes and $r \subseteq D_1^r \times \ldots \times D_k^r$. For example, adjacent $\subseteq$ locations $\times$ locations.

By definition, rigid relations are invariant for a given planning domain. Hence, they do not need to be stated in every state. They have to be specified in the problem statement, together with the specification of the various classes of the constants in the domain, e.g., locations(loc2), robots(r1), containers(c3), adjacent(loc1,loc2), adjacent(loc2,loc3), etc.

2.5.2 Operators and Actions

Let us define planning operators and actions for the state-variable representation.

Definition 2.10 A *planning operator* is a triple $o = (\text{name}(o), \text{precond}(o), \text{effects}(o))$ where:

- name(o) is a syntactic expression of the form $n(u_1, \ldots, u_k)$, where n is a symbol called an *operator symbol*, $u_1, \ldots, u_k$ are all of the object variable symbols that appear anywhere in o, and n is unique (i.e., no two operators can have the same operator symbol).
- precond(o) is a set of expressions on state variables and relations.
- effects(o) is a set of assignments of values to state variables of the form $x(t_1, \ldots, t_k) \leftarrow t_{k+1}$, where each t_i is a term in the appropriate range. ■

Example 2.15 Consider the simplified DWR domain in which there are no piles and no cranes; robots can load and unload containers autonomously. This simplified domain has only three operators.

move(r, l, m)
;; robot r at location l moves to an adjacent location m
precond: rloc(r) $= l$, adjacent(l, m)
effects: rloc(r) $\leftarrow m$

load(c, r, l)
;; robot r loads container c at location l
precond: rloc(r) $= l$, cpos(c) $= l$, rload(r) $=$ nil
effects: rload(r) $\leftarrow c$, cpos(c) $\leftarrow r$

unload(c, r, l)
;; robot r unloads container c at location l
precond: rloc(r) $= l$, rload(r) $= c$
effects: rload(r) $\leftarrow$ nil, cpos(c) $\leftarrow l$

Here, c, r, l, and m are object variables. There are three state variables in these operators, rloc(r), rload(r), and cpos(c):

rloc: robots $\times S \rightarrow$ locations
rload: robots $\times S \rightarrow$ containers $\cup$ {nil}
cpos: containers $\times S \rightarrow$ locations $\cup$ robots

There is one rigid relation: adjacent $\subseteq$ locations $\times$ locations. To keep the notation simple, the state argument in state variables is implicit: the conditions in precond(a) refer to the values of state variables in a state s, whereas the updates in effects(a) refer to the values in the state $\gamma(s, a)$. This is similar to the notation used in the set-theoretic and classical representations where the effects$^+$ and effects$^-$ of an action refer also to changes in $\gamma(s, a)$. Note that the types of object variables, here left implicit, can be specified in a straightforward way in precond(o) with unary rigid relations: locations(l), robots(r), containers(c), etc. ■

An action a is a ground operator o that meets the rigid relations in precond(o), i.e., every object variable in o is replaced by a constant of the appropriate class such that these constants meet the rigid relations in precond(o). For example, the ground operator move(r1,loc1,loc4) is not considered to be an action if adjacent(loc1,loc4) does not hold in the domain.[7]

An action a is applicable in a state s when the values of the state variables in s meet the conditions in precond(a). In that case, the state $\gamma(s, a)$ is produced by updating the values of the state variables according to the assignments in effects(a). For example, in the domain of Figure 2.2 adjacent(loc2,loc1) holds, hence move(r1,loc2,loc1) is an action; this action is applicable to the state s_1 because rloc(r1) $=$ loc2 in state s_1.

As in the classical representation, the set of states S is defined as the states that are reachable with the specified planning operators from some initial state, given the rigid relations of the problem.

A goal is given by specifying the values of one or more ground state variables. For example, $g =$ {cpos(c1) $=$ loc2, cpos(c2) $=$ loc3} specifies that the container c1 has to be brought to location loc2 and c2 to loc3. More generally, a goal can be specified with a set of expressions on state variables, as in the preconditions of operators.

2.5.3 Domains and Problems

Let us now summarize what has been introduced so far and define more formally planning domains and problems. A state-variable representation relies on the following ingredients.

---

7. This is a simple matter of economy because this ground operator cannot contribute to any state transition.

- *Constant symbols*, also called *object symbols*, are partitioned into disjoint classes corresponding to the objects of the domain, e.g., the finite sets of robots, locations, cranes, containers, and piles in the DWR domain.
- *Object variable symbols*: these are typed variables, each of which ranges over a class or the union of classes of constants, e.g., $r \in$ robots, $l \in$ locations, etc.
- *State variable symbols*: these are functions from the set of states and zero or more sets of constants into a set of constants, e.g., rloc, rload, and cpos.
- *Relation symbols*: these are rigid relations on the constants that do not vary from state to state for a given planning domain, e.g., adjacent(loc1,loc2), belong(pile1,loc1), attached(crane1,loc1).
- *Planning operators*: they have preconditions that are sets of expressions on state variables and relations plus effects that are sets of assignments of values to state variables, as illustrated in Example 2.15.

A planning language $\mathcal{L}$ in the state-variable representation is given by the definition of a finite set of state variables X, a finite set of rigid relations R, and the sets of constants that define their domains.

Let X be the set of all ground state variables of $\mathcal{L}$, i.e., if x is a k-ary state variable in X, then for every tuple $(c_1, \ldots, c_k) \in D_1^x \times \ldots \times D_k^x$ that meets the rigid relations in R, the ground state variables $x(c_1, \ldots, c_k) \in X$.

Definition 2.11 Let $\mathcal{L}$ be a planning language in the state-variable representation defined by X and R. A *planning domain* in $\mathcal{L}$ is a restricted state-transition system $\Sigma = (S, A, \gamma)$ such that:

- $S \subseteq \prod_{x \in X} D_x$, where D_x is the range of the ground state variable x; a state s is denoted $s = \{(x = c) \mid x \in X\}$, where $c \in D_x$.
- $A = \{$all ground instances of operators in O that meet the relations in $R\}$, where O is a set of operators as defined earlier; an action a is applicable to a state s iff every expression $(x = c)$ in precond(a) is also in s.
- $\gamma(s, a) = \{(x = c) \mid x \in X\}$, where c is specified by an assignment $x \leftarrow c$ in effects(a) if there is such an assignment, otherwise $(x = c) \in s$.
- S is closed under γ, i.e., if $s \in S$, then for every action a that is applicable to s, $\gamma(s, a) \in S$.

■

Definition 2.12 A *planning problem* is a triple $\mathcal{P} = (\Sigma, s_0, g)$, where s_0 is an initial state in S and the goal g is a set of expressions on the state variables in X.

■

The goal g may contain unground expressions; e.g., $g = \{$cpos$(c) =$ loc2$\}$ requires moving any container c to loc2. A state s satisfies a goal g if there is a substitution σ such that every expression of $\sigma(g)$ is in s. A goal g corresponds to a set of goal states S_g defined as follows:

$$S_g = \{s \in S \mid s \text{ satisfies } g\}$$

As in the classical representation, we can define the relevance of an action a for a goal g and $\gamma^{-1}(g, a)$. If we restrict for simplicity to ground goals, then an action a is relevant for g iff both of the following conditions hold:

- $g \cap \text{effects}(a) \neq \emptyset$.
- For every expression $(x = c)$ in g, effects(a) contains no assignment of the form $x \leftarrow d$ such that c and d are different constant symbols.

If a is relevant for g, then $\gamma^{-1}(g, a) = (g - \vartheta(a)) \cup \text{precond}(a)$, where $\vartheta(a) = \{(x = c) \mid (x \leftarrow c) \in \text{effects}(a)\}$.

Definition 2.13 The *statement* of a planning problem is a 4-tuple $P = (O, R, s_0, g)$, where O is the set of operators, R is the set of rigid relations, s_0 is the initial state, and g is the goal. ■

Note that the statement of a planning problem is here a 4-tuple, instead of a 3-tuple as in the previous representations. Because rigid relations are not explicit in the specification of the state, they cannot be deduced from s_0, hence we need the additional term R in P.

A state-variable representation is ground if no state variable has any arguments. As we will discuss in Section 2.6, ground state-variable representations are similar to set-theoretic representations, and unground state-variable representations are similar to classical representations. Note that a ground state-variable representation does not have rigid relations because it does not have object variables: these relations need to be specified implicitly through the actions in A.

As in the classical representation, a plan for a problem P is a sequence of actions $\pi = \langle a_1, \ldots, a_k \rangle$ such that a_1 is applicable to s_0, i.e., the conditions and relations in precond(a_1) are met in state s_0, a_2 is applicable in $\gamma(s_0, a_1), \ldots,$ and the conditions in the goal g are met in $\gamma(s_0, a_k)$.

2.5.4 Properties

We have not introduced logical connectors in preconditions or effects, neither in states or goals of this representation. Clearly, the lack of negation operators is not a restrictive assumption on the expressiveness of the representation.

- The negation in the effects of classical planning operators is already expressed here through the state-variable assignments because we are using functions instead of relations. For example, $\text{rloc}(r) \leftarrow m$ in the move operator of Example 2.15 corresponds to the two literals $\text{at}(r, m)$ and $\neg\, \text{at}(r, l)$ in the effects of that operator in Example 2.8.

- The negation in preconditions can be handled through a simple syntactical change, as discussed in the following section (in the comparison between the set-theoretic and the classical representations).

Furthermore, complex expressions on state variables, such as $\text{rload}(r) \neq \text{nil}$ or $\text{cpos}(c) \in \{\text{loc1}, \text{loc2}\}$, can easily be introduced in preconditions and goals, as will be illustrated in Section 8.3. Other extensions, similar to those discussed in Section 2.4, can also be added to the state-variable representation.

Recall that here a state s is a tuple $s \in \prod_{x \in X} D_x$: we said that s is specified by giving the value of every ground state variable in X. In order to avoid a fastidious enumeration of all the ground state variables,[8] it is possible to rely on a *default value assumption*, similar to the *closed-world assumption* that assumes the value false for every atom not explicitly stated as true. More interesting schemes are possible when the range of a state variable is an ordered set or a lattice.

Finally, let us go back to the advantages of the state-variable representation. In classical planning, these advantages are simply the conciseness of the functional notation. This conciseness goes beyond what has been illustrated up to here. For example, some of the axiomatic inference extensions of classical planning, discussed in Section 2.4.5, are already provided in the state-variable representation. An axiom such as Formula 2.2, which states that a crane is empty iff it is not holding anything, is simply expressed through a state variable. For example, $\text{holds}: \text{cranes} \times S \rightarrow \text{containers} \cup \{\text{nil}\}$ tells us that the crane k is empty iff $\text{holds}(k) = \text{nil}$. Similarly, a state variable that denotes what object, if any, is above a container, e.g., $\text{above}: (\text{containers} \cup \{\text{pallet}\}) \times S \rightarrow \text{containers} \cup \{\text{nil}\}$, tells us that a container c is at the top of a pile iff $\text{above}(c) = \text{nil}$. Hence, we do not need to manage explicitly state variables equivalent to the predicates empty and top. Other advantages of the state-variable representation will appear later, in particular in Part IV, when we will go beyond classical planning.

2.6 Comparisons

From a theoretical point of view, the classical and state-variable representation schemes have equivalent expressivity: a problem represented in one of them can easily be translated into the other with at most a linear increase in size. To translate a classical representation into a state-variable representation, replace every positive literal $p(t_1, \ldots, t_n)$ with a state-variable expression of the form $p(t_1, \ldots, t_n) = 1$ and every negative literal $\neg p(t_1, \ldots, t_n)$ with a state-variable expression of the form $p(t_1, \ldots, t_n) = 0$.

Here is how to translate a state-variable representation into a classical representation. First, in the initial state and the preconditions of all operators, replace every

8. For the same domain, there are in general fewer ground state variables than ground atoms in the classical representation: if $|D_x| = 2^m$ then x corresponds to m propositions.

state-variable expression $x(t_1, \ldots, t_n) = v$ with an atom of the form $x(t_1, \ldots, t_n, v)$. Next, for every state-variable assignment $x(t_1, \ldots, t_n) \leftarrow v$ that appears in the effects of an operator, replace it with a pair of literals $\neg x(t_1, \ldots, t_n, w)$ and $x(t_1, \ldots, t_n, v)$, and insert $x(t_1, \ldots, x_n, w)$ into the operator's preconditions.

Classical and state-variable representations are more expressive than set-theoretic representations. Although all three representation schemes can still represent the same set of planning domains, a set-theoretic representation of a problem may take exponentially more space than the equivalent classical and state-variable representations. For example, suppose we have a classical representation in which the number of constant symbols is k. Then each n-ary predicate corresponds to k^n propositions, and if a classical operator's preconditions and effects lists each contain two n-ary predicates, then the operator corresponds to $(4k)^n$ set-theoretic actions. For a more concrete example, see Example 2.5 (see page 25).

If we restrict all of the atoms and state variables to be ground, then from a theoretical point of view the set-theoretic, classical, and state-variable representation schemes are essentially equivalent: each can be translated into the other with at most a linear increase in size. More specifically:

- Ground classical and ground state-variable representations can be translated into each other as described earlier.
- To translate a set-theoretic representation into a ground classical representation, replace each action $a = (\text{precond}(a), \text{effects}^+(a), \text{effects}^-(a))$ with an operator whose preconditions and effects are $\text{precond}(a)$ and $\text{effects}^+(a) \cup \{\neg(e) \mid e \in \text{effects}^-(a)\}$.
- To translate a ground classical representation into a set-theoretic representation, do the following. First, for every negated atom $\neg e$ that appears anywhere as a precondition, create a new atom e', replace $\neg e$ with e' wherever the latter occurs as a precondition, add an additional effect $\neg e'$ to every operator whose effects include e, and add an additional effect e' to every operator whose effects include $\neg e$. Next, replace each ground atom $p(c_1, \ldots, c_n)$ (where each c_i is a constant symbol) with a proposition symbol $p_{c_1,\ldots,c_n}$. Next, replace each operator $(o, \text{precond}(o), \text{effects}(o))$ with an action $(\text{precond}(o), \text{effects}^+(o), \text{effects}^-(o))$.
- Ground state-variable representations can be translated into set-theoretic representations and vice versa by first translating them into classical representations and then translating them into the desired representation with one of the methods outlined earlier.

Beyond these theoretical considerations, there may be practical reasons why one or another of these representation schemes is preferable in a given domain. For example, if we want to express a concept that is essentially a single-valued function, e.g., the location of a robot r1, then it may be more convenient to use a state-variable representation (e.g., location(r1) = loc1) than a classical representation (e.g., location(r1,loc1)) because the former avoids the necessity of explicitly deleting location(r1,loc1) in order to assert location(r1,loc2).

2.7 Discussion and Historical Remarks

In the planning literature, there has often been confusion between the language for specifying a planning problem and the model of that problem (i.e., the state-transition system). This confusion is reflected in our somewhat awkward distinction between a planning problem and the statement of a planning problem (see Section 2.2.3).

Early work on automated planning was heavily influenced by work on automated theorem proving. One of the first formulations of automated planning [249] used an axiomatic description of the initial state, goal, and planning operators; used resolution theorem proving to produce a constructive proof that a plan exists; and then used answer extraction to find the actual plan (see Chapter 12). However, this approach was hampered by a problem that became known as the *frame problem* [383], which was the problem of specifying axiomatically not only what changes an operator would make to a state but also what elements of the state it would leave unchanged. One motivation for the development of the classical planning formulation was that it provided a simple solution to the frame problem: in the classical formulation, any atom not mentioned in an operator's effects remains unchanged.

The classical representation scheme is linked to STRIPS (see [189] and Chapter 4), an early automated planning system. In the original version of STRIPS, the states and planning operators were similar to those of classical planning, but the operators had more expressive power. Each operator had a precondition list, add list, and delete list, and these were allowed to contain arbitrary well-formed formulas in first-order logic. However, there were a number of problems with this formulation, such as the difficulty of providing a well-defined semantics for it [362].

In subsequent work, researchers restricted the representation so that the preconditions, add lists, and delete lists would contain only atoms. Nilsson used this formulation to describe STRIPS in his 1980 textbook [426]. Hence, the operators and the representation scheme became known as STRIPS-style operators and STRIPS-style planning, respectively.

In the UCPOP planner [436], Penberthy and Weld introduced a syntactic modification of STRIPS-style operators in which the operators did not have add lists and delete lists but instead had positive and negative effects. This representation is the basis of our classical planning operators. Classical planning and STRIPS-style planning have equivalent expressive power, in the sense that any classical planning problem can easily be translated into a STRIPS-style planning problem with the same set of solutions and vice versa (see Exercise 2.13).

The semantics of classical planning has been addressed by Lifschitz [362]. The community working on reasoning on action and change studies more ambitious representations in a logical framework, e.g., for handling the frame problem in general state-transition systems (without the restrictive assumptions A0 through A7 introduced in Chapter 1), for dealing with operators that may have implicit effects (the so-called ramification problem) and implicit preconditions (the qualification problem). A general framework for the study of the representations of actions is proposed by Sandewall [463].

The Action Description Language (ADL) representation, introduced by Pednault [434, 435], proposes a trade-off between the expressiveness of general logical formalism and the computation complexity of reasoning with that representation, i.e., computing the transition function γ. Starting from UCPOP [436], several planners [120, 142, 433, 438] were generalized to ADL or to representations close to ADL that handle most of the extensions introduced in Section 2.4. These extensions have been implemented in the PDDL planning language used in the AIPS (International Conference on AI Planning and Scheduling) planning competitions [196, 387].

Syntactic constructs similar to our state variables have been used in operations research for many years [422] and have been used indirectly in AI planning, e.g., to encode classical planning problems as integer programming problems [539]. The idea of using state variables rather than logical atoms directly in the planning operators was introduced in Bäckströms's planner SAS [38, 39, 40, 286] and in several other planners such as IxTeT [224]. We will come back to the latter in the temporal planning chapter (Chapter 14). The work on the former planner led to the extensive study of the complexity of several classes of state-variable planning, corresponding to a broad range of interesting syntactic and structural restrictions.

The set-theoretic, classical, and state-variable representation schemes all use a special case of the well-known *closed-world assumption*: the only atoms or state-variable expressions that are true in a state are the ones explicitly specified in the state.

The notion of two planning formalisms having "equivalent expressivity," which we discussed informally in Section 2.6, has been defined formally by Nebel [418], who defines two representation schemes to have equivalent expressivity if there are polynomial-time translations between them that preserve plan size exactly.

In this chapter, we have avoided discussing a plan's cost and whether it is optimal. This notion was not emphasized in the early years of research on classical planning because it was difficult enough to find a plan at all without worrying about whether the plan was optimal. However, some of the later formulations of classical planning (e.g., [560]) include cost explicitly. The usual way of doing this is to assume that each action has a cost and that the cost of a plan is the sum of the costs of its actions. However, this formulation is relatively limited in comparison with more sophisticated notions used in fields such as scheduling and operations research, such as monotonic cost functions, flexibility of a plan in order to allow for changes, penalties for achieving some but not all goals [355], and Pareto optimality [209].

2.8 Exercises

2.1 Here is a classical planning problem that involves moving blocks around on a table.

$s_0 = \{\mathsf{on(c1, table)}, \mathsf{on(c3, c1)}, \mathsf{clear(c3)}, \mathsf{on(c2, table)}, \mathsf{clear(c2)}\}$
$g = \{\mathsf{on(c2, c2)}, \mathsf{on(c3, c3)}\}$

pickup(x)
  precond: on(x,table), clear(x)
  effects: ¬on(x,table), ¬clear(x), holding(x)

putdown(x)
  effects: holding(x)
  precond: ¬holding(x), on(x,table), clear(x)

unstack(x, y)
  precond: on(x, y), clear(x)
  effects: ¬on(x, y), ¬clear(x), holding(x), clear(y)

stack(x, y)
  effects: holding(x), clear(y)
  precond: ¬holding(x), ¬clear(y), on(x,table), clear(x)

(a) Rewrite the problem as a set-theoretic planning problem.

(b) Why are there separate operators for pickup and unstack, rather than a single operator for both?

(c) In the DWR domain, why do we not need two operators analogous to pickup and unstack for taking containers from a pile with a crane?

(d) What else can you say about the similarities and differences between this formulation of the Sussman anomaly and the one in Example 4.3 (see page 23)?

(e) Rewrite the problem as a state-variable planning problem.

(f) Rewrite the problem as a state-variable planning problem in which no state variable has any arguments.

2.2 Let $P_1 = (O, s_0, g_1)$ and $P_2 = (O, s_0, g_2)$ be two classical planning problems that have the same operators and initial state. Let $\pi_1 = \langle a_1, \ldots, a_n \rangle$ be any solution for P_1, and $\pi_2 = \langle b_1, \ldots, b_n \rangle$ be any solution for P_2.

(a) If $\pi_1 \cdot \pi_2$ is executable in P_2, then is it a solution for P_2?

(b) If no operator has negative effects, then is $\langle a_1, b_1, a_2, b_2, \ldots, a_n, b_n \rangle$ a solution for $(O, s_0, g_1 \cup g_2)$?

(c) Suppose no operator has any negative effects, and let π_2' be any permutation of π_2. Is π_2' a solution for P_2?

2.3 Let $P = (O, s_0, g)$ be the statement of a classical planning problem. In each of the following, explain the reason for your answer.

(a) Let $\Pi = \{\pi \mid \pi \text{ is applicable to } s_0\}$. Is Π finite?

(b) Let $S = \{\gamma(s_0, \pi) \mid \pi \in \Pi\}$. Is S finite?

(c) Let $\Pi' = \{\pi \mid \pi$ is nonredundant and is applicable to $s_0\}$. Is Π' finite?

(d) Suppose no operator has any negative effects, and let π' be any permutation of π. Is π' a solution for P?

(e) If π_1 and π_2 are plans, then π_1 is a *subplan* of π_2 if all actions in π_1 also appear in π_2 in the same order (although possibly with other actions in between). If π is a solution for P, then will π have a subplan that is a shortest solution for P?

(f) Let π be a solution for P, and let $P' = (O, s_0, g')$, where $g \subseteq g'$. Is π a subplan of a solution for P'?

2.4 Let Σ be the planning domain described in Example 2.7 (see page 27). Suppose we map the classical representation of Σ into a set-theoretic representation as described in Section 2.6. How many states will the set-theoretic representation contain? How many actions will it contain?

2.5 Specify the operators of the DWR domain of Example 2.8 (see page 29) entirely in a state-variable representation. Apply this set of operators to the domain of Example 2.7 extended with a third pile p3 and a second crane, both in loc2. The initial state is as depicted in Figure 2.2 with p3 initially empty. The goal is to have all containers in pile p3 in the following order: pallet, c3, c2, c1.

2.6 In the planning domain described in Example 2.7 (see page 27), let s be a state that is missing one or more atoms of the form in(c, p), while the position of the containers is correctly specified by the on(c, c') predicates. Write a preprocessing procedure that will restore the missing atoms.

2.7 In the planning domain described in Example 2.7 (see page 27), let s be a state that is missing one or more atoms of the form top(c, p). Write a preprocessing procedure that will restore the missing atoms.

2.8 In the planning domain described in Example 2.7 (see page 27), let s be a state that is missing one or more atoms of the form on$(c$, pallet$)$. Write a preprocessing procedure that will restore the missing atoms.

2.9 Which of the three previous preprocessing procedures would also work correctly on goal formulas? Why?

2.10 How will it change the DWR domain if we redefine the take operator as follows?

take(k, l, c, d, p)
;; crane k at location l takes c off d in pile p
precond: belong(k, l), attached(p, l), empty(k),
in(c, p), top(c, p), on(c, d), in(d, p)
effects: holding(k, c), $\neg$ in(c, p), $\neg$ top(c, p),
$\neg$ on(c, d), top(d, p), $\neg$ empty(k)

2.11 In the definition of a classical operator, why did we require that each variable of precond(o) and effects(o) must be a parameter of o?

2.12 Give the statement of a classical planning problem and a solution π for the problem such that π is not redundant and not shortest.

2.13 Rewrite the DWR domain in the STRIPS-style planning formalism of Section 2.7. (Hint: Replace each negated atom with a new nonnegated atom.)

2.14 Let P be the statement of a classical planning problem in which all of the predicates are ground (i.e., there are no variable symbols). Write an algorithm for converting P into the statement of a set-theoretic planning problem.

2.15 Suppose a state of the world is an arbitrary pair of integer coordinates (x, y), and thus S is infinite. Suppose we have an action a such that $\gamma((x, y), a)$ is the state $(x + 1, y + 1)$. How many classical planning operators are needed to express a?

2.16 If we extended the classical representation scheme to allow function symbols, then how would your answer to Exercise 2.15 change?

2.17 Show that the total number of states for the domain corresponding to Figure 2.1 is $8n(n!)$ if there are $n > 0$ containers.

2.18 Prove Proposition 2.1 (see page 23).

2.19 Prove Proposition 2.2 (see page 23).

2.20 Prove Proposition 2.3 (see page 24).

2.21 How many classical planning operators would you need to represent the incr operator of Example 2.5 (see page 25)? How many conditional operators would you need?

2.22 One way function symbols can be used is to encode lists. For example, the list $\langle \mathsf{a}, \mathsf{b}, \mathsf{c} \rangle$ can be represented as cons(a, cons(b, cons(c, nil))), where cons is a binary function symbol and nil is a constant symbol. Write planning operators to put an element onto the front of a list and to remove the first element of a nonempty list.

CHAPTER 3

Complexity of Classical Planning

3.1 Introduction

Much planning research has been motivated by the difficulty of producing complete and correct plans. We now examine how the decidability and complexity of classical planning varies depending on a variety of conditions. The results in this chapter can be summarized as follows.

1. For classical planning, plan existence is *decidable*, i.e., it is possible to write an algorithm that takes as input a statement $P = (A, s_0, g)$ of a planning problem $\mathcal{P}$ and returns yes if $\mathcal{P}$ is solvable and no otherwise. This is independent of whether the statement of the problem uses the set-theoretic, classical, or state-variable representations.
2. There are a number of syntactic restrictions we can place on the planning operators to reduce the complexity of the planning problem. The computational complexity of classical planning varies from constant time to EXPSPACE-complete,[1] depending on which representation we use and which restrictions we make.
3. The classical and state-variable representation schemes can be extended to allow the terms to contain function symbols (e.g., see Section 2.4.6). Such an extension puts them outside of the set of restricted state-transition systems discussed in Chapter 2 because it means that the set of possible states can be infinite. In this case, plan existence is *semidecidable*. It is possible to write a procedure that always terminates and returns yes if $\mathcal{P}$ is solvable and never returns yes if $\mathcal{P}$ is unsolvable. However, if $\mathcal{P}$ is unsolvable, then there is no guarantee that the procedure will terminate. It remains semidecidable even if we make several restrictions on the planning operators.

1. See Appendix A.

4. All of these results are independent of whether or not we extend the planning operators to have conditional effects.

In this chapter, Section 3.3 discusses the decidability and undecidability results, Section 3.4 discusses the complexity results, Section 3.5 discusses the significance and limitations of the results, and Section 3.6 contains discussion and historical remarks. The results in this chapter are based largely on work by Bylander [100], Erol *et al.*[176], and Bäckström and Nebel [40].

3.2 Preliminaries

In order to analyze the decidability and complexity of planning problems, they must be reformulated as language-recognition problems. Appendix A discusses the details of how to do this. Given a set D of statements of planning problems, we let:

- PLAN-EXISTENCE(D) be the set of all statements $P \in D$ such that P represents a solvable planning problem; and
- PLAN-LENGTH(D) be the set of all statements $P \in D$ such that P represents a planning problem for which there is a solution that contains no more than k actions.

For example, D may be the set of all classical planning problems, or the set of all planning problems that can be obtained by extending the representation scheme to include function symbols, or the set of all classical problems in which none of the operators have negative effects, etc. When it is obvious what D is, we will omit it and just write PLAN-EXISTENCE or PLAN-LENGTH instead.

In our theorems and proofs, we will concentrate primarily on classical planning (i.e., on planning problems expressed using the classical representation scheme). However, in most cases this is sufficient to establish results for set-theoretic and state-variable planning as well because of the equivalences among them described in Section 2.6. Classical planning and state-variable planning are essentially equivalent; and set-theoretic planning, ground classical planning, and ground state-variable planning are all essentially equivalent.

We also consider a variety of syntactic extensions and restrictions on classical planning, such as allowing the terms to contain function symbols (see Section 2.4.6), not allowing the operators to have negative preconditions, not allowing them to have negative effects, and so forth. These extensions and restrictions are also applicable to set-theoretic planning, with one exception: it makes no sense to allow function symbols in set-theoretic planning because the latter does not have terms.

With one exception, equivalent extensions and restrictions can also be made for state-variable planning. As examples, both classical planning and state-variable planning can be extended to allow function symbols, and requiring classical planning operators to have no negative preconditions is equivalent to requiring state-variable planning operators to have no inequality preconditions.

The exception is that although we can restrict classical planning operators from having negative effects, there is no sensible way to accomplish the same thing in state-variable planning. If $x(v_1, \ldots, v_n) = c$ and a state-variable planning operator assigns $x(v_1, \ldots, v_n) \leftarrow d$, this automatically removes the old value, c.

Whenever the extensions and restrictions can sensibly be applied to set-theoretic and state-variable planning, our results for classical planning can be generalized to include them as well. We will point this out as appropriate.

3.3 Decidability and Undecidability Results

The decidability and undecidability results are summarized in Table 3.1. For ordinary classical planning, PLAN-EXISTENCE and PLAN-LENGTH are decidable. The same is true for both set-theoretic and state-variable planning. If we extend classical or state-variable planning to allow the terms to contain function symbols, then PLAN-LENGTH remains decidable, but PLAN-EXISTENCE becomes semidecidable. The latter is true even with several syntactic restrictions on the planning operators.

Table 3.1 Decidability of PLAN-EXISTENCE and PLAN-LENGTH.

Allow function symbols?	*Decidability of* PLAN-EXISTENCE	*Decidability of* PLAN-LENGTH
No[a]	Decidable	Decidable
Yes	Semidecidable[b]	Decidable

[a] This is ordinary classical planning.
[b] True even if we make several restrictions (see text).

PLAN-EXISTENCE becomes semidecidable. The latter is true even with several syntactic restrictions on the planning operators.

Proposition 3.1 *For classical, set-theoretic, and state-variable planning,* PLAN-EXISTENCE *is decidable.*

The above proposition is not hard to prove. For a classical planning problem, the number of possible states is finite, so it is possible to do a brute-force search to see whether a solution exists. The same is true of set-theoretic and state-variable planning.

Proposition 3.2 *If we extend classical planning or state-variable planning to allow the terms to contain function symbols, then* PLAN-LENGTH *is still decidable.*

Proof We present the proof only for classical planning; it is straightforward to generalize it to state-variable planning.

Let $P = (O, s_0, g)$ be the statement of a classical planning problem and k be a nonnegative integer. We can modify the **Lifted-backward-search** procedure of

Chapter 4 to exit with failure every time it reaches a plan of length k that is not a solution. It is not hard to see that this procedure is sound and is guaranteed to terminate. If we can also show that the procedure is complete, this will be sufficient to show that PLAN-LENGTH is decidable.

To show that the procedure is complete, let π be any solution for P of length k or less. If $|\pi| = 0$, then π is empty, so our procedure terminates immediately. Otherwise, let a_1 be the last action in π. Then a_1 is relevant for g, so it must be a substitution instance of some operator o_1 chosen in one of our procedure's nondeterministic traces. Thus, $\gamma^{-1}(g, a_1)$ is a substitution instance of $\gamma^{-1}(g, o_1)$. If $|\pi| = 1$, then s_0 satisfies $\gamma^{-1}(g, a_1)$, so it also satisfies $\gamma^{-1}(g, o_1)$, so the procedure terminates. Otherwise, let a_2 be the second-to-last action in π. Then a_2 is relevant for $\gamma^{-1}(g, a_1)$, so it must be a substitution instance of some operator o_2 chosen by one of our procedure's nondeterministic traces. Continuing in this manner, we can show that some execution trace of our procedure will terminate in $|\pi|$ iterations. ■

Proposition 3.3 *If we extend classical planning or state-variable planning to allow the terms to contain function symbols, then* PLAN-EXISTENCE *is semidecidable.*

Proof As before, we will present the proof just for classical planning.

Let $P = (O, s_0, g)$ be a statement of a planning problem. PLAN-EXISTENCE is no worse than semidecidable because **Lifted-backward-search**(P) will terminate if a solution exists for P.

To show that PLAN-EXISTENCE is not decidable, let $P = (O, s_0, g)$ be a statement of a planning problem such that each operator of O has no negative preconditions, no negative effects, and at most one positive effect. Then we can define a set of Horn clauses H_P as follows. Each atom $a \in s_0$ is also in H_P. Corresponding to the goal g, H_P includes the following Horn clause:

$$:\!-\ g$$

If $o \in O$ is an operator, there are atoms $p_1, \ldots, p_n, e$ such that precond(o) $= \{p_1, \ldots, p_n\}$ and effects(o) $= \{e\}$. Corresponding to this operator, H_P includes the following Horn clause:

$$e :\!-\ p_1, \ldots, p_n$$

It is straightforward to show that P and H_P are equivalent in the sense that P has a solution plan iff H_P is consistent. It is a well-known result of logic programming that it is not decidable whether H_P is consistent; thus it follows that it is not decidable whether P has a solution. ■

The same result holds regardless of whether or not the planning operators have negative preconditions, negative effects, more than one precondition, or conditional effects. The result is true even if the planning operators are fixed in advance (to enable the use of a domain-specific planning algorithm) or given as part of the input.

3.4 Complexity Results

As summarized in Table 3.2, the computational complexity for classical planning problems (and thus for most set-theoretic and state-variable planning problems)

Table 3.2 Complexity of classical planning.

Kind of representation	*How the operators are given*	*Allow negative effects?*	*Allow negative preconditions?*	*Complexity of* PLAN-EXISTENCE	*Complexity of* PLAN-LENGTH
Classical rep.	In the input	Yes	Yes/no	EXPSPACE-complete	NEXPTIME-complete
		No	Yes	NEXPTIME-complete	NEXPTIME-complete
		No	No	EXPTIME-complete	NEXPTIME-complete
			No[a]	PSPACE-complete	PSPACE-complete
	In advance	Yes	Yes/no	PSPACE[b]	PSPACE[b]
		No	Yes	NP[b]	NP[b]
			No	P	NP[b]
			No[a]	NLOGSPACE	NP
Set-theoretic or ground classical rep.	In the input	Yes	Yes/no	PSPACE-complete	PSPACE-complete
		No	Yes	NP-complete	NP-complete
			No	P	NP-complete
			No[a]/no[c]	NLOGSPACE-complete	NP-complete
	In advance	Yes/no	Yes/no	Constant time	Constant time
State-variable rep.	In the input	Yes[d]	Yes/no	EXPSPACE-complete	NEXPTIME-complete
	In advance	Yes[d]	Yes/no	PSPACE[b]	PSPACE[b]
Ground state-variable rep.	In the input	Yes[d]	Yes/no	PSPACE-complete	PSPACE-complete
	In advance	Yes[d]	Yes/no	Constant time	Constant time

[a] No operator has > 1 precondition.
[b] With PSPACE- or NP-completeness for some sets of operators.
[c] Each operator with > 1 precondition is the composition of other operators.
[d] There is no way to keep the operators from having negative effects.

varies from constant time to EXPSPACE-complete, depending on what kinds of restrictions we make. Rather than proving every entry in Table 3.2 (which would make for a very long chapter!), we will illustrate the proof techniques by proving the first entry in the table, which says that ordinary classical planning is EXPSPACE-complete.

The proof, which appears in Section 3.4.2, involves reducing a known EXPSPACE-complete language-recognition problem, the EXPSPACE-bounded Turing Machine problem, to classical planning. The proof depends on using function-free ground atoms to represent binary n-bit counters and function-free planning operators to increment and decrement these counters. Section 3.4.1 shows how this can be done.

3.4.1 Binary Counters

To represent a counter that can be incremented, we would like to have an atom $c(i)$ whose intuitive meaning is that the counter's value is i and an operator incr that deletes $c(i)$ and replaces it with $c(i+1)$. The problem is that without function symbols, we cannot directly represent the integer i nor the arithmetic operation on it. However, because we have the restriction $0 \leq i \leq 2^n - 1$ for some n, then we can achieve the same effect by encoding i in binary as

$$i = i_1 \times 2^{n-1} + i_2 \times 2^{n-2} + \cdots + i_{n-1} \times 2^1 + i_n,$$

where each i_k is either 0 or 1. Instead of the unary predicate $c(i)$, we can use an n-ary predicate $c(i_1, i_2, \ldots, i_n)$; and to increment the counter we can use the following operators:

$\mathsf{incr}_1(i_1, i_2, \ldots, i_{n-1})$
  precond: $c(i_1, i_2, \ldots, i_{n-1}, 0)$
  effects: $\neg c(i_1, i_2, \ldots, i_{n-1}, 0), c(i_1, i_2, \ldots, i_{n-1}, 1)$

$\mathsf{incr}_2(i_1, i_2, \ldots, i_{n-2})$
  precond: $c(i_1, i_2, \ldots, i_{n-2}, 0, 1)$
  effects: $\neg c(i_1, i_2, \ldots, i_{n-2}, 0, 1), c(i_1, i_2, \ldots, i_{n-2}, 1, 0)$

  $\vdots$

$\mathsf{incr}_n()$
  precond: $c(0, 1, 1, \ldots, 1)$
  effects: $c(0, 1, 1, \ldots, 1), c(1, 0, 0, \ldots, 0)$

For each $i < 2^n - 1$, exactly one of the incr_j will be applicable to $c(i_1, i_2, \ldots, i_n)$, and it will increment i by 1. If we also wish to decrement the counter, then similarly we can define a set of operators $\{\mathsf{decr}_k : k = 1, \ldots, n\}$ as follows:

$\mathsf{decr}_k(i_1, i_2, \ldots, i_{n-k+1})$
  precond: $c(i_1, i_2, \ldots, i_{n-k+1}, 1, 0, \ldots, 0)$

effects: $\neg c(i_1, i_2, \ldots, i_{n-k+1}, 1, 0, \ldots, 0)$,
$c(i_1, i_2, \ldots, i_{n-k+1}, 0, 1, \ldots, 1)$

For each $i > 0$, exactly one of the decr_k will be applicable to $c(i_1, i_2, \ldots, i_n)$, and it will decrement i by 1.

Suppose we want to have two n-bit counters having values $0 \le i \le 2^n$ and $0 \le j \le 2^n$ and an operator that increments i and decrements j simultaneously. If we represent the counters by n-ary predicates $c(i_1, i_2, \ldots, i_n)$ and $d(j_1, j_2, \ldots, j_n)$, then we can simultaneously increment i and decrement j using a set of operators $\{\mathsf{shift}_{hk} : h = 1, 2, \ldots, n,\ k = 1, 2, \ldots, n\}$ defined as follows:

$\mathsf{shift}_{hk}(i_1, i_2, \ldots, i_{n-h+1}, j_1, j_2, \ldots, j_{n-k+1})$
precond: $c(i_1, i_2, \ldots, i_{n-h+1}, 0, 1, 1, \ldots, 1)$,
$d(j_1, j_2, \ldots, j_{n-k+1}, 1, 0, 0, \ldots, 0)$
effects: $\neg\, c(i_1, i_2, \ldots, i_{n-h+1}, 0, 1, 1, \ldots, 1)$,
$\neg\, d(j_1, j_2, \ldots, j_{n-k+1}, 1, 0, 0, \ldots, 0)$,
$c(i_1, i_2, \ldots, i_{n-h+1}, 1, 0, 0, \ldots, 0)$,
$d(j_1, j_2, \ldots, j_{n-k+1}, 0, 1, 1, \ldots, 1)$

For each i and j, exactly one of the shift_{hk} will be applicable, and it will simultaneously increment i and decrement j.

For notational convenience, instead of explicitly defining a set of operators such as the set $\{\mathsf{incr}_h : h = 1, \ldots, n\}$ defined previously, we sometimes will informally define a single abstract operator such as:

$\mathsf{incr}(\underline{i})$
precond: $c(\underline{i})$
effects: $\neg c(\underline{i}), c(\underline{i+1})$

where $\underline{i}$ is the sequence $i_1, i_2, \ldots, i_n$ that forms the binary encoding of i. Whenever we do this, it should be clear from context how a set of actual operators could be defined to manipulate $c(i_1, i_2, \ldots, i_n)$.

3.4.2 Unrestricted Classical Planning

Proposition 3.4 *For classical planning,* PLAN-EXISTENCE *is* EXPSPACE*-complete.*

Proof In order to prove Proposition 3.4, it is necessary to prove (1) that PLAN-EXISTENCE is in EXPSPACE, and (2) that PLAN-EXISTENCE is EXPSPACE-hard. Here is a summary of each of those proofs.

The number of ground instances of predicates involved is exponential in terms of the input length. Hence the size of any state cannot be more than exponential. Starting from the initial state, we nondeterministically choose an operator and apply it. We do this repeatedly until we reach the goal, solving the planning problem in NEXPSPACE. NEXPSPACE is equal to EXPSPACE, hence our problem is in EXPSPACE.

To see that PLAN-EXISTENCE is EXPSPACE-hard, we define a polynomial reduction from the EXPSPACE-bounded Turing Machine problem, which is defined as follows:

> Given a Turing Machine M that uses at most an exponential number of tape cells in terms of the length of its input and an input string x, does M accept the string x?

To transform this into a planning problem, a Turing Machine M is normally denoted by $M = (K, \Sigma, \Gamma, \delta, q_0, F)$. $K = \{q_0, \ldots, q_m\}$ is a finite set of states. $F \subseteq K$ is the set of final states. Γ is the finite set of allowable tape symbols; we use # to represent the "blank" symbol. $\Sigma \subseteq \Gamma$ is the set of allowable input symbols. $q_0 \in K$ is the start state. δ, the next-move function, is a mapping from $K \times \Gamma$ to $K \times \Gamma \times \{\text{Left}, \text{Right}\}$.

Suppose we are given M and an input string $x = (x_0, x_2, \ldots, x_{n-1})$ such that $x_i \in \Sigma$ for each i. To map this into a planning problem, the basic idea is to represent the machine's current state, the location of the head on the tape, and the contents of the tape by a set of atoms.

The transformation is as follows.

Predicates: contains$(\underline{i}, c)$ means that c is in the ith tape cell, where $\underline{i} = i_1, i_2, \ldots, i_n$ is the binary representation of i. We can write c on cell i by deleting contains$(\underline{i}, d)$ and adding contains$(\underline{i}, c)$, where d is the symbol previously contained in cell i.

$State_F(q)$ means that the current state of the Turing Machine is q. $h(\underline{i})$ means that the current head position is i. We can move the head to the right or left by deleting $h(\underline{i})$ and adding $h(\underline{i+1})$ or $h(\underline{i-1})$. counter$(\underline{i})$ is a counter for use in initializing the tape with blanks. start() denotes that initialization of the tape has been finished.

Constant symbols: $\Gamma \cup K \cup \{0, 1\}$.

Operators: Each operator in this subsection that contains increment or decrement operations (such as mapping i to $i+1$ or $i-1$) should be expanded into n operators as described in Section 3.4.1.

Whenever $\delta(q, c)$ equals (s, c', Left), we create the following operator:

$L^{s,c'}_{q,c}(\underline{i})$
  precond: $h(\underline{i}), State_F(q)$, contains$(\underline{i}, c)$, start()
  effects: $\neg h(\underline{i}), \neg State_F(q), \neg$ contains$(\underline{i}, c)$,
  $h(\underline{i-1}), State_F(s)$, contains$(\underline{i}, c')$

Whenever $\delta(q, c)$ equals (s, c', Right), we create the following operator:

$R^{s,c'}_{q,c}(\underline{i})$
  precond: $h(\underline{i}), State_F(q)$, contains$(\underline{i}, c)$, start()
  effects: $\neg h(\underline{i}), \neg State_F(q), \neg$ contains$(\underline{i}, c)$,
  $h(\underline{i+1}), State_F(s)$, contains$(\underline{i}, c')$

We have the following operator that initializes the tape with blank symbols:

$I(\underline{i})$
precond: $\mathsf{counter}(\underline{i}), \neg\, \mathsf{start}()$
effects: $\mathsf{counter}(\underline{i+1}), \mathsf{contains}(\underline{i}, \#)$

The following operator ends the initialization phase:

$I^*()$
precond: $\mathsf{counter}(\underline{2^n-1}), \neg\, \mathsf{start}()$
effects: $\mathsf{contains}(\underline{2^n-1}, \#), \mathsf{start}()$

Finally, for each $q \in F$ we have this operator:

$F_q()$
precond: $State_F(q)$
effects: $\mathsf{done}()$

Initial state: $\{\mathsf{counter}(\underline{n}), State_F(q_0), h(\underline{0})\} \cup \{\mathsf{contains}(\underline{i}, x_i) : i = 0, \ldots, n-1\}$.

Goal condition: $\mathsf{done}()$.

The transformation is polynomial both in time and space. It directly mimics the behavior of the Turing Machine. Thus PLAN-EXISTENCE is EXPSPACE-hard. ■

3.4.3 Other Results

Using techniques like the ones in the previous sections, complexity results can be proved for PLAN-EXISTENCE and PLAN-LENGTH in a large variety of situations. As summarized in Table 3.2, the computational complexity varies from constant time to EXPSPACE-complete, depending on a wide variety of conditions: whether or not negative effects are allowed; whether or not negative preconditions are allowed; whether or not the atoms are restricted to be ground (which is equivalent to set-theoretic planning); and whether the planning operators are given as part of the input to the planning problem or instead are fixed in advance. Here is a summary of how and why these parameters affect the complexity of planning.

1. If no restrictions are put on the planning problem $\mathcal{P}$, then as shown in Section 3.4.2, an operator instance might need to appear many times in the same plan, forcing us to search through all the states. Because the size of any state is at most exponential, PLAN-EXISTENCE can be solved in EXPSPACE.
2. If the planning operators are restricted to have no negative effects, then any predicate instance asserted remains true throughout the plan, hence no operator instance needs to appear in the same plan twice. Because the number of operator instances is exponential, this reduces the complexity of PLAN-EXISTENCE to NEXPTIME.
3. If the planning operators are further restricted to have no negative preconditions, then no operator can ever delete another's preconditions. Thus the

order of the operators in the plan does not matter, and the complexity of PLAN-EXISTENCE reduces to EXPTIME.

4. In spite of the restrictions above, PLAN-LENGTH remains NEXPTIME. Because we try to find a plan of length at most k, which operator instances we choose and how we order them makes a difference.
5. If each planning operator is restricted to have at most one precondition, then we can do backward search, and because each operator has at most one precondition, the number of the subgoals does not increase. Thus both PLAN-EXISTENCE and PLAN-LENGTH with these restrictions can be solved in PSPACE.
6. If we restrict all atoms to be ground, the number of operator instances and the size of each state reduce from exponential to polynomial. The complexity results for this case (and hence for set-theoretic planning) are usually one level lower than the complexity results for the nonground case.

   We could get the same amount of reduction in complexity by placing a constant bound on the arity of predicates and the number of variables in each operator. Set-theoretic planning corresponds to the case where the bound is zero.
7. If the operator set is fixed in advance, then the arity of predicates and the number of variables in each operator are bound by a constant. Thus, the complexity of planning with a fixed set of operators is the same as the complexity of set-theoretic planning. For classical planning with a fixed set of operators, the complexity of planning is at most in PSPACE, and there exist such domains for which planning is PSPACE-complete.

Examination of Table 3.2 reveals several interesting properties.

1. Extending the planning operators to allow conditional effects does not affect our results. This should not be particularly surprising because conditional operators are useful only when we have incomplete information about the initial state of the world or the effects of the operators, so that we can try to come up with a plan that would work in any situation that is consistent with the information available. Otherwise, we can replace the conditional operators with a number of ordinary operators to obtain an equivalent planning domain.
2. Comparing the complexity of PLAN-EXISTENCE in the set-theoretic case with the classical case reveals a regular pattern. In most cases, the complexity in the classical case is exactly one level harder than the complexity in the corresponding set-theoretic case. We have EXPSPACE-complete versus PSPACE-complete, NEXPTIME-complete versus NP-complete, EXPTIME-complete versus polynomial.
3. If negative effects are allowed, then PLAN-EXISTENCE is EXPSPACE-complete but PLAN-LENGTH is only NEXPTIME-complete. Normally, one would not expect PLAN-LENGTH to be easier than PLAN-EXISTENCE. In this case, it

happens because the length of a plan can sometimes be doubly exponential in the length of the input. In PLAN-LENGTH we are given a bound k, encoded in binary, which confines us to plans of length at most exponential in terms of the input. Hence finding the answer is easier in the worst case of PLAN-LENGTH than in the worst case of PLAN-EXISTENCE.

We do not observe the same anomaly in the set-theoretic case because the lengths of the plans are at most exponential in the length of the input. As a result, giving an exponential bound on the length of the plan does not reduce the complexity of PLAN-LENGTH.

4. PLAN-LENGTH has the same complexity regardless of whether or not negated preconditions are allowed. This is because what makes the problem hard is how to handle *enabling-condition interactions*, which are situations where a sequence of actions that achieves one subgoal might also achieve other subgoals or make it easier to achieve them. Although such interactions do not affect PLAN-EXISTENCE, they do affect PLAN-LENGTH because they make it possible to produce a shorter plan. It is not possible to detect and reason about these interactions if we plan for the subgoals independently; instead, we have to consider all possible operator choices and orderings, making PLAN-LENGTH NP-hard.

5. Negative effects are more powerful than negative preconditions. Thus, if the operators are allowed to have negative effects, then whether or not they have negated preconditions has no effect on the complexity.

3.5 Limitations

The results in this chapter say that the worst-case computational complexity of classical planning is quite high, even if we make severe restrictions. However, since these results are worst-case results, they do not necessarily describe the complexity of any particular classical planning domain.

As an example, consider the DWR domain. Since the planning operators for this domain have both negative preconditions and negative effects, this puts the domain into the class of planning problems in the first line of Table 3.2, i.e., the class for which PLAN-EXISTENCE is EXPSPACE-complete and PLAN-LENGTH is NEXPTIME-complete. We can get a much more optimistic measure of the complexity by observing that the operators are fixed in advance: this puts the DWR domain into the class of domains given in the fifth line of the table, where PLAN-EXISTENCE and PLAN-LENGTH are both in PSPACE.

Furthermore, by devising a domain-specific planning algorithm, we can get an even lower complexity. In the DWR domain, PLAN-EXISTENCE can be determined in polynomial time, and PLAN-LENGTH is only NP-complete. Chapter 4 gives a fast domain-specific planning algorithm for a restricted case of the DWR domain.

3.6 Discussion and Historical Remarks

What we call set-theoretic planning is usually called *propositional planning*, and its complexity has been heavily studied. The best-known works on this topic and the sources of the set-theoretic planning entries in Table 3.2 are Bylander [101] and Erol *et al.* [176]. Bylander [101] has also studied the complexity of propositional planning extended to allow a limited amount of inference in the domain theory. His complexity results for this case range from polynomial time to PSPACE-complete.

Littman *et al.* [365, 366] have analyzed the complexity of propositional planning if it is extended to allow probabilistic uncertainty (see Chapter 16). Their complexity results range from NP-complete to EXPTIME-complete depending on what kinds of restrictions are imposed.

Most of our results for classical planning come from Erol *et al.* [176]. They also describe some restrictions under which planning remains decidable when the planning formulation is extended to allow function symbols.

Our results on state-variable planning come from Bäckström *et al.* [38, 39, 40, 286]. They also describe several other sets of restrictions on state-variable planning. Depending on the restrictions, the complexity ranges from polynomial to PSPACE-complete.

3.7 Exercises

3.1 Let $\mathcal{P}$ be a set-theoretic planning problem in which the number of proposition symbols is r, the number of actions is a, and each operator has at most p preconditions and e effects. Write an upper bound on the number of states in $\mathcal{P}$.

3.2 Let $\mathcal{P}$ be a classical planning problem in which the number of predicate symbols is r, each predicate takes at most a arguments, the number of constant symbols is c, the number of operators is o, and each operator has at most p preconditions and e effects. Write an upper bound on the number of states in $\mathcal{P}$.

3.3 Suppose we extend classical planning to include function symbols. Write an algorithm that, given the statement of a planning problem P, returns yes if P has a solution of length k or less and no otherwise.

3.4 PLAN-EXISTENCE is EXPSPACE-complete for classical planning. However, every classical planning problem can be rewritten as a set-theoretic planning problem, and PLAN-EXISTENCE is only PSPACE-complete for set-theoretic planning. Resolve the apparent contradiction.

3.5 A *blocks-world planning problem* is a classical planning problem whose statement is as follows: The operators are those of Exercise 2.1 (see page 50), and the initial state and the goal are arbitrary sets of ground atoms in which every atom has one of the following forms: clear(x), holding(x), on(x, y), ontable(x). Let B be the set of all blocks-world planning problems.

(a) Write a polynomial-time algorithm to solve PLAN-EXISTENCE(B), thereby showing that PLAN-EXISTENCE(B) is in P.

(b) Write a polynomial-time nondeterministic algorithm to solve PLAN-LENGTH (B), thereby showing that PLAN-LENGTH(B) is in NP.

(c) Which lines of Table 3.2 include PLAN-EXISTENCE(B) and PLAN-LENGTH(B)? Resolve the apparent contradiction between this information and the results you proved in parts a and b of this exercise.

3.6 Write the exact set of operators produced by the transformation in Section 3.4.2 for the case where $n = 3$. If $s_0 = \{c(0, 0, 0)\}$ and $g = \{c(1, 1, 1)\}$, then what is the size of the state space?

3.7 If we rewrite the planning problem of Section 3.4.2 as a set-theoretic planning problem, how many actions will there be?

CHAPTER 4

State-Space Planning

4.1 Introduction

The simplest classical planning algorithms are *state-space search algorithms*. These are search algorithms in which the search space is a subset of the state space: Each node corresponds to a state of the world, each arc corresponds to a state transition, and the current plan corresponds to the current path in the search space.

In this chapter, Section 4.2 discusses algorithms that search forward from the initial state of the world to try to find a state that satisfies the goal formula. Section 4.3 discusses algorithms that search backward from the goal formula to try to find the initial state. Section 4.4 describes an algorithm that combines elements of both forward and backward search. Section 4.5 describes a fast domain-specific forward-search algorithm.

4.2 Forward Search

One of the simplest planning algorithms is the Forward-search algorithm shown in Figure 4.1. The algorithm is nondeterministic (see Appendix A). It takes as input the statement $P = (O, s_0, g)$ of a planning problem $\mathcal{P}$. If $\mathcal{P}$ is solvable, then Forward-search(O, s_0, g) returns a solution plan; otherwise it returns failure.

The plan returned by each recursive invocation of the algorithm is called a *partial solution* because it is part of the final solution returned by the top-level invocation. We will use the term *partial solution* in a similar sense throughout this book.

Although we have written Forward-search to work on classical planning problems, the same idea can be adapted to work on any planning problem in which we can (1) compute whether or not a state is a goal state, (2) find the set of all actions applicable to a state, and (3) compute a successor state that is the result of applying an action to a state.

Example 4.1 As an example of how Forward-search works, consider the DWR problem whose initial state is the state s_5 shown in Figure 2.3 and whose goal formula is

```
Forward-search(O, s0, g)
    s ← s0
    π ← the empty plan
    loop
        if s satisfies g then return π
        applicable ← {a | a is a ground instance of an operator in O,
                          and precond(a) is true in s}
        if applicable = ∅ then return failure
        nondeterministically choose an action a ∈ applicable
        s ← γ(s, a)
        π ← π.a
```

Figure 4.1 A forward-search planning algorithm. We have written it using a loop, but it can easily be rewritten to use a recursive call instead (see Exercise 4.2).

$g = \{$at(r1, loc1), loaded(r1, c3)$\}$. One of the execution traces of Forward-search chooses $a =$ move(r1, loc2, loc1) in the first iteration of the loop and $a =$ load(crane1, loc1, c3, r1) in the second iteration of the loop, producing the state s_6 shown in Figure 2.4. Since this state satisfies g, the execution trace returns:

$$\pi = \langle \text{move(r1, loc2, loc1), load(crane1, loc1, c3, r1)} \rangle$$

There are many other execution traces, some of which are infinite. For example, one of them makes the following infinite sequence of choices for a:

move(r1, loc2, loc1)

move(r1, loc1, loc2)

move(r1, loc2, loc1)

move(r1, loc1, loc2)

...

■

4.2.1 Formal Properties

Proposition 4.1 Forward-search *is sound, so any plan π returned by* Forward-search(O, s_0, g) *is a solution for the planning problem* (O, s_0, g).

Proof The first step is to prove that at the beginning of every loop iteration:

$$s = \gamma(s_0, \pi)$$

For the first loop iteration, this is trivial since π is empty. If it is true at the beginning of the ith iteration, then because the algorithm has completed $i - 1$ iterations, there are actions $a_1, \ldots, a_{i-1}$ such that $\pi = \langle a_1, \ldots, a_{i-1} \rangle$ and states $s_1, \ldots, s_{i-1}$ such that for $j = 1, \ldots, i-1$, $s_j = \gamma(s_{j-1}, a_j)$. If the algorithm exits at either of the **return** statements, then there is no $(i + 1)$th iteration. Otherwise, in the last three steps of the algorithm, it chooses an action a_i that is applicable to s_{i-1}, assigns

$$
\begin{aligned}
s &\leftarrow \gamma(s_{i-1}, a_i) \\
&= \gamma(\gamma(s_0, \langle a_1, \ldots, a_{i-1} \rangle), a_i) \\
&= \gamma(s_0, \langle a_1, \ldots, a_i \rangle),
\end{aligned}
$$

and assigns $\pi \leftarrow \langle a_1, \ldots, a_i \rangle$. Thus $s = \gamma(s_0, \pi)$ at the beginning of the next iteration.

If the algorithm exits at the first **return** statement, then it must be true that s satisfies g. Thus, because $s = \gamma(s_0, \pi)$, it follows that π is a solution to (O, s_0, g). ■

Proposition 4.2 *Let $\mathcal{P} = (O, s_0, g)$ be a classical planning problem, and let Π be the set of all solutions to $\mathcal{P}$. For each $\pi \in \Pi$, at least one execution trace of* Forward-search(O, s_0, g) *will return π.*

Proof Let $\pi_0 = \langle a_1, \ldots, a_n \rangle \in \Pi$. We will prove that there is an execution trace such that for every positive integer $i \leq n + 1$, $\pi = \langle a_1, \ldots, a_{i-1} \rangle$ at the beginning of the ith iteration of the loop (which means that the algorithm will return π_0 at the beginning of the $(n + 1)$th iteration). The proof is by induction on i.

- If $i = 0$, then the result is trivial.
- Let $i > 0$, and suppose that at the beginning of the ith iteration, $s = \gamma(s_0, \langle a_1, \ldots, a_{i-1} \rangle)$. If the algorithm exits at either of the **return** statements, then there is no $(i + 1)$st iteration, so the result is proved. Otherwise, $\langle a_1, \ldots, a_n \rangle$ is applicable to s_0, so $\langle a_1, \ldots, a_{i-1}, a_i \rangle$ is applicable to s_0, so a_i is applicable to $\gamma(s_0, \langle a_1, \ldots, a_{i-1} \rangle) = s$. Thus $a_i \in E$, so in the nondeterministic choice, at least one execution trace chooses $a = a_i$. This execution trace assigns

$$
\begin{aligned}
s &\leftarrow \gamma(s_0, \gamma(\langle a_1, \ldots, a_{i-1} \rangle), a_i) \\
&= \gamma(s_0, \langle a_1, \ldots, a_{i-1}, a_i \rangle)
\end{aligned}
$$

so $s = \gamma(s_0, \langle a_1, \ldots, a_{i-1}, a_i \rangle)$ at the beginning of the $(i + 1)$st iteration. ■

One consequence of Proposition 4.2 is that Forward-search is complete. Another consequence is that Forward-search's search space is usually much larger than it needs to be. There are various ways to reduce the size of the search space by modifying the algorithm to *prune* branches of the search space (i.e., cut off search below these branches). A pruning technique is *safe* if it is guaranteed not to prune every solution; in this case the modified planning algorithm will still be complete. If we have some notion of plan optimality, then a pruning technique is *strongly safe* if there is at least one optimal solution that it doesn't prune. In this case, at least one trace of the modified planning algorithm will lead to an optimal solution if one exists.

Here is an example of a strongly safe pruning technique. Suppose the algorithm generates plans π_1 and π_2 along two different paths of the search space, and suppose π_1 and π_2 produce the same state of the world s. If π_1 can be extended to form some solution $\pi_1 \cdot \pi_3$, then $\pi_2 \cdot \pi_3$ is also a solution, and vice versa. Thus we can prune one of π_1 and π_2, and we will still be guaranteed of finding a solution if one exists. Furthermore, if we prune whichever of π_1 and π_2 is longer, then we will still be guaranteed of finding a shortest-length solution if one exists.

Although the above pruning technique can remove large portions of a search space, its practical applicability is limited due to the following drawback: it requires us to keep track of states along more than one path. In most cases, this will make the worst-case space complexity exponential.

There are safe ways to reduce the branching factor of Forward-search without increasing its space complexity, but most of them are problem-dependent. Section 4.5 is an example.

4.2.2 Deterministic Implementations

Earlier we mentioned that in order for a depth-first implementation of a nondeterministic algorithm to be complete, it needs to detect and prune all infinite branches. In the Forward-search algorithm, this can be accomplished by modifying the algorithm to incorporate a simple loop-checking scheme: Keep a record of the sequence $(s_0, s_1, \ldots, s_k)$ of states on the current path, and return failure whenever there is an $i < k$ such that $s_k = s_i$. This will prevent sequences of assignments such as the one described in Example 4.1 (see page 69), but there are some domains in which the second modification will prune infinite sequences sooner than the first one.

To show that the modification works correctly, we need to prove two things: (1) that it causes the algorithm to return failure on every infinite branch of the search space, and (2) that it does not cause the algorithm to return failure on every branch that leads to a shortest-length solution.

To prove (1), recall that classical planning problems are guaranteed to have only finitely many states. Thus, every infinite path must eventually produce some state s_k that is the same as a state s_i that previously occurred on that path—and whenever this occurs, the modified algorithm will return failure.

To prove (2), recall that if the modification causes the algorithm to return failure, then there must be an $i <, k$ such that $s_k = s_i$. If the current node in the search tree is part of a successful execution trace, then the sequence of states for that trace will be

$$\langle s_0, \ldots, s_{i-1}, s_i, s_{i+1}, \ldots, s_{k-1}, s_k, s_{k+1}, \ldots, s_n \rangle,$$

where n is the length of the solution. Let that solution be $p = \langle a_1, \ldots, a_n \rangle$, where $s_{j+1} = \gamma(s_j, a_{j+1})$ for $j = 0, \ldots, n-1$. Then it is easy to prove that the plan $p' = \langle a_1, \ldots, a_{i-1}, a_k, a_{k+1}, \ldots, a_n \rangle$ is also a solution (see Exercise 4.3). Thus, p cannot be a shortest-length solution.

4.3 Backward Search

Planning can also be done using a backward search. The idea is to start at the goal and apply inverses of the planning operators to produce subgoals, stopping if we produce a set of subgoals satisfied by the initial state. The set of all states that are predecessors of states in S_g is:

$$\Gamma^{-1}(g) = \{s \mid \text{there is an action } a \text{ such that } \gamma^{-1}(g, a) \text{ satisfies } g\}$$

This is the basis of the Backward-search algorithm shown in Figure 4.2. It is easy to show that Backward-search is sound and complete; the proof is analogous to the proof for Forward-search.

Example 4.2 As an example of how Backward-search works, consider the same DWR problem given in Example 4.1 (see page 69). Recall that in this problem, the initial state is the state s_5 of Figure 2.3, and the goal formula is $g = \{\text{at(r1, loc1)},$

```
Backward-search(O, s₀, g)
    π ← the empty plan
    loop
        if s₀ satisfies g then return π
        relevant ← {a | a is a ground instance of an operator in O
                              that is relevant for g}
        if relevant = ∅ then return failure
        nondeterministically choose an action a ∈ applicable
        π ← a.π
        g ← γ⁻¹(g, a)
```

Figure 4.2 A nondeterministic backward search algorithm.

loaded(r1, c3)}, which is a subset of the state s_6 of Figure 2.4. In one of the execution traces of Backward-search it does the following:

In the first iteration of the loop, it chooses $a =$ load(crane1, loc1, c3, r1) and then assigns:

$$\begin{aligned} g &\leftarrow \gamma^{-1}(g, a) \\ &= (g - \text{effects}^{+}(a)) \cup \text{precond}(a) \\ &= (\{\text{at(r1, loc1), loaded(r1, c3)}\} - \{\text{empty(crane1), loaded(r1, c3)}\}) \\ &\cup \{\text{belong(crane1, loc1), holding(crane1, c3), at(r1, loc1), unloaded(r1)}\} \\ &= \{\text{at(r1, loc1), belong(crane1, loc1), holding(crane1, c3), unloaded(r1)}\} \end{aligned}$$

In the second iteration of the loop, it chooses $a =$ move(r1, loc2, loc1) and then assigns:

$$\begin{aligned} g &\leftarrow \gamma^{-1}(g, a) \\ &= (g - \text{effects}^{+}(a)) \cup \text{precond}(a) \\ &= (\{\text{at(r1,loc1), belong(crane1,loc1), holding(crane1,c3), at(r1,loc1),} \\ &\quad \text{unloaded}(r1)\} - \{\text{ at(r1,loc1), occupied(loc1) }\}) \\ &\cup \{\text{adjacent(loc2,loc1), at(r1,loc2), } \neg \text{ occupied(loc1)}\} \\ &= \{\text{belong(crane1, loc1), holding(crane1, c3),} \\ &\text{unloaded(r1), adjacent(loc2, loc1), at(r1, loc2), occupied(loc1)}\} \end{aligned}$$

This time g is satisfied by s_5, so the execution trace terminates at the beginning of the fourth interation and returns the plan:

$$\pi = \langle(\text{move(r1, loc2, loc1), load(crane1, loc1, c3, r1)}\rangle$$

There are many other execution traces, some of which are infinite. For example, one of them makes the following infinite sequence of assignments to a:

load(crane1, loc1, c3, r1)
unload(crane1, loc1, c3, r1)
load(crane1, loc1, c3, r1)
unload(crane1, loc1, c3, r1)
...

■

Let $g_0 = g$. For each integer $i > 0$, let g_i be the value of g at the end of the ith iteration of the loop. Suppose we modify Backward-search to keep a record of the

```
Lifted-backward-search(O, s0, g)
    π ← the empty plan
    loop
        if s0 satisfies g then return π
        relevant ← {(o, σ) | o is an operator in O that is relevant for g,
                    σ1 is a substitution that standardizes o's variables,
                    σ2 is an mgu for σ1(o) and the atom of g that o is
                    relevant for, and σ = σ2σ2}
        if relevant = ∅ then return failure
        nondeterministically choose a pair (o, σ) ∈ relevant
        π ← σ(o).σ(π)
        g ← γ^{-1}(σ(g), σ(o))
```

Figure 4.3 Lifted version of Backward-search. *mgu* is an abbreviation for *most general unifier*; see Appendix B for details.

sequence of goal formulas $(g_1, \ldots, g_k)$ on the current path and to backtrack whenever there is an $i < k$ such that $g_i \subseteq g_k$. Just as with Forward-search, it can be shown that this modification causes Backward-search to return failure on every infinite branch of the search space and that it does not cause Backward-search to return failure on every branch that leads to a shortest-length solution (see Exercise 4.5). Thus, the modification can be used to do a sound and complete depth-first implementation of Backward-search.

The size of *relevant* can be reduced by instantiating the planning operators only partially rather than fully. Lifted-backward-search, shown in Figure 4.3, does this. Lifted-backward-search is a straightforward adaptation of Backward-search. Instead of taking a ground instance of an operator $o \in O$ that is relevant for g, it standardizes[1] o's variables and then unifies it with the appropriate atom of g.

The algorithm is both sound and complete, and in most cases it will have a substantially smaller branching factor than Backward-search.

Like Backward-search, Lifted-backward-search can be modified in order to guarantee termination of a depth-first implementation of it while preserving its soundness and completeness. However, this time the modification is somewhat trickier. Suppose we modify the algorithm to keep a record of the sequence of goal formulas $(g_1, \ldots, g_k)$ on the current path and to backtrack whenever there is an $i < k$ such that $g_i \subseteq g_k$. This is not sufficient to guarantee termination. The problem is that this time, g_k need not be ground. There are infinitely many possible unground

1. *Standardizing* an expression means replacing its variable symbols with new variable symbols that do not occur anywhere else.

atoms, so it is possible to have infinite paths in which no two nodes are the same. However, if two different sets of atoms are unifiable, then they are essentially equivalent, and there are only finitely many possible nonunifiable sets of atoms. Thus, we can guarantee termination if we backtrack whenever there is an $i < k$ such that g_i unifies with a subset of g_k.

4.4 The STRIPS Algorithm

With all of the planning algorithms we have discussed so far, one of the biggest problems is how to improve efficiency by reducing the size of the search space. The STRIPS algorithm was an early attempt to do this. Figure 4.4 shows a ground version of the algorithm; STRIPS is the lifted version (see Exercise 4.11).

STRIPS is somewhat similar to Backward-search but differs from it in the following ways.

- In each recursive call of the STRIPS algorithm, the only subgoals eligible to be worked on are the preconditions of the last operator added to the plan. This reduces the branching factor substantially; however, it makes STRIPS incomplete.
- If the current state satisfies all of an operator's preconditions, STRIPS commits to executing that operator and will not backtrack over this commitment.

```
Ground-STRIPS(O, s, g)
    π ← the empty plan
    loop
        if s satisfies g then return π
        A ← {a | a is a ground instance of an operator in O,
                  and a is relevant for g}
        if A = ∅ then return failure
        nondeterministically choose any action a ∈ A
        π' ← Ground-STRIPS(O, s, precond(a))
        if π' = failure then return failure
        ;; if we get here, then π' achieves precond(a) from s
        s ← γ(s, π')
        ;; s now satisfies precond(a)
        s ← γ(s, a)
        π ← π.π'.a
```

Figure 4.4 A ground version of the STRIPS algorithm.

This prunes a large portion of the search space but again makes STRIPS incomplete.

As an example of a case where STRIPS is incomplete, STRIPS is unable to find a plan for one of the first problems a computer programmer learns how to solve: the problem of interchanging the values of two variables.

Even for problems that STRIPS solves, it does not always find the best solution. Here is an example.

Example 4.3 Probably the best-known planning problem that causes difficulty for STRIPS is the Sussman anomaly, which was described in Exercise 2.1. Figure 4.5 shows a DWR version of this problem. In the figure, the objects include one location (loc1), one crane (crane1), three containers (c1, c2, c3), and five piles (p1, p2, q1, q2, q3). Although STRIPS's search space for this problem contains infinitely many solutions (see Exercise 4.15), none of them are nonredundant. The shortest solutions that STRIPS can find are all similar to the following:

⟨ take(c3,loc,crane,c1)	
put(c3,loc,crane,q1)	
take(c1,loc,crane,p1)	
put(c1,loc,crane,c2)	(STRIPS has achieved on(c1,c2).)
take(c1,loc,crane,c2)	
put(c1,loc,crane,p1)	
take(c2,loc,crane,p2)	
put(c2,loc,crane,c3)	(STRIPS has achieved on(c2,c3) but needs to reachieve on(c1,c2).)
take(c1,loc,crane,p1)	
put(c1,loc,crane,c2)⟩	(STRIPS has now achieved both goals.)

■

In both Example 4.3 and the problem of interchanging the values of two variables, STRIPS's difficulty involves *deleted-condition interactions*, in which the action chosen to achieve one goal has a side effect of deleting another previously achieved goal. For example, in the plan shown in Example 4.3, the action take(c1,loc,crane,c2) is necessary in order to help achieve on(c2,c3), but it deletes the previously achieved condition on(c1,c2).

One way to find the shortest plan for the Sussman anomaly is to interleave plans for different goals. The shortest plan for achieving on(c1,c2) from the initial state is:

⟨take(c3,loc,crane,c1), put(c3,loc,crane,q1), take(c1,loc,crane,p1), put(c1,loc,crane,c2)⟩

The shortest plan for achieving on(c2,c3) from the initial state is:

⟨take(c2,loc,crane,p2), put(c2,loc,crane,c3)⟩

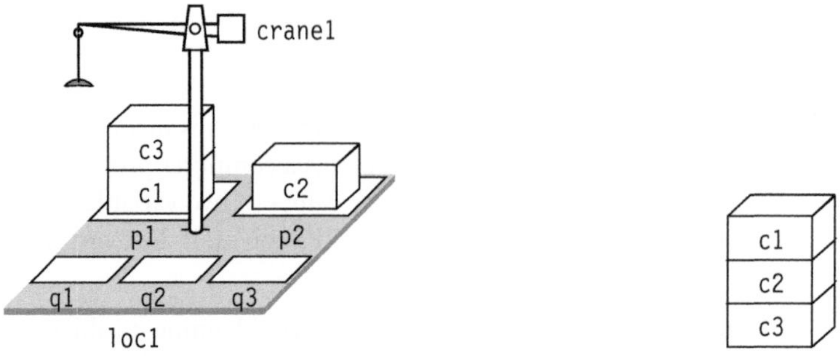

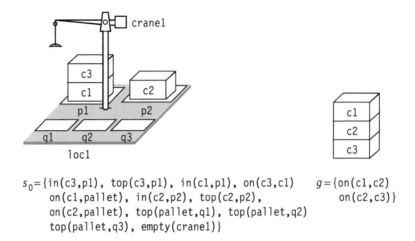

```
s0={in(c3,p1), top(c3,p1), in(c1,p1), on(c3,c1)      g={on(c1,c2)
    on(c1,pallet), in(c2,p2), top(c2,p2),                  on(c2,c3)}
    on(c2,pallet), top(pallet,q1), top(pallet,q2)
    top(pallet,q3), empty(crane1)}
```

Figure 4.5 A DWR version of the Sussman anomaly.

We can get the shortest plan for both goals by inserting the second plan between the second and third actions of the first plan.

Observations such as these led to the development of a technique called *plan-space planning*, in which the planning system searches through a space whose nodes are partial plans rather than states of the world, and a partial plan is a partially ordered sequence of partially instantiated actions rather than a totally ordered sequence. Plan-space planning is discussed in Chapter 5.

4.5 Domain-Specific State-Space Planning

This section illustrates how knowledge about a specific planning domain can be used to develop a fast planning algorithm that very quickly generates plans whose lengths are optimal or near optimal. The domain, which we call the *container-stacking domain*, is a restricted version of the DWR domain.

4.5.1 The Container-Stacking Domain

The language for the container-stacking domain contains the following constant symbols. There is a set of containers (c1, c2, ..., cn) and a set of piles (p1,p2, ..., pm, q1,q2, ..., ql), where n, m, and l may vary from one problem to

Table 4.1 Positions of containers in the initial state shown in Figure 4.5.

Container	*Position*	*Maximal?*	*Consistent with goal?*
c1	{on(c1,pallet)}	No	No: contradicts on(c1,c2)
c2	{on(c2,pallet)}	Yes	No: contradicts on(c2,c3)
c3	{on(c3,c1),on(c1,pallet)}	Yes	No: contradicts on(c1,c2)

another and $l \geq n$. There is one location loc, one crane crane, and a constant symbol pallet to represent the pallet at the bottom of each pile. The piles p1, ..., pm are the *primary piles*, and the piles q1, ..., ql are the *auxiliary piles*.

A container-stacking problem is any DWR problem for which the constant symbols are the ones just described and for which the crane and the auxiliary piles are empty in both the initial state and the goal. As an example, Figure 4.5 shows a container-stacking problem in which $n = 3$.

If s is a state, then a *stack* in s is any set of atoms $e \subseteq s$ of the form

$$\{\mathsf{in}(c_1, p), \mathsf{in}(c_2, p), \ldots, \mathsf{in}(c_k, p), \mathsf{on}(c_1, c_2), \mathsf{on}(c_2, c_3), \ldots, \mathsf{on}(c_{k-1}, c_k), \mathsf{on}(c_k, t)\},$$

where p is a pile, each c_i is a container, and t is the pallet. The top and bottom of e are c_1 and c_k, respectively. The stack e is *maximal* if it is not a subset of any other stack in s.

If s is a state and c is a container, then position(c, s) is the stack in s whose top is c. Note that position(c, s) is a maximal stack iff s contains the atom top(c, p); see Table 4.1 for examples.

From these definitions, it follows that in any state s, the position of a container c is consistent with the goal formula g only if the positions of all containers below c are also consistent with g. For example, in the container-stacking problem shown in Figure 4.5, consider the container c3. Because position(c1, s_0) is inconsistent with g and c3 is on c1, position(c1, s_0) is also inconsistent with g.

4.5.2 Planning Algorithm

Let $\mathcal{P}$ be a container-stacking problem in which there are m containers and n atoms. We can check whether $\mathcal{P}$ is solvable by checking whether g satisfies some simple consistency conditions. For example, g should not mention any containers not mentioned in s_0, g should not say that a container is sitting on two other containers at once, and so forth. It is not hard to write an algorithm to check these things in time $O(n \log n)$.

If $\mathcal{P}$ is solvable, then let $u_1, u_2, \ldots, u_k$ be all of the maximal stacks in g. It is easy to construct a plan that solves $\mathcal{P}$ by moving all containers to auxiliary pallets and then building each maximal stack from the bottom up. The length of this plan is at most $2m$ and it can be generated in time $O(n)$.

```
Stack-containers(O, s0, g):
  if g does not satisfy the consistency conditions then
    return failure       ;; the planning problem is unsolvable
  π ← the empty plan
  s ← s0
  loop
    if s satisfies g then return π
    if there are containers b and c at the tops of their piles such that
          position(c, s) is consistent with g and on(b, c) ∈ g
    then
      append actions to π that move b to c
      s ← the result of applying these actions to s
      ;; we will never need to move b again
    else if there is a container b at the top of its pile
          such that position(b, s) is inconsistent with g
          and there is no c such that on(b, c) ∈ g
    then
      append actions to π that move b to an empty auxiliary pile
      s ← the result of applying these actions to s
      ;; we will never need to move b again
    else
      nondeterministically choose any container c such that c is
          at the top of a pile and position(c, s) is inconsistent with g
      append actions to π that move c to an empty auxiliary pallet
      s ← the result of applying these actions to s
```

Figure 4.6 A fast algorithm for container stacking.

In general, the shortest solution length is likely to be much less than $2m$ because most of the containers will need to be moved only once or not at all. The problem of finding a shortest-length solution can be proved to be NP-hard, which provides strong evidence that it requires exponential time in the worst case. However, it is possible to devise algorithms that find, in low-order polynomial time, a solution whose length is either optimal or near optimal. One simple algorithm for this is the Stack-containers algorithm shown in Figure 4.6. Stack-containers is guaranteed to find a solution, and it runs in time $O(n^3)$, where n is the length of the plan it finds.

Unlike STRIPS, Stack-containers has no problem with deleted-condition interactions. For example, Stack-containers will easily find a shortest-length plan for the Sussman anomaly.

The only steps of Stack-containers that may cause the plan's length to be non-optimal are the ones in the else clause at the end of the algorithm. However, these steps usually are not executed very often because the only time they are needed is when there is no other way to progress toward the goal.

4.6 Discussion and Historical Remarks

Although state-space search might seem like an obvious way to do planning, it languished for many years. For a long time, no good techniques were known for guiding the search; and without such techniques, a state-space search can search a huge search space. During the last few years, better techniques have been developed for guiding state-space search (see Part III of this book). As a result, some of the fastest current planning algorithms use forward-search techniques [33, 271, 414].

The container-stacking domain in Section 4.5 is a DWR adaptation of a well-known domain called the *blocks world*. The blocks world was originally developed by Winograd [555] as a test bed for his program for understanding natural language, but it subsequently has been used much more widely as a test bed for planning algorithms.

The planning problem in Example 4.3 (see page 77) is an adaptation of a blocks-world planning problem originally by Allen Brown [540], who was then a Ph.D. student of Sussman. Sussman popularized the problem [501]; hence it became known as the Sussman anomaly.

In Fikes and Nilsson's original version of STRIPS [189], each operator had a precondition list, add list, and delete list, and these were allowed to contain arbitrary well-formed formulas in first-order logic. However, in the presentation of STRIPS in Nilsson's subsequent textbook [426], the operators were restricted to a format equivalent to our classical planning operators.

Stack-containers is an adaption of Gupta and Nau's blocks-world planning algorithm [253]. Although our version of this algorithm runs in $O(n^3)$ time, Slaney and Thiébaux [481] describe an improved version that runs in linear time. They also describe another algorithm that runs in linear time and finds significantly better plans.

4.7 Exercises

4.1 Here is a simple planning problem in which the objective is to interchange the values of two variables v1 and v2.

$$s_0 = \{\text{value(v1,3), value(v2,5), value(v3,0)}\}$$
$$g = \{\text{value(v1,5), value(v2,3)}\}$$

assign(v, w, x, y)
precond: value(v, x), value(w, y)
effects: $\neg$ value(v, x), value(v, y)

If we run Forward-search on this problem, how many iterations will there be in the shortest execution trace? In the longest one?

4.2 Show that the algorithm shown in Figure 4.7 is equivalent to Forward-search, in the sense that both algorithms will generate exactly the same search space.

4.3 Prove property (2) of Section 4.2.2.

4.4 Prove that if a classical planning problem $\mathcal{P}$ is solvable, then there will always be an execution trace of Backward-search that returns a shortest-length solution for $\mathcal{P}$.

4.5 Prove that if we modify Backward-search as suggested in Section 4.3, the modified algorithm has the same property described in Exercise 4.4.

4.6 Explain why Lifted-backward-search needs to standardize its operators.

4.7 Prove that Lifted-backward-search is sound and complete.

4.8 Prove that Lifted-backward-search has the same property described in Exercise 4.4.

4.9 Prove that the search space for the modified version of Lifted-backward-search never has more nodes than the search space for the modified version of Backward-search.

4.10 Why did Exercise 4.9 refer to the modified versions of the algorithms rather than the unmodified versions?

4.11 Write STRIPS, the lifted version of the STRIPS algorithm in Figure 4.4.

4.12 Trace the operation of the STRIPS algorithm on the Sussman anomaly to create the plan given in Section 4.4. Each time STRIPS makes a nondeterministic choice, tell what the possible choices are. Each time it calls itself recursively, give the parameters and the returned value for the recursive invocation.

```
Recursive-forward-search(O, s0, g)
    if s satisfies g then return the empty plan
    active ← {a | a is a ground instance of an operator in O
                    and a's preconditions are true in s}
    if active = ∅ then return failure
    nondeterministically choose an action a1 ∈ active
    s1 ← γ(s, a1)
    π ← Recursive-forward-search(O, s1, g)
    if π ≠ failure then return a1.p
    else return failure
```

Figure 4.7 A recursive version of Forward-search.

4.13 In order to produce the plan given in Section 4.4, STRIPS starts out by working on the goal on(c1,c2). Write the plan STRIPS will produce if it starts out by working on the goal on(c2,c3).

4.14 Trace the operation of STRIPS on the planning problem in Exercise 4.1.

4.15 Prove that STRIPS's search space for the Sussman anomaly contains infinitely many solutions and that it contains paths that are infinitely long.

4.16 Redo Exercises 4.12 through 4.14 using your lifted version of STRIPS.

4.17 Our formulation of the container-stacking domain requires n auxiliary piles. Will the nth pile ever get used? Why or why not? How about the $(n-1)$th pile?

4.18 Show that if we modify the container-stacking domain to get rid of the auxiliary piles, then there will be problems whose shortest solution lengths are longer than before.

4.19 Suppose we modify the notation for the container-stacking domain so that instead of writing, e.g.,

```
in(a,p1), in(b,p1), top(a,p1), on(a,b), on(b,pallet),
in(c,p2), in(d,p2), top(c,p2), on(c,d), on(d,pallet),
```

we would write

```
clear(a), on(a,b), on(b,p1), clear(c), on(c,d), on(c,p2).
```

(a) Show that there is a one-to-one correspondence between each problem written in the old notation and an equivalent problem written in the new notation.

(b) What kinds of computations can be done more quickly using the old notation than using the new notation?

4.20 If P is the statement of a container-stacking problem, what is the corresponding planning problem in the blocks-world domain described in Exercise 3.5? What things prevent the two problems from being completely equivalent?

4.21 Trace the operation of Stack-containers on the Sussman anomaly to show that this algorithm finds the shortest solution.

4.22 Find a container-stacking problem for which Stack-containers will not always find a shortest-length solution. Hint: You probably will need at least 13 containers.

CHAPTER 5

Plan-Space Planning

5.1 Introduction

In the previous chapter, we addressed planning as the search for a path in the graph Σ of a state-transition system. For state-space planning, the search space is given directly by Σ. Nodes are states of the domain; arcs are state transitions or actions; a plan is a sequence of actions corresponding to a path from the initial state to a goal state.

We shall be considering in this chapter a more elaborate search space that is not Σ anymore. It is a space where nodes are *partially specified plans*. Arcs are *plan refinement operations* intended to further complete a partial plan, i.e., to achieve an open goal or to remove a possible inconsistency. Intuitively, a refinement operation avoids adding to the partial plan any constraint that is not strictly needed for addressing the refinement purpose. This is called the *least commitment principle*. Planning starts from an initial node corresponding to an empty plan. The search aims at a final node containing a solution plan that correctly achieves the required goals.

Plan-space planning differs from state-space planning not only in its search space but also in its definition of a solution plan. Plan-space planning uses a more general plan structure than a sequence of actions. Here planning is considered as two separate operations: (1) the choice of actions, and (2) the ordering of the chosen actions so as to achieve the goal. A plan is defined as a set of planning operators together with ordering constraints and binding constraints; it may not correspond to a sequence of actions.

The search space is detailed in Section 5.2. Properties of solution plans are analyzed in Section 5.3; correctness conditions with respect to the semantics of state-transition systems are established. Algorithms for plan-space planning are proposed in Section 5.4. Several extensions are considered in Section 5.5. A comparison to state-space planning is offered in Section 5.6. The chapter ends with discussion and exercises.

5.2 The Search Space of Partial Plans

Generally speaking, a plan is a set of actions organized into some structure, e.g., a sequence. A partial plan can be defined as any subset of actions that keeps some useful part of this structure, e.g., a subsequence for state-space planning. All planning algorithms seen up to now extend step-by-step a partial plan. However, these were particular partial plans. Their actions are sequentially ordered. The total order reflects the intrinsic constraints of the actions in the partial plan and the particular search strategy of the planning algorithm. The former constraints are needed; a partial plan that is just an unstructured collection of actions would be meaningless because the relevance of a set of actions depends strongly on its organization. However, the constraints reflecting the search strategy of the algorithm are not needed. There can be advantages in avoiding them.

To find out what is needed in a partial plan, let us develop an informal planning step on a simple example. Assume that we already have a partial plan; let us refine it by adding a new action and let us analyze how the partial plan should be updated. We'll come up with four ingredients: adding actions, adding ordering constraints, adding causal relationships, and adding variable binding constraints.

Example 5.1 In the *DWR* domain, consider the problem where a robot r1 has to move a container c1 from pile p1 at location l1 to pile p2 and location l2 (see Figure 5.1). Initially r1 is unloaded at location l3. There are empty cranes k1 and k2 at locations l1 and l2, respectively. Pile p1 at location l1 contains only container c1; pile p2 at location l2 is empty. All locations are adjacent. ■

For Example 5.1, let us consider a partial plan that contains only the two following actions.

- take(k1,c1,p1,l1): crane k1 picks up container c1 from pile p1 at location l1.
- load(k1,c1,r1,l1): crane k1 loads container c1 on robot r1 at location l1.

Adding Actions. Nothing in this partial plan guarantees that robot r1 is already at location l1. Proposition at(r1,l1), required as a precondition by action load, is a *subgoal* in this partial plan. Let us add to this plan the following action.

- move(r1,*l*,l1): robot r1 moves from location l to the required location l1.

Adding Ordering Constraints. This additional move action achieves its purpose only if it is constrained to come *before* the load action. Should the move action come *before* or *after* the take action? Both options are feasible. The partial plan does not commit unnecessarily at this stage to either one. This follows the *least commitment principle* of not adding a constraint to a partial plan unless strictly needed. Here, the only needed constraint is to have move before load. Other constraints that may be

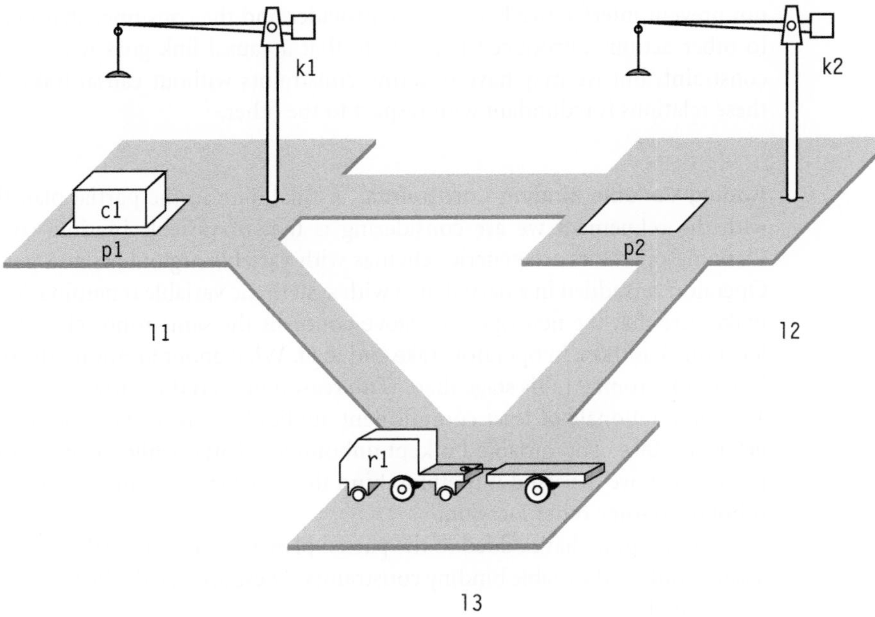

Figure 5.1 A simple DWR problem.

needed later while planning or even executing the plan may order move and take or may permit them to run concurrently.

Adding Causal Links. In the partial plan, we have added one action and one ordering constraint to another action already in the plan. Is that enough? Not quite. Because there is no explicit notion of a current state, an ordering constraint does not say that the robot stays at location l1 until the load action is performed. While pursuing the refinement of the partial plan, the planner may find other reasons to move the robot elsewhere, forgetting about the rationale for moving it to l1 in the first place. Hence, we'll be encoding explicitly in the partial plan the reason why action move was added: to satisfy the subgoal at(r1,l1) required by action load.

This relationship between the two actions move and load with respect to proposition at(r1,l1), is called a *causal link*. The former action is called the *provider* of the proposition, the later its *consumer*.[1] The precise role of a causal link is to state that a precondition of an action is *supported* by another action. Consequently, a precondition without a causal link is not supported. It is considered to be an open *subgoal* in the partial plan.

A provider has to be ordered before a consumer but not necessarily strictly before in a sequence: other actions may take place in between. Hence, a causal link does

1. Not in the sense of consuming a resource: load does not change this precondition.

not prevent interference between the provider and the consumer that may be due to other actions introduced later. Note that a causal link goes with an ordering constraint, but we may have ordering constraints without causal links. None of these relations is redundant with respect to the other.

Adding Variable Binding Constraints. A final item in the partial plan that goes with the refinement we are considering is that of variable binding constraints. Planning operators are generic schemas with variable arguments and parameters. Operators are added in a partial plan with systematic variable renaming. We should make sure that the new operator move concerns the same robot r1 and the same location l1 as those in operators take and load. What about location l the robot will be coming from? At this stage there is no reason to bind this variable to a constant. The same rationale of least commitment applies here as in the ordering between move and take. The variable l is kept unbounded. Later, while further refining the partial plan, we may find it useful to bind the variable to the initial position of the robot or to some other location.

To sum up, we have added to the partial plan an action, an ordering constraint, a causal link, and variable binding constraints. These are exactly the four ingredients of partial plans.

Definition 5.1 A *partial plan* is a tuple $\pi = (A, \prec, B, L)$, where:

- $A = \{a_1, \ldots, a_k\}$ is a set of partially instantiated planning operators.
- $\prec$ is a set of ordering constraints on A of the form $(a_i \prec a_j)$.
- B is a set of binding constraints on the variables of actions in A of the form $x = y$, $x \neq y$, or $x \in D_x$, D_x being a subset of the domain of x.
- L is a set of causal links of the form $\langle a_i \xrightarrow{p} a_j \rangle$, such that a_i and a_j are actions in A, the constraint $(a_i \prec a_j)$ is in $\prec$, proposition p is an effect of a_i and a precondition of a_j, and the binding constraints for variables of a_i and a_j appearing in p are in B.

■

A plan space is an implicit directed graph whose vertices are partial plans and whose edges correspond to refinement operations. An outgoing edge from a vertex π in the plan space is a *refinement operation* that transforms π into a successor partial plan π'. A refinement operation consists of one or more of the following steps.

- Add an action to A.
- Add an ordering constraint to $\prec$.
- Add a binding constraint to B.
- Add a causal link to L.

Planning in a plan space is a search in that graph of a path from an initial partial plan denoted π_0 to a node recognized as a solution plan. At each step, the planner has to choose and apply a refinement operation to the current plan π in order to achieve the specified goals. We now describe how goals and initial states are specified in the plan space.

Partial plans represent only actions and their relationships; states are not explicit. Hence, goals and initial states also have to be coded within the partial plan format as particular actions. Since preconditions are subgoals, the propositions corresponding to the goal g are represented as the preconditions of a dummy action, call it a_∞, that has no effect. Similarly, the propositions in the initial state s_0 are represented as the effects of a dummy action, a_0, that has no precondition. The initial plan π_0 is defined as the set $\{a_0, a_\infty\}$, together with the ordering constraint $(a_0 \prec a_\infty)$, but with no binding constraint and no causal link. The initial plan π_0 and any current partial plan represent goals and subgoals as preconditions without causal links.

Example 5.2 Let us illustrate two partial plans corresponding to Example 5.1 (see Figure 5.1). The goal of having container c1 in pile p2 can be expressed simply as in(c1,p2). The initial state is:

{adjacent(l1,l2), adjacent(l1,l3), adjacent(l2,l3),
adjacent(l2,l1), adjacent(l3,l1), adjacent(l3,l2),
attached(p1,l1), attached(p2,l2), belong(k1,l1), belong(k2,l2),
empty(k1), empty(k2), at(r1,l3), unloaded(r1), occupied(l3),
in(c1,p1), on(c1,pallet), top(c1,p1), top(pallet, p2)}

The first three lines describe rigid properties, i.e., invariant properties on the topology of locations, piles, and cranes; the last two lines define the specific initial conditions considered in this example.

A graphical representation of the initial plan π_0 corresponding to this problem appears in Figure 5.2. The partial plan discussed earlier with the three actions take, load, and move appears in Figure 5.3. In these figures, each box is an action

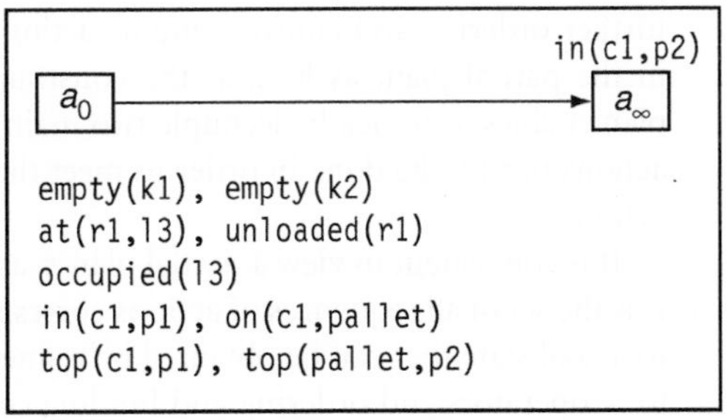

Figure 5.2 Initial plan π_0.

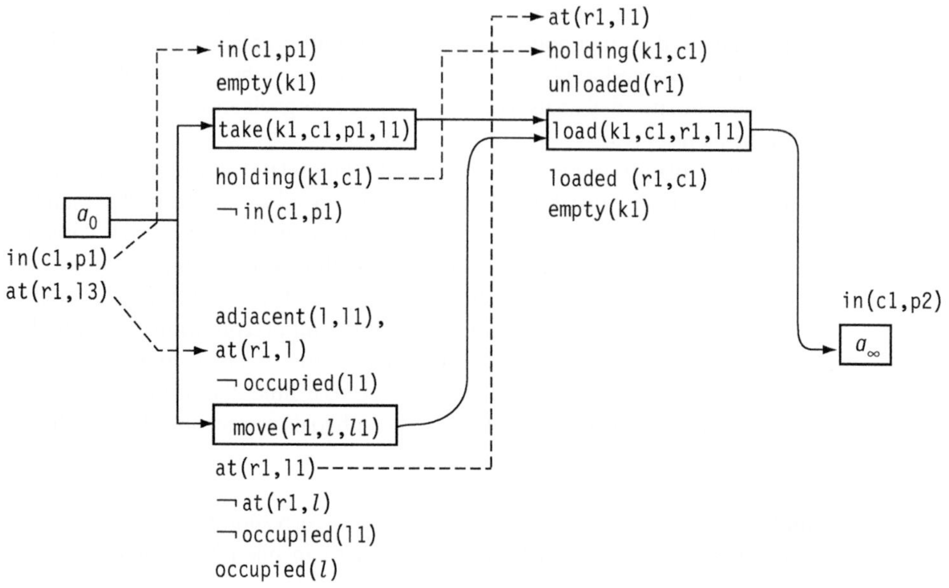

Figure 5.3 A partial plan.

with preconditions above and effects below the box. To simplify, rigid properties are not shown in the effects of a_0. Solid arrows are ordering constraints; dashed arrows are causal links; and binding constraints are implicit or shown directly in the arguments.

■

To summarize, a partial plan π is a structured collection of actions that provides the causal relationships for the actions in π, as well as their intrinsic ordering and variable binding constraints. A partial plan also provides subgoals in π as preconditions without causal links. A plan-space planner refines the partial plan by further ordering and constraining its actions or by adding new actions anywhere in the partial plan, as long as the constraints in π remain satisfiable. A partial plan enables us to neatly decouple two main issues in classical planning: (1) which actions need to be done in order to meet the goals, and (2) how to organize these actions.

It is convenient to view a partial plan π as representing a particular set of plans. It is the set of all sequences of actions corresponding to a path from the initial state to a goal state that can be obtained by refinement operations on π, i.e., by adding to π operators and ordering and binding constraints. A refinement operation on π reduces the set of plans associated with π to a smaller subset. This view will be formalized in the next section.

5.3 Solution Plans

In order to define planning algorithms in the plan space, we need to formally specify what is a solution plan in the plan space. A solution plan for a problem $P = (\Sigma, s_0, g)$ has been formally defined, with respect to the semantics of state-transition systems, as a sequence of ground actions from s_0 to a state in g (see Section 2.3.3). We now have to take into account that actions in a partial plan $\pi = (A, \prec, B, L)$ are only partially ordered and partially instantiated.

A consistent partial order $\prec$ corresponds to the set of all sequences of totally ordered actions of A that satisfy the partial order. Technically, these sequences are the topological orderings of the partial order $\prec$. There can be an exponential number of them. Note that a partial order defines a directed graph; it is consistent when this graph is loop free.

Similarly, for a consistent set of binding constraints B, there are many sequences of totally instantiated actions of A that satisfy B. These sequences correspond to all the ways of instantiating every unbounded variable x to a value in its domain D_x allowed by the constraints. The set B is consistent if every binding of a variable x with a value in the allowed domain D_x is consistent with the remaining constraints. Note that this is a strong consistency requirement.

Definition 5.2 A partial plan $\pi = (A, \prec, B, L)$ is a *solution plan* for problem $P = (\Sigma, s_0, g)$ if:

- its ordering constraints $\prec$ and binding constraints B are consistent; *and*
- every sequence of totally ordered and totally instantiated actions of A satisfying $\prec$ and B is a sequence that defines a path in the state-transition system Σ from the initial state s_0 corresponding to effects of action a_0 to a state containing all goal propositions in g given by preconditions of a_∞.

■

According to Definition 5.2, a solution plan corresponds to a set of sequences of actions, each being a path from the initial state to a goal state. This definition does not provide a computable test for verifying plans: it is not feasible to check all instantiated sequences of actions of A. We need a practical condition for characterizing the set of solutions. We already have a hint. Remember that a subgoal is a precondition without a causal link. Hence, a plan π meets its initial goals, and all the subgoals due to the preconditions of its actions, if it has a causal link for every precondition. However, this is not sufficient: π may not be constrained enough to guarantee that all possible sequences define a solution path in graph Σ.

Example 5.3 Consider Example 5.1, where we had a causal link from action move(r1,l,l1) to action load(k1,c1,r1,l1) with respect to proposition at(r1,l1). Assume that the final plan contains another action move(r,l',l''), without any ordering constraint that requires this action to be ordered before the previous move(r1,l',l1) or after

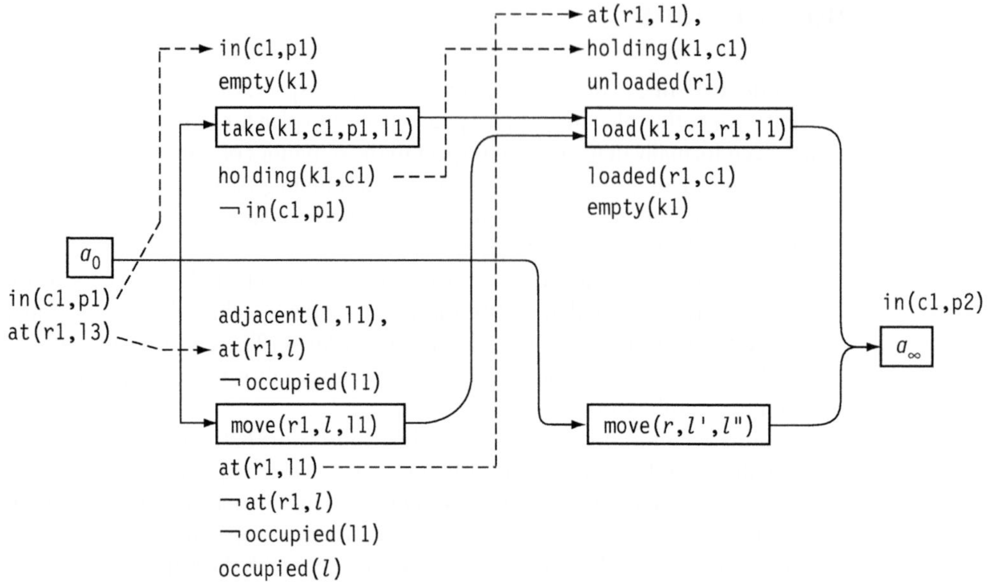

Figure 5.4 A plan containing an incorrect sequence.

action load, and without any binding constraint that requires r to be distinct from r1 or l' from l1 (Figure 5.4).

Among the set of totally ordered and instantiated sequences of actions of such a plan, there is at least one sequence that contains the subsequence

$$\langle \text{move(r1,}l\text{, l1)}, \ldots, \text{move(r1,l1,}l''\text{)}, \ldots, \text{load(k1,c1,r1,l1)} \rangle,$$

which is not a correct solution: the precondition at(r1,l1) is not satisfied in the state preceding action load. ■

Definition 5.3 An action a_k in a plan π is a *threat* on a causal link $\langle a_i \xrightarrow{p} a_j \rangle$ iff:

- a_k has an effect $\neg q$ that is possibly inconsistent with p, i.e., q and p are unifiable;
- the ordering constraints $(a_i \prec a_k)$ and $(a_k \prec a_j)$ are consistent with $\prec$; and
- the binding constraints for the unification of q and p are consistent with B. ■

Definition 5.4 A *flaw* in a plan $\pi = (A, \prec, B, L)$ is either:

- a subgoal, i.e., a precondition of an action in A without a causal link; or
- a threat, i.e., an action that may interfere with a causal link. ■

Proposition 5.1 *A partial plan $\pi = (A, \prec, B, L)$ is a solution to the planning problem $P = (\Sigma, s_0, g)$ if π has no flaw and if the sets of ordering constraints $\prec$ and binding constraints B are consistent.*

Proof Let us prove the proposition inductively on the number of actions in A.

Base step: For $A = \{a_0, a_1, a_\infty\}$, there is just a single sequence of totally ordered actions. Since π has no flaw, every precondition of a_1 is satisfied by a causal link with a_0, i.e., the initial state, and every goal or precondition of a_∞ is satisfied by a causal link with a_0 or a_1.

Induction step: Assume the proposition to hold for any plan having $(n-1)$ actions. Consider a plan π with n actions and without a flaw. Let $A_i = \{a_{i1}, \ldots, a_{ik}\}$ be a subset of actions whose only predecessor in the partial order $\prec$ is a_0. Every totally ordered sequence of actions of π satisfying $\prec$ starts necessarily with some action a_i from this subset. Since π has no flaw, all preconditions of a_i are met by a causal link with a_0. Hence every instance of action a_i is applicable to the initial state corresponding to a_0.

Let $[a_0, a_i]$ denote the first state of Σ after the execution of a_i in state s_0, and let $\pi' = (A', \prec', B', L')$ be the remaining plan. That is, π' is obtained from π by replacing a_0 and a_i with a single action (in the plan-space notation) that has no precondition and whose effects correspond to the first state $[a_0, a_i]$, and by adding to B the binding constraints due to this first instance of a_i. Let us prove that π' is a solution.

- $\prec'$ is consistent because no ordering constraint has been added from π to π'.
- B' is consistent because new binding constraints are consistent with B.
- π' has no threat because no action has been added in π, which had no threat.
- π' has no subgoal: every precondition of π that was satisfied by a causal link with an action $a \neq a_0$ is still supported by the same causal link in π'. Consider a precondition p supported by a causal link $\langle a_0 \xrightarrow{p} a_j \rangle$. Because a_i was not a threat in π, the effects of any consistent instance of a_i do not interfere with p. Hence condition p is satisfied in the first state $[a_0, a_i]$. The causal link in π' is now $\langle [a_0, a_i] \xrightarrow{p} a_j \rangle$.

Hence π' has $(n-1)$ actions without a flaw: by induction it is a solution plan. ∎

Example 5.4 Let us augment Example 5.3 with actions:

```
move(r1,l1,l2)
unload(k1,c1,r1)
put(k1,c1,p2,l2)
```

The corresponding plan (Figure 5.5, where causal links are not shown) is a solution. ∎

Finally, let us remark that Definition 5.2 and Proposition 5.1 allow for two types of flexibility in a solution plan: actions do not have to be totally ordered and they do not have to be totally instantiated. This remark applies also to a_∞ because all actions in a partial plan have the same syntactical status. In other words, the

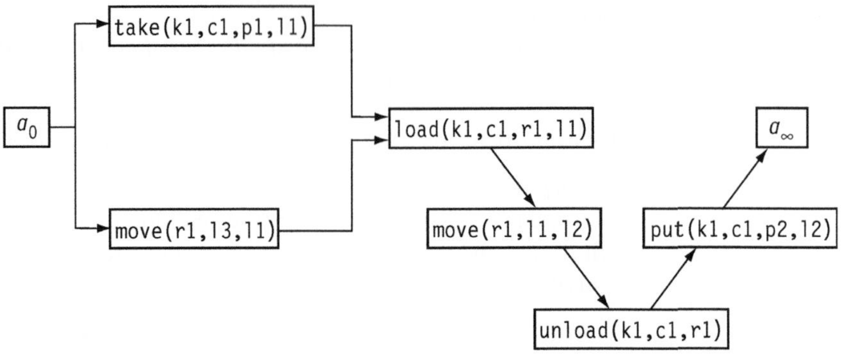

Figure 5.5 A solution plan.

flexibility introduced allows us to handle partially instantiated goals. Recall that variables in a goal are existentially quantified. For example, any state in which there is a container c in the pile p2 meets a goal such as in(c, p2) (see Exercise 5.4).

5.4 Algorithms for Plan-Space Planning

This section presents search procedures in the plan space. We first introduce a generic schema for planning in the plan space that clarifies the main ingredients of flaws and resolvers for flaws. We then introduce a particular control scheme that processes differently the two types of flaws in a partial plan.

5.4.1 The PSP Procedure

The characterization of the set of solution plans gives the elements needed for the design of planning algorithms in the plan space. Since π is a solution when it has no flaw, the main principle is to refine π, while maintaining $\prec$ and B consistent, until it has no flaw. The basic operations for refining a partial plan π toward a solution plan are the following.

- Find the flaws of π, i.e., its subgoals and its threats.
- Select one such flaw.
- Find ways to resolve it.
- Choose a resolver for the flaw.
- Refine π according to that resolver.

The resolvers of a flaw are defined so as to maintain the consistency of $\prec$ and B in any refinement of π with a resolver. When there is no flaw in π, then the conditions

```
PSP(π)
    flaws ← OpenGoals(π) ∪ Threats(π)
    if flaws = ∅ then return(π)
    select any flaw φ ∈ flaws
    resolvers ← Resolve(φ, π)
    if resolvers = ∅ then return(failure)
    nondeterministically choose a resolver ρ ∈ resolvers
    π' ← Refine(ρ, π)
    return(PSP(π'))
end
```

Figure 5.6 The PSP procedure.

of Proposition 5.1 are met, and π is a solution plan. Symmetrically, when a flaw has no resolver, then π cannot be refined into a solution plan.

Let us specify the corresponding procedure as a recursive nondeterministic schema, called PSP (for Plan-Space Planning). The pseudocode of PSP is given in Figure 5.6. The following variables and procedures are used in PSP.

- *flaws* denotes the set of all flaws in π provided by procedures OpenGoals and Threats; ϕ is a particular flaw in this set.
- *resolvers* denotes the set of all possible ways to resolve the current flaw ϕ in plan π and is given by procedure Resolve. The resolver ρ is an element of this set.
- π' is a new plan obtained by refining π according to resolver ρ, using for that procedure Refine.

The PSP procedure is called initially with the initial plan π_0. Each successful recursion is a refinement of the current plan according to a given resolver. The choice of the resolver is a *nondeterministic* step. The correct implementation of the nondeterministically choose step is the following.

- When a recursive call on a refinement with the chosen resolver returns a failure, then another recursion is performed with a new resolver.
- When all resolvers have been tried unsuccessfully, then a failure is returned from that recursion level back to a previous choice point. This is equivalent to an empty set of resolvers.

Note that the selection of a flaw (select step) is a *deterministic* step. All flaws need to be solved before reaching a solution plan. The order in which flaws are processed is very important for the efficiency of the procedure, but it is unimportant for its soundness and completeness. Before getting into the properties of PSP, let us detail the four procedures it uses.

OpenGoals (π). This procedure finds all subgoals in π. These are preconditions not supported by a causal link. This procedure is efficiently implemented with an *agenda* data structure. For each new action a in π, all preconditions of a are added to the agenda; for each new causal link in π, the corresponding proposition is removed from the agenda.

Threats (π). This procedure finds every action a_k that is a threat on some causal link $\langle a_i \xrightarrow{p} a_j \rangle$. This can be done by testing all triples of actions in π, which takes $O(n^3)$, n being the current number of actions in π. Here also an incremental processing is more efficient. For each new action in π, all causal links not involving that action are tested (in $O(n^2)$). For each new causal link, all actions in π, but not those of the causal link, are tested (in $O(n)$).

Resolve (ϕ, π). This procedure finds all ways to solve a flaw ϕ. If ϕ is a subgoal for a precondition p of some action a_j, then its resolvers are either of the following:

- A causal link $\langle a_i \xrightarrow{p} a_j \rangle$ if there is an action a_i already in π whose effect can provide p. This resolver contains three elements: the causal link, the ordering constraint $(a_i \prec a_j)$ if consistent with $\prec$, and the binding constraints to unify p with the effect of a_i.
- A new action a that can provide p. This resolver contains a together with the corresponding causal link and the ordering and binding constraints, including the constraints $(a_0 \prec a \prec a_\infty)$ required for a new action. Note that there is no need here to check the consistency of these constraints with $\prec$ and B.

If ϕ is a threat on causal link $\langle a_i \xrightarrow{p} a_j \rangle$ by an action a_k that has an effect $\neg q$, and q is unifiable with p, then its resolvers are any of the following:[2]

- The constraint $(a_k \prec a_i)$, if consistent with $\prec$, i.e., ordering a_k before the causal link.
- The constraint $(a_j \prec a_k)$, if consistent with $\prec$, i.e., ordering a_k after the causal link.
- A binding constraint consistent with B that makes q and p nonunifiable.

Note that another way to address a threat is to choose for a causal link an alternate provider a'_i that has no threat. Replacing a_i with a'_i as the provider for a_j can be done through backtracking.

---

2. These three resolvers are called respectively *promotion, demotion,* and *separation.*

Refine (ρ, π). This procedure refines the partial plan π with the elements in the resolver, adding to π an ordering constraint, one or several binding constraints, a causal link, and/or a new action. This procedure is straightforward: no testing needs to be done because we have checked, while finding a resolver, that the corresponding constraints are consistent with π. Refine just has to maintain incrementally the set of subgoals in the agenda and the set of threats.

The Resolve and Refine procedures perform several query and update operations on the two sets of constraints $\prec$ and B. It is preferable to have these operations carried out by specific *constraint managers*. Let us describe them briefly.

The Ordering constraint manager handles query and update operations. The former include operations such as querying whether a constraint $(a \prec a')$ is consistent with $\prec$ and asking for all actions in A that can be ordered after some action a. The update operations consist of adding a consistent ordering constraint and removing one or several ordering constraints, which is useful for backtracking on a refinement. The alternatives for performing these operations are either of the following:

- Maintain as an explicit data structure only input constraints. In that case, updates are trivial, in $O(1)$, whereas queries require a search in $O(n^2)$, n being the number of constraints in $\prec$.
- Maintain the transitive closure of $\prec$. This makes queries easy, in $O(1)$, but requires an $O(n^2)$ propagation for each new update; a removal is performed on the input constraints plus a complete propagation.

In planning there are usually more queries than updates, hence the latter alternative is preferable.

The Binding constraint manager handles three types of constraints on variables over finite domains: (1) unary constraints $x \in D_x$, (2) binary constraints $x = y$, and (3) $x \neq y$. Types 1 and 2 are easily managed through a Union-Find algorithm in time linear to the number of query and update operations, whereas type 3 raises a general NP-complete Constraint Satisfaction Problem (CSP).[3]

Figure 5.7 depicts the global organization of the PSP procedure. The correct behavior of PSP is based on the nondeterministic step for choosing a resolver for a flaw and for backtracking over that choice, when needed, through all possible resolvers. The order in which resolvers are tried is important for the efficiency of the algorithm. This choice has to be heuristically guided.

The order in which the flaws are processed (the step select for selecting the next flaw to be resolved) is also very important for the performance of the algorithm, even if no backtracking is needed at this point. A heuristic function is again essential for guiding the search.

---

3. For example, the well-known NP-complete graph coloring problem is directly coded with type 3 constraints.

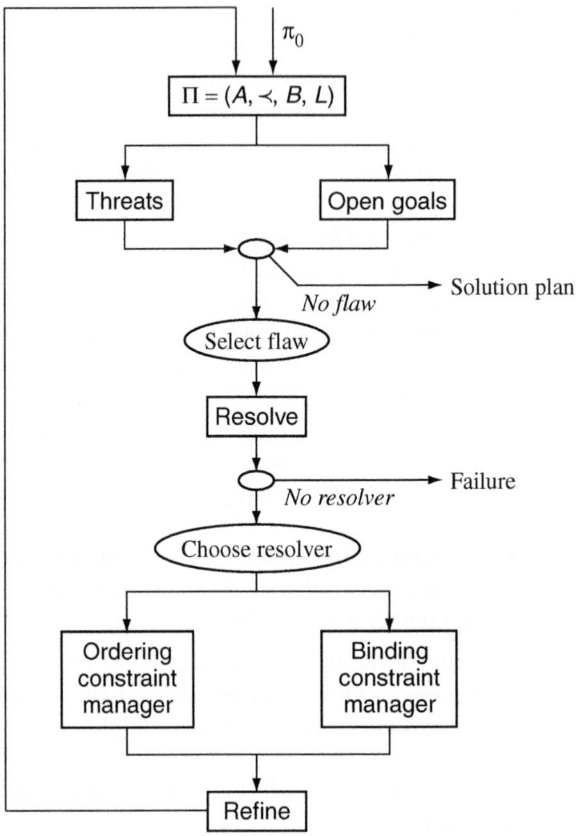

Figure 5.7 Organization of the PSP procedure.

Proposition 5.2 *The PSP procedure is sound and complete: whenever π_0 can be refined into a solution plan, PSP(π_0) returns such a plan.*

Proof Let us first prove the soundness, then the completeness.

In the initial π_0, the sets of constraints in $\prec$ and B are obviously consistent. The Resolve procedure is such that every refinement step uses a resolver that is consistent with $\prec$ and B. Consequently, the successful termination step of PSP returns a plan π that has no flaw and whose sets of constraints in $\prec$ and B are consistent. According to Proposition 5.1 (see page 93), π is a solution plan, hence PSP is sound.

In order to prove the completeness of this nondeterministic procedure, we must show that at least one of its execution traces returns a solution, when there is one. Let us prove it inductively on the length k of a solution plan.

Base step, for $k = 0$: If the empty plan is a solution to the problem, then π_0 has no flaw and PSP returns immediately this empty plan.

Induction step: Assume that PSP is complete for planning problems that have solutions of length $(k - 1)$, and assume that the problem at hand $P = (O, s_0, g)$ admits a solution $\langle a_1, \ldots, a_k \rangle$ of length k. Because a_k is relevant for the goal g, then there is at least one trace of PSP that chooses (and partially instantiates) an operator a'_k to address the flaws in π_0, such that a_k is an instance of a'_k. Let $[a'_k, a_\infty]$ be the set of goal propositions (in plan-space notation) corresponding to $\gamma^{-1}(g, a'_k)$. The next recursion of PSP takes place on a partial plan π_1 that has three actions $\{a_0, a'_k, a_\infty\}$. π_1 is equivalent to the initial plan of a problem from the state s_0 to a goal given by $[a'_k, a_\infty]$. This problem admits $\langle a_1, \ldots, a_{k-1} \rangle$ as a solution of length $(k - 1)$. By induction, the recursion of PSP on π_1 has an execution trace that finds this solution.

■

An important remark is in order. Even with the restrictive assumption of a finite transition system (assumption A0 in Section 1.5) the plan space is *not finite*. A *deterministic* implementation of the PSP procedure will maintain the completeness only if it guarantees to explore all partial plans, up to some length. It has to rely, e.g., on an iterative deepening search, such as IDA*, where a bound on the length of the sought solution is progressively increased.[4] Otherwise, the search may keep exploring deeper and deeper a single path in the search space, adding indefinitely new actions to the current partial plan and never backtracking. Note that a search with an A* algorithm is also feasible as long as the refinement cost from one partial plan to the next is not null.

5.4.2 The PoP Procedure

The PSP procedure is a generic schema that can be instantiated into several variants. Let us describe briefly one of them, algorithm PoP, which corresponds to a popular implementation for a planner in the plan space.

Figure 5.8 gives the pseudocode for PoP. It is specified as a nondeterministic recursive procedure. It has two arguments: (1) π, which is the current partial plan, and (2) *agenda*, which is a set of ordered pairs of the form $(a, p\hat{E})$, where a is an action in A and p is a precondition of a that is a subgoal. The arguments of the initial call are π_0 and an agenda containing a_∞ with all its preconditions.

PoP uses a procedure called Providers that finds all actions, either in A or in new instances of planning operators of the domain, that have an effect q unifiable with p. This set of actions is denoted *relevant* for the current goal.

There is a main difference between PSP and PoP. PSP processes the two types of flaws in a similar way: at each recursion, it selects heuristically a flaw from any type to pursue the refinement. The PoP procedure has a distinct control for subgoals and for threats. At each recursion, it first refines with respect to a subgoal, then it

4. See Appendix A.

```
PoP(π, agenda)          ;; where π = (A, ≺, B, L)
    if agenda = ∅ then return(π)
    select any pair (a_j, p) in and remove it from agenda
    relevant ← Providers(p, π)
    if relevant = ∅ then return(failure)
    nondeterministically choose an action a_i ∈ relevant
    L ← L ∪ {⟨a_i --p--> a_j⟩}
    update B with the binding constraints of this causal link
    if a_i is a new action in A then do:
        update A with a_i
        update ≺ with (a_i ≺ a_j), (a_0 ≺ a_i ≺ a_∞)
        update agenda with all preconditions of a_i
    for each threat on ⟨a_i --p--> a_j⟩ or due to a_i do:
        resolvers ← set of resolvers for this threat
        if resolvers = ∅ then return(failure)
        nondeterministically choose a resolver in resolvers
        add that resolver to ≺ or to B
    return(PoP(π, agenda))
end
```

Figure 5.8 The PoP procedure.

proceeds by solving all threats due to the resolver of that subgoal. Consequently, there are two nondeterministic steps: (1) the choice of a relevant action for solving a subgoal, and (2) the choice of an ordering constraint or a binding constraint for solving a threat.

Backtracking for these two nondeterministic steps is performed chronologically by going over all resolvers for a threat and, if none of them works, then backtracking to another resolver for the current subgoal. Note that a resolver for a threat is a single constraint to be added to either $\prec$ or B.

5.5 Extensions

The PoP procedure is a simplified version of a planner called UCPOP that implements many of the extensions of the classical representation introduced in Section 2.4. Let us mention here briefly how plan-space planning can handle some of these extensions.

Conditional Operators. Recall that a conditional operator has, in addition to normal preconditions and effects, some conditional effects that depend on whether an associated antecedent condition holds in the state s to which the operator is applied. In order to handle a conditional operator, two changes in the PoP procedure are required.

1. The Providers procedure may find an action that provides p conditionally. If this is the action chosen in *relevant*, then the antecedent on which p conditionally depends needs to be added to the *agenda*, along with the other unconditional preconditions of the action.

2. An action a_k can be a *conditional threat* on a causal link $\langle a_i \xrightarrow{p} a_j \rangle$ when the threatening effect is a conditional effect of a_k. In that case, there is another set of possible resolvers for this threat. In addition to ordering and binding constraints, here one may also solve the threat by adding to the *agenda*, as a precondition of a_k, the negation of a proposition in the antecedent condition of the threat. By making the antecedent condition false, one is sure that a_k cannot be a threat to the causal link. Note that there can be several such resolvers.

Disjunctive Preconditions. These correspond to a syntactical facility that allows one to specify in a concise way several operators into a single one. They are in principle easy to handle although they lead to an exponentially larger search space. Whenever the pair selected in the *agenda* corresponds to a disjunctive precondition, a nondeterministic choice takes place. One disjunct is chosen for which relevant providers are sought, and the procedure is pursued. The other disjuncts of the precondition are left as a possible backtrack point.

Quantified Conditional Effects. Under the assumption of a finite Σ, a quantified expression can be expanded into a finite ground expression. This expansion is made easier when each object in the domain is typed (see Section 2.4).

5.6 Plan-Space versus State-Space Planning

The search space is a critical aspect for the types of plans that can be synthesized and for the performance of a planner. Here are some of the ways in which plan-space planning compares to state-space planning.

- The state space is finite (under assumption A0), while the plan space is not, as discussed earlier.
- Intermediate states are explicit in state-space planning, while there are no explicit states in the plan space.
- A partial plan separates the choice of the actions that need to be done from how to organize them into a plan; it only keeps the intrinsic ordering and binding

constraints of the chosen actions. In state-space planning, the ordering of the sequence of actions reflects these constraints as well as the control strategy of the planner.

- The plan structure and the rationale for the plan's components are explicit in the plan space: causal links give the role of each action with respect to goals and preconditions. It is easy to explain a partial plan to a user. A sequence generated by a state-space planner is less explicit with regard to this causal structure.
- Nodes of the search space are more complex in the plan space than in states. Refinement operations for a partial plan take significantly longer to compute than state transitions or state regressions.

Despite the extra cost for each node, plan-space planning appeared for a while to be a significant improvement over state-space planning, leading to a search exploring smaller spaces for several planning domains [52, 544].

However, partial plans have an important drawback: the notion of explicit states along a plan is lost. Recent state-space planners have been able to significantly benefit from this advantage by making very efficient use of domain-specific heuristics and control knowledge. This has enabled state-space planning to scale up to very large problems. There are some attempts to generalize these heuristics and control techniques to plan-space planning [424]. However, it appears to be harder to control plan-space planners as efficiently as state-space ones because of the lack of explicit states.[5]

In summary, plan-space planners are not today competitive enough in classical planning with respect to computational efficiency. Nevertheless, plan-space planners have other advantages.

- They build partially ordered and partially instantiated plans that are more explicit and flexible for execution than plans created with state-space planners.
- They provide an open planning approach for handling several extensions to the classical framework, such as time, resources, and information gathering actions. In particular, planning with temporal and resource constraints can be introduced as natural generalization of the PSP schema (see Chapter 14).
- They allow distributed planning and multiagent planning to be addressed very naturally, since different types of plan-merging operations are easily defined and handled on the partial plan structure.

A natural question then arises: is it possible to blend state-space planning and plan-space planning into an approach that keeps the best of the two worlds?

5. For more detail, see Part III about heuristics and control issues, and in particular see Section 9.4 on heuristics for plan-space planning.

The planner called FLECS [527] provides an affirmative answer. The idea in FLECS is to combine the least commitment principle with what is called an *eager commitment strategy*. The former chooses new actions and constraints in order to solve flaws in a partial plan π, as is done PSP. The latter maintains a current state s; whenever there is in π an action a applicable to s that has no predecessor in $\prec$ except a_0, this strategy chooses to progress from s to the successor state $\gamma(s, a)$. Flaws are assessed with respect to this new current state. At each recursion, FLECS introduces a flexible choice point between eager and least commitment: it chooses nondeterministically either to progress on the current state or to solve some flaw in the current partial plan. The termination condition is an empty set of flaws. In a way, FLECS applies to plan-space planning the idea of the STRIPS procedure in state-space planning (see Exercise 5.10). However, unlike STRIPS, the procedure is sound and complete, provided that the flexible choice between eager and least commitment is a backtrack point. Several interesting heuristics for guiding this choice, and in particular an abstraction-driven heuristic, can be considered [524].

5.7 Discussion and Historical Remarks

The shift from state-space to plan-space planning is usually attributed to Sacerdoti [460], who developed a planner called NOAH [459] that has also been a seminal contribution to task reduction or Hierarchical Task Network (HTN) planning (see Chapter 11). Interestingly, the structure of a partial plan emerged progressively from another contribution to HTN planning, the Nonlin planner [503], which introduced causal links.[6] Nonlin raised the issue of *linear* versus *nonlinear* planning, which remained for a while an important and confusing debate issue in the field. The *linear* adjective for a planner referred confusingly in different papers either to the structure of the planner's current set of actions (a sequence instead of a partial order) or to a search strategy that addresses one goal after the previous one has been completely solved.

The issue of interacting goals in a planning problem and how to handle them efficiently has been a motivating concern for the study of the plan space. Starting from [502] and the so-called Sussman anomaly (see Example 4.3), several authors [51, 164, 267, 291] discussed this issue.

In the context of plan-space planning, Korf [336] introduced a distinction between problems with fully independent goals, serializable goals, and arbitrarily interacting goals. The first category is the easiest to handle. In the second category, there is an ordering constraint for solving the goals without violating the previously solved ones. If the goals are addressed in this correct order, then the planning complexity grows linearly in the number of goals. This goal dependence hierarchy is further refined in the context of plan-space planning by Barrett and

6. See [297] for a comparative analysis of plan-space and HTN planning.

Weld [52], where the authors introduce a planner-dependent notion of trivially and laboriously serializable goals. According to their analysis, plan-space planners have the advantage of more often leading to trivial serializable goals that are easily solved.

The truth criterion in a partial plan has been another major debate in the field. In state-space planning, it is trivial to check whether some condition is true or not in some current state. But plan-space planning does not keep explicit states. Hence it is less easy to verify whether a proposition is true before or after the execution of an action in a partially ordered and partially instantiated set of actions. The so-called Modal Truth Criterion (MTC) [120] provided a necessary and sufficient condition for the truth of a proposition at some point in a partial plan π. A planner called TWEAK relied at each recursion on the evaluation of this MTC criterion for synthesizing a plan in the plan space. It was shown that if π contains actions with conditional effects, then the evaluation of the MTC is an NP-hard problem. This complexity result led to a belief that plan-space planning with extended representation is impractical. However, this belief is incorrect because planning does not require a necessary and sufficient truth condition. It only has to enforce a sufficient truth condition, which basically corresponds in PSP to the identification and resolution of flaws, performed in polynomial time. A detailed analysis of the MTC in planning appears in Kambhampati and Nau [303].

The UCPOP planner of Penberthy and Weld [436, 544] has been a major contribution to plan-space planning. It builds on the advances brought by SNLP [381], an improved formalization of TWEAK, to propose a proven sound and complete planner able to handle most of the extensions to the classical representation introduced in the Action Description Language (ADL) of Pednault [433, 434]. The well-documented open-source Lisp implementation of UCPOP [50] offers several enhancements such as domain axioms and control rules. The latter even incorporate some of the learning techniques developed in the state-space planner PRODIGY [393, 524] for acquiring control knowledge.

The work on UCPOP opened the way to several other extensions such as handling incomplete information and sensing actions [183, 236, 438] and managing extended goals with protection conditions that guarantee a plan meeting some safety requirements [546] (see Part V). Issues such as the effects of domain features on the performance of the planner [327] and the role of ground actions (i.e., an early commitment as opposed to a late commitment strategy) [563] have been studied. Recent implementations, such as HCPOP [217], offer quite effective search control and pruning capabilities. The study of the relationship between state space and plan space exemplified in the FLECS planner [527] follows on several algorithmic contributions such as those by Minton *et al.* [392, 394] and on studies that relate the performance of PSP to specific features of the planning domain [327]. The work of Kambhampati *et al.* [296, 302] introduces a much wider perspective and a nice formalization that takes into account many design issues such as multiple contributors to a goal or systematicity [295], i.e., whether a planner is nonredundant and does not visit a partial plan in the space more than once.

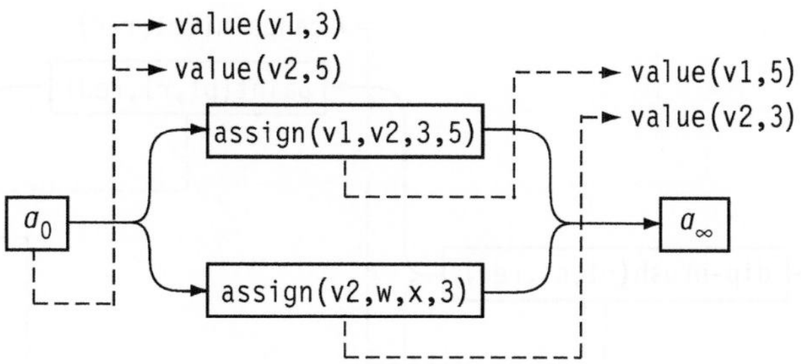

Figure 5.9 Partial plan for interchanging variables.

5.8 Exercises

5.1 Figure 5.9 shows a partial plan generated by PSP for the variable-interchange problem described in Exercise 4.1.

(a) How many threats are there?

(b) How many children (immediate successors) would this partial plan have?

(c) How many different solution plans can be reached from this partial plan?

(d) How many different nonredundant solution plans can be reached from this partial plan?

(e) If we start PSP running from this plan, can it ever find any redundant solutions?

(f) Trace the operation of PSP starting from this plan, along whichever execution trace finds the solution that has the smallest number of actions.

5.2 Trace the PSP procedure step-by-step on Example 5.1 (see page 86), from Figure 5.2 to Figure 5.5.

5.3 Trace the operation of PSP on the Sussman anomaly (Example 4.3; see page 86).

5.4 Trace the PSP procedure on the problem that has a single partially instantiated goal in(*c*,p2) with an initial state similar to that of Figure 5.1 except that location l1 has two piles p0 and p1, p0 has a single container c0, and p1 has a container c1.

5.5 Let $\mathcal{P}$ be a planning problem in which no operator has any negative effects.

(a) What part(s) of PSP will not be needed to solve $\mathcal{P}$?

(b) Suppose we run PSP deterministically, with a best-first control strategy. When, if at all, will PSP have to backtrack?

5.6 Consider the following "painting problem." We have a can of red paint (c1), a can of blue paint (c2), two paint brushes (r1, r2), and four unpainted blocks

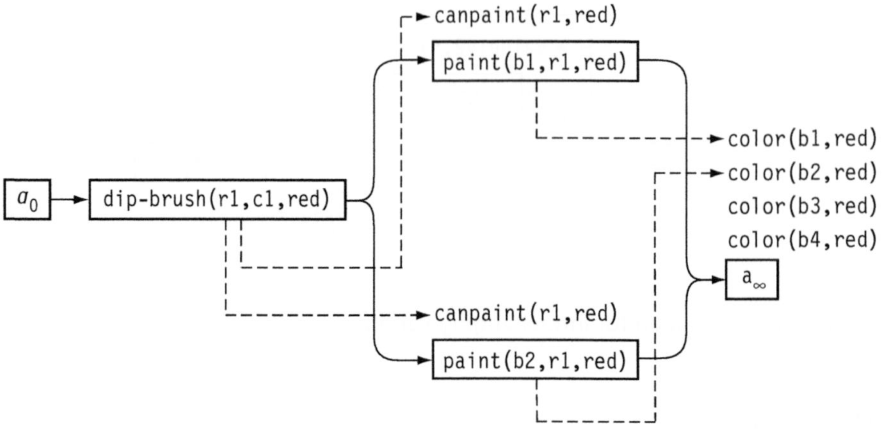

Figure 5.10 Partial plan for painting blocks.

(b1, b2, b3, b4). We want to make b1 and b2 red and make b3 and b4 blue. Here is a classical formulation of the problem:

s_0 = {can(c1), can(c2), color(c1,red), color(c2,blue), brush(r1), brush(r2), dry(r1), dry(r2), block(b1), block(b2), dry(b1), dry(b2), block(b3), block(b4), dry(b3), dry(b4)}

g = {color(b1,red), color(b2,red), color(b3,blue), color(b4,blue)}

dip-brush(r, c, k)
  precond: brush(r), can(c), color(c, k)
  effects: ¬dry(r), canpaint(r, k)

paint(b, r, k)
  precond: block(b), brush(r), canpaint(r, k)
  effects: ¬dry(b), color(b, k), ¬canpaint(r, k)

(a) In the paint operator, what is the purpose of the effect ¬canpaint(r,k)?

(b) Starting from the initial state, will PSP ever generate the partial plan shown in Figure 5.10? Explain why or why not.

(c) What threats are in the partial plan?

(d) Starting from the partial plan, resolve all of the open goals without resolving any threats. What threats are in the plan now?

(e) If we start PSP running with this plan as input, will PSP generate any successors? Explain why or why not.

(f) If we start PSP running with this plan as input, will PSP find a solution? Explain why or why not.

5.7 Dan wants to wash his clothes with a washing machine wm, wash his dishes in a dishwasher dw, and bathe in a bathtub bt. The water supply doesn't have enough pressure to do more than one of these activities at once. Here is a classical representation of the problem:

Initial state: status(dw,ready), status(wm,ready), status(bt,ready),
clean(dan,0), clean(clothes,0), clean(dishes,0),
loc(dishes,dw), loc(clothes,wm), loc(dan,bt), use(water,0)

Goal formula: clean(clothes,1), clean(dishes,1), clean(dan,1)

Operators:

```
start-fill(x)                                     end-fill(x)
  precond:  status(x,ready), use(water,0)           precond:  status(x,fill)
  effects:  status(x,fill),                         effects:  status(x,full),
            use(water,1)                                      use(water,0)

start-wash(x)                     end-wash(x, y)
  precond:  status(x,full)          precond:  status(x,wash)
  effects:  status(x,wash)          effects:  status(x,ready), clean(y,1)
```

(a) Let π_1 be the partial plan shown in Figure 5.11. What threats are in π_1?

(b) What flaws are in π_1 other than threats?

(c) How many different solutions can PSP find if we start it out with plan π_1 and do not allow it to add any new actions to the plan? Explain your answer.

(d) How many different solutions can PSP find if we do allow it to add new actions to π_1? Explain your answer.

5.8 Let $P = (O, s_0, g)$ and $P' = (O, s_0, g')$ be the statements of two planning problems having the same operators and initial state. Let B and B' be the search spaces for PSP on P and P', respectively.

(a) If $g \subseteq g'$, then is $B \subseteq B'$?

(b) If $B \subseteq B'$, then is $g \subseteq g'$?

(c) Under what conditions, if any, can we guarantee that B is finite?

(d) How does your answer to part (c) change if we run PSP deterministically with a breadth-first control strategy?

(e) How does your answer to part (c) change if we run PSP deterministically with a depth-first control strategy?

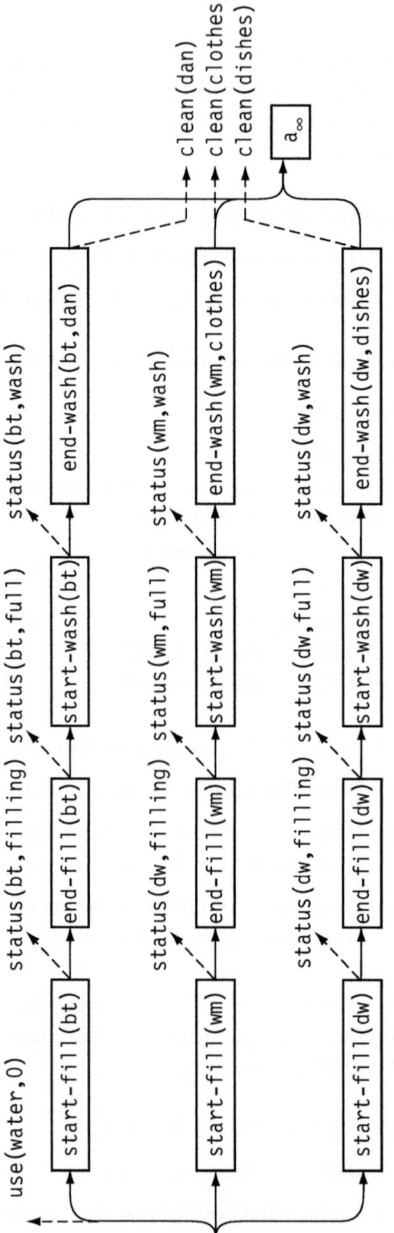

Figure 5.11 Partial plan for washing.

5.9 If $\mathcal{L}$ is a planning language in which the number of different ground atoms is n, then for any planning domain whose language is $\mathcal{L}$, the number of possible different states is at most 2^n. Use this upper bound on the number of states to create a simple loop-detection mechanism for PSP. Why is this loop-detection mechanism not very useful in practice?

5.10 Discuss the commonalities and differences of FLECS and STRIPS. Why is the former complete while the latter is not?

5.11 Download one of the public-domain plan-space planners, e.g., UCPOP[7] or HCPOP [217]. Test the full DWR example on several domains and problems with an increasing number of locations, robots, and containers. Discuss the practical range of applicability of this planner for the DWR application.

---

7. http://www.cs.washington.edu/ai/ucpop.html.

PART II

Neoclassical Planning

Neoclassical planning, like classical planning, is also concerned with restricted state-transition systems. We will be using here the classical representations developed in Chapter 2. However, at a time when classical planning appeared to be stalled for expressiveness as well as for complexity reasons, the techniques discussed in this part, that we qualify as *neoclassical*,[1] led to a revival of the research on classical planning problems. The development of neoclassical techniques brought new search spaces and search algorithms for planning that allowed directly (or indirectly through improvement of classical techniques) a significant increase on the size of classical problems that could be solved.

The main differences between classical and neoclassical techniques are the following.

- In classical planning, every node of the search space is a partial plan, i.e., a sequence of actions in the state space, or a partially ordered set of actions in the plan space; any solution reachable from that node contains *all* the actions of this partial plan.
- In neoclassical planning, every node of the search space can be viewed as a set of several partial plans. This set is either explicit or implicit in the data structures that make a search node, but it is evident in the fact that in the neoclassical approaches, not every action in a node appears in a solution plan reachable from that node.[2]

---

1. *Neoclassic: of or relating to a revival or adaptation of the classical style, especially in literature, art, or music* [Webster New Collegiate Dictionary]. Neoclassical has referred to slightly different meanings in planning literature depending on one's views of where and when the revival took place.
2. Because of this property, neoclassical planning approaches have sometimes been called *disjunctive-refinement approaches* [306].

We will come back to this common feature in Part III, once the reader has become familiar with the neoclassical techniques. Three such techniques will be studied here.

- *Planning-graph* techniques are based on a powerful reachability structure for a planning problem called a *planning graph*, which is used to efficiently organize and constrain the search space.
- *Propositional satisfiability* techniques encode a planning problem into a SAT problem and then rely on efficient SAT procedures for finding a solution, among which are complete methods based on the Davis-Putnam procedure and pseudorandom local search methods.
- *Constraint satisfaction* techniques similarly enable encoding a planning problem into a constraint satisfaction problem and also bring to the field a variety of efficient methods, in particular filtering and constraint propagation for disjunctive refinements in the plan space or within the planning-graph approaches.

These three techniques are described in Chapters 6, 7 and 8, respectively.

CHAPTER 6

Planning-Graph Techniques

6.1 Introduction

The *planning-graph techniques* developed in this chapter rely on the classical representation scheme.[1] These techniques introduce a very powerful search space called a *planning graph*, which departs significantly from the two search spaces presented earlier, the state space (Chapter 4) and the plan space (Chapter 5).

State-space planners provide a plan as a sequence of actions. Plan-space planners synthesize a plan as a partially ordered set of actions; any sequence that meets the constraints of the partial order is a valid plan. Planning-graph approaches take a middle ground. Their output is a sequence of sets of actions, e.g., $\langle\{a_1, a_2\}, \{a_3, a_4\}, \{a_5, a_6, a_7\}\rangle$, which represents all sequences starting with a_1 and a_2 in any order, followed by a_3 and a_4 in any order, followed by a_5, a_6, and a_7 in any order. A sequence of sets of actions is obviously more general than a sequence of actions: there are $2 \times 2 \times 6 = 24$ sequences of actions in the previous example. However, a sequence of sets is less general than a partial order. It can be expressed immediately as a partial order, but the converse is false, e.g., a plan with three actions a_1, a_2, and a_3 and a single ordering constraint $a_1 \prec a_3$ cannot be structured as a sequence of sets unless an additional constraint is added.

We have seen that the main idea behind plan-space planning is the *least commitment principle*: i.e., to refine a partial plan, one flaw at a time, by adding only the ordering and binding constraints needed to solve that flaw. Planning-graph approaches, on the other hand, make strong commitments while planning: actions are considered fully instantiated and at specific steps. These approaches rely instead on two powerful and interrelated ideas: *reachability analysis* and *disjunctive refinement.*

Reachability analysis addresses the issue of whether a state is reachable from some given state s_0. Disjunctive refinement consists of addressing one or several flaws

---

1. The Graphplan algorithm assumes, for notational convenience, a somewhat restricted but theoretically equivalent representation, with no negated literals in preconditions of operators nor in goals; this restriction is easily relaxed.

through a disjunction of resolvers. Because in general flaws are not independent and their resolvers may interfere, dependency relations are posted as constraints to be dealt with at a later stage.

Disjunctive refinement may not appear right away to the reader as the main motivation in planning-graph techniques. However, reachability analysis is clearly a driving mechanism for these approaches. Let us detail its principles and the planning-graph structure (Section 6.2) before getting into planning-graph algorithms (Section 6.3).

6.2 Planning Graphs

The planning-graph structure provides an efficient way to estimate which set of propositions[2] is possibly reachable from s_0 with which actions. We first discuss here the general notion of state reachability, which cannot be computed in a tractable way. We then introduce the relaxed reachability estimate provided by a planning graph. Then we detail the issues of independence between actions and mutual exclusion for actions and propositions in a planning graph.

6.2.1 Reachability Trees

Given a set A of actions, a state s is *reachable* from some initial state s_0 if there is a sequence of actions in A that defines a path from s_0 to s. Reachability analysis consists of analyzing which states can be reached from s_0 in some number of steps and how to reach them. Reachability can be computed *exactly* through a *reachability tree* that gives $\hat{\Gamma}(s_0)$, or it can be *approximated* through a planning graph developed as shown in this section. Let us first introduce an example.

Example 6.1 Consider a simplified DWR domain with no piles and no cranes where robots can load and unload autonomously containers and where locations may contain an unlimited number of robots. In this domain, let us define a problem (see Figure 6.1) with two locations (loc1 and loc2), two containers (conta and contb), and two robots (robr and robq). Initially, robr and conta are in location loc1, robq and contb are in loc2. The goal is to have conta in loc2 and contb in loc1. Here, the set A has 20 actions corresponding to the instances of the three operators in Figure 6.1.

To simplify the forthcoming figures, let us denote ground atoms by propositional symbols.

2. In the context of a first-order language classical planning, we will use the terms *ground atom* and *proposition* interchangeably.

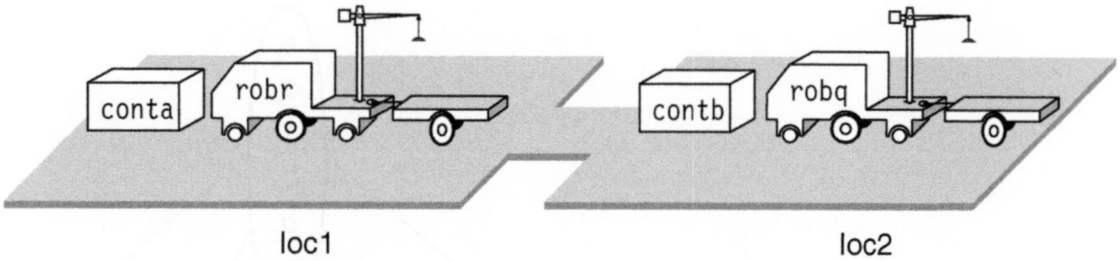

move(r, l, l') ;; robot r at location l moves to a connected location l'
  precond: at(r, l), adjacent(l, l')
  effects: at(r, l'), $\neg$ at(r, l)

load(c, r, l) ;; robot r loads container c at location l
  precond: at(r, l), in(c, l), unloaded(r)
  effects: loaded(r, c), $\neg$ in(c, l), $\neg$ unloaded(r)

unload(c, r, l) ;; robot r unloads container c at location l
  precond: at(r, l), loaded(r, c)
  effects: unloaded(r), in(c, l), $\neg$ loaded(r, c)

Figure 6.1 A simplified DWR problem.

- r_1 and r_2 stand for at(robr,loc1) and at(robr,loc2), respectively.
- q_1 and q_2 stand for at(robq,loc1) and at(robq,loc2), respectively.
- a_1, a_2, a_r, and a_q stand for container conta in location loc1, in location loc2, loaded on robr, and loaded on robq, respectively.
- b_1, b_2, b_r, and b_q stand for the possible positions of container contb.
- u_r and u_q stand for unloaded(robr) and unloaded(robq), respectively.

Let us also denote the 20 actions in A as follows.

- Mr12 is the action move(robr,loc1,loc2), Mr21 is the opposite move, and Mq12 and Mq21 are the similar move actions of robot robq.
- Lar1 is the action load(conta,robr,loc1). Lar2, Laq1, and Laq2 are the other load actions for conta in loc2 and with robq, respectively. Lbr1, Lbr2, Lbq1, and Lbq2 are the load actions for contb.
- Uar1, Uar2, Uaq1, Uaq2, Ubr1, Ubr2, Ubq1, and Ubq2 are the unload actions.

The reachability tree for this domain, partially developed down to level 2 from the initial state $\{r_1, q_2, a_1, b_2, u_r, u_q\}$, is shown in Figure 6.2. ■

A reachability tree is a tree T whose nodes are states of Σ and whose edges corresponds to actions of Σ. The root of T is the state s_0. The children of a node s are

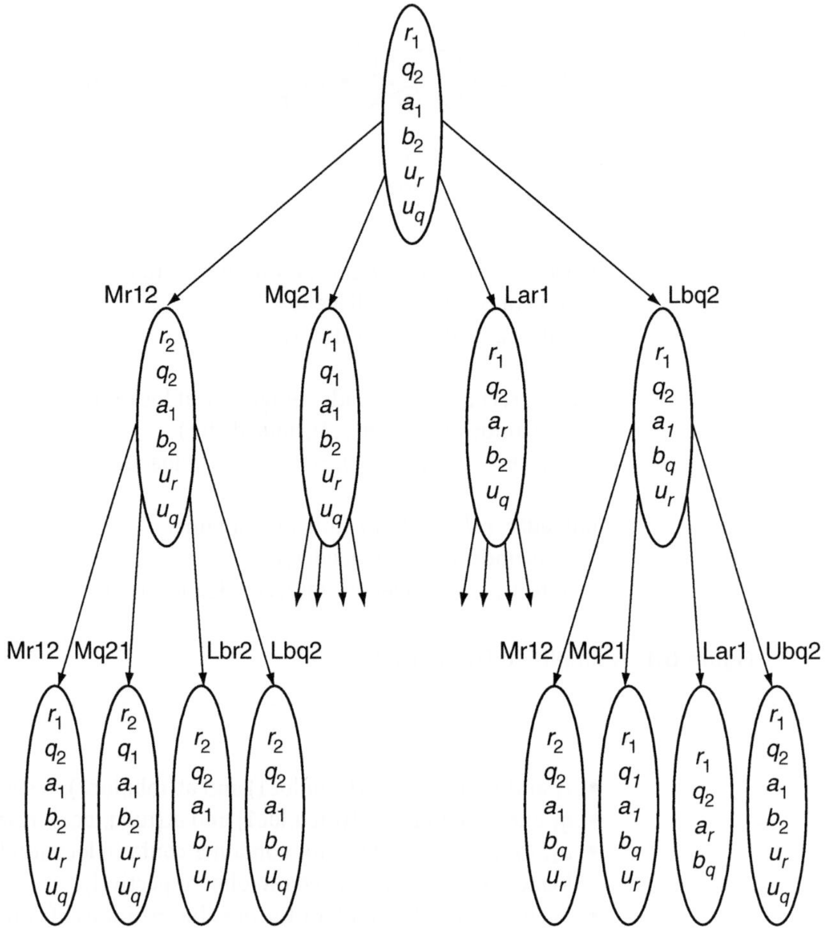

Figure 6.2 Reachability tree.

all the states in $\Gamma(s)$. A complete reachability tree from s_0 gives $\hat{\Gamma}(s_0)$. A reachability tree developed down to depth d solves *all* planning problems with s_0 and A, for *every* goal that is reachable in d or fewer actions: a goal is reachable from s_0 in at most d steps iff it appears in some node of the tree. Unfortunately, a reachability tree blows up in $O(k^d)$ nodes, where k is the number of valid actions per state.

Since some nodes can be reached by different paths, the reachability tree can be factorized into a graph. Figure 6.3 illustrates such a reachability graph down to level 2 for Example 6.1 (omitting for clarity most of the back arcs from a node to its parents). However, even this reachability graph would be a very large, impractical size, as large as the number of states in the domain.

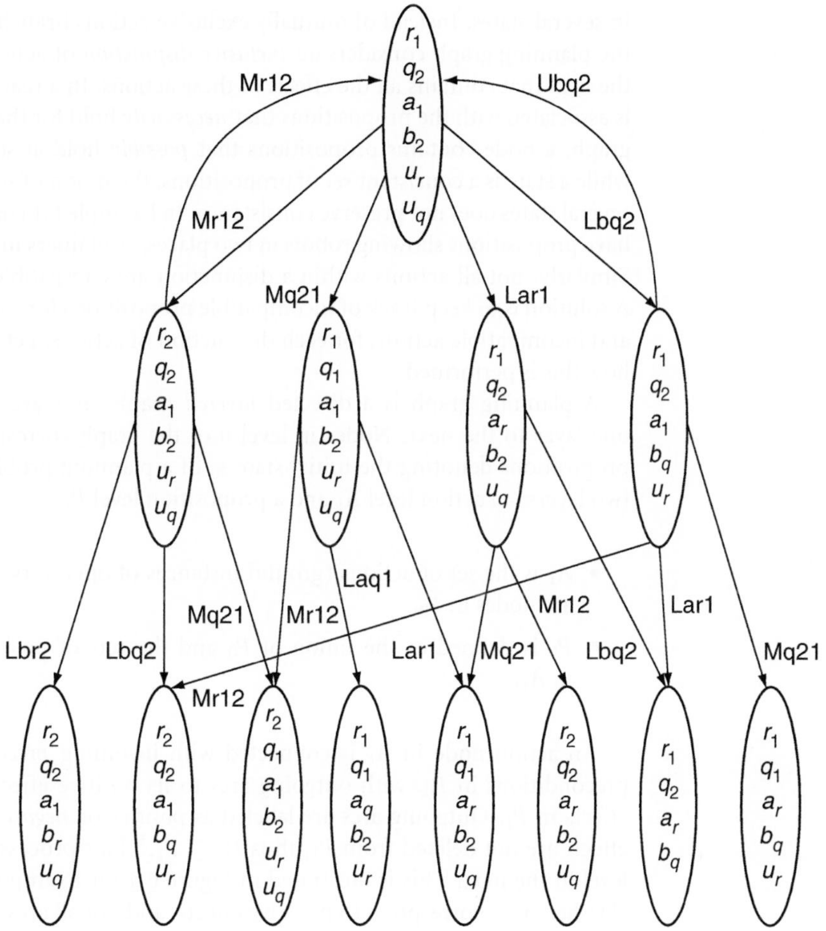

Figure 6.3 Reachability graph.

6.2.2 Reachability with Planning Graphs

A major contribution of the Graphplan planner is a relaxation of the reachability analysis. The approach provides an incomplete condition of reachability through a planning graph. A goal is reachable from s_0 *only if* it appears in some node of the planning graph. However, this is not a sufficient condition anymore. This weak reachability condition is compensated for by a low complexity: the planning graph is of polynomial size and can be built in polynomial time in the size of the input.

The basic idea in a planning graph is to consider at every level of this structure not individual states but, to a first approximation, the *union* of sets of propositions in several states. Instead of mutually exclusive actions branching out from a node, the planning graph considers an *inclusive disjunction* of actions from one node to the next that contains all the effects of these actions. In a reachability graph a node is associated with the propositions that *necessarily* hold for that node. In a planning graph, a node contains propositions that *possibly* hold at some point. However, while a state is a consistent set of propositions, the union of sets of propositions for several states does not preserve consistency. In Example 6.1 (see page 114) we would have propositions showing robots in two places, containers in several locations, etc. Similarly, not all actions within a disjunction are compatible; they may interfere. A solution is to keep track of incompatible propositions for each set of propositions and incompatible actions for each disjunction of actions. Let us explain informally how this is performed.

A planning graph is a directed *layered* graph: arcs are permitted only from one layer to the next. Nodes in level 0 of the graph correspond to the set P_0 of propositions denoting the initial state s_0 of a planning problem. Level 1 contains two layers: an action level A_1 and a proposition level P_1.

- A_1 is the set of actions (ground instances of operators) whose preconditions are nodes in P_0.
- P_1 is defined as the union of P_0 and the sets of positive effects of actions in A_1.

An action node in A_1 is connected with incoming *precondition arcs* from its preconditions in P_0, with outgoing arcs to its positive effects and to its negative effects in P_1. Outgoing arcs are labeled as *positive* or *negative*. Note that negative effects are not deleted from P_1, thus $P_0 \subseteq P_1$.[3] This process is pursued from one level to the next. This is illustrated in Figure 6.4 for Example 6.1 down to level 3. (Dashed lines correspond to negative effects, and not all arcs are shown.)

In accordance with the idea of inclusive disjunction in A_i and of union of propositions in P_i, a plan associated to a planning graph is no longer a sequence of actions corresponding directly to a path in Σ, as defined in Chapter 2. Here, a plan Π is *sequence of sets of actions* $\Pi = \langle \pi_1, \pi_2, \ldots, \pi_k \rangle$. It will be qualified as a *layered plan* since it is organized into levels corresponding to those of the planning graph, with $\pi_i \subseteq A_i$. The first level π_1 is a subset of independent actions in A_1 that can be applied in *any* order to the initial state and can lead to a state that is a subset of P_1. From this state, actions in $\pi_2 \subseteq A_2$ would proceed and so on until a level π_k, whose actions lead to a state meeting the goal. Let us define these notions more precisely.

3. The persistence principle or "frame axiom," which states that unless it is explicitly modified, a proposition persists from one state to the next, is modeled here through this definition that makes $P_0 \subseteq P_1$.

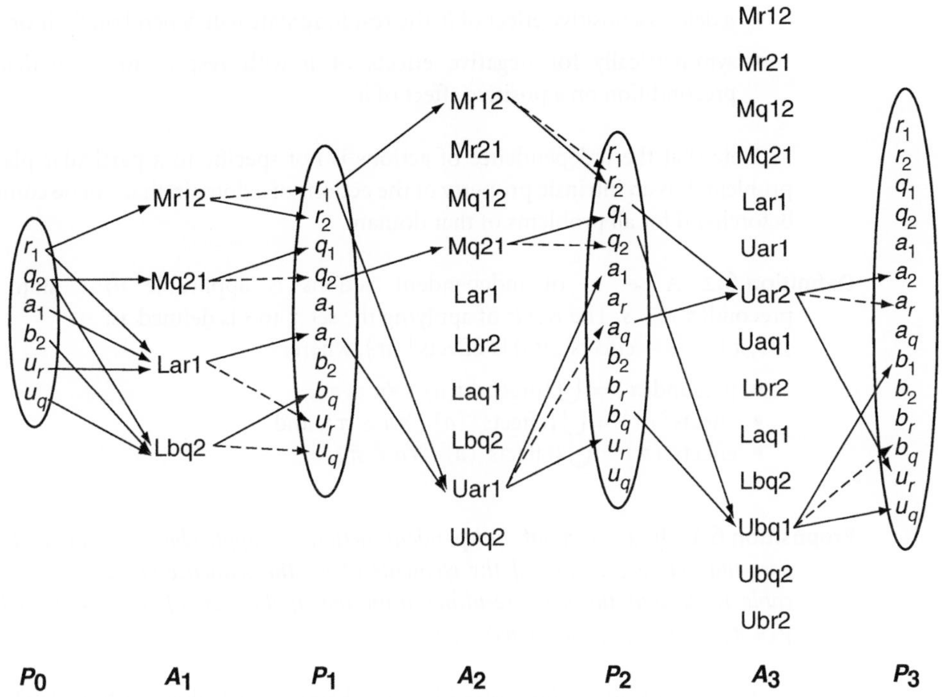

Figure 6.4 Planning graph.

6.2.3 Independent Actions and Layered Plans

In Example 6.1 (see page 114), the two actions Mr12 (i.e., move(robr, loc1, loc2)) and Mq21 in A_1 are *independent*: they can appear at the beginning of a plan in any order, and the two sequences ⟨Mr12, Mq21⟩ and ⟨Mq21, Mr12⟩ when applied to s_0 lead to the same state; similarly for the pair Mr12 and Lbq2. But the two actions Mr12 and Lar1 are not independent: a plan starting with Mr12 will be in a state where robr is in loc2, hence Lar1 is not applicable.

Definition 6.1 Two actions (a, b) are *independent* iff:

- $\text{effects}^-(a) \cap [\text{precond}(b) \cup \text{effects}^+(b)] = \emptyset$ and
- $\text{effects}^-(b) \cap [\text{precond}(a) \cup \text{effects}^+(a)] = \emptyset$.

A set of actions π is independent when every pair of π is independent. ■

Conversely, two actions a and b are *dependent* if:

- a deletes a precondition of b: the ordering $a \prec b$ will not be permitted; or

- a deletes a positive effect of b: the resulting state will depend on their order; or
- symmetrically for negative effects of b with respect to a: b deletes a precondition on a positive effect of a.

Note that the independence of actions is not specific to a particular planning problem: it is an intrinsic property of the actions of a domain that can be computed beforehand for all problems of that domain.

Definition 6.2 A set π of independent actions is applicable to a state s iff $\text{precond}(\pi) \subseteq s$. The *result* of applying the set π to s is defined as: $\gamma(s, \pi) = (s - \text{effects}^-(\pi)) \cup \text{effects}^+(\pi)$, where:

- $\text{precond}(\pi) = \bigcup\{\text{precond}(a) \mid \forall a \in \pi\}$,
- $\text{effects}^+(\pi) = \bigcup\{\text{effects}^+(a) \mid \forall a \in \pi\}$, and
- $\text{effects}^-(\pi) = \bigcup\{\text{effects}^-(a) \mid \forall a \in \pi\}$.

■

Proposition 6.1 *If a set π of independent actions is applicable to s then, for any permutation $\langle a_1, \ldots, a_k\rangle$ of the elements of π, the sequence $\langle a_1, \ldots, a_k\rangle$ is applicable to s, and the state resulting from the application of π to s is such that $\gamma(s, \pi) = \gamma(\ldots\gamma(\gamma(s, a_1), a_2)\ldots a_k)$.*

This proposition (whose proof is left as Exercise 6.6) allows us to go back to the standard semantics of a plan as a path in a state-transition system from the initial state to a goal.

Definition 6.3 A *layered plan* is a sequence of sets of actions. The layered plan $\Pi = \langle\pi_1, \ldots, \pi_n\rangle$ is a solution to a problem (O, s_0, g) iff each set $\pi_i \in \Pi$ is independent, and the set π_1 is applicable to s_0, π_2 is applicable to $\gamma(s_0, \pi_1)$, ..., etc., and $g \subseteq \gamma(\ldots\gamma(\gamma(s_0, \pi_1), \pi_2)\ldots\pi_n)$.

■

Proposition 6.2 *If $\Pi = \langle\pi_1, \ldots, \pi_n\rangle$ is a solution plan to a problem (O, s_0, g), then a sequence of actions corresponding to any permutation of the elements of π_1, followed by any permutation of π_2 ..., followed by any permutation of π_n is a path from s_0 to a goal state.*

This proposition follows directly from Proposition 6.1.

6.2.4 Mutual Exclusion Relations

Two dependent actions in the action level A_1 of the planning graph cannot appear simultaneously in the first level π_1 of a plan. Hence, the positive effects of two dependent actions in A_1 are incompatible propositions in P_1, unless these propositions are also positive effects of some other independent actions. In our example,

r_2 and a_r are the positive effects, respectively, of Mr12 and Lar1, and only of these dependent actions. These two propositions are incompatible in P_1 in the following sense: they cannot be reached through a single level of actions π_1, and similarly for q_1 and b_q.

Furthermore, negative and positive effects of an action are also incompatible propositions. This is the case for the pair (r_1, r_2), (q_1, q_2), (a_r, u_r), (b_q, u_q) in level P_1 of Figure 6.4. In order to deal uniformly with this second type of incompatibility between propositions, it is convenient to introduce for each proposition p a neutral *no-op* action, noted α_p, whose precondition and sole effect is p.[4] If an action a has p as a negative effect, then according to our definition, a and α_p are dependent actions; their positive effects are incompatible.

Dependency between actions in an action level A_i of the planning graph leads to incompatible propositions in the proposition level P_i. Conversely, incompatible propositions in a level P_i lead to additional incompatible actions in the following level A_{i+1}. These are the actions whose preconditions are incompatible. In Example 6.1, (r_1, r_2) are incompatible in P_1. Consequently, Lar1 and Mr21 are incompatible in A_2. Note that an action whose preconditions are incompatible is simply removed from A_{i+1}. This is the case for Uar2 (r_2 and a_r incompatible) and for Ubq2 in A_2. Indeed, while an incompatible pair in A_i is useful because one of its actions may be used in level π_i of a plan, there is no sense in keeping an impossible action.

The incompatibility relations between actions and between propositions in a planning graph, also called *mutual exclusion* or *mutex relations*, are formally defined as shown in Definition 6.4.

Definition 6.4 Two actions a and b in level A_i are *mutex* if either a and b are dependent or if a precondition of a is mutex with a precondition of b. Two propositions p and q in P_i are mutex if every action in A_i that has p as a positive effect (including no-op actions) is mutex with every action that produces q, and there is no action in A_i that produces both p and q. ■

Note that dependent actions are necessarily mutex. Dependency is an intrinsic property of the actions in a domain, while the mutex relation takes into account additional constraints of the problem at hand. For the same problem, a pair of actions may be mutex in some action level A_i and become nonmutex in some latter level A_j of a planning graph.

Example 6.2 Mutex relations for Example 6.1 (see page 114) are listed in Table 6.1, giving for each proposition or action at every level the list of elements that are mutually exclusive with it, omitting for simplicity the no-op actions. A star (*) denotes mutex actions that are independent but have mutex preconditions. ■

---

4. Hence, the result of no-op actions is to copy all the propositions of P_{i-1} into P_i: no-ops are also a way of modeling the persistence principle.

Table 6.1 Mutex actions and propositions.

Level	*Mutex elements*
A_1	{Mr12} × {Lar1}
	{Mq21} × {Lbq2}
P_1	$\{r_2\} \times \{r_1, a_r\}$
	$\{q_1\} \times \{q_2, b_q\}$
	$\{a_r\} \times \{a_1, u_r\}$
	$\{b_q\} \times \{b_2, u_q\}$
A_2	{Mr12} × {Mr21,Lar1,Uar1}
	{Mr21} × {Lbr2,Lar1*,Uar1*}
	{Mq12} × {Mq21,Laq1,Lbq2*,Ubq2*}
	{Mq21} × {Lbq2,Ubq2}
	{Lar1} × {Uar1,Laq1,Lbr2}
	{Lbr2} × {Ubq2,Lbq2,Uar1,Mr12*}
	{Laq1} × {Uar1,Ubq2,Lbq2,Mq21*}
	{Lbq2} × {Ubq2}
P_2	$\{b_r\} \times \{r_1, b_2, u_r, b_q, a_r\}$
	$\{a_q\} \times \{q_2, a_1, u_q, b_q, a_r\}$
	$\{r_1\} \times \{r_2\}$
	$\{q_1\} \times \{q_2\}$
	$\{a_r\} \times \{a_1, u_r\}$
	$\{b_q\} \times \{b_2, u_q\}$
A_3	{Mr12} × {Mr21,Lar1,Uar1,Lbr2*,Uar2*}
	{Mr21} × {Lbr2,Uar2,Ubr2}
	{Mq12} × {Mq21,Laq1,Uaq1,Ubq1,Ubq2*}
	{Mq21} × {Lbq2,Ubq2,Laq1*,Ubq1*}
	{Lar1} × {Uar1,Uaq1,Laq1,Uar2,Ubr2,Lbr2,Mr21*}
	{Lbr2} × {Ubr2,Ubq2,Lbq2,Uar1,Uar2,Ubq1*}
	{Laq1} × {Uar1,Uaq1,Ubq1,Ubq2,Lbq2,Uar2*}
	{Lbq2} × {Ubr2,Ubq2,Uaq1,Ubq1,Mq12*}
	{Uaq1} × {Uar1,Uar2,Ubq1,Ubq2,Mq21}*
	{Ubr2} × {Uar1,Uar2,Ubq1,Ubq2,Mr12}*
	{Uar1} × {Uar2,Mr21*}
	{Ubq1} × {Ubq2}
P_3	$\{a_2\} \times \{a_r, a_1, r_1, a_q, b_r\}$
	$\{b_1\} \times \{b_q, b_2, q_2, a_q, b_r\}$
	$\{a_r\} \times \{u_r, a_1, a_q, b_r\}$
	$\{b_q\} \times \{u_q, b_2, a_q, b_r\}$
	$\{a_q\} \times \{a_1, u_q\}$
	$\{b_r\} \times \{b_2, u_r\}$
	$\{r_1\} \times \{r_2\}$
	$\{q_1\} \times \{q_2\}$

In the rest of the chapter, we will denote the set of mutex pairs in A_i as μA_i, and the set of mutex pairs in P_i as μP_i. Let us remark that:

- dependency between actions as well as mutex between actions or propositions are *symmetrical* relations, and
- for $\forall i : P_{i-1} \subseteq P_i$, and $A_{i-1} \subseteq A_i$.

Proposition 6.3 *If two propositions p and q are in P_{i-1} and $(p, q) \notin \mu P_{i-1}$, then $(p, q) \notin \mu P_i$. If two actions a and b are in A_{i-1} and $(a, b) \notin \mu A_{i-1}$, then $(a, b) \notin \mu A_i$.*

Proof Every proposition p in a level P_i is supported by at least its no-op action α_p. Two no-op actions are necessarily independent. If p and q in P_{i-1} are such that $(p, q) \notin \mu P_{i-1}$, then $(\alpha_p, \alpha_q) \notin \mu A_i$. Hence, a nonmutex pair of propositions remains nonmutex in the following level. Similarly, if $(a, b) \notin \mu A_{i-1}$, then a and b are independent and their preconditions in P_{i-1} are not mutex; both properties remain valid at the following level. ■

According to this result, propositions and actions in a planning graph monotonically increase from one level to the next, while mutex pairs monotonically decrease. These monotonicity properties are essential to the complexity and termination of the planning-graph techniques.

Proposition 6.4 *A set g of propositions is reachable from s_0 only if there is in the corresponding planning graph a proposition layer P_i such that $g \in P_i$ and no pair of propositions in g are in μP_i.*

6.3 The Graphplan Planner

The Graphplan algorithm performs a procedure close to *iterative deepening*, discovering a new part of the search space at each iteration. It iteratively expands the planning graph by one level, then it searches backward from the last level of this graph for a solution. The first expansion, however, proceeds to a level P_i in which all of the goal propositions are included and no pairs of them are mutex because it does not make sense to start searching a graph that does not meet the necessary condition of Proposition 6.4.

The iterative loop of graph expansion and search is pursued until either a plan is found or a failure termination condition is met. Let us detail the algorithm and its properties.

6.3.1 Expanding the Planning Graph

Let (O, s_0, g) be a planning problem in the classical representation such that s_0 and g are sets of propositions, and operators in O have no negated literals in their preconditions. Let A be the union of all ground instances of operators in O and of all no-op actions α_p for every proposition p of that problem; the no-op action for p is defined as $\text{precond}(\alpha_p) = \text{effects}^+(\alpha_p) = \{p\}$, and $\text{effects}^- = \emptyset$. A planning graph for that problem expanded up to level i is a sequence of layers of nodes and of mutex pairs:

$$G = \langle P_0, A_1, \mu A_1, P_1, \mu P_1, \ldots, A_i, \mu A_i, P_i, \mu P_i \rangle$$

This planning graph does not depend on g; it can be used for different planning problems that have the same set of planning operators O and initial state s_0.

Starting initially from $P_0 \leftarrow s_0$, the expansion of G from level $i-1$ to level i is given by the Expand procedure (Figure 6.5). The steps of this procedure correspond to generating the sets A_i, P_i, μA_i, and μP_i, respectively, from the elements in the previous level $i-1$.

Let us analyze some properties of a planning graph.

Proposition 6.5 *The size of a planning graph down to level k and the time required to expand it to that level are polynomial in the size of the planning problem.*

Proof If the planning problem (O, s_0, g) has a total of n propositions and m actions, then $\forall i : |P_i| \leq n$, and $|A_i| \leq m + n$ (including no-op actions), $|\mu A_i| \leq (m+n)^2$, and $|\mu P_i| \leq n^2$. The steps involved in the generation of these sets are of polynomial complexity in the size of the sets.

Furthermore, n and m are polynomial in the size of the problem (O, s_0, g). This is the case because, according to classical planning assumptions, operators cannot

```
Expand(⟨P0, A1, μA1, P1, μP1, ..., A(i−1), μA(i−1), P(i−1), μP(i−1)⟩)
   Ai ← {a ∈ A | precond(a) ⊆ P(i−1) and precond²(a) ∩ μP(i−1) = ∅}
   Pi ← {p | ∃a ∈ Ai : p ∈ effects⁺(a)}
   μAi ← {(a, b) ∈ Ai², a ≠ b | effects⁻(a) ∩ [precond(b) ∪ effects⁺(b)] ≠ ∅
                or effects⁻(b) ∩ [precond(a) ∪ effects⁺(a)] ≠ ∅
                or ∃(p, q) ∈ μP(i−1) : p ∈ precond(a), q ∈ precond(b)}
   μPi ← {(p, q) ∈ Pi², p ≠ q | ∀a, b ∈ Ai, a ≠ b :
                p ∈ effects⁺(a), q ∈ effects⁺(b) ⇒ (a, b) ∈ μAi}
   for each a ∈ Ai do: link a with precondition arcs to precond(a) in P(i−1)
        positive arcs to effects⁺(a) and negative arcs to effects⁻(a) in Pi
   return(⟨P0, A1, μA1, ..., P(i−1), μP(i−1), Ai, μAi, Pi, μPi⟩)
end
```

Figure 6.5 Expansion of a planning graph.

create new constant symbols.[5] Hence, if c is the number of constant symbols given in the problem, $e = \max_{o \in O}\{|\,\mathrm{effects}^+(o)|\}$, and α is an upper bound on the number of parameters of any operator, then $m \leq |O| \times c^\alpha$, and $n \leq |s_0| + e \times |O| \times c^\alpha$. ■

Moreover, the number of distinct levels in a planning graph is bounded: at some stage, the graph reaches a *fixed-point level*, as defined next.

Definition 6.5 A *fixed-point level* in a planning graph G is a level κ such that for $\forall i, i > \kappa$, level i of G is identical to level κ, i.e., $P_i = P_\kappa$, $\mu P_i = \mu P_\kappa$, $A_i = A_\kappa$, and $\mu A_i = \mu A_\kappa$. ■

Proposition 6.6 *Every planning graph G has a fixed-point level κ, which is the smallest k such that $|P_{k-1}| = |P_k|$ and $|\mu P_{k-1}| = |\mu P_k|$.*

Proof To show that the planning graph has a fixed-point level, notice that (1) there is a finite number of propositions in a planning problem, (2) $\forall i$, $P_{i-1} \subseteq P_i$, and (3) if a pair $(p, q) \notin \mu P_{i-1}$, then $(p, q) \notin \mu P_i$. Hence, a proposition level P_i either has more propositions than P_{i-1} or it has as many propositions and, in that case, it has an equal number or fewer mutex pairs. Because these monotonic differences are bounded, at some point $(P_{i-1} = P_i)$ and $(\mu P_{i-1} = \mu P_i)$. Hence $(A_{i+1} = A_i)$ and $(\mu A_{i+1} = \mu A_i)$.

Now, suppose that $|P_{k-1}| = |P_k|$ and $|\mu P_{k-1}| = |\mu P_k|$; let us show that all levels starting at k are identical.

- Because $(|P_{k-1}| = |P_k|)$ and $\forall i$, $P_{i-1} \subseteq P_i$, it follows that $(P_{k-1} = P_k)$.
- Because $(P_{k-1} = P_k)$ and $(|\mu P_{k-1}| = |\mu P_k|)$, then $(\mu P_{k-1} = \mu P_k)$. This is the case because a nonmutex pair of propositions at $k - 1$ remains nonmutex at level k (Proposition 6.3).
- A_{k+1} depends only on P_k and μP_k. Thus $(P_{k-1} = P_k)$ and $(\mu P_{k-1} = \mu P_k)$ implies $(A_{k+1} = A_k)$, and consequently $(P_{k+1} = P_k)$. The two sets A_{k+1} and A_k have the same dependency constraints (that are intrinsic to actions) and the same mutex between their preconditions (because $\mu P_{k-1} = \mu P_k$), thus $\mu A_{k+1} = \mu A_k$. Consequently $\mu P_{k+1} = \mu P_k$.

Level $k+1$ being identical to level k, the same level will repeat for all i such that $i > k$. ■

6.3.2 Searching the Planning Graph

The search for a solution plan in a planning graph proceeds back from a level P_i that includes all goal propositions, no pair of which is mutex, i.e., $g \in P_i$ and $g^2 \cap \mu P_i = \emptyset$. The search procedure looks for a set $\pi_i \in A_i$ of nonmutex actions

5. This is due to assumption A0 about a finite Σ (see Chapter 1).

that achieve these propositions. Preconditions of elements of π_i become the new goal for level $i - 1$ and so on. A failure to meet the goal of some level j leads to a backtrack over other subsets of A_{j+1}. If level 0 is successfully reached, then the corresponding sequence $\langle \pi_1, \ldots, \pi_i \rangle$ is a solution plan.

Example 6.3 The goal $g = \{a_2, b_1\}$ of Example 6.1 (see page 114) is in P_3 without mutex (see Figure 6.6, where goal propositions and selected actions are shown in bold). The only actions in A_3 achieving g are, respectively, Uar2 and Uqb1. They are nonmutex, hence $\pi_3 = \{\text{Uar2, Ubq1}\}$.

At level 2, the preconditions of the actions in π_3 become the new goal: $\{r_2, a_r, q_1, b_q\}$. r_2 is achieved by α_{r_2} or by Mr12 in A_2; a_r by α_{a_r} or by Lar1. Out of the four combinations of these actions, three are mutex pairs: (Mr21,Lar1), (α_{r_2},Lar1), and (α_{r_2},α_{a_r}); the last two are mutex because they require mutex preconditions (r_1, r_2) and (r_2, a_r) in P_1. Similarly for the two couples of actions achieving q_1 and b_q: (Mq21,Lbq2), (α_{q_1},Lbq2), and (α_{q_1},α_{b_q}); are mutex pairs. Hence the only possibility in A_2 for achieving this subgoal is the subset $\pi_2 = \{\text{Mr12}, \alpha_{a_r}, \text{Mq21}, \alpha_{b_q}\}$.

At level 1, the new goal is $\{r_1, a_r, q_2, b_q\}$. Its propositions are achieved, respectively, by α_{r_1}, Lar1, α_{q_2}, and Lbq2.

Level 0 is successfully reached.

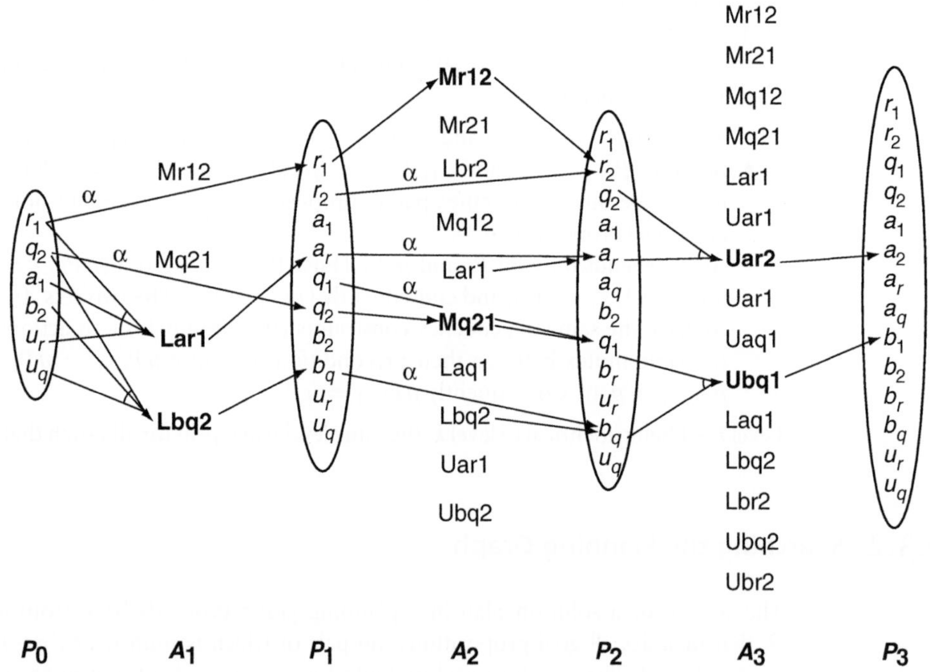

Figure 6.6 A solution plan.

The solution plan is thus the sequence of subsets, without no-op actions: $\Pi = \langle\{\text{Lar1}, \text{Lbq2}\}, \{\text{Mr12}, \text{Mq21}\}, \{\text{Uar2}, \text{Ubq1}\}\rangle$. ■

The extraction of a plan from a planning graph corresponds to a search in an AND/OR subgraph of the planning graph.

- From a proposition in goal g, *OR-branches* are arcs from all actions in the preceding action level that support this proposition, i.e., positive arcs to that proposition.
- From an action node, *AND-branches* are its precondition arcs (shown in Figure 6.6 as connected arcs).

The mutex relation between propositions provides only forbidden pairs, not tuples. But the search may show that a tuple of more than two propositions corresponding to an intermediate subgoal fails. Because of the backtracking and iterative deepening, the search may have to analyze that same tuple more than once. Recording the tuples that failed may save time in future searches. This recording is performed by procedure Extract (Figure 6.7) into a *nogood* hash-table denoted ∇. This hash table is indexed by the level of the failed goal because a goal g may fail at level i and succeed at $j > i$.

Extract takes as input a planning graph G, a current set of goal propositions g, and a level i. It extracts a set of actions $\pi_i \subseteq A_i$ that achieves propositions of g by recursively calling the GP-Search procedure (Figure 6.8). If it succeeds in reaching level 0, then it returns an empty sequence, from which pending recursions successfully return a solution plan. It records failed tuples into the ∇ table, and it checks each current goal with respect to recorded tuples. Note that a tuple g is added to the nogood table at a level i only if the call to GP-Search fails to establish g at this level from mutex and other nogoods found or established at the previous level.

```
Extract(G, g, i)
    if i = 0 then return (⟨⟩)
    if g ∈ ∇(i) then return(failure)
    π_i ← GP-Search(G, g, ∅, i)
    if π_i ≠ failure then return(π_i)
    ∇(i) ← ∇(i) ∪ {g}
    return(failure)
end
```

Figure 6.7 Extraction of a plan for a goal g.

```
GP-Search(G, g, π_i, i)
    if g = ∅ then do
        Π ← Extract(G, ⋃{precond(a) | ∀a ∈ π_i}, i − 1)
        if Π = failure then return(failure)
        return(Π.⟨π_i⟩)
    else do
        select any p ∈ g
        resolvers ← {a ∈ A_i | p ∈ effects+(a) and ∀b ∈ π_i : (a, b) ∉ μA_i}
        if resolvers = ∅ then return(failure)
        nondeterministically choose a ∈ resolvers
        return(GP-Search(G, g − effects+(a), π_i ∪ {a}, i))
end
```

Figure 6.8 Search for actions $\pi_i \in A_i$ that achieve goal g.

The GP-Search procedure selects each goal proposition p at a time, in some heuristic order. Among the *resolvers* of p, i.e., actions that achieve p and that are not mutex with actions already selected for that level, it nondeterministically chooses one action a that tentatively extends the current subset π_i through a recursive call at the same level. This is performed on a subset of goals minus p and minus all positive effect of a in g. As usual, a failure for this nondeterministic choice is a backtrack point over other alternatives for achieving p, if any, or a backtracking further up if all *resolvers* of p have been tried. When g is empty, then π_i is complete; the search recursively tries to extract a solution for the following level $i - 1$.

One may view the GP-Search procedure as a kind of CSP solver.[6] Here CSP *variables* are goal propositions, and their *values* are possible actions achieving them. The procedure chooses a value for a variable compatible with previous choices (nonmutex) and recursively tries to solve other pending variables. This view can be very beneficial if one applies to procedure GP-Search the CSP heuristics (e.g., for the ordering of variables and for the choice of values) and techniques such as intelligent backtracking or forward propagation. The latter is easily added to the procedure: before recursion, a potential value a for achieving p is propagated forward on *resolvers* of pending variables in g; a is removed from consideration if it leads to an empty *resolver* for some pending goal proposition.

We are now ready to specify the Graphplan algorithm (Figure 6.9) with the graph expansion, search steps, and termination condition. Graphplan performs an initial graph expansion until either it reaches a level containing all goal propositions without mutex or it arrives at a fixed-point level in G. If the latter happens first, then the goal is not achievable. Otherwise, a search for a solution is performed. If no

6. This view will be further detailed in Chapter 8.

```
Graphplan(A, s0, g)
    i ← 0,    ∇ ← ∅,    P0 ← s0
    G ← ⟨P0⟩
    until [g ⊆ Pi and g² ∩ μPi = ∅] or Fixedpoint(G) do
        i ← i + 1
        G ← Expand(G)
    if g ⊈ Pi or g² ∩ μPi ≠ ∅ then return(failure)
    Π ← Extract(G, g, i)
    if Fixedpoint(G) then η ← |∇(κ)|
    else η ← 0
    while Π = failure do
        i ← i + 1
        G ← Expand(G)
        Π ← Extract(G, g, i)
        if Π = failure and Fixedpoint(G) then
            if η = |∇(κ)| then return(failure)
            η ← |∇(κ)|
    return(Π)
end
```

Figure 6.9 The Graphplan algorithm.

solution is found at this stage, the algorithm iteratively expands, then searches the graph G.

This iterative deepening is pursued even *after* a fixed-point level has been reached, until success or until the termination condition is satisfied. This termination condition requires that the number of nogood tuples in $\nabla(\kappa)$ at the fixed-point level κ, stabilizes after two successive failures.

In addition to Expand and Extract, the Graphplan algorithm calls the procedure Fixedpoint(G) that checks the fixed-point condition; this procedure sets κ to the fixed-point level of the planning graph when the fixed-point level is reached.

6.3.3 Analysis of Graphplan

In order to prove the soundness, completeness, and termination of Graphplan, let us first analyze how the nogood table evolves along successive deepening stages of G. Let $\nabla_j(i)$ be the set of nogood tuples found at level i after the unsuccessful completion of a deepening stage down to a level $j > i$. The failure of stage j means that any plan of j or fewer steps must make at least one of the goal tuples in $\nabla_j(i)$ true at a level i, and that none of these tuples is achievable in i levels.

Proposition 6.7 *$\forall i, j$ such that $j > i$, $\nabla_j(i) \subseteq \nabla_{j+1}(i)$.*

Proof A tuple of goal propositions g is added as a nogood in $\nabla_j(i)$ only when Graphplan has performed an exhaustive search for all ways to achieve g with the actions in A_i and it fails: each set of actions in A_i that provides g is either mutex or involves a tuple of preconditions g' that was shown to be a nogood at the previous level $\nabla_k(i-1)$, for $i < k \leq j$. In other words, only the levels from 0 to i in G are responsible for the failure of the tuple g at level i. By iterative deepening, the algorithm may find that g is solvable at some later level $i' > i$, but regardless of how many iterative deepening stages are performed, once g is in $\nabla_j(i)$, it remains in $\nabla_{j+1}(i)$ and in the nogood table at the level i in all subsequent deepening stages. ■

Proposition 6.8 *The* Graphplan *algorithm is sound, and complete, and it terminates. It returns* failure *iff the planning problem (O, s_0, g) has no solution; otherwise, it returns a sequence of sets of actions Π that is a solution plan to the problem.*

Proof To show the soundness of the algorithm, assume that Graphplan returns the sequence $\Pi = \langle \pi_1, \ldots, \pi_n \rangle$. The set *resolvers*, as defined in GP-Search, is such that every set of actions $\pi_i \in \Pi$ is independent. Furthermore, the set of actions π_n achieves the set of problem goals, π_{n-1} achieves precond(π_n), etc. Finally, when GP-Search calls Extract on the recursion $i = 1$, we are sure that all precond(π_1) are in P_0. Hence the layered plan Π meets Definition 6.3 (see page 120) of a solution plan to the problem.

Suppose that instead of finding a solution, the algorithm stops on one of the two failure termination conditions, i.e., either the fixed point κ is reached before attaining a level i that contains all goal propositions (no pair of which is mutex) or there are two successive deepening stages such that $|\nabla_{j-1}(\kappa)| = |\nabla_j(\kappa)|$. In the former case G does not have a level that meets the necessary condition of Proposition 6.4 (see page 123), hence the problem is unsolvable.

In the latter case:

- $\nabla_{j-1}(\kappa) = \nabla_j(\kappa)$ because of Proposition 6.7.
- $\nabla_{j-1}(\kappa) = \nabla_j(\kappa + 1)$ because the last $i - \kappa$ levels are identical, i.e., $\nabla_{j-1}(\kappa)$ is to stage $j - 1$ what $\nabla_j(\kappa + 1)$ is to stage j.

These two equations entail $\nabla_j(\kappa) = \nabla_j(\kappa + 1)$: all unsolvable goal tuples at the fixed-point level (including the original goals of the problem) are also unsolvable at the next level $\kappa + 1$. Hence the problem is unsolvable.

Finally, we have to show that Graphplan necessarily stops when the planning problem is unsolvable. Because of Proposition 6.7, the number of nogood goal tuples at any level grows monotonically, and there is a finite maximum number of goal tuples. Hence, there is necessarily a point where the second failure termination condition is reached, if the first failure condition did not apply before. ■

To end this section, let us underline two main features of Graphplan.

1. The mutex relation on incompatible pairs of actions and propositions, and the weak reachability condition of Proposition 6.4 (see page 123), offer a very good insight about the interaction between the goals of a problem and about which goals are possibly achievable at some level.
2. Because of the monotonic properties of the planning graph, the algorithm is guaranteed to terminate; the fixed-point feature together with the reachability condition provide an efficient failure termination condition. In particular, when the goal propositions without mutex are not reachable, no search at all is performed.

Because of these features and its backward constraint-directed search, Graphplan brought a significant speed-up and contributed to the scalability of planning. Evidently, Graphplan does not change the intrinsic complexity of planning, which is PSPACE-complete in the set-theoretic representation. Since we showed that the expansion of the planning graph is performed in polynomial time (Proposition 6.5 (see page 124)), this means that the costly part of the algorithm is in the search of the planning graph. Furthermore, the memory requirement of the planning-graph data structure can be a significant limiting factor. Several techniques and heuristics have been devised to speed up the search and to improve the memory management of its data structure. They will be introduced in the next section.

6.4 Extensions and Improvements of Graphplan

The planning-graph techniques can be extended and improved along different directions. Several extensions to the planning language will be presented. Various improvements to planning-graph algorithms will then be discussed. Finally, the principle of independent actions in a graph layer will be relaxed to a less demanding relation.

6.4.1 Extending the Language

The planning algorithm described in Section 6.3.3 takes as input a problem (O, s_0, g), stated in a restricted classical representation, where s_0 and g are sets of propositions, and operators in O have no negated literals in their preconditions. A more expressive language is often desirable. Let us illustrate here how some of the extensions of the classical representation described in Section 2.4 can be taken into account in Graphplan.

Handling negation in the preconditions of operators and in goals is easily performed by introducing a new predicate *not-p* to replace the negation of a predicate p

in preconditions or goals (see Section 2.6). This replacement requires adding *not-p* in effects$^-$ when p is in effects$^+$ of an operator o and adding *not-p* in effects$^+$ when p is in effects$^-$ of o. One also has to extend s_0 with respect to the newly introduced *not-p* predicate in order to maintain a consistent and *closed*[7] initial world.

Example 6.4 The DWR domain has the following operator:

move(r, l, m) ;; robot r moves from location l to location m
  precond: adjacent(l, m), at(r, l), $\neg$ occupied(m)
  effects: at(r, m), occupied(m), $\neg$ occupied(l), $\neg$ at(r, l)

The negation in the precondition is handled by introducing the predicate not-occupied in the following way:

move(r, l, m) ;; robot r moves from location l to location m
  precond: adjacent(l, m), at(r, l), not $-$ occupied(m)
  effects: at(r, m), occupied(m), $\neg$ occupied(l), $\neg$ at(r, l),
    not-occupied(l), $\neg$not-occupied(m)

Furthermore, if a problem has three locations (l1, l2, l3) such that only l1 is initially occupied, we need to add to the initial state the propositions not-occupied(l2) and not-occupied(l3).

■

This approach, which rewrites a planning problem into the restricted representation required by Graphplan, can also be used for handling the other extensions discussed in Section 2.4. For example, recall that an operator with a conditional effect can be expanded into an equivalent set of pairs (precond$_i$, effects$_i$). Hence it is easy to rewrite it as several operators, one for each such pair. Quantified conditional effects are similarly expanded. However, such an expansion may lead to an exponential number of operators. It is preferable to generalize the algorithm for directly handling an extended language.

Generalizing Graphplan for directly handling operators with disjunctive preconditions can be done by considering the edges from an action in A_i to its preconditions in P_{i-1} as being a disjunctive set of *AND-connectors*, as in AND/OR graphs. The definition of mutex between actions needs to be generalized with respect to these connectors. The set of *resolvers* in GP-Search, among which a nondeterministic choice is made for achieving a goal, now has to take into account not the actions but their AND-connectors (see Exercise 6.11).

Directly handling operators with conditional effects requires more significant modifications. One has to start with a generalized definition of dependency between actions, taking into account their conditional effects. This is needed in order to keep the desirable result of Proposition 6.1 (see page 120), i.e., that an independent set of actions defines the same state transitions for any permutation of the set. One also has to define a new structure of the planning graph for handling the conditional effects, e.g., for propagating a desired goal at level P_i, which is a conditional effect,

7. That is, any proposition that is not explicitly stated is false.

over to its antecedent condition either in a positive or in a negative way. One also has to come up with ways to compute and propagate mutex relations and with a generalization of the search procedure in this new planning graph. For example, the planner called IPP labels an edge from an action to a proposition by the conditions under which this proposition is an effect of the action. These labels are taken into account for the graph expansion and search. However, they are not exploited for finding all possible mutex, hence leaving a heavier load on the search.

6.4.2 Improving the Planner

Memory Management. The planning-graph data structure makes explicit all the ground atoms and instantiated actions of a problem. It has to be implemented carefully in order to maintain a reasonable memory demand that is not a limiting factor on the planner's performance.

The monotonic properties of the planning graph are essential to this purpose. Because $P_{i-1} \subseteq P_i$ and $A_{i-1} \subseteq A_i$, one does not need to keep these sets explicitly but only to record for each proposition p the level i at which p appeared for the first time in the graph, and similarly for each action.

Because of Proposition 6.3 (see page 123), a symmetrical technique can be used for the mutex relations, that is, to record the level at which a mutex disappeared for the first time. Furthermore, there is no need to record the planning graph after its fixed-point level κ. One just has to maintain the only changes that can appear after this level, i.e., in the nogood table of nonachievable tuples. Here also the monotonic property of Proposition 6.7 (see page 130), i.e., $\nabla_j(i) \subseteq \nabla_{j+1}(i)$, allows incremental management.

Finally, several general programming techniques can also be useful for memory management. For example, the bitvector data structure allows one to encode a state and a proposition level P_i as a vector of n bits, where n is the number of propositions in the problem; an action is encoded as four such vectors, one for each of its positive and negative preconditions and effects.

Focusing and Improving the Search. The description of a domain involves rigid predicates that do not vary from state to state. In the DWR domain, e.g., the predicates adjacent, attached, and belong are rigid: there is no operator that changes their truth values. Once operators are instantiated into ground actions for a given problem, one may remove the rigid predicates from preconditions and effects because they play no further role in the planning process. This simplification reduces the number of actions. For example, there will be no action load(crane3,loc1,cont2,rob1) if belong(crane3,loc1) is false, i.e., if crane3 is not in location loc1. Because of this removal, one may also have flexible predicates that become invariant for a given problem, triggering more removals. There can be a great benefit in preprocessing a planning problem in order to focus the processing and the search on the sole relevant facts and actions. This preprocessing can be quite sophisticated and may allow one to infer nonobvious object types, symmetries, and invariant properties, such as permanent mutex relations, hence simplifying the mutex computation. It may even find mutex propositions that cannot be detected by Graphplan because of the binary propagation.

Nogood tuples, as well as mutex relations, play an essential role in pruning the search. However, if we are searching to achieve a set of goals g in a level i, and if $g' \in \nabla_i$ such that $g' \subset g$, we will not detect that g is not achievable and prune the search. The Extract procedure can be extended to test this type of set inclusion, but this may involve a significant overhead. It turns out, however, that the termination condition of the algorithm, i.e., $|\nabla_{j-1}(\kappa)| = |\nabla_j(\kappa)|$, holds even if the procedure records and keeps in ∇_i only nogood tuples g such that no subset of g has been proven to be a nogood. With this modification, the set inclusion test can be efficiently implemented.

In addition to pruning, the GP-Search procedure has to be focused with heuristics for selecting the next proposition p in the current set g and for nondeterministically choosing the action in *resolvers*. A general heuristics consists of selecting first a proposition p that leads to the smallest set of *resolvers*, i.e., the proposition p achieved by the smallest number of actions. For example, if p is achieved by just one action, then p does not involve a backtrack point and is better processed as early as possible in the search tree. A symmetrical heuristics for the choice of an action supporting p is to prefer no-op actions first. Other heuristics that are more specific to the planning-graph structure and more informed take into account the level at which actions and propositions appear for the first time in the graph. The later a proposition appears in the planning graph, the most constrained it is. Hence, one would select the latest propositions first. A symmetrical reasoning leads one to choose for achieving p the action that appears earliest in the graph.[8]

Finally, a number of algorithmic techniques allow one to improve the efficiency of the search. For example, one is the *forward-checking* technique: before choosing an action a in *resolvers* for handling p, one checks that this choice will not leave another pending proposition in g with an empty set of *resolvers*. Forward-checking is a general algorithm for solving constraint satisfaction problems. It turns out that several other CSP techniques apply to the search in a planning graph, which is a particular CSP problem.[9]

6.4.3 Extending the Independence Relation

We introduced the concept of layered plans with a very strong requirement of *independent* actions in each set π_i. In practice, we do not necessarily need to have *every* permutation of each set be a valid sequence of actions. We only need to ensure that there exists *at least one* such permutation. This is the purpose of the relation between actions called the *allowance relation*, which is less constrained than the independence relation while keeping the advantages of the planning graph.

---

8. This topic will be further developed in Chapter 9, which is devoted to heuristics.
9. This point is developed in Section 8.6.2 of the CSP chapter.

An action a allows an action b when b can be applied after a and the resulting state contains the union of the positive effects of a and b. This is the case when a does not delete a precondition of b and b does not delete a positive effect of a:

$$a \text{ allows } b \text{ iff } \text{effects}^-(a) \cap \text{precond}(b) = \emptyset \text{ and } \text{effects}^-(b) \cap \text{effects}^+(a) = \emptyset$$

Allowance is weaker than independence. Independence implies allowance: if a and b are independent, then a allows b and b allows a. Note that when a allows b but b does not allow a, then a has to be ordered before b. Note also that allowance is not a symmetrical relation.

If we replace the independence relation with the allowance relation in Definition 6.4 (see page 121) we can say that two actions a and b are mutex either

- when they have mutually exclusive preconditions, or
- when a does not allow b and b does not allow a.

This definition leads to fewer mutex pairs between actions, and consequently to fewer mutex relations between propositions. On the same planning problem, the planning graph will have fewer or at most the same number of levels, before reaching a goal or a fixed point, than with the independence relation.

Example 6.5 Let us illustrate the difference entailed by the two relations on a simple planning domain that has three actions (a, b, and c) and four propositions (p, q, r, and s).

$$\text{precond}(a) = \{p\}; \text{effects}^+(a) = \{q\}; \text{effects}^-(a) = \{\}$$

$$\text{precond}(b) = \{p\}; \text{effects}^+(b) = \{r\}; \text{effects}^-(b) = \{p\}$$

$$\text{precond}(c) = \{q, r\}; \text{effects}^+(c) = \{s\}; \text{effects}^-(c) = \{\}$$

Actions a and b are not independent (b deletes a precondition of a), hence they will be mutex in any level of the planning graph built with the independence relation. However, a allows b: these actions will not be mutex with the allowance relation. The two graphs are illustrated in Figure 6.10 for a problem whose initial state is $\{p\}$ and goal is $\{s\}$ (solution plans are shown in bold). In graph (i) with the independence relation, preconditions of c are mutex in P_1; because of the no-op α_q they become nonmutex in P_2. Action c appears in A_3 giving the goal in P_3. In graph (ii) with the allowance relation, q and r are nonmutex in P_1, and the goal is reached one level earlier.

■

The benefit of the allowance relation, i.e., fewer mutex pairs and a smaller fixed-point level, has a cost. Since the allowance relation is not symmetrical, a set of pairwise nonmutex actions does not necessarily contain a "valid" permutation. For example, if action a allows b, b allows c, and c allows a but none of the opposite relations holds, then the three actions a, b, and c can be nonmutex (pending

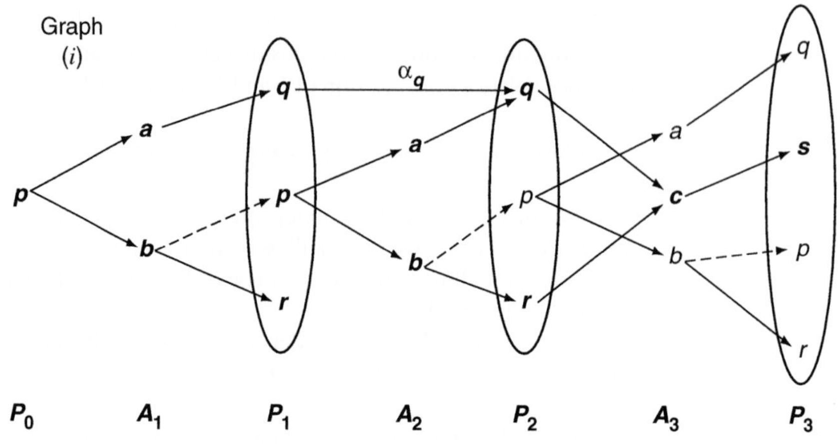

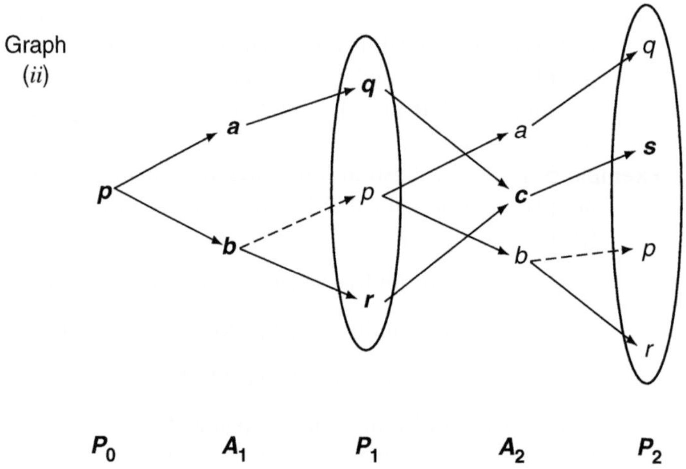

Figure 6.10 Planning graphs for independence (*i*) and allowance (*ii*) relations.

nonmutex preconditions), but there is no permutation that gives an applicable sequence of actions and a resulting state corresponding to the union of their positive effects. While earlier a set of nonmutex actions was necessarily independent and could be selected in the search phase for a plan, here we have to add a further requirement for the allowance relation within a set.

A permutation $\langle a_1, \ldots, a_k \rangle$ of the elements of a set π_i is allowed if every action allows all its followers in the permutation, i.e., $\forall j, k$: if $j < k$, then a_j allows a_k. A set is allowed if it has at least one allowed permutation.

The state resulting from the application of an allowed set can be defined as in Section 6.3: $\gamma(s, \pi_i) = (s - \text{effects}^-(\pi_i)) \cup \text{effects}^+(\pi_i)$. All propositions of Section 6.2.3 can be rephrased for an allowed set and for a layered plan whose levels are allowed sets by just replacing "any permutation" with "any allowed permutation" (see Exercise 6.14).

In order to compute $\gamma(s, \pi_i)$ and to use such a set in the GP-Search procedure, one does not need to produce an allowed permutation and to commit the plan to it—one just needs to check its existence. We already noticed that an ordering constraint "*a* before *b*" would be required whenever *a* allows *b* but *b* does not allow *a*. It is easy to prove that a set is allowed if the relation consisting of all pairs (a, b) such that "*b* does not allow *a*" is cycle free. This can be checked with a topological sorting algorithm in complexity that is linear in the number of actions and allowance pairs. Such a test has to take place in the GP-Search procedure right before recursion on the following level:

GP-Search(G, g, π_i, i)
  if $g = \emptyset$ then do
    if π_i is not allowed then return(failure)
    $\Pi \leftarrow$ Extract(G, $\bigcup \{\text{precond}(a) \mid \forall a \in \pi_i\}, i-1$)
  ...etc. (as in Figure 6.8)

It is easy to show that with the above modification and the modification in Expand for the definition of allowance in μA_i, the Graphplan algorithm keeps the same properties of soundness, completeness, and termination. The allowance relation leads to fewer mutex pairs, hence to more actions in a level and to fewer levels in the planning graph. The reduced search space pays off in the performance of the algorithm. The benefit can be very significant for highly constrained problems where the search phase is very expensive.

6.5 Discussion and Historical Remarks

The Graphplan planner attracted considerable attention from the research community. The original papers on this planner [74, 75] are among the most cited references in AI planning. One reason for that was the spectacular improvement in planning performance introduced by Graphplan in comparison with the earlier plan-space planners. The other and probably more important reason is the richness of the planning-graph structure, which opened the way to a broad avenue of research and extensions. For several years, a significant fraction of the papers in every planning conference was concerned with planning-graph techniques. An extensive survey of these papers is beyond the scope of this section. Let us discuss a few illustrative contributions.

The analysis of the planning graph as a reachability structure is due to Kambhampati *et al.* [305], who introduced three approximations of the reachability tree (the "unioned plangraph," where every level is the union of states in the corresponding level of the reachability tree; the "naive plangraph" that does not take into account mutex in action levels; and the planning graph). They also proposed a backward construction of the planning graph starting from the goal. This paper relied on previous work (e.g., [306]) to analyze Graphplan as a disjunctive refinement planner and to propose CSP techniques for improving it [158]. Some CSP techniques, such as forward-checking, were already in the initial Graphplan article [75]. But other contributions (e.g., [299, 300]) elaborated further by showing that a planning graph is a dynamic CSP and by developing intelligent backtracking and efficient recording and management of failure tuples.

The proposal for translating into the restricted language of Graphplan a classical planning problem with some of the extensions of Section 6.4.1 is due to Gazen and Knoblock [213]. Several contributions for handling directly and efficiently extended constructs, like conditional effects, have also been developed [20, 332]. Some of the improvements to the encoding, memory management, and algorithms of the planning-graph techniques (see Section 6.4.2) appeared in other sources [192, 489]. A significant part of the work for extending the language or improving the algorithms took part along with the development of two Graphplan successors, the IPP [331] and STAN [367] planners. Several domain analysis techniques [218, 420, 565] for removing nonrelevant propositions and action instances and for detecting symmetries and invariance properties were proposed in order to focus the graph and the search. Domain analysis techniques have been extensively developed in a system called the Type Inference Module [192] and integrated to STAN [193].

Several articles on the planning-graph techniques insisted on plans with *parallel* actions as an important contribution of Graphplan. We carefully avoided mentioning parallelism is this chapter because there is no semantics of concurrency in layered plans.[10] This is clearly illustrated in the extension from the independence to the allowance relations, i.e., the requirement to have all permutations of actions in a layer π_i equivalent, and the weaker requirement that there is at least one permutation that achieves the effects of π_i from its preconditions. This extension from independence to allowance is due to Cayrol *et al.* [112] for a planner called LCGP.

The work on LCGP led also to contributions on level-based heuristics for Graphplan [111]. Similar heuristics were independently proposed by Kambhampati and Nigenda [304]. More elaborated heuristics relying on local search techniques were proposed in the LPG planner [220] and led to significant performances, as illustrated in AIPS'02 planning competition results [195]. A related issue that arose at that time (and to which we will return in Chapter 9) is the use of Graphplan not as a planner but as a technique to derive heuristics for state-based planners [271, 423, 425].

The relationship between two techniques that were developed in parallel, the planning graph and the SAT-based techniques (see Chapter 7) have been analyzed by several authors (e.g., [42, 316]).

---

10. See Chapter 14, and particularly Section 14.2.5, which is devoted to concurrent actions with interfering effects.

Many other extensions to the planning-graph techniques have been studied, e.g., handling resources [330], dealing with uncertainty [73, 554], and managing a partial specification of the domain [488].

6.6 Exercises

6.1 Suppose we run Graphplan on the painting problem described in Exercise 5.6.

(a) How many actions does it generate at level 1 of the planning graph? How many of these are maintenance actions?

(b) Expand the planning graph out to two levels, and draw the result.

(c) What is the first level at which Graphplan calls Extract?

(d) At what level will Graphplan find a solution? What solution will it find?

(e) If we kept generating the graph out to infinity rather than stopping when Graphplan finds a solution, what is the first level of the graph at which the number of actions would reach its maximum?

6.2 Redo Exercise 6.1 on the washing problem described in Exercise 5.7.

6.3 How many times will Graphplan need to do graph expansion if we run it on the Sussman anomaly (see Example 4.3)?

6.4 How much time (give big-O figures) do Expand and Extract procedures take? Give answers for both (a) the amount of time needed during a single iteration of Graphplan's while loop and (b) the cumulative time needed over all iterations of Graphplan's while loop.

6.5 Let $P = (O, s_0, g)$ and $P' = (O, s_0, g')$ be the statements of two solvable planning problems such that $g \subseteq g'$. Suppose we run Graphplan on both problems, generating planning graphs G and G'. Is $G \subseteq G'$?

6.6 Prove Proposition 6.1 (see page 120) about the result of a set of independent actions.

6.7 Prove Proposition 6.4 (see page 123) about the necessary condition for reaching a goal in a planning graph.

6.8 Show that the definition of P_i in the Expand procedure can be modified to be

$$P_i \leftarrow [P_{i-1} - \bigcap \{\text{effects}^-(a) \mid a \in A_i\}] \bigcup \{\text{effects}^+(a) \mid a \in A_i)\}.$$

Discuss how this relates to the usual formula for the transition function, i.e., $\gamma(a, s) = (s - \text{effects}^-(a)) \cup \text{effects}^+(a)$.

6.9 Specify the Graphplan algorithm, including the procedures Expand, Extract, and GP-Search, without the no-op actions. Discuss whether this leads to a benefit in the presentation and/or in the implementation of the algorithm.

6.10 Suppose we want to modify Graphplan so that it can use the following operators to increment and decrement a register r that contains some amount v:

add1(r, v)
  precond: contains(r, v)
  effects: $\neg$contains(r, v), contains$(r, v + 1)$
sub1(r, v)
  precond: contains(r, v)
  effects: $\neg$contains(r, v), contains$(r, v - 1)$

We could modify Graphplan to instantiate these operators by having it instantiate v and then compute the appropriate value for $v + 1$ or $v - 1$.

(a) What modifications will we need to make to Graphplan's graph-expansion subroutine, if any?

(b) Suppose we have the following initial state and goal:

$$s_0 = \{\text{contains(r1, 5), contains(r2, 8)}\}$$

$$g = \{\text{contains(r1, 8), contains(r2, 7)}\}$$

How many operator instances will we have at level 1 of the planning graph?

(c) What atoms will we have at level 2 of the planning graph?

(d) At what level of the planning graph will we start calling the solution-extraction subroutine?

(e) What modifications will we need to make to Graphplan's solution-extraction subroutine, if any?

(f) Why wouldn't it work to have the following operator to add an integer amount w to a register r?

addto(r, v, w)
  precond: contains(r, v)
  effects: $\neg$contains(r, v), contains$(v, v + w)$

6.11 Detail the modifications required for handling operators with disjunctive preconditions in the modification of mutex relations and in the planning procedures.

6.12 Apply the Graphplan algorithm to a modified version of the problem in Example 6.1 (see page 114) in which there is only one robot. Explain why the problem with two robots is simpler for Graphplan than the problem with just one robot.

6.13 Apply Graphplan with the allowance relation to the same planning problem mentioned in Exercise 6.12. Compare the two planning graphs and the obtained solutions.

6.14 In Propositions 6.1 and 6.2 (see page 120), replace the expression "any permutation" with "any allowed permutation" and prove these new propositions.

6.15 Discuss the structure of plans as output by Graphplan with the allowance relation. Compare these plans to sequences of independent sets of actions, to plans that are simple sequences of actions, and to partially ordered sets of actions.

6.16 Download one of the public-domain implementations of Graphplan, e.g., the original Graphplan,[11] IPP,[12] STAN,[13] or SGP.[14] Test the full DWR example on several domains and problems with an increasing number of locations, robots, and containers. Discuss the practical range of applicability of this planner for the DWR application.

11. http://www-2.cs.cmu.edu/afs/cs.cmu.edu/usr/avrim/Planning/Graphplan/
12. http://www.informatik.uni-freiburg.de/ koehler/ipp/IPPcode4.1.tar.gz
13. http://planning.cis.strath.ac.uk/STAN
14. ftp://ftp.cs.washington.edu/pub/ai/sgp.tgz

CHAPTER 7

Propositional Satisfiability Techniques

7.1 Introduction

The general idea underlying the "planning as satisfiability" approach is to map a planning problem to a well-known problem for which there exist effective algorithms and procedures. A plan is then extracted from the solution to the new problem. More specifically, the idea is to formulate a planning problem as a *propositional satisfiability problem*, i.e., as the problem of determining whether a propositional formula is satisfiable. The approach follows this outline.

- A planning problem is *encoded* as a propositional formula.
- A *satisfiability decision procedure* determines whether the formula is satisfiable by assigning truth values to the propositional variables.
- A plan is *extracted* from the assignments determined by the satisfiability decision procedure.

Recent improvements in the performance of general purpose algorithms for propositional satisfiability provide the ability to scale up to relatively large problems. The ability to exploit the efforts and the results in a very active field of research in computer science is indeed one of the main advantages of this approach.

In this chapter, we focus on the encoding of planning problems into satisfiability problems and describe some existing satisfiability procedures that have been used in planning. We first discuss a way to translate a planning problem to a propositional formula (Section 7.2). Then we show how standard decision procedures can be used as planning algorithms (Section 7.3). We then discuss some different ways to encode a planning problem into a satisfiability problem (Section 7.4).

In this chapter we focus on classical planning problems, with all the restrictions described in Chapter 1. The "planning as satisfiability" approach has been recently extended to different kinds of planning problems, most notably to the problem of planning in nondeterministic domains. These extensions are described in Part V, Chapter 18.

7.2 Planning Problems as Satisfiability Problems

We consider a classical planning problem $\mathcal{P}$ as defined in Sections 2.1 and 2.2, where $\mathcal{P} = (\Sigma, s_0, S_g)$; $\Sigma = (S, A, \gamma)$ is the planning domain, S the set of states, A the set of actions, γ the deterministic transition function, s_0 the initial state, and S_g the set of goal states.

In the "planning as satisfiability" approach, a classical planning problem is encoded as a propositional formula with the property that any of its models correspond to plans that are solutions to the planning problem. A *model* of a propositional formula is an assignment of truth values to its variables for which the formula evaluates to true.[1] A *satisfiability problem* is the problem of determining whether a formula has a model. We say that a formula is *satisfiable* if a model of the formula exists.

In the following subsections we describe how a planning problem can be translated to the problem of determining whether a propositional formula is satisfiable. The two key elements that need to be translated to propositional formulas are states and state transitions. We first provide some guidelines on how states and state transitions can be translated to propositional formulas (Sections 7.2.1 and 7.2.2, respectively). We then describe the encoding of a planning problem to a satisfiability problem (Section 7.2.3). The size of the encoding, i.e., the number of propositional variables and the length of the formula, are critical. Sizes of different encodings are discussed in Section 7.4.

7.2.1 States as Propositional Formulas

Similar to the set-theoretic representation (Section 2.2), we use propositional formulas to represent facts that hold in states. For instance, consider a simple domain where we have a robot r1 and a location l1. The states where the robot is unloaded and at location l1 can be represented with the following formula:

$$\mathsf{at(r1,l1)} \wedge \neg\mathsf{loaded(r1)} \tag{7.1}$$

If we consider at(r1, l1) and loaded(r1) as propositional variables, Formula 7.1 is a propositional formula. A model of Formula 7.1 is the one that assigns true to the

1. See Appendix B for a review of basic concepts in propositional logic, e.g., propositional formulas, propositional variables, and models.

propositional variable at(r1, l1), and false to loaded(r1). Let us call this model μ. More formally, μ can be written as:

$$\mu = \{\mathsf{at(r1, l1)} \leftarrow \mathit{true}, \mathsf{loaded(r1)} \leftarrow \mathit{false}\} \tag{7.2}$$

Consider now the case where we have two locations l1 and l2. As a consequence we have, beyond the propositional variables at(r1, l1) and loaded(r1), the propositional variable at(r1, l2), which intuitively represents the fact that robot r1 is at location l2. Suppose we want to represent the fact that the robot is unloaded and at location l1. Formula 7.1 does not "exactly" entail this. Indeed, we have two models:

$$\mu_1 = \{\mathsf{at(r1, l1)} \leftarrow \mathit{true}, \mathsf{loaded(r1)} \leftarrow \mathit{false}, \mathsf{at(r1, l2)} \leftarrow \mathit{true}\}$$

$$\mu_2 = \{\mathsf{at(r1, l1)} \leftarrow \mathit{true}, \mathsf{loaded(r1)} \leftarrow \mathit{false}, \mathsf{at(r1, l2)} \leftarrow \mathit{false}\}$$

μ_2 is the *intended model*, i.e., intuitively, the model we have in mind when we write Formula 7.1 because we think that a robot cannot stay in two locations at the same time. μ_1 is an *unintended model*, i.e., an assignment to the formula that we do not have in mind but makes the formula true. Formally, nothing distinguishes μ_1 from μ_2. They are both models. In order to avoid the unintended model, we have to add to Formula 7.1 a proposition that represents an obvious fact for us, i.e., the fact that the robot cannot be at location l2:

$$\mathsf{at(r1, l1)} \land \neg\mathsf{at(r1, l2)} \land \neg\mathsf{loaded(r1)} \tag{7.3}$$

The only model of Formula 7.3 is μ_2, i.e., the intended model.

A propositional formula can represent sets of states rather than a single state. For instance,

$$(\mathsf{at(r1, l1)} \land \neg\mathsf{at(r1, l2)}) \lor (\neg\mathsf{at(r1, l1)} \land \mathsf{at(r1, l2)}) \land \neg\mathsf{loaded(r1)} \tag{7.4}$$

represents both the state where the robot is at l1 and the one where it is at l2.

Encoding states as propositional formulas is therefore rather straightforward. However, notice that a propositional formula represents a state (or a set of states) without encoding the dynamics of the system. We need some different kind of propositional formulas to represent the fact that a system evolves from a state to another state.

7.2.2 State Transitions as Propositional Formulas

The behavior of deterministic actions is described by the transition function $\gamma : S \times A \rightarrow S$. Figure 7.1 depicts the state transition of an action move(r1,l1,l2)

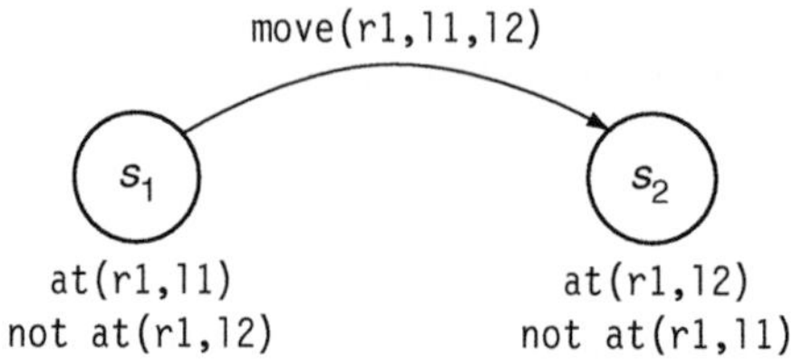

Figure 7.1 An example of state transition.

such that $\gamma(s_1, \mathsf{move(r1,l1,l2)}) = s_2$. In s_1, the robot r1 is at location l1, while in s_2 it is at l2. States s_1 and s_2 could be represented by Formulas 7.5 and 7.6, respectively:

$$\mathsf{at(r1,l1)} \land \neg\mathsf{at(r1,l2)} \tag{7.5}$$

$$\neg\mathsf{at(r1,l1)} \land \mathsf{at(r1,l2)} \tag{7.6}$$

However, these formulas cannot be used to represent the fact that the system evolves from state s_1 to state s_2. We need a propositional formula to assert that, in state s_1, before executing the action, Formula 7.5 holds, and in state s_2, after the execution of the action, Formula 7.6 holds. We need different propositional variables that hold in different states to specify that a fact holds in one state but does not hold in another state.

For instance, we can have two distinct propositional variables at(r1, l1, s1) and at(r1, l2, s2). The first one intuitively means that the robot is at location l1 in state s_1, while the second means that the robot is at location l2 in state s_2. They are different and can be assigned different truth values. The transition in Figure 7.1, i.e., the fact that the system evolves from state s_1 to state s_2, can be represented by the following propositional formula:

$$\mathsf{at(r1,l1,s1)} \land \neg\mathsf{at(r1,l2,s1)} \land \neg\mathsf{at(r1,l1,s2)} \land \mathsf{at(r1,l2,s2)} \tag{7.7}$$

where at(r1,l1,s1), at(r1,l2,s1), at(r1,l1,s2), and at(r1,l2,s2) are four different propositional variables.[2] A model of Formula 7.7 is

$$\begin{aligned}\mu_3 = \{\, & \mathsf{at(r1,l1,s1)} \leftarrow \mathit{true}, \\ & \mathsf{at(r1,l2,s1)} \leftarrow \mathit{false}, \\ & \mathsf{at(r1,l1,s2)} \leftarrow \mathit{false}, \\ & \mathsf{at(r1,l2,s2)} \leftarrow \mathit{true} \,\}\end{aligned}$$

Formula 7.7 encodes the transition from state s_1 to state s_2. We can now represent the fact that it is the action move(r1,l1,l2) that causes this transition. One possible

2. Notice that Formula 7.7 encodes the transition from state s_2 to s_1 as well.

way to do this is to encode move(r1,l1,l2) as a propositional variable. We always have to take into account the fact that we need to distinguish when the action is executed in state s_1 from when it is executed in another state. We therefore introduce a propositional variable, move(r1,l1,l2,s1), whose intended meaning is that the action is executed in state s_1. The function $\gamma(s_1, \text{move}(r1, l1, l2))$ can therefore be encoded as

$$\text{move}(r1, l1, l2, s1) \wedge \text{at}(r1, l1, s1) \wedge \neg\text{at}(r1, l2, s1) \wedge \neg\text{at}(r1, l1, s2) \wedge \text{at}(r1, l2, s2) \quad (7.8)$$

We have one model of Formula 7.8:

$$\begin{aligned}\mu_4 = \{\ & \text{move}(r1, l1, l2, s1) \leftarrow \textit{true}, \\ & \text{at}(r1, l1, s1) \leftarrow \textit{true}, \\ & \text{at}(r1, l2, s1) \leftarrow \textit{false}, \\ & \text{at}(r1, l1, s2) \leftarrow \textit{false}, \\ & \text{at}(r1, l2, s2) \leftarrow \textit{true}\ \}\end{aligned}$$

This encoding is similar to the situation calculus representation (see Chapter 12). The main difference is that situation calculus allows for variables denoting states, called *situations*, in a first-order logical language, while propositional satisfiability encodes the planning problem with propositions.

Notice also that this encoding is conceptually different from the set-theoretic representation (Section 2.2), where state transitions are represented as operators, i.e., as functions that map states to states that are represented as sets of propositions. Here the encoding represents the state transition as a formula in propositional logic.

7.2.3 Planning Problems as Propositional Formulas

Given the fact that we can encode states and state transitions as propositional formulas (Sections 7.2.1 and 7.2.2), we can then encode a planning problem to a propositional formula, say, Φ. The construction of Φ is based on two main ideas.

- Restrict the planning problem to the problem of finding a plan of known length n for some fixed n. This problem is called the *bounded planning problem*. We call each i, $0 \leq i \leq n$, a *step* of the planning problem.
- Transform the bounded planning problem into a satisfiability problem. The description of states and actions of the bounded planning problem are mapped to propositions that describe states and actions at each step, from step 0 (corresponding to the initial state) to step n (corresponding to the goal state).

Technically, each predicate symbol with k arguments is translated into a symbol of $k+1$ arguments, where the last argument is the step. In the case of predicate symbols describing the state such as at(r1,l1) we have at(r1,l1,i), $0 \leq i \leq n$. The intended meaning is that the robot r1 is at location l1 at step i. We call *fluents* the ground atomic formulas that describe states at a given step, e.g., at(r1,l1,i).[3] In the case of actions, such as move(r1,l1,l2), we have move(r1,l1,l2,i), $0 \leq i \leq n-1$. The intended meaning is that the robot r1 moves from location l1 at step i and gets to l2 at step $i+1$. Intuitively, the proposition encoding an action at step i represents an action that is executed at step i and its effects hold at step $i+1$.

A bounded planning problem can be easily extended to the problem of finding a plan of length $\leq n$, for some fixed n, with the use of a dummy action that does nothing. In principle, if a solution plan exists, the plan has a maximum length less than or equal to the number of all states, i.e., $|S|$, which is a double exponential in the number of constant symbols and predicate arity: $n \leq 2^{|D|^{A_p}}$, where $|D|$ is the number of constants in the domain and A_p is the maximum arity of predicates. However, this is of little practical relevance because such a bound is too large, and looking for plans of such length leads to failure. The hope is that there might exist a plan with a relatively short length so that it will not be necessary to go through this large space. In practice, therefore, the plan length is not known in advance. Since the "planning as satisfiability" approach can deal only with bounded planning problems, the execution of planning algorithms based on this approach needs to be repeated for different tentative lengths, e.g., with a binary search on plan lengths. For instance, the algorithm can be iteratively run (e.g., each time with plan length fixed at 2, 4, 8, etc.) until a plan is found.

The formula Φ encoding a bounded planning problem can be constructed as the conjunction of formulas describing the initial and goal states (where atoms are instantiated at steps 0 and n, respectively) and formulas describing the behavior of actions (e.g., preconditions and effects) through the n steps.

Here we describe one of the possible ways to construct a formula Φ that encodes a bounded planning problem into a satisfiability problem. (Section 7.4 discusses different possibilities.) We write as f_i a fluent at step i. For instance, if f is at(r1,l1), we write at(r1,l1,i) as f_i. We write as a_i the propositional formula representing the action executed at step i. For instance, if a is move(r1,l1,l2), we write move(r1,l1,l2,i) as a_i.

Φ is built with the following five kinds of sets of formulas.

1. The *initial state* is encoded as a proposition that is the conjunction of fluents that hold in the initial state and of the negation of those that do not hold, all of them instantiated at step 0.

$$\bigwedge_{f \in s_0} f_0 \wedge \bigwedge_{f \notin s_0} \neg f_0 \qquad (7.9)$$

The initial state is thus fully specified.

3. Fluents here are propositional variables; this notion is therefore different from the notion of fluent introduced in Chapter 2. There is also a difference with the fluents introduced in Chapter 12, where fluents are terms in first-order logic.

2. The *set of goal states* is encoded as a proposition that is the conjunction of fluents that must hold at step n.

$$\bigwedge_{f \in g^+} f_n \wedge \bigwedge_{f \in g^-} f_n \tag{7.10}$$

The goal state is partially specified by the conjunction of the fluents that hold in all the goal states.

3. The fact that *an action, when applicable, has some effects* is encoded with a formula that states that if the action takes place at a given step, then its preconditions must hold at that step and its effects will hold at the next step. Let A be the set of all possible actions. For each $a \in A$ and for each $0 \leq i \leq n-1$, we have:

$$a_i \Rightarrow \left(\bigwedge_{p \in \mathsf{precond}(a)} p_i \wedge \bigwedge_{e \in \mathsf{effects}(a)} e_{i+1} \right) \tag{7.11}$$

4. We need to state that *an action changes only the fluents that are in its effects.* For instance, moving a container does not change the position of other containers. The need for formalizing and reasoning about this fact is known as the *frame problem* (see also Chapter 2). This fact can be reformulated equivalently in a slightly different way as the fact that, *if a fluent changes, then one of the actions that have that fluent in its effects has been executed.* More precisely, if a fluent f, which does not hold at step i, holds instead at step $i+1$, then one of the actions that has f in its positive effects has been executed at step i. Similarly, in the case that f holds at step i and not at step $i+1$, an action that has f in its negative effects has been executed. We have therefore a set of propositions that enumerate the set of actions that could have occurred in order to account for a state change. These formulas are called *explanatory frame axioms.* For each fluent f and for each $0 \leq i \leq n-1$, we have:

$$\begin{aligned} \neg f_i \wedge f_{i+1} &\Rightarrow \left(\bigvee_{a \in A | f_i \in \mathsf{effects}^+(a)} a_i \right) \wedge \\ f_i \wedge \neg f_{i+1} &\Rightarrow \left(\bigvee_{a \in A | f_i \in \mathsf{effects}^-(a)} a_i \right) \end{aligned} \tag{7.12}$$

5. The fact that only one action occurs at each step is guaranteed by the following formula, which is called the *complete exclusion axiom.* For each $0 \leq i \leq n-1$, and for each distinct $a_i, b_i \in A$, we have:

$$\neg a_i \vee \neg b_i \tag{7.13}$$

The propositional formula Φ encoding the bounded planning problem into a satisfiability problem is the conjunction of Formulas 7.9 through 7.13.

Example 7.1 Consider a simple example where we have one robot r1 and two locations l1 and l2. Let us suppose that the robot can move between the two locations. In the initial state, the robot is at l1; in the goal state, it is at l2. The operator that moves the robot is:

move(r, l, l')
  precond: at(r, l)
  effects: at(r, l'), $\neg$ at(r, l)

In this planning problem, a plan of length 1 is enough to reach the goal state. We therefore fix the length of the plan to $n = 1$. The initial and goal states are encoded as formulas (init) and (goal), respectively:

(init) at(r1,l1,0) $\wedge\neg$ at(r1,l2,0)
(goal) at(r1,l2,1) $\wedge\neg$ at(r1,l1,1)

The action is encoded as:

(move1) move(r1, l1, l2, 0) $\Rightarrow$ at(r1, l1, 0) $\wedge$ at(r1, l2, 1) $\wedge$ $\neg$at(r1, l1, 1)
(move2) move(r1, l2, l1, 0) $\Rightarrow$ at(r1, l2, 0) $\wedge$ at(r1, l1, 1) $\wedge$ $\neg$at(r1, l2, 1)

The explanatory frame axioms are:

(at1) $\neg$at(r1, l1, 0) $\wedge$ at(r1, l1, 1) $\Rightarrow$ move(r1, l2, l1, 0)
(at2) $\neg$at(r1, l2, 0) $\wedge$ at(r1, l2, 1) $\Rightarrow$ move(r1, l1, l2, 0)
(at3) at(r1, l1, 0) $\wedge$ $\neg$at(r1, l1, 1) $\Rightarrow$ move(r1, l1, l2, 0)
(at4) at(r1, l2, 0) $\wedge$ $\neg$at(r1, l2, 1) $\Rightarrow$ move(r1, l2, l1, 0)

The complete exclusion axioms are:

$\neg$move(r1, l1, l2, 0) $\vee$ $\neg$move(r1, l2, l1, 0)

■

We can easily extract a plan from the model of Φ. Given a bounded planning problem of length n, we take a sequence of propositional variables $\langle a_1(0), \ldots, a_n(n-1)\rangle$, where $a_i(j)$ is the propositional variable representing action a_i at step j, such that the model assigns true to all $a_{i+1}(i)$, $0 \leq i \leq n-1$. The plan that can be extracted is $\langle a_1, \ldots, a_n\rangle$.

Example 7.2 Consider Example 7.1. A model of the formula Φ assigns true to move(r1,l1,l2,0). The plan of length 1 that is extracted is move(r1,l1,l2). Suppose we now have a different planning problem where the robot can move from/to the two locations and load and unload containers. In the initial state, we have the robot r1 at location l1, the robot is unloaded, and a container c1 is in location l1. The goal is to move container c1 to l2. We fix the bound to three steps. The encoded planning problem has a model that assigns true to:

move(r1,l1,l2,1), load(l1,c1,r1,0), unload(l1,c1,r1,2)

The plan that is extracted is the sequence:

$\langle$ load(l1,c1,r1), move(r1,l1,l2), unload(l1,c1,r1) $\rangle$

■

We can now formalize the notion of encoding correctly a planning problem into a satisfiability problem. Let $\Sigma = (S, A, \gamma)$ be a deterministic state-transition system (as described in Section 1.4). Let $\mathcal{P} = (\Sigma, s_0, S_g)$ be a classical planning problem, where s_0 and S_g are the initial and goal states, respectively. Let Enc be a function that takes a planning problem $\mathcal{P}$ and a length bound n and returns a propositional formula Φ: $\mathsf{Enc}(\mathcal{P}, n) = \Phi$.

Definition 7.1 Enc *encodes the planning problem* $\mathcal{P}$ *to a satisfiability problem* when the following holds: Φ is satisfiable iff there exists a solution plan of length n to $\mathcal{P}$. We say, in short, that Enc encodes planning to satisfiability. ■

Proposition 7.1 *The encoding defined by Formulas 7.9 through 7.13 encodes planning to satisfiability.*

See Kautz *et al.* [312] for a proof of this proposition.

7.3 Planning by Satisfiability

Once a bounded planning problem is encoded to a satisfiability problem, a model for the resulting formula can be constructed by a satisfiability decision procedure. A variety of different procedures have been devised in the literature. In this section we describe some of the procedures that have been used extensively for planning. We describe mainly two different kinds of procedures.

1. The algorithms based on the *Davis-Putnam procedure* are sound and complete. A satisfiability procedure is *sound* if every input formula on which it returns a model is satisfiable; it is *complete* if it returns a model on every satisfiable input formula. When a bounded planning problem of length n is encoded as a satisfiability problem, this means that the returned plans are solution plans and that if no solution plan of length n exists, they can tell you that no plan exists. Note that soundness and completeness hold for *bounded* planning problems. The fact that a plan does not exist for a bounded planning problem does not imply that no plan exists for the original planning problem.
2. The procedures based on the idea of randomized local search, called *stochastic procedures*, are sound but not complete. This means that even for a bounded planning problem they cannot return failure and guarantee therefore that a plan does not exist. However, these procedures can sometimes scale up better than complete algorithms to large problems in the case a solution does exist.

7.3.1 Davis-Putnam Procedure

The Davis-Putnam procedure, one of the first decision procedures, is still one of the most effective and widely used in the "planning as satisfiability" approach. A version of the Davis-Putnam procedure is shown in Figure 7.2. Calling Davis-Putnam(Φ,$\emptyset$), where Φ is a propositional formula, returns a model $\mu \neq \emptyset$ if Φ is satisfiable; otherwise, it returns $\mu = \emptyset$. We suppose Φ to be in Conjunctive Normal Form (CNF),[4] i.e., it is a conjunction of clauses, where a clause is a disjunction of literals. A *literal* is a propositional variable (positive literal) or its negation (negative literal). A *unit clause* is a clause with one literal. A CNF formula can thus be represented as a set of clauses, where each clause is represented as a set of literals. The model μ is represented as a set of of literals, with positive and negative literals corresponding to assignments to true and false, respectively.

Davis-Putnam performs a depth-first search through the space of all possible assignments until either it finds a model or explores the entire search space without finding any. Unit-Propagate eliminates in one shot all that can be eliminated and returns a smaller formula. Indeed, for any unit clause in the formula, i.e., for every clause composed by a single literal, if the literal is positive (negative), Unit-Propagate sets the literal to true (false) and simplifies. This step is called *unit propagation*. Then, Davis-Putnam selects a variable P to be simplified and recourses sequentially first

```
Davis-Putnam(Φ,μ)
    if ∅ ∈ Φ then return
    if Φ = ∅ then exit with μ
    Unit-Propagate(Φ,μ)
    select a variable P such that P or ¬P occurs in φ
    Davis-Putnam(Φ ∪ {P},μ)
    Davis-Putnam(Φ ∪ {¬P},μ)
end

Unit-Propagate(Φ,μ)
    while there is a unit clause {l} in Φ do
        μ ← μ ∪ {l}
        for every clause C ∈ Φ
            if l ∈ C then Φ ← Φ − {C}
            else if ¬l ∈ C then Φ ← Φ − {C} ∪ {C − {¬l}}
end
```

Figure 7.2 The Davis-Putnam satisfiability decision procedure.

4. There is a well-known transformation to convert any satisfiability problem to CNF form; see, e.g., Plaisted [442].

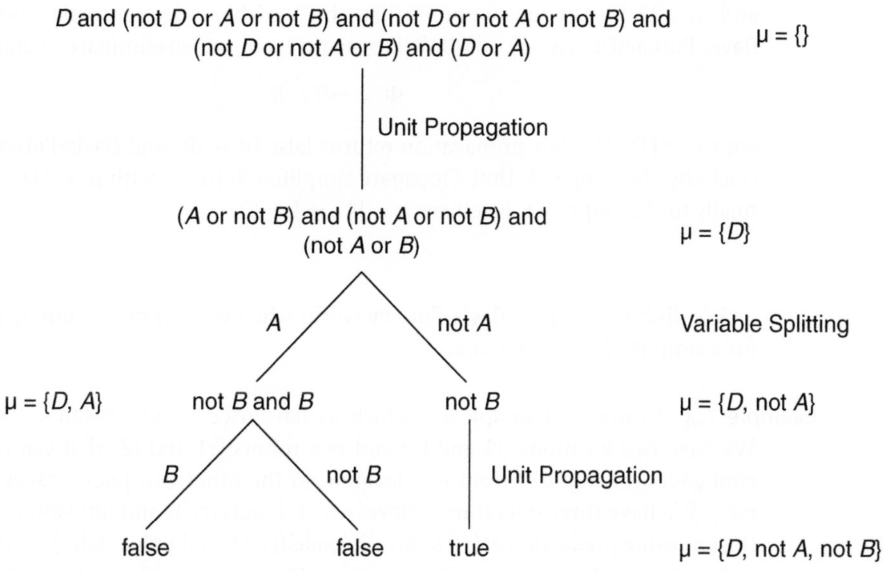

Figure 7.3 An example of a search tree constructed by Davis-Putnam.

with $P = true$ and then, if this choice fails, with $P = false$. The sequential choice of the truth assignment is a particular implementation of a nondeterministic step, where the nondeterminism resides in whether to assign true or false to the selected variable. This step is called *variable selection.*

The variable selection rule may be as simple as choosing the first remaining variable in Φ, or it may be quite sophisticated. For instance, it can select a variable occurring in a clause of minimal length, or it can select a variable with a maximum number of occurrences in minimum-size clauses. These heuristics try to eliminate clauses as early as possible in the search.

Example 7.3 Consider the following propositional formula in CNF:

$$\Phi = D \wedge (\neg D \vee A \vee \neg B) \wedge (\neg D \vee \neg A \vee \neg B) \wedge (\neg D \vee \neg A \vee B) \wedge (D \vee A)$$

In Figure 7.3 we depict the search tree dynamically constructed by Davis-Putnam. We label each node with the formula Φ that gets simplified step-by-step and with the current assignment μ. Edges represent either unit propagation or recursive calls to Davis-Putnam with a variable selection. We label edges with the literal that is selected. Given Φ and $\mu = \emptyset$, Unit-Propagate eliminates in one step the unit clause D. It returns

$$\Phi = (A \vee \neg B) \wedge (\neg A \vee \neg B) \wedge (\neg A \vee B)$$

and $\mu = \{D\}$. Let us suppose that the variable selection rule chooses A. Davis-Putnam($\Phi \cup A$, μ) calls Unit-Propagate again, which eliminates A and returns

$$\Phi = \neg B \wedge B$$

with $\mu = \{D, A\}$. Unit propagation returns false ($\emptyset \in \Phi$) and Davis-Putnam backtracks by choosing $\neg A$. Unit-Propagate simplifies Φ to $\neg B$ with $\mu = \{D, \neg A\}$, and finally to the empty set. It returns $\mu = \{D, \neg A, \neg B\}$. ■

We discuss now how Davis-Putnam works when we encode a planning problem for a simplified DWR domain.

Example 7.4 Consider[5] Example 6.1, which we have used for Graphplan in Chapter 6. We have two locations (l1 and l2) and two robots (r1 and r2) that can transport containers (c1 and c2) from one location to the other (no piles, cranes, pallets, etc.). We have three operators—move(r,l,l'), load(c,r,l), and unload(c,r,l)—and the following predicates: at(r,l), in(c,l), loaded(c,r), and unloaded(r). In the initial state we have the container c1 at location l1, and c2 at l2. In the goal state we want the position of the containers to be exchanged, i.e., c1 at l2, and c2 at l1. In this simple case we know that a plan of length 6 is enough to solve the problem; therefore, we fix the plan length to $n = 6$. We encode the planning problem with Formulas 7.9 through 7.13 described in Section 7.2.3.

Davis-Putnam first applies Unit-Propagate to the unit clauses in the encoding of the initial state and of the goal states. This first step rules out the propositional variables corresponding to the actions that are not applicable in the initial state at step 0 and the actions at step 5 that do not lead to the goal state at step 6. For instance, consider one of the formulas for the operator move that is instantiated at step 0 according to formulas like Formula 7.11:

$$\text{move(r1, l2, l1, 0)} \Rightarrow \text{at(r1, l2, 0)} \wedge \text{at(r1, l1, 1)} \wedge \neg\text{at(r1, l2, 1)} \tag{7.14}$$

Because in the initial state we have the unit clause ¬at(r1, l2, 0), it is easy to verify that unit propagation simplifies the CNF version of Formula 7.14 to ¬move(r1, l2, l1, 0). Then μ, at the second iteration of unit propagation, assigns false to move(r1,l2,l1,0). This corresponds to the fact that move(r1,l2,l1,0) is not applicable in the initial state. Consider now one of the formulas for the operator unload that is instantiated at step 5 according to formulas like Formula 7.11:

$$\begin{aligned} &\text{unload(c1, r1, l1, 5)} \Rightarrow \\ &\quad \text{loaded(c1, r1, 5)} \wedge \text{at(r1, l1, 5)} \wedge \\ &\quad \text{unloaded(r1, 6)} \wedge \text{in(c1, l1, 6)} \wedge \neg\text{loaded(c1, r1, 6)} \end{aligned} \tag{7.15}$$

5. This example is available at http://www.laas.fr/planning/.

Because in the goal state we have the unit clause $\neg\mathsf{in}(\mathsf{c1}, \mathsf{l1}, 6)$, it is easy to verify that unit propagation simplifies the CNF version of Formula 7.15 to $\neg\mathsf{unload}(\mathsf{c1}, \mathsf{r1}, \mathsf{l1}, 5)$. Then μ, at the second iteration of unit propagation, assigns false to unload(c1,r1,l1,5). This corresponds to the fact that unload(c1,r1,l1,5) does not lead to the goal; indeed, c1 is required to be in l2 in the goal state.

Unit propagation[6] in its first step also simplifies frame axioms. For instance, the frame axiom

$$\neg\mathsf{at}(\mathsf{r1}, \mathsf{l1}, 0) \wedge \mathsf{at}(\mathsf{r1}, \mathsf{l1}, 1) \Rightarrow \mathsf{move}(\mathsf{r1}, \mathsf{l2}, \mathsf{l1}, 0) \tag{7.16}$$

gets simplified to true by the unit clause at(r1,l1,0), while the frame axiom

$$\neg\mathsf{at}(\mathsf{r1}, \mathsf{l2}, 0) \wedge \mathsf{at}(\mathsf{r1}, \mathsf{l2}, 1) \Rightarrow \mathsf{move}(\mathsf{r1}, \mathsf{l1}, \mathsf{l2}, 0) \tag{7.17}$$

gets simplified by the unit clause $\neg\mathsf{at}(\mathsf{r1}, \mathsf{l2}, 0)$ to

$$\mathsf{at}(\mathsf{r1}, \mathsf{l2}, 1) \Rightarrow \mathsf{move}(\mathsf{r1}, \mathsf{l1}, \mathsf{l2}, 0) \tag{7.18}$$

A similar simplification is performed for frame axioms that involve instantiations at step 6.

Complete exclusion axioms get simplified at the second iteration of unit propagation. For instance, since the first iteration has simplified to $\neg\mathsf{move}(\mathsf{r1}, \mathsf{l2}, \mathsf{l1}, 0)$, complete exclusion axioms like

$$\neg\mathsf{move}(\mathsf{r1}, \mathsf{l2}, \mathsf{l1}, 0) \vee \neg\mathsf{move}(\mathsf{r2}, \mathsf{l1}, \mathsf{l2}, 0) \tag{7.19}$$

simplify to true. This intuitively corresponds to the fact that since move(r1,l2,l1,0) corresponds to an action that is not applicable in the initial state, we do not need to eliminate the case in which it could get applied in the same step with another action, in this case, move(r2,l1,l2,0).

The first call to Unit-Propagate eliminates all these possible facts. When unit propagation terminates, the variable selection phase has to select a variable to eliminate. We can choose among different propositional variables that correspond to different applications of actions in different steps or to different propositions that may hold in different steps. How the search will proceed depends on this choice. Variable selection may end up in two main cases, depending on whether it chooses a variable instantiated at step i that will actually correspond or will not correspond to either an action of a solution plan at step $i-1$ or a fact that holds after executing an action of a solution plan at step $i-1$. If this is done at each recursive call of Davis-Putnam, then the recursive application of Davis-Putnam will lead to a solution plan. Otherwise, Davis-Putnam will need to backtrack.

For instance, let us suppose that variable selection chooses move(r1,l1,l2,0) its first time (the robot needs to be loaded first). This is an unlucky choice because it

6. Here, for simplicity, we do not write formulas in the CNF version.

rules out the possibility of finding a solution plan of length 6. Davis-Putnam is called recursively until it discovers that and has to backtrack.

A good choice is instead load(c1,r1,l1,0) because the solution plan of length 6 must first load one of the two robots. Unit propagation does its job by ruling out all the actions that are not applicable after loading the robot, e.g., load(c1,r1,l1,1). Some good alternatives to load(c1,r1,l1,0) are load(c2,r2,l1,0) (loading the other robot as the first action), move(r1,l1,l2,1) (moving the first robot as the second action), unload(r2,2) (unloading the second robot as the second action), and so on. Alternative good choices for predicates are loaded(c1,r1,1), ¬unloaded(r1, 1), at(r1,l1,1), etc.

Of course, the procedure does not have to choose first the propositions instantiated at step 0, then those at step 1, etc. The first (good) choice can be, for instance, unload(c2,r2,l1,5).

In our example, Davis-Putnam, depending on the choice of variables, can return many different totally ordered plans corresponding to different possible models. Here are two possibilities:

load(c1, r1, l1, 0), move(r1, l1, l2, 1), unload(c1, r1, l2, 2),

load(c2, r2, l2, 3), move(r2, l2, l1, 4), unload(c2, r2, l1, 5)

and

load(c2, r2, l2, 0), load(c1, r1, l1, 1), move(r2, l2, l1, 2),

move(r1, l1, l2, 3), unload(c2, r2, l1, 4), unload(c1, r1, l2, 5)

Notice that in this case a partially ordered plan (in the style of Graphplan) would help a lot to keep the planning length shorter. Indeed, we could devise a partially ordered plan of length 3: we load, move, and unload the two robots. The use of complete exclusion axioms prevents the possibility of searching for partially ordered plans. In Section 7.4 we will describe a different kind of encoding that allows for partially ordered plans. This encoding is called *conflict exclusion* and is similar in spirit to the mutual exclusion (mutex) relations of Graphplan. ■

Proposition 7.2 *Davis-Putnam is sound and complete.*

7.3.2 Stochastic Procedures

Davis-Putnam works with *partial assignments*: at each step, not all the variables are assigned a truth value. At the initial step, μ is empty; then it is incrementally constructed by adding assignments to variables. An alternative idea is to devise algorithms that work from the beginning on *total assignments*, i.e., on assignments to all the variables in Φ. A trivial algorithm based on this idea is the one that randomly selects an initial total assignment, checks whether there is a model, and, if not, iteratively selects a different total assignment until a model is found or the space of all possible total assignments is exhausted. This is of course a sound and complete procedure, but it is of no practical use because it searches randomly through the huge space of all possible assignments. However, it can be used as the basic idea underlying a set of *incomplete satisfiability decision procedures* that have been shown experimentally to scale up to rather large problems.

Typically, incomplete procedures employ some notion of *randomized local search.* Figure 7.4 presents an algorithm based on randomized local search. Local-Search-SAT selects randomly a total assignment μ and, if it is not a model, tries to improve the choice by replacing it with a "better" assignment μ'. The assignment is "better" according to a function cost Cost(μ,Φ) that typically is the number of clauses of Φ that are not satisfied by μ. Condition $|\mu - \mu'| = 1$ imposes that the search is local because μ and μ' must differ for the assignment to one variable. In other words, μ' is obtained from μ by *flipping* one variable, i.e., by changing the assignment to one variable in Φ. It is easy to show that Local-Search-SAT is sound and incomplete. Incompleteness is due to the possible existence of local minima.

A widely used variation of Local-Search-SAT is the GSAT algorithm. A basic version of GSAT is presented in Figure 7.5. At each step of Basic-GSAT, one variable is flipped: Flip(P, μ) returns the truth assignment obtained by flipping the variable P (this is equivalent to computing a μ' at hamming distance 1 from μ, see Local-search-SAT). The new truth assignment is selected by flipping the variable that leads to the best neighboring assignment: arg $\min_{\mu_P}$ Cost(μ_P, Φ) returns a μ_P such that Cost(μ_P, Φ) is minimal. Notice that, unlike Local-Search-SAT, Basic-GSAT does not impose any condition on the fact that the assignment must be improved, i.e., it does not impose that the number of unsatisfied clauses decreases. Indeed, even the best flip can increase the number of unsatisfied clauses. In this aspect, Basic-GSAT differs significantly from the classical notion of local search, in which an improvement is made at every step and search is terminated when no improving

```
Local-Search-SAT(Φ)
   select a total assignment μ for Φ randomly
   while μ does not satisfy Φ do
      if ∃μ' s.t. Cost(μ',Φ) < Cost(μ,Φ) and |μ − μ'| = 1
         then μ ← μ'
         else return failure
   return μ
```

Figure 7.4 A SAT algorithm based on randomized local search.

```
Basic-GSAT(Φ)
    select μ randomly
    while μ does not satisfy Φ do
        for every P ∈ Φ, μ_P ← Flip(P,μ)
        μ ← arg min_{μ_P} Cost(μ_P, Φ)
    return μ
```

Figure 7.5 A basic version of GSAT.

step is possible. One motivation for this choice is that it helps avoid local minima. Experimental results have indeed shown that GSAT manages often to avoid local minima, while procedures restricted to improving steps (like Local-Search-SAT) perform poorly. Basic-GSAT is not guaranteed to terminate. In the real implementations of GSAT, the algorithm *restarts* with a new initial guess after a maximum number of flips and terminates after a maximum number of restarts. Moreover, many different variations have been devised to try to avoid the local minima problem, including backtracking, different heuristics for restarts, and random flips.

Other alternative incomplete methods, still based on local search, are the algorithms based on the so-called *iterative repair approach*. The basic idea is to iteratively modify a truth assignment such that it satisfies one of the unsatisfied clauses selected according to some criterion. An unsatisfied clause is seen as a "fault" to be "repaired." This approach differs from local search in that, at every step, the number of unsatisfied clauses (the typical cost) may increase. In Figure 7.6, we present a generic algorithm based on this idea. It is easy to show that Iterative-Repair is sound and incomplete.

A well-known version of an iterative repair algorithm is Random-walk, which implements the step "modify μ to satisfy C" in a way that resembles GSAT, i.e., by

```
Iterative-Repair(Φ)
    select any μ
    while μ does not satisfy Φ do
        if iteration limit exceeded then return failure
        select any clause C ∈ Φ not satisfied by μ
        modify μ to satisfy C
    return μ
```

Figure 7.6 A general iterative repair algorithm.

flipping iteratively one variable in C. While Random-walk can be shown to solve any satisfiable CNF formula, it has been shown experimentally to suffer several problems on formulas of a certain complexity. However, a variation of Random-walk called Walksat has been shown experimentally to perform better than local search and GSAT. Walksat is a "probabilistically greedy" version of Random-walk. After C is selected randomly, Walksat selects randomly the variable to be flipped among the two following possibilities: (1) a random variable in C or (2) the variable in C that leads to the greatest number of satisfied clauses when flipped. The intuition underlying Walksat is that mixing up randomly nongreedy (case 1) and greedy (case 2) choices provides the ability to move toward a better choice while avoiding local minima as much as possible.

Conceptually, Walksat has similarities with another incomplete method, Simulated-Annealing, which has been shown to perform comparably. Simulated-Annealing is a method for finding global minima of an energy function. It was originally devised as a method for combinatorial optimization (i.e., for determining the minimum value of a function with several independent variables) and has been applied for the analysis of the equations of state in n-body systems (e.g., to analyze how liquids freeze or metals recrystallize during the process of annealing). In the satisfiability problem, the value of the energy can be seen as the number of unsatisfied clauses in the propositional formula. Simulated-Annealing performs the following steps.

1. Select an initial assignment randomly.
2. Select randomly any variable P.
3. Compute δ, i.e., the change in the number of unsatisfied clauses when P is flipped.
4. If $\delta \leq 0$, make the flip.
5. If $\delta > 0$, make the flip with probability $e^{\delta/T}$, where T is the temperature and is usually a decreasing function of the number of steps taken. For instance, the temperature $T(1)$ at the first step can be a predefined high value (the maximal temperature), and the temperature at step $i + 1$ can be computed as

$$T(i+1) = T(i) - \frac{\Delta T}{i}$$

where ΔT is the difference between the maximal value of the temperature (i.e., $T(1)$) and a predefined minimal value.

Example 7.5 Consider the same propositional formula used in Example 7.3:

$$\Phi = D \wedge (\neg D \vee A \vee \neg B) \wedge (\neg D \vee \neg A \vee \neg B) \wedge (\neg D \vee \neg A \vee B) \wedge (D \vee A)$$

We describe some of the possible executions of the different stochastic procedures discussed in this section.

- Local-Search-SAT selects a random total assignment first. Let us suppose the assignment is $\mu = \{D, A, B\}$. Under this assignment, the only unsatisfied clause is $(\neg D \vee \neg A \vee \neg B)$, and therefore Cost($\mu$,$\Phi$) $= 1$. There is no μ' such that $|\mu - \mu'| = 1$ and Cost(μ,Φ) < 1. Local-Search-SAT terminates execution with failure. It behaves differently if the initial guess is different, for instance, if $\mu = \{\neg D, A, \neg B\}$, then it finds the model in one iteration step.
- Basic-GSAT selects a random total assignment. Let us suppose it starts also with the initial guess $\mu = \{D, A, B\}$. Different than Local-Search-SAT, Basic-GSAT has two alternatives. It can flip either variable D or B because the corresponding cost is 1 (flipping A has a cost of 2). If D is flipped, then the alternative is to flip D again or to flip B. If B is flipped, then one of the alternatives is to flip A. If this alternative is taken, the solution is found.
- Iterative-Repair, with the same initial guess, has to repair clause $(\neg D \vee \neg A \vee \neg B)$. Different assignments can repair this clause. One is the solution $\mu = \{D, \neg A, \neg B\}$. If this is not selected, Iterative-Repair has to reiterate. Let us suppose $\mu = \{\neg D, \neg A, \neg B\}$ is selected. We then have two clauses to repair: D and $(D \vee A)$. If D is selected, then Iterative-Repair finds the solution by repairing it. If $D \vee A$ is selected, then Iterative-Repair has two different possibilities, and one of them leads to the solution.

■

7.4 Different Encodings

In Section 7.2, we presented one particular encoding of a bounded planning problem to a satisfiability problem. The encoding determines the number of propositional variables and the number of clauses in the satisfiability problem, i.e., the variables and the clauses in the formula Φ that is generated. Since the efficiency of satisfiability decision procedures (both complete and incomplete ones) depends on the number of variables and clauses (e.g., Walksat takes time exponential in the number of variables), the choice of encoding is critical. The encoding in Section 7.2 is based on two main choices.

1. The *encoding of actions.* Each ground action is represented by a different logical variable at each step. For instance, we encode operator move(r,l,l') with the propositional variables move(r1,l1,l2,i), move(r1,l2,l1,i), etc. This results in $|A| = n|O||D|^{A_0}$ variables, where n is the number of steps, $|O|$ is the number of operators, $|D|$ is the number of constants in the domain, and A_0 is the maximum arity of operators. One could devise a different type of encoding, e.g., provide m bits that can encode each ground action. This encoding is called "bitwise." For example, if we have four ground actions—a_1 = move(r1,l1,l2,i), a_2 = move(r1,l2,l1,i), a_3 = move(r2,l1,l2,i), and a_4 = move(r2,l2,l1,i)—we can use just two bits: bit1(i) and bit2(i).

The formula $\text{bit1}(i) \wedge \text{bit2}(i)$ can represent a_1, $\text{bit1}(i) \wedge \neg\text{bit2}(i)$ represents a_2, etc. This reduces the number of variables to $\lceil \log_2 |A| \rceil$.

2. The *encoding of the frame problem.* We have chosen *explanatory frame axioms,* i.e., formulas that, for each fluent, enumerate the set of actions that could have occurred in order to account for a state change (see Formula 7.12). We could have used the most natural way to formalize the fact that actions change only the values of fluents that are in their effects by generating formulas that, for each action, state that the fluents that do not appear in their effects remain the same. For instance, for action move(r1,l1,l2), we could have a formula like $\text{unloaded}(\text{r1}, i) \wedge \text{move}(\text{r1}, \text{l1}, \text{l2}, i) \Rightarrow \text{unloaded}(\text{r1}, i+1)$, which states that moving an unloaded robot leaves the robot unloaded. The formulas resulting from this way of encoding are called *classical frame axioms.* In the case of classical frame axioms, the number of clauses in Φ is $O(n, |F|, |A|)$, where $|F|$ is the number of ground fluents. In the case of explanatory frame axioms, we have just $O(n, |F|)$ clauses if actions are represented as described in Section 7.2.

Different encodings can be classified depending on how actions are represented and how the frame problem is formalized. In the following we review some of the main alternatives proposed in the literature.

7.4.1 Action Representation

We discuss four alternatives for encoding actions.

Regular. This is the encoding proposed in Section 7.2: each ground action is represented by a different logical variable. It results in $|A| = n|O||D|^{A_0}$ variables.

Simple Operator Splitting. The idea is to replace each n-ary action ground proposition with n unary ground propositions. For instance, the propositional variable move(r1,l1,l2,i), resulting from the regular action representation, is replaced by $\text{move1}(\text{r1}, i) \wedge \text{move2}(\text{l1}, i) \wedge \text{move3}(\text{l2}, i)$. Intuitively, the advantage is that instances of each operator share the same variables. For instance, the same variable move2(l1,i) is used to represent move(r1,l1,l2,i) can be reused to represent move(r2,l1,l3,i) without generating a number of variables that is exponential on the arity of an operator. In other words, the same variable can be used to represent different cases where the starting location of the move operation is the same. Consider, for instance, the case in which we have three robots and three locations. We need $3^3 = 27$ variables in the regular representation, while we need just $3 + 3 + 3 = 9$ variables with the simple operator splitting. In general, simple operator splitting results in $n|O||D|A_0$ variables.

Overloaded Operator Splitting. This generalizes the idea of simple operator splitting by allowing different operators to share the same variable. This is done by representing the action (e.g., move) as the argument of a general action predicate Act. For instance, move(r1,l1,l2,i) is replaced by Act(move, i) $\wedge$ Act1(r1, i) $\wedge$ Act2(l1, i) $\wedge$ Act3(l2, i). Notice that a different action, like fly(r1,l1,l2,i), can share the same variables of move(r1,l1,l2,i): Act(fly, i) $\wedge$ Act1(r1, i) $\wedge$ Act2(l1, i) $\wedge$ Act3(l2, i). Overloaded splitting further reduces the number of variables to $n(|O| + |D|A_0)$.

Bitwise. This is the technique already introduced in this section. $n\lceil \log_2 |A| \rceil$ propositional variables can be used in a sort of binary encoding. For instance, in order to represent 30 ground actions, we need just 5 bits because $2^5 = 32$.

The conclusion of this analysis on action representation could let us think that the bitwise encoding is the most convenient. This is not true! The number of variables is not the only cause of complexity that satisfiability decision procedures have to deal with. The complexity depends also on the number of clauses generated, their length, and other factors. Moreover, action representation is not the only choice we have. Depending on the frame axioms we choose, one or another action representation might be more or less convenient. In the next subsection, we proceed along the other dimension of the space of encodings: frame axioms.

7.4.2 Frame Axioms

Let us discuss in more detail the two different possibilities we have already introduced: classical and explanatory frame axioms.

Classical Frame Axioms. This is the most obvious formalization of the fact that actions change only what is explicitly stated. With this choice, formulas like Formula 7.12 are replaced with formulas of the following kind. For each action a, for each fluent $f \notin$ effects(a), and for each $0 \leq i \leq n-1$, we have:

$$f_i \wedge a_i \Rightarrow f_{i+1} \qquad (7.20)$$

However, such a replacement is not enough. Indeed, notice that if action a_i does not occur at step i, a_i is false and Formula 7.20 is trivially true. Classical frame axioms do not constrain the value of f_{i+1}, which can therefore take an arbitrary value. The final consequence is that we have unintended models. For instance, consider this classical frame axiom:

$$\text{unloaded}(\text{r1}, i) \wedge \text{move}(\text{r1}, \text{l1}, \text{l2}, i) \Rightarrow \text{unloaded}(\text{r1}, i) \qquad (7.21)$$

When the robot is not moved from l1 to l2 at step i the robot might become loaded "magically." We do not want this! A solution is to add the *at-least-one axioms*, i.e., a disjunction of every possible ground action at step i, that assures that at least one action is performed:[7]

$$\bigvee_{a \in A} a_i \tag{7.22}$$

While classical frame axioms force us to add at-least-one axioms, they avoid complete exclusion axioms (Formula 7.13) when we need to state that just one action occurs at a time. Indeed, classical frame axioms like Formula 7.20 combined with the axioms on action preconditions and effects (Formula 7.11) ensure that any two actions that occur at step i lead to an identical state at step $i + 1$. Therefore, if more than one action occurs in a step, then either one can be selected to form a valid plan.

Explanatory Frame Axioms. We used this kind of axiom in Section 7.3, Formula 7.12. No at-least-one axioms are required. On the other hand, we need to state complete exclusion axioms (Formula 7.13) to ensure that just one action occurs at a given step. The result is that we are searching for totally ordered plans, which might not be the best thing to do. We have seen that other planning approaches (e.g., Graphplan) take strong advantage of searching in the space of partial-ordered plans. While classical frame axioms impose total order, explanatory frame actions can allow for partial order. This can be done by limiting exclusion axioms to *conflicting actions*. The notion of conflicting actions is similar to the one provided in Graphplan: two actions are conflicting if one's precondition is inconsistent with the other's effect. We have axioms of the form $\neg a_i \vee \neg b_i$ only if a and b are conflicting. This form of encoding is called *conflict exclusion*, as opposed to *complete exclusion*.

In Figure 7.7, we report the worst-case size for the different possible encodings of actions and frame axioms. The size of the encoding is measured in terms of number of variables and number of clauses. The conversion, compared with the original problem statement (see Chapter 2), grows the size of the problem statement exponentially. Figure 7.7 gives an idea of the complexity of the formula resulting from the encodings. However, as reported in Ernst *et al.* [172], practical experimentation shows that some of the expectations from this complexity analysis are not fulfilled. From several experiments in planning domains from the literature, regular explanatory and simple splitting explanatory encodings are the smallest ones. Indeed, explanatory frame axioms are in practice smaller than classical ones because they state only what changes, rather than what does not change, when an action occurs, and an action usually affects just a few fluents. Regular explanatory encodings allow for parallel actions and as a consequence for shorter plans. Moreover, conflict exclusion axioms are a subset of complete exclusion axioms. It is surprising that bitwise encoding does not give advantages in practice. In the worst

7. Axioms like Formula 7.22 are not necessary with a bitwise representation of actions because all the models must assign values to bit1(i) such that at least one action is executed.

Actions	Number of variables
Regular	$n\|F\| + n\|O\|\|D\|^{A_0}$
Simple splitting	$n\|F\| + n\|O\|\|D\|A_0$
Overloaded splitting	$n\|F\| + n(\|O\| + \|D\|A_0)$
Bitwise	$n\|F\| + n\lceil \log_2 \|O\|\|D\|^{A_0} \rceil$

Action	Frame axiom	Number of clauses
Regular	Classical	$O(n\|F\|\|A\|)$
Regular	Explanatory	$O(n\|F\|\|A\| + n\|A\|^2)$
Simple splitting	Classical	$O(n\|F\|\|A\|A_0 + n\|A\|A_0{}^{\|A\|})$
Simple splitting	Explanatory	$O(n\|F\|A_0{}^{\|A\|} + n(\|A\|A_0)^2)$
Overloaded splitting	Classical	$O(n\|F\|\|A\|A_0 + n\|A\|A_0{}^{\|A\|})$
Overloaded splitting	Explanatory	$O(n\|F\|(\|A\|A_0)^2 + n\|F\|\|A\|A_0{}^{\|A\|})$
Bitwise	Classical	$O(n\|F\|\|A\| \log_2 \|A\|)$
Bitwise	Explanatory	$O(n\|F\|\|A\|(\log_2 \|A\|)^{\|A\|})$

Figure 7.7 Size of the different encodings: n is the number of steps of the plan; $|F|$ is the number of fluents, with $|F| = |P||D|^{A_p}$, where $|P|$ is the number of predicate symbols, $|D|$ is the number of constants in the domain, and A_p is the maximum arity of predicates; $|O|$ is the number of operators; A_0 is the maximum arity of operators; and $|A| = |O||D|^{A_0}$ is the number of ground actions.

case, it has the smallest number of variables. A possible explanation is that bitwise encoding cannot take advantage of possible simplifications during the search. Operator splitting allows for reasoning about parts of actions, which represent a sort of generalization of many possible instantiations. It is possible to deduce more from generalized formulas than from fully instantiated ones.

7.5 Discussion and Historical Remarks

The original idea of "planning as satisfiability" is due to Kautz and Selman [313, 314] and was subsequently incorporated into a planner called BlackBox [315]. Different possible encodings were first investigated by the work by Kautz, McAllester, and Selman [312]. A rationalization and further investigation of the encoding problem and of its automatic generation is due to Ernst, Millstein, and Weld [172]. Along these lines, different methods and encodings have been proposed (e.g., [232]). The ability to add control knowledge to gain efficiency has been shown in two papers [122, 315]. Finally, the approach has been extended to resource handling [556]. A good survey of complete and incomplete methods for deciding satisfiability can be found in Cook and Mitchell [132]. A detailed description and discussion of the simulated annealing method can be found in other sources [62, 284, 469].

The "planning as satisfiability" approach has demonstrated that general purpose logic-based reasoning techniques can be applied effectively to plan synthesis.[8] In early attempts, general purpose logic-based planning was done by deduction, e.g., by first-order resolution theorem proving (see the seminal work by Green in 1969 [249]). Deduction, however, could not compete with algorithms designed specifically for planning, such as search-based algorithms in the state or plan space. In the first AIPS Planning Competition in 1998, the BlackBox planning system [315] was competitive with the most efficient planners, including Graphplan and planners that do heuristic search. This was mainly for two main reasons: (1) the ability to exploit recent improvements in the performance of general purpose algorithms for propositional satisfiability [244, 469], and (2) probably most importantly, the use of an encoding based on conflict exclusion axioms based on the idea of mutex in Graphplan, called *Graphplan-based encoding* (see Section 7.4). Graphplan has since actually been used to efficiently generate the SAT encoding [41, 316].

In this chapter we have focused on planning in classical planning problems. The approach has been extended to deal with different kinds of problems (see Chapter 18). Finally, note that the SAT encoding is a particular case of the CSP encoding (see Chapter 8).

7.6 Exercises

7.1 Are the following formulas satisfiable?

$$(\neg D \vee A \vee \neg B) \wedge (\neg D \vee \neg A \vee \neg B) \wedge (\neg D \vee \neg A \vee B) \wedge (D \vee A)$$

$$(D \rightarrow (A \rightarrow \neg B)) \vee (D \wedge (\neg A \rightarrow \neg)B) \wedge (\neg D \vee \neg A \vee B) \wedge (D \rightarrow A)$$

Run the Davis-Putnam procedure on them and explain the result. Also run a stochastic procedure.

7.2 Complicate Example 7.1 (see page 150) with a loading and unloading operation. Describe the regular, explanatory, and complete exclusion encodings. How many clauses do the encodings generate?

7.3 Consider Example 7.1 (see page 150) with two robots. Write the different possible encodings.

7.4 Describe the different possible encodings of the complete DWR example. For each encoding, how many clauses do we have?

7.5 Can conflict exclusion be used with simple and overloading action representation? Why?

7.6 Can you find an example of a planning problem where Davis-Putnam is more effective than the stochastic procedures? Vice versa?

8. Notice, however, that the reasoning technique used in SAT is much closer to, indeed a particular case of, CSP techniques (see Chapter 8) than logical deduction.

7.7 In Example 7.1 (see page 150), suppose you do not know in which location the robot is initially. Suppose the planning problem is to find a plan such that no matter where the robot is initially, the plan leads to the goal "the robot must be in l2." Can you find an encoding such that the problem can be formulated as a satisfiability problem?

7.8 Run BlackBox (http://www.cs.washington.edu/homes/kautz/blackbox) on the DWR domain. Check the size of the encoding.

7.9 Describe the possible encodings of the planning problem described in Exercise 2.1. Run BlackBox on this planning problem.

Chapter 8
Constraint Satisfaction Techniques

8.1 Introduction

Constraint satisfaction is a general and powerful problem-solving paradigm that is applicable to a broad set of areas, ranging from planning and scheduling to computer vision, pattern recognition, CAD, modeling, and decision support systems.

The general formulation of a constraint satisfaction problem (CSP) is as follows. Given (1) a set of variables and their respective domains, and (2) a set of constraints on the compatible values that the variables may take, the problem is to find a value for each variable within its domain such that these values meet all the constraints.

Three instances of this general problem are of special interest to planning.

- Boolean values and Boolean constraints, dealt with in the previous chapter on SAT techniques (Chapter 7).
- Variables ranging over real values or integer values with linear constraints. This is the case of the *linear programming* or *integer programming techniques.* We will refer to these mainly in Chapter 15 on planning and resource scheduling.
- Finite domains and finite tuples of constraints.

CSPs over finite domains can be used in planning in two different ways:

1. Directly, by stating a planning problem as a CSP. It is indeed possible to follow an approach similar to that of SAT, i.e., to encode a planning problem into a CSP and to rely entirely on CSP tools for planning.
2. Indirectly, by using CSP techniques within approaches specific to planning.

This latter use of CSPs in planning is much more frequent and broader than the former direct encoding. We already met several instances of particular constraint satisfaction problems in previous chapters. CSP techniques are even more important in plan-space or Graphplan approaches within the disjunctive-refinement framework. Other instances of CSP techniques will be discussed in the rest of book, in particular with regard to planning with time and resources (Part IV). CSPs are also relevant for planning because several planning heuristics (Chapter 9) and extensions to classical planning, in particular, can rely on CSP techniques.

This chapter provides a general introduction to CSP techniques, as well as some developments on their specific use in planning. The chapter first reviews the essential definitions and concepts of CSPs over finite domains (Section 8.2). It then presents an approach for encoding a planning problem into a CSP and extracting a plan from the solution of that CSP (Section 8.3). Algorithms for solving a CSP and filtering techniques for testing its consistency are introduced (Section 8.4). The chapter briefly discusses two particular classes of CSPs of relevance to planning: active CSPs and valued CSPs (Section 8.5). CSP techniques in the plan-space approach and the Graphplan approach are discussed in Section 8.6. The chapter ends with a discussion and exercises.

8.2 Constraint Satisfaction Problems

A CSP over finite domains is defined to be a triple $\mathcal{P} = (X, \mathcal{D}, \mathcal{C})$ where:

- $X = \{x_1, \ldots, x_n\}$ is a finite set of n variables.
- $\mathcal{D} = \{D_1, \ldots, D_n\}$ is the set of finite domains of the variables, $x_i \in D_i$.
- $\mathcal{C} = \{c_1, \ldots, c_m\}$ is a finite set of constraints. A constraint c_j of some arity k restricts the possible values of a subset of k variables $\{x_{j1}, \ldots, x_{jk}\} \subseteq X$. c_j is defined as a subset of the cartesian product: $c_j \subseteq D_{j1} \times \ldots \times D_{jk}$, i.e., as the set of tuples of values allowed by this constraint for its variables: $\{(v_{j1}, \ldots, v_{jk}) \in D_{j1} \times \ldots \times D_{jk} \mid (v_{j1}, \ldots, v_{jk}) \in c_j\}$.

Definition 8.1 A *solution* to a CSP $(X, \mathcal{D}, \mathcal{C})$ is an n-tuple $\sigma = (v_1, \ldots, v_n)$ such that $v_i \in D_i$ and the values of the variables $x_i = v_i$, for $1 \leq i \leq n$, meet *all* the constraints in $\mathcal{C}$. A CSP is *consistent* if such a solution σ exists. ■

A tuple σ is a solution iff for every constraint $c_j \in \mathcal{C}$, the values specified in σ for the variables $x_{j1}, \ldots, x_{jk}$ of c_j correspond to a tuple $(v_{j1}, \ldots, v_{jk}) \in c_j$.

A set of constraints is interpreted throughout this book as a *conjunction* of the constraints, unless explicitly stated otherwise. We will say that the set of constraints $\{c_1, \ldots, c_m\}$ is consistent or, equivalently, that the conjunction $c_1 \wedge \ldots \wedge c_m$ holds, when there is a solution σ that meets every constraint in the set. Note that an empty set of constraints always holds because it is met by every tuple of values, whereas a set containing an empty constraint never holds.

A constraint can be specified *explicitly* by listing the set of its allowed tuples or the complementary set of forbidden tuples. It can also be specified *implicitly* by using one or more relation symbols, e.g., $x_i \neq x_j$. The tuples in a constraint may be conveniently denoted by giving the variables and their values, e.g., $(x_i = v_i, x_j = v_j)$. We will often refer to the *universal constraint*, which is satisfied by every tuple of values of its variables, i.e., a constraint $c_j = D_{j1} \times \ldots \times D_{jk}$. If there is no constraint between a subset of variables, then this is equivalent to the universal constraint on these variables. We will also refer to the *empty constraint*, which forbids all tuples and cannot be satisfied.

A CSP is *binary* whenever all its constraints are binary relations. A binary CSP can be represented as a constraint network, i.e., a graph in which each node is a CSP variable x_i labeled by its domain D_i, and each edge (x_i, x_j) is labeled by the corresponding constraint on the two variables x_i and x_j. In a binary CSP, a constraint on x_i and x_j is simply denoted c_{ij}.

The symmetrical relation of a binary constraint c is the set of pairs $c' = \{(w, v) \mid (v, w) \in c\}$. A binary CSP is *symmetrical* if for every constraint $c_{ij} \in \mathcal{C}$, the symmetrical relation c'_{ji} is in $\mathcal{C}$. A symmetrical CSP $\tilde{P} = (X, D, \tilde{C})$ can be defined from $\mathcal{P} = (X, \mathcal{D}, \mathcal{C})$ by letting $\forall i, j, \tilde{c}_{ij} = c_{ij} \cap c'_{ji}$.

A unary constraint c_i on a variable x_i is simply a subset of D_i, the domain of x_i. One can replace D_i with c_i and remove this unary constraint. Hence, if a CSP involves unary and binary constraints, it is simple to express the former directly as reduced domains, keeping only binary constraints. In the remainder of this chapter, we'll focus mainly on binary symmetrical CSPs. Many popular puzzles and combinatorial problems, such as the eight-queens problem (place eight queens on a chessboard without threats between them) and the map coloring problem, are easily formalized as binary CSPs.

Let us illustrate the forthcoming definitions with a simple example.

Example 8.1 A constraint network for a symmetrical binary CSP that has five variables $\{x_1, \ldots, x_5\}$ and eight constraints $\{c_{12}, c_{13}, \ldots, c_{45}\}$ is given in Figure 8.1. All the variables have the same domain: $D_i = \{\alpha, \beta, \gamma\}, 1 \leq i \leq 5$. A solution to this CSP is, e.g., the tuple $(\alpha, \gamma, \beta, \gamma, \alpha)$, which satisfies all eight constraints:

$$(\alpha,\gamma) \in c_{12}; \quad (\alpha,\beta) \in c_{13}; \quad (\alpha,\gamma) \in c_{14}; \quad (\alpha,\alpha) \in c_{15}$$
$$(\gamma,\beta) \in c_{23}; \quad (\gamma,\gamma) \in c_{24}; \quad (\beta,\alpha) \in c_{35}; \quad (\gamma,\alpha) \in c_{45}$$

The other solutions are $(\alpha, \beta, \beta, \alpha, \beta)$, $(\alpha, \gamma, \beta, \alpha, \beta)$, and $(\beta, \gamma, \gamma, \alpha, \gamma)$. ■

It is convenient to consider a constraint network for a binary CSP as a *complete* directed graph. If it is not complete, then a missing edge from x_i to x_j corresponds implicitly to the symmetrical relation of c_{ji} if edge (x_j, x_i) exists in the network, or to the universal constraint if (x_j, x_i) does not exist. In Example 8.1, the edge (x_2, x_1) is implicitly labeled with the symmetrical relation of c_{12}, and the edge (x_2, x_5) is labeled with the universal constraint.

Definition 8.2 Two CSPs $\mathcal{P}$ and $\mathcal{P}'$ on the same set of variables X are *equivalent* if they have the same set of solutions. ■

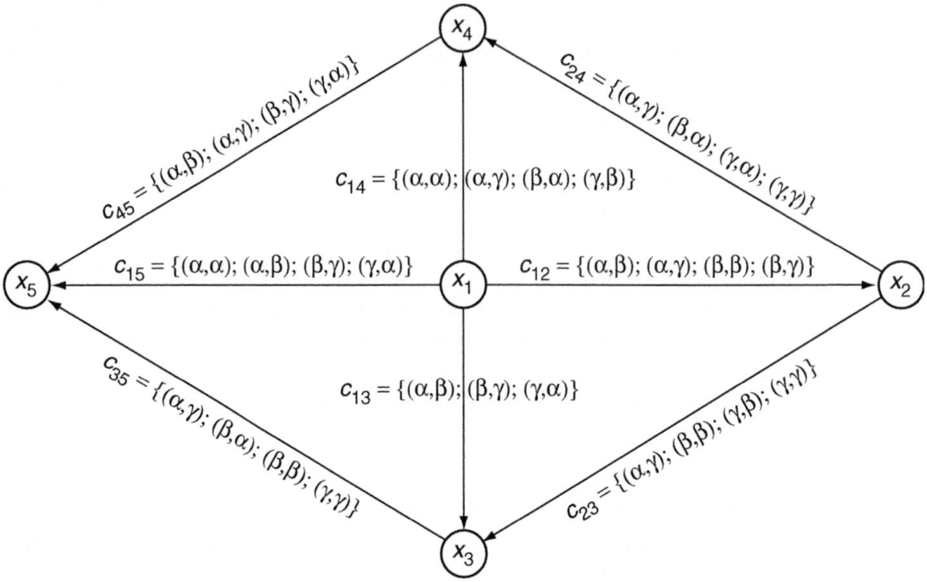

Figure 8.1 A CSP network.

For example, a binary CSP $\mathcal{P}$ and the symmetrical CSP $\tilde{\mathcal{P}}$ obtained from $\mathcal{P}$ are equivalent (see Exercise 8.2). Given a CSP $\mathcal{P}$, one may prefer to solve an equivalent CSP $\mathcal{P}'$ if $\mathcal{P}'$ appears simpler, e.g., if $\mathcal{P}'$ has smaller domains or fewer constraints than $\mathcal{P}$. These extra values are said to be redundant in $\mathcal{P}$ and the extra constraints to be entailed from the other constraints.

Definition 8.3 A value v in a domain D_i is *redundant* if it does not appear in any solution; a tuple in a constraint c_j is redundant if it is not an element of any solution. ■

Example 8.2 Assume that the only solutions of the CSP in Figure 8.1 are the four tuples given in Example 8.1. It is easy to check that the value γ is redundant in D_1, α is redundant in D_2, the pair (β, β) is redundant in c_{12}, and (α, γ) is redundant in c_{13}. ■

The removal of a value from a domain or a tuple from a constraint corresponds to *tightening* the CSP unless that value or tuple is redundant. The removal of a redundant value from a domain or a redundant tuple from a constraint gives an equivalent CSP because it does not change the solution set. Note that if all values in a domain or if all tuples in a constraint are redundant, then the corresponding CSP is not consistent.

Definition 8.4 A CSP is *minimal* if it has no redundant values in the domains of $\mathcal{D}$ *and* no redundant tuples in the constraints of $\mathcal{C}$. ■

Definition 8.5 A set of constraints $\mathcal{C}$ is *consistent with* a constraint c iff the following holds: when $(X, \mathcal{D}, \mathcal{C})$ is consistent, then $(X, \mathcal{D}, \mathcal{C} \cup \{c\})$ is also consistent. ■

In other words, when the CSP $(X, \mathcal{D}, \mathcal{C})$ has a solution and the additional constraint c does not reduce its set of solutions to the empty set, then $\mathcal{C}$ is consistent with c.

Example 8.3 The constraint $c_{25} = \{(\alpha,\alpha),(\beta,\beta),(\gamma,\gamma)\}$ is consistent with the CSP in Figure 8.1: it leaves the tuples $(\alpha,\beta,\beta,\alpha,\beta)$ and $(\beta,\gamma,\gamma,\alpha,\gamma)$ as solutions to $(X, \mathcal{D}, \mathcal{C} \cup \{c_{25}\})$. ■

Definition 8.6 A set of constraints $\mathcal{C}$ *entails* a constraint c, denoted as $\mathcal{C} \models c$, iff the CSP $(X, \mathcal{D}, \mathcal{C})$ is equivalent to $(X, \mathcal{D}, \mathcal{C} \cup \{c\})$, i.e., the two CSPs have the *same* set of solutions. ■

In other words, $\mathcal{C}$ entails c when c does not restrict the set of solutions further than the constraints in $\mathcal{C}$. This is the case, e.g., for constraints that are transitive relations over an ordered domain: $\{x < y, y < z\}$ entails the constraint $x < z$. Note that an entailed constraint c may or may not be in $\mathcal{C}$: if c belongs to $\mathcal{C}$, then it is trivially entailed by $\mathcal{C}$. Note also that if $\mathcal{C}$ entails c, then $\mathcal{C}$ is consistent with c.

Example 8.4 The constraint $c_{25} = \{(\alpha,\alpha),(\beta,\beta),(\gamma,\gamma)\}$ given in Example 8.3 is not entailed by $\mathcal{C}$ because it reduces the set of solutions: the two tuples $(\alpha,\gamma,\beta,\gamma,\alpha)$ and $(\alpha,\gamma,\beta,\alpha,\beta)$ are not consistent with c_{25}. However, the constraint $c'_{25} = \{(\beta,\beta),(\gamma,\gamma),(\gamma,\alpha),(\gamma,\beta)\}$ is entailed by $\mathcal{C}$ because the four solution tuples are consistent with this constraint. ■

Definition 8.7 A constraint $c \in \mathcal{C}$ is *redundant* iff the CSP $(X, \mathcal{D}, \mathcal{C})$ is equivalent to $(X, \mathcal{D}, \mathcal{C} - c)$, i.e., the removal of c from $\mathcal{C}$ does not change the set of solutions. ■

Example 8.5 In the CSP of Figure 8.1, the constraint c_{13} is redundant. ■

In general, removing a constraint c from $\mathcal{C}$ or adding tuples to c corresponds to *relaxing* the CSP problem unless that constraint c is redundant. Contrarily, removing tuples from a constraint corresponds to *tightening* the problem unless that tuple is redundant. Note that removing a redundant constraint from a set $\mathcal{C}$ is equivalent to replacing it with the universal constraint. This is due to the notion of removing a redundant tuple within a constraint. In a symmetrical binary CSP, for each (i, j) either c_{ij} or c_{ji} are redundant. Hence, when a binary CSP is transformed into a symmetrical CSP, one may keep only one edge and one constraint between each pair of nodes.

Given a CSP, one may be interested in addressing: (1) a *resolution* problem: finding a solution tuple; (2) a *consistency* problem: checking whether such a solution exists; (3) a *filtering* problem: removing some redundant values from domains or some redundant tuples from constraints; and (4) a *minimal reduction* problem: removing every redundant value and redundant tuple.

One may define several levels of filtering, but filtering is weaker than minimal reduction because remaining values in a filtered domain may or may not belong to a solution. Minimal reduction solves the consistency problem because a CSP has no solution iff minimal reduction reduces a domain or a constraint to an empty set. Minimal reduction greatly simplifies the resolution problem, providing potentially all solutions.

The consistency problem of a binary CSP over finite domains is NP-complete. Resolution and minimal reduction are NP-hard problems. Filtering is a polynomial problem. Its practical efficiency makes it desirable as an approximation to consistency checking: it provides a *necessary* but not a *sufficient* condition of consistency. If filtering reduces a domain or a constraint to an empty set, then the CSP is inconsistent, but the converse is not true. Filtering is useful in particular when a CSP is specified incrementally, as is typical for CSPs in planning, by adding at each step new variables and constraints. One needs to check whether a step is consistent before pursuing it further. This incremental checking can be approximated by filtering techniques.

8.3 Planning Problems as CSPs

This section presents a technique for encoding a bounded planning problem[1] P into a constraint satisfaction problem P'. This encoding has the following property: given P and a constant integer k, there is a one-to-one mapping between the set of solutions of P of length $\leq k$ and the set of solutions of P'. From a solution of the CSP problem P', if any, the mapping provides a solution plan to planning problem P. If P' has no solution, then there is no plan of length $\leq k$ for the problem P.

We will focus here on encoding classical planning problems. However we will not rely on the two popular representations we have been using so far, the set-theoretic or the classical representation, but on the state-variable representation introduced in Section 2.5. The state-variable representation is convenient for our purpose because it leads to a compact encoding into CSPs.

Recall that a state-variable representation for planning relies on the following elements.

- *Constant symbols* are partitioned into disjoint classes corresponding to the objects of the domain, e.g., the classes of robots, locations, cranes, containers, and piles in the DWR domain.

---

1. As defined in Section 7.2.3, a bounded planning problem is restricted to the problem of finding a plan of length at most k for an a priori given integer k.

- *Object variable symbols* are typed variables; each ranges over a class or the union of classes of constants, e.g., $r \in$ robots, $l \in$ locations, etc.
- *State variable symbols* are functions from the set of states and one or more sets of constants into a set of constants, such as:

  rloc: robots $\times S \rightarrow$ locations
  rload: robots $\times S \rightarrow$ containers $\cup$ {nil}
  cpos: containers $\times S \rightarrow$ locations $\cup$ robots

- *Relation symbols* are *rigid* relations on the constants that do not vary from state to state for a given planning domain, e.g., adjacent(loc1,loc2), belong(pile1,loc1), attached(crane1,loc1). The type of an object variable can also be specified with a rigid relation, e.g., locations(l), robots(r).

A planning operator is a triple: $o = $ (name(o),precond(o),effects(o)) where precond(o) is a set of expressions that are conditions on state variables and on rigid relations, and effects(o) is a set of assignments of values to state variables. The statement of a bounded planning problem is $P = (O, R, s_0, g, k)$, where O, s_0, and g are as usual, R is the set of rigid relations of the domain, and k is the length bound.

The encoding of a planning problem into a CSP will be illustrated on a simple example that we presented earlier (Example 2.8).

Example 8.6 This simplified DWR domain has no piles and no cranes, and robots can load and unload autonomously containers. The domain has only three operators:

move(r, l, m)
  ;; robot r at location l moves to an adjacent location m
  precond: rloc(r) $= l$, adjacent(l, m)
  effects: rloc(r) $\leftarrow m$

load(c, r, l)
  ;; robot r loads container c at location l
  precond: rloc(r) $= l$, cpos(c) $= l$, rload(r) $=$ nil
  effects: rload(r) $\leftarrow c$, cpos(c) $\leftarrow r$

unload(c, r, l)
  ;; robot r unloads container c at location l
  precond: rloc(r) $= l$, rload(r) $= c$
  effects: rload(r) $\leftarrow$ nil, cpos(c) $\leftarrow l$

The domain has three state variables, i.e., rloc(r), rload(r), and cpos(c), and a rigid relation adjacent(l, m). To keep the notation simple, the state argument in state variables is implicit. The expressions in precond(a) for an action a refer to the values of state variables in a state s, whereas the updates in effects(a) refer to the values in the state $\gamma(s, a)$. ■

8.3.1 Encoding a Planning Problem into a CSP

A bounded planning problem $P = (O, R, s_0, g, k)$ in the state-variable representation is encoded into a constraint satisfaction problem P' in four steps corresponding respectively to (1) the definition of the CSP variables of P', (2) the definition of the constraints of P' encoding the initial state s_0 and the goal g, (3) the encoding of the actions that are instances of operators in O, and (4) the encoding of the frame axioms.

This encoding of $P = (O, R, s_0, g, k)$ is with respect to the given integer k: the set of solutions of the CSP P' is intended to correspond to the set of plans $\langle a_1, \ldots, a_k \rangle$ of P of length $\leq k$. We are interested in characterizing the sequences of states $\langle s_0, s_1, \ldots, s_k \rangle$ corresponding to such plans. For convenience, let us refer to the state s_j in this sequence by its index j, for $0 \leq j \leq k$.

Step 1: CSP Variables. The CSP variables of P' are defined as follows.

- For each ground state variable x_i of P ranging over D_i and for each $0 \leq j \leq k$, there is a CSP variable of P', $x_i(j, v_u, \ldots, v_w)$ whose domain is D_i.
- For each $0 \leq j \leq k - 1$, there is a CSP variable of P', denoted act(j), whose domain is the set of all possible actions in the domain, in addition to a no-op action that has no preconditions and no effects, i.e., $\forall s, \gamma(s, \text{noop}) = s$. More formally:

  $$\text{act}: \{0, \ldots, k-1\} \rightarrow D_{\text{act}}$$
  $$D_{\text{act}} = \{a(v_u, \ldots, v_w) \text{ ground instance of } o \in O\} \cup \{\text{noop}\}$$

Hence, the CSP variables are all the ground state variables of P, plus one variable act($\hat{j}$) whose value corresponds to the action carried out in state j.

Example 8.7 Let $P = (O, R, s_0, g)$, where O are the operators given in Example 8.6 for a simplified DWR domain with one robot (r1), three containers (c1, c2, c3), and three locations (l1, l2, l3). Let s_0 be the state s_0 = {rloc(r1) = l1, rload(r1) = nil, cpos(c1) = l1, cpos(c2) = l2, cpos(c3) = l2}; and let g = {cpos(c1) = l2, cpos(c2) = l1}. Assume that we are seeking a plan of at most $k = 4$ steps. The corresponding CSP P' has the following set of variables:

- rloc(j,r1) $\in$ {l1, l2, l3}, for $0 \leq j \leq 4$
- rload(j,r1) $\in$ {c1, c2, c3, nil}, for $0 \leq j \leq 4$
- cpos(j, c) $\in$ {l1, l2, l3, r1}, for $c \in$ c1, c2, c3 and $0 \leq j \leq 4$
- act(j) $\in$ {move(r, l, m), load(c, r, l), unload(c, r, l), no-op}, for all the possible instances of these operators and for $0 \leq j \leq 3$

Note that act(k) is not a variable in P'. In this problem there are $6 \times 5 - 1 = 29$ CSP variables.

■

Now that we have the CSP variables in P', the constraints of P' will enable us to encode the initial state s_0, the goal g, the actions, and the frame axioms.

Step 2: Constraints Encoding s_0 and g. The encoding of the state s_0 and the goal g into constraints follows directly from the definition of the CSP variables.

Every ground state variable x_i whose value in s_0 is v_i is encoded into a unary constraint of the corresponding CSP variable for $j = 0$ of the form:

$$(x_i(0) = v_i) \tag{8.1}$$

Every ground state variable x_i whose value is v_i in the goal g is encoded into a unary constraint of the corresponding CSP variable for $j = k$:

$$(x_i(k) = v_i) \tag{8.2}$$

Note that there is no constraint for s_0 and g on the CSP variables act(j).

Example 8.8 The state s_0 of Example 8.7 is translated into the following constraints:
rloc(0,r1) = l1, rload(0,r1) = nil, cpos(0,c1) = l1, cpos(0,c2) = l2, cpos(0,c3) = l2.
The goal g is translated into the two constraints:
cpos(4,c1) = l2, and cpos(4,c2) = l1. ■

Step 3: Constraints Encoding Actions. This encoding step translates the actions of the planning problem P into binary constraints of P'. Let $a(v_u, \ldots, v_w)$ be an action instance of some operator $o \in O$ such that the constants $v_u, \ldots, v_w$ meet the rigid relations in the preconditions of a. Then, $\forall j, 0 \leq j \leq k-1$:

- Every condition of the form $(x_i = v_i)$ in precond(a) is translated into a constraint with a single tuple of the form:

$$(\mathsf{act}(j) = a(v_u, \ldots, v_w), x_i(j) = v_i) \tag{8.3}$$

- Every condition of the form $(x_i \in D'_i)$ in precond(a) is translated into a constraint corresponding to the set of pairs:

$$\{(\mathsf{act}(j) = a(v_u, \ldots, v_w), x_i(j) = v_i) \mid v_i \in D'_i\} \tag{8.4}$$

- Every assignment $x_i \leftarrow v_i$ in effects(a) is translated into a constraint with a single tuple:

$$(\mathsf{act}(j) = a(v_u, \ldots, v_w), x_i(j+1) = v_i) \tag{8.5}$$

We can write these sets of constraints with arguments that are object variables instead of constants. However, we restrict the instances of these object variables to tuples that meet the rigid relation in the preconditions. This is illustrated in the following example with the adjacent relation.

Example 8.9 Let us give the constraints translating the move and load operators in Example 8.7. The move operator has only one condition and one effect; it is encoded into the following constraints:

$$\{(\mathsf{act}(j) = \mathsf{move}(r, l, m), \mathsf{rloc}(j, r) = l) \mid \mathsf{adjacent}(l, m) \wedge 0 \le j \le 3\}$$
$$\{(\mathsf{act}(j) = \mathsf{move}(r, l, m), \mathsf{rloc}(j+1, r) = m) \mid \mathsf{adjacent}(l, m) \wedge 0 \le j \le 3\}$$

The operator load has three conditions and two effects, which are encoded into the following constraints:

$$\{(\mathsf{act}(j) = \mathsf{load}(c, r, l), \mathsf{rloc}(j, r) = l) \mid 0 \le j \le 3\}$$
$$\{(\mathsf{act}(j) = \mathsf{load}(c, r, l), \mathsf{rload}(j, r) = \mathsf{nil}) \mid 0 \le j \le 3\}$$
$$\{(\mathsf{act}(j) = \mathsf{load}(c, r, l), \mathsf{cpos}(j, c) = l) \mid 0 \le j \le 3\}$$
$$\{(\mathsf{act}(j) = \mathsf{load}(c, r, l), \mathsf{rload}(j+1, r) = c) \mid 0 \le j \le 3\}$$
$$\{(\mathsf{act}(j) = \mathsf{load}(c, r, l), \mathsf{cpos}(j+1, c) = r) \mid 0 \le j \le 3\}$$

■

Step 4: Constraints Encoding Frame Axioms. This final step encodes the frame axioms constraints. A frame axiom constraint says that any state variable that is invariant for an action a (i.e., not explicitly modified in an assignment in effects(a)) remains unchanged between s and $\gamma(s, a)$. A frame axiom is encoded into a *ternary* constraint involving three variables: act(j) and the invariant state variable but of in state j and in state $j + 1$. More precisely: for every action $a(v_u, \ldots, v_w)$ and every state variable x_i that is invariant for a, we have a constraint with the following set of triples:

$$\{(\mathsf{act}(j) = a(v_u, \ldots, v_w),\ x_i(j) = v_i,\ x_i(j+1) = v_i) \mid v_i \in D_i\} \tag{8.6}$$

Note that no-op has no action constraint, since it has no precondition and no effect, but every state variable is invariant for no-op.

Example 8.10 In Example 8.7, two state variables are a-invariant with respect to action move: rload and cpos. Consequently, the frame axioms for this operator are the following constraints, for $0 \le j \le 3$:

$$\{(\mathsf{act}(j) = \mathsf{move}(r, l, m), \mathsf{rload}(j, r) = v, \mathsf{rload}(j+1, r) = v) \mid \mathsf{adjacent}(l, m) \wedge v \in D_{\mathsf{rload}}\}$$
$$\{(\mathsf{act}(j) = \mathsf{move}(r, l, m), \mathsf{cpos}(j, c) = v, \mathsf{cpos}(j+1, c) = v) \mid \mathsf{adjacent}(l, m) \wedge v \in D_{\mathsf{cpos}}\}$$

where $D_{\mathsf{rload}} = \{\mathsf{c1, c2, c3, nil}\}$ and $D_{\mathsf{cpos}} = \{\mathsf{l1, l2, l3, r1}\}$.

■

Plan Extraction. We have encoded a planning problem P and an integer k into a CSP P'. Let us assume that we have a tool for solving CSPs. Given P' as input, this CSP solver returns a tuple σ as a solution of P' or failure if P' has no solution. The tuple σ gives a value to every CSP variable in P', in particular to the variables act(j). Let these values in σ be: $\mathsf{act}(j) = a_{j+1}$, for $0 \le j \le k - 1$. Each a_j is an action of P, and the sequence $\pi = \langle a_1, \ldots, a_k \rangle$ is a valid plan of P that possibly includes no-op actions.

Proposition 8.1 *There is a one-to-one mapping between the set of plans of length $\leq k$ that are solutions of a bounded planning problem P and the set of solutions of the CSP problem P' encoding P.*

Proof Let σ be a tuple solution of P'. The value in σ of the variable $\text{act}(0) = a_1$ meets all the constraints, in particular those specified in Formulas 8.3 and 8.4, for every condition in $\text{precond}(a_1)$: $x_i(0) = v_i$. These values of $x_i(0)$ also meet the unary constraints in Formula 8.1 for state s_0. Consequently, action a_1, whose preconditions are met in state s_0, is applicable to s_0.

Consider now the state s_1 corresponding to the state variables defined by the values of $x_i(1)$ in the solution σ. These values of $x_i(1)$ meet all the constraints, in particular those of Formulas 8.5 and 8.6 for $j = 0$. This is exactly the definition of the state resulting from applying a_1 to s_0, hence $s_1 = \gamma(s_0, a_1)$.

The same argument can be repeated for $\text{act}(1) = a_2$ and $s_2 = \gamma(s_1, a_2)$, ..., till $\text{act}(k-1) = a_k$ and $s_k = \gamma(s_{k-1}, a_k)$. Now, the values $x_i(k) = v_i$ meet also the unary constraints of Formula 8.2, i.e., the goal g is satisfied in s_k. Hence $\pi = \langle a_1, \ldots, a_k \rangle$ is a valid plan of P.

Conversely, let $\pi = \langle a_1, \ldots, a_k \rangle$ be a solution plan of P and let $s_1 = \gamma(s_0, a_1), \ldots, s_k = \gamma(s_{k-1}, a_k)$ be the corresponding sequence of states. Consider the tuple σ that gives to every CSP variable $x_i(j)$ the value corresponding to that of the state variable x_i in state s_j, for $0 \leq j \leq k$, and $\text{act}(j) = a_{j+1}$, for $0 \leq j \leq k-1$. It is straightforward to show that σ meets all the constraints of P', hence it is a solution of P'.

This proof also shows that there is no plan of length $\leq k$ for the planning problem P iff the CSP P' is inconsistent.

■

8.3.2 Analysis of the CSP Encoding

It is interesting to compare the encoding of a planning problem P into a CSP to the encoding of P into a SAT problem (see Section 7.2.3). The two encodings are very similar except for the specific properties of the state-variable representation used here, which relies on functions instead of relations. Indeed, the encoding steps used here are similar to those used in SAT for encoding states, goals, actions, and the frame axioms. However, the encoding step in SAT called the *complete exclusion axioms* (Formula 7.13), which requires that only one action is performed per state, is not needed here, thanks to the state-variable representation. The act variables correspond to functions from states to possible actions. Hence, they take one and only one value for each state. Similarly, the encoding of a state is simpler than in SAT encoding, which required a specific formula (Formula 7.3) to restrict valid models to intended models. Other more elaborate SAT encodings were discussed in Section 7.4.2; they can also be considered for the CSP encoding in the state-variable representation.

The encoding of a planning problem into a CSP requires $m = k(n+1) - 1$ CSP variables, where n is the number of state variables and k is the bound on the plan length. However, the domain of each CSP variable can be quite large. It is important to remark that both CSP and SAT are NP-complete problems, whereas planning, and more precisely the PLAN-LENGTH problem which is of interest to us here, is PSPACE- or NEXPTIME-complete (see Section 3.3 and Table 3.2). This is explained by the fact that the two encodings of planning, into SAT or into a CSP, lead to a blowup in the size of the resulting problem. For SAT, this blowup results in an exponential number of Boolean variables. For the CSP encoding, the number of variables remains linear in the size of P, but the total size of the CSP P' is exponential, i.e., it is $d = \prod_{i=1}^{i=m} |D_i|$, where D_i is the domain of the CSP variable x_i.

For the same value of d, it is often easier to solve a CSP that has a small number of CSP variables (small m) ranging over large domains than a CSP that has a large number of binary variables. However, this depends largely on the constraints involved.

A related issue here is that the frame axioms are encoded into ternary constraints. CSP solvers have less efficient techniques for handling ternary constraints than binary constraints. Ternary constraints can be translated into binary ones [35, 149], but at the expense of an increase in the size of the problem.

An interesting property of the CSP encoding is that the problem P' remains close enough to the original planning problem P to allow embedding in the CSP solver domain-specific control knowledge for planning, if such knowledge is available, in addition to general CSP heuristics.

8.4 CSP Techniques and Algorithms

This section is devoted to a brief presentation of the main algorithms used for handling a CSP, either for solving it (Section 8.4.1) or for filtering its domains and constraints (Section 8.4.2). These algorithms are the backbones of general CSP solvers over finite domains. They can also be useful for designing a constraint manager for a planner.

For simplicity, this section focuses on algorithms for binary CSPs. The management of higher arity constraints will be briefly discussed in Section 8.7.

8.4.1 Search Algorithms for CSPs

A backtracking search algorithm that solves a CSP is given in Figure 8.2. It is a nondeterministic recursive procedure. Its arguments are σ, the tuple of values corresponding to the current partial solution, and X, the set of remaining variables for which a value has to be found. Starting from an empty σ and the full set X of n variables, the procedure heuristically selects the next variable x_i. Then it propagates previous choices of the values in σ on the domain of x_i. This is done by reducing

```
Backtrack(σ, X)
    if X = ∅ then return(σ)
    select any x_i ∈ X
    for each value v_j in σ do
        D_i ← D_i ∩ {v ∈ D_i | (v, v_j) ∈ c_ij}
    if D_i = ∅ then return(failure)
    nondeterministically choose v_i ∈ D_i
    Backtrack(σ.(v_i), X − {x_i})
end
```

Figure 8.2 Backtracking search algorithm for a CSP.

D_i to the sole values consistent with those already in σ. In this reduced domain, a value v_i for x_i is nondeterministically chosen. This value is added to σ in a recursive call on remaining variables.

In a deterministic implementation, the nondeterministic step would be associated to a backtracking point over other untried values in the reduced D_i, if any, or a backtracking point further up in the recursion tree if needed, as for an empty D_i. Note that the step select is not a backtracking point: all variables have to be processed, and the order in which they are selected affects the efficiency of the algorithm, not its completeness (see Appendix A).

This algorithm is sound and complete. It runs in time $O(n^d)$ for $d = max_i\{|D_i|\}$. Its practical performance depends essentially on the quality of the heuristics used for ordering the variables and for choosing their values.

- *Heuristics for variable ordering* rely on the idea that a backtrack deep in the search tree costs more than an early backtrack. Hence the principle is to choose first the most constrained variables in order to backtrack, if needed, as early as possible in the search tree. These most constrained variables are heuristically evaluated by the cardinality of their domains. The heuristic chooses the variable x_i with the smallest $|D_i|$.
- *Heuristics for the choice of values* apply the opposite principle of preferring the least constraining value v_i for a variable x_i. These least constraining values v_i are heuristically evaluated by the number of pairs in constraints c_{ij} in which v_i appears. The heuristics chooses the most frequent v_i.

Both types of heuristics can be computed *statically*, before the algorithm starts, or *dynamically* at each recursion node, taking into account current domains and constraints as reduced by earlier choices. Heuristics computed dynamically are more informed than static ones.

Another improvement to the Backtrack algorithm is to propagate a potential choice v_i for x_i on the domains of remaining variables before committing to that choice in the following recursions. Propagation consists of removing values inconsistent with v_i. It is preferable to find out at this point whether such a propagation leads to an empty domain D_j than to discover it much later in the recursion tree, when x_j is considered. The algorithm implementing this technique is called Forward-Checking. It is given in Figure 8.3. Forward-Checking has been shown empirically and analytically to be a faster algorithm than backtracking [334].

Other improvements to backtrack search are based on *intelligent backtracking* or *dependency-directed backtracking* and on *learning techniques.* These techniques can be seen as *look-back improvements* of the search, while Forward-Checking provides a *look-ahead improvement.* The principle of intelligent backtracking is to identify at a failure position the variables that can be usefully backtracked to. If a failure occurs at x_i with an empty D_i, then there is no need to backtrack to the next previous point x_j if the value v_j in σ did not contribute toward reducing D_i. The *conflict set* at a failure position corresponds to the tuple included in σ that made D_i empty. The algorithm called Backjumping [148] backtracks to the next previous variable within the conflict set. Learning relies on recording and analyzing these conflict sets as nogood tuples never to be committed to again [148, 298].

8.4.2 Filtering Techniques

Despite good heuristics and many improvements, the resolution of a CSP remains in general a costly combinatorial problem. However, it is possible to test the consistency of a CSP with fast algorithms that provide a necessary but not a sufficient condition of consistency. These algorithms address the *filtering problem* introduced earlier, i.e., they remove redundant values from domains or redundant tuples from constraints. When such a removal leads to an empty domain or to an empty constraint, then the CSP is inconsistent.

Filtering techniques rely on a *constraint propagation operation.* Propagating a constraint on a variable x consists of computing its local effects on variables adjacent

```
Forward-Checking(σ, X)
    if X = ∅ then return(σ)
    select any x_i ∈ X
    nondeterministically choose v_i ∈ D_i
    for each x_j ∈ X, j ≠ i do
        D_j ← D_j ∩ {v ∈ D_j | (v_i, v) ∈ c_ij}
        if D_j = ∅ then return(failure)
    Forward(σ.(v_i), X − {x_i})
end
```

Figure 8.3 Forward-checking search algorithm for a CSP.

to x in the constraint network, removing redundant values and tuples. This removal in turn leads to new constraints that need to be propagated. Hence, filtering is a *local propagation operation* that is pursued until no further change occurs, i.e., until a fixed-point termination condition.

Filtering through constraint propagation is particularly adequate when a CSP is defined incrementally by adding to it new variables and constraints, as in many planning systems. Incremental filtering algorithms allow a fast although partial testing of the consistency of the current state of a CSP.

Arc Consistency. A straightforward filter, called *arc consistency*, consists of removing from a domain D_i any value that does not satisfy constraints c_{ij} involving x_i. Such a value is redundant because it necessarily violates a constraint.

A naive algorithm for arc consistency is to perform an iteration over all pairs of variables, (x_i, x_j), $i \neq j$, with the two following updates:

$$D_i \leftarrow \{v \in D_i \mid \exists v' \in D_j\colon (v, v') \in c_{ij}\};$$

$$D_j \leftarrow \{v' \in D_j \mid \exists v \in D_i\colon (v, v') \in c_{ij}\}.$$

Once a pair of variables (x_i, x_j) is filtered out, the next pair involving one of these two variables, e.g., (x_i, x_k), may further reduce D_i. This may entail other redundant values in D_j and so on. One may keep repeating the naive iteration until a fixed point is reached. Such a fixed point is a complete iteration during which no domain is reduced. At this point, one is sure that the only values left in a domain D_i meet all the constraints involving variable x_i. If a domain D_i is reduced to an empty set, then the CSP is inconsistent. If no D_i is reduced to an empty set, then the CSP is said to be *arc-consistent* or *2-consistent*. Arc-consistent CSPs are not necessarily consistent.

Example 8.11 In the CSP of Example 8.1, filtering out the variables (x_1, x_2) reduces the two domains to $D_1 = \{\alpha, \beta\}$ and $D_2 = \{\beta, \gamma\}$ because no pair in c_{12} starts with a γ or ends with an α.

■

A better arc-consistency algorithm, called AC3 (Figure 8.4), keeps a list L of pairs of variables whose domains have to be filtered. Initially L is the set of all constrained pairs in the CSP, i.e., $L = \{(x_i, x_j) \mid c_{ij} \text{ or } c_{ji} \text{ are in } \mathcal{C}\}$. L is updated whenever filtering reduces a domain, which may entail further filtering. Note that when (x_i, x_j) is in L, then (x_j, x_i) is also in L. Hence the two domains D_i and D_j are both filtered out.

AC3 runs in time $o(md^2)$, where $m = |\mathcal{C}|$ and $d = max_i\{|D_i|\}$. It is an *incremental* algorithm: it can filter out a CSP to which variables and constraints are added incrementally. In that case, L is initially the set of pairs concerned with newly added variables and constraints. Other arc-consistency algorithms, improving on the idea of AC3, have been developed, e.g., algorithm AC4 [399].

Path Consistency. A more thorough filter, called *path consistency*, consists of testing all triples of variables x_i, x_j, and x_k, checking that they have values that meet the

```
AC3(L)
    while L ≠ ∅ do
        select any pair (x_i, x_j) in L and remove it from L
        D ← {v ∈ D_i | ∃v' ∈ D_j : (v, v') ∈ c_ij}
        if D ≠ D_i then do
            D_i ← D
            L ← L ∪ {(x_i, x_k), (x_k, x_i) | ∃c_ik or c_ki ∈ C, k ≠ j}
end
```

Figure 8.4 An arc-consistency algorithm.

three constraints c_{ij}, c_{jk}, and c_{ik}. A pair of values (v_i, v_j) can be part of a solution if it meets the constraint c_{ij} and if there is a value v_k for x_k such that (v_i, v_k) meets c_{ik} and (v_k, v_j) meets c_{kj}. In other words, the two constraints c_{ik} and c_{kj} entail by transitivity a constraint on c_{ij}.

Let us define a composition operation between constraints, denoted $\bullet$:

$$c_{ik} \bullet c_{kj} = \{(v, v'), v \in D_i, v' \in D_j \mid \exists w \in D_k\text{: } (v, w) \in c_{ik} \text{ and } (w, v') \in c_{kj}\}.$$

The composition $c_{ik} \bullet c_{kj}$ defines a constraint from x_i to x_j entailed by the two constraints c_{ik} and c_{kj}. For example, in Figure 8.1, $c_{24} \bullet c_{45} = \{(\alpha, \alpha), (\beta, \beta), (\beta, \gamma), (\gamma, \beta), (\gamma, \gamma), (\gamma, \alpha)\}$.

A pair (v_i, v_j) has to meet c_{ij} as well as the composition $c_{ik} \bullet c_{kj}$ for every k; otherwise, it is redundant. Hence the filtering operation here is:

$$c_{ij} \leftarrow c_{ij} \cap [c_{ik} \bullet c_{kj}], \text{ for every } k \neq i, j$$

When the filterings lead to an empty constraint, then the CSP is inconsistent. Note that while arc consistency removes redundant values from domains, path consistency removes redundant tuples from constraints.

Example 8.12 In the CSP of Figure 8.1, $c_{14} \bullet c_{45} = \{(\alpha, \alpha), (\alpha, \beta), (\alpha, \gamma), (\beta, \gamma)\}$; hence $c_{15} \cap [c_{14} \bullet c_{45}]$ filters out the tuple (γ, α). ■

A simple algorithm called PC (Figure 8.5) filters out constraints for all triples (x_i, x_j, x_k) on the basis of this operation until a fixed point with no further possible reduction is reached. This algorithm assumes a complete symmetrical graph, or a graph implicitly completed for missing edges with the symmetrical constraint or with the universal constraint. Note that the symmetrical of $[c_{ik} \bullet c_{kj}]$ is $[c_{jk} \bullet c_{ki}]$.

```
PC(C)
    until stabilization of all constraints in C do
        for each k : 1 ≤ k ≤ n do
            for each pair i, j : 1 ≤ i < j ≤ n, i ≠ k, j ≠ k do
                c_ij ← c_ij ∩ [c_ik • c_kj]
                if c_ij = ∅ then exit(inconsistent)
end
```

Figure 8.5 Path consistency in a CSP

A CSP is said to be *path-consistent* or *3-consistent* if a path-consistency algorithm does not detect an inconsistency. However, algorithm PC, as any other filtering algorithm, is not complete for consistency checking: it may not detect an inconsistent network, as illustrated in the following example.

Example 8.13 Consider the graph coloring problem, i.e., assigning distinct colors to adjacent vertices in a graph, for a complete graph with four vertices and only three colors. This is a CSP with four variables that range over a set of three colors; the six constraints require different colors at their vertices. This CSP is obviously inconsistent although it is path-consistent. ■

Furthermore, a network that is initially arc-consistent may not be arc-consistent after being filtered out by PC because several redundant tuples have been removed from constraints. It is easy to extend this algorithm for maintaining both path and arc consistency through a uniform representation obtained by defining $c_{ii} = D_i^2$ and modifying the filtering operation as follows:

$$c_{ij} \leftarrow c_{ij} \cap [c_{ik} \bullet c_{kk} \bullet c_{kj}] \text{ for all triples, including for } i = j$$

An incremental version of algorithm PC (Figure 8.6) works like AC3 by updating the list of constraints to be filtered out. This *Updatelist* is initialized to the entire set C or to the subset of newly added or modified constraints. The filtering operation is performed by procedure Revise, which returns either the constraint to be added to *Updatelist* or $\emptyset$ if no updating is needed. An improved path-consistency algorithm, called PC3 [399], runs in $O(n^3 d^3)$.

Other filters can be defined by checking the consistency of all k-tuples. A CSP is said to be *k-consistent* if for any subset of k variables $\{x_1, \ldots, x_k\}$ and for any tuple of $(k-1)$ consistent values $\sigma = (v_1, \ldots, v_{k-1})$ there is a value for variable x_k that is consistent with σ. A CSP is *strongly k-consistent* if for all i: $1 \leq i \leq k$ the CSP is i-consistent. Note that for $k = n$, strong n-consistency is equivalent to consistency [150]. In practice, filtering techniques are useful mainly for $k = 2$

```
IPC(Updatelist)
    while Updatelist ≠ ∅ do
    select any c_ij in Updatelist and remove it from Updatelist
    for each k : 1 ≤ k ≤ n and k ≠ i, j do
        Updatelist ← Updatelist ∪ Revise(i, k, [c_ij • c_jk])
        Updatelist ← Updatelist ∪ Revise(j, k, [c_ji • c_ik])
end
```

```
Revise(i, j, c)
    c ← c ∩ c_ij
    if c = ∅ then exit(inconsistent)
    if c = c_ij then return(∅)
    c_ij ← c
    return(c_ij)
end
```

Figure 8.6 Incremental path-consistency algorithm.

(arc consistency) and $k = 3$ (path consistency). They are seldom used for higher levels of k-consistency, giving the computational cost that grows exponentially with k and the incompleteness of filtering.

8.4.3 Local Search Techniques and Hybrid Approaches

Local search methods present an alternative to filtering techniques for the same purpose of avoiding the combinatorial explosion of a complete search. Local search methods are not complete: they can fail to find a solution when there is one. But they may find a solution very efficiently.

The main ingredient of a local search method is a neighborhood $\mathcal{N}(\sigma)$ of a candidate solution tuple $\sigma = (v_1, \ldots, v_n)$. $\mathcal{N}(\sigma)$ is a set of other tuples that can be obtained easily from σ, e.g., by changing the value of one variable x_i.

A local search algorithm starts from some initial σ_0. If this tuple does not meet the constraints, then it moves to another candidate tuple $\sigma \in \mathcal{N}(\sigma_0)$ that appears closer to a solution according to some distance estimate, i.e., σ meets more constraints than the initial tuple. Local search follows basically a local gradient according to this distance estimate. It may rely on several stochastic strategies, such as simulated annealing and tabu search as illustrated in Section 7.3.2 for SAT.

Hybrid techniques perform a combination of filtering, local search, and systematic search. For example, a systematic search may rely on filtering or local search at some node of the search tree for pruning and/or choosing the next step.

Alternatively, a local search may use a bounded systematic search for assessing a local neighborhood. For example, Jussien and Lhomme [292] propose a technique called decision-repair: at some node of the search a value is chosen for a variable. Filtering is applied from this partial tuple, and if an inconsistency is detected, a local search is performed to improve the current tuple. Good results on several CSP applications have been reported for these hybrid techniques [292, 470].

8.5 Extended CSP Models

The standard CSP model discussed so far can be extended in several ways. Two such extensions, *active CSPs* and *valued CSPs*, of interest to planning are briefly introduced here. A third extension, called *mixed CSPs* or *stochastic CSPs*, which involves normal CSP variables linked with constraints to contingent random variables whose values cannot be chosen by the CSP solver, will be briefly discussed in Section 8.7 and in the chapters on temporal constraints and temporal planning (see Part IV).

8.5.1 Active CSPs

The *active CSP* model extends the constraint satisfaction model with a notion of *activity* for variables.[2] The set X is partitioned into *active* and *inactive* variables. Initially, a subset of variables is active. Other inactive variables may become active depending on the values chosen for the already active variables. This is stated by a set of activity constraints of the form:

$$(x_i = v_i) \wedge \ldots \wedge (x_j = v_j) \Rightarrow x_k, \ldots, x_l \text{ are active}$$

One has to solve the CSP of finding consistent values only for active variables—those initially active and those that become active because of the triggered activity constraints.

Example 8.14 Let us modify three constraints in the network of Figure 8.1 as follows: remove the pair (β, α) from c_{35}, remove (α, β) from c_{45}, and remove (β, γ) from c_{15}. This leads to the network in Figure 8.7, which is an inconsistent CSP.

Assume now that this is an active CSP with the following activity constraints:

$(x_1 = \alpha) \Rightarrow x_2$ and x_3 active
$(x_2 = \beta) \Rightarrow x_4$ and x_5 active
$(x_3 = \beta) \Rightarrow x_4$ active

2. This type of CSP is often referred to in the literature as *dynamic CSPs*. In the context of planning, it is preferable to reserve the latter expression for the case where the CSP variables evolve dynamically as functions of time and where the problem is to find a set of such functions that meet all the constraints.

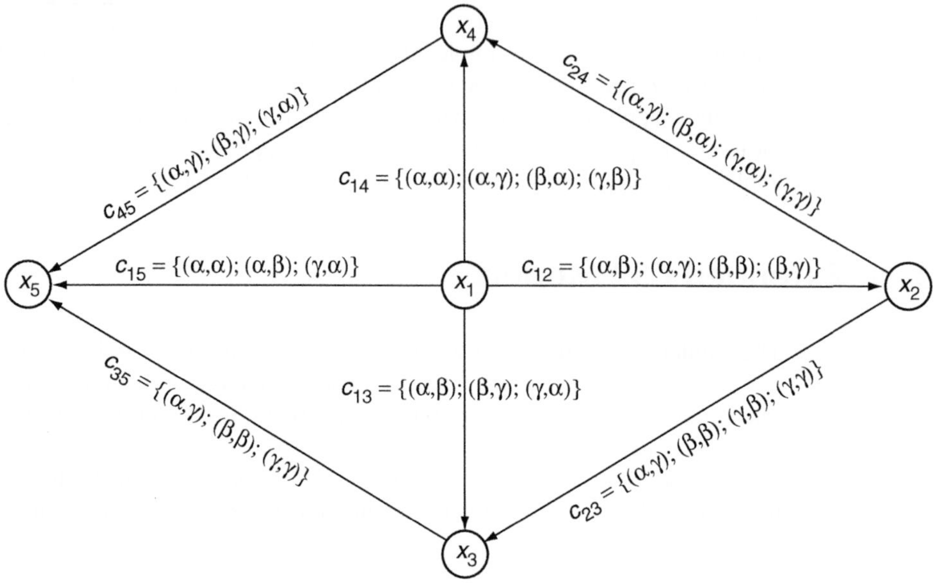

Figure 8.7 An active CSP network.

If only x_1 is initially active, then this active CSP has a single solution: $(x_1 = \alpha, x_2 = \beta, x_3 = \beta, x_4 = \alpha)$.

■

Search algorithms such as Backtrack and Forward-Checking can be extended to handle active CSPs. For example, in Backtrack one restricts the set X to the variables initially active. X is updated according to activity constraints whenever a value is chosen for a variable. Forward-Checking requires an additional restriction of the domains of newly active variables to values compatible with the current σ; it also requires a careful management of backtracking steps.

Instead, one may transform an active CSP into a normal CSP and apply to it all the standard resolution algorithms or filtering techniques and known heuristics. This transformation proceeds as follows.

- Extend the domain of every initially inactive variable with a particular value called inactive.
- Rewrite the activity constraints as normal constraints of the form:
  $(x_i = v_i) \wedge \ldots \wedge (x_j = v_j) \Rightarrow (x_k \neq \text{inactive}) \wedge \ldots \wedge (x_l \neq \text{inactive})$

This transformation of an active CSP into a normal one allows the direct use of all the algorithms, heuristics, and software tools developed for CSPs.

8.5.2 Valued CSPs

The *valued CSP* model extends the model of constraint satisfaction with utilities and an optimization criteria. A *utility value* is attached to each constraint. An n-tuple $\sigma = (v_1, \ldots, v_n)$ that meets a subset of the constraints in C has a utility $U(\sigma)$ equal to the sum of the utilities of the constraints satisfied by σ. The problem is to find a solution that maximizes the criteria U. A dual formulation is to associate costs to constraints and to seek a tuple that minimizes the sum of the costs of violated constraints.

Exact resolution techniques for valued CSPs are based on the Branch-and-Bound algorithm. Basically, one extends the search algorithm with heuristics and bounding estimates in order to prune the search tree.

The *local search techniques* offer approximation approaches that are more tractable for large problems with hundred of variables and constraints. One searches locally in the neighborhood of an n-tuple σ through local modifications in order to improve the criteria. Random techniques such as simulated annealing, tabu search, and genetic algorithms are examples of these approximation techniques.

8.6 CSP Techniques in Planning

As explained in Section 8.1, the use of CSP techniques within approaches specific to planning is much more frequent and broader than the direct encoding of a planning problem into a CSP. We already encountered constraint satisfaction issues in plan-space and planning-graph planning (Chapters 5 and 6, respectively). In the forthcoming chapters, particularly for planning with time and resources (Part IV), we will rely extensively on CSPs. Let us revisit here briefly the plan-space and planning-graph approaches in order to review possible improvements in the light of CSP techniques.

8.6.1 CSPs in Plan-Space Search

In plan-space planning, a partial plan involves precedence constraints between actions and binding constraints between variables. The precedence constraints define a very specific CSP that is efficiently handled with the usual graph-search techniques. The binding constraints, however, correspond to a general CSP.[3] It can be very time-consuming to check the consistency of these constraints at each step of the planner, when new binding constraints are added or modified. One may rely on filtering techniques to perform partial tests at each incremental refinement of a partial plan. A complete consistency check can be performed at regular stages, at least when a plan has been found. Here, backtracking will be more difficult to manage.

---

3. For example, a graph coloring problem is directly coded with binding constraints of the form $x \neq y$.

The relationship between plan-space planning and CSPs is more important if one generalizes the *flaw-repair refinement* framework of a plan-space algorithm. Recall that this framework involves three steps:

1. Analyze flaws, i.e., goals and threats.
2. Find resolvers for each flaw.
3. Choose one resolver for a flaw and refine the current plan with that resolver.

In plan-space procedures such as PSP (Figure 5.6), this last step is a nondeterministic branching point where backtracking occurs whenever needed. In a more general framework, called *disjunctive refinement*, one does not branch nondeterministically on the choice of a particular resolver for a flaw. Instead one keeps as much as possible the entire disjunction of resolvers. This leads to a refinement *without* branching. The current node is refined with the disjunction of resolvers. Hence, a node is not a partial plan anymore but a disjunction of partial plans.

The main idea, introduced in the Descartes planner, is to associate with each flaw a CSP variable whose domain is the set of resolvers for that variable. One has to manage variables associated with threats differently than those associated with open goals. This is because a refinement for a threat adds only constraints to a node; it does not add new resolvers to other pending flaws. But a refinement for an open goal may add new resolvers to other flaws. We will explore more details on these techniques in the context of temporal planning (Section 14.3.5).

Finally, as a transition to the next section, let us mention some recent improvements of plan-space planning that involve CSP techniques as well as Graphplan-based distance heuristics [424].

8.6.2 CSPs for Planning-Graph Techniques

Graphplan already handles the mutex relations between propositions and actions in every level as binary constraints. In our discussion of this algorithm and its improvements (Section 6.4.2), we referred to several CSP techniques and heuristics for Graphplan, such as look-ahead enhancements, e.g., through forward-checking, or look-back improvements, e.g., through intelligent backtracking and learning.

But one may go even further in the use of CSP techniques and tools by encoding the planning graph for a given planning problem into a CSP, as proposed in the GP-CSP planner. Along that view, the graph expansion phase corresponds to the encoding of the problem into a particular CSP, while the graph extraction phase is the resolution of that CSP. In this encoding, the following conditions are met.

- Each proposition $p \in P_i$ is a CSP variable.
- The values in the variable p are the actions in A_i supporting p.
- The constraints between CSP variables are given by the mutex relations between actions. If a and b are two mutex actions, then for every p and q

supported respectively by a and b, we have a constraint that forbids the pair $(p = a, q = b)$.

This encoding leads to an active CSP. The goal propositions are the variables initially active. Activity constraints say that when a proposition p is associated to a value a, then all preconditions of a in the previous level become active, unless a is in the first level A_1 (because we do not need to support the propositions in s_0). Finally, mutex relations between propositions are encoded into constraints on activities: if p and q are mutex in some level, then we have the constraint $\neg(active(p) \wedge active(q))$.

A further encoding step makes it possible to transform this active CSP into a normal CSP, as explained in Section 8.5.1, and to run a standard CSP solver for its resolution. The iterative deepening procedure of Graphplan (which is equivalent to considering bounded planning problems over increasing bounds) and the termination condition can be directly handled in this encoding framework.

There can be several benefits in compiling a planning graph into a CSP and solving it with standard CSP tools. Among the benefits are the availability of several CSP filtering and local search techniques that can speed up the search and provide heuristics, pruning, and control information; the capability to perform a nondirectional search (unlike Graphplan, whose search follows the graph levels in decreasing order) as directed by available control information; and the potential to integrate planning to other problems that are naturally solved with CSP tools, such as scheduling and design.

Finally, there are also several techniques in constraints programming that enable one to provide additional control knowledge as constraints and to guide the search in an interactive user-oriented framework.

8.7 Discussion and Historical Remarks

CSPs were developed very early in the history of computer science within particular application areas such as CAD and pattern recognition. There is the well-known contribution of Waltz [542] for line labeling in computer vision, which started constraint propagation techniques, and the contribution of Stallman and Sussman [497] in CAD circuit analysis, which introduced intelligent backtracking techniques.

The pioneering work of Montanari [400] established CSPs as a generic problem-solving paradigm. There is now a very wide range of literature in this area. Several surveys [151, 339] offer a good introduction to the field. Russel and Norvig devote a chapter to CSPs in the new edition of their textbook [458]. The monographs of Tsang [515] and Mariott and Stuckey [379] detail extensively most of the CSP techniques we have discussed. This last reference develops CSPs as a paradigm for programming, following on a long tradition of work on logic programming and logic and constraints programming. Constraint programming is successfully used today for addressing resource allocation and scheduling problems [45, 178].

Search techniques for CSPs have been studied and improved through many contributions [148, 201, 373]. Montanari [400] started filtering techniques. Arc consistency received considerable attention, e.g., the AC3 algorithm is due to Mackworth [373], AC4 to Mohr and Henderson [399], and AC6 to Bessiere and Cordier [67]. More general *k*-consistency techniques are due to Freuder [202]. Heuristics for CSP have been proposed and analyzed in two sources [153, 395]. The performance of several search techniques has been studied empirically [34] and theoretically [334].

Local search methods for CSPs started with Kirkpatrick *et al.* [324], within an optimization framework, followed by several other contributions, in particular to hybrid approaches [292, 470].

The extended CSP models, such as active and valued CSPs, have attracted many contributions (e.g., [466, 529]). The work on the so-called mixed CSPs or stochastic CSPs, which involve normal CSP variables linked with constraints to contingent random variables whose values cannot be chosen by the CSP solver, is more recent (e.g., [185, 541]). It certainly is of relevance for planning, in particular for the management of temporal constraints (see Part IV).

Constraints in planning appeared quite early. For example, the Molgen planner [498] provides a good illustration of the management of binding constraints. Several HTN planners, particularly UMCP [174], make extensive use of CSP techniques to manage state, variable binding, and ordering constraints.

Advanced CSP techniques in plan-space planning were introduced in the Descartes planner [289, 290] for handling threats and open goals. The use of CSPs for managing threats or causal constraints has been analyzed [296]. CSPs for Graphplan have been discussed [305]; look-back enhancements such as data-directed backtracking and learning have been introduced [298, 299, 300]. The idea has been further developed for both types of flaws in the Descartes planner.

The encoding of a planning problem into a CSP has been explored in particular [158, 519, 539, 556]. The paper by van Beck and Chen [519] proposes a constraint programming approach in which the planning problem is directly specified by the user as a CSP problem. Two other approaches [539, 556] use encodings into Integer Linear Programming (ILP), a special class of CSP with integer variables and linear constraints (see Section 24.3). The approach of Do and Kambhampati [158], summarized in Section 8.6.2, encodes the planning graph into a CSP. It led to a planner called GP-CSP that relies on the CSPLIB software library [518]. Do and Kambhampati report a more compact and efficient encoding than the SAT-based or ILP-based encodings and a significant speedup with respect to standard Graphplan.

8.8 Exercises

8.1 In the CSP of Figure 8.1, find all the redundant values in D_i, $1 \leq i \leq 5$, and all the redundant tuples in the constraints.

8.2 Prove that a binary CSP $\mathcal{P}$ and the symmetrical CSP $\tilde{P}$ obtained from $\mathcal{P}$ are equivalent.

8.3 Define the five operators of the DWR domain in the state-variable representation (see the three operators of the simplified DWR of Example 8.6; see page 173).

8.4 Define a planning problem P in the state-variable representation for the DWR domain of the previous exercise, with three locations, five containers initially in loc1, and one robot in loc2, with the goal of having all containers in loc3. Encode P into a CSP.

8.5 Run the Forward-Checking algorithm on the CSP of Example 8.1 (see page 169). Modify the pseudocode of this algorithm (given in Figure 8.3) so as to find all solutions and run it on this CSP. Compare with the four solutions given in Example 8.1 (see page 169).

8.6 Run the AC3 algorithm on the CSP of Example 8.1 (see page 169). What are the filtered domains of the variables?

8.7 Modify the pseudocode of algorithm PC (Figure 8.5) so as to filter with both arc and path consistency, i.e., to test for strong 3-consistency. Run this algorithm on the two networks in Figures 8.1 and 8.7.

8.8 Dowload the GP-CSP planner.[4] Run it on the same DWR domains and problems used for Exercise 6.16. Discuss the practical range of applicability of this planner for the DWR application.

8.9 Compare the performances of GP-CSP on the DWR domain with those of the Graphplan planner from Exercise 6.16.

8.10 Compare the performances of GP-CSP on the DWR domain with those of the HSPOP planner from Exercise 5.11.

---

4. See http://rakaposhi.eas.asu.edu/gp-csp.html.

PART III
Heuristics and Control Strategies

Although planning systems have become much more efficient over the years, they still suffer from combinatorial complexity. As described in Chapter 3 on the complexity of planning, even relatively restricted planning domains can be intractable in the worst case.

The four chapters in this part of the book are devoted to several approaches for improving the efficiency of planning. To provide a foundation for presenting these approaches, we now describe an abstract common framework for the planning procedures presented earlier in the book.

Nearly all of the planning procedures in Parts I and II of this book can be viewed as instances of the Abstract-search procedure shown in Figure III.1. The objective of Abstract-search is to find at least one solution, if a solution exists, without enumerating all of the set explicitly.

Abstract-search nondeterministically searches a space in which each node u represents a set of solution plans Π_u, namely, the set of all solutions that are reachable from u. A node u is basically a structured collection of actions and constraints.

- In state-space planning, u is simply a sequence of actions. Every solution reachable from u (i.e., every plan in Π_u) contains this sequence as either a prefix or a suffix, depending on whether we are doing a forward search or a backward search.
- In plan-space planning, u is a set of actions together with causal links, ordering constraints, and binding constraints. Every solution reachable from u contains all the actions in u and meets all the constraints.

- In the Graphplan algorithm, u is a subgraph of a planning graph, i.e., a sequence of sets of actions, together with constraints on preconditions, effects, and mutual exclusions. Each solution reachable from u contains the actions in u corresponding to the solved levels and at least one action from each level of the subgraph that has not been solved yet in u.
- In SAT-based planning, u is a set of assigned literals and remaining clauses, each of which is a disjunction of literals that describe actions and states. Each solution reachable from u corresponds to an assignment of truth values to the unassigned literals such that all of the remaining clauses are satisfied.
- In CSP-based planning, u is a set of CSP variables and constraints, some variables having already assigned values. Each solution reachable from u includes these assigned variables and assignments to all other CSP variables that satisfy the constraints.

In state-space and plan-space planning, u is a partial plan; every action in u belongs to any solution plan in Π_u. But in the latter three approaches just listed, not every action in u appears in a solution plan in Π_u.[1] For example, several actions may achieve a propositional goal in a planning graph, but perhaps only one of them will be needed in a solution plan in Π_u.

The Abstract-search procedure involves three main steps in addition to a termination step.

1. A *refinement step* consists of modifying the collection of actions and/or constraints associated with a node u. In a refinement of u, the set Π_u of solutions corresponding to u remains *unchanged*. For example, if we find out that there is only one action a that meets a particular constraint in u, then we might make a an explicit part of u and remove the constraint.
2. A *branching step* generates one or more children of u; these nodes will be the *candidates* for the next node to visit. Each child v of the node u represents a *subset* of solution $\Pi_v \subseteq \Pi_u$. For example, in a forward state-space search, each child would correspond to appending a different action to the end of a partial plan. Branching does not need to generate explicitly all the child nodes of u.
3. A *pruning step* consists of removing from the set of candidate nodes $\{u_1, \ldots, u_k\}$ some nodes that appear to be unpromising for the search. For example, we might consider a node to be unpromising if we have a record of having already visited that node or if we have some domain-specific reasons to believe that it is unlikely to contain any desirable solutions.[2]

---

1. Because of this property, the latter three approaches have sometimes been called *disjunctive-refinement approaches* [306].
2. What constitutes a "desirable" solution depends largely on the planning domain. Sometimes a planning problem can be viewed as an optimization problem involving a numeric objective function such as the "cost" or "utility" of a plan. In other cases, it may be a Pareto optimization problem [209] that

```
Abstract-search(u)
    if Terminal(u) then return(u)
    u ← Refine(u)          ;; refinement step
    B ← Branch(u)          ;; branching step
    C ← Prune(B)           ;; pruning step
    if C = ∅ then return(failure)
    nondeterministically choose v ∈ C
    return(Abstract-search(v))
end
```

Figure III.1 An abstract search procedure that provides a general framework for describing classical and neoclassical planning procedures.

In some planning procedures, the order of these three steps may be different. For example, a procedure might do branching, then pruning, then refinement. Also, some planning procedures may extend Abstract-search to use a control mechanism such as heuristic search or iterative deepening (see Appendix A).

Here is a brief discussion of how the refinement, branching, pruning, and termination steps of Abstract-search relate to previous planning procedures.

In plan-space planning, branching consists of selecting a flaw and finding its resolvers; refinement consists of applying such a resolver to the partial plan; and there is no pruning step. Termination occurs when no flaws are left in the plan. Since paths in the plan space are likely to be infinite, a control strategy such as best-first search or iterative deepening should be used.

The relationship between Abstract-search and state-space planning is also very direct: branches are actions; pruning removes candidate nodes corresponding to cycles; and termination occurs when the plan goes all the way from the initial state to a goal.

Graphplan corresponds to using Abstract-search with an iterative-deepening control strategy. Refinement consists of propagating constraints for the actions chosen in the branching step. Branching identifies possible actions that achieve subgoals. Pruning uses the recorded nogood tuples of subgoals that failed in some layer. Termination occurs if the solution-extraction process succeeds.

In SAT planning, refinement is exactly the Unit-Propagate procedure. Branching consists of selecting some proposition and calling Davis-Putnam with both of the possible truth values (true and false) for that proposition. Termination occurs if no clause remains unsatisfied.

---

involves several competing objective functions (e.g., cost, time, number of goals achieved). In other cases, a plan's desirability may depend on things like how easily it can be modified during execution to accomodate unforeseen events (e.g., unanticipated delays or failures, new goals to achieve).

Finally, CSP-based planning branches over the consistent values in the domain of a CSP variable; the refinement step consist of propagating the chosen value for that variable over remaining constraints.

Note that we may need to extend Abstract-search with some type of iterative-deepening control mechanisms in order to model the expansion phase of Graphplan or the control needed for handling the infinite search space in plan-space planning, for example.

Abstract-search includes a nondeterministic step that chooses among the current node's nonpruned children, if any, to get the next node to visit in the search space. As discussed in Chapter 4 and Appendix A, this essential step is usually implemented as a depth-first backtracking search. Thus, a *node-selection function* Select(C) is needed to choose which child $u \in C$ to visit next, i.e., in place of the nondeterministic choice in Figure III.1 we will have a step such as $v \leftarrow$ Select(C).

In general, the search procedure will perform well if the Refine, Branch, Prune, and Select procedures can do a good job of organizing the search space and guiding the search. A number of heuristic techniques have been developed to try to accomplish this.

Sometimes, the heuristics are *domain-independent*, i.e., intended for use in many different planning domains. Chapter 9 describes several domain-independent heuristics for node selection.

Alternatively, the heuristics may be *domain-specific*, i.e., tailor-made for a particular kind of domain. One way to reduce the effort needed to write these heuristics is to provide a domain-independent planning engine plus a language in which to write the heuristics. Chapter 10 describes how to use *temporal logic* to write node-pruning rules that focus the search. Chapter 11 describes how to use *task decomposition* to write branching rules. Chapter 12 describes how to specify search strategies in two different logic formalisms: situation calculus and dynamic logic. The formalisms described in these chapters have expressive power that goes substantially beyond classical planning: they can accommodate numeric computations, external function calls, axiomatic inference, time durations, and overlapping actions.

Although it can take some effort to write and tune domain-specific heuristics, the case for doing so is quite strong. In the last two AI planning competitions [28, 195], the systems that were fastest, could solve the hardest problems, and could handle the widest variety of planning domains all incorporated domain-specific control of the planning process. Furthermore, nearly every successful planning system for real-world applications incorporates domain-specific heuristics or even domain-specific algorithms.

To end this introduction, here is a brief discussion of other proposed unifying frameworks for planning.

A general formulation of planning as a *refinement search* has been proposed and analyzed in [302, 306]. The notion of refinement used in that work is slightly different from ours, since it includes branching and pruning. However some of the notions described there can be transported easily to Abstract-search. Examples include *completeness*, i.e., the property that every solution in u is included in at least one of the nodes of B', and *systematicity*, i.e., the property that the nodes of B' define a partition of the set of solutions in u. It is important to note that completeness requires that only nodes in B corresponding to an empty set of solutions can be pruned.

Another unifying framework [427] views planning as a *branch-and-bound* search. Branch-and-bound is a widely known technique for *optimization problems*. It maintains an upper bound λ on the cost of the optimal solution, which can simply be the cost of the best solution found so far. When the procedure visits a new node u in its search space, it calls a domain-specific lower bound function $l(u)$ that returns a lower bound on the cost of the best solution in Π_u. If $l(u) > \lambda$, then the procedure prunes the node u; if u is terminal, then the procedure updates λ and decides either to stop or to pursue some promising open node. More generally, branch-and-bound can incorporate an abstract pruning function similar to our Prune function, which can prune nodes based on criteria other than just bounding [415]. Our Abstract-search procedure can be viewed as a version of such a branch-and-bound procedure.

Chapter 9

Heuristics in Planning

9.1 Introduction

The introduction to this part described a conceptual view of planning as an abstract search problem in which the steps include refinement, branching, and pruning. The introduction pointed out that in order to implement the search deterministically, a node-selection function Select(C) is needed to choose which node u to visit next from a set of candidate nodes C. Often, although not always, the deterministic search is done in a depth-first manner; Figure 9.1 gives an abstract example. This chapter focuses on heuristic techniques for node selection.

The outline of the chapter is as follows. We first discuss the notion of relaxation as a general principle for designing heuristics (Section 9.2). We then detail several heuristics for state-space planning and relate them to the planning-graph techniques (Section 9.3). We finally present heuristics for flaw selection and resolver selection in plan-space planning (Section 9.4). The chapter ends with a discussion section and exercises.

9.2 Design Principle for Heuristics: Relaxation

A *node-selection heuristic* is any way of ranking a set of nodes in order of their relative desirability. We will model this heuristic as a function h that can be used to compute a numeric evaluation $h(u)$ for each candidate node $u \in C$, with a convention that says that the preferred node $u \in C$ is the one that has the smallest $h(u)$, i.e., Select(C) = $\text{argmin}\{h(u) \mid u \in C\}$.

Node-selection heuristics are used for resolving nondeterministic choices. If there is a known deterministic technique for choosing at each choice point the right node for solving the problem, one would just integrate that way into a deterministic algorithm and we would not call it a heuristic. Hence, a node-selection heuristic is usually not foolproof, in the sense that the node recommended by the heuristic is not always guaranteed to be the best choice: this node may not always lead to the best

```
Depth-first-search(u)
    if Terminal(u) then return(u)
    u ← Refine(u)          ;; refinement step
    B ← Branch(u)          ;; branching step
    C ← Prune(B)           ;; pruning step
    while C ≠ ∅ do
        v ← Select(C)      ;; node-selection step
        C ← C − {v}
        π ← Depth-first-search(v)
        if π ≠ failure then return(π)
    return(failure)
end
```

Figure 9.1 Abstract version of a depth-first search procedure.

solution or even to a solution at all. However, we would like the heuristic to be as *informative* as possible, i.e., to be as close as possible to an *oracle* that knows the right choice. The smaller the number of incorrect choices a node-selection heuristic h makes, the more informative it is. We also want h to be easily computable, so that there will be a clear benefit in computing it and using it for making choices rather than, say, making random choices or doing a brute-force search that tries all alternatives. There is usually a trade-off between how informative h is and how easy it is to compute.

Node-selection heuristics are often based on the following *relaxation principle*: in order to assess how desirable a node u is, one considers a simpler problem that is obtained from the original one by making simplifying assumptions and by relaxing constraints. One estimates how desirable u is by using u to solve the simpler relaxed problem and using that solution as an estimate of the solution one would get if one used u to solve the original problem. The closer the relaxed problem is to the original one, the more informative the estimate will be. On the other hand, the more simplified the relaxed problem is, the easier it will be to compute the heuristic. Unfortunately, most of the time it is not easy to find the best trade-off between relaxation and informativeness of the heuristic: to do that requires a knowledge of the structure of the problem.

We close this section with another property of node-selection heuristics that is desirable if one seeks a solution that is *optimal* with respect to some cost criterion. In this case, a candidate node u is preferred if it leads to a lower-cost solution, and $h(u)$ is an estimate of the minimum possible cost $h^*(u)$ of any solution reachable from u (with $h^*(u) = \infty$ if no solution is reachable from u). In this case, a heuristic function h is *admissible* if it is a lower bound estimate of the cost of a minimal solution reachable from u, i.e., if $h(u) \leq h^*(u)$. Heuristic search algorithms, such as the iterative-deepening scheme, are usually able to guarantee an optimal solution when guided with an admissible node-selection heuristic. But quite often, one may have to trade admissibility for informativeness.

9.3 Heuristics for State-Space Planning

This section presents several node-selection heuristics for state-space planning. We start with a simple heuristic function and present its use in guiding a forward-search backtracking algorithm, then a backward-search procedure. We then develop several more elaborate heuristics and discuss their properties. Finally, the relationship between these heuristics and the planning-graph techniques is discussed.

9.3.1 State Reachability Relaxation

Let us consider a planning domain in the set-theoretic representation (Section 2.2), and let us focus on a forward-search procedure in the state space. At some point the candidate nodes are the successor states of the current state s, for the actions applicable to s. In order to choose the most preferable one, we need to assess how close each action may bring us to the goal.

For any action a applicable to a state s, the next state is given by the transition function: $\gamma(s, a) = (s - \text{effects}^-(a)) \cup \text{effects}^+(a)$. Although this is a very simple set operation for each elementary transition, $\gamma(s, a)$ does not allow an easy prediction of distances to a goal: even if $\text{effects}^+(a)$ brings us apparently closer by adding some of the goal propositions to s, we may still be getting off track with an action a because of its $\text{effects}^-(a)$.

A very intuitive relaxation idea for the classical planning search is to neglect $\text{effects}^-(a)$. This simplified $\gamma(s, a)$ involves only a *monotonic* increase in the number of propositions from s to $\gamma(s, a)$. Hence, it is easier to compute distances to goals with such a simplified γ. The following heuristic functions are based on this relaxation idea.

Definition 9.1 Let $s \in S$ be a state, p a proposition, and g a set of propositions. The *minimum distance* from s to p, denoted by $\Delta^*(s, p)$, is the minimum number of actions required to reach from s a state containing p. The *minimum distance* from s to g, $\Delta^*(s, g)$, is the minimum number of actions required to reach from s a state containing *all* propositions in g. ■

Let $\Delta(s, p)$ be an estimate of $\Delta^*(s, p)$, and $\Delta(s, g)$ be an estimate of $\Delta^*(s, g)$. In the remaining sections, we will be defining several instances of the estimate Δ, denoted by $\Delta_0, \Delta_1, \ldots, \Delta_k$, and Δ_g, as well as heuristic functions obtained from these estimates, denoted by $h_0, \ldots, h_k$. These estimates will rely on different relaxations of the planning problem. Let us focus on the estimate Δ_0, which ignores effects$^-(a)$ for all a and which approximates the distance to g as the sum of the distances to the propositions in g. This estimate is based on the intuitive relaxation discussed previously. Δ_0 is given by the following equations.

$$
\begin{array}{ll}
\Delta_0(s,p) = 0 & \text{if } p \in s \\
\Delta_0(s,p) = \infty & \text{if } \forall a \in A, p \notin \text{effects}^+(a) \\
\Delta_0(s,g) = 0 & \text{if } g \subseteq s \\
\text{otherwise:} & \\
\Delta_0(s,p) = \min_a\{1 + \Delta_0(s, \text{precond}(a)) \mid p \in \text{effects}^+(a)\} & \\
\Delta_0(s,g) = \sum_{p \in g} \Delta_0(s,p) &
\end{array}
\tag{9.1}
$$

These equations give an estimate of the distance to g in the relaxed problem, and this value is an estimate of the distance to g in the unrelaxed problem. The first two equations are simple termination conditions. The third one says that p is not reachable from s if the domain contains no action that produces p. The fourth equation defines $\Delta_0(s,p)$ recursively with respect to $\Delta_0(s,g)$. It states that if a is applicable to s' and produces p, then it takes just one step to reach p from s', precond$(a) \subseteq s'$, and Δ_0 is the minimum distance to reach any such s'. The last equation states that the distance to g is the sum of the distances to its propositions. It follows the relaxation intuition that each proposition in g can be reached *independently* of the others. This follows the independence relaxation. Note that Formulas 9.1 do ignore the effects$^-$ of actions.

We can now define a heuristic function $h_0(s)$ that gives an estimate of the distance from a node s to a node that satisfies the goal g of a planning problem $\mathcal{P} = (\Sigma, s_0, g)$:

$$h_0(s) = \Delta_0(s,g)$$

Figure 9.2 shows an algorithm that computes $h_0(s)$ by using Formulas 9.1 to compute $\Delta_0(s,p)$ for every proposition p in the domain. It is similar to a minimum-distance graph-searching algorithm: starting from the state s, it proceeds through each action whose preconditions have been reached, until a fixed point is reached. The algorithm is polynomial in the number of propositions and actions.

If we are given a planning problem where each action a has a cost $cost(a)$, then we will define the distance to a proposition p or to a goal g to be the cost of achieving p or g, and we will try to estimate such a distance. This can be done easily when the cost of a sequence of actions is the sum of the individual costs. In that case, in Formulas 9.1 and in the Delta algorithm, we just need to replace the digit "1" with $cost(a)$. The same is true for the other node-selection heuristics that we will define later in Formulas 9.3 through 9.5.

A state-space algorithm that is heuristically guided with h_0 is given in Figure 9.3. This algorithm does a recursive backtracking search. Among the children of each node s, it first goes to the child whose Δ_0 value is best. If backtracking is required, then the algorithm tries the second-best child, then the third-best child,

```
Delta(s)
    for each p do: if p ∈ s then Δ0(s,p) ← 0, else Δ0(s,p) ← ∞
    U ← {s}
    iterate
        for each a such that ∃u ∈ U, precond(a) ⊆ u do
            U ← {u} ∪ effects+(a)
            for each p ∈ effects+(a) do
                Δ0(s,p) ← min{Δ0(s,p), 1 + Σ_{q∈precond(a)} Δ0(s,q)}
    until no change occurs in the above updates
end
```

Figure 9.2 Algorithm for computing heuristic estimates of distances from a state s to propositions.

```
Heuristic-forward-search(π, s, g, A)
    if s satisfies g then return π
    options ← {a ∈ A | a applicable to s}
    for each a ∈ options do Delta(γ(s,a))
    while options ≠ ∅ do
        a ← argmin{Δ0(γ(s,a), g) | a ∈ options}
        options ← options − {a}
        π' ← Heuristic-forward-search(π.a, γ(s,a), g, A)
        if π' ≠ failure then return(π')
    return(failure)
end
```

Figure 9.3 Heuristically guided forward-search algorithm.

and so forth. The argument π is the current partial plan; thus the initial call is Heuristic-forward-search($\langle\rangle, s_0, g, A$), where $\langle\rangle$ is the empty plan.

One may also use h_0 with a greedy search algorithm or with a best-first search that keeps all candidate nodes and chooses at each step the best one. Variants that are less memory intensive than a best-first search can be a mixture between greedy and best-first (keep a greedy strategy unless its choice is too far from the best candidate node) or an iterative-deepening algorithm.

The generalization of Delta and the above procedure to the classical planning representation with predicate symbols in planning operators is quite easy. In such a representation, a state s is a set of ground atoms, and a goal formula g is a set of ground literals. Along with the relaxation principle, we estimate the distances to the goal by approximating g to g^+, its set of positive atoms. We do not need to compute the distances $\Delta_0(s, p)$ for all ground instances of predicate symbols in the domain but only for those needed to get the sum: $\sum_{p \in g^+} \Delta_0(s, p)$.

9.3.2 Heuristically Guided Backward Search

Although the Delta algorithm is very efficient, it will be heavily used in the Heuristic-forward-search algorithm because it has to be run for every applicable action of every visited state. By doing a backward search instead of a forward search, we can use the node-selection heuristic more economically in the number of calls to Delta.

A backward search would proceed by regressing the current goal g through an action a that is relevant for g until the initial state s_0 is reached.[1] According to the definition of γ^{-1}, the heuristic distances are with respect to various current goals and a single initial state s_0. We may run Delta initially and compute, *just once*, $\Delta_0(s_0, p)$ for every p. In backward search, the current node is a current goal g. The heuristic estimate of g is given from the precomputed values by $\Delta_0(s_0, g) = \sum_{p \in g} \Delta_0(s_0, p)$.

The guided backward-search procedure is specified in Figure 9.4. It does not include any call to procedure Delta, but it relies on an initial run of Delta(s_0). After this run, the procedure is called initially with Backward-search($\langle\rangle, s_0, g, A$).

We close this section with two remarks. First, a goal regression does not involve effects$^-(a)$ because $\gamma^{-1}(g, a) = (g - \text{effects}^+(a)) \cup \text{precond}(a)$. In a sense, the goal regression achieved by not taking into account effects$^-$ is similar to the relaxation used here in Delta. However, recall that the definition of a *relevant* action

```
Backward-search(π, s0, g, A)
    if s0 satisfies g then return(π)
    options ← {a ∈ A | a relevant for g}
    while options ≠ ∅ do
        a ← argmin{Δ0(s0, γ^-1(g, a)) | a ∈ options}
        options ← options − {a}
        π' ← Backward-search(a.π, s0, γ^-1(g, a), A)
        if π' ≠ failure then return(π')
    return failure
end
```

Figure 9.4 Heuristically guided backward-search algorithm.

1. Recall that the regression of a goal g for an action a *relevant* to g, as defined in Section 2.2.2, is $\gamma^{-1}(g, a) = (g - \text{effects}^+(a)) \cup \text{precond}(a)$.

(and consequently the set *options* in the above procedure) does involve effects$^-(a)$ because we defined a to be relevant for g iff $g \cap \text{effects}^+(a) \neq \emptyset$ and $g \cap \text{effects}^-(a) = \emptyset$.

Second, in the classical representation, goals are ground literals, including negated literals. The generalization of this approach to the classical representation requires neglecting the atoms in g^- but also taking into account unground atoms that may appear in γ^{-1} because of precond(a). In that case, $\Delta_0(s_0, p)$ can be defined as the minimal distance to any ground instance of p. The initial run of algorithm Delta is pursued until $\Delta_0(s_0, g)$ can be computed, for the initial goal g. This run is resumed incrementally whenever a new set of atoms g' requires the value of not yet computed distances $\Delta_0(s_0, p)$.

9.3.3 Admissible State-Space Heuristics

The heuristic h_0 is not admissible. In other words, the estimate $\Delta_0(s, g)$ is not a lower bound on the true minimal distance $\Delta^*(s, g)$. This is easily verified. For example, assume a problem where there is an action a such that precond$(a) \subseteq s_0$, effects$^+(a) = g$, and $s_0 \cap g = \emptyset$. In this problem the distance to the goal is 1, but $\Delta_0(s_0, g) = \sum_{p \in g} \Delta_0(s_0, p) = |g|$.

It can be desirable to use admissible heuristic functions for two reasons. We may be interested in getting the shortest plan, or there may be explicit costs associated with actions and we are using a best-first algorithm and requiring an optimal or near optimal plan. Furthermore, admissible heuristics permit a *safe pruning*: if Y is the length (or the cost) of a known plan and if $h(u) > Y$, h being admissible, then we are sure that no solution of length (or cost) smaller than Y can be obtained from the node u. Pruning u is safe in the sense that it does not affect the completeness of the algorithm.

It is very simple to obtain an admissible heuristic by modifying the estimate Δ_0 given earlier. Instead of estimating the distance to a set of propositions g to be the *sum* of the distances to the elements of g, we estimate it to be the *maximum* distance to its propositions. This leads to an estimate, denoted Δ_1, which is defined by changing the last equation of Formulas 9.1 to the following:

$$\Delta_1(s, g) = \max\{\Delta_1(s, p) \mid p \in g\} \tag{9.2}$$

The heuristic function associated with this estimate is $h_1(s) = \Delta_1(s, g)$.

The Delta algorithm is easily changed for computing h_1: the update step for each $p \in \text{effects}^+(a)$ is now:

$$\Delta_1(s, p) \leftarrow \min\{\Delta_1(s, p), 1 + \max\{\Delta_1(s, q) \mid q \in \text{precond}(a)\}\}$$

The heuristic h_1 can be used, like h_0 was used, to guide a state-space search algorithm in a forward or backward manner. In addition, it allows a safe pruning with respect to an a priori given upper bound. However, experience shows that h_1 is not as informative as h_0. It usually leads to a much less focused search.

The idea behind h_1 can be extended in order to produce a more informative heuristic that is still admissible. Instead of considering that the distance to a set g is the maximum distance to a proposition $p \in g$, we estimate it to be the maximum distance to a *pair of propositions* $\{p, q\} \in g$. This new estimate Δ_2 is defined according to the three following recursive equations (in addition to the termination cases that remain as in Formulas 9.1):

$$\begin{aligned}
\Delta_2(s,p) &= \min_a\{1 + \Delta_2(s, \text{precond}(a)) \mid p \in \text{effects}^+(a)\} \\
\Delta_2(s,\{p,q\}) &= \min\{ \\
&\quad \min_a\{1 + \Delta_2(s, \text{precond}(a)) \mid \{p,q\} \subseteq \text{effects}^+(a)\} \\
&\quad \min_a\{1 + \Delta_2(s, \{q\} \cup \text{precond}(a)) \mid p \in \text{effects}^+(a)\} \\
&\quad \min_a\{1 + \Delta_2(s, \{p\} \cup \text{precond}(a)) \mid q \in \text{effects}^+(a)\}\} \\
\Delta_2(s,g) &= \max_{p,q}\{\Delta_2(s,\{p,q\}) \mid \{p,q\} \subseteq g\}
\end{aligned} \tag{9.3}$$

The first equation gives, as before, the value of Δ_2 for a single proposition p. The second equation states that a pair $\{p, q\}$ can be reached in one step from a state s' to which is applicable an action a that produces both p and q, when $\text{precond}(a) \subseteq s'$; or it can be reached in one step from a state s'' by an action a that produces either p or q when s'' contains the other proposition q or p and the preconditions of a. The last equation states the relaxation condition: it estimates the distance from s to g as the longest distance to the pairs in g. This new estimate Δ_2 leads to the heuristic function $h_2(s) = \Delta_2(s, g)$.

The heuristic h_2 is admissible (see Exercise 9.3) and is significantly more informative than h_1. It takes longer to compute. However, the backward-search procedure devised with h_0, which relies on precomputed distances from s_0, is applicable to h_2. In this scheme, we modify the Delta algorithm to compute distances from s_0 to pairs of propositions, and we either run it just once to reach every pair or run it incrementally when the backward search reaches a pair whose distance from s_0 is not already precomputed (see Exercise 9.4).

It is interesting to note that the relaxation idea in the heuristic h_2 can be generalized. Instead of estimating the distance from s to g through the pairs in g, we may rely on the triples of g or on its k-tuples for any k.

Recall that $\Delta^*(s, g)$ is the true minimal distance from a state s to a goal g. Δ^* can be computed (albeit at great computational cost) according to the following equations:

$$\Delta^*(s,g) = \begin{cases} 0 & \text{if } g \subseteq s, \\ \infty & \text{if } \forall a \in A, a \text{ is not relevant for } g, \text{ and} \\ \min_a\{1 + \Delta^*(s, \gamma^{-1}(g,a)) \mid a \text{ relevant for } g\} & \\ & \text{otherwise.} \end{cases} \tag{9.4}$$

From Δ^*, let us define the following family Δ_k, for $k \geq 1$, of heuristic estimates:

$$\Delta_k(s,g) = \begin{cases} 0 & \text{if } g \subseteq s, \\ \infty & \text{if } \forall a \in A, a \text{ is not relevant for } g, \\ \min_a\{1 + \Delta^*(s, \gamma^{-1}(g,a)) \mid a \text{ relevant for } g\} & \\ \quad \text{if } |g| \leq k, & \\ \max_{g'}\{\Delta_k(s,g') \mid g' \subseteq g \text{ and } |g'| = k\} & \\ \quad \text{otherwise.} & \end{cases} \tag{9.5}$$

The third equation in Formula 9.5 says that when g has at most k propositions, we take the exact value Δ^*; otherwise, the relaxation approximates the distance Δ_k to g as the maximum distance to its k-tuple. The corresponding heuristic function is $h_k(s) = \Delta_k(s,g)$.

The heuristic h_k is very informative, but it also incurs a high computational cost, having a complexity of at least $O(n^k)$ for a problem with n propositions. When $k = \max_a\{|g|, |\text{precond}(a)|\}$, with g being the goal of the problem, getting the heuristic values requires solving the planning problem first! For the family of admissible heuristics $h_1, h_2, \ldots, h_k$, the quality of the heuristic estimate and its computational cost increase with larger values of k. The natural question is how to find the best trade-off. Most published results and experimental data are for low values of k, typically $k \leq 2$; beyond that the overhead seems to be too high.

9.3.4 Graphplan as a Heuristic Search Planner

The Backward-search procedure of Section 9.3.2 relies on an initial run of the algorithm Delta that computes, in a forward manner, the distances from state s_0; Backward-search then uses these distances in a backward-search manner to find a solution. The Graphplan procedure (Chapter 6) follows a similar approach. Indeed, Graphplan also runs a forward expansion of polynomial complexity, namely the Expand algorithm (Figure 6.5), before starting a backward search with the procedure GP- Search (Figure 6.8) that relies on the result of the first phase.

The two algorithms Delta and Expand both perform a reachability analysis. The main difference is that Expand builds a data structure, the planning graph, which provides more information attached to propositions than just the distances to s_0.

Indeed, these distance estimates are directly explicit in the planning graph. Let $\Delta^G(s_0, p)$ be the level i of the first layer P_i such that $p \in P_i$. Then $\Delta^G(s_0, p)$ is an estimate of $\Delta^*(s_0, p)$ that is very similar to previously defined estimates. Their differences are clarified in the next step.

The planning graph provides not only these distance estimates from s_0 to every reachable proposition but also the mutual exclusion relations μP_i. Recall that the GP- Search procedure of Graphplan selects a set of propositions g in a layer only if no pair of elements in g is mutex. Furthermore, we showed that if a pair is not mutex in a layer, then it remains nonmutex in the following layers: if p and q are in P_{i-1} and $(p,q) \notin \mu P_{i-1}$, then $(p,q) \notin \mu P_i$. Consequently, we can consider that the planning-graph structure approximates the distance $\Delta^*(s_0, g)$ with an estimate $\Delta^G(s_0, g)$ that is the level of the first layer of the graph such that $g \subseteq P_i$ and no pair of g is in μP_i. This is very close to Δ_2, as defined in Formulas 9.3. The difference between $\Delta^G(s_0, p)$ and Δ_0 is that Δ_2 counts each action individually with a cost of 1, because it is a state-space distance, whereas $\Delta^G(s_0, g)$ counts all the independent actions of a layer with a total cost of 1.

It is simple to modify Formulas 9.3 to get exactly the distance estimates $\Delta^G(s_0, g)$ defined from the planning-graph structure. We modify the second equation to state that a pair (p, q) is reachable in *one* step if either there is a single action achieving both propositions or there are two *independent* actions achieving each one. This modification gives a more informed node-selection heuristic in a domain where independence between actions is important.

Consequently, Graphplan can be viewed as a heuristic search planner that first computes the distance estimates $\Delta^G(s_0, g)$ in a forward propagation manner and then searches backward from the goal using an iterative-deepening approach (i.e., the planning graph is deepened if needed) augmented with a learning mechanism corresponding to the nogood hash table of previously failed sets of propositions.

9.4 Heuristics for Plan-Space Planning

Plan-space planning (e.g., the PSP procedure described in Chapter 5) searches a search space whose nodes are partial plans and finds solutions by repairing flaws in these plans. This search space can be viewed as a search in an AND/OR tree (see Figure 9.5). The flaws in a plan correspond to an AND-branch because all of them must eventually be resolved in order to find a solution. For each flaw, the possible resolvers correspond to an OR-branch because only one of them is needed in order to find a solution. Each solution corresponds to a *solution tree* that starts at the root of the tree and includes one edge at each OR-branch and edges at each AND-branch. As an example, Figure 9.5 shows one of the solution trees in boldface.

Thus, plan-space planning leaves room for two types of node-selection heuristics: heuristics for selecting the next flaw, and heuristics for choosing the resolver of the selected flaw. Section 9.4.1 discusses the former type of heuristic, while the latter is discussed in Section 9.4.2.

9.4.1 Flaw-Selection Heuristics

Since a plan-space planner such as PSP repairs flaws one at a time, this means that in effect it searches a *serialization* of the AND/OR tree. The flaws that are not explored immediately do not appear at the top of the serialized tree but instead appear lower in that tree. For example, consider the AND-branch at the top of Figure 9.5. This branch represents three flaws in the partial plan π. Suppose PSP chooses to resolve

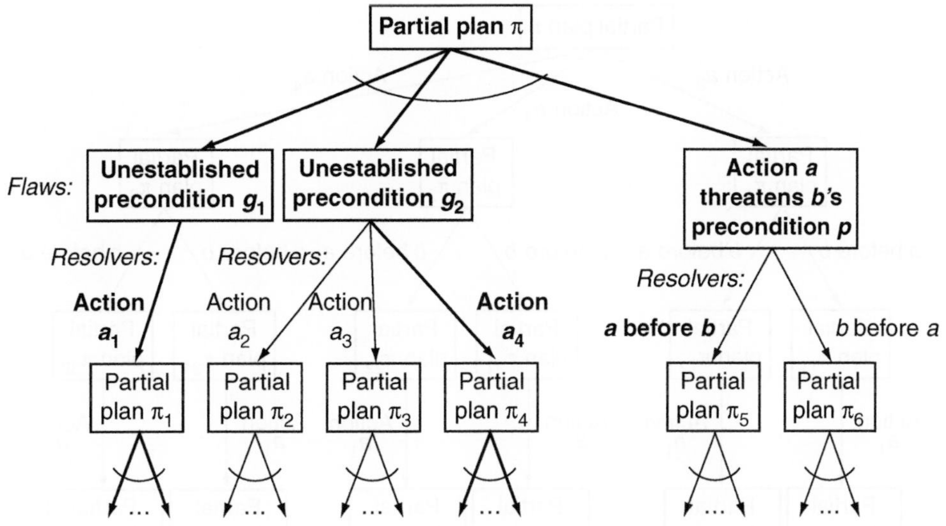

Figure 9.5 An AND/OR tree for flaw repair. Each set of flaws corresponds to an AND-branch, and each set of resolvers corresponds to an OR-branch. A solution tree is shown in boldface.

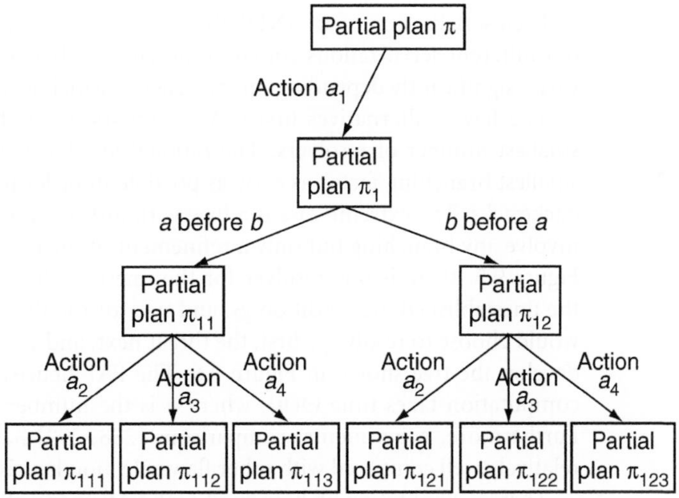

Figure 9.6 A serialization of the AND/OR tree shown in Figure 9.5.

these flaws in the following order: first find an establisher for g_1, then resolve the threat, and then find an establisher for g_2. Then PSP will develop the serialized tree shown in Figure 9.6. However, if PSP chooses to resolve these flaws in the opposite order, then it will explore the tree shown in Figure 9.7. Both of these trees are serializations of the AND/OR tree in Figure 9.5.

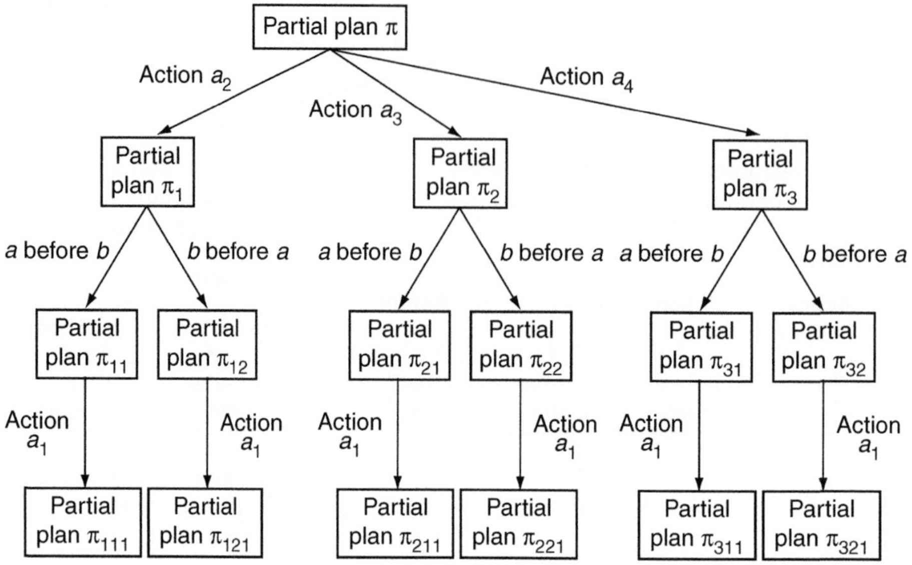

Figure 9.7 Another serialization of the AND/OR tree.

Each serialization of an AND/OR tree leads to exactly the same set of solutions, but different serializations contain different numbers of nodes. The speed of PSP varies significantly depending on the order in which it selects flaws to resolve.

The fewest alternatives first (FAF) heuristic is to choose the flaw having the smallest number of resolvers. The rational for that is to work on flaws with the smallest branching factor as early as possible in order to limit the cost of eventual backtracks. The extreme case is a flaw with just one resolver: such a flaw does not involve any branching but only a refinement of the current node. For example, in Figure 9.5, there is one resolver for the unestablished precondition g_1, three for the unestablished precondition g_2, and two for the threat. Thus, the FAF heuristic would choose to resolve g_1 first, the threat next, and g_2 last. In this case, PSP would develop the tree shown in Figure 9.6. The FAF heuristic is easy to compute: the computation takes time $\Theta(n)$, where n is the number of flaws in a partial plan. Furthermore, experimental comparisons [288, 290] have shown that FAF works relatively well compared with other flaw-selection heuristics.

There is a limitation on how good a job FAF or any other flaw-selection heuristic can do: if $n_{\min}$ and $n_{\max}$ are, respectively, the sizes of the smallest and largest serializations of an AND/OR graph, then no resolver-selection heuristic can reduce the size of the search space by more than $n_{\max} - n_{\min}$. To get an idea of this limitation, suppose we take the pattern shown in Figure 9.8(a), and use it repeatedly to form an AND/OR tree $G_{b,k}$ of height $2k$, as shown in Figure 9.8(b). In $G_{b,k}$, the number of occurrences of the pattern is

$$c_{b,k} = 1 + (b+1) + (b+1)^2 + \ldots + (b+1)^{k-1} = \Theta(bk),$$

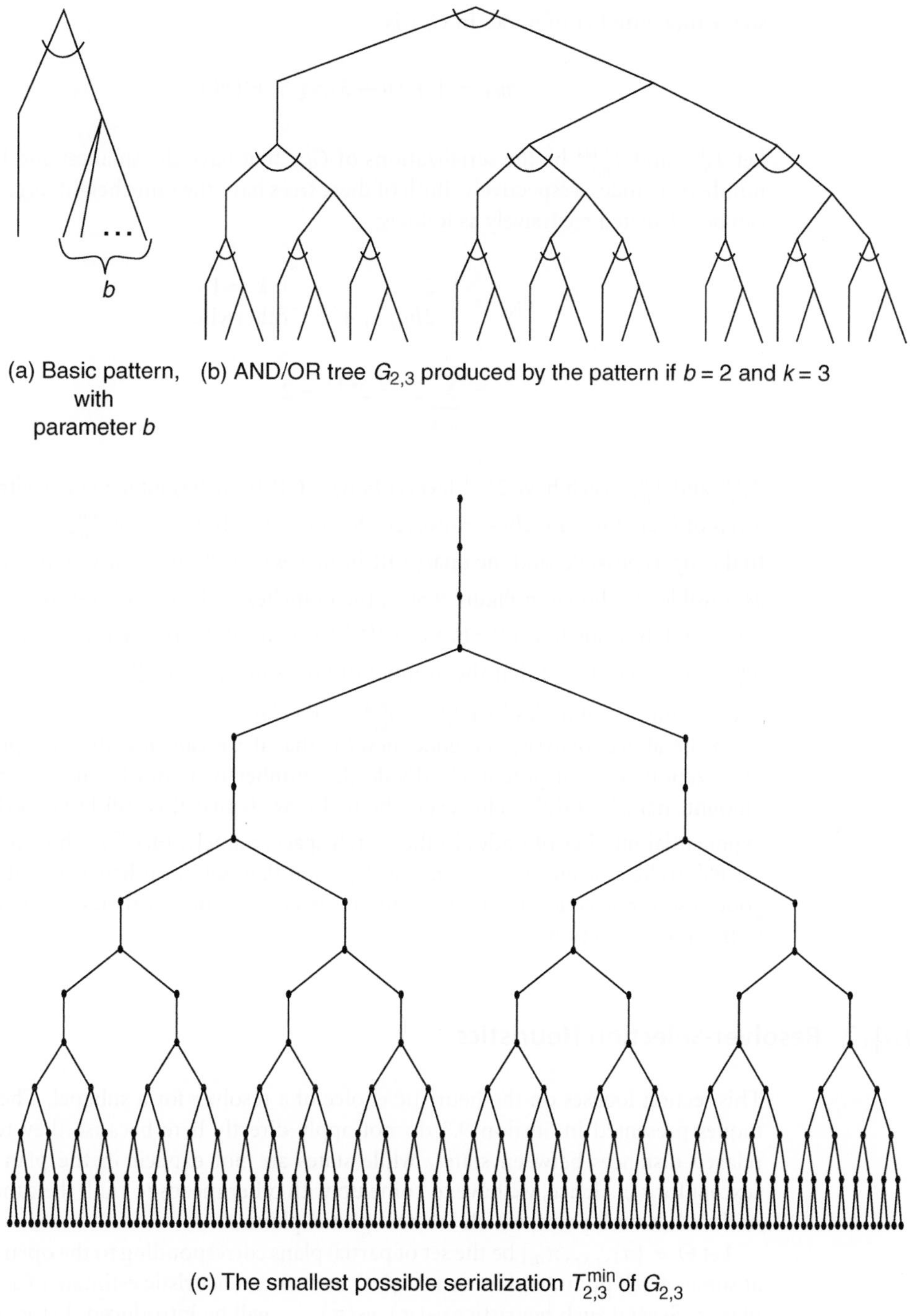

b
(a) Basic pattern, with parameter b
(b) AND/OR tree $G_{2,3}$ produced by the pattern if b = 2 and k = 3
(c) The smallest possible serialization $T^{min}_{2,3}$ of $G_{2,3}$

Figure 9.8 A basic pattern (a), an AND/OR tree formed by repetitions of the pattern (b), and the smallest possible serialization of the AND/OR tree (c).

so the total number of nodes in $G_{b,k}$ is

$$n_{b,k} = 1 + (b+3)c_{b,k} = \Theta(bk).$$

Let $T^{\min}_{b,k}$ and $T^{\max}_{b,k}$ be the serializations of $G_{b,k}$ that have the smallest and largest numbers of nodes, respectively. Both of these trees have the same height $h_{b,k}$, which can be calculated recursively as follows:

$$\begin{aligned} h_{b,k} &= \begin{cases} 2 & \text{if } k = 1 \\ 2h_{b,k-1} + 2 & \text{otherwise} \end{cases} \\ &= \sum_{i=1}^{k} 2^i = 2^{k+1} - 2 \end{aligned}$$

$T^{\min}_{b,k}$ and $T^{\max}_{b,k}$ each have 2^{k-1} levels of unary OR-branches interspersed with 2^{k-1} levels of b-ary OR-branches. However, the unary OR-branches of $T^{\min}_{b,k}$ are as near to the top as possible, and the unary OR-branches of $T^{\min}_{b,k}$ are as near to the bottom as possible. As shown in Figure 9.8(c), the branches at the top k levels of $T^{\min}_{b,k}$ are unary and the branches at the bottom 2^{k-1} levels are all b-ary; the reverse is true for $T^{\max}_{b,k}$. It can be shown that the number of nodes in $T^{\min}_{b,k}$ is $n^{\min}_{b,k} = \Theta(b^{2^k})$ nodes and the number of nodes in $T^{\max}_{b,k}$ is $n^{\max}_{b,k} = \Theta(2^k b^{2^k})$.

In the above analysis, the good news is that if we can find the best possible serialization, we can potentially divide the number of nodes by an exponential amount, namely, $\Theta(2^k)$. However, the bad news is that this still leaves a doubly exponential number of nodes in the search space, namely, $\Theta(b^{2^k})$. Thus, in order for PSP to be efficient, it needs not just a good flaw-selection heuristic but also a good resolver-selection heuristic. Some resolver-selection heuristics are described in the next subsection.

9.4.2 Resolver-Selection Heuristics

This section focuses on the heuristic choice of a resolver for a subgoal. The techniques presented in Section 9.3 do not apply directly here because they rely on relaxed distances between states, while states are not explicit in the plan space (except for s_0). Hence, we have to come up with other means to rank the candidate nodes at a search point, which are here partial plans.

Let $\Theta = \{\pi_1, \ldots, \pi_m\}$ be the set of partial plans corresponding to the open nodes at some search point, and let us use $\eta(\pi)$ to denote a heuristic estimate of a partial plan π. Several such heuristics $\eta_0(\pi), \eta_1(\pi), \ldots,$ will be introduced. Let g_π be the set of subgoals in partial plan $\pi \in \Theta$. Remember that g_π is the set of propositions in π without causal links. A very simple and intuitive heuristic is to choose in Θ the partial plan π that has the smallest set g_π, i.e., $\eta_1(\pi) = |g_\pi|$. However, this heuristic is not very informative.

A more informed heuristic involves building from each g_π an AND/OR graph, along regression steps defined by γ^{-1} down to some fixed level k. Let $\eta_k(g_\pi)$ be the weighted sum of: (1) the number of actions in this graph that are not in π, and (2) the number of subgoals remaining in its leaves that are not in the initial state s_0. Then $\eta_k(g_\pi)$ gives an estimate of how far g_π is from s_0, given π. The procedure then chooses the following partial plan: $\pi \leftarrow \text{argmin}\{\eta_k(\pi) \mid \pi \in \Theta\}$.

The heuristic η_k is more informative than η_0. It can be tuned for various values of the depth k of the AND/OR graph explored to assess g_π. However, η_k incurs a significant computational overhead.

A more efficient way to assess the distance in π between g_π and s_0 relies on the planning-graph data structure. Let us define $\delta_\pi(a)$ to be the set of actions *not* in π, i.e., $\delta_\pi(a) = 0$ when a is in π, and $\delta_\pi(a) = 1$ otherwise. This heuristic estimate $\eta(g_\pi)$ can be specified recursively as follows:

$$\eta(g_\pi) = \begin{cases} 0 & \text{if } g_\pi \subseteq s_0, \\ \infty & \text{if } \forall a \in A, a \text{ is not relevant for } g, \\ \max_p\{\delta_\pi(a) + \eta(\gamma^{-1}(g_\pi, a)) \mid p \in g_\pi \cap \text{effects}^+(a) & \\ \quad \text{and } a \text{ relevant for } g_\pi\} \text{ otherwise.} & \end{cases} \tag{9.6}$$

To compute η, we first run an expansion phase that gives the planning graph for the problem at hand, once and for all, down to a level containing the goal propositions without mutex. Let $l(p)$ be the level of the first layer of the graph containing proposition p. Given g for some partial plan, we find the proposition $p \in g$ that has the highest level $l(p)$. We then apply, backward from p, the recursive definition of η for an action a that provides p, which may be already in π. The heuristic η is quite similar to η_k, but it is computed more efficiently because it relies on a planning graph computed once.

9.5 Discussion and Historical Remarks

Distance-based heuristics were initially proposed for a plan-space temporal planner called IxTeT [224], which introduced flaw-selection as well as resolver-selection heuristics relying on relaxation techniques for estimating the distances to the goal. A more systematic characterizations of the usefulness of distance-based heuristics in planning is due to the work of Bonet and Geffner on the HSP planner [81]. At a time were state-space planning was thought to be too simple to be efficient, this planner, with heuristics h_0 and a best-first search algorithm, outperformed several elaborate planners in the AIPS '99 planning competition. The backward-search improvement and the admissible heuristics [260] brought other improvements, with further extension for dealing with time and resources [261]. The relationship between these heuristics and Graphplan was identified very early [81].

Distance-based goal-ordering heuristics for Graphplan were proposed in several sources [304, 423, 425].

The success of HSP inspired Hoffmann's development of the Fast-Forward planning system [271, 272].[2] Fast-Forward's heuristic estimate is based on the same relaxation as HSP's, but Fast-Forward computes an explicit solution to the relaxed planning problem and uses information about this solution both to compute its heuristic estimate h and to prune some of the current state's successors. Fast-Forward also incorporates some modifications to its hill-climbing algorithm in an effort to prevent getting trapped in local minima [270]. These modifications worked well for Fast-Forward; it outperformed HSP in the AIPS '00 planning competition [28].

For plan-space planning, Pollack *et al.* [444] have done experimental comparisons of several different flaw-selection heuristics. In their experimental results, the FAF heuristic performed well, but no one flaw-selection heuristic consistently dominated the others. Our analysis of the limitations of flaw-selection heuristics for PSP is adapted from the one by Tsuneto *et al.* [517]. Aside from being viewed as a state-space planning algorithm, forward search can alternatively be viewed as a flaw-selection heuristic for plan-space planning: the next flaw to be selected is the one that will occur first in the plan being developed. Although forward search is not particularly effective by itself, it has the advantage that the current state is known at each point in the planning process. This enables the use of the node-selection functions discussed above, as well as the use of some powerful domain-dependent pruning rules, which are discussed in Chapter 10. In HTN planning, which will be introduced in Chapter 11, the flaws to be resolved include unachieved subtasks and constraints that have not yet been enforced. Tsuneto *et al.* have shown that the FAF heuristic works well here but that it is helpful to supplement FAF with an analysis of the preconditions of tasks in the task network [516, 517].

Analogously to forward search, the forward-decomposition approach to HTN planning (see Chapter 11) can be viewed as a flaw-selection heuristic in which the next flaw to be selected is the one that will occur first in the resulting plan. As with forward search, forward decomposition has the advantage that the current state is known at each point in the planning process.

9.6 Exercises

9.1 Compute the values of h_0, h_1, and h_2 at level P_2 of the planning graph in Figure 6.4. Compare these values with each other and with the true distance to a solution.

9.2 Compute the values of h_0, h_1, and h_2 at level P_1 of the planning graph in Figure 6.4. Compare these values with each other and with the true distance to a solution.

9.3 Prove directly that the heuristic functions h_k, for $k \geq 1$, are admissible.

---

2. See http://www.informatik.uni-freiburg.de/~hoffmann/ff.html.

9.4 Modify the Delta algorithm to compute distances from s_0 to pairs of propositions either systematically to every pair or incrementally. Detail a backward-search procedure with heuristic h_2 that uses this modified Delta.

9.5 Let $\mathcal{P}$ be a planning problem whose state space is a binary tree T whose root node is the initial state s_0. Suppose that every node at depth d is a leaf node, and no other nodes are leaf nodes. Suppose that there is exactly one node s_g that is a goal node and that this node is a leaf of T. Suppose we have a heuristic function h such that at each node s that is an ancestor of s_g, there is a probability of 0.9 that h will recommend the action that takes us toward s_g. Suppose a Heuristic-forward-search algorithm starts at s_0 and uses h to decide which action to choose at each node.

(a) What is the probability that s_g will be the first leaf node visited by the algorithm?

(b) What is the probability that the algorithm will visit all of the other leaf nodes before visiting s_g?

(c) On average, how many other leaf nodes will the algorithm visit before visiting s_g?

9.6 How many different serializations are there for the AND/OR tree in Figure 9.5?

9.7 Let T be a binary AND/OR tree in which the topmost branch is an AND-branch, every node at depth d is a leaf node, and no other nodes are leaf nodes.

(a) How many leaf nodes are there in any serialization of T?

(b) How many different serializations are there for T?

(c) What are the smallest and largest possible numbers of leaf nodes in any serialization of T?

(d) Let e be an edge at the bottom of the tree. Then e will correspond to several different edges in any serialization of T. What are the smallest and largest possible values for this number of edges?

Chapter 10
Control Rules in Planning

10.1 Introduction

In the Abstract-search procedure in Figure III.1, the purpose of the Prune function is to detect unpromising nodes and prune them from the search space. The efficiency of a planning procedure can often be improved dramatically if a good way can be found to do this—for example, in some cases it may enable a procedure to solve problems in polynomial time that might otherwise take exponential time.

Deciding whether a node can be pruned often involves a collection of highly domain-specific tests to detect situations in which we can be confident that the solutions that lie below a node are less desirable than the solutions that lie below nodes elsewhere in the search space. Here is an example.

Example 10.1 Suppose we want to solve a container-stacking problem (see Section 4.5) using a modified version of Forward-search that includes a Prune function to prune undesirable nodes. Recall that each node corresponds to a state s, and the node's children are produced by applying actions to s. If we consider long plans to be less desirable than short ones, then here are some situations in which some of those children can be pruned.

1. Suppose that in the state s there is a container c whose position is consistent with the goal g. Then c will never need to be moved. For any action a that moves c and any solution plan π that applies a to s, there is a shorter solution π' that does not apply a to s. Thus the state $\gamma(s, a)$ can be pruned.
2. Suppose c's position is inconsistent with g but there is an action a that moves c to a position consistent with g. Then for any action b that moves c to a position inconsistent with g and for any solution plan π that applies b to s, there is a shorter solution π' that applies a to s instead. Thus we can prune $\gamma(s, b)$.

If we modify Forward-search to prune nodes in these situations and a few others, it will search the same search space as the Stack-containers procedure of Section 4.5. Thus it will find near-optimal solutions in low-order polynomial time. ■

In order to write pruning rules like the ones above, we need a language for expressing relationships among properties of the current state and properties of subsequent states. This chapter describes such a language and a planning algorithm based on it. Our presentation is based loosely on ideas developed by Bacchus and Kabanza [33].

Section 10.2 describes a language for writing control rules, Section 10.3 describes a procedure for evaluating control rules written in that language, and Section 10.4 describes a planning procedure based on the inference procedure. Section 10.5 describes ways to extend the approach. Section 10.6 discusses how to handle certain kinds of extended goals.

10.2 Simple Temporal Logic

This section describes a logical formalism that we will call *Simple Temporal Logic* (STL). STL extends first-order logic to include some *modal operators* that express relationships among the current state and subsequent states.

Let $\mathcal{L}$ be any function-free first-order language. Then $\mathcal{L}_\mathcal{T}$, the STL language based on $\mathcal{L}$, includes all the symbols of $\mathcal{L}$ plus the following:

- The propositional constants true, which is an atom that is always true, and false, which is an atom that is always false.
- The modal operators $\cup$ (until), $\square$ (always), $\diamond$ (eventually), $\bigcirc$ (next), and GOAL. These operators have the following syntax. If ϕ_1 and ϕ_2 are formulas, then so are $\phi_1 \cup \phi_2$, $\square\, \phi_1$, $\diamond\, \phi_1$, and $\bigcirc\, \phi_1$. If ϕ_1 contains no modal operators, then $\text{GOAL}(\phi_1)$ is a formula.

Below are the rules for how to interpret a formula ϕ of $\mathcal{L}_\mathcal{T}$. The interpretation of ϕ involves not just the current state as in classical planning (see Chapter 2) but instead a triple (S, s_i, g), where $S = \langle s_0, s_1, \ldots\rangle$ is an infinite sequence of states, $s_i \in S$ is the current state, and g is a goal formula.

The case that will interest us, of course, is where $\mathcal{L}_\mathcal{T}$ is based on the language $\mathcal{L}$ of some planning domain $\mathcal{D}$, and S is the sequence of states produced by a plan. One difficulty is that a finite plan $\pi = \langle a_1, a_2, \ldots, a_n\rangle$ produces only a finite sequence of states $S_\pi = \langle s_0, \ldots, s_n\rangle$, where $s_1 = \gamma(s_0, a_1), s_2 = \gamma(s_1, a_2), \ldots, s_n = \gamma(s_{n-1}, a_n)$. The work-around is to consider the infinite sequence of states $\hat{S}_\pi = \langle s_0, s_1, \ldots, s_{n-1}, s_n, s_n, s_n, \ldots\rangle$. Intuitively, this is the sequence of states that we get by executing π and then doing nothing forever afterward.

Definition 10.1 Let ϕ be an STL formula, $S = \langle s_0, s_1, \ldots\rangle$ be an infinite sequence of states, and g be a goal formula like the ones in Chapter 2. Then here are the rules that define whether $(S, s_i, g) \models \phi$.

- If ϕ is a ground atom, then $(S, s_i, g) \models \phi$ iff $s_i \models \phi$. In other words, ϕ is true if it is true in the current state.

- Quantifiers and logical connectives have the same semantic rules as in first-order logic. For example, $(S, s_i, g) \models \phi_1 \wedge \phi_2$ iff both $(S, s_i, g) \models \phi_1$ and $(S, s_i, g) \models \phi_2$.
- $(S, s_i, g) \models \Box\phi$ iff $(S, s_j, g) \models \phi$ for every $j \geq i$. For example, if ϕ contains no modal operators, then $\Box\phi$ is true iff ϕ is true in s_i and all subsequent states.
- $(S, s_i, g) \models \bigcirc\phi$ iff $(S, s_{i+1}, g) \models \phi$, i.e., $\bigcirc\phi$ is true iff ϕ is true in s_{i+1}.
- $(S, s_i, g) \models \Diamond\phi$ iff there is a $j \geq i$ such that $(S, s_j, g) \models \phi$, i.e., $\Diamond\phi$ is true iff ϕ is true in some state s_j that is after s_i.
- $(S, s_i, g) \models \phi_1 \cup \phi_2$ iff there is a $j \geq i$ such that $(S, s_k, g) \models \phi_1$ for $k = i, \ldots, j-1$ and $(S, s_j, g) \models \phi_2$, i.e., $\phi_1 \cup \phi_2$ is true if ϕ_1 is true in all states from s_i up until the first state (if any) in which ϕ_2 is true.
- $(S, s_i, g) \models \textsc{goal}(\phi)$ iff $\phi \in g$. In other words, $\textsc{goal}(\phi)$ is true if ϕ is a goal.

If ϕ contains no occurrences of the GOAL operator, then g is irrelevant, and in this case we will write $(S, s_i) \models \phi$ to mean $(S, s_i, g) \models \phi$. ■

Example 10.2 Let $S = \langle s_0, s_1, s_2, \ldots \rangle$ be a sequence of DWR states. Then:

- Each of the following means that on(c1,c2) and on(c2,c3) are true in s_2:

$$s_2 \models \mathsf{on(c1,c2)} \wedge \mathsf{on(c2,c3)}$$
$$(S, s_0) \models \bigcirc\bigcirc(\mathsf{on(c1,c2)} \wedge \mathsf{on(c2,c3)})$$
$$(S, s_1) \models \bigcirc(\mathsf{on(c1,c2)} \wedge \mathsf{on(c2,c3)})$$
$$(S, s_2) \models (\mathsf{on(c1,c2)} \wedge \mathsf{on(c2,c3)})$$

- $(S, s_i) \models \Box\neg\mathsf{holding(crane1,c1)}$ means that holding(crane1, c1) is false in all of $s_i, s_{i+1}, \ldots$.
- $(S, s_i) \models \forall x(\mathsf{on}(x,\mathsf{c1}) \rightarrow \Box\,\mathsf{on}(x,\mathsf{c1}))$ means that if another container is on c1 in s_i, then the same container is on c1 in all subsequent states. $(S, s_i) \models \forall x\ \Box(\mathsf{on}(x,\mathsf{c1}) \rightarrow \bigcirc\,\mathsf{on}(x,\mathsf{c1}))$ has the same meaning.
- $(S, s_i, g) \models \forall y\,(\mathsf{on}(y,\mathsf{pallet}) \wedge \textsc{goal}(\mathsf{on}(y,\mathsf{pallet})) \rightarrow \bigcirc\,\mathsf{on}(y,\mathsf{pallet}))$ means that for every container that is at the bottom of a pile in both s_i and the goal, it is also at the bottom of a pile in s_{i+1}. ■

The next example illustrates how to use STL to write a *control formula* describing situations where states can be pruned.

Example 10.3 Here is how to write an STL formula ϕ that encodes item 1 in Example 10.1. First, here is a formula $\phi_1(c, d, p)$ that holds if it is acceptable for the container c to be on the item d (which may be either a container or a pallet) in the pile p, i.e., if there is no goal requiring c to be in another pile or on top of something else:

$$\begin{aligned}\phi_1(c,d,p) = {} & [\textsc{goal}(\mathsf{in}(c,p)) \vee \neg\exists q\ \textsc{goal}(\mathsf{in}(c,q))] \\ & \wedge [\textsc{goal}(\mathsf{on}(c,d)) \vee \neg\exists e\ \textsc{goal}(\mathsf{on}(c,e))]\end{aligned}$$

Here is a formula $\phi_2(c,p)$ saying that $\mathsf{ok}(c,p)$ holds iff c is in the pile p and c's position is consistent with the goal:

$$\phi_2(c,p) \;=\; \mathsf{ok}(c,p) \leftrightarrow [\mathsf{same}(p,\mathsf{pallet}) \vee \exists d\,(\phi_1(c,d,p) \wedge \mathsf{ok}(d,p))]$$

Here is a formula $\phi_3(c)$ that holds iff c's position is consistent with the goal:

$$\phi_3(c) \;=\; \exists p\,(\phi_2(c,p) \wedge \mathsf{ok}(c,p))$$

Finally, here is a formula ϕ that holds iff for every container c whose position is consistent with g, c will never be moved, i.e., c will always remain in the same pile and on the same item in that pile:

$$\phi \;=\; \forall c\,[\phi_3(c) \rightarrow \exists p \exists d\; \Box(\mathsf{in}(c,p) \wedge \mathsf{in}(c,d))]$$

■

10.3 Progression

In order to use control formulas to prune nodes during planning, one of the key ideas is to compute the *progression* of a control formula ϕ from a state s_i to the next state s_{i+1}. The progression of ϕ is a formula progress (ϕ, s_i) that is true in s_{i+1} iff ϕ is true in s_i.

First, we define a formula progr (ϕ, s_i) recursively as follows. If ϕ contains no modal operators, then:

$$\mathrm{progr}(\phi, s_i) = \begin{cases} \mathsf{true} & \text{if } s_i \models \phi \\ \mathsf{false} & \text{if } s_i \not\models \phi \end{cases}$$

Logical connectives are handled in the usual fashion:

$$\mathrm{progr}(\phi_1 \wedge \phi_2, s_i) = \mathrm{progr}(\phi_1, s_i) \wedge \mathrm{progr}(\phi_2, s_i)$$
$$\mathrm{progr}(\neg\phi, s_i) = \neg\mathrm{progr}(\phi, s_i)$$

Quantifiers are handled as follows. Because $\mathcal{L}_\mathcal{T}$ has no function symbols, its only ground terms are $c_1, \ldots, c_k$. For $j = 1, \ldots, k$, let θ_j be the substitution $\{x \leftarrow c_j\}$. Then:

$$\mathrm{progr}(\forall x\phi, s_i) = \mathrm{progr}(\theta_1(\phi), s_i) \wedge \ldots \wedge \mathrm{progr}(\theta_k(\phi), s_i)$$
$$\mathrm{progr}(\exists x\phi, s_i) = \mathrm{progr}(\theta_1(\phi), s_i) \vee \ldots \vee \mathrm{progr}(\theta_k(\phi), s_i)$$

Modal operators are handled as follows:

$$\mathrm{progr}(\bigcirc\,\phi, s_i) = \phi$$
$$\mathrm{progr}(\phi_1 \cup \phi_2, s_i) = ((\phi_1 \cup \phi_2) \wedge \mathrm{progr}(\phi_1, s_i)) \vee \mathrm{progr}(\phi_2, s_i)$$
$$\mathrm{progr}(\Diamond\,\phi, s_i) = (\Diamond\,\phi) \vee \mathrm{progr}(\phi, s_i)$$
$$\mathrm{progr}(\Box\,\phi, s_i) = (\Box\,\phi) \wedge \mathrm{progr}(\phi, s_i)$$

Next, progress(ϕ, s_i) is the formula produced from progr(ϕ, s) by performing the usual simplifications (i.e., replace true $\wedge\, d$ with d, true $\vee\, d$ with true, $\neg$true with false, false $\wedge\, d$ with false, and so forth).

progr(ϕ, s) and progress(ϕ, s) can be computed in low-order polynomial time[1] by writing algorithms that directly implement their definitions (see Exercise 10.1). Proposition 10.1 says that progress(ϕ, s) means what it is supposed to mean.

Proposition 10.1 $(S, s_i, g) \models \phi$ *iff* $(S, s_{i+1}, g) \models \text{progress}(\phi, s_i)$.

The proof is by induction (Exercise 10.10), but here is a simple example.

Example 10.4 Here is a proof for the special case where $\phi = \Box\,\mathsf{on(c1,c2)}$. There are two cases. The first one is where $s_i \models \mathsf{on(c1,c2)}$. In this case, $s_i \models \phi$ iff $s_{i+1} \models \phi$, so:

$$\begin{aligned}\text{progress}(\phi, s_i) &= \Box\,\mathsf{on(c1,c2)} \wedge \text{progress}(\mathsf{on(c1,c2)}, s_i)\\ &= \Box\,\mathsf{on(c1,c2)} \wedge \mathsf{true}\\ &= \phi\end{aligned}$$

The second case is where $s_i \models \neg\mathsf{on(c1,c2)}$. In this case, $s_i \not\models \phi$, so:

$$\begin{aligned}\text{progress}(\phi, s_i) &= \Box\,\mathsf{on(c1,c2)} \wedge \text{progress}(\mathsf{on(c1,c2)}, s_i)\\ &= \Box\,\mathsf{on(c1,c2)} \wedge \mathsf{false}\\ &= \mathsf{false}\end{aligned}$$

Thus, $s_i \models \phi$ iff $s_{i+1} \models \text{progress}(\phi, s_i)$. ■

If ϕ is a closed formula and $S = \langle s_0, \ldots, s_n \rangle$ is any finite sequence of states (e.g., the sequence of states produced by a plan), then we define progress(ϕ, S) to be the result of progressing ϕ through all of those states:

$$\text{progress}(\phi, S) = \begin{cases} \phi & \text{if } n = 0 \\ \text{progress}(\text{progress}(\phi, \langle s_0, \ldots, s_{n-1} \rangle), s_n) & \text{otherwise} \end{cases}$$

The following two propositions tell how to use a control formula to prune nodes during planning. Proposition 10.2 can be proved by induction (see Exercise 10.11), and Proposition 10.3 follows as a corollary (see Exercise 10.12).

Proposition 10.2 *Let* $S = \langle s_0, s_1, \ldots \rangle$ *be an infinite sequence of states and* ϕ *be an STL formula. If* $(S, s_0, g) \models \phi$*, then for every finite truncation* $S' = \langle s_0, s_1, \ldots, s_i \rangle$ *of* S, progress(ϕ, S') $\neq$ false.

1. Readers who are familiar with model checking will note that this is much lower than the exponential time complexity for progression in model checking.

Proposition 10.3 *Let s_0 be a state, π be a plan applicable to s_0, and $S = \langle s_0, \ldots, s_n \rangle$ be the sequence of states produced by applying π to s_0. If ϕ is an STL formula and* $\text{progress}(\phi, S) = \text{false}$, *then S has no extension $S' = \langle s_0, \ldots, s_n, s_{n+1}, s_{n+2}, \ldots \rangle$ such that $(S', s_0, g) \models \phi$.*

Example 10.5 Let s_0 and g be be the initial state and goal formula, respectively, for a container-stacking problem whose constant symbols are $c_1, \ldots, c_k$. Let ϕ_1, ϕ_2, ϕ_3, and ϕ be as in Example 10.3 (see page 219). Then:

$$\begin{aligned}\text{progress}(\phi, s_0) &= \text{progress}(\forall c\,[\phi_3(c) \rightarrow \exists p \exists d\ \Box(\text{in}(c,p) \wedge \text{in}(c,d))], s_0)\\ &= \text{progress}([\phi_3(c_1) \rightarrow \exists p \exists d\ \Box(\text{in}(c_1,p) \wedge \text{in}(c_1,d))], s_0)\\ &\quad \wedge \text{progress}([\phi_3(c_2) \rightarrow \exists p \exists d\ \Box(\text{in}(c_2,p) \wedge \text{in}(c_2,d))], s_0)\\ &\quad \wedge \ldots\\ &\quad \wedge \text{progress}([\phi_3(c_k) \rightarrow \exists p \exists d\ \Box(\text{in}(c_k,p) \wedge \text{in}(c_k,d))], s_0)\end{aligned}$$

Suppose that in s_0, there is exactly one container c_1 whose position is consistent with g. Then $s_0 \models \phi_3(c_1)$, and $s_0 \not\models \phi_3(c_i)$ for $i = 2, \ldots, k$. Suppose also that in s_0, c_1 is on item d_1 in pile p_1. Then:

$$\begin{aligned}\text{progress}(\phi, s_0) &= \text{progress}(\exists p \exists d\ \Box(\text{in}(c_1,p) \wedge \text{in}(c_1,d)), s_0)\\ &= \text{progress}(\Box(\text{in}(c_1,p_1) \wedge \text{in}(c_1,d_1)), s_0)\\ &= \Box(\text{in}(c_1,p_1) \wedge \text{in}(c_1,d_1))\end{aligned}$$

Let a be an action applicable to s_0. If a moves c_1, then c_1 will no longer be on item d_1 in pile p_1, whence $\gamma(s_0, a) \not\models \text{progress}(\phi, s_0)$. Thus $\gamma(s_0, a)$ can be pruned. ■

10.4 Planning Procedure

It is straightforward to modify the Forward-search procedure of Chapter 4 to prune any partial plan π such that $\text{progress}(\phi, S_\pi) = \text{false}$. Furthermore, there is an easy way to optimize the computation of $\text{progress}(\phi, S_\pi)$, by setting $\phi \leftarrow \text{progress}(\phi, s)$ each time through the loop. The optimized procedure, STL-plan, is shown in Figure 10.1.

The soundness of STL-plan follows directly from the soundness of Forward-search. Proposition 10.4 establishes a condition on ϕ that is sufficient to make STL-plan complete.

Proposition 10.4 *Let (O, s_0, g) be the statement of a solvable planning problem $\mathcal{P}$ and ϕ be an STL formula such that $(\hat{S}_\pi, s_0, g) \models \phi$ for at least one solution π of $\mathcal{P}$. Then* $\text{STL-plan}(O, s_0, g, \phi)$ *is guaranteed to return a solution for $\mathcal{P}$.*

Proof From the condition on ϕ, we know there is at least one solution π for $\mathcal{P}$ such that $(\hat{S}_\pi, s_0, g) \models \phi$. Thus from Proposition 10.2, it follows that STL-plan will not

```
STL-plan(O, s0, g, φ)
  s ← s0
  π ← the empty plan
  loop
    if φ = false then return failure
    if s satisfies g then return π
    A ← {a | a is a ground instance of an operator in O
              and precond(a) is true in s}
    if A = ∅ then return failure
    nondeterministically choose an action a ∈ A
    s ← γ(s, a)
    π ← π.a
    φ ← progress(φ, s)
```

Figure 10.1 STL-plan, a modified version of Forward-search that prunes any plan π such that $\text{progress}(\phi, S_\pi) = \text{false}$.

prune any state along the path generated by π. Thus at least one of STL-plan's nondeterministic traces will return π. Other nondeterministic traces may possibly return other plans, but it follows from the soundness of Forward-search that any plan returned by STL-plan will be a solution. ∎

In some cases it can be proved that a control formula ϕ satisfies the requirements of Proposition 10.4 (e.g., see Exercise 10.13). However, in general, writing a good control formula is much more of an *ad hoc* activity. A control formula is basically a computer program in a specialized programming language; thus control formulas need to be debugged just like any other computer programs.

10.5 Extensions

Section 2.4 discussed how to augment classical planning to incorporate extensions such as axioms, function symbols, and attached procedures. Similar extensions can be made to STL and to the STL-plan procedure, with a few restrictions as described in this section.

Function Symbols. Recall from Section 10.3 that we defined $\text{progr}(\forall x \phi)$ and $\text{progr}(\exists x \phi)$ to be conjunctions and disjunctions over all of the ground terms of $\mathcal{L}_\mathcal{T}$. If we add function symbols to $\mathcal{L}$, then these definitions become uncomputable because there are infinitely many ground terms. One way around this difficulty is to restrict every universally quantified formula to have the form $\forall x\,(a \rightarrow \phi)$ and every existentially quantified formula to have the form $\exists x\,(a \wedge \phi)$, where a is an atom known to be true for only finitely many values of x. Then instead of evaluating ϕ for every possible value of x, we only need to consider the values of x that make a true.[2]

Axioms. To include axioms, we need a way to perform axiomatic inference. The easiest approach is to restrict the axioms to be Horn clauses, and use a Horn-clause theorem prover. If an operator or method has a positive precondition p, then we take p to be true iff it can be proved from the current state s.

In some planning domains, it is useful to allow negated conditions to occur in the tails of the Horn clauses and in the preconditions of the planning operators. If we do this, then there is a problem with what it means for a condition to be satisfied by a state because there is more than one possible semantics for what logical entailment might mean [500]. However, if we restrict the set of Horn-clause axioms to be a stratified logic program, then the two major semantics for logical entailment agree with each other [46], and in this case the inference procedure will still be sound and complete.

Attached Procedures. It is easy to generalize STL-plan and similar planning procedures to allow some of the function symbols and predicate symbols to be evaluated as attached procedures. In some cases, restrictions can be put on the attached procedures that are sufficient to preserve soundness and completeness. In the most general case, soundness and completeness cannot be preserved, but attached procedures are nevertheless quite useful for practical problem solving.

Time. It is possible to generalize STL-plan and similar procedures to do certain kinds of temporal planning, e.g., to deal with actions that have time durations and may overlap with each other. The details are beyond the scope of this chapter, but some references are given in Section 10.7.

10.6 Extended Goals

By using STL, we can extend the classical planning formalism to allow a much larger class of extended goals than the ones that can be translated into ordinary classical planning problems. We do this by defining an *STL planning problem* to be a 4-tuple (O, s_0, g, ϕ), where ϕ is a control formula expressed in STL. A *solution* to an STL

---

2. In practice, a similar restriction is normally used even if $\mathcal{L}$ is function-free, in order to alleviate the combinatorial explosion that occurs when a formula contains multiple quantifiers. For example, if $\phi = \forall x_1 \forall x_2 \ldots \forall x_n\, \phi'$ and there are k different possible values for each variable x_i, then progr(ϕ) is a conjunct of k^n different instances of ϕ. The restriction can decrease the complexity of this computation in the same way as if we had decreased the value of k.

planning problem is any plan $\pi = \langle a_1, \ldots, a_k \rangle$ such that the following conditions are satisfied.

- π is a solution to the classical planning problem (O, s_0, g).
- For $i = 1, \ldots, k$, let $s_i = \gamma(s_{i-1}, a_i)$. Then the infinite sequence of states $\langle s_0, s_1, \ldots, s_k, s_k, s_k, \ldots \rangle$ satisfies ϕ.

Here are examples of how to encode several kinds of extended goals in STL planning problems.

- Consider a DWR domain in which there is some location bad-loc to which we never want our robots to move. To express this as a classical planning domain, it is necessary to add an additional precondition to the move operator (see Section 2.4.8). For STL planning, such a change to the move operator is unnecessary because we can instead use the control rule

  $$\phi = \Box \neg \mathrm{at(r1, bad\text{-}loc)}.$$

- Suppose that r1 begins at location loc1 in the initial state, and we want r1 to go from loc1 to loc2 and back exactly twice. In Section 2.4.8, we said that this kind of problem cannot be expressed as a classical planning problem. However, it can be expressed as an STL planning problem by using this control rule:

  $$\phi = (\bigcirc\, \mathrm{at(loc2)}) \wedge (\bigcirc \bigcirc\, \mathrm{at(loc1)}) \wedge (\bigcirc \bigcirc \bigcirc\, \mathrm{at(loc2)}) \wedge (\bigcirc \bigcirc \bigcirc \bigcirc \Box\, \mathrm{at(loc1)})$$

- To require that every solution reach the goal in five actions or fewer, we can use this control rule:

  $$\phi = g \vee (\bigcirc g) \vee (\bigcirc \bigcirc g) \vee (\bigcirc \bigcirc \bigcirc g) \vee (\bigcirc \bigcirc \bigcirc \bigcirc g)$$

- Suppose we want to require that the number of times r1 visits loc1 must be at least three times the number of times it visits loc2. Such a requirement cannot be represented directly in an STL planning problem. However, it can be represented using the same approach we described for classical planning in Section 2.4.8: extend STL planning by introducing the predicate symbols, function symbols, and attached procedures needed to perform integer arithmetic, modify the move operator to maintain atoms in the current state that represent the number of times we visit each location, and modify the goal to include the required ratio of visits. Unlike most classical planning procedures, STL-plan can easily accommodate this extension. The key is to ensure that all of the variables of an attached procedure are bound at the time the procedure is called. This is easy to accomplish in STL-plan because it plans forward from the initial state.

Because STL-plan returns only plans that are finite sequences of actions, there are some kinds of extended goals it cannot handle. Here is an example.

Example 10.6 Consider an STL planning problem $\mathcal{P}$ in which $s_0 = \{p\}$, $g = \emptyset$, $\phi = \square(\diamond p \wedge \diamond \neg p)$, and O contains the following operators:

off	on	no-op
precond: p	precond: ¬p	precond: *(none)*
effects: ¬p	effects: p	effects: *(none)*

Now, consider the infinite sequence of actions:

$$\pi = \langle \text{off}, \text{on}, \text{off}, \text{on}, \text{off}, \text{on}, \ldots \rangle$$

Our formal definitions do not admit π as a solution, nor will STL-plan return it. However, there are situations in which we would want to consider π to be a solution for a planning problem. We might consider modifying STL-plan to print out π one action at a time. However, because STL-plan is nondeterministic, there is no guarantee that it would print out π rather than, say:

$$\langle \text{no-op}, \text{no-op}, \text{no-op}, \ldots \rangle$$

Part V describes some nonclassical planning formalisms and algorithms that address problems like these. ∎

10.7 Discussion and Historical Remarks

One of the earliest planning systems to incorporate search-control rules was PRODIGY [105, 524, 525].[3] Unlike the approach described in this chapter, in which the control rules are written by a human, PRODIGY's rules are designed to be learned automatically. They are not written in a logical formalism like STL but instead act like expert-system rules for guiding algorithmic choices made by the search algorithm. Although PRODIGY's planning speed is not competitive with more recent control-rule planners such as TLPlan and TALplanner (discussed next), it can use its learning techniques to improve its efficiency on various classical planning problems [105].

STL is a simplification of the version of the Linear Temporal Logic that Bacchus and Kabanza used in their TLPlan system [33].[4] Similarly, STL-plan is a simplification of TLPlan's planning algorithm. TLPlan incorporates most or all of the extensions we described in Section 10.5. If it is given a good set of domain-specific control rules to guide its search, TLPlan can outperform all of the classical planning systems described in Parts I and II. TLPlan won one of the top two prizes in the 2002 International Planning Competition [195].

STL's modal operators are similar to those used in model checking, but they are used in a different way. In STL-plan, modal formulas are used to prune paths in a forward-search algorithm. In model checking (see Appendix C), the objective is to determine whether a modal formula will remain true throughout all possible

3. For a downloadable copy of PRODIGY, see http://www-2.cs.cmu.edu/afs/cs.cmu.edu/project/prodigy/Web/prodigy-home.html.
4. For a downloadable copy of TLPlan, see http://www.cs.toronto.edu/~fbacchus/tlplan.html.

behaviors of a nondeterministic finite-state system, and the algorithms for doing this are rather different than forward search. However, these algorithms can also be used to do planning (see Chapter 17).

Doherty and Kvarnström's TALplanner [160, 342] has a planning algorithm similar to TLPlan's but uses a different temporal logic. TALplanner has capabilities and efficiency similar to those of TLPlan; TALplanner won one of the top two prizes in the AIPS '00 Planning Competition [28]. Both TLPlan and TALplanner can do certain kinds of temporal planning [29, 342]. See Long and Fox [368] for a discussion of some of the issues involved.

Advantages and Disadvantages. Compared to classical and neoclassical planners, the primary advantage of planners such as TLPlan and TALplanner is their sophisticated knowledge representation and reasoning capabilities. They can represent and solve a variety of nonclassical planning problems, and with a good set of control rules they can solve classical planning problems orders of magnitude more quickly than classical or neoclassical planners. The primary disadvantage of TLPlan and TALplanner is the need for the domain author to write not only a set of planning operators but also a set of control rules.

10.8 Exercises

10.1 Write pseudocode for computing progr(ϕ, S), and analyze its worst-case time complexity.

10.2 Consider the painting problem described in Exercise 5.6.

(a) Suppose we run STL-plan on this problem without any control rules. How many nodes will there be at depth 3 of the search space?

(b) Write a control rule to prevent brushes from being dipped first into one can and then into the other.

(c) Suppose we run STL-plan on this problem with your control rule. How many nodes will there be at depth 3 of the search space?

10.3 Consider the washing problem described in Exercise 5.7.

(a) Suppose we run STL-plan on this problem without any control rules. How many nodes will there be at depth 3 of the search space?

(b) Write control rules to ensure that once we start filling an object x, we will not try to fill any other object y until we are finished filling x.

(c) Will your control rule make any difference in what set of states STL-plan visits? Why or why not?

10.4 Write the rest of the rules needed for the pruning function in Example 10.1 (see page 217).

10.5 Encode the second rule in Example 10.1 as a set of STL formulas similar to those in Example 10.3 (see page 219).

10.6 The first rule in Example 10.1 (see page 217) is not strong enough to express the idea that if c's position is consistent with g, then c should not be moved at all. Write a set of STL formulas to represent this.

10.7 For the variable-interchange problem described in Exercise 4.1, do the following.

(a) Write a control rule saying that STL-plan should never assign a value into v1 until it has copied the value of v1 into some other variable.

(b) Generalize the rule so that it applies to both v1 and v2.

(c) Trace the execution of STL-plan on the variable-interchange problem using the control rule you wrote in part (b), going along the shortest path to a goal state. For each node you visit, write the associated control rule.

(d) With the control rule in part (b), are there any paths in STL-plan's search space that do not lead to goal nodes? If so, write a control rule that will be sufficient to prune those paths without pruning the path you found in part (c).

10.8 Give an example of a situation in which both Proposition 10.2 (see page 221) and its converse are true.

10.9 Give an example of a situation in which the converse of Proposition 10.2 (see page 221) is false.

10.10 Prove Proposition 10.1 (see page 221).

10.11 Prove Proposition 10.2 (see page 221).

10.12 Prove Proposition 10.3 (see page 222).

10.13 Let ϕ be the control formula in Example 10.4 (see page 221). Prove that for any container-stacking problem, there is at least one solution π such that $(\hat{S}_\pi, s_0, g) \models \phi$.

10.14 Professor Prune says, "Under the conditions of Proposition 10.10, STL-plan(O, s_0, g, ϕ) will return a solution π such that $(\hat{S}_\pi, s_0, g) \models \phi$." Prove that Professor Prune is wrong.

10.15 Download a copy of TLPlan from http://www.cs.toronto.edu/~fbacchus/tlplan.html.

(a) Write several planning problems for TLPlan in the blocks world (see Section 4.6), including the one in Exercise 2.1, and run TLPlan on them using the blocks-world domain description that comes with it.

(b) Rewrite TLPlan's blocks-world domain description as a domain description for the container-stacking domain (See Section 4.5). Rewrite your blocks-world planning problems as container-stacking problems, and run TLPlan on them.

CHAPTER 11

Hierarchical Task Network Planning

11.1 Introduction

Hierarchical Task Network (HTN) planning is like classical planning in that each state of the world is represented by a set of atoms, and each action corresponds to a deterministic state transition. However, HTN planners differ from classical planners in what they plan for and how they plan for it.

In an HTN planner, the objective is not to achieve a set of goals but instead to perform some set of *tasks*. The input to the planning system includes a set of operators similar to those of classical planning and also a set of *methods*, each of which is a prescription for how to decompose some task into some set of *subtasks* (smaller tasks). Planning proceeds by decomposing *nonprimitive tasks* recursively into smaller and smaller subtasks, until *primitive tasks* are reached that can be performed directly using the planning operators. An HTN planner will apply an operator only if directed to do so by a method; thus in the terminology of Figure III.1, each method is part of the specification of the Branch function.

HTN planning has been more widely used for practical applications than any of the other planning techniques described in this book. This is partly because HTN methods provide a convenient way to write problem-solving "recipes" that correspond to how a human domain expert might think about solving a planning problem. Here is a simple example that we will refer to several times in this chapter.

Example 11.1 Figure 11.1 shows a DWR problem in which three stacks of containers need to be moved from the piles p1a, p2a, and p3a to the piles p1c, p2c, and p3c in a way that preserves the ordering of the containers, i.e., each container should be on top of the same container that it was on originally. Here is an informal description of some methods for solving this problem.

- To accomplish the task of moving all three of the stacks in a way that preserves the containers' ordering, we can do the following for each stack: Move it to an intermediate pile (which will reverse the order of the containers), then move

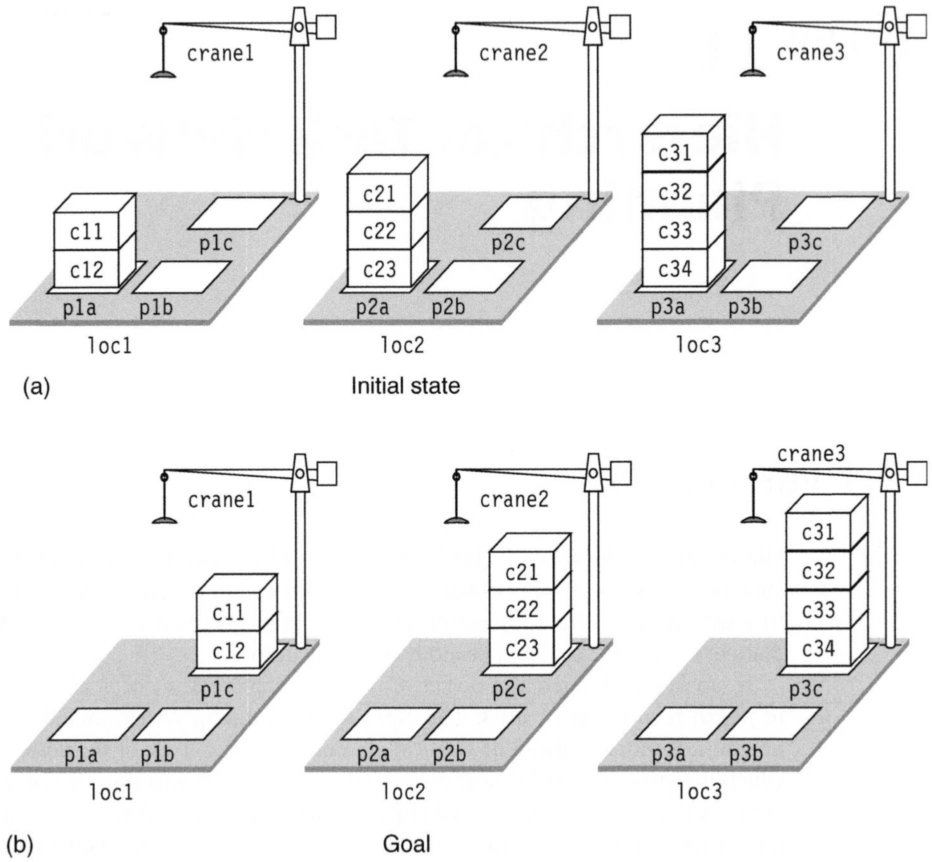

Figure 11.1 A DWR problem in which several stacks of containers need to be moved to different piles.

it to the desired pile (which will put the containers back into their original order).

- To accomplish the task of moving a stack of containers from a pile p to another pile q, we can do the following until p is empty: repeatedly move the topmost container of p to q.
- To accomplish the task of moving the topmost container of a pile p to another pile q, we can use the DWR domain's take operator to remove the container from p and use the put operator to put it on top of q.

An HTN description of the problem would include the DWR operators, the initial state, the task of moving the three stacks in a way that preserves their ordering, and a formal description of the methods just listed. These methods make it much easier to solve the planning problem because they generate only plans that are solutions to the problem. ■

This chapter describes ways to represent HTN planning problems and algorithms for solving the problems. The presentation draws loosely from ideas developed by Sacerdoti [460], Tate [503], Wilkins [549], Erol *et al.* [174], and Nau *et al.* [413, 414].

Sections 11.2 through 11.4 discuss a simplified version of HTN planning that we will call Simple Task Network (STN) planning. Section 11.2 describes the representation scheme, Section 11.3 discusses a planning procedure for a case in which the tasks are totally ordered, and Section 11.4 describes a planning procedure for a more general case in which the tasks may be partially ordered (e.g., to specify that we don't care about the order in which the stacks are moved). Section 11.5 discusses HTN planning, in full generality, including its representation scheme and planning procedures. Section 11.6 discusses the expressivity and complexity of HTN planning; it can express planning problems that cannot be expressed as classical planning problems. Section 11.7 discusses how to extend HTN planning to include extensions like the ones in Section 2.4, and Section 11.8 covers extended goals. Section 11.9 contains discussion and historical remarks.

11.2 STN Planning

This section describes a language for a simplified version of HTN planning called Simple Task Network (STN) planning. Our definitions of terms, literals, operators, actions, and plans are the same as in classical planning. The definition of $\gamma(s, a)$, the result of applying an action a to a state s, is also the same as in classical planning. However, the language also includes tasks, methods, and task networks, which are used in the definitions of a planning problem and its solutions.

11.2.1 Tasks and Methods

One new kind of symbol is a *task symbol.* Every operator symbol is a task symbol, and there are some additional task symbols called *nonprimitive task symbols.* A *task* is an expression of the form $t(r_1, \ldots, r_k)$ such that t is a task symbol, and $r_1, \ldots, r_k$ are terms. If t is an operator symbol, then the task is *primitive*; otherwise, the task is *nonprimitive.* The task is *ground* if all of the terms are ground; otherwise, it is *unground.* An action $a = (\text{name}(a), \text{precond}(a), \text{effects}(a))$ *accomplishes* a ground primitive task t in a state s if $\text{name}(a) = t$ and a is applicable to s.

Definition 11.1 A *simple task network* (or, for short, a *task network*) is an acyclic digraph $w = (U, E)$ in which U is the node set, E is the edge set, and each node $u \in U$ contains a task t_u. w is *ground* if all of the tasks $\{t_u \mid u \in U\}$ are ground; otherwise, w is *unground.* w is *primitive* if all of the tasks $\{t_u \mid u \in U\}$ are primitive; otherwise, w is *nonprimitive.* ∎

The edges of w define a partial ordering of U, namely, $u \prec v$ iff there is a path from u to v. If the partial ordering is total, then we say that w is *totally ordered*. In this case, we will sometimes dispense with the graph notation for w and instead write w as the sequence of tasks, namely, $w = \langle t_1, \ldots, t_k \rangle$, where t_1 is the task in the first node of U, t_2 is the task in the second node of U, and so forth. Note that if w is ground, primitive, and totally ordered, and if there are actions $a_1, \ldots, a_k$ whose names are $t_1, \ldots, t_k$, then w corresponds to the plan $\pi_w = \langle a_1, \ldots, a_k \rangle$.

Example 11.2 In the DWR domain, let $t_1 =$ take(crane2, loc1, c1, c2, p1) and $t_2 =$ put(crane2, loc2, c3, c4, p2). Let $t_3 =$ move-stack(p1, q), where move-stack is a nonprimitive task symbol. Then t_1 and t_2 are primitive tasks, and t_3 is a nonprimitive task. Let u_1, u_2, and u_3 be nodes such that $t_{u_i} = t_i \ \forall i$. Let $w_1 = (\{u_1, u_2, u_3\}, \{(u_1, u_2), (u_2, u_3)\})$ and $w_2 = (\{u_1, u_2\}, \{(u_1, u_2)\})$. Then w_1 and w_2 are task networks. Since w_2 is totally ordered, we would usually write it as $w_2 = \langle t_1, t_2 \rangle$. Since w_2 also is ground and primitive, it corresponds to the plan $\langle a_1, a_2 \rangle$, where a_1 and a_2 are the actions whose names are t_1 and t_2, respectively. Since we normally use the names of actions to refer to the actions themselves, we usually would say that this is the plan ⟨take(crane2, loc1, c1, c2, p1), put(crane2, loc2, c3, c4, p2)⟩. ■

We also will include in the planning language a new set of symbols called *method symbols*.

Definition 11.2 An *STN method*[1] is a 4-tuple

$$m = (\text{name}(m), \text{task}(m), \text{precond}(m), \text{network}(m))$$

in which the elements are described as follows.

- name(m), the *name* of the method, is a syntactic expression of the form $n(x_1, \ldots, x_k)$, where n is a unique method symbol (i.e., no two methods have the same value for n), and $x_1, \ldots, x_k$ are all of the variable symbols that occur anywhere in m.
- task(m) is a nonprimitive task.
- precond(m) is a set of literals called the method's *preconditions*.
- network(m) is a task network whose tasks are called the *subtasks* of m. ■

In Definition 11.2, name(m) has the same purpose as the name of a classical planning operator: it lets us refer unambiguously to substitution instances of the method, without having to write the preconditions and effects explicitly. task(m) tells what kind of task m can be applied to, precond(m) specifies what conditions the current state must satisfy in order for m to be applied, and network(m) specifies the subtasks to accomplish in order to accomplish task(m).

1. As usual, we will abbreviate this and other terms by omitting adjectives such as STN and HTN when we can do so unambiguously.

A method m is *totally ordered* if network(m) is totally ordered. In this case, rather than specifying the digraph network(m) explicitly, it is simpler to specify subtasks(m), the sequence of subtasks in network(m). For example, if we write

$$\text{subtasks}(m) = \langle t_1, \ldots, t_k \rangle,$$

then this means that

$$\text{network}(m) = (\{u_1, \ldots, u_k\}, \{(u_1, u_2), (u_2, u_3), \ldots, (u_{k-1}, u_k)\})$$

where each u_i is a node such that $t_{u_i} = t_i$.

Rather than writing methods as 4-tuples, we usually will write them in the format shown in the following example.

Example 11.3 Here are formal descriptions of the methods mentioned in Example 11.1 (see page 229). We need two methods for the task of moving a stack of containers: one for the case where the stack is nonempty, and one for the case where it is empty.

The subtasks of the first three methods are totally ordered, so for each of them we specify subtasks(m) rather than network(m). In the last method, the subtasks are partially ordered, so we need to specify its task network explicitly. We do this by naming each of the nodes and using those names to specify the edges.

```
take-and-put(c, k, l1, l2, p1, p2, x1, x2):
   task:      move-topmost-container(p1, p2)
   precond:   top(c, p1), on(c, x1),       ; true if p1 is not empty
              attached(p1, l1), belong(k, l1),   ; bind l1 and k
              attached(p2, l2), top(x2, p2)      ; bind l2 and x2
   subtasks:  ⟨take(k, l1, c, x1, p1), put(k, l2, c, x2, p2)⟩

recursive-move(p, q, c, x):
   task:      move-stack(p, q)
   precond:   top(c, p), on(c, x)    ; true if p is not empty
   subtasks:  ⟨move-topmost-container(p, q), move-stack(p, q)⟩
              ;; the second subtask recursively moves the rest of the stack

do-nothing(p, q)
   task:      move-stack(p, q)
   precond:   top(pallet, p)    ; true if p is empty
   subtasks:  ⟨⟩   ; no subtasks because we are done

move-each-twice()
   task:      move-all-stacks()
   precond:     ; no preconditions
   network:     ; move each stack twice:
              u1 = move-stack(p1a,p1b), u2 = move-stack(p1b,p1c),
              u3 = move-stack(p2a,p2b), u4 = move-stack(p2b,p2c),
```

$u_5 =$ move-stack(p3a,p3b), $u_6 =$ move-stack(p3b,p3c),
$\{(u_1, u_2), (u_3, u_4), (u_5, u_6)\}$

■

Definition 11.3 A method instance m *is applicable* in a state s if $\text{precond}^+(m) \subseteq s$ and $\text{precond}^-(m) \cap s = \emptyset$.

■

For planning, we will be interested in finding method instances that are both applicable in the current state and relevant for some task we are trying to accomplish. We now formalize what we mean by relevance.

Definition 11.4 Let t be a task and m be a method instance (which may be either ground or unground). If there is a substitution σ such that $\sigma(t) = \text{task}(m)$, then m is *relevant* for t, and the *decomposition* of t by m under σ is $\delta(t, m, \sigma) = \text{network}(m)$. If m is totally ordered, we may equivalently write $\delta(t, m, \sigma) = \text{subtasks}(m)$.

■

Example 11.4 Continuing Example 11.3, let t be the nonprimitive task move-stack (p1a, q), s be the state of the world shown in Figure 11.1(a), and m be the method instance recursive-move(p1a, p1b, c11, c12). Then m is applicable in s, is relevant for t under the substitution $\sigma = \{q \leftarrow \text{p1b}\}$, and decomposes t into:

$$\delta(t, m, \sigma) = \langle\text{move-topmost-container(p1a,p1b)move-stack(p1a,p1b)}\rangle$$

As shown in Figure 11.2, we can draw the decomposition as an AND-branch.[2] The next section discusses how to combine such branches into tree structures that represent derivations of plans.

■

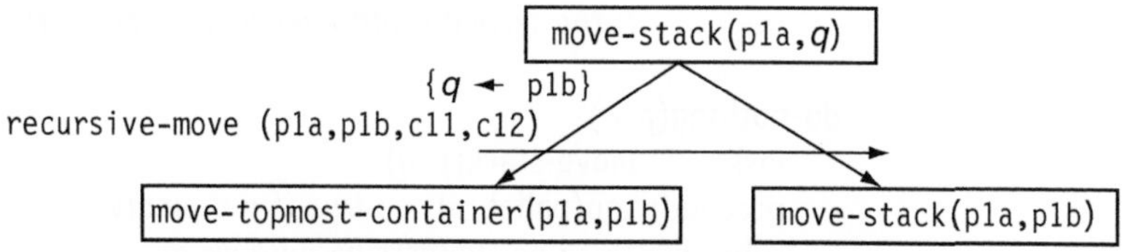

Figure 11.2 An AND-branch depicting the decomposition of the task move-stack(p1a,q) using the method instance recursive-move(p1a,p1b,c11,c12). The branch is labeled with the substitution and the name of the method instance. The rightward-pointing arrow represents the ordering of the subtasks.

2. For background material on AND/OR trees, see Appendix A.

When we use a method m to decompose a task t, usually this task will be part of a node u in a task network w, in which case we will get a new task network $\delta(w, u, m, \sigma)$ as defined in Definition 11.5. The formal definition of $\delta(w, u, m, \sigma)$ is somewhat complicated, but the intuitive idea is simple: u is removed from w, a copy of subtasks(m) is inserted into w in place of u, and every ordering constraint that formerly applied to u now applies to every node in the copy of subtasks(m).[3]

The complication arises from the need to *enforce* precond(m) in the new task network, i.e., the need to ensure that even after subsequent task decompositions, precond(m) still remains true at the correct place in the network. The point where precond(m) is supposed to be true is just before the first task in subtasks(m), and we need to insert additional ordering constraints into the task network to ensure that this will happen (see Example 11.17 later in this chapter). Because subtasks(m) is partially ordered, there may be more than one possible candidate for the first task in subtasks(m). Thus $\delta(w, u, m, \sigma)$ needs to be a set of alternative task networks: one for each possible candidate for the first task in subtasks(m).

Definition 11.5 Let $w = (U, E)$ be a task network, u be a node in w that has no predecessors in w, and m be a method that is relevant for t_u under some substitution σ. Let $succ(u)$ be the set of all immediate successors of u, i.e., $succ(u) = \{u' \in U \mid (u, u') \in E\}$. Let $succ_1(u)$ be the set of all immediate successors of u for which u is the *only* predecessor. Let (U', E') be the result of removing u and all edges that contain u. Let (U_m, E_m) be a copy of network(m). If (U_m, E_m) is nonempty, then the result of decomposing u in w by m under σ is this set of task networks:

$$\delta(w, u, m, \sigma) = \{(\sigma(U' \cup U_m), \sigma(E_v)) \mid v \in \text{subtasks}(m)\}$$

where

$$E_v = E_m \cup (U_m \times succ(u)) \cup \{(v, u') \mid u' \in succ_1(u)\}$$

Otherwise, $\delta(w, u, m, \sigma) = \{(\sigma(U'), \sigma(E'))\}$ ■

11.2.2 Problems and Solutions

We now discuss STN planning domains, planning problems, and solutions.

Definition 11.6 An *STN planning domain* is a pair

$$\mathcal{D} = (O, M), \tag{11.1}$$

3. The reason for using a copy of subtasks(m) rather than subtasks(m) itself is basically the same as the reason for repeatedly renaming variables in resolution theorem proving: to avoid potential problems if we want to apply m more than once.

where O is a set of operators and M is a set of methods. $\mathcal{D}$ is a *total-order planning domain* if every $m \in M$ is totally ordered. ■

Definition 11.7 An *STN planning problem* is a 4-tuple

$$\mathcal{P} = (s_0, w, O, M), \tag{11.2}$$

where s_0 is the initial state, w is a task network called the *initial task network*, and $\mathcal{D} = (O, M)$ is an STN planning domain. $\mathcal{P}$ is a *total-order planning problem* if w and $\mathcal{D}$ are totally ordered. ■

We now define what it means for a plan $\pi = \langle a_1, \ldots, a_n \rangle$ to be a solution for a planning problem $\mathcal{P} = (s_0, w, O, M)$, or equivalently, what it means for π to *accomplish* w. Intuitively, it means that there is a way to decompose w into π in such a way that π is executable and each decomposition is applicable in the appropriate state of the world. The formal definition is recursive and has three cases.

Definition 11.8 Let $\mathcal{P} = (s_0, w, O, M)$ be a planning problem. Here are the cases in which a plan $\pi = \langle a_1, \ldots, a_n \rangle$ is a *solution* for $\mathcal{P}$.

- **Case 1:** w is empty. Then π is a solution for $\mathcal{P}$ if π is empty (i.e., $n = 0$).
- **Case 2:** There is a primitive task node $u \in w$ that has no predecessors in w. Then π is a solution for $\mathcal{P}$ if a_1 is applicable to t_u in s_0 and the plan $\pi = \langle a_2, \ldots, a_n \rangle$ is a solution for this planning problem:

$$\mathcal{P}' = (\gamma(s_0, a_1), w - \{u\}, O, M)$$

  Intuitively, $\mathcal{P}'$ is the planning problem produced by executing the first action of π and removing the corresponding task node from w.
- **Case 3:** There is a nonprimitive task node $u \in w$ that has no predecessors in w. Suppose there is an instance m of some method in M such that m is relevant for t_u and applicable in s_0. Then π is a solution for $\mathcal{P}$ if there is a task network $w' \in \delta(w, u, m, \sigma)$ such that π is a solution for (s_0, w', O, M).

Note that if w is not totally ordered, then w may contain more than one node that has no predecessors. Thus, cases 2 and 3 are not necessarily mutually exclusive. ■

If π is a solution for (s_0, w, O, M), then for each task node $u \in U$ there is a *decomposition tree* whose leaf nodes are actions of π. The decomposition tree is composed of AND-branches like the ones in Figure 11.12. If u is primitive, then t_u is the name of an action in π, so the decomposition tree consists just of u. Otherwise, if u decomposes into a task network $\delta(w, u, m, \sigma)$ (see case 3 of Definition 11.8),

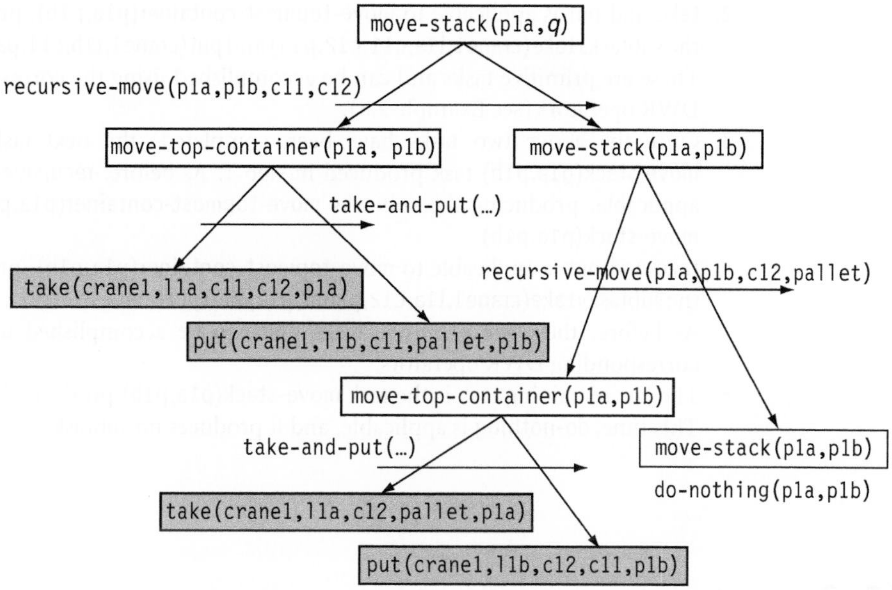

Figure 11.3 The decomposition tree for the task move-stack(p1a,p1b).The left-to-right arrows below each node indicate the ordering of the children. The plan for the task consists of the shaded nodes. No edges are shown for do-nothing(p1a,p1b) because it has no subtasks.

then the root of the decomposition tree is u, and its subtrees are the decomposition trees for the nodes of $\delta(w, u, m, \sigma)$.

Example 11.5 Let $\mathcal{P} = (s_0, w, O, M)$, where s_0 = the state shown in Figure 11.1 (a), $w = \langle$move-stack(p1a,p1b)$\rangle$, O is the usual set of DWR operators, and M is the set of methods given in Example 11.3. Then there is only one solution for $\mathcal{P}$, namely, the following plan:

$$\begin{aligned}\pi = \langle & \text{take(crane1, l1a, c11, c12, p1a)},\\ & \text{put(crane1, l1b, c11, pallet, p1b)},\\ & \text{take(crane1, l1a, c12, pallet, p1a)},\\ & \text{put(crane1, l1b, c12, c11, p1b)}\rangle\end{aligned}$$

The decomposition tree for move-stack(p1a,p1b) is shown in Figure 11.3. Here are the details of how it is produced:

1. Since p1 is nonempty in the initial state, do-nothing is not applicable. However, recursive-move is applicable, producing the subtasks move-topmost-container(p1a,p1b) and move-stack(p1a,p1b).

2. take-and-put is applicable to move-topmost-container(p1a,p1b), producing the subtasks take(crane1,l1a,c11,c12,p1a) and put(crane1,l1b,c11,pallet,p1b). These are primitive tasks and can be accomplished using the corresponding DWR operators (see Example 2.8).
3. Once the above two tasks have been completed, the next task is the move-stack(p1a,p1b) task produced in step 1. As before, recursive-move is applicable, producing the subtasks move-topmost-container(p1a,p1b) and move-stack(p1a,p1b).
4. take-and-put is applicable to move-topmost-container(p1a,p1b), producing the subtasks take(crane1,l1a,c12,pallet,p1a) and put(crane1,l1b,c12,c11,p1b). As before, these are primitive tasks that can be accomplished using the corresponding DWR operators.
5. The last remaining task is the task move-stack(p1a,p1b) produced in step 3. This time, do-nothing is applicable, and it produces no subtasks. ■

11.3 Total-Order STN Planning

Figure 11.4 shows the TFD (Total-order Forward Decomposition) procedure for solving total-order STN problems. The procedure is based directly on the definition of a solution for an STN planning problem; this makes it easy to show that it is sound and complete for all total-order STN planning problems (Exercises 11.6 and 11.7).

Example 11.6 All of the methods in Example 11.3 (see page 233) are totally ordered except for move-each-twice. If we omit this method, we have a total-order STN domain. In this planning domain, suppose we invoke TFD on the planning problem described in Example 11.13. Then one of its execution traces will carry out the steps described in that example, producing the decomposition tree shown in Figure 11.3. ■

Example 11.7 In order to use TFD to solve the planning problem shown in Figure 11.1, we need a totally ordered version of the move-each-twice method. We can write one by specifying an order in which to move the three stacks of containers.

```
move-each-twice()
    task:      move-all-stacks()
    precond:   ; no preconditions
    subtasks:  ⟨move-stack(p1a,p1b), move-stack(p1b,p1c),
                move-stack(p2a,p2b), move-stack(p2b,p2c),
                move-stack(p3a,p3b), move-stack(p3b,p3c)⟩
```
■

```
TFD(s, ⟨t1, ..., tk⟩, O, M)
   if k = 0 then return ⟨⟩ (i.e., the empty plan)
   if t1 is primitive then
      active ← {(a, σ) | a is a ground instance of an operator in O,
                         σ is a substitution such that a is relevant for σ(t1),
                         and a is applicable to s}
      if active = ∅ then return failure
      nondeterministically choose any (a, σ) ∈ active
      π ← TFD(γ(s, a), σ(⟨t2, ..., tk⟩), O, M)
      if π = failure then return failure
      else return a.π
   else if t1 is nonprimitive then
      active ← {m | m is a ground instance of a method in M,
                    σ is a substitution such that m is relevant for σ(t1),
                    and m is applicable to s}
      if active = ∅ then return failure
      nondeterministically choose any (m, σ) ∈ active
      w ← subtasks(m).σ(⟨t2, ..., tk⟩)
      return TFD(s, w, O, M)
```

Figure 11.4 The TFD procedure for total-order STN planning.

Here are some comparisons between TFD and the Forward-search and Backward-search procedures described in Chapter 4.

- Like Forward-search, TFD considers only actions whose preconditions are satisfied in the current state. However, like Backward-search, it considers only operators that are relevant for what it is trying to achieve. This combination can greatly increase the efficiency of the search.
- Like Forward-search, TFD generates actions in the same order in which they will be executed. Thus, each time it plans how to accomplish a task, it has already planned everything that comes before that task, so it knows the current state of the world. Section 11.7 discusses some ways to take advantage of this property.
- Just as Backward-search can create unnecessarily many ground instances of operators, TFD can create unnecessarily many ground instances of methods. Just as before, the cure is to "lift" the procedure, i.e., to modify it so that it only partially instantiates the methods. The resulting Lifted-TFD procedure (see Exercises 11.9 and 11.10) has some properties analogous to those of Lifted-backward-search: it works correctly even when the initial task list is not ground, and it has a smaller branching factor than TFD because it does not instantiate variables except when necessary.

11.4 Partial-Order STN Planning

In Example 11.6, it was easy to rewrite the planning domain of Example 11.3 (see page 233) as a total-order STN domain. However, not all planning domains can be rewritten so easily.

Example 11.8 Consider a DWR problem where we start with the initial state shown in Figure 11.5, and we want to use r1 to move the two containers to location loc2. It is easy (see Exercise 11.3) to write totally ordered methods that produce a decomposition tree like the one in Figure 11.6.

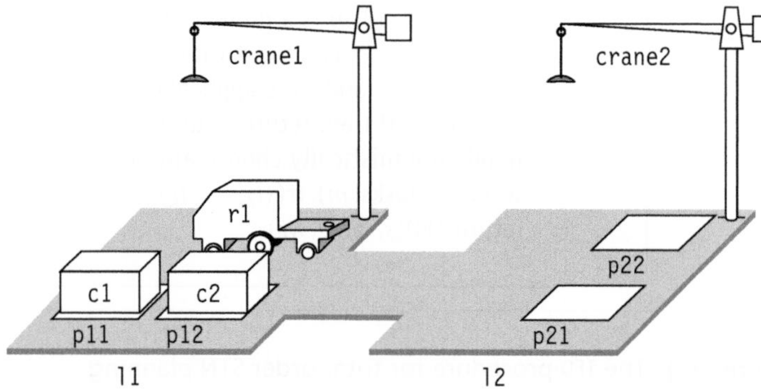

Figure 11.5 Initial state for a DWR problem in which two containers need to be moved from one location to another.

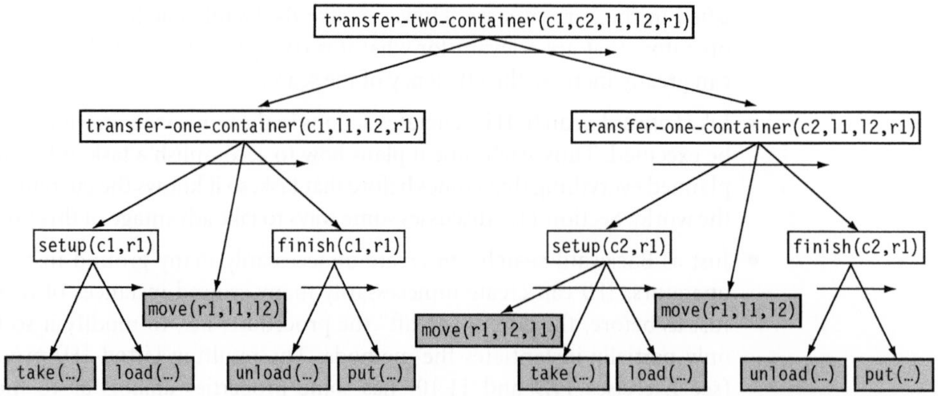

Figure 11.6 Decomposition tree for the DWR problem of Figure 11.5. To keep the figure simple, the labels on the branches have been omitted.

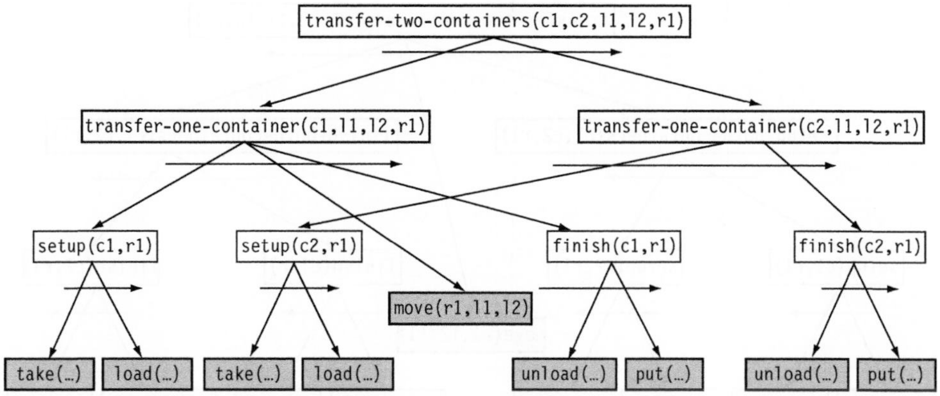

Figure 11.7 An interleaved decomposition tree for the case where r1 can carry more than one container at once. The subtasks of the root are unordered, and their subtasks are interleaved. Decomposition trees like this one can occur in a partial-order STN domain but not in a total-order one.

Next, consider a modified version of the problem in which r1 can carry many containers at once. In this case, we would probably prefer to get a solution tree like the one in Figure 11.7, in which the plans for the two containers are interleaved so that the robot can move both containers at once. Here are some methods for doing that.

transfer2(c_1, c_2, l_1, l_2, r) *; method to transfer c_1 and c_2*
  task: transfer-two-containers(c_1, c_2, l_1, l_2, r)
  precond: *; none*
  subtasks: ⟨transfer-one-container(c_1, l_1, l_2, r),
  transfer-one-container(c_2, l_1, l_2, r)⟩

transfer1(c, l_1, l_2, r) *; method to transfer c*
  task: transfer-one-container(c, l_1, l_2, r)
  precond: *; none*
  network: u_1 = setup(c, r), u_2 = move-robot(r, l_1, l_2),
  u_3 = finish(c,r), $\{(u_1, u_2), (u_2, u_3)\}$

move1(r, l_1, l_2) *; method to move r if it is not at l_2*
  task: move-robot(l_1, l_2)
  precond: at(r, l_1)
  subtasks: ⟨move(r, l_1, l_2)⟩

move0(r, l_1, l_2) *; method to do nothing if r is already at l_2*
  task: u_0 = move-robot(l_1, l_2)
  precond: at(r, l_2)
  subtasks: ⟨⟩ *; i.e., no subtasks*

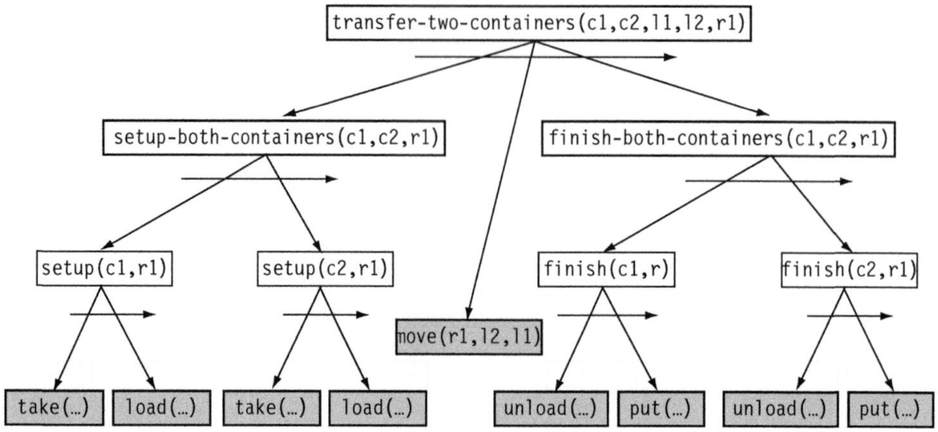

Figure 11.8 A noninterleaved decomposition tree for the case where r1 can carry two containers side by side.

do-setup(c, d, k, l, p, r) *; method to prepare for moving a container*
task: setup(c, r)
precond: on(c, d), in(c, p), belong(k, l), *;attached(p,l), at (r,l)*
network: $u_1 =$ take(k, l, c, d, p), $u_2 =$ load(k, l, c, r), $\{(u_1, u_2)\}$

unload-robot(c, d, k, l, p, r) *; method to finish after moving a container*
task: finish(c, r)
precond: attached(p, l), loaded(r,c), top(d, p), belong(k, l), at (r,l)
network: $u_1 =$ unload(k, l, c, r), $u_2 =$ put(k, l, c, d, p), $\{(u_1, u_2)\}$

Not all of these methods are totally ordered. Furthermore, the decomposition tree in Figure 11.7 cannot be produced by a set of totally ordered methods because the total-ordering constraints would prevent subtasks of different tasks from being interleaved. With totally ordered methods the best one could do would be to write methods that generate a noninterleaved decomposition tree such as the one in Figure 11.8 (see Exercise 11.4). ■

Example 11.9 Here is an example to illustrate the need for the set of edges $\{(v, u') \mid u' \in succ_1(u)\}$ in Definition 11.5 (see page 235).

In the decomposition tree shown in Figure 11.7, consider how to use the transfer1 method from the previous example to decompose the task transfer-one-container(c2,l1,l2,r1) into the subtasks setup(c2,r1) and finish(c2,r1). The transfer1 method has no preconditions—but if it did, they would need to be evaluated in the same state of the world as the preconditions of the first action in the subtree rooted at transfer1(c2). The additional edges inserted by δ provide ordering constraints to guarantee that this will occur. ■

```
PFD(s, w, O, M)
    if w = ∅ then return the empty plan
    nondeterministically choose any u ∈ w that has no predecessors in w
    if t_u is a primitive task then
        active ← {(a, σ) | a is a ground instance of an operator in O,
                           σ is a substitution such that name(a) = σ(t_u),
                           and a is applicable to s}
        if active = ∅ then return failure
        nondeterministically choose any (a, σ) ∈ active
        π ← PFD(γ(s, a), σ(w − {u}), O, M)
        if π = failure then return failure
        else return a.π
    else
        active ← {(m, σ) | m is a ground instance of a method in M,
                         σ is a substitution such that name(m) = σ(t_u),
                         and m is applicable to s}
        if active = ∅ then return failure
        nondeterministically choose any (m, σ) ∈ active
        nondeterministically choose any task network w' ∈ δ(w, u, m, σ)
        return(PFD(s, w', O, M)
```

Figure 11.9 The PFD procedure for STN planning.

Figure 11.9 shows the PFD (Partial-order Forward Decomposition) procedure. PFD is a generalization of the TFD procedure so that STN planning problems do not have to be total-order problems. PFD is a direct implementation of the definition of a solution to an STN planning problem, so it is not hard to show that it is sound and complete.

Like TFD, PFD can be lifted to produce a Lifted-PFD procedure (see Exercise 11.18) that will search a smaller search space.

Example 11.10 Here is how to use the methods listed previously to produce the decompositions shown in Figure 11.7. First, start with the task network $w_1 = (\{u\}, \emptyset)$, where t_u = transfer-two-containers(c1,c2,l1,l2,r1). Next, apply the method transfer2 to u, to produce the task network $w_2 = (\{u_1, u_2\}, \emptyset)$, where t_{u_1} = transfer-one-container(c1,l1,l2,r1) and t_{u_2} = transfer-one-container(c2,l1,l2,r1). Next, apply the method transfer1 to u_1 to produce the task network $w_3 = (\{u_2, u_3, u_4, u_5\}, \{(u_3, u_4), (u_4, u_5)\})$, where:

$$t_{u_3} = \text{setup(c1,r1)}$$

$$t_{u_4} = \text{move(r1,l1,l2)}$$

$$t_{u_5} = \text{finish(c1,r1)}$$

These are the first two decompositions. The rest of the decomposition tree can be produced in a similar manner. ■

11.5 HTN Planning

In STN planning, we associated two kinds of constraints with a method: ordering constraints and preconditions. We represented ordering constraints explicitly in the task network as edges of a digraph. We did not keep track of these preconditions explicitly in the task network: instead, we *enforced* the preconditions by constructing task networks that were guaranteed to satisfy them. This was the purpose of the set of edges $\{(v, u') \mid u' \in succ_1(u)\}$ in Definition 11.5 (see page 235).

Probably the only kind of planning procedure that is feasible for use with Definition 11.5 is a forward-decomposition procedure such as TFD or PFD. However, there are cases where one may not want to use a forward-decomposition procedure. HTN planning is a generalization of STN planning that gives the planning procedure more freedom about how to construct the task networks.

In order to provide this freedom, a bookkeeping mechanism is needed to represent constraints that the planning algorithm has not yet enforced. The bookkeeping is done by representing the unenforced constraints explicitly in the task network.

11.5.1 Task Networks

The HTN-planning definition of a task network generalizes the definition used in STN planning.

Definition 11.9 A *task network* is a pair $w = (U, C)$, where U is a set of task nodes and C is a set of constraints as described in the text.[4] ■

Each constraint in C specifies a requirement that must be satisfied by every plan that is a solution to a planning problem. Here is some notation that will be useful in describing the constraints. Let π be a solution for w, $U' \subseteq U$ be a set of task nodes in w, and A be the set of all actions $a_i \in \pi$ such that in π's decomposition tree, a_i is a descendant of a node in U'. Then first(U', π) is the action $a_i \in A$ that occurs first, i.e., $i \leq j$ for every $a_j \in A$; and last(U', π) is the action $a_k \in A$ that occurs last, i.e., $k \geq j$ for every $a_j \in A$.

---

4. It is straightforward to extend this definition to allow C to be a Boolean combination of constraints, but we have restricted it to be a conjunct in order to simplify the presentation.

Here are the kinds of constraints we will consider.[5]

- A *precedence constraint* is an expression of the form $u \prec v$, where u and v are task nodes. Its meaning is identical to the meaning of the edge (u, v) in STN planning: it says that in every solution π for $\mathcal{P}$, the action last$(\{u\}, \pi)$ must precede the action first$(\{v\}, \pi)$. For example, if $t_u =$ move(r2,l2,l3) and $t_v =$ move(r1,l1,l2), then the constraint $u \prec v$ says that r2 must be moved from l2 to l3 before r1 is moved from l1 to l2.
- A *before-constraint* is a generalization of the notion of a precondition in STN planning. It is a constraint of the form before(U', l), where $U' \subseteq U$ is a set of task nodes and l is a literal. It says that in any solution π for $\mathcal{P}$, the literal l must be true in the state that occurs just before first(U', π). For example, suppose u is a task node for which $t_u =$ move(r2,l2,l3). Then the constraint

$$\text{before}(\{u\}, \text{at}(r2, l2))$$

  says that r2 must be at l2 just before we move it from l2 to l3.
- An *after-constraint* has the form after(U', l). It is like a before-constraint except that it says l must be true in the state that occurs just after last(U', π).
- A *between-constraint* has the form between(U', U'', l). It says that the literal l must be true in the state just after last(U', π), the state just before first(U'', π), and all of the states in between.

11.5.2 HTN Methods

The definition of a method in HTN planning generalizes the definition used in STN planning.

Definition 11.10 An *HTN method* is a 4-tuple

$$m = (\text{name}(m), \text{task}(m), \text{subtasks}(m), \text{constr}(m))$$

in which the elements are described as follows.

- name(m) is an expression of the form $n(x_1, \ldots, x_k)$, where n is a unique method symbol (i.e., no two methods in the planning domain can have the same method symbol), and $x_1, \ldots, x_k$ are all of the variable symbols that occur anywhere in m.

5. These are merely suggestive of the kinds of constraints that an HTN planner may handle. Some planners do not handle all of the constraints listed here. Others handle various generalizations of the constraints, such as before(first(U'), l) or before(last(U'), l) to say that l must hold before the first or last action in A, or they allow additional kinds of constraints, such as the binding constraints described in Chapter 5.

- task(m) is a nonprimitive task.
- (subtasks(m), constr(m)) is a task network. ■

Suppose that $w = (U, C)$ is a task network, $u \in U$ is a task node, t_u is its task, m is an instance of a method in M, and task$(m) = t_u$. Then m *decomposes* u into subtasks(m'), producing the task network

$$\delta(w, u, m) = ((U - \{u\}) \cup \text{subtasks}(m'), C' \cup \text{constr}(m')),$$

where C' is the following modified version of C.

- For every precedence constraint that contains u, replace it with precedence constraints containing the nodes of subtasks(m'). For example, if subtasks$(m') = \{u_1, u_2\}$, then we would replace the constraint $u \prec v$ with the constraints $u_1 \prec v$ and $u_2 \prec v$.
- For every before-, after-, or between-constraint in which there is a set of task nodes U' that contains u, replace U' with $(U' - \{u\}) \cup$ subtasks(m'). For example, if subtasks$(m') = \{u_1, u_2\}$, then we would replace the constraint before$(\{u, v\}, l)$ with the constraint before$(\{u_1, u_2, v\}, l)$.

Example 11.11 Here is a rewrite of the STN methods of Example 11.8 (see page 240) as HTN methods. In each method's task and subtask lists, each u_i is a label for a task; it is used to refer to the task in the method's constraint list.

transfer2(c_1, c_2, l_1, l_2, r) *;; method to move c_1 and c_2 from pile p1 to pile p2*
task: transfer-two-containers(c_1, c_2, l_1, l_2, r)
subtasks: u_1 = transfer-one-container(c_1, l_1, l_2, r),
u_2 = transfer-one-container(c_2, l_1, l_2, r)
constr: $u_1 \prec u_2$

transfer1(c, l_1, l_2, R) *;; method to transfer c*
task: transfer-one-container(c, l_1, l_2, r)
subtasks: u_1 = setup(c, r), u_2 = move-robot(r, l_1, l_2), u_3 = finish(c, r)
constr: $u_1 \prec u_2$, $u_2 \prec u_3$

move1(r, l_1, l_2) *;; method to move r if it is not at l_2*
task: move-robot(l_1, l_2)
subtasks: u_1 = move(r, l_1, l_2)
constr: before$(\{u_1\}$, at$(r, l_1))$

move0(r, l_1, l_2) *;; method to do nothing if r is already at l_2*
task: u_0 = move-robot(l_1, l_2)
subtasks: *;; no subtasks*
constr: before$(\{u_0\}$, at$(r_1, l_2))$

do-setup(c, d, k, l, p, r) ;; *method to prepare for moving a container*
task: setup(c, r)
subtasks: $u_1 =$ take(k, l, c, d, p), $u_2 =$ load(k, l, c, r)
constr: $u_1 \prec u_2$, before$(\{u_1\}$, on$(c, d))$, before$(\{u_1\}$, attached$(p, l))$,
before$(\{u_1\}$, in$(c, p))$, before$(\{u_1\}$, belong(k, l), before$(\{u_1\})$, at$(r, l))$

unload-robot(c, d, k, l, p, r) ;; *method to finish after moving a container*
task: finish(c, r)
subtasks: $u_1 =$ unload(k, l, c, r), $u_2 =$ put(k, l, c, d, p)
constr: $u_1 \prec u_2$, before$(\{u_1\}$, attached$(p, l))$, before$(\{u_1\}$, loaded$(r, c))$,
before $(\{u_1\}$, top$(d, p))$ before$(\{u_1\})$, belong(k, l),
before$(\{u_1\}$, at$(r, l))$

Here is how to use the above methods to produce the decompositions shown in Figure 11.7. First, start with a task network $w_1 = (\{u\}, \emptyset)$, where u is a node such that $t_u =$ transfer-two-containers(c1,c2,l1,l2,r1). Next, apply the method transfer2 to u to produce a task network $w_2 = (\{u_1, u_2\}, \emptyset)$ such that $t_{u_1} =$ transfer-one-container(c1,l1,l2,r1) and $t_{u_2} =$ transfer-one-container(c2). Next, apply the instance transfer1 to u_1 to produce a task network $w_3 = (\{u_2, u_3, u_4, u_5\}, C_3)$ such that:

$$t_{u_3} = \text{setup(c1)}$$
$$t_{u_4} = \text{get-r1-to-p2()}$$
$$t_{u_5} = \text{finish(c1)}$$
$$C_3 = \{u_3 \prec u_4,\ u_4 \prec u_5\}$$

These are the first two decompositions. The rest of the decomposition tree can be produced in a similar manner. ■

11.5.3 HTN Problems and Solutions

HTN planning domains are identical to STN planning domains except that they use HTN methods.

Definition 11.11 An *HTN planning domain* is a pair

$$\mathcal{D} = (O, M),$$

and an *HTN planning problem* is a 4-tuple

$$\mathcal{P} = (s_0, w, O, M),$$

where s_0 is the initial state, w is the initial task network, O is a set of operators, and M is a set of HTN methods. ■

We now define what it means for a plan π to be a solution for $\mathcal{P}$. There are two cases, depending on whether w is primitive or nonprimitive.

Definition 11.12 If $w = (U, C)$ is primitive, then a plan $\pi = \langle a_1, a_2, \ldots, a_k \rangle$ is a *solution* for $\mathcal{P}$ if there is a ground instance (U', C') of (U, C) and a total ordering $\langle u_1, u_2, \ldots, u_k \rangle$ of the nodes of U' such that all of the following conditions hold.

- The actions in π are the ones named by the nodes $u_1, u_2, \ldots, u_k$, i.e., $\text{name}(a_i) = t_{u_i}$ for $i = 1, \ldots, k$.
- The plan π is executable in the state s_0.
- The total ordering $\langle u_1, u_2, \ldots, u_k \rangle$ satisfies the precedence constraints in C', i.e., C' contains no precedence constraint $u_i \prec u_j$ such that $j \leq i$.
- For every constraint before(U', l) in C', l holds in the state s_{i-1} that immediately precedes the action a_i, where a_i is the action named by the first node of U' (i.e., the node $u_i \in U'$ that comes earliest in the total ordering $\langle u_1, u_2, \ldots, u_k \rangle$).
- For every constraint after(U', l) in C', l holds in the state s_j produced by the action a_j, where a_j is the action named by the last node of U' (i.e., the node $u_j \in U'$ that comes latest in the total ordering $\langle u_1, u_2, \ldots, u_k \rangle$).
- For every constraint between(U', U'', l) in C', l holds in every state that comes between a_i and a_j, where a_i is the action named by the last node of U', and a_j is the action named by the first node of U''.

If $w = (U, C)$ is nonprimitive (i.e., at least one task in U is nonprimitive), then π is a *solution* for $\mathcal{P}$ if there is a sequence of task decompositions that can be applied to w to produce a primitive task network w' such that π is a solution for w'. In this case, the *decomposition tree* for π is the tree structure corresponding to these task decompositions. ■

Example 11.12 Let $\mathcal{P} = (s_0, (\{u\}, \emptyset), O, M)$, where s_0 is the state shown in Figure 11.5, u is a task node such that $t_u =$ transfer-two-containers(c1,c2), O is the usual set of DWR operators, and M is the set of methods given in Example 11.11. Then the solution plan and its decomposition tree are the same as in Example 11.5 (see page 237). ■

11.5.4 Planning Procedures

HTN planning procedures must both instantiate operators and decompose tasks. Because there are several different ways to do both of these things, the the number of different possible HTN planning procedures is quite large. Abstract-HTN, shown in Figure 11.10, is an abstract procedure that includes many (but not necessarily

```
Abstract-HTN(s, U, C, O, M)
   if (U, C) can be shown to have no solution
      then return failure
   else if U is primitive then
      if (U, C) has a solution then
         nondeterministically let π be any such solution
         return π
      else return failure
   else
      choose a nonprimitive task node u ∈ U
      active ← {m ∈ M | task(m) is unifiable with t_u}
      if active ≠ ∅ then
         nondeterministically choose any m ∈ active
         σ ← an mgu for m and t_u that renames all variables of m
         (U', C') ← δ(σ(U, C), σ(u), σ(m))
         (U', C') ← apply-critic(U', C') ;; this line is optional
         return Abstract-HTN(s, U', C', O, M)
      else return failure
```

Figure 11.10 The Abstract-HTN procedure. An mgu is a most-general unifer (see Appendix B).

all) of them. For example, Abstract-HTN is general enough to accommodate HTN versions of both TFD and PFD.

When Abstract-HTN chooses a nonprimitive task $u \in U$, this is not a nondeterministic choice (i.e., it is not a backtracking point) because every task in U must eventually be decomposed before we can find a solution. The size of the decomposition tree will differ depending on the order in which the tasks are decomposed. Because the smallest possible decomposition tree can be exponentially smaller than the biggest one [517], a good HTN planning procedure will try to choose an ordering that generates a small decomposition tree rather than a large one. As an example, the approach used in TFD and PFD is to decompose the tasks in the same order that they will later be executed.

As written, Abstract-HTN is a "lifted" procedure: when it computes *active*, it does not fully instantiate a method unless it absolutely needs to. We could just as easily have written the procedure to use ground instances of the methods, but the lifted version will usually generate a much smaller search space.

The assignment $(U', C') \leftarrow$ apply-critic(U', C') formalizes the notion of a *critic*, which is a function that can make an arbitrary modification to a task network. Critics can be useful for performing application-specific computations that would be difficult to represent within the planning formalism itself—for example, in a manufacturing planning domain, a critic might invoke a computational package that determines an appropriate trajectory for a manufacturing tool. However, critics must be written carefully if one wants to preserve soundness and completeness. Formally, the Abstract-HTN procedure will be sound if every solution to apply-critic(U', C') is also a solution to (U', C'), and it will be complete if apply-critic(U', C') has at least one solution whenever (U', C') has at least one solution.

11.6 Comparisons

We now compare HTN planning to STN planning and compare both to the control-rule techniques described in Chapter 10. The comparisons involve the expressivity of the formalisms and the computational complexity of the problems they can express.

11.6.1 HTN Planning versus STN Planning

STN planning (and thus HTN planning because it is a generalization of STN planning) can be used to encode undecidable problems. In fact, undecidable problems can even be encoded as STN planning problems that contain no variable symbols. We will skip the details, but the proof involves expressing the problem of determining whether two context-free languages have a nonempty intersection—a problem that is known to be undecidable—as an STN planning problem.

From the above, it follows that STN and HTN planning are more expressive than classical planning because the latter cannot express undecidable problems. Furthermore, STN and HTN planning are more expressive than classical planning even if we require that the tasks in every task network be totally ordered. The details of the proof depend on the theory of formal languages [175]. However, the basic idea is that the set of solutions for a classical planning problem is a regular language, the set of solution for a total-order STN planning problem is a context-free language, and there are context-free languages that are not regular languages.

Example 11.13 Here is a total-order STN planning problem in which the set of solutions is a context-free language that is not a regular language. The initial state is empty, the initial task list is ⟨task1()⟩, and the methods and operators are as follows.

method1():
task: task1()
precond: *(no preconditions)*
subtasks: op1(), task1(), op2()

method2():
task: task1()
precond: *(no preconditions)*
subtasks: *(no subtasks)*

```
op1():
    precond: (no preconditions)
    effects: (no effects)

op2():
    precond: (no preconditions)
    effects: (no effects)
```

The solutions to this problem are as follows:

$$\pi_0 = \langle\rangle$$
$$\pi_1 = \langle \texttt{op1()}, \texttt{op2()} \rangle$$
$$\pi_2 = \langle \texttt{op1()}, \texttt{op1()}, \texttt{op2()}, \texttt{op2()} \rangle$$
$$\pi_3 = \langle \texttt{op1()}, \texttt{op1()}, \texttt{op1()}, \texttt{op2()}, \texttt{op2()}, \texttt{op2()} \rangle$$
$$\ldots$$

■

Example 11.13 depends on the ability of methods (such as method1) to recursively invoke each other or themselves an unlimited number of times. It is possible to formulate an "acyclicity" restriction to ensure that there is a finite bound on the maximum number of times such recursions can occur. However, even with this restriction, total-order STN (and thus HTN) planning is more expressive than classical planning. Given an acyclic total-order STN planning problem, it is possible to rewrite it as an equivalent classical planning problem—but in the worst case, the statement of the classical planning problem will be exponentially larger than the statement of the total-order STN planning problem.

If we restrict total-order STN planning even further, by requiring the initial task list and each method's subtask list to be "regular" (i.e., the list can contain at most only one nonprimitive task, and this task must be at the very end of the list), then this makes the expressive power the same as that of classical planning. Table 11.1 gives the complexity of STN planning in this and several other cases.

11.6.2 HTN Methods versus Control Rules

TFD and PFD are similar in several respects to the STL-plan procedure described in Chapter 10. In both cases, planning is done forward from the initial state, and control knowledge is used to restrict which operators to apply. However, there is a difference in how the control knowledge is represented.

Consider a state space that begins with the initial state and contains all possible sequences of operator applications. STL-plan's rules tell it what parts of this state space to avoid; it can explore any part of the search space that avoids the "bad" states and their successors. In contrast, TFD's and PFD's HTN methods tell them which

Table 11.1 Complexity of PLAN-EXISTENCE for HTN planning.

Restrictions on nonprimitive tasks	*Must the HTNs be totally ordered?*	*Are variables allowed?* No	*Are variables allowed?* Yes
None	No	Undecidable[a]	Undecidable[a,b]
	Yes	In EXPTIME; PSPACE-hard	in DEXPTIME;[d] EXPSPACE-hard
"Regularity" (≤ 1 nonprimitive task, which must follow all primitive tasks)	Does not matter	PSPACE-complete	EXPSPACE-complete[c]
No nonprimitive tasks	No	NP-complete	NP-complete
	Yes	Polynomial time	NP-complete

[a] Decidable if we impose acyclicity restrictions.
[b] Undecidable even when the planning domain is fixed in advance.
[c] In PSPACE when the planning domain is fixed in advance, and PSPACE-complete for some fixed planning domains.
[d] DEXPTIME means double-exponential time.

parts of this state space to explore. They can apply only actions that are reachable using their HTN methods.

Without the extensions discussed in Sections 10.5, control-rule planning is restricted to solving just classical planning problems. In this case, Section 11.6 shows that HTN planning has more expressive power than control-rule planning. However, several of the extensions in Section 10.5 are used in nearly all control-rule planners, and analogous extensions (see Section 11.7) are used in most HTN planners. With these extensions, both formalisms are capable of representing undecidable problems.

It is hard to say which type of control knowledge (methods or control rules) is more effective. Most researchers would probably agree that both types are useful in different situations and that combining them is a useful topic for future research.

11.7 Extensions

Section 2.4 discussed how to augment classical planning languages to incorporate extensions such as axioms, function symbols, and attached procedures. Both these and several other kinds of extensions have been widely used in HTN planning procedures.

11.7.1 Extensions from Chapter 2

It is especially easy to incorporate the extensions into the TFD and PFD procedures. Since these procedures both plan forward from the initial state, they both know the complete current state of the world at each step of the planning process. This makes it easy to do arbitrary computations involving the current state, including complicated numeric computations, axiomatic inference, and calls to domain-specific software packages such as engineering modelers, database systems, and probabilistic reasoners. Here is a discussion of some of the issues involved.

Function Symbols. If we allow the planning language to contain function symbols, then the arguments of an atom or task are no longer restricted to being constant symbols and variable symbols. Instead, they may be arbitrarily complicated terms. This causes a problem in a planning procedure like TFD and PFD that works with ground instances of operators and methods because there may be infinitely many ground method instances or ground operator instances that are applicable to a given state of the world. In order to make those sets finite, the solution is to use the lifted procedures, Lifted-TFD and Lifted-PFD.

In the lifted versions, the current state still will be completely ground; thus using the lifted versions does not make it any more difficult to incorporate the other extensions mentioned earlier.

Axioms. To incorporate axiomatic inference, we will need to use a theorem prover as a subroutine of the planning procedure. The easiest approach is to restrict the axioms to be Horn clauses and use a Horn-clause theorem prover. If an operator, method, or axiom has a positive precondition p, then we can take p to be true iff p can be proved in the current state s. If we also want to allow negative preconditions, then there is a question about what it means for a condition to be satisfied by a state because there is more than one possible semantics for what logical entailment might mean [500]. However, if we restrict the set of Horn-clause axioms to be a stratified logic program, then the two major semantics for logical entailment agree with each other [46], and in this case the inference procedure will still be sound and complete.

Attached Procedures. We can modify the precondition evaluation algorithm (which, if we have incorporated axiomatic inference, would be the Horn-clause theorem prover) to recognize that certain terms or predicate symbols are to be evaluated by using attached procedures rather than by using the normal theorem-proving mechanism. In the most general case, such an extension would make it impossible to prove soundness and completeness. However, let us consider two of the main situations in which we might want to use attached procedures: (1) to provide a way to do numeric computations, and (2) to allow queries to external information sources. Provided that certain restrictions are satisfied, both of these things are possible to accomplish in a way that is both sound and complete [157].

Example 11.14 If we extend STN planning to incorporate the extensions described previously, then we can write methods, operators, and axioms that encode the container-stacking procedure of Section 4.5.

In the HTN representation of a container-stacking problem (O, s_0, g), we will want the initial task to be the task of achieving a state in which all of the conditions in g are simultaneously true. For this purpose, we will need to represent a list of the conditions in g. We will use a constant symbol nil to represent the empty list and a binary function symbol cons such that cons(a, l) represents the list in which a is the first element and l is a list of the remaining elements.[6] For example, the list ⟨a, b, c⟩ will be represented as cons(a, cons(b, cons(c, nil))). The Horn-clause axioms for list manipulation are as follows.

```
;; x is a member of any list whose head is x
member(x,cons(x, y))

;; if x is a member of v, then x is a member of cons(u, v)
member(x,cons(u, v)) :- member(x, v)

;; g is the result of removing a from the front of the list cons(a, g)
remove(a,cons(a, g),g)

;; if removing a from g leaves h, then removing a from cons(b, g)
   leaves cons(b, h)
remove(a,cons(b, g),cons(b, h)) :- remove(a, g, h)
```

Here are some axioms to describe situations in which containers need to be moved. All of the above are Horn clauses except for the axiom for different.

```
;; x needs to be moved if there's a goal saying it should be elsewhere
need-to-move(x, h) :- on(x, y), member(on(x, z),h), different(y, z)

;; x needs to be moved if something else should be where x is
need-to-move(x, h) :- on(x, z), member(on(y, z),h), different(x, y)

;; x needs to be moved if x is on y and y needs to be moved
need-to-move(x, h) :- on(x, y), need-to-move(y, h)

same(x, x)                          ;; any term is the same as itself
different(x, y) :- ¬same(x, y)     ;; two terms are different if they are not
   the same

;; find a goal on(x, y) that we can achieve immediately
can-achieve(on(x, y),h, r) :- remove(on(x, y),h, r), top(x, p), top(y, q),
                              ¬need-to-move(y, r)

;; return true if we can proceed, false if we need to move a container out of
   the way
can-proceed(h) :- can-achieve(on(x, y),h, r)
```

The initial task list will contain a single task h of the form cons(a_1,cons(a_2,...)), where $a_1, a_2, \ldots$ are terms that are syntactically identical to the atoms in the goal g. Here are the methods for accomplishing h.

6. The names cons and nil are inspired, of course, by the Lisp programming language.

```
transfer1(h, r, c, d, e, p, q, k, l) ;; method to achieve a goal on(c, d) by moving c
task:      achieve-goals(h)
precond:   can-achieve(on(c, d),h, r), need-to-move(c, h),
subtasks:  take(k, l, c, e, p), put(k, l, c, d, q),  ;; move c to its final position
           achieve-goals(r)                          ;; achieve the rest of the goals

move0(h, c, d, r)           ;; method for when a goal on(c, d) is already true
task:      achieve-goals(h)
precond:   can-achieve(on(c, d),h, r), ¬need-to-move(c, h)
subtasks:  achieve-goals(r)      ;; just achieve the rest of the goals

move-out-of-way(h, c, d, p, q, k, l)  ;; method to move c out of the way
task:      achieve-goals(h)
precond:   ¬can-proceed(h), need-to-move(c, h),   ;; there's an impasse
           top(c, p), ¬on(c,pallet),               ;; moving c will resolve it
subtasks:  take(k, l, c, d, p), put(k, l, c, pallet, q),  ;; move c to an empty pile q
           achieve-goals(h)                        ;; achieve the remaining goals

do-nothing()                ;; the "base case," i.e., no goals to achieve
task:      achieve-goals(nil)
precond:   ;; no preconditions
subtasks:  ;; no subtasks
```

■

11.7.2 Additional Extensions

High-Level Effects. Some HTN planners allow the user to declare in the planner's domain description that various nonprimitive tasks, or the methods for those tasks, will achieve various effects. Such planners can use these high-level effects to establish preconditions and can prune the partial plan if a high-level effect threatens a precondition. In practical applications, declarations of high-level effects can be useful for improving the efficiency of planning—but we did not include them in our formal model because their semantics can be defined in several ways, some of which can make it difficult to ensure soundness and completeness.

External Preconditions. Suppose that to decompose some task t, we decide to use some method m. Furthermore, suppose that there is some condition c such that regardless of what subplan we produce below m, at least one action in the subplan will require c as a precondition and the subplan will contain no action that achieves c. In this case, in order for the subplan to appear as part of a solution plan π, the precondition c must somehow be achieved elsewhere in π. Thus, we say that the precondition c is *external* to the method m. Some HTN planning systems allow users to state explicitly in the planner's domain description that certain conditions are external. Also, in some cases it is possible to detect external preconditions (even when they have not been declared) by analyzing the planning domain.

Time. It is possible to generalize PFD and Abstract-HTN to do certain kinds of temporal planning, e.g., to deal with actions that have time durations and may overlap with each other. The details are beyond the scope of this chapter, but some references are given in Section 11.19.

Planning Graphs. This extension is different from the others because it is an extension to the planning algorithm but not the HTN representation: it is possible to modify Abstract-HTN to make use of planning graphs like those described in Chapter 6. The modified algorithm generates both a decomposition tree and a planning graph. The size of the planning graph is reduced by generating only those actions that match tasks in the decomposition tree, and the size of the decomposition tree is reduced by decomposing a task only if the planning graph can accomplish all of its predecessors. In empirical studies [370], an implementation of such an algorithm performed significantly better than an implementation of Abstract-HTN.

11.8 Extended Goals

HTN planning can easily accommodate (or be extended to accomodate) certain kinds of extended goals. Here are some examples:

- Consider a DWR domain in which there is some location bad-loc to which we never want our robots to move. To express this as a classical planning domain, it is necessary to add an additional precondition $\neg$ at(r, bad-loc) to the move operator. In HTN planning, such a change to the move operator is unnecessary. We will never put the move operator into a plan unless it appears in the subtasks of one or more methods—thus if we prefer, we can instead put the precondition into the methods that call the move operator rather than into the move operator itself.
- Suppose that r1 begins at location loc1 in the initial state, and we want r1 to go from loc1 to loc2 back exactly twice. In Section 2.4.8, we said that this kind of problem cannot be expressed as a classical planning problem. It can be expressed as an STN planning problem in which the initial task network is ⟨solve-problem()⟩ and the only method relevant for this task is the following.

```
two-round-trips()
    task:      solve-problem()
    precond:   ;;no preconditions
    subtasks:  move(r1,loc1,loc2), move(r1,loc2,loc1),
               move(r1,loc1,loc2), move(r1,loc2,loc1)
```

- Suppose we want to require that every solution reach the goal in five actions or fewer. In HTN planning without any extensions, this can be ensured in a domain-specific way by limiting the number of actions that each method can generate. For example, the two-round-trips method of the previous scenario will never generate a plan of more than four actions. However, this approach is less satisfying than the domain-independent control rule that can be written in STL planning (see Section 10.6). A more general solution would be to extend the planning language to include the predicate symbols, function symbols, and attached procedures needed to perform integer arithmetic. If we do this, then we can put into the initial state the atom count(0) and modify every operator to have the preconditions count(i) and $i \leq 5$. This is basically the same approach that we proposed for classical planning in Section 2.4.8.

- Suppose we want to require that the number of times r1 visits loc1 must be at least three times the number of times it visits loc2. Such a requirement cannot be represented directly in an STL planning problem. However, it can be represented using the same approach that we described for classical planning in Section2.4.8: extend HTN planning by introducing the predicate symbols, function symbols, and attached procedures needed to perform integer arithmetic, modify the move operator to maintain atoms in the current state that represent the number of times we visit each location, and modify the goal to include the required ratio of visits.

Two of the above examples required extending HTN planning to accommodate function symbols and integer arithmetic. The key is to ensure that all of the variables of an attached procedure are bound at the time the procedure is called. This is easy to accomplish in planning algorithms such as TFD and PFD that plan forward from the initial state.

Like STL planning (see Example 10.6), HTN planning would have difficulty accommodating extended goals that require infinite sequences of actions.

11.9 Discussion and Historical Remarks

The basic ideas of HTN planning were first developed more than 25 years ago in work by Sacerdoti [460] and in Tate's Nonlin planner [503]. HTN planning has been more widely used in planning applications than any of the other planning techniques described in this book [551]. Examples include production-line scheduling [549], crisis management and logistics [72, 135, 504], planning and scheduling for spacecraft [1, 180, see next page], equipment configuration [3], manufacturing process planning [494], evacuation planning [406], the game of bridge [495], and robotics [401, 402]. Some of these applications will be discussed in Chapters 19 and 22.

In a complex application, an HTN planner may generate plans that contain thousands of nodes. Plans this large are very difficult for humans to understand without a natural pictorial representation. Several HTN planners (e.g., SIPE-2 and O-Plan) provide GUIs to aid in generating plans, viewing them, and following and controlling the planning processes [551]. Particularly useful for visualizing the plan derivation and structure is the ability to view its decomposition tree at various levels of abstraction.

The first steps toward a theoretical model of HTN planning were taken by Yang [558] and Kambhampati and Hendler [301]. A complete model was developed by Erol *et al.* [174]. This model provided the basis for complexity analysis [175] and the first provably correct HTN planning procedure, UMCP [174]. Our model of HTN planning in Section 11.5 is based on theirs, as are our complexity results for HTN planning in Section 11.6.

We have described HTN methods as a modification to the branching function of Abstract-search. An alternative model [49, 53] is to use the branching function of classical planning and consider the methods to be a pruning function. This model is appealing in that it provides a clear relation to classical planning. However, the limitation of this model is that it is only capable of expressing classical planning problems.

The best-known domain-independent HTN planning systems are listed here.

- Nonlin [503][7] is one of the first HTN planning systems.
- SIPE-2 [550][8] has been used in many application domains.
- O-Plan [135, 504][9] has also been used in many application domains.
- UMCP [174][10] is an implementation of the first provably sound and complete HTN planning algorithm.
- SHOP2 [413][11] is an efficient planning system which won one of the top four prizes in the 2002 International Planning Competition [195].

Several of these systems incorporate most of the extensions described in Section 11.7.

Our Lifted-PFD procedure is a simplified version of SHOP2, our Lifted-TFD procedure is a simplified version of SHOP2's predecessor SHOP, and our Abstract-HTN procedure is a simplified version of UMCP.

High-level effects were first described by Tate [503], and the conditions necessary to achieve soundness with them were explored by Bacchus and Yang [36] and Young *et al.* [564]. The semantics of high-level effects are defined in two different ways in the literature: either as effects in addition to the ones asserted by the planning operators (e.g., [36]) or as contraints that must be satisfied in order for a task to be achieved or a method to succeed (e.g., [173]). These two approaches result in very different planning algorithms.

Declarations of external preconditions have been used in the Nonlin [503] and SIPE-2 [550] planning systems. Algorithms for finding external preconditions automatically have been developed for use in the UMCP system [516].

---

7. A copy of Nonlin can be downloaded at http://www.aiai.ed.ac.uk/project/nonlin.
8. A copy of SIPE-2 can be downloaded at http://www.ai.sri.com/~sipe if the user has a license.
9. A copy of O-Plan can be downloaded at http://www.aiai.ed.ac.uk/oplan.
10. A copy of UMCP can be downloaded at http://www.cs.umd.edu/projects/plus/umcp.
11. A copy of SHOP2 can be downloaded at http://www.cs.umd.edu/projects/shop.

O-Plan, SIPE-2, and SHOP2 can each do certain kinds of temporal planning. For details, see the web sites for O-Plan and SIPE-2, and see Nau *et al.* [413] for SHOP2.

Advantages and Disadvantages. Compared with classical planners, the primary advantage of HTN planners is their sophisticated knowledge representation and reasoning capabilities. They can represent and solve a variety of nonclassical planning problems; with a good set of HTNs to guide them, they can solve classical planning problems orders of magnitude more quickly than classical or neoclassical planners. The primary disadvantage of HTN planners is the need for the domain author to write not only a set of planning operators but also a set of methods.

Comparing HTNs to the control rules described in Chapter 10, it is hard to say which type of control knowledge is more effective. HTN planners have been much more widely used in practical applications, but that is partly because they have been around longer. HTNs give a planner knowledge about what options to consider, and control rules give a planner knowledge about what options *not* to consider. Probably most researchers would agree with Bacchus and Kabanza [33] that the two types of knowledge are useful in different situations and that combining them is a useful topic for future research.

11.10 Exercises

11.1 Draw the decomposition tree produced by TFD on the planning problem in Figure 11.1, using the methods listed in Example 11.7 (see page 238).

11.2 Since TFD is a nondeterministic procedure, it may have several different execution traces that solve the same planning problem. How many such execution traces are there in Exercise 11.1?

11.3 Write totally ordered methods and operators to produce a decomposition tree similar to the one shown in Figure 11.6.

11.4 Write totally ordered methods to generate the noninterleaved decomposition tree shown in Figure 11.8.

11.5 Let c be any positive integer, and let $\mathcal{P}$ be any HTN planning problem for which the height of $\mathcal{P}$'s search space is no greater than c. Can $\mathcal{P}$ be expressed as a classical planning problem? If so, how? If not, why not?

11.6 Prove that TFD is sound.

11.7 Prove that TFD is complete for all total-order STN planning problems.

11.8 Suppose we write a deterministic implementation of TFD that does a depth-first search of its decomposition tree. Is this implementation complete? Why or why not?

11.9 Write the Lifted-TFD procedure described near the end of Section 11.3.

11.10 Prove that Lifted-TFD is sound and complete for all total-order STN planning problems.

11.11 Give a way to rewrite any classical planning problem as a total-order STN planning problem.

11.12 Trace the operation of PFD on the planning problem in Figure 11.1, using the methods listed in Example 11.3 (see page 233). Draw the decomposition tree.

11.13 Since PFD is a nondeterministic procedure, it may have several different execution traces that solve the same planning problem. How many such execution traces are there in Exercise 11.12?

11.14 To make the painting problem of Exercise 5.6 into a total-order STN problem, let's add these atoms to the initial state:

need-color(b1,red), need-color(b2,red),

need-color(b3,blue), need-color(b4,blue)

The initial task network is $w = \langle \text{paint1}(w), \text{paint1}(x), \text{paint1}(y), \text{paint1}(z) \rangle$. The operators are unchanged, and there is just one method:

method1(b, r, c, k)
  task: paint1(b)
  precond: need-color(b, k)
  subtasks: dip(r, c, k), paint(b, r, k)

(a) How many different possible solutions are there?

(b) How many method and operator applications will a depth-first implementation of TFD do in the best case? In the worst case?

(c) How can the domain description be modified to make the worst case more efficient?

(d) To introduce partial ordering into the planning problem, suppose we redefine the initial task network to be $w = (\{u_1, u_2, u_3, u_4\}, \emptyset)$, where $u_1 =$ paint1(b1), $u_2 =$ paint1(b2), $u_3 =$ paint1(b3), and $u_4 =$ paint1(b4). What problem will occur if we do this, and how can it be fixed?

11.15 Consider the washing problem described in Exercise 5.7.

(a) To turn the problem domain into a total-order STN domain, write a method called do-wash that will decompose a task wash(x, y) into the totally ordered sequence of tasks $\langle$start-fill(x), end-fill(x), start-wash(x), end-wash(x, y)$\rangle$. Include preconditions sufficient to guarantee that if do-wash is applicable, then start-fill(x) can be accomplished.

(b) Is do-wash's precondition sufficient to guarantee that if do-wash is applicable, then all of its subtasks can be accomplished? Explain your answer.

(c) Suppose we run TFD with the method you wrote in part (a), the same initial state and operators as in Exercise 5.7, and the initial task network

⟨wash(wm,clothes), wash(dw,dishes), wash(bt,dan)⟩. Are there any solution plans that TFD will be unable to find that PSP was able to find? Explain your answer.

(d) Suppose we run PFD with the same information as in part (c), except that the intial task network is an unordered set of tasks {wash(wm,clothes), wash(dw,dishes), wash(bt,dan)}. Are there any solution plans that PFD will be unable to find that PSP was able to find? Explain your answer.

(e) Is do-wash's precondition still sufficient to guarantee that if do-wash is applicable, then all of its subtasks can be accomplished? Explain your answer.

11.16 In Example 11.3 (see page 233), suppose we allow the initial state to contain an atom need-to-move(p, q) for each stack of containers that needs to be moved from some pile p to some other pile q. Rewrite the methods and operators so that instead of being restricted to work on three stacks of containers, they will work correctly for an arbitrary number of stacks and containers.

11.17 Prove that PFD is sound and complete for all STN planning problems.

11.18 Write the Lifted-PFD procedure described near the end of Section 11.4. (Hint: Take a look at the Abstract-HTN procedure.)

11.19 Prove that Lifted-PFD is sound and complete for all STN planning problems.

11.20 Modify PFD to work for HTN planning problems in which there are no constraints of the form after(U', l) and between(U', U'', l).

11.21 Modify the procedure you developed in Exercise 11.20 to work for HTN planning problems in which there are constraints of the form after(U', l) and between(U', U'', l).

11.22 Trace how Example 11.14 (see page 253) would work on the DWR version of the Sussman anomaly (Example 4.3).

11.23 Using the domain description given in Example 11.14 (see page 253), is there ever a possibility of TFD finding any redundant solutions? Why or why not?

11.24 Is there a way to rewrite Example 11.14 (see page 253) so that all of the axioms are Horn clauses? If so, what is it? If not, why not?

11.25 In Exercise 11.16, suppose the planning language includes a single binary function symbol. Do the exercise without allowing the additional atoms in the initial state. (Hint: Use the function symbol to create a task whose argument represents a list of containers to be moved.)

11.26 Download a copy of SHOP2 from http://www.cs.umd.edu/projects/shop.

(a) Write several planning problems for it in the blocks world (see Section 4.6), including the one in Exercise 2.1, and run SHOP2 on them using the blocks-world domain description that comes with it.

(b) Encode the domain description of Example 11.8 (see page 240) as a SHOP2 domain description. Run it on several problems in that domain, including the one in Example 11.1.

CHAPTER 12

Control Strategies in Deductive Planning

12.1 Introduction

In deductive planning, a planning problem is seen as a deduction problem, i.e., as a problem of proving a theorem in a logical framework. The main difference between classical planning and deductive planning is that in the former each action is specified with a triple of preconditions, positive effects, and negative effects, whereas in the latter actions are specified with logical formulas. In classical planning, state transitions are computed directly by adding positive effects and deleting negative ones. Deductive planning uses deduction for computing state transitions. Plan generation is done by logical deduction, i.e., by applying the inference rules of the logic, rather than by state-space or plan-space search. Given a description of the planning domain as a set of formulas and a goal as a formula, then a solution plan is generated by a proof in the logic.

The consequence is twofold. From the positive side, the main advantage of deductive planning is its expressiveness. Depending on the logic that is chosen, most of the restrictive assumptions of classical planning can be released. For instance, both of the approaches presented in this chapter, situation calculus and dynamic logic, can easily represent infinite state-transition systems, nondeterminism, partial observability, conditional and iterative plans, and extended goals.

From the negative side, planning-specific search techniques have been shown to be more practical than deduction to solve classical planning problems. The main bottleneck in deductive planning is the lack of automatic procedures to generate plans. The reactions to this problem have been along two main lines. One approach is to limit the expressiveness of the logic to special cases for which there are efficient decision procedures, such as the "planning as satisfiability" techniques described in Chapter 7. Another approach, which is the focus of the current chapter, is to keep the logic expressive but allow the user to write domain-dependent control strategies that can reduce the burden of searching for a proof. We focus on two main paradigms.

1. *Plans as programs.* In this approach, the user does not specify a goal and ask the theorem prover to find a plan by deduction. One rather writes programs in a logical language that are *possibly incomplete* specifications of plans. This can reduce significantly the search for a proof because the theorem prover needs to find a proof only for those parts of the plan that are not fully specified. For instance, rather than giving to the planner the goal "the robot should be loaded at a target location," the user can write a program "move the robot to an intermediate location, find a plan for loading the robot and move the robot to the target location."
2. *Tactics.* Tactics are user-defined programs that specify which inference rules should be applied in a deduction process and how inference rules should be combined to generate a proof. This approach is conceptually different than the previous one. The user specifies the goal and then writes a program that guides the search for a proof of that goal. Thus, for instance, if the goal is "the robot should be loaded at a target location," and this is represented as a conjunction of two formulas, "the robot is loaded" and "the robot is at target location," a tactic can specify that the theorem prover should search for two proofs for the two conjuncts and then apply a simple inference rule that proves the conjunction.

Very expressive deductive planning frameworks have been proposed that support either the approach based on plans as programs or the one based on tactics. In this chapter, we describe the "plans as programs" paradigm in Section 12.2 and tactics in Section 12.3. For both of them, we focus on a basic and simple framework mostly for classical planning. This framework has been extended significantly in the literature to deal with different kinds of planning problems (see Section 12.4).

12.2 Situation Calculus

Situation calculus is a first-order language for representing states and actions that change states. Section 12.2.1 introduces the notion of *situation*, Section 12.2.2 shows how actions are represented, and Section 12.2.3 describes planning domains, problems, and solutions in situation calculus. Section 12.2.4 introduces the "plans as programs" paradigm in situation calculus. These sections provide an informal introduction to the topic. See the discussion and historical remarks in Section 12.4 for some main references to formal accounts.

12.2.1 Situations

In classical planning, each state s corresponds to a *different* logical theory whose axioms are the atoms in s (see Chapter 2). Rather than atoms, we could even have axioms that are of a more general form, e.g., any kind of formula in first-order logic (see Section 2.4).

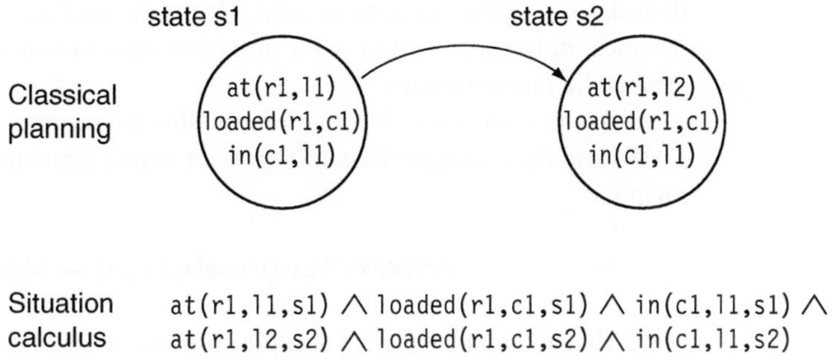

Figure 12.1 Situation calculus versus classical planning.

In situation calculus there is only *one* logical theory, and different states are represented by including the "name" of each state as an extra argument to each atom that is true in the state. For example, to say that s is a state in which at(r1,l1) holds, one would write at(r1,l1,s). The term s is called a *situation*. Figure 12.1 shows the conceptual difference in representation between classical planning and situation calculus.

The language $\mathcal{L}$ of situation calculus is a first-order language that includes terms that are situations. All the expressive power of a first-order language can then be used to describe a planning domain. This means that atoms holding in some states need not be mentioned explicitly; they just need to be entailed by the theory. Thus, for instance, we can state that:

$$\forall r \forall l \forall c \forall s (\mathsf{at}(r, l, s) \wedge \mathsf{loaded}(r, c) \rightarrow \mathsf{in}(c, l, s))$$

Given at(r1,l1,s1) and loaded(r1,c1), then in(c1,l1,s1) is entailed by the theory, and this is true for all the possible instantiations of the variables r, l, c, and s.

Terms and formulas containing a situation are called *fluents*. For example, at(r1,l1,s1) and at(r,l,s), are fluents.

12.2.2 Actions

In classical planning, atoms in different states are described in a restricted first-order language L, and actions are described by operators that are elements of a separate "planning language" based on L. In contrast to classical planning, in situation calculus actions are represented as terms in the same first-order language $\mathcal{L}$ in which states are represented. For instance, the terms move(r1,l1,l2) and move(r,l,l') of $\mathcal{L}$ denote actions. The situation resulting after the execution of an action is represented by means of the special function symbol do. If α is a variable denoting an action, then $\mathsf{do}(\alpha,s)$ is the situation resulting from the execution of α in situation s. For instance, $\mathsf{do}(\mathsf{move}(r,l,l'),s)$ is the situation after executing the action denoted by $\mathsf{move}(r,l,l')$ in situation s.

Action preconditions in situation calculus are represented in the same language $\mathcal{L}$. We use the predicate Poss to represent action preconditions. For instance, the formula

$$\forall r \forall l \forall l' \forall s(\mathsf{Poss}(\mathsf{move}(r,l,l'),s) \leftrightarrow \mathsf{at}(r,l,s)) \tag{12.1}$$

states that action $\mathsf{move}(r,l,l')$ is applicable to a situation s iff the robot is at location l in s ($\mathsf{at}(r,l,s)$). These formulas are called *action precondition axioms.* They are generalizations of action preconditions in classical planning because they can be any first-order formula. For instance, preconditions can be defined with existential quantifiers, disjunctions, etc., as in the following precondition of action transport,

$$\forall c \forall l(\mathsf{Poss}(\mathsf{transport}(c,l),s) \leftrightarrow \exists l' \exists r(\mathsf{adjacent}(l,l') \wedge \mathsf{at}(r,l') \wedge \mathsf{loaded}(r,c))) \tag{12.2}$$

which states that a container can be transported to a location if there is a robot loaded with that container in an adjacent location.

In situation calculus, action effects are described by formulas of $\mathcal{L}$. For instance, the formula

$$\forall r \forall l \forall l' \forall s(\mathsf{Poss}(\mathsf{move}(r,l,l'),s) \rightarrow \mathsf{at}(r,l',\mathsf{do}(\mathsf{move}(r,l,l'),s))) \tag{12.3}$$

states that the effect of moving a robot from l to l' is that the robot is at l'. Formula 12.3 describes a *positive effect,* i.e., the fact that a fluent becomes true. We also have to take into account *negative effects,* i.e., the case where an action causes a fluent to become false. For instance, the formula

$$\forall r \forall l \forall l' \forall s(\mathsf{Poss}(\mathsf{move}(r,l,l'),s) \rightarrow \neg \mathsf{at}(r,l,\mathsf{do}(\mathsf{move}(r,l,l'),s))) \tag{12.4}$$

describes a negative effect. The action effects we have described so far are analogous to the effects represented in classical planning. In situation calculus, however, we can use all the expressiveness of first-order logic to describe effects. For instance, we can also have *conditional effects,* i.e., effects that depend on the situation. For instance, the formula

$$\forall r \forall l \forall l' \forall c \forall s((\mathsf{Poss}(\mathsf{move}(r,l,l'),s) \wedge \mathsf{loaded}(r,c,s)) \rightarrow \mathsf{in}(c,l',\mathsf{do}(\mathsf{move}(r,l,l'),s))) \tag{12.5}$$

states that if the robot is loaded with a container and the robot moves to a destination, then the container is at the destination.

Different than classical planning, situation calculus must take into account the *frame problem,* i.e., the problem of describing what actions do not change.

For instance, in classical planning, if loaded(r1,c1) is true in a state s, and the robot moves to a different location, then loaded(r1,c1) is still true in the new state s'. In situation calculus, because state transitions are computed by deduction, if loaded(r1,c1,s) is true, we cannot conclude that loaded(r1,c1,s') is true unless there is an axiom saying so. For instance, the formula

$$\forall r \forall l \forall l' \forall s(\mathsf{Poss}(\mathsf{move}(r,l,l'),s) \rightarrow (\mathsf{loaded}(r,\mathsf{do}(\mathsf{move}(r,l,l'),s) \leftrightarrow \mathsf{loaded}(r,s))) \quad (12.6)$$

states that, if the action move(r,l,l') is applicable in s, then, if the robot is loaded in s, the robot will still be loaded after moving, and it will not be loaded if it is not loaded in s. These kinds of formulas must be axioms of the logical theory and are called *frame axioms.*

12.2.3 Planning Domains, Problems, and Solutions

Given the proper constants, function symbols, and predicate symbols, a *planning domain* in situation calculus is described by $D = (Ax_p, Ax_e, Ax_f)$, where the elements are defined as follows.

- Ax_p is a set of action precondition axioms.
- Ax_e is a set of action effect axioms.
- Ax_f is a set of frame axioms.

We need to define what *plans* are in situation calculus. In order to do this we introduce a function symbol ; in $\mathcal{L}$. We use an infix notation for ; rather than ordinary prefix notation, i.e., we write $x;y$ in place of $;(x,y)$.[1] Then any term denoting an action is a *plan*. If π_1 and π_2 are plans, then $\pi_1;\pi_2$ is also a plan. The intended meaning of ; is sequential composition: in $\pi_1;\pi_2$ we first execute π_1 and then π_2. This definition of *plan* implies totally ordered plans.

The execution of a plan π is defined through the symbol Exec. Intuitively, Exec(π,s,s') holds if the plan π leads from situation s to situation s'. Let α be a variable denoting an action and π_1 and π_2 be variables denoting plans. Then we can use the following notation to abbreviate some of the expressions of $\mathcal{L}$[2]:

$$\mathsf{Exec}(\alpha,s,s') \text{ means } \mathsf{Poss}(\alpha,s) \wedge s' = \mathsf{do}(\alpha,s)$$

$$\mathsf{Exec}(\pi_1;\pi_2,s,s') \text{ means } \exists s''(\mathsf{Exec}(\pi_1,s,s'') \wedge \mathsf{Exec}(\pi_2,s'',s')$$

---

1. We should also introduce the fundamental axioms that allow us to prove that $(x;y);z = x;(y;z)$. We refer to Levesque *et al.* [360] for a formal account.
2. Formally, the abbreviation Exec(α,s,s') should take into account the need for restoring the situation arguments to any functional fluent of α in Poss(α,s).

In order to define a classical planning problem, we need to represent initial and goal states. Initial states are denoted by a constant s0 in the language called the *initial situation*. The initial situation is described by a formula called the *initial situation axiom* Ax_0. It is a formula of $\mathcal{L}$ that either does not contain any situation or contains only the situation s0. Thus, for instance, the formula at(r1,l1,s0) $\wedge$ $\neg$loaded(r1,s0) describes an initial situation where the robot r1 is at location l1 and is not loaded. Goal states are described by a formula $\Phi_g(s)$ called the *goal formula*. $\Phi_g(s)$ is a formula whose only free variable is s. Thus, for instance, the formula at(r1,l2,s) $\wedge$ loaded(r1,s) describes the goal of reaching a state where the robot r1 is at location l2 and is loaded.

A *planning problem* $(D, Ax_0, \Phi_g(s))$ is a planning domain D, an initial situation Ax_0, and a goal formula $\Phi_g(s)$. A *solution* to a planning problem $(D, Ax_0, \Phi_g(s))$ is a plan π such that

$$\exists s(\mathsf{Exec}(\pi, \mathsf{s0}, s) \wedge \Phi_g(s))$$

is entailed[3] by D and Ax_0.[4]

Example 12.1 Consider the DWR example where we have one robot r1, two adjacent locations l1 and l2, and the actions move(r1,l1,l2), move(r1,l2,l1), and load(r1). The action precondition axioms are:

$$\forall r \forall l \forall l' \forall s(\mathsf{Poss}(\mathsf{move}(r,l,l'),s) \leftrightarrow \mathsf{at}(r,l,s))$$

$$\forall r \forall l \forall l' \forall s(\mathsf{Poss}(\mathsf{load}(r),s) \leftrightarrow \neg \mathsf{loaded}(r,s))$$

The action effect axioms are:

$$\forall r \forall l \forall l' \forall s(\mathsf{Poss}(\mathsf{move}(r,l,l'),s) \rightarrow \mathsf{at}(r,l',\mathsf{do}(\mathsf{move}(r,l,l'),s)))$$

$$\forall r \forall l \forall l' \forall s(\mathsf{Poss}(\mathsf{move}(r,l,l'),s) \rightarrow \neg \mathsf{at}(r,l,\mathsf{do}(\mathsf{move}(r,l,l'),s)))$$

$$\forall r \forall l \forall l' \forall s(\mathsf{Poss}(\mathsf{load}(r),s) \rightarrow \mathsf{loaded}(r,\mathsf{do}(\mathsf{load}(r),s)))$$

The frame axioms are:

$$\forall r \forall l \forall l' \forall s(\mathsf{Poss}(\mathsf{move}(r,l,l'),s) \rightarrow (\mathsf{loaded}(r,\mathsf{do}(\mathsf{move}(r,l,l'),s)) \leftrightarrow \mathsf{loaded}(r,s)))$$

$$\forall r \forall l \forall l' \forall s(\mathsf{Poss}(\mathsf{load}(r,s)) \rightarrow (\mathsf{at}(r,l,l',\mathsf{do}(\mathsf{load}(r),s)) \leftrightarrow \mathsf{at}(r,l,l',s)))$$

The initial situation axiom is:

$$\mathsf{at}(\mathsf{r1},\mathsf{l1},\mathsf{s0}) \wedge \neg \mathsf{loaded}(\mathsf{r1},\mathsf{s0})$$

The goal formula is:

$$\mathsf{at}(\mathsf{r1},\mathsf{l2},s) \wedge \mathsf{loaded}(\mathsf{r1},s)$$

---

3. See Appendix B for a formal notion of entailment in first-order logic.
4. In this informal presentation, we skip the discussion of *fundamental axioms*, i.e., domain independent axioms, such as unique name axioms for actions and situations. See Levesque *et al.* [360] for a detailed description of fundamental axioms.

We can then use a first-order logic theorem prover to obtain the plan that achieves the goal described by the goal formula. ■

12.2.4 Plans as Programs in Situation Calculus

This section describes how to generalize the definition of a plan to allow plans that are not necessarily sequential. We discuss this extension briefly and informally through some examples; see Levesque *et al.* [360] for formal definitions.

Test actions are introduced through the symbol ?:

$$\text{Exec(at(r1,l1)?,}s,s') \text{ means } \text{at(r1,l1,}s) \wedge s = s'$$

The formula Exec(at(r1,l1)?,s,s') is true only if the test at(r1,l1)? succeeds in s and the resulting state is s'. Note, however, that the test at(r1,l1)? does not *change* s. Thus Exec(at(r1,l1)?,s,s') is true if and only if at(r1,l1,s) is true and $s = s'$.

Nondeterministic choices are expressed through the symbol |:

$$\text{Exec(move(r1,l1,l2) | move(r1,l1,l3),}s,s') \text{ means}$$
$$\text{(Exec(move(r1,l1,l2),}s,s') \vee \text{Exec(move(r1,l1,l3),}s,s'))$$

The formula Exec(move(r1,l1,l2) | move(r1,l1,l3),s,s') is true if s' is the resulting state of executing either move(r1,l1,l2) or move(r1,l1,l3) in s.

Nondeterministic iterations are expressed through the symbol $*$. For instance, Exec(load(r1,c1)$*$,s,s') means that executing load(r,c) zero or more times in s produces s'.

Nondeterministic iteration and test actions can be used to define the usual programming constructs for conditionals and loops. Let ϕ be a formula, and let π, π_1, and π_2 be plans. Then:

$$\text{if } \phi \text{ then } \pi_1 \text{ else } \pi_2 \text{means } (\phi?;\pi_1)|(\neg\phi?;\pi_2)$$
$$\text{while } \phi \text{ do } \pi \text{ means } (\phi?;\pi)*;\neg\phi?$$

if ϕ then π_1 can be defined analogously. The above planning constructs can then be used by the user to write programs that specify plans.

The logical language described here can be viewed as a high-level programming language. Planning in this framework is equivalent to executing the logical program. The program in the following example is a complete specification of a plan.

Example 12.2 In the DWR domain, we can instantiate the following formula

$\forall l \forall l'$ if at(r1,l') then
  while $\exists c$ in(c,l) do
    move(r1,l',l);load(r1,c);move(r1,l;l');unload(r1,c)

to a plan that moves iteratively the robot r1 to transport all the containers in a given location to the original location where the robot comes from. ■

The language allows for incomplete specifications of plans, in which case ordinary first-order theorem proving is used to generate the plan.

Example 12.3 In situation calculus, it is possible to write the following program

$$\forall l \forall l' \ \texttt{if at}(\texttt{r1},l') \ \texttt{then}$$
$$\texttt{while} \ \exists c \ \texttt{in}(c,l) \ \texttt{do}$$
$$\texttt{move}(\texttt{r1},l',l);\pi;\texttt{move}(\texttt{r1},l;l');\texttt{unload}(\texttt{r1},c)$$

with a condition that states that π should lead from a situation where r1 is unloaded in l' to a situation where r1 is loaded in l' with a container c. In this case, the plan π has to be generated by deduction. Fortunately, this is a rather easy task because the plan is just one action, load(r1,c).[5] ■

Example 12.4 As an extreme case, we may leave the theorem prover a harder task and write the following program with a proper initial and goal condition for π.

$$\forall l \forall l' \ \texttt{if at}(\texttt{r1},l') \ \texttt{then}$$
$$\texttt{while} \ \exists c \ \texttt{in}(c,l) \ \texttt{do} \ \pi$$

■

12.3 Dynamic Logic

Dynamic logic, like situation calculus, is a logic for reasoning about states and actions that change states. In dynamic logic, states are represented in *one* logical theory as well. However, contrary to situation calculus, states are not represented explicitly in the language of the logic. Which atoms hold in different states is stated through modal operators, similar to those of temporal logics, like LTL (see Chapter 10) and CTL (see Chapter 17). While temporal logics have been devised to reason about temporal evolutions, dynamic logic is used to reason about actions (or programs) that change the state. For this reason, modal operators are "parameterized" with actions. If a is an action, then $[a]$ and $\langle a \rangle$ are modal operators that state what is true after action a is executed. For example, to say that at(r1,l2) is true in a state after the execution of action move(r1,l1,l2), one would write move(r1,l1,l2) > at(r1,l2). Figure 12.2 shows the conceptual difference in representation between classical planning, situation calculus, and dynamic logic.

In this section, we first define the language of a very simple fragment of dynamic logic (Section 12.3.1), its semantics (Section 12.3.2), and its deductive machinery,

---

5. In order to present all of this formally, we would need the introduction of procedures in the logical framework [360].

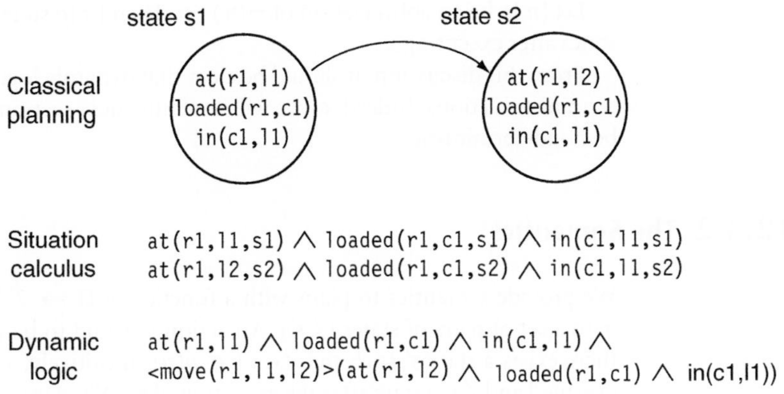

Figure 12.2 Classical planning, situation calculus, and dynamic logic.

i.e., axioms and inference rules (Section 12.3.3). These are the basic ingredients of planning domains, problems, and solutions in dynamic logic (Section 12.3.4). We start with a rather simple framework, in which plans are restricted to be sequences of actions, and we then extend it to represent plans involving control structures, such as conditional and iterative plans (Section 12.3.5). We finally give some guidelines on how deductive planning can be guided by user-defined control strategies (Section 12.3.6).

12.3.1 The Language of the Logic

The set of plans Π includes the set of basic actions Π_0. For instance, the basic action move(r1,l1,l2) is a plan. Furthermore, for every pair of plans π_1 and π_2, the plan $\pi_1;\pi_2$ is also in Π. The set of formulas Φ is inductively defined starting from a set of atomic propositions Φ_0 and the set of plans Π.

- True and False are formulas in Φ.
- $\Phi_0 \subseteq \Phi$.
- If p and q are formulas in Φ, then $\neg p$ and $p \wedge q$ are also formulas in Φ.
- If p is a formula in Φ and π is a plan in Π, then $\langle\pi\rangle p$ is a formula in Φ.

The formula $\langle\pi\rangle p$ states that p is true in *at least one* of the possible states that result from the execution of π. For example, the intended meaning of the formula

$$\langle \text{move(r1,l1,l2); load(r1)} \rangle (\text{at(r1,l2)} \wedge \text{loaded(r1)})$$

is that if we first move the robot r1 to location l2 and then we load it, then the robot is at l2 and is loaded.

Let $[\pi]p$ be an abbreviation of $\neg\langle\pi\rangle\neg p$. Then $[\pi]p$ states that p holds in *all* the states after executing π.

From this discussion, it should be clear that dynamic logic can represent nondeterministic actions. Indeed, as we will see in the next section, actions and plans can be nondeterministic.

12.3.2 The Semantics

We provide semantics to plans with a function $\rho:\Pi \rightarrow 2^{S\times S}$, which maps a plan π to a set of pairs of states (s, s'). An action a is said to be *applicable* to a state s if there exists a state s' such that $(s, s') \in \rho(a)$. Intuitively, s is the state where π is executed and s' is a state after the execution of π. When we concatenate sequentially two actions, we get the pairs with the initial states of the first action and the final states of the second action, provided that the first one leads to states where the second one is applicable:

$$\rho(\pi_1;\pi_2) = \{(s,t) \in S \times S \mid \exists s' \in S.\, (s,s') \in \rho(\pi_1) \wedge (s',t) \in \rho(\pi_2)\}$$

Let a proposition p be true in a state s. Then we write $p \in s$. The set of states in which $\langle\pi\rangle p$ is true is the following:

$$\{s \in S \mid \exists s'.\, (s,s') \in \rho(\pi) \wedge p \in s'\}$$

Figure 12.3 describes the semantics of formulas of the form $\langle\pi\rangle p$. If $\langle a\rangle p$ holds in state s_1, i.e., $s_1 \in \tau(\langle a\rangle p)$, and a leads from s_1 to s_2, i.e., $(s_1, s_2) \in \rho(a)$, then p holds in s_2, i.e., $s_2 \in \tau(p)$. Notice that in the example in Figure 12.3, we suppose that s_2 is the only state such that $(s_1, s_2) \in \rho(a)$, i.e., a is deterministic when applied to s_1. If there are more than one pair, then p holds in at least one of the resulting states. If $\langle a;b\rangle p$ holds in s_1, i.e., $s_1 \in \tau(\langle a;b\rangle p)$, and a leads from s_1 to s_2, i.e., $(s_1, s_2) \in \rho(a)$, and b leads from s_2 to s_3, i.e., $(s_2, s_3) \in \rho(b)$, then p holds in s_3, i.e., $s_3 \in \tau(p)$.

An *interpretation* is a triple $M = (S, \tau, \rho)$. A formula $p \in \Phi$ is *valid in an interpretation* $M = (S, \tau, \rho)$ (written $M \models p$) if and only if $\tau(p) = S$; p is *valid* (written $\models p$) if it is valid in every interpretation.

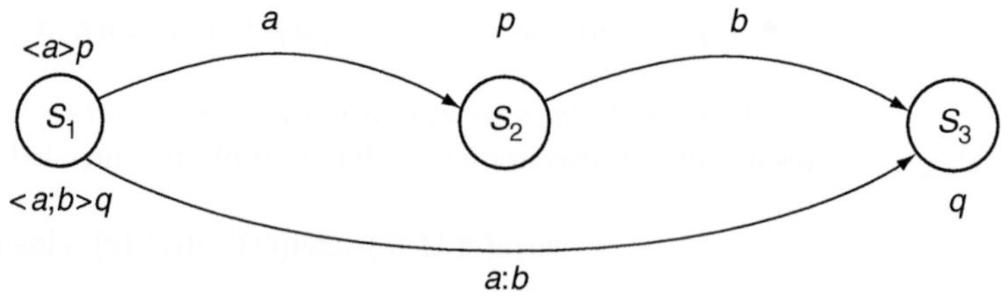

Figure 12.3 Semantics of formulas and plans.

12.3.3 The Deductive Machinery

The deductive machinery of the logic is based on a set of axioms and a set of inference rules. Any axiom of the propositional calculus is an axiom of the logic.[6] Moreover, we have the following axioms:

$$\langle \pi_1; \pi_2 \rangle p \leftrightarrow \langle \pi_1 \rangle (\langle \pi_2 \rangle p)$$
$$\langle \pi \rangle (p \vee q) \leftrightarrow (\langle \pi \rangle p \vee \langle \pi \rangle q)$$

It is easy to show that these formulas are valid. We have two inference rules.

1. From $p, p \rightarrow q$, derive q. This is the usual modus ponens rule.
2. From p, derive $\neg\langle a \rangle \neg p$. This rule, which is called necessitation, states that if p holds in all states, then the negation of p cannot hold in any of the states reached by a.

If a formula p follows from the axioms under the rules of inference, we say it is *provable* and write $\vdash p$. If p follows from a formula q, we say that it is *derivable* from q and we write $q \vdash p$.

12.3.4 Planning Domains, Problems, and Solutions

A *planning domain* is a triple $(\Phi_0, \Pi_0, Ax_{\Pi_0})$, where Φ_0 is a set of atomic propositions, Π_0 is the set of actions, and Ax_{Π_0} is the union of the following three disjoint sets.

1. A set of propositional formulas called *domain axioms.*
2. A set of formulas called *action axioms* that describe the action preconditions and effects. They are of the form $p \rightarrow \langle a \rangle q$ or of the form $p \rightarrow [a]q$, where a is any basic action in Π_0, and p and q are any propositional formulas. We call p the preconditions and q the effects.
3. *Frame axioms,* which describe what actions do not change. See Section 12.2 for a discussion of why frame axioms are needed.

Example 12.5 Consider a DWR example where we have one robot r1, two adjacent locations l1 and l2, and the actions move(r1,l1,l2), move(r1,l2,l1), and load(r1). The set of basic propositions and actions are:

$$\Phi_0 = \{\texttt{at(r1,l1)}, \texttt{at(r1,l2)}, \texttt{loaded(r1)}\}$$
$$\Pi_0 = \{\texttt{move(r1,l1,l2)}, \texttt{move(r1,l2,l1)}, \texttt{load(r1)}\}$$

6. See Appendix B for a description of the axioms of propositional and first-order logic and for a definition of interpretation.

The set Ax_{Π_0} contains the following formulas:

$$
\begin{aligned}
\neg\texttt{at(r1,l2)} &\leftrightarrow \texttt{at(r1,l1)}\ \texttt{(domain)}\\
\texttt{at(r1,l1)} &\rightarrow \langle\texttt{move(r1,l1,l2)}\rangle\texttt{at(r1,l2)}\ \texttt{(move l2)}\\
\texttt{at(r1,l2)} &\rightarrow \langle\texttt{move(r1,l2,l1)}\rangle\texttt{at(r1,l1)}\ \texttt{(move 2l)}\\
\neg\texttt{loaded(r1)} &\rightarrow \langle\texttt{load(r1)}\rangle\texttt{loaded(r1)}\ \texttt{(load)}\\
\texttt{loaded(r1)} &\rightarrow \langle\texttt{move(r1,l1,l2)}\rangle\texttt{loaded(r1)}\ \texttt{(frame 1)}\\
\texttt{loaded(r1)} &\rightarrow \langle\texttt{move(r1,l2,l1)}\rangle\texttt{loaded(r1)}\ \texttt{(frame 2)}\\
\neg\texttt{loaded(r1)} &\rightarrow \langle\texttt{move(r1,l1,l2)}\rangle\neg\texttt{loaded(r1)}\ \texttt{(frame 3)}\\
\neg\texttt{loaded(r1)} &\rightarrow \langle\texttt{move(r1,l2,l1)}\rangle\neg\texttt{loaded(r1)}\ \texttt{(frame 4)}\\
\texttt{at(r1,l1)} &\rightarrow \langle\texttt{load(r1)}\rangle\texttt{at(r1,l1)}\ \texttt{(frame 5)}\\
\texttt{at(r1,l2)} &\rightarrow \langle\texttt{load(r1)}\rangle\texttt{at(r1,l2)}\ \texttt{(frame 6)}\\
\neg\texttt{at(r1,l1)} &\rightarrow \langle\texttt{load(r1)}\rangle\neg\texttt{at(r1,l1)}\ \texttt{(frame 7)}\\
\neg\texttt{at(r1,l2)} &\rightarrow \langle\texttt{load(r1)}\rangle\neg\texttt{at(r1,l2)}\ \texttt{(frame 8)}
\end{aligned}
$$

The domain axiom (domain) states that a robot is in only one of the two possible locations at a time. The formulas (move12), (move21), and (load) describe the preconditions and effects of the actions. The other formulas, (frame1) through (frame8), are called *frame axioms.* They describe what does not change after an action is executed.

■

A planning problem is (D, Φ_0, Φ_g), where D is a planning domain, Φ_0 is a propositional formula describing the initial state, and Φ_g is a propositional formula describing the goal state. A *solution* to a planning problem is a plan $\pi \in \Pi$ such that

$$Ax_{\Pi_0} \vdash \Phi_0 \rightarrow \langle\pi\rangle\Phi_g$$

Example 12.6 Consider Example 12.5. Let Φ_0 be at(r1,l1) $\wedge$ ¬loaded(r1) and Φ_g be at(r1,l2) $\wedge$ loaded(r1). From (move12), (load), and (domain) we derive:

$$(\texttt{at(r1,l1)} \wedge \neg\texttt{loaded(r1)}) \rightarrow \langle\texttt{move(r1,l1,l2);load(r1)}\rangle\texttt{at(r1,l2)} \wedge \texttt{loaded(r1)}$$

■

12.3.5 Extensions

In the previous sections we have discussed deductive planning within a very small subset of Propositional Dynamic Logic (PDL) [259]. PDL can express plans that include control structures like conditionals and loops, defined on the basis of nondeterministic choices, tests, and repetitions. Plans and formulas are defined inductively as follows.

- *True*, *False* $\in \Phi$, $\Phi_0 \subseteq \Phi$.
- If $p, q \in \Phi$, then $\neg p \in \Phi$ and $p \wedge q \in \Phi$.
- If π_1 and π_2 are plans in Π, then the following hold.
  - $\pi_1; \pi_2$ is a plan in Π (sequence).
  - $\pi_1 \cup \pi_2$ is a plan in Π (nondeterministic choice).
  - π^* is a plan in Π (nondeterministic repetition).
- If $p \in \Phi$, then $p? \in \Pi$ (test).
- If $\alpha \in \Pi$, then $\langle \alpha \rangle p \in \Phi$.

According to the definition above, plans can be obtained as sequences of actions, $\alpha; \beta$(do α and then β); nondeterministic choices, $\alpha \cup \beta$(do α or β, nondeterministically); nondeterministic repetitions, α^*(do α zero or more times); and tests, $p?$ (if p is true, then proceed with the execution of the plan; otherwises, stop execution). This allows us to define conditionals and loops. For any $p \in \Phi$ and $\pi, \pi_1, \pi_2 \in \Pi$, we define:

- **if** p **then** π_1 **else** $\pi_2 = p?; \pi_1 \cup (\neg p)?; \pi_2$
- **while** p **do** $\pi = (p?; \alpha)^*; (\neg p)?$

12.3.6 User-Defined Control Strategies as Tactics

In deductive planning, plan generation is done by searching for a proof. A lot of effort has been devoted to finding domain-independent heuristics for this search problem. However, automatic theorem proving is well known to be very hard, e.g., semidecidable in first-order logic. It is unlikely that automatic theorem proving can be used to solve planning problems of realistic complexity. For this reason, an alternative approach has been devised where the user can specify control knowledge for the search of a proof. This approach is called *tactical theorem proving*, and the user-defined control strategies are called *tactics*.

Tactics are programs that control a theorem prover by telling which are the inference rules to use, to which formulas they should be applied, and in which order. Tactics are either primitive or compound. *Primitive tactics* are programs that apply basic inference rules, i.e., basic proof steps. If a rule is applicable, then the corresponding tactic returns the formula that is the conclusion of the rule; if it is not applicable, it returns failure. This is how tactics deal with "wrong" attempts to generate a proof, i.e., attempts to apply inference rules that are not applicable. Indeed, when writing a tactic that has to deal with a large or complex proof, the user may not know whether a rule is applicable at a certain point in the proof search. As an example, consider the basic rule of modus ponens: from a formula A and a formula $A \rightarrow B$, the rule derives B. The corresponding primitive tactic `modus-ponens-tac`

```
modus-ponens-tac(φ1,φ2)                ;; primitive tactic for modus ponens
    if premise(φ1,φ2)                  ;; rule preconditions
        then return conclusion(φ2)     ;; rule application
        else exit with "failure"       ;; failure generation
end
```

Figure 12.4 A primitive tactic.

is shown in Figure 12.4. The primitive tactic modus-ponens-tac tests whether the rule is applicable. The function premise(ϕ_1,ϕ_2) tests whether ϕ_1 is a premise of ϕ_2, namely, whether ϕ_2 is $\phi_1 \rightarrow \phi_3$, where ϕ_3 is any formula. If it is, then the tactic returns the conclusion of the rule, i.e., ϕ_3. It fails otherwise.

Compound tactics are compositions of primitive tactics through operators called *tacticals.* Some of the possible tacticals are the following.

- then(tac1,tac2) applies tac1. If tac1 fails, then the tactical fails; otherwise, it applies tac2.
- orelse(tac1,tac2) applies tac1. If tac1 fails, then the tactical applies tac2.
- try(tac1) applies tac1. If tac1 fails, then the tactical returns the original formula it is applied to.
- repeat(tac1) applies tac1 until the tactical fails.

Example 12.7 Consider the tactic conjunction-tac(ϕ,ψ) that always returns $\phi \wedge \psi$. Then

$$\text{orelse(modus-ponens-tac,conjunction-tac)}(B, A \rightarrow B)$$

returns $B \wedge (A \rightarrow B)$.

As a further example, the application of the following tactic

$$\text{repeat(tac1)}(A, A \rightarrow (A \rightarrow (A \rightarrow B)))$$

returns B. ■

12.4 Discussion and Historical Remarks

In this section, we discuss some relations with the other approaches that are described in this part of the book, we discuss the main pros and cons of deductive planning, and we provide some historical remarks.

The "plans as programs" approach is somewhat analogous to HTN planning (see Chapter 11). In HTN planning, each method corresponds roughly to an incomplete plan. The main difference is that in the "plans as program" approach, one can do operations that are analogous to HTN decomposition and also operations that are analogous to state-space search. This is both an advantage and a disadvantage. The advantage is the expressiveness in specifying control strategies, the disadvantage in the loss of efficiency.

The "plans as programs" approach has been proposed in other logical frameworks than situation calculus, e.g., in dynamic logic [496], in process logic [510], and in programming logics that have been extended with temporal operators [499].

The main conceptual difference of the tactics-based approach with respect to other approaches, such as plans as programs and HTN planning, is that tactics are programs whose basic constructs are the basic routines of the theorem prover. They are not specific to planning but are general techniques for theorem proving.

The main advantage of deductive planning is its expressiveness. Compared with classical planning, deductive planning allows for relaxing most of the restrictions described in Chapter 1. This is true even in the very simple logical frameworks we have presented in this chapter. We can use logics that are expressive enough to represent nonfinite state-transition systems, nondeterminism, partial observability, and extended goals.

Nonfinite state-transition systems can be of interest, e.g., in the case new objects are introduced in the domain. For instance, we may not know a priori how many containers are in a DWR domain because new containers can be delivered by boats. Nonfinite state systems are also useful when we have variables that range over real values.

Both situation calculus and dynamic logic can represent and reason about actions with nondeterministic effects, which can be represented with disjunctive formulas. Dynamic logic has modal operators that can distinguish when an effect holds in all the resulting states ($[a]p$) and in at least one state ($\langle a \rangle p$). Partial observability has also been represented through knowledge or sensing actions, e.g., in the situation calculus approach [359] and in the dynamic logic approach [496]. Extended goals can be expressed, e.g., in frameworks that combine temporal and programming logic [499].

Another advantage of deductive planning is that further functionalities like plan verification are given for free. Given a plan, one can prove properties of the plan, e.g., that it achieves a desired goal, that it preserves a given property, and so on. While this feature is not much relevant in classical planning, it is important in cases where plan validation is not trivial, as in planning under uncertainty with extended goals. However, it should be noted that other frameworks for planning under uncertainty, such as those based on model checking, allow for automatic plan validation (see Chapter 17).

In spite of all these potential advantages, the planning technique matured outside of the deductive approach. Indeed, most of the issues discussed previously (e.g., nondeterminism, plan verification) have been tackled with different techniques. Indeed, the major problem of deductive planning is the lack of procedures that generate plans automatically. This is due mainly to the expressiveness of the logic. The work described in this chapter is an attempt to deal with this problem by allowing for user-defined strategies in the logical framework. Important sources in this area are the work on tactics-based deductive planning [54, 71], and on GOLOG [360].

The situation calculus approach was the first to be used for planning. In his seminal work, Green [249] proposes a situation calculus for modeling planning domains and a general purpose resolution theorem prover for generating plans. Manna and Waldinger [377] proposed a theory where recursive plans are generated by deduction in a resolution-based and induction-based tableau calculus. The framework allows for plans involving programming control structures, such as conditionals, loops, and recursion. The early work on program synthesis [378] is very close to this idea.

The "plans as programs" approach relies on modal logic and specifically on dynamic and temporal logic. The modal logic approach was first proposed in early work by Rosenschein [457], within a framework based on Propositional Dynamic Logic [259], and then extended by Kautz to first-order dynamic logic [318]. In these papers the plan generation process is still algorithmic rather than deductive.

A more recent approach to deductive planning has been introduced by W. Stephan and S. Biundo [499]. In this work, actions are composed out of add and delete operations (somehow similar to Strips), plans are combined with control structures including nondeterministic choice and recursion. This approach was the first to provide an efficient solution to the frame problem in the "plans as programs" paradigm. The framework has been implemented within a theorem prover for dynamic logic where users can specify strategies, called tactics in theorem proving. The idea of using hand-coded and reusable theorem-proving strategies (tactics) was first proposed in the PHI system [54, 71], a theorem prover based on a modal interval-based logic, called LLP (Logical Language for Planning), which combines dynamic logic and temporal logic. Interestingly enough, not only does the logical framework allow for plan generation by deduction but it also provides the ability to do plan recognition by means of abduction and to combine plan recognition with plan generation [329].

A different line of research pursues planning based on linear logic [69], which has received some recent attention in the work by Cresswell [134]. Moreover, there is an active line of research on the use of situation calculus as a programming language, in the style of logic programming. GOLOG [360] is a programming language based on situation calculus. The GOLOG approach was first used in cognitive robotics [359] and is recently being used in planning for information gathering and planning for the web.

12.5 Exercises

12.1 Formalize the planning problem described in Example 7.1 in situation calculus and in dynamic logic. Provide a sketch of the proofs that generate a solution plan.

12.2 Write a tactic that automates the generation of a solution plan for a dynamic logic formulation of the planning problem in Example 7.1.

12.3 Write a plan-as-program in situation calculus that automates the generation of a solution plan for a situation calculus formulation of the planning problem in Example 7.1.

12.4 Complicate Example 7.1 with a loading and unloading operation. Formalize the example in situation calculus and in dynamic logic. Provide a sketch of the proofs that generate a solution plan. Write a tactic and a plan-as-program that generate a solution plan.

12.5 Formalize the full DWR domain in situation calculus and in dynamic logic. Formalize some planning problems.

12.6 In Example 7.1, suppose you do not know in which location the robot is initially. Suppose the planning problem is to find a plan such that, no matter where the robot is initially, the plan leads you to the same goal of Example 7.1 (the robot must be in l2). Formalize the planning problem in situation calculus and in dynamic logic, and provide a sketch of the proofs that generate solution plans.

12.7 Provide a situation calculus formulation of the DWR domain with the following modifications.

- The number of containers is c, with $c > 0$.
- The number of robots is r, with $r > 0$.
- The number of locations is l, with $l \geq r$.

Then formalize a planning problem where in the initial state all the containers are in location l_i and in the goal state all the containers must be in location l_j, with $l_j \neq l_i$. Provide a high-level sketch of the proof that generates a solution plan.

12.8 Provide a dynamic logic formulation of the DWR domain with the following modification: If we have containers in more than one pile in the same location, then the loading operation may load a wrong container, i.e., it may load a container different from the designated one (e.g., the container loaded is one at the top of a different pile in the same location). Consider then the goal where you have to move a container to a different location. Does a solution exist? Show with a proof that there is or is not a solution.

Part IV
Planning with Time and Resources

This part of the book is devoted to planning with time and resources. We will be relaxing assumption A6 (Section 1.5), i.e., we will make time explicit in the representation. However, we will keep assuming a deterministic system with complete knowledge and no uncertainty (these three assumptions will be relaxed in Part V). Part IV includes three chapters, on temporal reasoning, temporal planning, and resource handling. In this introduction, we motivate the need for explicit time and give an overview of the representation and approaches detailed in Chapters 13, 14, and 15.

The conceptual model for planning described in Section 1.4 is mainly a general model for a dynamic system. Up to here we relied on the model of state-transition systems with the restrictive assumption of implicit time (assumption A6). In this model the dynamics are represented as a sequence of states; actions and events are instantaneous state transitions; the planning goals are not constrained in time. This restricted model is quite useful for studying the logics and computational aspects of planning with simple state-transition operators. However, in many applications, it is not realistic.

In reality, actions do occur over a time span. A finer model of an action should account not only for the preconditions *before* the action starts but also for other conditions that should prevail *while* it is taking place. Such a model should represent the effects of an action throughout its duration and the delayed effects after the action has finished. For example, consider the move action in the DWR domain, which requires free space for the robot at its destination. In the real domain, this condition is needed not when the action starts but only when the robot reaches its destination. The effect of allowing free space in the origin location does not take place when the action ends but as soon as the robot leaves. Actions may overlap even if their conditions and effects are not independent.[1] In such a case, concurrency of actions is more realistically handled with an explicit time representation.

Furthermore, often goals in a plan are meaningful only if achieved within a time bound. In a dynamic environment, various events may be expected to occur at future time periods. Hence, actions have to be located in time with respect to expected events and to goals. Time is required in two forms: (1) *qualitatively*, to handle synchronization between actions and with events, e.g., to plan for a robot to move to a destination that is not yet free; and (2) *quantitatively*, as a resource, to model the duration of actions with respect to deadlines or cost functions, e.g., to plan how to load or unload all the containers of a ship before its departure.

The main reasons for making time explicit in planning can be summarized as the following list of actions one can perform.

- Model the durations of actions, e.g., to treat time as a resource.
- Model the effects and conditions of an action at various points along its duration, including delayed effects.
- Handle goals with relative or absolute temporal constraints.
- Take into account the dynamics of a domain, i.e., events expected to occur at some future time that are not the results of planned actions.
- Plan with actions that *maintain* a value while being executed, as opposed to just changing that value, e.g., tracking a moving target or keeping a spring latch compressed.
- Plan with overlapping actions that have *interacting* and *joint effects*. For example, a door that has a knob and a spring latch that controls the knob requires two actions to be opened: (1) pushing and maintaining the latch *while* (2) turning the knob.

An explicit representation of time can significantly extend the expressiveness of the planning model. One may pursue such an extension in either of the following two ways.

1. Keep the notion of global states of the world and include time explicitly in the representation of state-transition systems, e.g., as in timed automata. This approach will not be developed here. This state-oriented view models the dynamics of the world as a sequence of global states or snapshots of the entire domain.
2. Take another view that deals not with a set of states but with a set of functions of time describing parallel evolutions. This time-oriented view represents the dynamics of the world as a collection of partial functions of time describing local evolutions of a state variable.

1. In classical planning, only independent actions, as defined in Chapters 5 and 6, are allowed to overlap.

These two views are represented in Figure IV.1, where time is the horizontal axis and state variables are along the vertical axis. In the state-oriented view, the elementary component is a state, i.e., a "vertical slice" or snapshot that gives a complete description of the domain at a single time point. In the time-oriented view, the building block is a function of time, i.e., a "horizontal slice" that focuses on just one state variable and gives its evolution along the time line.

Example IV.1 The state-oriented view, on which we relied up to now, is illustrated in Figure 1.1 for the DWR domain as a set of six states. One possible *trajectory* for this dynamic system is, e.g., the sequence of states $\langle s_0, s_2, s_3, s_4 \rangle$. In the time-oriented view, the same trajectory can be described, informally and qualitatively, as three concurrent functions of time for three variables describing, respectively, the behavior of the robot, the crane, and the container.

- The robot moves from location 1 to location 2 unloaded, then it gets loaded with the container, then it moves to location 2.
- The crane picks up the container and puts it on the robot when the robot is at location 1.
- The container is on top of the pallet in location 1, then it gets loaded onto the robot at that location and gets moved to location 2.

■

This part of the book introduces a shift of focus. We will be moving from the state-oriented view to the time-oriented view. Although there are some approaches to temporal planning that rely on timed extensions of state-transition systems (e.g., [24, 374, 376]), most approaches adopt the time-oriented view that appears more natural and conceptually simpler.

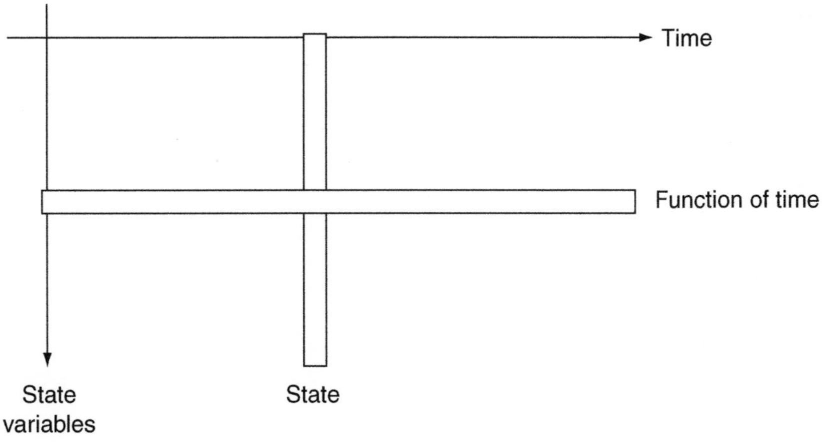

Figure IV.1 From a state-oriented to a time-oriented view of the dynamics.

An appealing advantage of this time-oriented view is that it makes use of well-developed representations of time and temporal reasoning techniques. Chapter 13 is entirely devoted to these techniques. Temporal planning is addressed in Chapter 14.

Another good reason for adopting the time-oriented view is its closeness to scheduling techniques. This makes it possible to integrate the synthesis of plans to the scheduling of actions and resource allocation. Chapter 15 is devoted to planning and resource scheduling.

CHAPTER 13

Time for Planning

13.1 Introduction

The purpose of this chapter is to present temporal representations and temporal reasoning techniques that are useful to planning with time and resources. Temporal planning itself will not be covered until the next chapter.

The mathematical structure of time is generally a set with a transitive and asymmetric ordering operation. It can be discrete, dense or continuous, bounded or unbounded, totally ordered or branching.[1] We will rely here on a simple structure of time as modeled by the set $\Re$ of real numbers.

The chapter introduces, informally through examples, temporal references and temporal relations (Section 13.2). Temporal references are instants or intervals. Relations are, for example, before, overlap, or a numerical relation. In planning, temporal relations can be conveniently represented and handled with CSP-based approaches and techniques.[2] Two main formalisms for qualitative relations are developed: the time-point algebra, in Section 13.3.1, and the interval algebra in Section 13.3.2. The relationships between these two formalisms are discussed in Section 13.3.4. Finally, the quantitative temporal constraint networks are introduced in Section 13.4. The chapter ends with a discussion and exercises.

13.2 Temporal References and Relations

Consider the following assertion: "`crane2` loads `container5` onto `robot1` during interval *i*." This assertion can be analyzed from the causal point of view: *what* changes are entailed by the assertion and *what* conditions are required for it to hold consistently. But it can also be analyzed from the temporal point of view: *when* other related assertions can or cannot take place. These *what* and *when* issues may or may not be decomposed into two separate computational processes, but they need to

---

1. For a discussion of the mathematical structure of time, see [474, 520].
2. Refer to Chapter 8 for a review of CSP concepts and algorithms.

be distinguished conceptually. Temporal planning, as any other form of temporal reasoning, has to deal with these two distinct issues.

1. *What*: reasoning about *change* and *causality* relations entailed by actions and events.
2. *When*: dealing with *temporal references* of propositions and temporal relations, our purpose in this chapter. These temporal references are time periods during which a proposition holds or time points at which a state variable changes its value. They are represented as instants or intervals. An *instant* is a variable ranging over the set $\Re$ of real numbers. An *interval* is a pair (x, y) of reals, such that $x \leq y$.

Typically, a planner that reasons about time operates on a temporal database that maintains temporal references for every domain proposition that varies in time: when does it hold or when does it change. These are the temporal references of the proposition. The planner asserts relations among these temporal references. The temporal database has to provide functions for querying, for updating, and for maintaining the consistency of the database. Let us illustrate through a few examples the different types of temporal references and relations we are considering.

Example 13.1 In the DWR domain, consider the operation of loading the container cont onto a robot rob at location loc.

- Let t_1 be the instant at which the robot enters the location loc, t_2 the instant at which the robot stops in loc,[3] and let i_1 be the interval $[t_1, t_2]$ corresponding to the robot *entering* loc.
- Let t_3 be the instant at which the crane starts picking up the container, t_4 the instant at which the crane finishes putting down the container onto the robot, and i_2 the interval $[t_3, t_4]$ corresponding to the crane *picking up and loading* cont.
- Let t_5 be the instant at which the container cont is loaded onto the robot, t_6 the instant at which the container stops being loaded onto the robot, and i_3 the interval $[t_5, t_6]$ corresponding to the container staying *loaded* on rob.

Let us assume that the crane can start picking up a container as soon as the robot on which it is to be loaded has entered the location. One possible position in time for these instants and intervals is depicted in Figure 13.1. Other possibilities would be to have $t_3 = t_1$ or $t_3 = t_2$ or $t_2 < t_3 < t_5$. Here we assume that the container is loaded as soon as the crane finishes putting it down, i.e., $t_4 = t_5$. The example does not mention any reason for the end of i_3; i.e., the value of t_6 can be arbitrarily large. ■

In this example, the set of instants $\{t_1, \ldots, t_6\}$ and the set of intervals $\{i_1, i_2, i_3\}$ are *temporal references* that specify when domain propositions are true. Here, these two

3. Presumably there is a specific loading/unloading position in loc at which the robot stops.

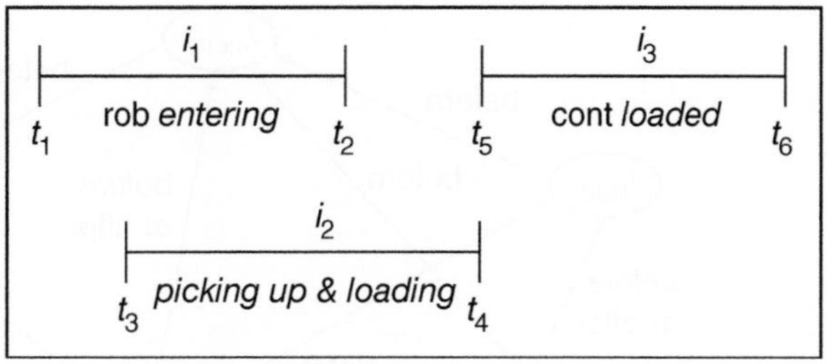

Figure 13.1 Entering and loading operations.

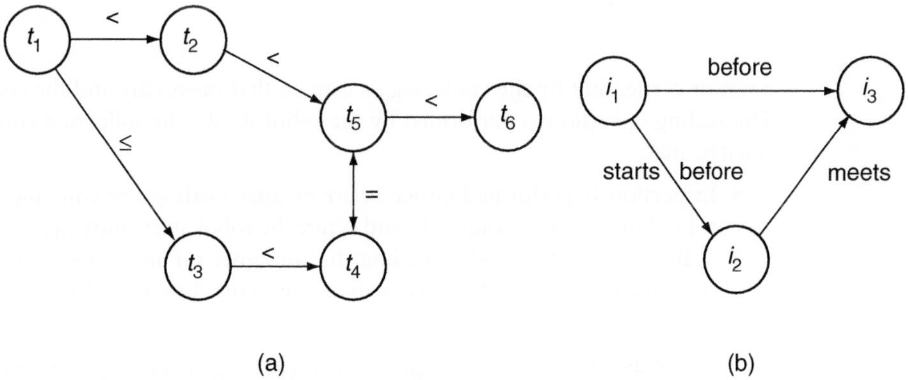

Figure 13.2 Networks of constraints over instants (a) and intervals (b).

sets play the same role. We may describe this example using just the three intervals: the *entering* of the robot during i_1, the *picking up and loading* of the container during i_2, and the container staying *loaded* during i_3. Intervals i_1 and i_2 refer to *activities*, while interval i_3 refers to a *proposition*. Note that the example does not give metrical information about duration or about absolute time positions: it is a qualitative representation.

The temporal relations between these temporal references can be expressed as binary constraints between instants or between intervals. The constraints for Example 13.1 are expressed in the two networks over instants and intervals, Figures 13.2(a) and (b), respectively. In these networks, nodes are labeled by temporal references, and arcs are labeled by temporal constraints (to be defined formally in upcoming sections), which express precedence and equality of time points or the relative positions of intervals.

Example 13.2 Consider a DWR domain where security is an important concern: every moved container has to be *inspected* and *sealed*. The inspection operation uses

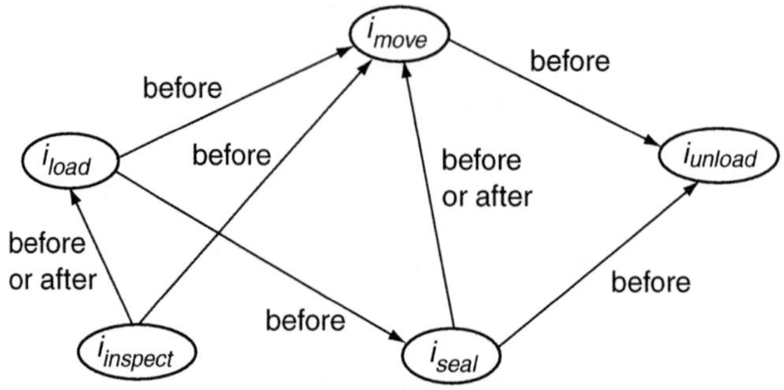

Figure 13.3 Network of constraints over intervals.

a sensor carried out by the crane, e.g., a camera that moves around the container. The sealing operation is performed by the robot itself. The following constraints must be met.

- Inspection is performed either *before or after* loading the container on the robot but *not while* holding it, and *before* the robot starts moving.
- Sealing is performed *after* loading the container on and *before* unloading it from the robot, and either *before or after* moving it to its destination, but *not while* in motion.

We may use five intervals (i_{load}, i_{move}, i_{unload}, $i_{inspect}$, and i_{seal}) to denote the *loading, moving, unloading, inspection,* and *sealing* operations, respectively. These intervals are nodes of a constraint network (Figure 13.3) whose arcs are labeled by the binary constraints between the intervals. The set of solutions of this constraint net corresponds to all feasible organizations of these five activities that meet the constraints.

■

An interval i is described by its two end points, noted i^- and i^+, together with the constraint $[i^- \leq i^+]$.[4] One could specify this example with a network of ten instants. A constraint such as $[i_{load}$ before $i_{move}]$ is translated into the conjunction of three constraints: $[i^+_{load} < i^-_{move}]$, $[i^-_{load} \leq i^+_{load}]$, and $[i^-_{move} \leq i^+_{move}]$. However, the constraint $[i_{move}$ before or after $i_{seal}]$ requires a more complex expression involving four instants: $[(i^+_{move} < i^-_{seal})$ or $(i^+_{seal} < i^-_{move})]$. This disjunction cannot be expressed into a single binary relation because it involves four instants; hence it cannot correspond to the label of an arc of a network of instants. Although the two networks of Figure 13.2 are equivalent, in general not every network of interval constraints can be translated into a network of instants (this will be detailed in Section 13.3.4). There are ways to combine instants and intervals into a general representation; however,

4. We will denote temporal constraints in the infix notation within square brackets as delimiters.

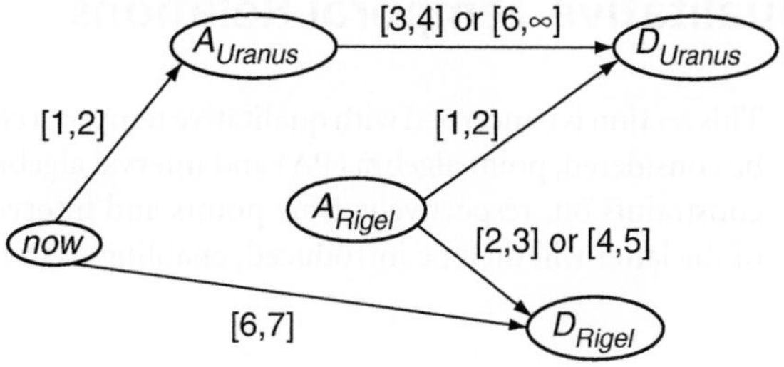

Figure 13.4 Network of numerical constraints over instants.

most temporal planning languages choose either instants or intervals for temporal references.

Let us now illustrate another type of *quantitative* temporal relation.

Example 13.3 Consider a DWR domain in which ships to be loaded and unloaded are not on dock indefinitely. The planner also may have to consider their schedules. Assume that two ships, the *Uranus* and the *Rigel*, are scheduled to be serviced. The *Uranus* arrival is expected within one or two days; it will leave either with a light cargo (then it will have to stay docked three to four days) or with a full load (then it will have to stay docked at least six days). The *Rigel* can be serviced either on an express dock (then it will stay docked two to three days) or on a normal dock (then it will stay four to five days).

Assume further that the *Uranus* has to depart one to two days after the arrival of the *Rigel*, which in turn has to depart six to seven days from now. Questions such as when the *Rigel* should arrive, whether it can be serviced on a normal dock, and whether the *Uranus* can take a full load can be answered by solving the constraint network in Figure 13.4. This network has five instants corresponding to the arrival and departure of the two ships (noted, respectively, A_{Rigel} and D_{Rigel} and similarly for the *Uranus*) and to the current time (noted *now*). It relates these instants with arcs labeled by numerical intervals or by disjunction of intervals, e.g., $(2 \leq D_{Rigel} - A_{Rigel} \leq 3) \vee (4 \leq D_{Rigel} - A_{Rigel} \leq 5)$. ■

To summarize, these examples illustrated two ways to express temporal information about activities and propositions of a planning domain: either with *instants* or with *intervals*. The first two examples consider *qualitative* constraints to relate two instants or two intervals, whereas this last example introduces *quantitative* and *absolute* time constraints. As illustrated in Example 13.2, intervals can be translated into instants, but some binary constraints on intervals cannot be translated into binary constraints on instants.

In the following sections, we will detail more formally how to manage qualitative constraints on instants and on intervals and quantitative constraints on instants.

13.3 Qualitative Temporal Relations

This section is concerned with qualitative temporal constraints. Two approaches will be considered, point algebra (PA) and interval algebra (IA), dealing with qualitative constraints on, respectively, time points and intervals. A geometric interpretation of the latter will then be introduced, enabling us to relate the two representations.

13.3.1 Point Algebra

Point algebra (PA) is a symbolic calculus that enables us to relate in time a set of instants with qualitative constraints without necessarily ordering them.

Two instants t_1 and t_2 that are set in time, with real values, can be related in only three possible ways: $[t_1 < t_2]$, $[t_1 > t_2]$, or $[t_1 = t_2]$. Two instants whose values are not known and whose relative positions are not precisely specified may be constrained, as in $[t_1 \leq t_2]$, $[t_1 \geq t_2]$, $[t_1 \neq t_2]$.

Let $P = \{<, =, >\}$ be the set of *primitive relation symbols* between instants (*primitives* for short). PA relies on the following set of qualitative constraints:

$$R = 2^P = \{\emptyset, \{<\}, \{=\}, \{>\}, \{<, =\}, \{>, =\}, \{<, >\}, P\}$$

Here, "$\emptyset$" denotes the empty constraint that cannot be satisfied and P the universal constraint.

Each element $r \in R$ is a set of primitives; r is a constraint interpreted as the *disjunction* of these primitives. For example, $[t \neq t']$ is denoted $[t\ r\ t']$ for $r = \{<, >\}$.

The usual operations on sets apply to R: $\cap, \cup$, etc. In addition, a composition operation, noted $\bullet$, is defined to handle transitivity:

$$\text{for } r, q \in R: \text{ if } [t_1\ r\ t_2] \text{ and } [t_2\ q\ t_3], \text{ then } [t_1\ r \bullet q\ t_3].$$

This operation is computed according to the composition table for the three primitives (Figure 13.5) and to the distributivity property:

$$\text{for } r, s, q \in R: (r \cup q) \bullet s = (r \bullet s) \cup (q \bullet s), \text{ and similarly for } s \bullet (r \cup q).$$

Finally, the symmetrical constraint of $[t_1\ r\ t_2]$ is the constraint r' such that $[t_2\ r'\ t_1]$ iff $[t_1\ r\ t_2]$. r' is obtained by replacing in the set r the primitive $<$ by $>$ and symmetrically, while $=$ remains unchanged. Note that $(r \bullet q)' = q' \bullet r'$.

The set R with the two operations $(R, \cup, \bullet)$ is an *algebra* in the following sense: It is closed under the two operations, $\cup$ is an associative and commutative operation whose identity is $\emptyset$ (i.e., $(R, \cup)$ is a semigroup with a unit element), $\bullet$ is an associative operation whose identity is $\{=\}$, and the two operations are distributive.

•	<	=	>
<	<	<	P
=	<	=	>
>	P	>	>

Figure 13.5 Composition table for time-point algebra.

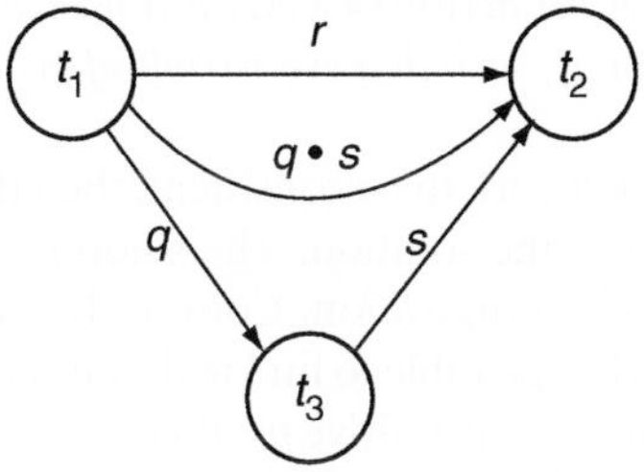

Figure 13.6 Transitive composition and conjunction.

However, the most useful operations, within a CSP framework, are $\cap$ and $\bullet$. Indeed, constraint propagation and consistency checking proceed by combining a given constraint r with the constraint entailed by transitive composition (Figure 13.6):

$$\text{if } [t_1 \ r \ t_2] \text{ and } [t_1 \ q \ t_3] \text{ and } [t_3 \ s \ t_2], \text{ then } [t_1 \ r \cap (q \bullet s) \ t_2].$$

If $r \cap (q \bullet s) = \emptyset$, then the constraints r, q, and s are inconsistent.

Example 13.4 Let us make explicit a few constraints in the PA network of Figure 13.2 (a) that are entailed by transitive composition.

$$(t_4, t_6) : [t_4 = t_5] \bullet [t_5 < t_6] \Rightarrow [t_4 < t_6]$$
$$(t_2, t_3) : [t_2 > t_1] \bullet [t_1 \leq t_3] \Rightarrow [t_2 \ P \ t_3]$$
$$(t_2, t_4) : [t_2 < t_5] \bullet [t_5 = t_4] \Rightarrow [t_2 < t_4]$$

Another path $\langle t_2, t_3, t_4 \rangle$ gives for (t_2, t_4):

$$[t_2 \ P \ t_3] \bullet [t_3 < t_4] \Rightarrow [t_2 \ P \ t_4]$$

and the conjunction for the two constraints on (t_2, t_4) is $P \cap \{<\} = \{<\}$. ■

More generally, let $X = \{t_1, t_2, \ldots, t_n\}$ be a set of instant variables, where the domain of each t_i is the set $\Re$ of real numbers. A *binary constraint network* for the point algebra is defined as a directed graph (X, C) where each arc in C is labeled by a constraint $r_{ij} \in R$: $[t_i \; r_{ij} \; t_j]$. We assume (X, C) to be symmetrical CSP, i.e., for all $i, j : r_{j,i} = r'_{ij}$. Note that if $(t_i, t_j) \notin C$, i.e., there is no explicit constraint in (X, C) between t_i and t_j, then $r_{ij} = P$, the universal constraint.

A tuple of reals $(v_1, \ldots, v_n)$ is a *solution* of (X, C) iff the n values $t_i = v_i$ satisfy all the constraints of C. The PA network (X, C) is *consistent* when a solution exists. Every pair (t_i, t_j) in a solution is related by a *single primitive relation* $p_{ij} \in P$ because it corresponds to a pair of $\Re^2$. This set of primitives characterizes entirely the relative positions of instants in a solution.

Proposition 13.1 *A PA network (X, C) is consistent iff there is a set of primitives $p_{ij} \in r_{ij}$, for each pair (i, j), such that every triple of primitives verifies $p_{ij} \in (p_{ik} \bullet p_{kj})$.*

Proof Assume the network to be consistent; then the set p_{ij} follows directly from the real values (v_i, v_j) of the solution. The solution meets all the constraints: $p_{ij} \in r_{ij}$; it also meets their composition. Conversely, assume that there is a set of primitives $p_{ij} \in r_{ij}$; then it is possible to find real values v_i, for $1 \leq i \leq n$, such that each pair of values is related by a primitive p_{ij}: there cannot be a conflict because $p_{ij} \in (p_{ik} \bullet p_{kj})$, and this set of values meets all the constraints. ■

In this qualitative calculus, we will not be interested in the real values of a solution but only in a set of primitives that meets the consistency condition.

Note that a PA network departs from the standard CSPs over finite domains because here the variable domains are not finite. However, most CSP definitions are easily extended to this case by viewing a constraint r_{ij} as a finite domain from which we are seeking a single element and a solution as being the set of primitives $p_{ij} \in r_{ij}$ meeting the consistency condition. In particular, we'll say that

- a primitive in $r_{ij} \in C$ is *redundant* if there is no solution where (t_i, t_j) are related by this primitive, and
- a network is *minimal* if it has no redundant primitive in a constraint.

Redundant primitives can be filtered out on the basis of the transitive closure propagation with a path-consistency algorithm in $O(n^3)$ (Figure 8.5). If the filtering leads to an empty constraint, r_{ij}, then the network is necessarily inconsistent. It turns out that this necessary condition is also a sufficient condition in this case: algorithm PC, incomplete in the general case, is complete for PA networks. Hence, a PA network (X, C) is consistent iff algorithm PC(X, C) does not return inconsistent. In planning, we will generate incrementally a network (X, C) by adding new instants and constraints while searching for a plan. In order to keep the current net consistent, we can use IPC, the incremental version of path consistency (Figure 8.6).

However, the path-consistency algorithms do not provide, after filtering, a minimal network. Indeed, the network in Figure 13.7 is path-consistent but the primitive $[t_1 = t_4]$ is redundant: there is no solution in which these two instants are equal. A 4-consistency algorithm is required for obtaining a minimal network [537, 538].

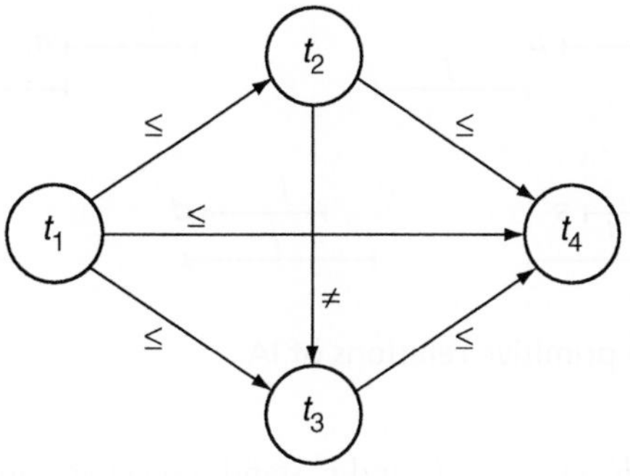

Figure 13.7 A path-consistent PA network.

Alternatively, one may restrict the set of constraints to $R - \{<, >\}$. The corresponding algebra, noted PA_c, is said to be convex. It is closed for the intersection and composition operations. Path consistency provides minimal networks for PA_c.

A more efficient approach for checking the consistency and for obtaining minimal PA networks is to use graph connectivity techniques. The *precedence graph* associated with a PA network (X, C) is a directed graph $G = (X, E)$ with the same set of vertices and with edges defined as follows.

- If r_{ij} is $\{<\}$ or $\{<, =\}$, then $(t_i, t_j) \in E$.
- If r_{ij} is $\{=\}$, then both $(t_i, t_j) \in E$ and $(t_j, t_i) \in E$.

E does not contain edges associated with the constraints $\neq$ or P. It can be shown that a PA network is consistent iff for any pair (t_i, t_j) such that $\{=\} \subseteq r_{ij}$, then t_i and t_j are in the same strongly connected component of G, i.e., there is a path in G from t_i to t_j and a path from t_j to t_i. Hence, consistency checking can be performed by computing strongly connected components of G and testing each constraint in C; both tasks require $O(|C|)$.

13.3.2 Interval Algebra

Interval algebra (IA) is similar to PA except that it deals with intervals instead of points. IA is a symbolic calculus that enables us to relate in time a set of intervals with qualitative constraints.

Two intervals i and j whose end points are precisely set in $\Re$ can be related qualitatively in only thirteen possible ways, seven of which are shown in Figure 13.8. These primitive relations correspond to all consistent cases, in PA, of precedence or equality of the four endpoints i^-, i^+, j^-, and j^+ of i and j, with the constraints $[i^- < i^+]$ and $[j^- < j^+]$. The thirteen relations are the following.

- b, m, o, s, d, and f stand respectively for *before, meet, overlap, start, during,* and *finish.*

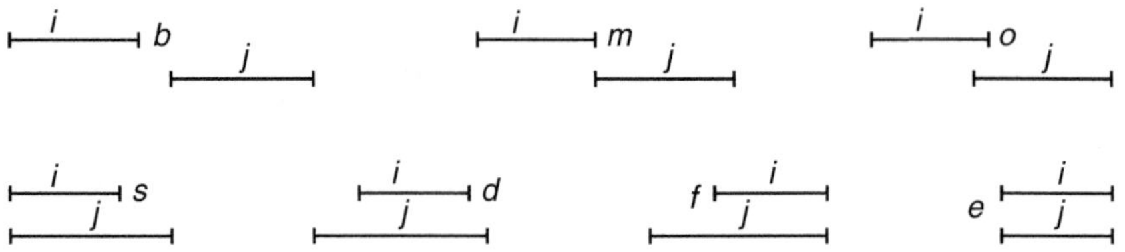

Figure 13.8 Seven primitive relations of IA.

- b', m', o', s', d', and f' stand respectively for *after, is-met-by, is-overlapped-by, is-started-by, includes,* and *is-finished-by*. These are the symmetrical relations of b, m, o, s, d, and f, i.e., $[i\ b'\ j]$ when $[j\ b\ i]$, $[i\ m'\ j]$ when $[j\ m\ i]$, etc.
- e stands for *equal*, which is identical to the symmetrical relation e'.

Two intervals whose relative positions are not precisely known can be related by any *disjunction* of such primitive relations.

Let $P = \{b, m, o, s, d, f, e, b', m', o', s', d', f'\}$ be the set of *primitive relation symbols* between intervals (*primitives* for short). IA relies on the following set of qualitative constraints:

$$R = 2^P = \{\emptyset; \{b\}; \{m\}; \{o\}; \ldots; \{b, m\}; \{b, o\}; \ldots; \{b, m, o\}; \ldots; P\}.$$

Each element $r \in R$ is a set of primitives; r is a constraint interpreted as the *disjunction* of these primitives. For example, $[i\ \{b, m\}\ i']$ denotes $[(i\ b\ i') \vee (i\ m\ i')]$. As in the previous section, "$\emptyset$" is the constraint that cannot be satisfied and P the universal constraint, which is always satisfied. Out of the 2^{13} constraints in R, one may select a subset of constraints that are useful for some applications and/or have a particular semantics, and give the constraints mnemonic names, e.g., while $= \{s, d, f\}$, disjoint $= \{b, b'\}$, and joint $= \{m, m', o, o', s, s', f, f', d, d', e\} = P -$ disjoint, etc.

The usual operations on sets apply to R: $\cap, \cup$, etc., as well as the composition operation, noted $\bullet$, for transitivity:

$$\text{for } r_{1,2}, r_{2,3} \in R\text{: if } [i_1\ r_{1,2}\ i_2] \text{ and } [i_2\ r_{2,3}\ i_3], \text{ then } [i_1\ (r_{1,2} \bullet r_{2,3})\ i_3].$$

This operation is computed from a composition table for the 13 primitives and from the distributivity property:

$$\text{for } r_1, r_2, r_3 \in R\text{: } (r_1 \cup r_2) \bullet r_3 = (r_1 \bullet r_2) \cup (r_2 \bullet r_3),$$

and similarly for $r_3 \bullet (r_1 \cup r_2)$.

Finally, the symmetrical constraint of $[i_1\ r\ i_2]$, i.e., r' such that $[i_2\ r'\ i_1]$, is obtained by replacing in r every primitive by its symmetrical primitive, i.e., b by b', o by o', etc.

$\bullet$	b	m	o	s	d	f	b'	d'	f'
b	b	b	b	b	$u \cup v$	$u \cup v$	P	b	b
m	b	b	b	m	v	v	$u' \cup v'$	b	b
o	b	b	u	o	v	v	$u' \cup v'$	$u \cup w'$	u
s	b	b	u	s	d	d	b'	$u \cup w'$	u
d	b	b	$u \cup v$	d	d	d	b'	P	$u \cup v$
f	m	m	v	d	d	f	b'	$u' \cup v'$	x
b'	P	$w \cup u'$	$w \cup u'$	$w \cup u'$	$w \cup u'$	b'	b'	b'	b'
d'	$u \cup w'$	v'	$o' \cup w'$	$o \cup w'$	y	v'	$u' \cup v'$	d'	d'
f'	b	m	o	o	v	x	$u' \cup v'$	d'	f'
s'	$u \cup w'$	$o \cup w'$	$o \cup w'$	$\{s,e,s'\}$	$o' \cup w$	o'	b'	d'	d'

Figure 13.9 Part of the composition table for IA.

Part of the composition table is given in Figure 13.9 where, for simplicity, curly brackets for sets are implicit and the following constraints in R are named: $u = \{b, m, o\}$; $v = \{o, s, d\}$; $w = \{d, f\}$; $x = \{f, e, f'\}$; and $y = P - \{b, m, b', m'\}$. Some (but not all) of the missing composition operations in the table can be completed with the general property of symmetrical constraints: $(r \cup q)' = q' \cup r'$, and by denoting that $\{e\}$ is the identity element for the composition.

Note that $\bullet$ is not a commutative operation in IA. For example, Figure 13.10 illustrates on the left of the figure. $\{d\} \cup \{b\} = \{b\}$; whereas on the right, $\{b\} \cup \{d\} = \{b, m, o, s, d\}$. This is because $[(i\ d\ j) \wedge (j\ b\ k)]$ constrains k to a single position with

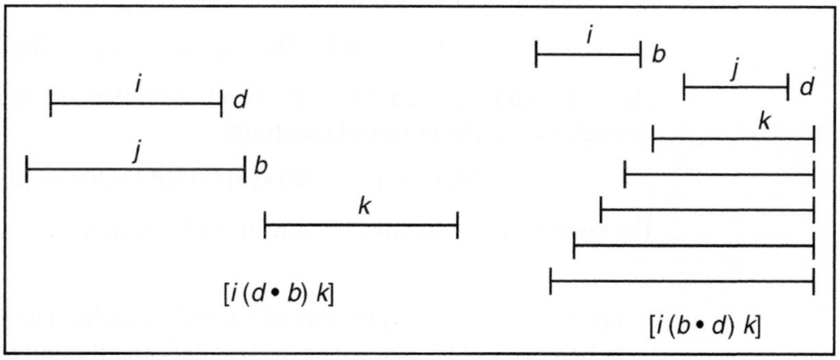

Figure 13.10 Two composition operations.

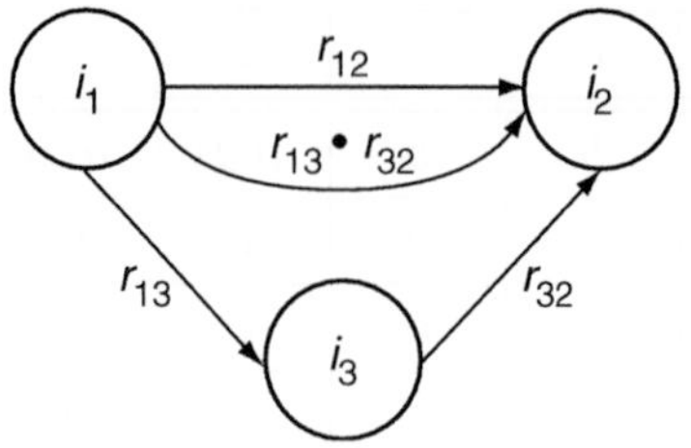

Figure 13.11 Transitive composition and conjunction over intervals.

respect to i, whereas $[(i\ b\ j) \wedge (j\ d\ k)]$ leaves five possibilities for k (drawn in the figure as separate segments) with respect to i. Each cell in the composition table can be obtained by just looking at the possible configurations of three intervals, i, j, and k. It can also be obtained with a PA net over the six end points i^-, i^+, j^-, j^+, k^-, and k^+ by finding all its subnetworks between i^-, i^+, k^-, and k^+ that correspond to valid PA networks for primitives in P.

As for PA, the set R in IA with the two operations $(R, \cup, \bullet)$ is an *algebra*: it is closed under two operations: $\cup$ is an associative and commutative operation, with identity $\emptyset$; $\bullet$ is associative, with identity $\{e\}$. The two operations are distributive.

Here also, the useful operation for constraint satisfaction relies on the transitive closure propagation (Figure 13.11, similar to Figure 13.6 for PA):

$$\text{if } [i_1\ r\ i_2] \text{ and } [i_1\ p\ i_3] \text{ and } [i_3\ q\ i_2], \text{ then } [i_1\ r \cap (p \bullet q)\ i_2].$$

If $r \cap (p \bullet q) = \emptyset$, then the three constraints are inconsistent.

Example 13.5 In the IA network for the situation described in Example 13.2 (see page 287) (Figure 13.12), suppose we want to know the constraint between the *inspect* and *unload* intervals. By transitivity through i_{move} we have:

$$[i_{inspect}\ (\{b\} \bullet \{b\})\ i_{unload}] = [i_{inspect}\ \{b\}\ i_{unload}].$$

The constraint between the *inspect* and *seal* intervals, computed by transitivity through i_{load}, is the universal constraint:

$$\{b, b'\} \bullet \{b\} = (\{b\} \bullet \{b\}) \cup (\{b'\} \bullet \{b\}) = \{b\} \cup P = P.$$

The same result is obtained by transitivity through i_{move}. ■

Let $X = \{i_1, i_2, \ldots, i_n\}$ be a set of interval variables. The domain of each interval is the half plane of $\Re^2$ defined by the inequality on the end points $i^- \leq i^+$. A *binary constraint network for interval algebra* is a directed graph (X, C) where each arc in C is labeled by a constraint $r_{ij} \in R$: $[i\ r_{ij}\ j]$. We assume (X, C) to be a symmetrical

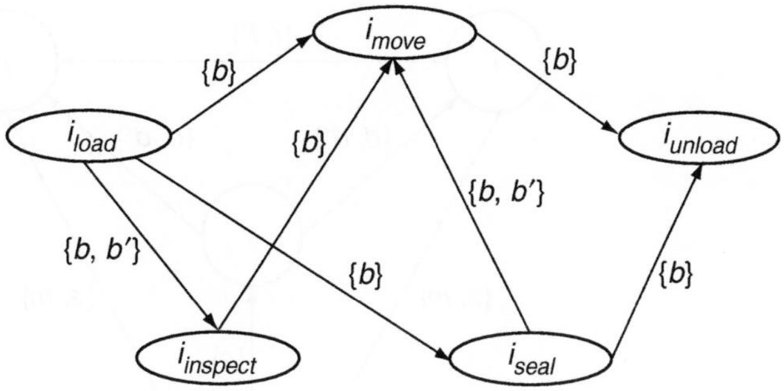

Figure 13.12 An IA network.

CSP, i.e., for all $i, j \in X : r_{j,i} = r'_{ij}$. Note that if $(i, j) \notin C$, i.e., there is no explicit constraint in (X, C) between intervals i and j, then $r_{ij} = P$, the universal constraint.

A tuple of pairs of reals $((i_1^-, i_1^+), \ldots, (i_n^-, i_n^+))$, with $i^- \leq i^+$, is a *solution* of (X, C) iff the n intervals $i = [i^-, i^+]$ satisfy all the constraints of C. The IA network (X, C) is *consistent* when a solution exists. Every pair (i, j) in a solution is related by a *single primitive relation* $p_{ij} \in P$.

Proposition 13.2 *An IA network (X, C) is consistent iff there is a set of primitives $p_{ij} \in r_{ij}$, for each pair (i, j), such that every triple of primitives verifies $p_{ij} \in (p_{ik} \bullet p_{kj})$.*

The proof is a direct transposition of the proof of Proposition 13.1 (see page 292) to IA. Note that it is essential in Proposition 13.2 that p_{ij} are *primitives*; in particular, the proposition does not hold if the intervals are related by a set of constraints meeting $r_{ij} \in (r_{ik} \bullet r_{kj})$.

The notions of redundant primitives in a constraint and of minimal networks for IA nets are as defined in standard CSPs. Redundant primitives can be filtered out by the transitive closure propagation with the path-consistency algorithm in $O(n^3)$. If the filtering leads to an empty constraint, then the network is necessarily inconsistent. However, this is no longer a sufficient condition: the path-consistency algorithm is not complete for IA networks. A counterexample is the network of Figure 13.13, which is path-consistent but is not consistent. Indeed, the consistency checking of IA networks is an NP-complete problem, as for general CSPs.

One may use the standard CSP algorithms such as backtrack search and forward checking (Figures 8.2 and 8.3, respectively) with some slight modifications: instead of choosing at each step a value for a variable, one chooses nondeterministically a primitive in a constraint and propagates this choice.

Let us close this section with some useful properties for temporal planning, with respect to the constraint in R that we proposed to name joint $= \{m, m', o, o', s, s', f, f', d, d', e\} = P - \{b, b'\}$. This constraint characterizes the case where intervals can have a nonempty intersection and enables us to detect various types of conflicts.

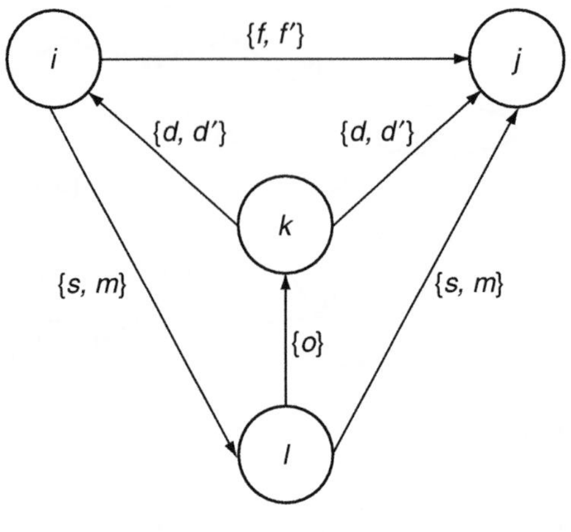

Figure 13.13 An inconsistent IA network.

Definition 13.1 Let (X, C) be a consistent IA network. Two interval variables $i, j \in X$ are *necessarily intersecting* iff for every solution of the network, the two corresponding intervals of $\Re$, $[i^-, i^+]$ and $[j^-, j^+]$, have a nonempty intersection, i.e., $[i^-, i^+] \cap [j^-, j^+] \neq \emptyset$. The two interval variables i and j are *possibly intersecting* iff there is a solution of the network that meets this equation. ■

Proposition 13.3 *Let r_{ij} be a constraint between two interval variables i and j in a consistent IA network (X, C). If $r_{ij} \subseteq$ joint, then i and j are necessarily intersecting.*

Proof For every solution of the network (X, C), the pair (i, j) is related by a primitive p_{ij} which is, by definition, included in the minimal constraint $\hat{r}_{ij}$ between i and j. Furthermore, in that solution, $[i^-, i^+] \cap [j^-, j^+] \neq \emptyset$ iff the corresponding primitive is neither b nor b'; any other primitive in joint corresponds to a nonempty intersection. Now, assume $r_{ij} \subseteq$ joint, because $\hat{r}_{ij} \subseteq r_{ij}$, then for every solution, the corresponding p_{ij} is neither b nor b', hence i and j are necessarily intersecting. ■

The converse of this proposition is weaker: if i and j are necessarily intersecting, then $\hat{r}_{ij} \subseteq$ joint, hence $r_{ij} \cap$ joint $\neq \emptyset$.

Proposition 13.4 *A pair (i, j) in a consistent IA network (X, C) is possibly intersecting iff the constraint $[i$ joint $j]$ is consistent with C, iff $C \not\models [i\ \{b, b'\}\ j]$.*

Proof When $[i$ joint $j]$ is consistent with the network, then $\hat{r}_{ij} \cap$ joint $\neq \emptyset$, hence there is a solution related by a primitive in joint. Conversely, if there is such a solution, then $\hat{r}_{ij} \cap$ joint $\neq \emptyset$. The second *iff* follows from the equivalence between $C \not\models [i\ \{b, b'\}\ j]$ and $\hat{r}_{ij} \cap$ joint $\neq \emptyset$. ■

Let us now generalize Definition 13.1 to a subset of interval variables.

Definition 13.2 A subset $I \subseteq X$ of interval variables is *necessarily intersecting* iff for every solution of the network $\bigcap_{i \in I}[i^-, i^+] \neq \emptyset$. The subset I is *possibly intersecting* iff there is a solution of the network for which $\bigcap_{i \in I}[i^-, i^+] \neq \emptyset$. ■

Proposition 13.5 *A subset of interval variables $I \subseteq X$ is necessarily intersecting iff every pair $i, j \in I$ is necessarily intersecting; I is possibly intersecting iff every pair in I is possibly intersecting.*

Proof The *only-if* part follows directly from the definition. Let us show the converse. Consider a solution in which the intervals $[i^-, i^+]$ are pairwise intersecting for all pairs in I. This means that the interval variables in I cannot be related in that solution with primitives b_{ij} or b'_{ij}. Hence the constraint $[i^+ < j^-]$, for any pair i and j in I, is inconsistent with the PA network corresponding for that solution to the set of end points of X. However, it is simple to show that the constraints $[i^- < j^+]$, for all pairs i and j in I, are consistent with this network. Let $\hat{\epsilon}^-$ be the biggest start point in I and $\hat{\epsilon}^+$ the smallest end point. We have $[\hat{\epsilon}^- < \hat{\epsilon}^+]$, $[i^- < \hat{\epsilon}^+]$, and $[\hat{\epsilon}^- < i^+]$ for every $i \in I$. Consequently, the intersection $\bigcap_{iC \in I}[i^-, i^+] \neq \emptyset$. ■

Proposition 13.5 enables us to reduce a global k-ary property of a subset of k interval variables to a local property of pairs.

13.3.3 A Geometric Interpretation of Interval Algebra

IA has a nice geometric model that helps in clarifying its relationship to PA. A temporal interval i is a geometric point in the Cartesian plane $(i^-, i^+) \in \Re^2$, with $i^- \leq i^+$. Conversely, a point (x, y) of the plane, with $x \leq y$, corresponds to a temporal interval. A set of points of the plane meeting $x \leq y$, such as a segment, a line, or a two-dimensional area, is associated with a set of temporal intervals. Hence, the relative position of two intervals can be described from the relative position of two geometric points in this plane.

In addition to a geometric point, six areas and six lines of the plane are defined with respect to an interval i, delimited with the x, y axes and the diagonal line $y = x$. These six areas, six lines, and a point are the thirteen zones labeled with the thirteen primitives of P (see Figure 13.14). Each zone delimits a set of intervals that have a particular relationship with i. For example, an interval j whose geometric mapping in the plane falls into the area labeled b with respect to i has its two end points before i^-, hence, by definition $[j\ b\ i]$. Similarly, an interval k whose geometric point falls in area d is such that $i^- < k^-$ and $k^+ < i^+$, i.e., $[k\ d\ i]$. Similar remarks explain the labeling of the other areas.

Among these zones, a line corresponds to a set of intervals that has one end point fixed as being equal to a end point of i and the other end point varying.

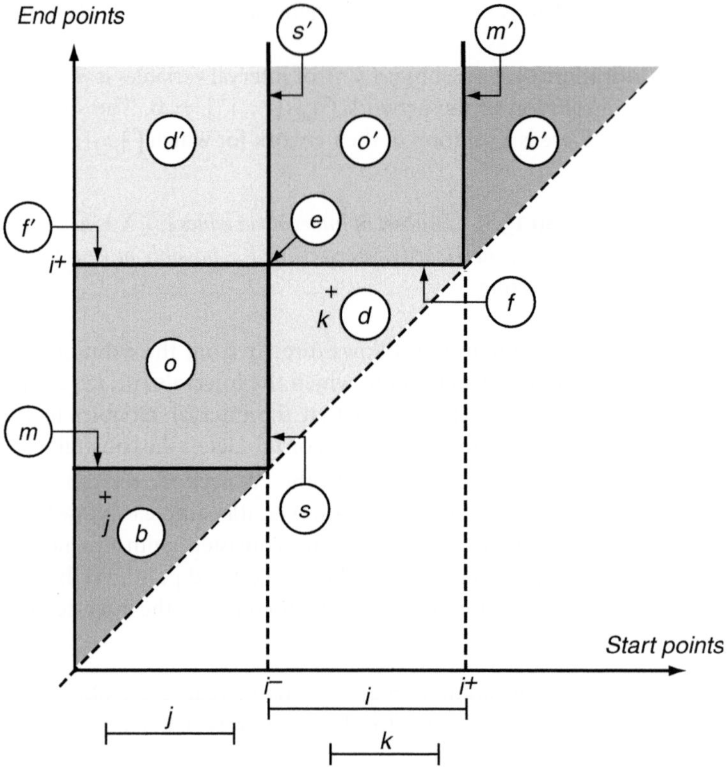

Figure 13.14 A geometric interpretation of interval algebra.

For example, the segment labeled s corresponds to the set of temporal intervals $\{j \mid j^- = i^-,\ j^+ > i^+\}$. A two-dimensional zone corresponds to a set of intervals whose two end points vary, e.g., the area labeled o corresponds to the intervals $\{j \mid j^- < i^-,\ i^- < j^+ < i^+\}$. Finally, the point labeled e is of dimension zero; it is the point i itself, and any interval mapped to this point is necessarily equal to i.

The position of an interval j that is not precisely known with respect to i can be modeled as one or several geometric zones (areas or lines) in the plane that are defined as the set of corresponding geometric points when j varies between some extreme positions. The intersection between these zones and the point, lines, and areas characteristic of i gives a disjunction of primitives corresponding to the constraint between i and j.

Example 13.6 In Figure 13.14, assume that an interval u starts with interval j and ends at some unknown point: it corresponds to a vertical half line starting at point j which crosses successively b, m, o, f', and d'; the constraint between u and i is thus $[u\ \{b, m, o, f', d'\}\ i]$. Similarly, an interval v that ends with k and starts at some unknown point will be described as a horizontal segment ending at point k that crosses the zones o, s, and d, hence $[v \{o, s, d\} i]$.

Consider an interval w that starts anywhere between the start points of j and k and ends between their end points, i.e., $j^- \leq w^- \leq k^-$ and $j^+ \leq w^+ \leq k^+$. Interval w corresponds to an area delimited by the equation $x \leq y$ and by the rectangle that has the line from point j to point k as one of its diagonals. This area intersects the zones labeled b, m, o, s, and d. Hence $[w \{b, m, o, s, d\} i]$. ■

It is interesting to note that the area associated with w in Example 13.6 is convex in the usual geometric sense, i.e., any point in a straight line between two points of the area belongs to it. Not every interval is mapped to a convex zone, i.e., an interval that is either entirely before or after i corresponds to the nonconvex union of the two zones labeled b and b'.

13.3.4 Interval Algebra versus Point Algebra

The convexity property of zones of the plane associated with intervals has an interesting and useful implication on IA. Let us define a graph G_{IA} that has 13 vertices labeled with the 13 primitives of P and that has an edge between two primitives iff the corresponding geometric zones are adjacent in the plane (Figure 13.15). A constraint $r \in R$ is said to be *convex* iff for any two primitives p_1 and p_2 in r all primitives along every shortest path in G_{IA} between p_1 and p_2 are also in r.

Example 13.7 $\{b, m, o, s, d\}$ is convex; $\{b, m, o, s, d, f\}$ is not convex because a minimal path from b to f goes through e and f'; but $\{b, m, o, s, d, f, e, f'\}$ is convex. ■

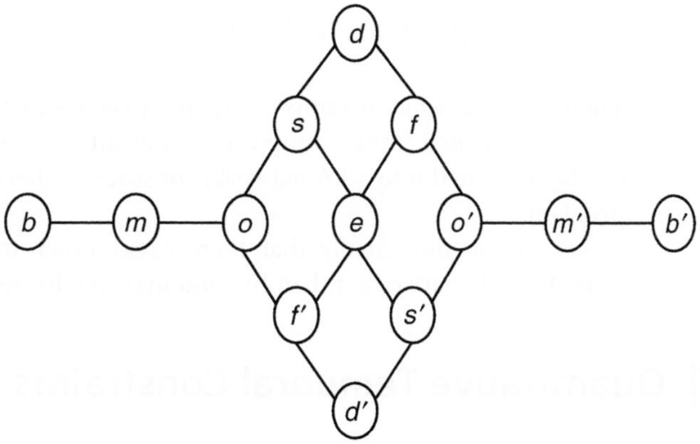

Figure 13.15 G_{IA} graph for convex constraints in interval algebra.

It can be shown that a constraint r is convex iff for every i and j such that $[j\ r\ i]$ the zone defined by j with respect to i is a convex zone in the plane.

As mentioned earlier, IA_c is the subset of the interval algebra restricted to convex constraints. Out of the 2^{13} constraints in IA, just 82 constraints are convex. IA_c is closed under the composition and intersection operations. Furthermore, checking the consistency of an IA_c network is a problem of polynomial complexity for which the path-consistency algorithm is complete and provides minimal networks.

A similar notion of convexity has been defined for PA. A constraint r in PA is said to be convex iff the set of points t that meet $[t\ r\ t_0]$, for t_0 fixed, is a convex part of $\Re$. It is easy to see that the only nonconvex constraint in PA is $\{<, >\}$. This explains the already introduced restriction of PA to the set $R - \{<, >\}$, denoted PA_c, which is closed under the composition and intersection operations.

Each of the 82 constraints in IA_c can be expressed as a conjunction of PA_c constraints. For example:

$$[i\ \{b, m, o\}\ j] \equiv [i^- < i^+] \wedge [j^- < j^+] \wedge [i^- < j^-] \wedge [i^+ < j^+].$$

Hence an IA_c network can be translated into a PA_c network. It is no surprise that we have the same computational properties for IA_c as for PA_c, namely, minimal nets obtained with path consistency.

Similarly, one may define another subset of IA by reference to the full PA. Let IA_p be the subset of IA constraints that can be expressed as conjunctions of PA constraints. For example:

$$[i\ \{b, o\}\ j] \equiv [i^- < i^+] \wedge [j^- < j^+] \wedge [i^- < j^-] \wedge [i^+ < j^+] \wedge [i^+ \neq j^-].$$

$\{b, o\}$ is an element of IA_p, but clearly it is not in IA_c (from the last constraint $[i^+ \neq j^-]$, or directly from Figure 13.15, which shows that $\{b, o\}$ is not convex). Furthermore, there are elements of IA that are not in IA_p. For example:

$$[i\ \{b, b'\}\ j] \equiv [i^- < i^+] \wedge [j^- < j^+] \wedge ([i^+ < j^-] \vee [j^+ \neq i^-]).$$

There are only 187 constraints in IA_p. It is easy to show $IA_c \subset IA_p \subset IA$. The subset IA_p is also closed under composition and intersection. Because an IA_p network can be translated into a PA network, consistency checking for IA_p is a polynomial problem.

Let us mention finally that there exists other tractable subsets of IA, e.g., [163, 419], that are richer than IA_p and maximal for set inclusion.

13.4 Quantitative Temporal Constraints

The temporal primitive in this section is again the time point. We'll be developing a calculus for relating a set of instants with quantitative, absolute, and relative numerical constraints. We'll first consider the simple case where every constraint is a simple interval, and then we'll move to the general case where disjunctions of intervals are allowed.

13.4.1 Simple Temporal Constraints

Let $X = \{t_1, t_2, \ldots, t_n\}$ be a set of time-point variables; the domain of each t_i is the set $\Re$ of real numbers. Each t_i can be subjected to

- a unary constraint of the form $a_i \leq t_i \leq b_i$ and to
- binary constraints of the form $a_{ij} \leq t_j - t_i \leq b_{ij}$,

with $a_i, b_i, a_{ij}, b_{ij} \in \Re$.

Let us take an origin reference point t_0 such as to rewrite every unary constraint $a_i \leq t_i \leq b_i$ as a binary one: $a_i \leq t_i - t_0 \leq b_i$. Furthermore, in order to retrieve the general framework set in the two previous sections, let us denote a binary constraint on a pair (t_i, t_j) as a constraint $r_{ij} = [a_{ij}, b_{ij}]$ corresponding to an interval of reals.

A simple temporal constraint problem (STP) is a pair (X, C), where each element in C is an interval r_{ij} that constrains the relative distance of a pair of instants (t_i, t_j). The composition and intersection operations for STPs are defined as follows.

- Composition: $r_{ij} \bullet r_{jk} = [a_{ij} + a_{jk}\ ,\ b_{ij} + b_{jk}]$, which corresponds to the sum of the two constraints $a_{ij} \leq t_j - t_i \leq b_{ij}$ and $a_{jk} \leq t_k - t_j \leq b_{jk}$.
- Intersection: $r_{ij} \cap r'_{ij} = [max\{a_{ij} + a'_{ij}\}\ ,\ min\{b_{ij} + b'_{ij}\}]$ which denotes the conjunction of $a_{ij} \leq t_j - t_i \leq b_{ij}$ and $a'_{ij} \leq t_j - t_i \leq b'_{ij}$.

Note that the symmetrical of r_{ij} is $r_{ji} = [-b_{ij}, -a_{ij}]$.

An STP (X, C) is consistent if there is a solution that satisfies all the constraints. It is minimal if every point in an interval r_{ij} belongs to some solution. Constraints can be reduced with the familiar transitive closure propagation operation: $r_{ij} \leftarrow r_{ij} \cap (r_{ik} \bullet r_{kj})$.

The path-consistency algorithm is complete for STPs. Furthermore, the algorithm reaches a fixed point after a single iteration over all triples i, j, k (see the simplified version of the algorithm in Figure 13.16). This fixed point corresponds to the minimal network.

Example 13.8 Returning to the situation in Example 13.3 (see page 289), assume that the *Uranus* ship takes a light load and that the *Rigel* is serviced on a normal dock. This reduces the network of Figure 13.4 to a simple net, shown in Figure 13.17. We can apply the path-consistency algorithm to this network to discover that it is consistent and that the *Rigel* arrives one or two days after the arrival of the *Uranus* and departs two to three days after the *Uranus* departs. ■

It is interesting to note that the path-consistency algorithm verifies these nice properties of completeness and reaching a minimal network after a single iteration

```
PC(X, C)
    for each k : 1 ≤ k ≤ n do
        for each pair i, j : 1 ≤ i < j ≤ n, , i ≠ k, j ≠ k do
            r_ij ← r_ij ∩ [r_ik • r_kj]
            if r_ij = ∅ then exit(inconsistent)
end
```

Figure 13.16 Path consistency algorithm for STPs.

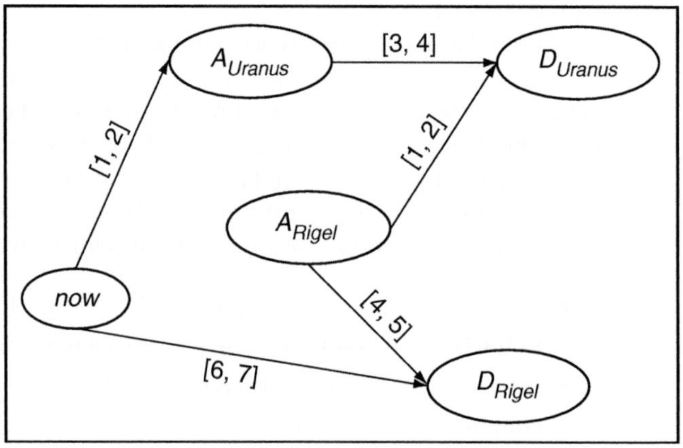

Figure 13.17 A simple temporal network.

whenever the transitive closure propagation uses a composition operation that distributes over an intersection, i.e., $r \bullet [r' \cap r''] = [r \bullet r'] \cap [r \bullet r'']$.

Distributivity is easily checked in STPs because

$$a + max\{a', a''\} = max\{a + a', a + a''\}$$

and similarly for *min*. Unfortunately, the distributivity property of $\bullet$ over $\cap$ does not hold, neither for PA nor for IA (see Exercises 13.9 and 13.10).

Another approach to consistency checking and finding minimal nets in STPs is the all-pairs minimal distance algorithm, Floyd-Warshall. Here, a network (X, C) is transformed into a distance graph $G = (X, E)$ as follows. Each constraint $r_{ij} = [a_{ij}, b_{ij}]$ of the network defines two labeled arcs in G: from t_i to t_j, labeled $l_{ij} = b_{ij}$, and from t_j to t_i, labeled $l_{ij} = -a_{ij}$. The algorithm (Figure 13.18) computes the minimal distances $d(i, j)$ between all pairs of vertices in G. The original network is inconsistent iff there is a negative cycle in G, i.e., a vertex i such that $d(i, i) < 0$.

```
Floyd-Warshall(X, E)
    for each i and j in X do
        if (i,j) ∈ E then d(i,j) ← l_ij else d(i,j) ← ∞
        d(i,i) ← 0
    for each i,j,k in X do
        d(i,j) ← min{d(i,j), d(i,k) + d(k,j)}
end
```

Figure 13.18 Minimal distance algorithm.

Floyd-Warshall has a complexity of $O(n^3)$, as does PC. Path consistency remains more convenient when the network is incrementally maintained.

13.4.2 Temporal Constraint Networks

We consider here the general case of quantitative temporal constraint network problems, called TCSPs, where disjunctions of constraints are allowed on the distances between pairs of instants, as illustrated in Example 13.3 (see page 289). In a TCSP network, the constraint between a pair (t_i, t_j) corresponds to the disjunction $(a_1 \leq t_j - t_i \leq b_1)$ or ... or $(a_m \leq t_j - t_i \leq b_m)$. It is denoted $r = \{[a_1, b_1], \ldots, [a_m, b_m]\}$.

Union, intersection, and composition operations are easily generalized to these extended constraints. Let $r = \{I_1, \ldots, I_h\}$, $q = \{J_1, \ldots, J_l\}$, where $I_i = [a_i, b_i]$ and $J_j = [c_j, d_j]$ are intervals on the reals.

- Union: $r \cup q = \{I_1, \ldots, I_h, J_1, \ldots, J_l\}$.
- Intersection: $r \cap q = \{K_1, \ldots, K_p\}$, where $p \leq h + l$ and each $K_k = I_i \cap J_j$ whenever this intersection is not empty.
- Composition: $r \bullet q = \{K_1, \ldots, K_p\}$, where $p \leq h \times l$ and each $K_k = I_i \bullet J_j = [a_i + c_j, b_i + d_j]$.

The symmetrical constraint of r is $r' = \{[-b_1, -a_1], \ldots, [-b_m, -a_m]\}$.

The consistency and minimality of a TCSP network are defined as in the previous section. Here also the transitive closure propagation can be applied. However, the path-consistency algorithm is no longer complete. Nonetheless, this algorithm has been proved to terminate whenever the interpretation domain of time is the natural or the rational numbers and to provide a path-consistent network in a time complexity of $O(n^3 d^3)$, where n is the number of instants and d is the maximum range of any constraint. However, path consistency does not guarantee in general the consistency of the network.

A straightforward approach for solving a TCSP is the following.

- Decompose it into several simple networks by choosing one disjunct for each constraint.
- Solve each simple net by finding the corresponding minimal network.
- Combine the results with the union of the minimal intervals.

This systematic enumeration can be improved with a backtrack-search algorithm on a meta-CSP. Every variable in the meta-CSP is a constraint in the original TCSP, such as $r = \{I_1, \ldots, I_h\}$, whose domain is that set of intervals. Constraints of the meta-CSP are given implicitly by stating that any partial assignment should correspond to a consistent simple network. Each solution of the meta-CSP defines directly a solution of the temporal network. By using standard CSP heuristics and improvements, such as forward checking, backjumping, and intelligent backtracking, this backtrack-search algorithm can be reduced to a time complexity of $O(n^2 w^{|C|})$, where w is the maximum number of intervals in a disjunct.

13.5 Discussion and Historical Remarks

Time is an essential component for reasoning about action and change. Temporal reasoning has been extensively studied in AI from the viewpoint of the knowledge representation and nonmonotonic reasoning techniques for dealing with change, events, actions, and causality [12, 386, 473, 474, 475, 536].

This chapter and the rest of the discussion are focused on a relatively narrow aspect of temporal reasoning, namely, how to describe and manage consistently a set of temporal references to a set of propositions and objects and the constraints between these references. The propositions and objects are dealt with by a specialized system, such as a planner, while the task of the temporal reasoner is to maintain, through queries and consistent updates, the set of temporal references to these objects and their constraints. This task is of interest in planning and in several other applications areas, such as temporal databases [97], diagnosis [96], multimedia document management [2, 184], and process supervision [161].

As usual, the problem for this reasoning task is to find a good trade-off between the expressiveness of a representation and the computational complexity of handling it. The literature can be classified into approaches involving intervals or time points, qualitative or quantitative constraints, approaches integrating intervals and points, qualitative and quantitative models, and various generalization efforts, e.g., handling imprecise constraints or contingent temporal variables.

Interval algebra was introduced by Allen [16], who proposed a path-consistency filtering algorithm for handling it. Vilain and Kautz [537] introduced point algebra and showed that the consistency-checking problem of the IA is an NP-complete problem, while PA is a tractable problem. With van Beek, they considered the subset

PA_c and solved it by path consistency; they proposed a 4-consistency algorithm for the full IA calculus [538]. It turns out that an $O(n^2)$ algorithm is sufficient for the full IA [388]. Techniques such as minimal indexed spanning trees [225] enable an average-case linear performance for the incremental consistency checking of PA_c and IA_c. Efficient techniques for handling disjunction of constraints in PA have also been proposed [216].

A number of tractable subclasses of IA that are larger than IA_c and IA_p have been identified (e.g., [163, 419]). Starting from the work of Ligozat [363], several models integrating PA and IA have been proposed [242, 243], and their tractable subclasses have been characterized [287].

Early work on quantitative models, such as Malik and Binford [375], relied on linear equations and linear programming. The TCSP and STP models were introduced by Dechter *et al.* [152]. They are widely used, and several improvements have been proposed, e.g., to the STP management algorithms [114]. More recent approaches generalize these models to allow disjunctions of constraints on points, intervals, and durations [95, 250]. Uncertainty in quantitative temporal constraints has been studied by several authors [165, 166, 323, 534].

Among a number of models integrating qualitative and quantitative constraints, there are the proposals of Ghallab and Vidal [226], Meiri [389], and Pujari and Sattar [449]. Disjunctions of constraints in the integrated qualitative and quantitative framework are further introduced by Barber [47] within a general scheme called *labeled constraints* (where each disjunct is associated with a unique label).

An important issue for planning is that of *contingent* temporal variables, which are random variables that cannot be freely constrained, as normal CSP variables are, when propagating constraints and checking their consistency. For example, in a temporal network dealing with starting and ending points of actions, the former are controllable CSP variables, i.e., one controls the triggering point of actions, while the latter are contingent variables: they can be observed but usually they cannot be planned for, unless one assumes that there is a precise model of action durations. Models handling hybrid CSPs with controllable and contingent variables have been studied [533]; good solutions have been proposed [403, 530, 531, 532].

13.6 Exercises

13.1 Reformulate the path-consistency algorithm in Figure 8.5 and its incremental version in Figure 8.6 for PA networks. Filter the network of Figure 13.7 using this algorithm, and show that this network is path-consistent.

13.2 In Figure 13.7, relabel the constraint to be $[t_1 = t_4]$ and show that this leads to an inconsistent network.

13.3 Prove that the path-consistency algorithm is complete for PA networks.

13.4 Show that in PA the composition operation does not distribute over intersection, i.e., $r \bullet [r' \cap r''] \neq [r \bullet r'] \cap [r \bullet r'']$.

13.5 Perform Exercise 13.4 for IA.

13.6 Prove that the IA of Figure 13.13 is path-consistent but is not consistent.

13.7 Apply the path-consistency algorithm to the simple temporal constraint network of Figure 13.17. Show that the resulting network is minimal.

13.8 Modify the network of Figure 13.4 by considering that the *Uranus* ship takes a full load while the *Rigel* is serviced on a normal dock. Using the path-consistency algorithm, show that the network is inconsistent. Is it possible to meet all the constraints by serving the *Rigel* on an express dock while still providing a full load to the *Uranus*? If not, which constraint needs to be relaxed to provide a full load to the *Uranus*?

13.9 For the three PA constraints $r = \{<, >\}$, $r' = \{<, =\}$, and $r'' = \{=, >\}$, compare $r \bullet [r' \cap r'']$ to $[r \bullet r'] \cap [r \bullet r'']$.

13.10 Find three constraints r, r', and r'' in IA that provide a counterexample for the distributivity of $\bullet$ over $\cap$ in IA, i.e., $r \bullet [r' \cap r''] \neq [r \bullet r'] \cap [r \bullet r'']$.

13.11 Show that the composition operation does not distribute over intersection in general temporal constraint networks.

13.12 Prove that the consistency problem of general constraint networks is NP-hard. (Hint: Use reduction from the three-coloring problem.)

13.13 Detail explicitly the proof of Proposition 13.5 (see page 299) by showing (*ad absurdum*) that the constraints $[i^- < j^+]$, for all pairs i and j in I, are consistent with the PA network corresponding to the considered solution.

Chapter 14

Temporal Planning

14.1 Introduction

The previous chapter was devoted to temporal reasoning techniques for planning. This chapter builds on that material by presenting some adequate representations for planning involving explicit time and by developing two related approaches to temporal planning. Time will be dealt with mainly within point algebra (PA) (Section 13.3.1) and the simple temporal networks (Section 13.4.1). Other approaches that rely on interval algebra (IA) will be discussed. We will focus on temporal planners that extend the planning techniques developed earlier in the book. However, as explained in the introduction to Part IV, we will depart significantly from the model of state-transition systems considered so far. We will view an action not as a single state transition but as a collection of local change and persistence conditions that are spread out in time but are focused on just a few state variables or propositions.

Such a view offers several advantages in expressiveness, which have been introduced earlier. In particular, explicit time is essential for handling properly the interaction of concurrent actions. For example, consider a door with a spring lock that controls the turning of the knob. Two synchronized actions are required for opening the door: (1) pushing the spring lock and maintaining the pressure, and (2) turning the knob and pulling open the door. It is not very satisfactory to represent this domain with two operators for these two actions (which may be needed separately for other tasks) and a third specific operator corresponding to their concurrent use. An adequate representation would enable reasoning on the concurrent execution of the two actions and their joint effects.

In previous chapters we considered plans that are more general than a strict sequence of actions: a partial-order plan in plan-space and HTN planning or a sequence of subsets of actions in planning-graph approaches. However, in all the algorithms presented earlier, only *independent* actions are left unordered and can occur concurrently. Their joint effects are simply the union of their individual effects. The additional combined effects of two concurrent actions cannot be expressed in classical planning unless we allow for a separate operator to represent the combined actions. Joint effects of concurrent and interfering actions will be dealt with here.

In order to specify a temporal planning domain and a problem as input to a planner, one needs a language. The purpose of this chapter is not to formalize such a language but instead to focus on the semantics of its underlying representation and to present temporal planning techniques. Two closely related approaches will be considered. The first one relies on extending the usual planning operators to include temporal preconditions and effects. That approach has a pedagogical merit: it introduces progressively most of the concepts needed in this chapter while keeping a representation as close as possible to that of classical planning, with propositions that hold over periods of time but with no logical connectives. The second approach may appear less familiar to the reader because it does not distinguish explicitly between preconditions and effects of actions. It specifies explicitly change and persistence constraints over time.

In both approaches, the underlying representation and semantics are those of CSPs, i.e., sets of constrained variables ranging over some domains. However, while in a CSP the variables are static and get single values in a solution, here the variables get different values at different time points, i.e., they are functions of time. The second approach relies on the state-variable representation that makes these functions of time explicit.

These two approaches are presented in Sections 14.2 and 14.3, respectively. The chapter ends with a discussion that briefly introduces other temporal planning techniques, followed by exercises.

14.2 Planning with Temporal Operators

Earlier in this book we viewed the dynamics of a domain as a sequence of states, and we had a way to tell which propositions are true in a given state and which are false. Here we will qualify each proposition of the domain with respect to the time periods during which the proposition is true, and we will build up a way to tell when a proposition is true and when it ceases to be true. This will be done through *temporally qualified expressions* in *temporal databases.*

14.2.1 Temporal Expressions and Temporal Databases

Let us define a representation scheme for specifying a temporal planning domain whose building blocks are finite sets of constant symbols, variable symbols, relation symbols, and constraints as described here.

The *constant symbols* are partitioned into disjoint classes corresponding to the objects of the domain, e.g., the classes of robots, locations, cranes, containers, and piles in the DWR domain.

The *variable symbols* are either *object variables* that are typed variables ranging over the classes or union of classes of constants or *temporal variables* ranging over the reals $\Re$. Object and temporal variables are viewed as CSP variables whose sets of possible values within their respective domains are constrained.

The *relation symbols* can be of two types.

- *Rigid relation symbols* represent relations that do not vary in time for a given planning problem, e.g., adjacent(loc1,loc2), belong(pile1,loc1), attached(crane1,loc1).
- *Flexible relation symbols*, also called *fluents*, represent relations on the constants of the domain that may or may not hold at some instant for a planning problem, e.g., at(robot1,loc1), in(cont1,pile1).

The *constraints* can also be of two types.

- *Temporal constraints* reside within the symbolic *PA* algebra calculus (see Section 13.3.1). Hence temporal variables will not be instantiating into numerical values[1] but is kept as a consistent set of constrained variables.
- *Binding constraints* on object variables are expressions of the form $x = y$, $x \neq y$, and $x \in D$, D being a set of constant symbols.

This representation scheme has time-invariant expressions and time-dependent expressions. The former are rigid relations and binding constraints; both will be referred to as *object constraints*. The latter are flexible relations and temporal constraints. These relations and constraints are used to specify temporally qualified expressions and temporal databases.

A *temporally qualified expression (tqe)* is an expression of the form:

$$p(\zeta_i, \ldots, \zeta_k)@[t_s, t_e)$$

where p is a flexible relation, $\zeta_i, \ldots, \zeta_k$ are constants or object variables, and t_s, t_e are temporal variables such that for $t_s < t_e$. A *tqe* $p(\zeta_i, \ldots, \zeta_k)@[t_s, t_e)$ asserts that $\forall t$ such that for $t_s \leq t < t_e$, the relation $p(\zeta_i, \ldots, \zeta_k)$ holds at the time t. For convenience reasons, to be illustrated in the following example, the interval $[t_s, t_e)$ qualifying a *tqe* is semi-open: the relation $p(\zeta_i, \ldots, \zeta_k)$ holds at t_s but not necessarily at t_e.

A *temporal database* is a pair $\Phi = (\mathcal{F}, \mathcal{C})$, where $\mathcal{F}$ is a finite set of *tqe*s and $\mathcal{C}$ is a finite set of temporal and object constraints; $\mathcal{C}$ is required to be consistent in the CSP sense, i.e., there exist values for the variables that meet all the constraints.

Example 14.1 In the DWR domain, suppose that a robot rob1 remains in a location loc1 and another robot rob2 moves from a location loc2 to an adjacent location loc3.

1. The use of numerical temporal constraint networks is discussed in Section 13.4.

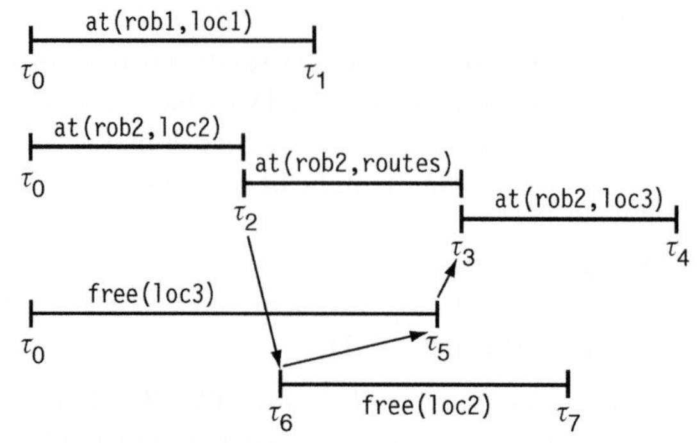

Figure 14.1 A picture of a temporal database.

We can express precisely an instance of this scenario with the following temporal database (Figure 14.1):

$$\begin{aligned}\Phi = (\{&\text{at(rob1, loc1)}@[\tau_0, \tau_1), \text{at(rob2, loc2)}@[\tau_0, \tau_2),\\ &\text{at(rob2, routes)}@[\tau_2, \tau_3), \text{at(rob2, loc3)}@[\tau_3, \tau_4),\\ &\text{free(loc3)}@[\tau_0, \tau_5), \text{free(loc2)}@[\tau_6, \tau_7)\},\\ \{&\text{adjacent(loc1, loc2)}, \text{adjacent(loc2, loc3)}, \tau_2 < \tau_6 < \tau_5 < \tau_3\})\end{aligned}$$

Φ says that robot rob1 is located at loc1 from time τ_0 to τ_1. Robot rob2 is at loc2 at time τ_0; it leaves that location at time τ_2 heading for an adjacent location loc3 that it reaches at time τ_3, where it stays till τ_4. Location loc3 is free from τ_0 till rob2 reaches it; loc2 becomes free when rob2 leaves it. The constant routes refers to all possible routes between locations because we are assuming that we do not need to specify a particular route.[2] We are assuming that a location can hold only one robot at a time: the relation free means that the location is not occupied. The temporal constraints require the destination location loc3 to remain free until rob2 gets into it ($\tau_5 < \tau_3$), while loc2 becomes free when rob2 leaves it and before it reaches loc3 ($\tau_2 < \tau_6 < \tau_5$). Because of the semiopen intervals in *tqes*, there is no ambiguity about the actual location of rob2 at the time points τ_2 and τ_3. Finally, note that the variables τ_0, τ_4, and τ_7 remain unconstrained, except for the implicit constraints on the end points of intervals qualifying *tqes*, i.e., $\tau_0 < \tau_1$, $\tau_3 < \tau_4$, $\tau_6 < \tau_7$, etc. ■

A temporal database Φ represents assertions about how the world changes over time. From these assertions in Φ we are going to deduce other assertion supported by Φ. Note that the representation does not have logical connectives. In particular, we are not using negated atoms. We rely on a variant of the closed-world assumption: a flexible relation holds in a temporal database Φ only during the periods of time explicitly stated by *tqes* in Φ; a rigid relation holds iff it is in Φ.

2. This constant is like the constant pallet used in previous chapters.

The intuition for a set of *tqe*s supported by a temporal database is the following: suppose we are given the database Φ illustrated in Example 14.1 and the following *tqe*: $\mathsf{free}(l)@[t, t')$. This *tqe* holds with respect to what is asserted in Φ provided that the interval $[t, t')$ can fit into one of the two intervals of Φ for which the flexible relation free is asserted, with a consistent binding for the variable l (see Figure 14.1). In other words, this *tqe* holds with respect to Φ if one of the two sets of constraints can be met: either $\{l = \mathsf{loc3}, \tau_0 \leq t, t' \leq \tau_5\}$ or $\{l = \mathsf{loc2}, \tau_6 \leq t, t' \leq \tau_7\}$. Note that we do not require the interval $[t, t')$ to be *equal* to the interval of the corresponding *tqe* in Φ, e.g., to $[\tau_0, \tau_5)$ or to $[\tau_6, \tau_7)$, because by definition a *tqe* holds for any subinterval of $[\tau_s, \tau_e)$. We will say that $\mathsf{free}(l)@[t, t')$ is *supported* by $\mathcal{F}$; the two sets of constraints are its *enabling conditions*, and one of them needs to be consistent with $\mathcal{C}$.

Definition 14.1 A set $\mathcal{F}$ of *tqes supports* a *tqe* $e = p(\zeta_i, \ldots, \zeta_k)@[t_1, t_2)$ iff there is in $\mathcal{F}$ a *tqe* $p(\zeta'_i, \ldots, \zeta'_k)@[\tau_1, \tau_2)$ and a substitution σ such that $\sigma(p(\zeta_i, \ldots, \zeta_k)) = \sigma(p(\zeta'_i, \ldots, \zeta'_k))$. An *enabling condition* for e in $\mathcal{F}$ is the conjunction of the two temporal constraints $\tau_1 \leq t_1$ and $t_2 \leq \tau_2$, together with the binding constraints of σ. ■

In general, an enabling condition for e in $\mathcal{F}$ is not unique because several *tqe*s in $\mathcal{F}$ may be unifiable with e. The set of all possible enabling conditions is denoted by $\theta(e/\mathcal{F})$. This set is empty when $\mathcal{F}$ does not support e.

Similarly, $\mathcal{F}$ supports a set of *tqes* $\mathcal{E}$ iff there is a substitution σ that unifies every element of $\mathcal{E}$ with an element of $\mathcal{F}$. An enabling condition for $\mathcal{E}$ in $\mathcal{F}$ is the conjunction of enabling conditions for the elements of $\mathcal{E}$. The set of all possible enabling conditions for $\mathcal{E}$ in $\mathcal{F}$ is denoted by $\theta(\mathcal{E}/\mathcal{F})$. This set is empty when $\mathcal{E}$ is not supported by $\mathcal{F}$.

Definition 14.2 A temporal database $\Phi = (\mathcal{F}, \mathcal{C})$ *supports* a set of *tqes* $\mathcal{E}$ when $\mathcal{F}$ supports $\mathcal{E}$ and there is an enabling condition $c \in \theta(\mathcal{E}/\mathcal{F})$ that is consistent with $\mathcal{C}$. $\Phi = (\mathcal{F}, \mathcal{C})$ *supports* another temporal database $(\mathcal{F}', \mathcal{C}')$ when $\mathcal{F}$ supports $\mathcal{F}'$ and there is an enabling condition $c \in \theta(\mathcal{F}'/\mathcal{F})$ such that $\mathcal{C}' \cup c$ is consistent with $\mathcal{C}$. ■

The following definition generalizes to temporal databases the notion of entailed constraints, as defined in Chapter 8.

Definition 14.3 A temporal database $\Phi = (\mathcal{F}, \mathcal{C})$ *entails* another temporal database $(\mathcal{F}', \mathcal{C}')$ iff $\mathcal{F}$ supports $\mathcal{F}'$ and there is an enabling condition $c \in \theta(\mathcal{F}'/\mathcal{F})$ such that $\mathcal{C} \models \mathcal{C}' \cup c$. ■

This definition requires a set of *tqe*s to be supported and one of its enabling conditions, as well as $\mathcal{C}'$, to be entailed by the constraints of Φ. Note that c is not a single constraint but a set of binding and temporal constraints.

When Φ supports a set of *tqes*, then we can consider these *tqes* to hold with respect to Φ only if we *augment* the constraints of Φ with an enabling condition consistent with $\mathcal{C}$. However, when Φ entails $(\mathcal{F}', \mathcal{C}')$, then the *tqes* of $\mathcal{F}'$ and the constraints of $\mathcal{C}'$ already hold with respect to Φ. This distinction is useful because we will be planning by performing successive refinements of a database, each refinement adding to it new *tqes* and constraints.

14.2.2 Temporal Planning Operators

We are now ready to define temporal planning operators and domains. Let us first introduce an example.

Example 14.2 In the DWR domain, we would like to specify a move operator for a robot r that leaves one location l at time t_s and reaches another adjacent location l' at time t_e. Figure 14.2 illustrates a possible definition of this operator with the intervals involved with respect to the duration of the action. When an end point of an interval is not constrained, e.g., t_1, t_5, t_3, it is left without a vertical bar (these are free variables in the operator).

The two preconditions of the operator require that the robot r should be at location l during some interval of time until t_s and that there should be free space available in location l' during some interval ending at t_e because a location can hold only one robot at a time.

The effects of the move operator are to have the robot on the way (constant routes) from t_s to t_e, to have it at l' at some interval starting in t_e, and to have space available in l starting at a time point t_4 between t_s and t_2, i.e., before space is required in l'.

The operator requires the two locations to be adjacent[3] and to have free space at the destination only after making the origin location free, i.e., $t_s < t_4 < t_2$. Note that the precondition $\mathsf{at}(r, l)@[t_1, t_s)$ does not mean that r is not at location l outside of $[t_1, t_s)$; it only requires r to be there during this interval: any *tqe* $\mathsf{at}(r, l)@[\tau_i, \tau_j)$ in a temporal database that may support this precondition will not be affected, at this point, by what is stated in the operator. Similarly, the precondition $\mathsf{free}(l')@[t_2, t_e)$ does not put any requirement on the location l' outside of the interval $[t_2, t_e)$, which is after the starting point of the action. The constraints for the end points of the intervals are implicit: $t_s < t_e$, $t_1 < t_s$, $t_2 < t_e$, $t_e < t_3$, and $t_4 < t_5$. ■

A *temporal planning operator* is a tuple $o = (\text{name}(o), \text{precond}(o), \text{effects}(o), \text{const}(o))$, where:

- $\text{name}(o)$ is an expression of the form $o(x_1, \ldots, x_k, t_s, t_e)$ such that o is an operator symbol, and $x_1, \ldots, x_k$ are all the object variables that appear in o,

3. The relations adjacent and free apply here to locations. We assume the constant routes to be always free and adjacent to and from every location.

move(r, l, l')@$[t_s, t_e)$
  precond: at(r, l)@$[t_1, t_s)$
    free(l')@$[t_2, t_e)$
  effects: at$(r$, routes$)$@$[t_s, t_e)$
    at(r, l')@$[t_e, t_3)$
    free(l)@$[t_4, t_5)$
  const: $t_s < t_4 < t_2$
    adjacent(l, l')

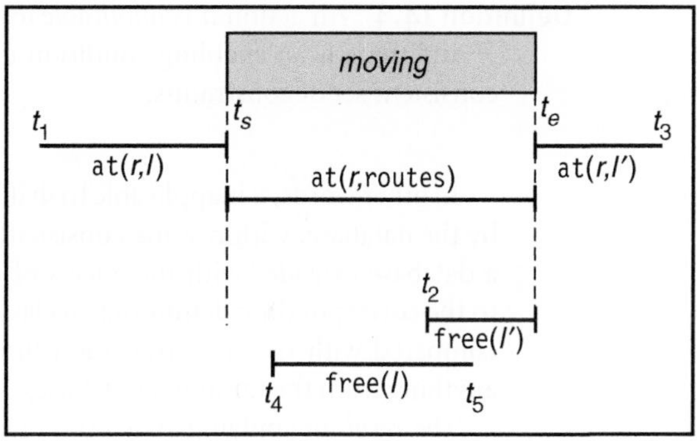

Figure 14.2 A temporal planning move operator.

together with the temporal variables in const(o). The other unconstrained temporal variables in o are *free variables.*

- precond(o) and effects(o) are *tqes*.
- const(o) is a conjunction of temporal constraints and object constraints, the latter being either rigid relations or binding constraints on object variables of the form $x = y$, $x \neq y$, or $x \in D$, with D being a set of constants.

Rather than writing an operator as a tuple, we use the format shown in Figure 14.2, where the temporal variables t_s, t_e, t_2, and t_4 are implicit parameters of the operator, while t_1, t_3, and t_5 are free variables.

An *action* is a partially instantiated planning operator $a = \sigma(o)$ for some substitution σ. The intended semantics is that if the preconditions and the constraints of an action hold with respect to some database, then the action is applicable. It will run from time t_s to t_e. The new *tqes* resulting from its execution are described by its effects. An important point to notice here is that the other changes due to the action, such as *tqes* that no longer hold, are not explicit in this representation. We have not introduced here the equivalent of effects$^-$, which would be needed in order to state explicitly, e.g., that r ceases to be at l at time t_s or that l' is not free anymore after t_e. This will become clear with the introduction of domain axioms in Section 14.2.3.

Let us now define the applicability of an action more precisely. Given a temporal database $\Phi = (\mathcal{F}, \mathcal{C})$, the preconditions of an action a are *supported* by $\mathcal{F}$ (according to Definition 14.1) iff there is a substitution σ such that for each p@$[t_1, t_2) \in$ precond(a), there is a *tqe* q@$[\tau_1, \tau_2) \in \mathcal{F}$ with $\sigma(p) = \sigma(q)$. An enabling condition for precond(a) is a conjunction, over all preconditions of a, of the two temporal constraints $\tau_1 \leq t_1$, $t_2 \leq \tau_2$, and the binding constraints in σ. This enabling condition is not unique because there can be more than one *tqe* in $\mathcal{F}$ unifiable with a condition. The set of all enabling conditions for precond(a) is denoted $\theta(a/\mathcal{F})$.

Definition 14.4 An action a is *applicable* to $\Phi = (\mathcal{F}, \mathcal{C})$ iff precond(a) is supported by $\mathcal{F}$ and there is an enabling condition c in $\theta(a/\mathcal{F})$ such that $\mathcal{C} \cup \text{const}(a) \cup c$ is a consistent set of constraints.

■

In other words, a is applicable to Φ if instances of its preconditions are supported by the database, within some consistent constraints. A result of applying a to Φ is a database *extended* with the effects of a and with other constraints. This is close to the corresponding definitions in classical planning, but the important difference compared with the state-transition function γ is that here we are not removing anything from the temporal database.

The *result* of applying an action a to a database Φ is a *set* of possible databases. Let us introduce a provisional definition of the result of a in Φ (we will refine it in Section 14.2.3):

$$\gamma_0(\Phi, a) = \{(\mathcal{F} \cup \text{effects}(a), \mathcal{C} \cup \text{const}(a) \cup c) \mid c \in \theta(a/\mathcal{F})\} \tag{14.1}$$

This result is empty whenever a is not applicable to Φ. Otherwise the set $\gamma_0(\Phi, a)$ may contain several possible databases because $\theta(a/\mathcal{F})$ is not a singleton. Each such resulting database is obtained by *consistently adding* to Φ the set of *tqe*s in effects(a) and the set of constraints const(a) $\cup\, c$ for some $c \in \theta(a/\mathcal{F})$.

It is important to note that the result of applying an action a is defined as being a set of databases. This is not due to nondeterminism; actions here are deterministic. This is because an action a can be applied in different ways and at different times in Φ, and we want to refer to the set of all these possibilities.

Example 14.3 Consider the temporal database of Figure 14.1. The action move(rob1,loc1,loc2)@$[t_s, t_e)$ is applicable to Φ. This is because the *tqe* at(rob1,loc1)@$[\tau_0, \tau_1)$ supports at(r, l)@$[t_1, t_s)$ when r = rob1, l = loc1, $\tau_0 \leq t_1$ and $t_s \leq \tau_1$; the *tqe* free(loc2)@$[\tau_6, \tau_7)$ supports free(l')@$[t_2, t_e)$ when l' = loc2 $\tau_6 \leq t_2$, and $t_e \leq \tau_7$. An enabling condition of this move action is thus:

$$c = \{r = \text{rob1}, l = \text{loc1}, l' = \text{loc2}, \tau_0 \leq t_1, t_s \leq \tau_1, \tau_6 \leq t_2, t_e \leq \tau_7\}$$

Note that the constraints in const(o), i.e., $t_s < t_4 < t_2$, are consistent with Φ and c because, in particular, τ_6 is not constrained with respect to τ_1.

If we had in Φ another *tqe* asserting rob1 in loc1, e.g., at(rob1,loc1)@$[\tau_8, \tau_9)$, we would have another instance of move(rob1,loc1,loc2)@$[t'_s, t'_e)$ applicable to Φ at different time periods than the previous instance, provided that the constraints are consistent.

If we also assume adjacent(loc3,loc2) in Φ, then there is another enabling condition for move, corresponding to moving rob2 from loc3 to loc2. Similarly, adjacent(loc1,loc3) would allow for another way to apply this operator, by moving rob1 from loc1 to loc3.

■

At this point, let us discuss the intended semantics of the variables in a temporal planning operator. For object variables, there are no major differences between a classical planning operator and a temporal one. All such variables appearing in an operator are existentially quantified parameters of the operator, ranging over finite domains. In classical planning, these parameters are instantiated with respect to atoms in a state. Here, they are instantiated with respect to *tqes* in a temporal database. Note, however, that a temporal database corresponds to a consistent collection of states.

The temporal parameters are also existentially quantified variables, but they range over the infinite set of real numbers. Hence, an applicable action has an infinite number of instances, e.g., for the action move(rob1,loc1,loc2)@$[t_s, t_e)$ in the previous example, each consistent tuple of values of its temporal parameters t_s, t_e, t_2, and t_4 defines a different instance. In this section we are using the *PA* symbolic calculus (i.e., we are not instantiating temporal variables into numerical values), so all these instances are equivalent.[4] Note that the free variables of the operator—t_1, t_3, and t_5 in the previous example—play no particular role in the sense that an instance of the action does not depend on the values of these variables.

14.2.3 Domain Axioms

The representation described in this section has no logical connectives. The "negative" effects of an action are not made explicit in the definition of the operator. Indeed, this definition asserts only what holds as an effect of an action—it does not say what does not hold anymore. For example, the move operator in Figure 14.2 does not say that the robot is no longer at location l starting at t_s; neither does it specify that location l' is not free starting at t_e. These effects will result from domain axioms on *tqes*.

A domain axiom is a conditional expression of the form:

$$\rho = \text{cond}(\rho) \rightarrow \text{disj}(\rho)$$

where:

- cond(ρ) is a set of *tqes*.
- disj(ρ) is a *disjunction* of temporal and object constraints.

Example 14.4 An axiom is required to specify that an object cannot be in two distinct places at the same time. For example, for the move operator in Figure 14.2 we write:

$$\{\mathtt{at}(r, l)@[t_s, t_e), \mathtt{at}(r', l')@[t'_s, t'_e)\} \rightarrow (r \neq r') \vee (l = l') \vee (t_e \leq t'_s) \vee (t'_e \leq t_s)$$

If the two *tqes* in cond(ρ) hold, then either we have two distinct robots, or one robot is in the same location, or the two intervals of these *tqes* are disjoint.

---

4. We will discuss in Section 14.3.4 the issues involved for instantiating temporal parameters.

Furthermore, we assume that there is space for just one robot at a time in a given location. However, the previous move operator does not prevent several robots from moving into the same location at the same time. The following axiom asserts this restriction:

$$\{\text{at}(r,l)@[t_1,t_1'), \text{free}(l')@[t_2,t_2')\} \rightarrow (l \neq l') \vee (t_1' \leq t_2) \vee (t_2' \leq t_1)$$

■

The semantics of domain axioms is given by Definition 14.5.

Definition 14.5 Let ρ be an axiom, $\Phi = (\mathcal{F},\mathcal{C})$ be a database such that cond(ρ) is supported by $\mathcal{F}$, and $\theta(\rho/\mathcal{F})$ be the set of enabling conditions for cond(ρ) in $\mathcal{F}$. Φ is *consistent* with ρ iff for each enabling condition $c_1 \in \theta(\rho/\mathcal{F})$, there is at least one disjunct $c_2 \in$ disj(ρ) such that $\mathcal{C} \cup c_1 \cup c_2$ is a consistent set of constraints.

■

In other words, this definition requires that for every way of enabling cond(ρ), there is at least one disjunct in disj(ρ) that is consistent with Φ.

A database Φ is consistent with a set X of axioms if it is consistent with every axiom in X.

Example 14.5 Consider the database of Example14.1 augmented with the effects of move(rob1,loc1,loc2)@$[t_s, t_e)$, whose sole enabling condition, as given in Example 14.3, is $\{r = \text{rob1}, l = \text{loc1}, l' = \text{loc2}, \tau_0 \leq t_1, t_s \leq \tau_1, \tau_6 \leq t_2, t_e \leq \tau_7\}$.

The first axiom of the previous example is supported for $r = r' = \text{rob1}$, $l = \text{loc1}$, and $l' = \text{routes}$. Consequently, $(t_e \leq \tau_0) \vee (\tau_1 \leq t_s)$ holds. But $(t_e \leq \tau_0)$ entails $t_1 < t_s < t_e \leq \tau_0 < \tau_1$, which is inconsistent with $\tau_0 \leq t_1$. However, $(\tau_1 \leq t_s)$ is consistent with Φ. Furthermore, because in Φ $t_s \leq \tau_1$, then $\tau_1 = t_s$. This means that the *tqe* at(rob1,loc1)@$[\tau_0, \tau_1)$ ends exactly at t_s, the starting point of the move.[5]

The second axiom is also supported for $l = l' = \text{loc2}$. Hence $(t_3 \leq \tau_6) \vee (\tau_7 \leq t_e)$ holds. Here also $(t_3 \leq \tau_6)$ contradicts $\tau_6 \leq t_2 < t_e \leq \tau_7$. But $(\tau_7 \leq t_e)$ is consistent with Φ, and together with $t_e \leq \tau_7$, it entails $\tau_7 = t_e$. This means that loc2 ceases to be free at exactly the end of the action.

■

A *consistency condition* for Φ with respect to a set of axioms X is the following union over all axioms $\rho \in X$ and over all enabling conditions in $\theta(\rho/\mathcal{F})$:

$$\varpi(c_2) = \bigcup_{\rho \in X, c_1 \in \theta(\rho/\mathcal{F})} \{c_1 \cup c_2 \mid c_2 \in \text{disj}(\rho)\} \tag{14.2}$$

5. A finer model of move may allow for some time between t_s and the moment at which rob1 leaves loc1, i.e., the time to get out of the initial location. This can easily be done with a slight modification in the definition of the operator (see Exercise 14.1).

There can be several such consistency conditions because each disj(ρ) may contain more than one constraint c_2. Let $\theta(X/\Phi) = \cup_{c_2}\varpi(c_2)$, i.e., the set of all consistency conditions of Φ with respect to X. Φ is consistent with the axioms of X iff *either* of the following holds:

- $\theta(X/\Phi)$ is empty, i.e., no axiom has its conditions supported.
- There is a consistency condition $c \in \theta(X/\Phi)$ that is consistent with $\mathcal{C}$.

In other words, Φ *satisfies* X iff either $\theta(X/\Phi)$ is empty or there is such a condition c that is *entailed* by $\mathcal{C}$.

A consistency condition gives, for all supported axioms, a set of constraints that needs to be met in order to enforce the consistency of every possible instance of Φ with the axioms. When Φ satisfies X, then this database will always remain consistent with X whatever constraints are consistently added to it. When Φ is consistent with X but does not satisfy X, then the constraints of Φ need to be augmented with a constraint $c \in \theta(X/\Phi)$ in order to maintain this consistency for every instance of Φ. The set of all databases obtained from Φ that satisfies the axioms X is thus:

$$\psi(\Phi, X) = \{(\mathcal{F}, \mathcal{C} \cup c) \mid c \in \theta(X/\Phi)\} \tag{14.3}$$

This set is empty when Φ is not consistent with X.

Having specified a set X of domain axioms, we'll restrict our interest solely to the databases that satisfy X. According to the preliminary definition of the result of an action, the set $\gamma_0(\Phi, a)$ of databases resulting from an action a may contain several databases that are not consistent with the axioms of X. Consequently, we will refine the definition of the result of applying an action a to Φ (as given by γ_0 in Equation 14.1) by restricting it to contain only databases that are consistent with X and that are augmented with the constraints needed to satisfy X. The result of applying to Φ an action a with respect to X is now the set of databases:

$$\gamma(\Phi, a) = \bigcup_i \{\psi(\Phi_i, X) | \Phi_i \in \gamma_0(\Phi, a)\} \tag{14.4}$$

$\gamma(\Phi, a)$ is empty whenever a is not applicable to Φ or cannot lead to a database consistent with X. Otherwise, $\gamma(\Phi, a)$ may contain several possible databases, each being a pair $(\mathcal{F} \cup \text{effects}(a), \mathcal{C} \cup \text{const}(a) \cup c \cup c')$, where $c \in \theta(a/\mathcal{F})$ is an enabling condition for precond(a) and $c' \in \theta(X/\Phi)$ is a consistency condition.

Finally, let us remark that axioms have been illustrated in this section mainly to constrain *tqe*s to intervals consistent with the specifications of the domain. But we can also use axioms to specify time-invariant properties, as in classical planning. For example, a DWR domain where the adjacency relation between locations is symmetrical may contain the axiom $\{\texttt{adjacent}(l, l')\} \rightarrow \texttt{adjacent}(l', l)$.

14.2.4 Temporal Planning Domains, Problems, and Plans

We are now ready to define temporal planning domains, problems, and their solutions.

A temporal planning *domain* is a triple $\mathcal{D} = (\Lambda_\Phi, \mathcal{O}, X)$, where:

- Λ_Φ is the set of all temporal databases that can be defined with the constraints and the constant, variable, and relation symbols in our representation.
- $\mathcal{O}$ is a set of temporal planning operators.
- X is a set of domain axioms.

A temporal planning *problem* in $\mathcal{D}$ is a tuple $\mathcal{P} = (\mathcal{D}, \Phi_0, \Phi_g)$, where:

- $\Phi_0 = (\mathcal{F}, \mathcal{C})$ is a database in Λ_Φ that satisfies the axioms of X. Φ_0 represents an initial scenario that describes not only the initial state of the domain but also the evolution predicted to take place independently of the actions to be planned.
- $\Phi_g = (\mathcal{G}, \mathcal{C}_g)$ is a database that represents the goals of the problem as a set $\mathcal{G}$ of *tqe*s together with a set $\mathcal{C}_g$ of objects and temporal constraints on variables of $\mathcal{G}$.

The *statement* of a problem $\mathcal{P}$ is given by $P = (\mathcal{O}, X, \Phi_0, \Phi_g)$.

A plan is a set $\pi = \{a_1, \ldots, a_k\}$ of actions, each being a partial instance of some operator in $\mathcal{O}$.[6]

We would like to define the result of applying a plan π to a database Φ *independently of the order* in which the actions are considered during the planning process. A tentative definition (to be refined in Section 14.2.5) of the result of π could be the following:

$$\begin{aligned} \gamma(\Phi, \{\}) &= \{\Phi\} \\ \gamma(\Phi, \pi \cup \{a\}) &= \textstyle\bigcup_i \{\gamma(\Phi_i, a) \mid \Phi_i \in \gamma(\Phi, \pi)\} \end{aligned} \tag{14.5}$$

such that π is a *solution* for a problem $P = (\mathcal{O}, X, \Phi_0, \Phi_g)$ iff there is a database in $\gamma(\Phi_0, \pi)$ that entails Φ_g.

However, this definition of $\gamma(\Phi, \pi)$ is not correct because the applicability of actions, as defined earlier, may depend on the order in which actions are considered, even though the actions are situated in time. This is dealt with in the next section, which generalizes the applicability conditions of actions.

---

6. Note that a plan is a set, not a sequence, because the actions in π are already situated in time.

14.2.5 Concurrent Actions with Interfering Effects

In classical planning, one cannot cope with concurrent and interfering actions unless one specifies an *ad hoc* operator for each useful combination of two operators a_1 and a_2, in order to express their joint conditions and effects. In HTN planning, an explicit method is also required for decomposing a task into the joint application of the two operators a_1 and a_2. A representation that requires the explicit definition of a_1, a_2, and a joint operator $a_1 \oplus a_2$, whenever such a join is useful, is less expressive than a representation that can reason on the joint applicability and joint effects of a given set of planning operators. The latter may solve more problems than the former.

The representation described here has such a capability. For example, it can manage the case of two actions a_1 and a_2 such that neither is applicable individually to a temporal database Φ but there is a joint combination of the two that is applicable and achieves a joint effect.

Example 14.6 Consider a DWR domain with just two locations loc1 and loc2 and two robots r1 and r2 that are initially in loc1 and loc2, respectively. The action move(r1,loc1,loc2)@$[t_s, t_e)$ is not applicable any time for lack of space in loc2. Similarly, move(r2,loc2,loc1) is not applicable because loc1 is not free. However, the DWR domain puts no space restriction on the routes between locations. Consequently, these two actions can be combined in time into two applicable and synchronized moves, as shown in Figure 14.3. The constraints required to make these two moves compatible are the following.

- When r1 gets to loc2, then r2 should have already left this location, i.e., $t'_4 \leq t_2$, and when r1 finishes moving into loc2, loc2 is no longer free, i.e., $t'_5 = t_e$.
- Similarly for r2 with respect to loc1: $t_4 \leq t'_2$ and $t_5 = t'_e$.

Note that t_s may take place before or after t'_s, and similarly for t_e and t'_e. ■

It is possible to view the set $\{a_1, a_2\}$ as a single joint operator

- whose effects are the union of the effects of a_1 and a_2;
- whose preconditions are the union of precond(a_1) minus the preconditions supported by effects(a_2), and of precond(a_2) minus the preconditions supported by effects(a_1); and
- whose constraints are the union of the two sets of constraints augmented with the constraints required to support preconditions of a_1 by effects(a_2) and preconditions of a_2 by effects(a_1).

This can be achieved by defining the applicability and effects $\gamma(\Phi, \pi)$ of a set of actions π as follows.

A pair of actions $\{a_1, a_2\}$ is applicable to $\Phi = (\mathcal{F}, \mathcal{C})$ when:

- $\mathcal{F} \cup$ effects(a_2) supports precond(a_1),

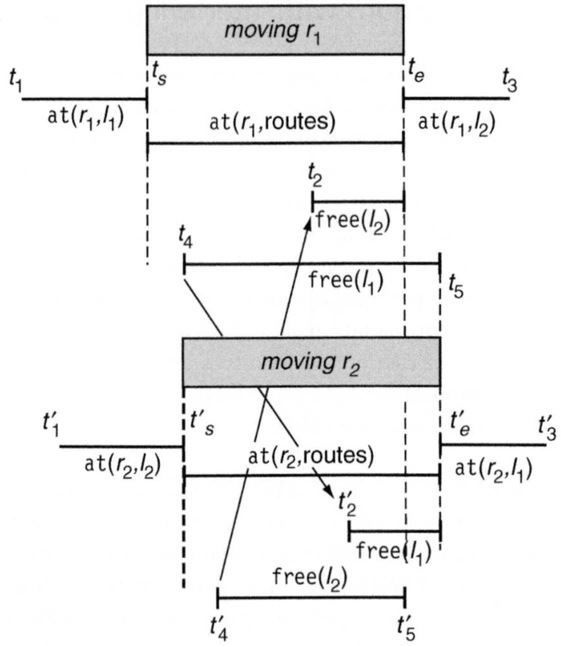

Figure 14.3 Two concurrent actions with interfering effects. Moving r_1 from l_1 to l_2 can take place only if the action is concurrent with the symmetrical move of r_2 and if the precedence constraints shown are met.

- $\mathcal{F} \cup \text{effects}(a_1)$ supports $\text{precond}(a_2)$,
- there is an enabling condition $c_1 \in C(a_1/\mathcal{F} \cup \text{effects}(a_2))$, and
- there is an enabling condition $c_2 \in C(a_2/\mathcal{F} \cup \text{effects}(a_1))$,

such that $\mathcal{C} \cup \text{const}(a_1) \cup c_1 \cup \text{const}(a_2) \cup c_2$ is a consistent set.[7]

The set of databases resulting from the application of the pair $\{a_1, a_2\}$ is:

$$\gamma(\Phi, \{a_1, a_2\}) = \bigcup_i \{\psi(\Phi_i, X) | \Phi_i \in \gamma_0(\Phi, \{a_1, a_2\})\},$$

where:

$$\begin{aligned}\gamma_0(\Phi, \{a_1, a_2\}) = \ & \{(\mathcal{F} \cup \text{effects}(a_1) \cup \text{effects}(a_2), \\ & \quad \mathcal{C} \cup \text{const}(a_1) \cup c_1 \cup \text{const}(a_2) \cup c_2 \\ & \mid c_1 \in \theta(a_1/\mathcal{F} \cup \text{effects}(a_2)), c_2 \in \theta(a_2/\mathcal{F} \cup \text{effects}(a_1))\}.\end{aligned}$$

7. This explains the advantage of distinguishing between $\mathcal{F}$ and $\mathcal{C}$ and of defining the enabling condition to be a function only of $\mathcal{F}$, not of $\mathcal{C}$.

This definition is easily generalized to any finite set of actions. Let π be a set of actions and let us denote effects(π_{-a})$= \bigcup_{a' \in \pi - \{a\}}$ effects(a').

The set π is applicable to Φ iff the following conditions hold for $\forall a \in \pi$:

- $\mathcal{F} \cup$ effects(π_{-a}) supports precond(a), and
- there is an enabling condition $c_a \in \theta(a/\mathcal{F} \cup \text{effects}(\pi_{-a}))$,

such that $\mathcal{C} \bigcup_{a \in \pi}(\text{const}(a) \cup c_a)$ is a consistent set.

The sets $\gamma_0(\Phi, \pi)$ and $\gamma(\Phi, \pi)$ are now defined as follows:

$$\begin{aligned} \gamma_0(\Phi, \pi) = \; & \{(\mathcal{F} \textstyle\bigcup_{a \in \pi} \text{effects}(a),\ \mathcal{C} \bigcup_{a \in \pi}(\text{const}(a) \cup c_a)) \mid \\ & c_a \in \theta(a/\mathcal{F} \cup \text{effects}(\pi_{-a}))\} \end{aligned} \tag{14.6}$$

and

$$\gamma(\Phi, \pi) = \bigcup_i \{\psi(\Phi_i, X) \mid \Phi_i \in \gamma_0(\Phi, \pi)\}. \tag{14.7}$$

To summarize, the applicability of an action a is defined with respect to $\mathcal{F}$ augmented with the effects of *all* other actions in the plan. This is an essential feature of the approach that needs to be taken into account by planning algorithms, as illustrated by the procedure of the next section.

14.2.6 A Temporal Planning Procedure

Given a planning problem $P = (\mathcal{O}, X, \Phi_0, \Phi_g)$, we now concentrate on finding a set π of actions that are instances of operators in $\mathcal{O}$, such that there is a database $(\mathcal{F}, \mathcal{C}) \in \gamma(\Phi_0, \pi)$ that entails $\Phi_g = (\mathcal{G}, \mathcal{C}_g)$, i.e., such that every element of $\mathcal{G}$ is supported by $(\mathcal{F}, \mathcal{C} \cup \mathcal{C}_g)$. For any practical purpose, a planner has to exhibit not only the set π but also a database $(\mathcal{F}, \mathcal{C})$ in $\gamma(\Phi_0, \pi)$ that entails Φ_g. A natural approach for addressing this problem relies on

- a search space similar to that of partial plans (Chapter 5) that is naturally close to this representation and
- the CSP-based techniques and algorithms (Chapter 8)needed to handle the temporal and domain constraints that are essential in this representation.

A nondeterministic planning procedure called TPS implements such an approach. It generalizes the PSP procedure developed earlier (Figures 5.6 and 5.7). TPS proceeds as follows (see Figure 14.4).

```
TPS(Ω)
    flaws ← OpenGoals(Ω) ∪ UnsatisfiedAxioms(Ω) ∪ Threats(Ω)
    if flaws = ∅ then return(Ω)
    select any flaw φ ∈ flaws
    resolvers ← Resolve(φ, Ω)
    if resolvers = ∅ then return(failure)
    nondeterministically choose a resolver ρ ∈ resolvers
    Ω' ← Refine(ρ, Ω)
    return(TPS(Ω'))
end
```

Figure 14.4 TPS, a temporal planning procedure.

- It maintains a data structure, Ω, which defines the current *processing stage* of the planning problem. Ω contains *flaws* as long as a solution plan has not been found.
- It selects a flaw and finds all its resolvers (i.e., all ways to resolve the flaw), if there are any.
- It nondeterministically chooses one or several resolvers for that flaw. If needed, it eventually backtracks on this choice.
- It refines Ω with respect to the chosen resolvers.

This schema will be made precise by specifying the set of flaws (as computed by the OpenGoals, UnsatisfiedAxioms, and Threats subroutines) and how flaws are handled by the Resolve and Refine subroutines. The processing stage of the planning problem is a 4-tuple $\Omega = (\Phi, G, \mathcal{K}, \pi)$, where:

- $\Phi = (\mathcal{F}, \mathcal{C})$ is the current temporal database, as refined with the effects and constraints of planned actions.
- G is a set of *tqe*s corresponding to the current open goals.
- $\mathcal{K} = \{C_1, \ldots, C_i\}$ is a set of pending sets of enabling conditions of actions and pending sets of consistency conditions of axioms.
- π is a set of actions corresponding to the current plan.

Given the problem $P = (\mathcal{O}, X, \Phi_0, \Phi_g)$, where $\Phi_0 = (\mathcal{F}_0, \mathcal{C}_0)$, and $\Phi_g = (\mathcal{G}, \mathcal{C}_g)$, we first check whether the set of the goal constraints $\mathcal{C}_g$ is consistent with $\mathcal{C}_0$. If $\mathcal{C}_0 \cup \mathcal{C}_g$ is inconsistent, then the problem has no solution. Otherwise, the initial resolution stage Ω has the following components: $\Phi = (\mathcal{F}_0, \mathcal{C}_0 \cup \mathcal{C}_g)$, $G = \mathcal{G}$, $\pi = \emptyset$, and $\mathcal{K} = \emptyset$.

If the problem P is successfully solved, then the final values in Ω will be the following: $G = \mathcal{K} = \emptyset$, π is a set of actions that are instances of operators in $\mathcal{O}$, and $\Phi \in \gamma(\Phi_0, \pi)$ is such that Φ entails Φ_g.

The temporal planning procedure TPS (Figure 14.4) recursively refines Ω. TPS selects a flaw and finds its resolvers (branching step). It nondeterministically chooses a resolver and updates Ω with respect to the chosen resolver (refinement step). This is performed for three types of flaws: *open goals*, *unsatisfied axioms*, and *threats*, according to the following definitions of the resolvers of these flaws and the refinement operations.

Open Goals. If $G \neq \emptyset$, then every element $e \in G$ is a goal expression that is not yet supported by Φ. A resolver for such a flaw is either of the following.

- A *tqe* in $\mathcal{F}$ that can support e. Such a resolver will exist if $\theta(e/\mathcal{F})$ is not empty and contains at least one enabling condition that is consistent with $\mathcal{C}$. The refinement of Ω in this case is the following updates:

$$\mathcal{K} \leftarrow \mathcal{K} \cup \{\theta(e/\mathcal{F})\}$$
$$G \leftarrow G - \{e\}.$$

- An action a that is an instance of some operator in o, such that effects(a) supports e and const(a) is consistent with $\mathcal{C}$. In this case, the refinement of Ω consists of the following updates:

$$\pi \leftarrow \pi \cup \{a\}$$
$$\mathcal{F} \leftarrow \mathcal{F} \cup \text{effects}(a)$$
$$\mathcal{C} \leftarrow \mathcal{C} \cup \text{const}(a)$$
$$G \leftarrow (G - \{e\}) \cup \text{precond}(a)$$
$$\mathcal{K} \leftarrow \mathcal{K} \cup \{\theta(a/\Phi)\}$$

Note that we are requesting a to be relevant for e but not necessarily to be supported by the current stage of the database. Hence, in the last update listed, $\theta(a/\Phi)$ is a set of pending consistency conditions.

Unsatisfied Axioms. These flaws are possible inconsistencies of instances of Φ with respect to the axioms of X. That is, a flaw here is any axiom ρ such that cond(ρ) is supported by $\mathcal{F}$. A resolver is any consistency condition in $\theta(X/\Phi)$. The refinement of Ω is the update of $\mathcal{K}$ with this set of consistency conditions:

$$\mathcal{K} \leftarrow \mathcal{K} \cup \{\theta(X/\Phi)\}$$

Threats. If $\mathcal{K} \neq \emptyset$, then every $C_i \in \mathcal{K}$ is a pending set of consistency conditions or enabling conditions that are not yet entailed by the database Φ. A resolver for this flaw is a constraint $c \in C_i$ that is consistent with $\mathcal{C}$. The refinement of Ω consists of the following updates:

$$\mathcal{C} \leftarrow \mathcal{C} \cup c, \text{ for some } c \in C_i \text{ that is consistent with } \mathcal{C}$$
$$\mathcal{K} \leftarrow \mathcal{K} - \{C_i\}$$

The TPS procedure is a general schema. It is able to handle concurrent actions with interfering effects (see Exercise 14.6). It can be instantiated into a broad class of planning algorithms. For example, one may consider flaws in some particular order, either systematic and/or according to heuristics for guiding the search. One may work on several resolvers at a time by updating Ω with a *disjunction* of resolvers along the disjunctive-refinement framework. Finally, one should devise efficient ways to handle the various types of constraints involved in the TPS procedure. For example, the handling of threats may benefit from a forward-checking type of constraint management (see Figure 8.3). That is, at each time a resolver $c \in C_i$ is added to $\mathcal{C}$, the corresponding constraints are propagated and the remaining C_j in $\mathcal{K}$ are reduced to conditions that are consistent with Φ. If a C_j is reduced to an empty set, then this is a backtrack point; if a C_j is reduced to a single condition, then this condition is further propagated.

We will present such algorithms in Section 14.3, within a different and somewhat simpler representation.

14.3 Planning with Chronicles

This section presents another approach to temporal planning that also follows the time-oriented view of a dynamic system. We will rely on the state-variable representation, in which a domain is described by a set of state variables, each being a function of time. This representation extends the state-variable representation introduced earlier for classical planning (Sections 2.5 and 8.3).

The chronicle approach differs from the temporal database approach mainly because of the use of the state-variable representation, which offers some advantages in expressiveness and conciseness. For example, an axiom such as "an object is at a single place at one time," as in Example 14.4, is no longer needed because of the use of state variables, i.e., functions of time instead of relations. Another difference with respect to Section 14.2 is the lack of an explicit separation between preconditions and effects in operators: a condition and an effect of an action can be represented through a single expression. But here, as in the previous section, we will use the *PA* symbolic calculus without instantiating temporal variables into numerical values.

14.3.1 State Variables, Timelines, and Chronicles

Recall that some relations of a planning domain are *rigid* and invariant in time, while others are *flexible* and vary over time. Because time is now an explicit variable of the representation, it can be convenient to rely on the usual mathematical representation for handling a variation that is dependent on some variable, i.e., as a function of that variable. The representation of this section relies on a finite set of *state variables*, each being a function from time into some finite domain.

Example 14.7 In the DWR domain, the position of a container c1 ranges over the union of the sets of piles, cranes, and robots. Similarly, the location of a robot r1 ranges over the set of locations (for simplicity we assume that the constant routes belongs to this set). These two state variables can be described by the two function symbols

position-c1 : time → piles ∪ cranes ∪ robots and
location-r1 : time → locations,

where time is the interpretation domain for temporal variables, taken here to be the set of real numbers $\Re$.

It can be convenient to use function symbols of more than one argument, i.e., of object variables and time. In order to refer to any container or to any robot in the domain, we can have

cpos : containers × time → piles ∪ cranes ∪ robots and
rloc : robots × time → locations.

Hence rloc(r), for $r \in$ robots, refers to the finite set of state variables that define the locations of the robots in the domain. Note that function symbols of more than one argument are only a syntactic facility of the representation because we are assuming that all of the object variables have finite domains. ■

Formally, let D be the set of all constant symbols in a planning domain partitioned into various *classes* of constants, such as the classes of robots, locations, cranes, and containers. The representation describes a domain with a finite set of n-ary state variables where each $x(v_1, \ldots, v_n)$ denotes an element of a function

$$x : D_1^x \times \ldots \times D_n^x \times \text{time} \rightarrow D_{n+1}^x,$$

where each $D_i^x \subseteq D$ is the union of one or more classes. All state variables are functions of time. Unless needed, the $(n+1)$th argument of an n-ary state variable will be left implicit.

These state variables will be used as *partially specified functions*. We do not need a complete knowledge of the value of each x for each time point. Planning will proceed from a partial specification by further refinement, i.e., by augmenting and constraining that specification with some change and persistence conditions over the state variables in order to achieve the objectives. In particular, there can be "holes" in the predicted evolution, i.e., time periods during which the value of some

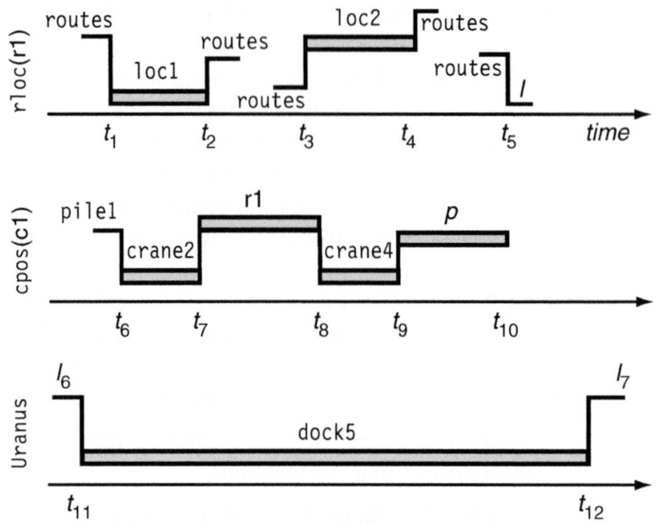

Figure 14.5 Three state variables as partial functions of time. (Persistent values are drawn as dashed rectangles while changes of values are represented as steps.)

x_i is unknown because it is not strictly needed for the plan. A state variable may have an imprecise or incomplete specification, i.e., $x(t) = v$, where v is an object variable whose value is not known but only constrained with respect to other object variables, and where the time point t is constrained with respect to other instants.

Example 14.8 Consider a DWR domain involving, among other objects, a robot r1, a container c1, and a ship Uranus, as well as several locations and cranes. A scenario partially specifying the whereabouts of r1, c1, and Uranus is represented with three state variables (Figure 14.5).

1. The first function says that r1 is in location loc1 at time t_1. It leaves loc1 at time t_2, enters loc2 at t_3, leaves loc2 at time t_4, and at t_5 enters location l.
2. The second function states that container c1 is in pile1 until t_6. It is held by crane2 from t_6 to t_7. Then it sits on r1 until t_8, at which point it is taken by crane4, which puts it on p at t_9, where it stays at least until t_{10}.
3. The last function says that the ship Uranus stays at location dock5 from t_{11} until t_{12}.

The object variable l is of type locations; it can be constrained but may remain unspecified even in a final plan. Similarly, the object variable p can be any pile in some location, e.g., if the goal is to have c1 anywhere in that location.

The temporal variables $t_1, \ldots, t_{12}$ are time points used to specify constraints. For example, the following constraints specify that the crane can start picking up a container when the destination robot enters the location: $t_1 \leq t_6$, $t_7 < t_2$, $t_3 \leq t_8$, and $t_9 < t_4$. Here, all the time points within a function are totally ordered, e.g., $t_1 < t_2 < t_3 < t_4 < t_5$, but the respective position of two time points in two different functions may remain unspecified, e.g., t_6 and t_{12} can be in any order.

There are several respects in which these functions are only partially specified. For example, the whereabouts of r1 are unknown from t_2 to t_3 and from t_4 to t_5. We know about the arrival of r1 to l at t_5, but nothing constrains it to stay there after t_5. The position of c1 is constrained to remain in p from t_9 at least until t_{10}, but it could stay there forever because the figure does not specify any change after this *persistence requirement.*

■

The three state variables in this example are *piecewise constant functions.* They can be specified with a set of temporal assertions using only two primitives, called *events* and *persistence conditions.* Both are primitives for describing the dynamics of a system due to actions or to predicted contingent events (e.g., the predicted arrival of Uranus, over which the planner has no control). These two primitives are defined as follows.

Definition 14.6 A *temporal assertion* on a state variable x is either an *event* or a *persistence condition* on x.

- An *event,* denoted as $x@t{:}(v_1, v_2)$, specifies the instantaneous *change* of the value of x from v_1 to v_2 at time t, with $v_1 \neq v_2$.
- A *persistence condition,* denoted as $x@[t_1, t_2){:}v$, specifies that the value of x *persists* as being equal to v over the interval $[t_1, t_2)$.

In this definition, t, t_1, and t_2 are constants or temporal variables, and v, v_1, and v_2 are constants or object variables in the domain of x.

■

As earlier, we have restricted intervals to be semi-open to avoid any confusion about the value of the state variable at a time t for an event $x@t{:}(v_1, v_2)$, or at the end of an interval for a persistence condition:

$$\begin{aligned}
x@[t_1, t_2){:}v \quad &\equiv \forall t\ (t_1 \leq t < t_2) \quad \wedge (x(t) = v)\\
x@t{:}(v_1, v_2) \quad &\equiv \exists t_0\ \forall t'(t_0 < t' < t) \quad \wedge (x(t') = v_1)\\
&\qquad \wedge (x(t) = v_2)
\end{aligned}$$

These two types of assertions are related:

$$\begin{aligned}
x@t{:}(v_1, v_2) \quad &\equiv \exists t_1, t_2\ (t_1 < t < t_2) \quad \wedge\ x@[t_1, t){:}v_1\\
&\qquad \wedge\ x@[t, t_2){:}v_2\\
&\qquad \wedge\ v_1 \neq v_2
\end{aligned}$$

The set of functions that can be described with the events and persistence conditions is limited to piecewise constant functions. This may seem very restricted as compared with the set of usual mathematical functions. Indeed, there are cases where one does need to reason about a continuous change from one value to another for a state variable ranging over a continuous domain. (The use of piecewise linear functions is discussed briefly in Section 14.4.) However, the restriction to piecewise constant functions, which is compatible with state variables ranging over finite domains, is often adequate given the abstraction level taken in planning where one leaves the precise values and the change of values to be taken care of at the execution level.

For example, the localization of a robot in a topological graph that has a finite set of locations and routes is not precise. One needs a more precise metrical localization for path planning and for controlling the robot along planned trajectories (see Chapter 20). However, a topological graph can be sufficient for planning the robot's mission. In that case it is reasonable to consider only discrete values for the state variable rloc(r1) and hence a piecewise constant function to describe its evolution; similarly for the state variable cpos(c1).

Definition 14.7 A *chronicle* for a set of state variables $\{x_i, \ldots, x_j\}$ is a pair $\Phi = (\mathcal{F}, \mathcal{C})$, where $\mathcal{F}$ is a set of temporal assertions, i.e., events and persistence conditions about the state variables $x_i, \ldots, x_j$, and $\mathcal{C}$ is a set of object constraints and temporal constraints. A *timeline* is a chronicle for a single state variable x. ■

Example 14.9 The timeline for the state variable rloc(r1) in Figure 14.5 is described by the following pair:

$$
\begin{aligned}
(\{ \quad & \mathsf{rloc(r1)}@t_1 : (l_1, \mathsf{loc1}),\\
& \mathsf{rloc(r1)}@[t_1, t_2) : \mathsf{loc1},\\
& \mathsf{rloc(r1)}@t_2 : (\mathsf{loc1}, l_2),\\
& \mathsf{rloc(r1)}@t_3 : (l_3, \mathsf{loc2}),\\
& \mathsf{rloc(r1)}@[t_3, t_4) : \mathsf{loc2},\\
& \mathsf{rloc(r1)}@t_4 : (\mathsf{loc2}, l_4),\\
& \mathsf{rloc(r1)}@t_5 : (l_5, \mathsf{loc3}) \ \},\\
\{ \quad & \mathsf{adjacent}(l_1, \mathsf{loc1}), \mathsf{adjacent}(\mathsf{loc1}, l_2),\\
& \mathsf{adjacent}(l_3, \mathsf{loc2}), \mathsf{adjacent}(\mathsf{loc2}, l_4), \mathsf{adjacent}(l_5, \mathsf{loc3}),\\
& t_1 < t_2 < t_3 < t_4 < t_5 \ \})
\end{aligned}
$$

This timeline for the state variable rloc(r1) refers to constants (loc1, loc2, etc.), object variables (l_1, l_2, etc.), and temporal variables (t_1, t_2, etc.). ■

A chronicle Φ can be seen as composed of several timelines, one for each state variable, and several constraints. It describes through these timelines and the constraints $\mathcal{C}$ how the world changes over time. The chronicle is interpreted as a *conjunction* of temporal assertions and temporal and object constraints. The object constraints in a chronicle are restricted to unary or binary constraints over finite domains on object variables. These are constraints of the form $x \in D$, $x = y$, $x \neq y$, conditional expressions such as "if $x \in D_1$ then $y \in D_2$," and pairs of allowed values for two variables, e.g., as defined by a rigid relation. The temporal constraints are here those of the point algebra *PA*. Hence, we will not instantiate temporal variables into numerical values. Other temporal constraint formalisms can be used in the chronicle representation; in particular, the use of TCSPs and the STPs will be discussed in Section 14.3.4.

A timeline Φ for a state variable x is used as a partial specification of a function that gives the value of x over time. Several such functions may correspond to Φ. Intuitively, a timeline Φ is *consistent* when the set of functions specified by Φ is not empty. This will be the case if no pair of assertions in the timeline conflicts, i.e., no specification leaves two possibly distinct values of the same state variable at the same time. We can avoid such a conflict by requiring a timeline to contain, either explicitly or implicitly, *separation constraints* that make each pair of assertions nonconflicting.

Definition 14.8 A timeline $\Phi = (\mathcal{F}, \mathcal{C})$ for the state variable x is *consistent* iff $\mathcal{C}$ is consistent and every pair of assertions in Φ is either disjoint or refers to the same value and/or the same time points.

- If two persistence conditions $x@[t_1, t_2){:}v_1$ and $x@[t_3, t_4){:}v_2$ are in $\mathcal{F}$, then one of the following sets of separation constraints is entailed by $\mathcal{C}$: $\{t_2 \leq t_3\}$, $\{t_4 \leq t_1\}$, or $\{v_1 = v_2\}$.
- If an event $x@t{:}(v_1, v_2)$ and persistence condition $x@[t_1, t_2){:}v$ are in $\mathcal{F}$, then one of the following sets of separation constraints is entailed by $\mathcal{C}$: $\{t < t_1\}$, $\{t_2 < t\}$, $\{t_1 = t, v = v_2\}$, or $\{t_2 = t, v = v_1\}$.
- If two events $x@t{:}(v_1, v_2)$ and $x@t'{:}(v_1', v_2')$ are in $\mathcal{F}$, then one of the following sets of separation constraints is entailed by $\mathcal{C}$: $\{t \neq t'\}$ or $\{v_1 = v_1', v_2 = v_2'\}$.

A chronicle Φ is consistent iff the timelines for all the state variables in Φ are consistent.

■

Recall that an n-ary state variable, e.g., rloc(r), is also a function of object variables. Consequently, two assertions on the same n-ary state variable in a chronicle may also be made disjoint by requiring their arguments to be distinct. For example, two events on rloc(r) and rloc(r') are made disjoint with the constraint $r \neq r'$. This additional constraint also has to be taken into account among the possible separation constraints for maintaining the consistency of a chronicle.

Note that the notion of a consistent chronicle is different from the usual notion of a consistent set of constraints. This definition requires a set of separation constraints to be entailed by $\mathcal{C}$, i.e., to be in $\mathcal{C}$ either explicitly or implicitly through other constraints. This is stronger than requiring only the possible consistency of a set of separation constraints with $\mathcal{C}$, which would make Φ only *possibly* consistent. Definition 14.8 requires $\mathcal{C}$ to be *necessarily* consistent with the separation constraints.

Example 14.10 Let $\mathcal{F}$ be the three timelines of Figure 14.5 and $\mathcal{C} = \{t_1 \leq t_6, t_7 < t_2, t_3 \leq t_8, t_9 < t_4, \mathsf{attached}(p, \mathsf{loc2})\}$. This last constraint means that pile p belongs to location loc2. The pair $(\mathcal{F}, \mathcal{C})$ is a consistent chronicle because in each timeline all pairs of assertions are either disjoint or they refer to the same value at the same time point. ∎

In Example 14.10, the time points in different timelines remain unordered with respect to each other, although within each timeline they are required to be totally ordered. This latter condition obviously simplifies checking the consistency of the chronicle, but even such a total order is not a sufficient consistency condition. For example, the chronicle $(\{x@[t', t):v, x@t:(v_1, v_2)\}, \emptyset)$ has its time points totally ordered but is not consistent because the constraint $(v = v_1)$ is not entailed from the chronicle.

Similarly to timelines, a chronicle is a partial specification for a collection of functions of time. We can refine such a specification by adding to a chronicle new temporal assertions and constraints, while keeping it consistent.

In order to do that precisely, let us define union and inclusion operations on chronicles. Because a chronicle is a pair of sets $(\mathcal{F}, \mathcal{C})$, the union of $\Phi = (\mathcal{F}, \mathcal{C})$ and $\Phi' = (\mathcal{F}', \mathcal{C}')$ is $\Phi \cup \Phi' = (\mathcal{F} \cup \mathcal{F}', \mathcal{C} \cup \mathcal{C}')$. The inclusion $\Phi \subseteq \Phi'$ holds iff $\mathcal{F} \subseteq \mathcal{F}'$ and $\mathcal{C} \subseteq \mathcal{C}'$.

We now define the notion of a chronicle *supporting* other chronicles, which is a notion quite different from that defined for temporal databases. Φ *supports* an assertion α when there is another assertion β in Φ that can be used as a causal support for α and when α can be added to Φ consistently. More precisely, when α asserts a value v or a change of value from v to some v' at time t for a state variable x, we require that β *establish* this value v for x at a time τ before t and that this value can *persist* consistently until t.

Definition 14.9 A consistent chronicle $\Phi = (\mathcal{F}, \mathcal{C})$ *supports* an assertion α (α being an event $\alpha = x@t:(v, v')$ or a persistence condition $\alpha = x@[t, t'):v$) iff there is in $\mathcal{F}$ an assertion β that asserts a value w for x (i.e., $\beta = x@\tau:(w', w)$ or $\beta = x@[\tau', \tau):w$) and there exists a set of separation constraints c such that $\Phi \cup (\{\alpha, x@[\tau, t):v\}, \{w = v, \tau < t\} \cup c)$ is a consistent chronicle. ∎

This definition requires β to establish the value v of x, needed by α, at some time τ prior to t, and that the persistence of this value from τ to t and the assertion α itself, together with separation constraints, can be added consistently to Φ. Here, β

is called the *support* of α in Φ. The pair $\delta = (\{\alpha,\ x@[\tau, t){:}v\},\ \{w = v, \tau < t\} \cup c)$ is an *enabler* of α in Φ. Several remarks are in order:

- This definition requires Φ to be consistent before enabling α.
- The enabler δ is a chronicle: its assertions are α itself and a persistence condition for the value v; its constraints are the precedence and binding constraints from β to α, as well as the separation constraints c required to make the new assertions nonconflicting with those of Φ.
- For an event $\alpha = x@t{:}(v, v')$, we are requiring a support in Φ only for the value v, not for v', and only *before* t. This is because the support will be used as a *causal explanation* for α, to appear before α because time orders causality.[8] The change from v to v' will be explained by an action.
- There can be several ways to enable an assertion α in Φ: the support β and the separation constraints c are not unique, hence the enabler is not unique.

Example 14.11 The chronicle Φ of Example 14.10 supports in two different ways the event α = rloc(r1)@t:(routes,loc3) with the following two supports:

$$\beta = \text{rloc(r1)@t}_2 : (\text{loc1, routes})$$

$$\beta = \text{rloc(r1)@t}_4 : (\text{loc2, routes})$$

An enabler for this latter case is:

$$\delta = (\{\text{rloc(r1)@}[t_4, t) : \text{routes}, \text{rloc(r1)@}t : (\text{routes, loc3})\}, \{t_4 < t < t_5\}$$

■

Let $\mathcal{E} = \{\alpha_1, \ldots, \alpha_k\}$ be a set of assertions. Assume that for each α_i in $\mathcal{E}$ there is a support β_i in $\mathcal{F} \cup \mathcal{E}$, $\beta_i \neq \alpha_i$, and an enabler δ_i. Let ϕ be the union of all these enablers: $\phi = \cup_i \delta_i$. Then we can create a new definition.

Definition 14.10 A consistent chronicle $\Phi = (\mathcal{F}, \mathcal{C})$ *supports* a set of assertions $\mathcal{E}$ iff each assertion α_i in $\mathcal{E}$ is supported by $(\mathcal{F} \cup \mathcal{E} - \{\alpha_i\}, \mathcal{C})$ with an enabler δ_i such that $\Phi \cup \phi$ is a consistent chronicle, where $\phi = \cup_i \delta_i$.

■

This definition allows an assertion $\alpha_i \in \mathcal{E}$ to support another assertion $\alpha_j \in \mathcal{E}$, $\alpha_j \neq \alpha_i$, with respect to Φ, as long as the union of the enablers is consistent with Φ. This union ϕ is called the *enabler* of $\mathcal{E}$ in Φ. Note that the assertions of ϕ include the set $\mathcal{E}$. Furthermore, ϕ is not unique because each α_i in $\mathcal{E}$ may have several supports and separation constraints with respect to Φ.

Example 14.12 The chronicle $\Phi = (\mathcal{F}, \mathcal{C})$ of Example 14.10 supports the pair of assertions $\{\alpha_1$ = rloc(r1)@t:(routes, loc3), α_2 = rloc(r1)@$[t', t'')$:loc3$\}$ in four different ways: with the two supports of Example 14.11 for α_1; and in each case α_2 can be

---

8. This is similar to causal links for preconditions in plan-space planning (Chapter 5).

supported either by α_1 or by the event in Φ: β = rloc(r1)@t_5:(routes,l), with the binding l=loc3. ∎

Let $\Phi' = (\mathcal{F}', \mathcal{C}')$ be a chronicle such that Φ supports $\mathcal{F}'$, and let $\theta(\Phi'/\Phi)$ be the set of all possible enablers of $\mathcal{F}'$ in Φ augmented with the constraints $\mathcal{C}'$ of Φ', i.e., $\theta(\Phi'/\Phi) = \{\phi \cup (\emptyset, \mathcal{C}') \mid \phi \text{ is an enabler of } \mathcal{F}'\}$. $\theta(\Phi'/\Phi)$ is empty when Φ does not support $\mathcal{F}'$. Note that every element of $\theta(\Phi'/\Phi)$ is a chronicle that contains Φ'; it is also called an *enabler* for Φ'.

Definition 14.11 A consistent chronicle $\Phi = (\mathcal{F}, \mathcal{C})$ *supports* a chronicle $\Phi' = (\mathcal{F}', \mathcal{C}')$ iff Φ supports $\mathcal{F}'$ and there is an enabler $\phi \in \theta(\Phi'/\Phi)$ such that $\Phi \cup \phi$ is a consistent chronicle. Chronicle Φ *entails* Φ' iff it supports Φ' and there is an enabler $\phi \in \theta(\Phi'/\Phi)$ such that $\phi \subseteq \Phi$. ∎

14.3.2 Chronicles as Planning Operators

We are now ready to use chronicles as building blocks for temporal planning.

Let $X = \{x_1, \ldots, x_n\}$ be a set of state variables. A chronicle planning operator on X is a pair $o = (\text{name}(o), (\mathcal{F}(o), \mathcal{C}(o))$, where:

- name(o) is a syntactic expression of the form $o(t_s, t_e, t_1, \ldots, v_1, v_2, \ldots)$, where o is an operator symbol, and $(t_s, t_e, t_1, \ldots, v_1, v_2, \ldots)$ are all the temporal and object variables in o.
- $(\mathcal{F}(o), \mathcal{C}(o))$ is a chronicle on the state variables of X.

Instead of such a pair, we will write operators as illustrated in the following example.

Example 14.13 A move operator for the DWR domain can be defined as follows (see Figure 14.6).

$$
\begin{aligned}
\mathsf{move}(t_s, t_e, t_1, t_2, r, l, l') = \{\ & \mathsf{rloc}(r)@t_s && : (l, \mathsf{routes}),\\
& \mathsf{rloc}(r)@[t_s, t_e) && : \mathsf{routes},\\
& \mathsf{rloc}(r)@t_e && : (\mathsf{routes}, l'),\\
& \mathsf{contains}(l)@t_1 && : (r, \mathsf{empty}),\\
& \mathsf{contains}(l')@t_2 && : (\mathsf{empty}, r),\\
& t_s < t_1 < t_2 < t_e, &&\\
& \mathsf{adjacent}(l, l')\ \} &&
\end{aligned}
$$

Here, rloc : robots × time → locations ∪ {routes}, where routes refers to any route between locations; contains : locations × time → robots ∪ {empty}, where empty means a free location. Note that the object variables r and l in rloc and contains, respectively, are both arguments of a state variable and values of another state variable.

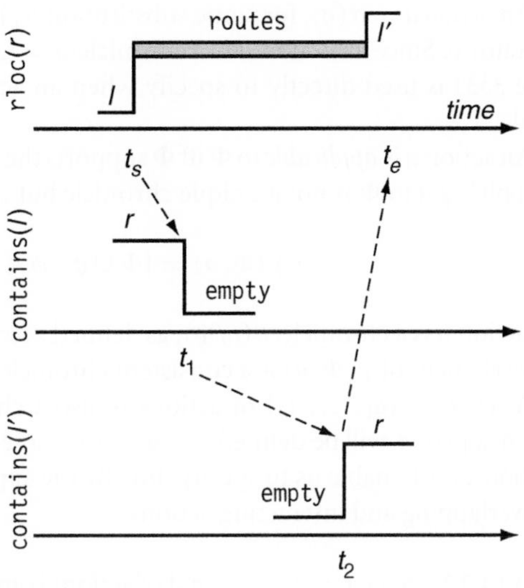

Figure 14.6 A planning operator as a chronicle. The figure depicts three timelines for the three state variables for this operator and temporal constraints on four time points. Note the the first timeline on rloc involves two events and a persistence condition.

These specifications are conservative in the sense that an origin location becomes empty *after* the robot leaves it ($t_s < t_1$), and a destination location ceases to be empty after the origin is free and *before* the robot enters it ($t_1 < t_2 < t_e$). ■

A chronicle planning operator o departs significantly from a classical planning operator.

- o does not specify preconditions and effects explicitly and separately. For example, contains$(l)@t_1 : (r,$ empty$)$ is both a precondition and an effect. It is a precondition for the value contains$(l) = r$, for which a support will be required for the action to be applicable. It is an effect for the value contains$(l) =$ empty, which can be used as a support for other actions.
- o is applied not to a state but to a chronicle. The applicability of o is defined with respect to an entire chronicle.
- The result of applying an instance of o to a chronicle is not unique; it is a set of chronicles.

Note that all object and temporal variables in o are parameters of o existentially quantified with respect to a chronicle. As in Section 14.3.1, temporal variables will not be instantiated into numerical values.

An *action* $a = \sigma(o)$, for some substitution σ, is a partially instantiated planning operator o. Since an action a is a chronicle $a = (\mathcal{F}(a), \mathcal{C}(a))$, Definition 14.10 (see page 333) is used directly to specify when an action is applicable and what is its result.

An action a is *applicable* to Φ iff Φ supports the chronicle $(\mathcal{F}(a), \mathcal{C}(a))$. The result of applying a to Φ is not a unique chronicle but a set:

$$\gamma(\Phi, a) = \{\Phi \cup \phi \mid \phi \in \theta(a/\Phi)\}$$

An action a is a chronicle, $\theta(a/\Phi)$, as defined according to Definition 14.11. Hence, every element of $\gamma(\Phi, a)$ is a consistent chronicle.

A set $\pi = \{a_1, \ldots, a_n\}$ of actions is also a chronicle $\Phi_\pi = \bigcup_i(\mathcal{F}(a_i), \mathcal{C}(a_i))$. Again, a plan π will be defined as a set, not as a sequence. The general constructs of Section 14.3.1 enable us to specify directly the applicability and the result of a set π of overlapping and interacting actions.

Definition 14.12 A set $\pi = \{a_1, \ldots, a_n\}$ of actions is applicable to Φ iff Φ supports $\Phi_\pi = \bigcup_i(\mathcal{F}(a_i), \mathcal{C}(a_i))$. The result of π is the set of chronicles $\gamma(\Phi, \pi) = \{\Phi \cup \phi \mid \phi \in \theta(\Phi_\pi/\Phi)\}$.

■

It is important to underline that the definition of a chronicle supporting another chronicle allows some assertions of Φ_π to be supported by other assertions of Φ_π (see Definition 14.10 (see page 333)). Hence, we can handle concurrent actions with interfering effects.

14.3.3 Chronicle Planning Procedures

It is now easy to pursue an approach similar to that developed for temporal databases in order to define with chronicles temporal planning domains, problems, and solution plans.

A temporal planning *domain* is a pair $\mathcal{D} = (\Lambda_\Phi, \mathcal{O})$ where $\mathcal{O}$ is a set of chronicle planning operators, and Λ_Φ is the set of all chronicles that can be defined with assertions and constraints on the state variables of X using the constants and the temporal and object variables of the representation.

A temporal planning *problem* on $\mathcal{D}$ is a tuple $\mathcal{P} = (\mathcal{D}, \Phi_0, \Phi_g)$, where Φ_0 is a consistent chronicle that represents an initial scenario describing the rigid relations, the initial state of the domain, and the expected evolution that will take place independently of the actions to be planned, and Φ_g is a consistent chronicle that represents the goals of the problem. The *statement* of a problem $\mathcal{P}$ is given by $P = (\mathcal{O}, \Phi_0, \Phi_g)$.

A *solution plan* for a problem P is a set $\pi = \{a_1, \ldots, a_n\}$ of actions, each being an instance of an operator in $\mathcal{O}$, such that there is a chronicle in $\gamma(\Phi, \pi)$ that entails Φ_g. We will require a planner to find not only the set π but also a chronicle in $\gamma(\Phi, \pi)$ that entails Φ_g.

The approach to planning appears here simpler than in Section 14.2 because we have not introduced domain axioms. This is due to the functional representation and to the fact that every change and persistence effect of an action is specified explicitly in its description as a chronicle. We are going to present a planning procedure for chronicles that refines the TPS schema using CSP-based techniques and a search space similar to that of partial plans.

The TPS procedure of Figure 14.4 and the notations of Section 14.2.6 apply here with the following modifications: only two types of flaws have to be considered (open goals and threats) and enablers are here chronicles, not just constraints.

The resolution stage of the planning problem is now the tuple $\Omega = (\Phi, G, \mathcal{K}, \pi)$, where $\Phi = (\mathcal{F}, \mathcal{C})$ is the current chronicle, G is a set of assertions corresponding to the current open goals, $\mathcal{K} = \{C_1, \ldots, C_i\}$ is a set of pending sets of enablers, and π is the current plan.

For the problem $P = (\mathcal{O}, \Phi_0, \Phi_g)$, where $\Phi_0 = (\mathcal{F}_0, \mathcal{C}_0)$ and $\Phi_g = (\mathcal{G}, \mathcal{C}_g)$, we start initially with $\Phi = (\mathcal{F}_0, \mathcal{C}_0 \cup \mathcal{C}_g)$, $G = \mathcal{G}$, $\pi = \emptyset$, and $\mathcal{K} = \emptyset$. The current chronicle Φ is then refined until it has no flaw.

If P is successfully solved, then in the final stage $G = \mathcal{K} = \emptyset$, π is a set of actions that are instances of operators in $\mathcal{O}$, and $\Phi \in \gamma(\Phi_0, \pi)$ such that Φ entails Φ_g. Actions in the final plan π are partially instantiated and their time points are partially constrained.

The two types of flaws are processed as follows.

Open Goals. If $G \neq \emptyset$, then every assertion $\alpha \in G$ is a goal not yet supported by Φ.

- If $\theta(\alpha/\Phi) \neq \emptyset$, then there is in Φ a support for α. A resolver for this flaw is an enabler consistent with Φ. The refinement of Ω consist of the following updates:

$$\mathcal{K} \leftarrow \mathcal{K} \cup \{\theta(\alpha/\Phi)\}$$
$$G \leftarrow G - \{\alpha\}$$

- Otherwise, a resolver for the flaw is an action a that is relevant for this flaw, i.e., there is a support for α in $\mathcal{F}(a)$. The procedure chooses nondeterministically such an action and refines Ω with the following updates:

$$\pi \leftarrow \pi \cup \{a\}$$
$$\Phi \leftarrow \Phi \cup (\mathcal{F}(a), \mathcal{C}(a))$$
$$G \leftarrow G \cup \mathcal{F}(a)$$
$$\mathcal{K} \leftarrow \mathcal{K} \cup \{\theta(a/\Phi)\}$$

Notice that we are not requesting a to be supported by the current stage of Φ but only to be relevant for α. Hence, in the latter update of $\mathcal{K}$, $\theta(a/\Phi)$ is not necessarily completely defined at that stage; it remains as a set of pending consistency conditions.

```
CP(Φ, G, K, π)
    if G = K = ∅ then return(π)
    perform the two following steps in any order
        if G ≠ ∅ then do
            select any α ∈ G
            if θ(α/Φ) ≠ ∅ then return(CP(Φ, G − {α}, K ∪ θ(α/Φ), π))
            else do
                relevant ← {a | a contains a support for α}
                if relevant = ∅ then return(failure)
                nondeterministically choose a ∈ relevant
                return(CP(Φ ∪ (F(a), C(a)), G ∪ F(a), K ∪ {θ(a/Φ)}, π ∪ {a}))
        if K ≠ ∅ then do
            select any C ∈ K
            threat-resolvers ← {φ ∈ C | φ consistent with Φ}
            if threat-resolvers = ∅ then return(failure)
            nondeterministically choose φ ∈ threat-resolvers
            return(CP(Φ ∪ φ, G, K − C, π))
end
```

Figure 14.7 CP, a chronicle planning procedure.

Threats. If $\mathcal{K} \neq \emptyset$, then every $C \in \mathcal{K}$ is a pending set of enablers that are not yet entailed by the chronicle Φ. A resolver for this flaw is an enabler $\phi \in C$ that is consistent with Φ. The procedure chooses nondeterministically such an enabler if it exists and refines Ω with the following updates:

$$\mathcal{K} \leftarrow \mathcal{K} - \{C\}$$

$$\Phi \leftarrow \Phi \cup \phi \quad \text{for } \phi \in C \text{ consistent with } \Phi$$

Backtracking is needed when a flaw has no resolver. The corresponding procedure, called CP, for *Chronicle Planning*, is given in Figure 14.7. At each recursion, CP performs a termination test and addresses one particular flaw. Either it checks for open goals first, then deals with threats if there are no open goals, or it focuses on threats first.

For an implementation of CP, several steps in the above pseudocode can be refined.

- The choice of a relevant action for an open goal has to be heuristically guided but also restricted to actions that are consistent with the current stage of Φ.
- When an action a is added to the current plan, the update of G can be restricted to the sole assertions of $\mathcal{F}(a)$ that are not supported by a itself.

- The link between a support brought by an action and the assertion α can be performed immediately when a is added to the current π, enabling one to remove α from G.

In addition, the implementation of CP into a practical planner requires two important design steps: how to handle the constraints and how to control the search.

14.3.4 Constraint Management in CP

Two types of constraints are involved in this representation: temporal constraints and object constraints. Here, these two types of constraints are *decoupled*: no constraint in the representation introduced so far restricts the value of a time point as a function of object variables or vice versa. In other words, a set of constraints $\mathcal{C}$ in a chronicle $\Phi = (\mathcal{F}, \mathcal{C})$ is consistent iff the temporal constraints in $\mathcal{C}$ are consistent and the object constraints in $\mathcal{C}$ are consistent.[9] Consequently, constraint handling relies on two independent constraint managers for the two types of constraints.

The Time-Map Manager. Here we have to rely on the techniques developed in Chapter 13 in order to handle the temporal constraints. For simplicity we used the symbolic calculus. However, more expressive constraints would be needed in a practical planner. Simple temporal networks (the STPs of Section 13.4.1) allow for all of the *PA* constraints as well as for quantitative constraints. Minimal STP networks can be maintained, enabling the computation of queries in $O(1)$ and incremental updates in $O(n^2)$. The more expressive TCSPs with disjunctive quantitative constraints allow for a richer planning language but also for a disjunctive-refinement process. Although they are more complex to maintain, they may be a viable alternative if the control benefits from a disjunctive-refinement procedure.

However, the use of quantitative constraints and the instantiation of temporal variables into numerical values raises another important issue. According to the semantics of existentially quantified parameters of planning operators, the planner is free to choose any value for its temporal parameters that meets the specified constraints. One way to view this is to proceed with temporal variables as with object variables. For example, in the DWR operator take(k, l, c, d, p) (Example 2.8), variables c and d are existentially quantified, but because of the relation on(c, d), the container d is a function of c. Hence, choosing c fixes d.

If we are going to instantiate numerically the temporal variables according to such an approach, we would obviously need to specify additional knowledge in a temporal operator in order to predict precisely, according to the physics of the world, the duration of an action and the other temporal periods involved in it. In the move operator of Example 14.13 (see page 334), we would need to predict how long

9. Note that a consistent $\mathcal{C}$ does not guarantee a consistent Φ, as defined in Definition 14.8.

it takes to leave the initial location, to travel the routes, and to enter the destination location. The additional constraints would make t_e, t_1, and t_2 functions of t_s and other domain features, leaving the value of the starting point t_s as the only temporal choice point available to the planner among the set of possible instances.

Because a precise model of an action cannot be achieved, in practice one relies on conservative estimates that may provide for some robustness in the action models. These estimates are not easy to assess. Furthermore, conservative estimates for each action may make the planner fail to find a plan for a time-constrained goal even though such a goal is most often achievable.

A more reasonable approach would not need precise predictive knowledge but only prediction about possible intervals, leaving a margin for uncertainty. This approach requires the introduction of another category of temporal variables that cannot be determined and instantiated at planning time but can only be *observed* at execution time. These *contingent temporal variables* can be considered as random variables ranging in some intervals specified in the operator constraints. They are not existentially quantified parameters but universally quantified variables, distinct from free variables in the sense that whatever their observed values at execution time, within their allowed intervals of uncertainty the plan should meet all its constraints. This issue of contingent temporal variables and constraints was briefly discussed Section 13.5 and requires further extension to planning procedures and to the STP techniques for handling these contingent constraints and variables.

The Object Constraints Manager. This manager handles unary and binary constraints on object variables that come from binding and separation constraints it also handles rigid relations. Here we have to maintain a general CSP over finite domains, whose consistency checking is an NP-complete problem. There appears to be no useful restriction of the constraint language to a tractable CSP for object constraints. Indeed, the separation constraints of type $x \neq y$ make consistency checking NP-complete.[10] Filtering techniques, such as incremental arc consistency, are not complete. Nonetheless, they are very efficient, and they offer a reasonable trade-off for testing the consistency of object constraint networks. They may be used jointly with complete resolution algorithms, such as Forward-checking, at regular stages of the search with a risk of late backtracking.

In addition to the temporal and object constraints, other constraint managers can be useful if planning proceeds along a disjunctive-refinement scheme. The disjunction of resolvers for a flaw can be handled with a meta-CSP. Here a flaw is a variable whose domain is the set of resolvers of that flaw. The technique for managing this meta-CSP is similar to that illustrated (in Section 13.4.2) for TCSPs and in Section 8.6.1.

A Meta-CSP for Pending Enablers. Let us explain briefly how a meta-CSP can be used for handling the set $\mathcal{K}$ of pending sets of enablers. $\mathcal{K}$ will be associated with a network denoted $X_{\mathcal{K}}$, where each CSP variable x_C corresponds to a set of enablers

10. Graph coloring, an NP-complete problem, gives a good example of a CSP with such a constraint.

C in $\mathcal{K}$. At an update such as $\mathcal{K} \leftarrow \mathcal{K} \cup \{C\}$, if C is not yet known explicitly, it is left pending.[11] Otherwise, the consistency of each enabler $\phi \in C$ is checked with respect to the current Φ; ϕ is removed from C if ϕ is not consistent with Φ. At the end, one of the following occurs.

- If $C = \emptyset$, then this is a backtracking point.
- If $|C| = 1$, then there is a single enabler. Its constraints are directly added to the temporal network and to the object variable network, with the corresponding updates for $\mathcal{K}$ and Φ.
- Otherwise, the meta-CSP $X_{\mathcal{K}}$ is updated with a new variable x_C, whose domain is the set of remaining enablers in C.

Consistent tuples of values of the variables in $X_{\mathcal{K}}$ are conjunctions of enablers consistent with Φ. The management of the meta-CSP $X_{\mathcal{K}}$ may rely on incremental arc consistency, performed when a new variable is added to $X_{\mathcal{K}}$. If filtering leads to inconsistency, then backtracking is needed. If filtering reduces the domain of a variable to a single possible resolver, that variable is removed from the CSP network and the corresponding constraints are added to the temporal network and to the object variable network. Otherwise, inconsistent pairs of enablers are explicitly recorded in order to avoid using them in resolving future flaws.

The principle of managing disjunctions with a meta-CSP may be used at even a finer level for handling the set $\mathcal{K}$. Each enabler ϕ corresponds to a set of possible supports β_i for the assertions supported by ϕ and to separation constraints. Each such set of supports may have several sets of separation constraints. Hence it can be worthwhile to manage separately in two meta-CSPs the disjunctions over a set of supports and the disjunctions over separation constraints. The relations between the two are kept as binary constraints. Here also the consistency of each disjunction is checked separately with respect to the temporal and object networks. Inconsistent disjunctions are filtered out. Arc-consistency checking may further reduce disjunctions.

14.3.5 Search Control in CP

The control of the search proceeds here, as in plan space, along the principle of least commitment. This means that no action and no temporal or object constraint in enablers is added to the current Ω unless strictly needed to solve a flaw. This principle is very appealing because it involves no unnecessary nondeterministic choices that may lead to conflicts and to backtracking. Furthermore, least commitment leads to a final plan that remains as flexible as possible for execution, with partially instantiated and partially constrained actions.

11. This is the case for an action a not yet supported by the current Φ.

However, the least commitment principle alone is too general and insufficient to focus the search. It has to be combined with more informed and/or problem-specific strategies and heuristics for ordering flaws and choosing resolvers.

The principles for designing flaw-ordering heuristics are similar to those used in the resolution of CSPs for variable ordering. The idea is to start with the most constrained flaws that have the smallest number of resolvers in order to backtrack, if needed, as early as possible. If the quality of each resolver can be assessed, more complex flaw-selection heuristic functions that combine the number of resolvers and their quality are possible. These heuristics, however, require finding and assessing all resolvers for all flaws. They involve a significant overhead.

If disjunctive-refinement techniques are used for managing threats, we are left only with open goal flaws. Because a resolver for a threat does not introduce new open goals, a possible strategy is to solve all open goals, then to address threats with CSP resolution and filtering techniques. In this strategy, the search has two distinct phases: the open goal phase, while posting disjunctive constraints, and the threat resolution phase, which solves these constraints. This two-phases strategy is effective as long as there is no backtracking from the second phase back to the first. This can be assisted during the open goal phase with the filtering techniques for the disjunctive refinement in order to find inconsistent constraints as early as possible.

The resolution of open goals requires flaw-ordering heuristics and resolver-selection heuristics. A good compromise for flaw-ordering heuristics is to select the assertion α that correspond to the smallest set of relevant actions that have a support for α. Resolver-selection heuristics are the most important control element for the efficiency of the search. Good distance-based heuristics, as discussed in Chapter 9, rely on a trade-off between relaxation and regression.

The *relaxation principle* here is to ignore the consistency constraints between assertions of $\Phi \cup (\mathcal{F}(a), \mathcal{C}(a))$. Hence an action a is evaluated only with respect to what assertions are possibly supported by a, as compared to what new assertions a adds to the open goals. Furthermore, the binding and temporal constraints are not taken into account in this evaluation, whereas the role variable instantiations due to the partial instantiation of a with the current open goal of interest are.

The *regression principle* may rely on a heuristic evaluation of the cost of solving an open goal α defined as follows:

$$h(\alpha) = \min_{a \in relevant} \{\text{cost}(a) + \sum_{\alpha_i \in \mathcal{F}(a)} h(\alpha_i)\}$$

In this expression, the sum can be restricted to the sole assertions in $\mathcal{F}(a)$ that are not supported by a itself; cost(a) can be either a unit cost for all actions or a user-given value that reflects the cost of planning with a.[12] The regression may proceed along an a priori bounded AND/OR graph whose root is the assertion α. Or-branches correspond to actions relevant for α. From such an action, AND-branches are the assertions of a for which there is no support, neither in Φ nor in

12. This cost should not be confused with the cost of executing a within a plan.

the current AND/OR graph. At some maximal depth, the formula is computed with heuristics estimates for leaf assertions and regressed backward until the root. The action corresponding to the minimum is chosen for resolving the current flaw.

A final element for controlling the search may rely on a partial order on the state variables. Flaws are processed according to this order: no flaw is considered for the state variable x until all flaws for all state variables that precede x have been addressed. This scheme works as long as the resolution of flaws on x does not introduce new flaws for state variables that precede x. It is easy to synthesize automatically a partial order that guarantees this property for a particular chronicle planning problem. The techniques for this are similar to those used in classical planning for generating hierarchies with the ordered monotonic property [325] (see Section 24.6).

14.4 Discussion and Historical Remarks

As discussed in the introduction to Part IV, an explicit representation of time in planning extends the expressiveness of planning models. In particular, concurrent actions that are not independent and have interfering effects can be dealt with. Note, however, that this capability is limited to effects explicit in the action models: we have not addressed the much more general *ramification problem*, where additional effects are deduced from explicit effects and a general world model [463].

Temporal planning can be pursued either along the state-oriented view or along the time-oriented view. The early work on temporal planning, as well as most of the more recent temporal planners, adopt the state-oriented view. This can be explained mainly because this view is much closer to the classical planning paradigm, and thus it is easier to integrate with classical planning techniques and to benefit from any new progress in these techniques. The state-oriented approach was taken by several planners.

- In state-space planning, following on the early work on Deviser [528], several recent heuristically guided planners have been generalized to handle time, e.g., TLplan and following planners [29, 32], TALplanner [160, 342, 343], and the HS planner [261].
- In plan-space planning, the ZENO system [437] introduced a rich representation with variable durations and linear constraints.
- In the planning-graph approaches, planners such as TGP [489], SAPA [159], and TPSYS [208] handle durations and other temporal constructs.
- In HTN planning, several planners such as O-Plan [135], SIPE [549], and SHOP2 [416] integrate time windows and constraints in their representations and search processes.

Among these approaches, several of the recent planners have been shown to be quite efficient and to allow a reasonable scaling up (e.g., see the AIPS'02 planning competition [195]). However, most often these approaches lead to restricted models of concurrency of actions. The assumptions usually made are that an action has a duration but there is no possible reference to intermediate time points during this duration interval. Preconditions and effects are specified at the end points of the interval, with eventually invariant conditions that should prevail during the duration (along the model of Sandewall and Rönnquist [464]). These assumptions are discussed in the specification of the PDDL2.1 domain description language [196]. They lead to a weak notion of concurrency that basically requires independence between actions, as in layered plans. Interfering effects, as discussed in Section 14.2.5, need additional modeling efforts, e.g., adding specific actions and states, or constructs such as the processes and events proposed in PDDL+ [194].

Planning along the time-oriented view followed the pioneering work of Allen [18]. The example of a door with a spring lock[13] and similar interfering actions are discussed and correctly handled through the planner of [13, 17]. This planner is based on Allen's interval algebra (Section 13.3.2) for handling qualitative temporal constraints between propositions that are conditions and effects of actions, anywhere during their duration intervals. The planner does a plan-space search in which causal links are handled through *IA* constraints.

Another significant contribution to planning along the time-oriented view is the Time-Map Manager of Dean and McDermott [145] and several planners based on it [78, 143]. These planners handle what we presented here as temporal databases and implement several variants of the techniques described in Section 14.2.

Planning with chronicles started with the IxTeT system [223, 224], whose kernel is an efficient manager of the *PA* and STP temporal constraints [225]. This system seeks a compromise between efficiency and expressiveness for handling concurrency and interfering actions, external events, and goals situated in time. Distance-based heuristics were originally proposed within IxTeT, which also integrates several extensions to the abstraction techniques of plan-space planning [205]. However, this planner still remains noncompetitive with the most efficient state-based or HTN temporal planners.

Several other planners adopt variants of the chronicle-based approach. These are notably ParcPlan [170, 361], and RAP and its follower EUROPA [198, 285, 409]. We will come back to the latter planners in Chapter 19 because these planners enabled a major planning application. ParcPlan has a control strategy that handles open goals in a simplified manner, then it manages threats with a meta-CSP technique, along the lines of the two-stages control technique discussed earlier.

Several temporal planners are able to handle more complex temporal constraints than those of *IA*, *PA*, STP and TCSP (Chapter 13). For example, in the state-oriented view, ZENO handles linear constraints; the planner of Dimopoulos and Gerevini [155] relies on mixed linear and integer programming techniques. In the time-oriented view, even if most temporal planners rely basically on piecewise constant functions, generalization to piecewise linear functions appears feasible in many cases [512].

---

13. This example is known as the "University of Rochester CS Building door"; see Exercise 14.7.

The issue of robust estimates for temporal periods and other parameters is well known in scheduling and is being explored in planning (e.g., [139]). The problem of contingent temporal variables and constraints is fairly well addressed [403, 530, 531, 532]. But a good integration of the proposed techniques into planning procedures remain to be further explored, eventually within the wider context of CSPs with contingent variables along approaches such as [185, 542].

The two approaches presented in this chapter are very close and involve similar techniques. The temporal database representation has didactic merits because its operators are closer to the familiar classical planning operators and it allows an easier introduction to the main concepts. The chronicle-based approach benefits from the state-variable representation and the lack of domain axioms in conciseness and probably also efficiency.

14.5 Exercises

14.1 Modify the move operator of Figure 14.2 to take into account within this action the time it takes the robot to get out of its initial location, i.e., between t_s and the moment at which the robot leaves location l. Work out the consistency constraints with domain axioms of Example 14.5 (see page 318) for this modified operator.

14.2 Using the representation of Figure 14.2, define temporal planning operators for the actions load, unload, take, and put of the DWR domain.

14.3 Define domain axioms corresponding to the operators of Exercise 14.2.

14.4 Extend the database of Example 14.1 (see page 311) to include two containers, respectively in loc1 and loc2, and apply the operators and axioms of the previous exercises to achieve the goal of permuting the positions of these two containers. Develop two possible plans, one that assumes a domain with three adjacent locations, and one restricted to only two locations.

14.5 Consider a DWR domain where each robot is equipped with a container fixture that guides the loading of a container on the robot with a crane and that maintains the container in position while the robot is moving. This fixture remains closed; it can be opened by the robot, but it closes as soon as the opening action ceases. With such a system, a robot has to open its container fixture and maintain it open during the load and unload operations. Define an open-fixture operator and revise the load and unload operators to have the desired joint effects of loading and fixing a container, or freeing and unloading it.

14.6 In the TPS procedure (Section 14.2.6), analyze the processing of open goal flaws. Explain how this processing makes TPS consistent with the definition of an applicable set of concurrent actions with interfering effects.

14.7 Consider two operators open and unlock for handling the "University of Rochester CS Building door" domain: open turns the knob and pushes the door but requires

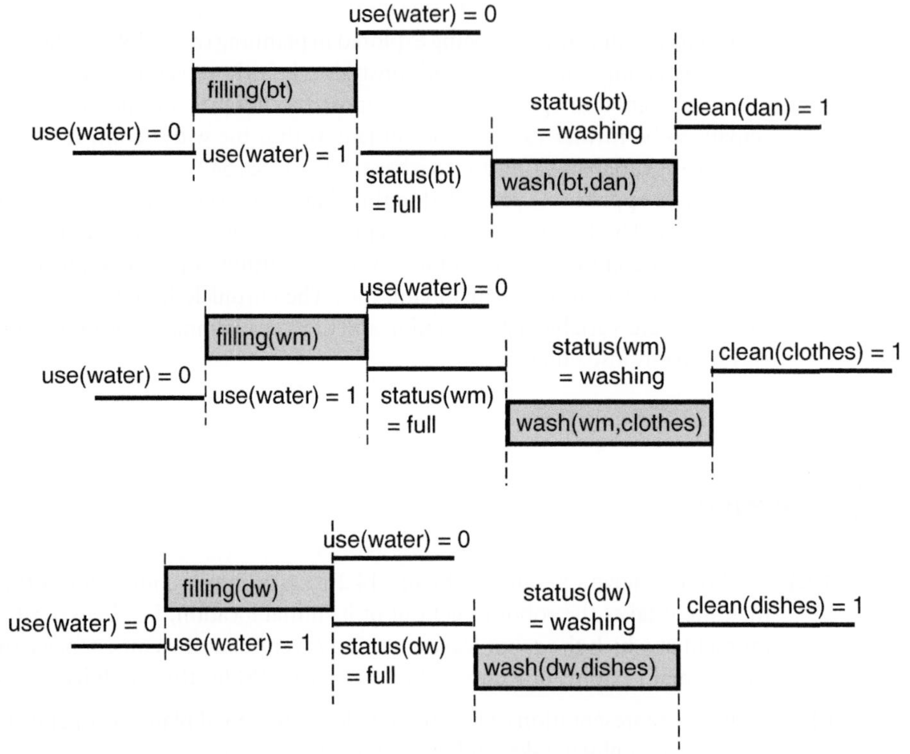

Figure 14.8 A chronicle for a washing problem.

the lock to be unlocked when turning; unlock pushes a spring and maintains it to keep the lock unlocked. Define these two operators in the temporal database approach and in the chronicle approach. Compare the two models.

14.8 Using the representation of Example 14.13 (see page 334), define four chronicle operators for the actions load, unload, take, and put of the DWR domain.

14.9 Extend the domain of Example 14.8 (see page 328) by considering that the ship Uranus contains two containers c2 and c3 that need to be unloaded, and the container c1 has to be loaded on Uranus while the ship is on dock. Assume that crane4 belongs to dock5. Find a plan for this problem.

14.10 Extend the chronicle planning representation to include numerical temporal constraints of the STP type. Discuss the required change in the CP procedure.

14.11 Here is a temporal planning adaptation of the planning problem described in Exercise 5.7. Dan wants to make a plan to wash his clothes with a washing machine wm, wash his dishes in a dishwasher dw, and bathe in a bathtub bt. The water supply doesn't have enough pressure to do more than one of these activities at once. Here are the operators for the planning domain:

fill(t_s, t_e, x)
  status(x)@t_s : (ready,filling)
  status(x)@[t_s, t_e) : (filling)
  status(x)@t_e : (filling,full)
  use(water)@t_s : (0,1)
  use(water)@[t_s, t_e) : 1
  use(water)@t_e : (1,0)
  $t_s < t_e$

wash(t_s, t_e, x, y)
  status(x)@t_s : (full,washing)
  status(x)@[t_s, t_e) : (washing)
  status(x)@t_e : (washing,ready)
  clean(y)@t_e : (0,1)
  $t_s < t_e$

(a) Write the initial chronicle for the planning problem.

(b) Figure 14.8 is a depiction of a chronicle at an intermediate point in the planning process. What are all of the flaws in this chronicle?

(c) Write the chronicle as a set of temporal assertions and a set of constraints.

(d) How many solution plans can be generated from the chronicle? Write one of them.

(e) How (if at all) would your answer to part (c) change if the planning domain also included operators to make everything dirty again?

14.12 Redo Exercise 14.11 using a temporal database representation.

CHAPTER 15

Planning and Resource Scheduling

15.1 Introduction

Scheduling addresses the problem of how to perform a given set of actions using a limited number of resources in a limited amount of time. A *resource* is an entity that one needs to borrow or to consume (e.g., a tool, a machine, or energy) in order to perform an action. An action may have the choice between several alternate resources, and a resource may be shared between several actions. The main decision variables for scheduling a given action are which resources should be allocated to the action and when to perform it. A solution *schedule*[1] has to meet a number of constraints (e.g., on deadlines, on the ordering of actions, on the type and amount of resources they require, and on the availability of resources). In addition, there is usually an optimization requirement in scheduling: one would like to minimize a cost criteria such as achieving all actions as early as possible or using the least costly resources.

Planning and scheduling are closely related problems. In a simple decomposition scheme, planning appears to be an upstream problem that needs to be solved before scheduling. Planning focuses on the causal reasoning for finding the set of actions needed to achieve the goal, while scheduling concentrates on time and resource allocation for this set of actions. Indeed, a plan given as output by a planner is usually a structured or partially ordered set of actions that does not specify the resources and a precise schedule for its actions.

Along with this decomposition scheme, a scheduled plan is synthesized in two steps (see Figure 15.1): (1) *what* to do, and (2) *when* and *how* to do it. Planning addresses the issue of what has to be done, while scheduling focuses on when and how to do it.

---

1. In the usual scheduling terminology, an action is called an *activity* or a *task*, and a solution is a *schedule*. We will keep here the planning terminology for actions, but we will use the word *schedule* to emphasize a plan with scheduled resources.

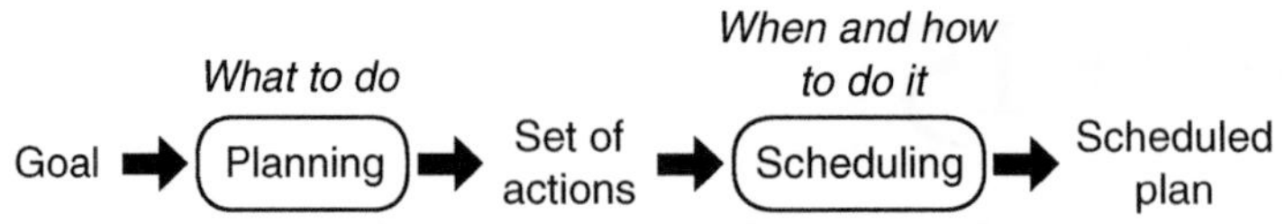

Figure 15.1 Planning and scheduling: a simple decomposition scheme.

Very often, planning and scheduling have been addressed as two separate problems.

1. In "*pure scheduling*" problems (e.g., for organizing jobs in a factory), there is a limited number of possible types of jobs. The set of actions required to process a job is known because the *what* issue has been addressed separately (e.g., as part of the initial design of the factory). The problem of interest is to find an optimal schedule for the jobs at hand.
2. In "*pure planning*" problems (e.g., for controlling an autonomous agent), the usual agent has few intrinsic resources, such as for moving around and handling objects. There is not much choice about the resources to allocate to actions and not much concurrency and resource sharing between actions. The concern is more about finding the right actions for achieving a goal than about finding an optimal schedule for sharing resources between actions and agents.

However, few practical planning problems are "pure planning" problems, and there is more and more demand for scheduling problems to handle planning issues as well. There is a need for both planning and scheduling, when the problem at hand is to organize the activity of a complex system (e.g., one with alternate resources, resource-sharing requirements, and a large set of possible goals), in particular when it is not feasible to cache the plans for each type of goal beforehand. For example, this is the case in factory organization with flexible manufacturing, in management of large infrastructure operations such as a rescue operation, and in the control of autonomous agents whose actions require and share a variety of resources.

Some of these complex applications may possibly be addressed along the simple decomposition scheme of Figure 15.1. However, considering planning and scheduling as two successive independent steps is, in general, too restrictive and oversimplifying. On the one hand, the decomposition scheme may not work when the constraints are too tight (e.g., when there are many plans but very few that have a feasible schedule). On the other hand, modeling resources and taking them into account as fluents can be highly inefficient.

A given set of objects in a planning domain can be modeled either as a resource or as a set of constants. In the latter case, these objects will be referred to *individually*, through the names of the constants, whereas in the former case they will be referred to *indiscriminately*, as the number of objects available at some time point. For example, if a location in a DWR scenario contains five identical cranes, then planning a `load` action with a particular crane introduces a decision point that may be unnecessary: if one is not interested in distinguishing between these five cranes, backtracking on this choice is meaningless. If this set of cranes is modeled as a resource, then a load action reduces during its duration the *number* of available cranes by one. The choice of which of the five cranes will be used is not a decision point at planning time. The set of robots in the DWR domain can also be modeled as a resource if they are considered to be identical or as several resources corresponding to the different types of available robots (see Section 20.4). Containers, on the other hand, cannot be modeled as a resource as long as one needs to refer to a container individually: its current location and its desired goal location.

The main difference between a state variable and a resource is not the types of their domains (usually symbolic and numeric, respectively).[2] It is the fact that an action modifies the value of a state variable in an *absolute* way, whereas an action changes a resource variable in a *relative* way. As an example of an action that can have effects on both state variables and resources, move(r, l, l') modifies the robot's location from the absolute value l to l', while it reduces the level of energy available on the robot in a relative way, from its current level before the action to some final level.

Furthermore, several *concurrent* actions may use the same resource; their cumulative effects shape the total evolution of that resource. For example, this is the case if the robot performs, while moving, some surveillance and communication actions that are not strictly required for its motion but that draw on its available energy.

We will be pursuing in this chapter an integrated approach that searches for a scheduled plan in which the resource allocation and the action scheduling decision are taken into account while planning. This approach, presented in Section 15.4, will be developed as a continuation of the temporal planning techniques of Chapter 14, where we addressed the temporal issues of planning and scheduling. This state-variable approach is not the only satisfactory way to tackle the integration of planning and scheduling. Other techniques, in particular HTN-based techniques, have been pursued successfully and are discussed in Section 15.5.

Before that, we introduce scheduling terminology and concepts (Section 15.2). We very briefly survey different types of machine scheduling problems and some of the mathematical programming techniques used specifically for scheduling (Section 15.3). These two sections remain quite informal; more precise notations and definitions are given in Section 15.4. The chapter ends with a discussion and exercises.

15.2 Elements of Scheduling Problems

A scheduling problem is specified by giving

- a set of resources and their future availability,
- a set of actions that needs to be performed and their resource requirements,

2. Hence, the extension of the PDDL to numerical variables does not strictly cover resources.

- a set of constraints on those actions and resources, and
- a cost function.

A schedule is a set of allocations of resources and start times to actions that meet all resource requirements and constraints of the problem. An optimal schedule optimizes the cost function.

There are different types of scheduling problems depending on the nature of the resources, the type of actions and their resource requirements, the type of constraints used, and the uncertainty explicitly modeled in the problem specification. Let us review informally some of the main classes of scheduling problems while focusing on the deterministic case, i.e., without uncertainty.

15.2.1 Actions

Usually in scheduling, actions have more restricted models than in planning. In particular, the state-transition function, which is essential in planning models, is usually implicit in scheduling, the emphasis being more on the resource and time needed by an action.

An action a is simply specified with its resource requirements (discussed in Section 15.2.2) and three variables ranging over the real numbers: its start time $s(a)$, its end time $e(a)$, and its duration $d(a)$. Usually $s(a)$ and $e(a)$ are specified within upper and lower bounds: $s(a) \in [s_{min}(a), s_{max}(a)]$ and $e(a) \in [e_{min}(a), e_{max}(a)]$.

Two types of actions are considered in scheduling: *preemptive actions* and *nonpreemptive actions*. A nonpreemptive action has to be executed continuously, without interruption; in that case, $d(a) = e(a) - s(a)$.

A preemptive action can be interrupted a number of times and resumed after a while. While interrupted, a preemptive action releases its resources that can be allocated to another action. Here $d(a) = \sum_I d_i(a) \leq e(a) - s(a)$, where the values of $d_i(a)$ are the durations of intervals during which a is executed. These execution intervals are not given as input (otherwise, a decomposes trivially into a finite sequence of actions). They have to be found as part of a solution schedule. Constraints can be associated with these execution intervals, e.g., fixed constraints such as "a requires daylight; if needed, the action must be interrupted during the night," and resource constraints such as "any action using resource r for an hour has to release it for at least half an hour." There can also be a cost associated with each interruption. In the rest of this chapter, we will consider only nonpreemptive actions, except when stated otherwise.

15.2.2 Resources

A resource is something needed in order to achieve an action. In addition to the usual preconditions and effects, the resource requirements of an action specify which

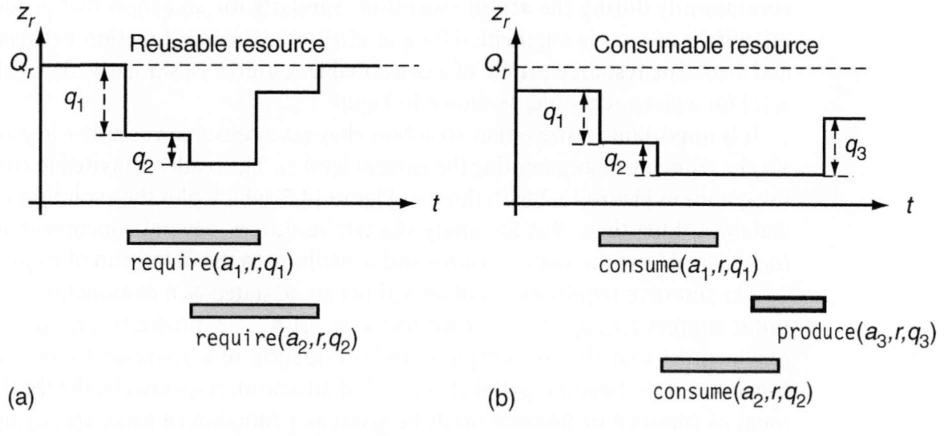

Figure 15.2 Examples of resource profiles.

resources and what quantities of each resource are needed for that action. Two main classes of resources can be distinguished: *reusable resources* and *consumable resources*.

A reusable resource is "borrowed" by an action during its execution. The resource is released, unchanged, when the action is completed or is interrupted. Typical examples of reusable resources are tools, machines, and cranes in some locations of the DWR domain. A reusable resource r has a total capacity Q_r and a current level $z_r(t) \in [0, Q_r]$. For example, if there is a total of five cranes at some location, then $Q_r = 5$ for that resource; its level $5 \geq z_r(t) \geq 0$ gives the number of available cranes at time t in that location.

An action a that requires during its execution a quantity q of the resource r decreases the current level of r at time $s(a)$ by an amount q; at time $e(a)$ it increases the current level by the same amount. For a given schedule, the function $z_r(t)$ is referred to as the *resource profile* of r. Figure 15.2 (a) illustrates a profile of a resource r that has two requirements, require(a_1, r, q_1) and require(a_2, r, q_2), by two overlapping actions. A reusable resource can be *discrete* (e.g., a finite set of tools) or *continuous*, (e.g., the electrical power in an outlet). A particular case is when r has a unit capacity, i.e., $Q_r = 1$: only one action at a time may use it. In the DWR domain, a single crane attached to a location can be modeled as a unary discrete resource.

A consumable resource is consumed by an action during its execution. Bolts, energy, and fuel are typical examples of consumable resources. A consumable resource may also be produced by other actions (e.g., refueling, which increases the amount of fuel in the tank of a robot). Such a resource r can be modeled as a *reservoir* of maximal capacity Q_r and of current level $z_r(t) \in [0, Q_r]$. An action a that consumes a quantity q of r reduces z_r by q. For example, this reduction can be modeled as a step function at the start time $s(a)$ if that resource is consumed all at once or as a linear function from $s(a)$ to $e(a)$ if the consumption takes place continuously during the action execution. Similarly for an action that produces a quantity q of r: z_r is augmented by q at $e(a)$ or as a linear function between $s(a)$ and $e(a)$. The resource profile of a consumable resource is, similarly, the evolution $z_r(t)$ for a given schedule, as shown in Figure 15.2 (b).

It is important to stress that an action changes a resource variable r in a *relative way* by reducing or augmenting the current level z_r. The reader is invited to compare the graphs in Figure 15.2 with those of Figure 14.5, which plot the evolution of state variables along time. But for unary discrete resources, several concurrent actions may share or use the same resource and contribute to the definition of its profile.

The resource requirements of an action can be stated as a conjunction of assertions: $\text{require}(a, r_i, q_i) \wedge \ldots \wedge \text{consume}(a, r_j, q_j) \wedge \ldots \wedge \text{produce}(a, r_k, q_k)$. Unless one assumes that the consumption and production of a resource happen as step functions at the beginning and at the end of an action, respectively, the third argument of consume or produce needs be given as a function of time, specifying how the resource is consumed or produced between the time points $s(a)$ and $e(a)$.

Furthermore, alternative resources can be specified for an action as a disjunction of assertions: $\text{require}(a, r_1, q_1) \vee \ldots \vee \text{require}(a, r_m, q_m)$. More generally, a set of alternative resources can be specified for all actions by defining a class of equivalent resources: $\text{resource-class}(s) = \{r_1, \ldots, r_m\}$. A requirement such as $\text{require}(a, s, q)$ is equivalent to the disjunction $\text{require}(a, r_1, q) \vee \ldots \vee \text{require}(a, r_m, q)$. It can be met by allocating to a a quantity q of any resource in this set. In the case of alternate resources, one has to distinguish between the resource requirements of an action a and the resources actually allocated to it by a schedule.

A resource may have a finite set of possible states. For example, this is the case for a refrigerated container that has different temperature settings, or a machine tool that can be set with different tools. A requirement for such a resource has to specify which particular state of the resource is required. Two actions may share the resource only if they require it to be in the same state. Changing the state of a resource has a cost and takes time.

Finally, an efficiency parameter can be associated with a resource r: the duration of an action using r varies as a function of that parameter.

15.2.3 Constraints and Cost Functions

Temporal constraints in scheduling problems are usually expressed within a framework equivalent to the quantitative temporal constraint networks (Section 13.4.2). Most often, simple temporal constraints (STPs, see Section 13.4.1) are used. Bounds on the distance between start points and end points of actions are specified in either of two ways:

- With respect to an absolute reference time, e.g., in order to specify a *deadline* for an action a, $e(a) \leq \delta_a$ (i.e., $e(a) \in (-\infty, \delta_a]$), or a *release* date for a before which the action cannot start, $s(a) \geq \rho_a$ (i.e., $s(a) \in [\rho_a, \infty)$)

- With respect to relative instants, e.g., in order to specify the *latency* between two actions a and b, $s(b) - e(a) \in [\lambda_{a,b}, \mu_{a,b}]$, or the total extent of a preemptive action c, $e(c) - s(c) \leq \nu_c$

Constraints can be associated with a resource, such as a reduced availability during some period. For example, a radio link resource of a satellite has *visibility windows*, which are intervals of time during which communication with the satellite is possible. Generally, an initial availability profile can be expressed for each resource by giving initial values to z_r as a function of time. Other constraints may link resource allocations to time bounds. For example, if two actions a and b use the same resource r, then there will be a latency, or required period of time between the two actions, of at least δ_r: if allocate(r, a) and allocate(r, b) then $s(b) - e(a) \geq \delta_r$ or $s(a) - e(b) \geq \delta_r$.

Several types of costs can be considered in scheduling. The cost for using or consuming a resource can be fixed or can be a function of the quantity and duration required by an action. A resource can have an additional *setup cost,* or cost of making the resource available after a use, which may depend on the previous action that used the resource or the previous state of the resource. For example, if action b follows action a in using the unary resource r, then this allocation has a cost of $c_r(a, b)$ and takes a duration of $d_r(a, b)$, i.e., $s(b) \geq e(a) + d_r(a, b)$. Different penalty costs can be specified, usually with respect to actions that do not meet their deadlines.

The objective criteria in scheduling is to minimize a function f of the various costs and/or the end time of actions in a schedule. The most frequent criteria to minimize are:

- the makespan or maximum ending time of the schedule, i.e., $f = max_i\{e(a_i) \mid a_i \in A\}$,
- the *total weighted completion time*, i.e., $f = \Sigma_i w_i e(a_i)$, where the constant $w_i \in \Re^+$ is the weight of action a_i,
- the maximum tardiness, i.e., $f = max\{\tau_i\}$, where the tardiness τ_i is the time distance to the deadline δ_{a_i} when the action a_i is late, i.e., $\tau_i = max\{0, e(a_i) - \delta_{a_i}\}$,
- the total weighted tardiness, i.e., $f = \Sigma_i w_i \tau_i$,
- the total number of late actions, i.e., for which $\tau_i > 0$,
- the weighted sum of late actions, i.e., $f = \Sigma_i w_i u_i$, where $u_i = 1$ when action i is late and $u_i = 0$ when i meets its deadline,
- the total cost of the schedule, i.e., the sum of the costs of allocated resources, of setup costs, and of penalties for late actions,
- the peak resource usage, and
- the total number of resources allocated.

Other criteria may also be considered, such as scheduling a maximum number of the given set A of actions, while taking into account all constraints, including the deadlines.

15.3 Machine Scheduling Problems

Machine scheduling is a well-studied generic class of scheduling problems. The class includes the *flow-shop*, the *open-shop*, and the *job-shop* scheduling problems. This section presents machine scheduling problems and their various special cases. It then discusses the complexity of machine scheduling and introduces briefly approaches for solving these problems and for integrating planning and machine scheduling.

15.3.1 Classes of Machine Scheduling Problems

A *machine* is a resource of unit capacity that is either available or not available at some time point. A *job* j is a partially ordered set of one or several actions, $a_{j1}, \ldots, a_{jk}$. It is analogous to what we have been calling a *plan*; it is partially ordered, and the resources needed by its actions, i.e., machines, are left uninstantiated. In a machine scheduling problem, we are given n jobs and m machines. A schedule specifies a machine i for each action a_{jk} of a job j and a time interval during which this machine processes that action. A machine cannot process two actions at the same time, and a job cannot be processed by two machines at once. In other words, two time intervals corresponding to the same machine or to the same job should not overlap.

Actions in different jobs are completely independent—they can be processed in any order. But actions in the same job cannot be processed concurrently, and they may have ordering constraints. One can think of a job as the same physical object, e.g., an engine in an assembly line, being processed at different stages through different actions or operations performed by different machines. This explains the constraint of no overlap in time of two actions of the same job.

In *single-stage* machine scheduling problems, each job corresponds to a single action, i.e., it requires a single operation and can be processed by *any* of the m machines. One may consider the following types of machines.

- For *identical parallel machines*, the processing time p_j of job j is independent of the machine allocated to j. The m machines can be modeled as a single discrete resource of capacity m.
- For *uniform parallel machines*, a machine i has a speed $\mathsf{speed}(i)$; the processing time of job j on the machine i is the ratio of p_j to the speed of i.

- For *unrelated parallel machines*, the $n \times m$ processing times p_{ij} have independent values.

In *multiple-stage* machine scheduling problems, a job corresponds to several actions, each requiring a particular machine. Here, the m machines have different functions. There are two particular cases and one general case of multi-stage machine scheduling problems.

- In *flow-shop* problems, each job j has exactly m actions. Action a_{ji} needs to be processed by machine i, and the actions have to be processed in the order $1, 2, \ldots, m$.
- *Open-shop problems*, are similar to flow-shop problems, but the m actions of a job can be processed in any order.
- *Job-shop problems* correspond to the general case in which each job has a number of actions with specific requirements on the needed machines for each action and the processing order of actions.

In addition to these features, a machine scheduling problem is characterized by the constraints associated with the set of jobs. One may specify deadlines and/or release dates for each job, setup times for the actions of a job j that depend on the allocated machine and/or the preceding action scheduled on this machine, and precedence constraints between jobs.

Finally, a machine scheduling problem is also characterized by the optimization criteria specified for that problem, e.g., makespan, maximum tardiness, weighted completion time, weighted tardiness, etc. However, here deadlines and end times of interest in the optimization criteria are those of jobs, not of their individual actions.

Example 15.1 Let us consider a job-shop problem with three machines (m_1, m_2, and m_3) and five jobs ($j_1, \ldots, j_5$). The first job j_1 has three actions. It requires successively the machine m_2 during three units of time for its first action, then the machine m_1 during three units for its second action, and then m_3 during six units for its last action. This is denoted as:

$j_1 : \langle m_2(3), m_1(3), m_3(6) \rangle$

The four other jobs are similarly specified:

$j_2 : \langle m_2(2), m_1(5), m_2(2), m_3(7) \rangle$
$j_3 : \langle m_3(5), m_1(7), m_2(3) \rangle$
$j_4 : \langle m_2(4), m_3(6), m_1(7), m_2(4) \rangle$
$j_5 : \langle m_2(6), m_3(2) \rangle$

A schedule for this problem is given in Figure 15.3. The horizontal axes represent time; each bar denotes which machine is allocated to a job and when it is allocated.

■

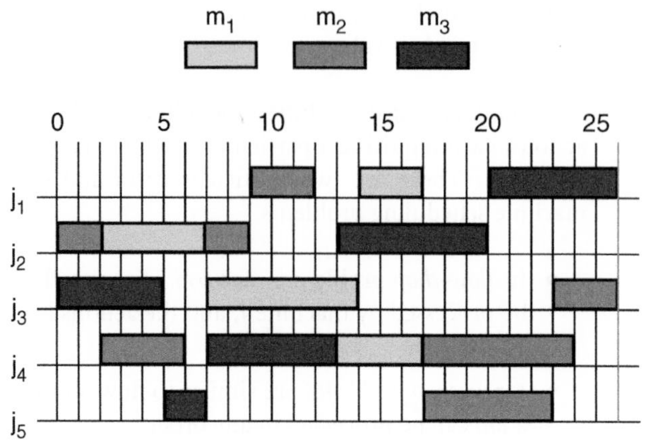

Figure 15.3 A schedule for a job-shop problem.

A standard notation, introduced in the survey of Graham *et al.* [247], is widely used in the literature for designating different machine scheduling problems. It has three descriptors, noted as $\alpha|\beta|\gamma$, where:

- α gives the type of the problem, denoted as P, U, and R for, respectively, identical parallel, uniform parallel, and unrelated parallel machines, and F, O, and J for, respectively, flow-shop, open-shop, and job-shop problems. α also gives the number of machines when the class of problem is specified with a fixed number of machines.
- β indicates the characteristics of the jobs, i.e., the jobs' deadlines, setup times, and precedence constraints. This descriptor field is left empty when there are no constraints on jobs, i.e., $\alpha||\gamma$.
- γ gives the objective function.

For example, $Pm|\delta_j|\Sigma_j w_j e_j$ is the class of problems with a fixed number of m parallel machines, deadlines on jobs, and the objective of minimizing the weighted completion time. $J|prec|makespan$ is the class of job-shop problems on an arbitrary number of machines with precedence constraints between jobs and the objective of minimizing the makespan of the schedule.

15.3.2 Complexity of Machine Scheduling

Only a few machine scheduling problems have been solved efficiently with polynomial algorithms. For example, the single-stage, one-machine problem, $1||max\text{-}tardiness$, can be solved in $O(n\log n)$: its solution is a sequence of jobs

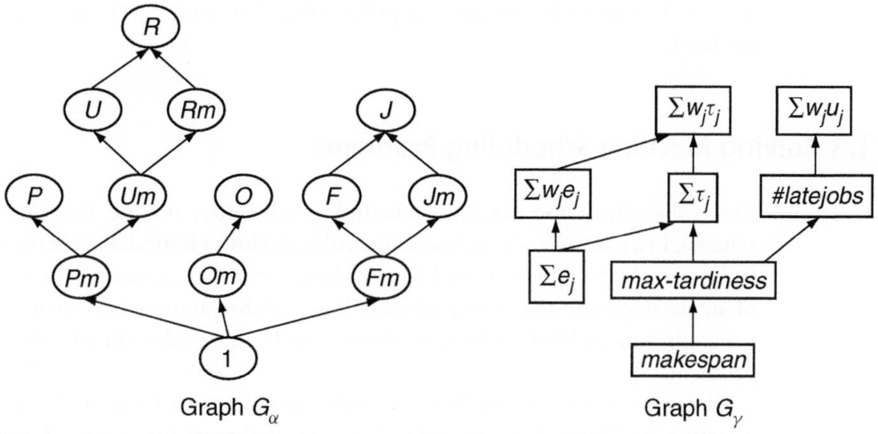

Figure 15.4 Reductions between machine scheduling problems.

as processed by the available machine; the optimal sequence is simply obtained by ordering the jobs in nondecreasing due dates. Similarly, the problem $1||\Sigma_j w_j e_j$ is solved by ordering jobs in nondecreasing ratios p_j/w_j. The flow-shop problem $F2||$*makespan* or the open-shop problem $O2||$*makespan* are also polynomial.

Other than these few cases, most machine scheduling problems have been shown to be of high complexity. For example, the problems $1|$*release-dates*$|$*max-tardiness*, $J2||$*makespan*, $J2||$*max-tardiness*, and $O3||$*makespan* are NP-hard.

As one may easily imagine, there are many polynomial reductions[3] among the various types of machine scheduling problems. A partial view of these reductions is illustrated through the two graphs shown in Figure 15.4, which correspond, respectively, to the α and γ descriptors introduced earlier: vertices in graph G_α are labeled with the α descriptor, and vertices in graph G_γ are labeled with the γ descriptor. If two classes of problems $P = \alpha|\beta|\gamma$ and $P' = \alpha'|\beta|\gamma$ are such that there is a path in G_α from the vertex labeled α to the vertex labeled α', then the class P reduces to the class P'. For example, the class $P_m|\beta|\gamma$ reduces to the class $U|\beta|\gamma$, and similarly for two classes of problems $P = \alpha|\beta|\gamma$ and $P' = \alpha|\beta|\gamma'$ with respect to paths in graphs G_γ. If P reduces to P', then when P' is polynomial so is P, and when P is NP-hard, so is P'. This general property simplifies the characterization of the complexity of machine scheduling problems.

Using these two graphs, and others for the β descriptors, and relying on known results of the complexity of some classes of problems, it is possible to derive automatically the complexity status of many problems. The survey of Lawler *et al.* [355] refers to a database of 4,536 classes of machine scheduling problems, out of which

3. See Appendix A, Section A.5.

417 are known to be solvable in polynomial time and 3,821 have been proven NP-hard.

15.3.3 Solving Machine Scheduling Problems

Exact algorithms for machine scheduling rely often on the *branch-and-bound* schema. In a few cases, clever branching rules and lower bounds enable the technique to be scaled up to address problems of large size, such as several NP-hard classes of single-stage one-machine problems [106]. Other approaches, such as dynamic programming and integer programming, have been found useful in some particular problems.

However, in general, machine scheduling problems are hard combinatorial optimization problems. For example, the state of the art for exact solutions of the $J||makespan$ problem is still open for instances of 10 to 20 jobs and 10 machines. Hence, approximation techniques are the most widely used ones for addressing practical problems, among which local search methods and randomized algorithms have been found successful (see Anderson *et al.* [21] for a survey on local search in machine scheduling). The characterization of these approximation techniques aims at establishing bounds of the quality of the solution with respect to the optimum.

15.3.4 Planning and Machine Scheduling

Some planning problems can be modeled as machine scheduling problems. This usually requires several simplifying assumptions and a significant change of focus. The planning actors intended to perform the actions of the plan are considered here to be machines. Instead of focusing on finding what each actor should do, machine scheduling focuses on deciding which machine should be allocated to which job and when. This is easily illustrated in the so-called logistic planning domains, such as transportation problems, where a set of trucks, airplanes, and other means of transportation is used to carry parcels between cities and locations. The DWR domain can provide a good example.

Example 15.2 A very simple version of the DWR domain, viewed in machine scheduling terms, considers the problem of using m identical robots to transport n containers between distinct locations. Here, a machine is a robot. A job, denoted by container-transportation(c, l, l'),[4] consists of moving a container c from l to l'. A job requires and is assumed to be entirely processed by a single robot. The robot allocated to a job has to go to location l, pick up and load container c, move to location l', and unload the container. There are no precedence constraints between jobs, but there can be release dates, e.g., a container is available for transportation

4. This notation is similar to the one used in Chapter 11 to denote tasks in HTN planning.

only when the ship carrying it arrives at the harbor. Jobs may also have deadlines, e.g., for the expected departure times of ships.

The duration of a job is the time it takes to go from l to l', plus the time for loading and unloading. To model the time it takes a robot to move from the destination of job k to the origin location of the next job j, we can introduce a setup time t_{ikj} if the robot i is allocated to a job j after performing a job k. Finally, if we are interested in minimizing the weighted completion time of the schedule, then this DWR problem is modeled as a problem of the class $P|r_j\delta_j t_{ikj}|\Sigma_j w_j e_j$, where r_j, δ_j, and t_{ikj} denote, respectively, the release date, the deadline, and the setup times of job j. ■

This simplified formulation of the DWR domain as a machine scheduling problem does not take into account cranes for loading and unloading containers nor the arrangement of containers into piles. The following example introduces a richer specification of the domain.

Example 15.3 Here the job container-transportation(c, l, l') decomposes into four actions: goto(l), load(c), move(l, l'), and unload(c). There are two types of resources: m robots and k_l cranes in location l. The four actions in each job require a robot, and the load and unload actions require cranes at locations l and l', respectively. The *same* robot should be allocated to the four actions of a job j because it does not make sense to use different robots for the same container transportation job.

Furthermore, precedence constraints between jobs can be used to take into account the relative positions of containers in piles: whenever c is on c', the transportation job of c should be ordered to start before that of c'. Similarly, one may specify precedence constraints on the end times of jobs to reflect the final positions of containers. This is not a general translation of the relation on(c, c') but only a limited way to handle it in scheduling terms. These constraints do not model the case of interfering containers that are in the initial or final piles but do not need to be transported between two locations. In order to do that, one has to introduce some *ad hoc* jobs, such as unstack(c, p), to remove c from a pile p, and stack(c, p), assuming unlimited free space in each location. These jobs should be added for every interfering container, in addition to precedence constraints between jobs that model the required initial and final positions of containers in piles. ■

Several remarks on the two previous examples are in order. First, machine scheduling handles requirements about which machines are needed for which actions in a job. There is also the requirement that although any robot can be allocated to the actions of a job it should be the *same* robot for *all* actions in a job is beyond the standard classes of machine scheduling problems.

Also note that not only are the precedence constraints on end times of jobs beyond standard classes, but it is hardly acceptable in practice. Even if one accepts a deterministic model without uncertainty in the durations of actions, at execution time it makes sense to control the start times of actions, but it is quite difficult to control their end times. A way to avoid this problem is to assume that the final position of containers within a pile is irrelevant. If these positions are important for the problem at hand, then the earlier machine scheduling formulation is not adequate.

Even this *ad hoc* machine scheduling model of the DWR domain ignores several resource constraints, such as the space in a location being limited to at most one robot at a time.

In conclusion, machine scheduling is a fairly restricted model with respect to the needs of planning. However, these well-studied classes of problems, which already have a high computational complexity, are very rich in heuristics and approximation techniques that can be beneficial for planning with resources using the approach presented in the next section.

15.4 Integrating Planning and Scheduling

We already discussed in the introduction of this chapter the limitations of separating planning from scheduling, and we motivated the need for an integrated approach when resources are involved in the problem at hand. The two frameworks presented in Chapter 14—temporal databases and chronicles—are both suitable for developing a planner that handles resources. In both cases the flaw-repair paradigm in the plan space within a CSP-based approach is applicable. Let us present in this section a *chronicle-based planner* that extends the material presented in Chapter 14 in order to integrate causal reasoning and resource reasoning.[5]

15.4.1 Representation

Recall from Chapter 14 that a chronicle representation is based on a set $X = \{x_1, \ldots, x_n\}$ of *state variables.* Each x_i is a function from time to some finite domain describing how the value of a state property evolves along time. To take resources into account, we further consider as part of the definition of a domain a finite set $Z = \{z_1, \ldots, z_m\}$ of *resource variables.* Each resource r is described by a resource variable z_r, which is a function of time that gives the resource profile of r.[6] In the rest of this chapter, we will focus on discrete *reusable* resources. Thus, each resource variable is a function $z_r : \mathsf{time} \rightarrow \{0, 1, \ldots, Q_r\}$, where Q_r is the total capacity of the resource r.

As we did with state variables, it can be convenient to describe generically a set of resource variables with a function of several arguments, of the form

5. This section relies on the material presented in the two previous chapters, in particular in Sections 13.3.2 and 14.3.

6. As for state variables, the time argument of the function z_r is not explicit in our notation.

$f : D \times \mathsf{time} \rightarrow \{0, 1, \ldots, Q\}$, such that D is a finite domain, and for any $v \in D, f(v)$ is a resource variable of Z. For example, in a DWR domain in which every location has Q identical cranes, we can model cranes as resources and use a function $\mathsf{cranes}(l)$ to describe the number of available cranes at location l at some time point t.

Because we are considering only discrete reusable resources, a resource is not consumed but only borrowed at the beginning of an action and released after its use. We will model the use of resources in a chronicle with temporal assertions, similar to those used for state variables, that express the amount of and the time at which the available quantity of a resource changes, or the interval during which some amount is used.

Definition 15.1 A *temporal assertion* on a resource variable z whose total capacity is Q is either:

- the instantaneous *decrease* of the resource profile of z at a time t by a *relative* quantity q, where q is an integer in the range $1 \leq q \leq Q$, when an amount q of z is borrowed at t,
- the instantaneous *increase* of the resource profile of z at a time t by a *relative* quantity q, when an amount q of z is released at t, or
- the *use* of a quantity q of the resource z during an interval $[t, t'), t < t'$, when an amount q is borrowed during the interval $[t, t')$.

These temporal assertions are denoted, respectively:

$$z@t : -q \qquad z@t : +q \qquad z@[t, t') : q$$

■

As for state variables, these types of assertions are directly related:

$$z@[t, t') : q \text{ is equivalent to } z@t : -q \wedge z@t' : +q$$

Furthermore, borrowing a resource *ad infinitum* is like consuming it: one may express the instantaneous *decrease* of the available quantity of a resource as a *use* of that resource over an infinite interval of time:

$$z@t : -q \text{ is equivalent to } z@[t, \infty) : q$$

Similarly, the *increase* of z at t by an amount $+q$ is equivalent to considering that a higher initial capacity $Q' = Q + q$ at time 0 and that the amount q of z was in use during the interval $[0, t)$:

$$z@t : +q \text{ is equivalent to } z@0 : +q \wedge z@[0, t) : q$$

For example, in Figure 15.2 (b) we can rewrite $\mathsf{produce}(a_3, r, q_3)$ as an initial capacity of $Q_r + q_3$ together with $\mathsf{require}(a', r, q_3)$ for a virtual action a' that starts at time 0 and ends at the end of action a_3. Note that this does not change the profile of the resource r nor in particular its maximal value.

Consequently, every set of temporal assertions about a resource z can be expressed in a uniform way as a set of *use assertions* over intervals of the form $\{z@[t_1, t'_1):q_1, \ldots, z@[t_n, t'_n):q_n\}$. This is a standard way to represent resource assertions.

From now on, let us assume that all assertions on resource variables are of this form. Let us also extend the notion of temporal assertions in a chronicle (Definition 14.6) to include both temporal assertions on state variables and temporal assertions on resource variables. The definition of a chronicle on a set of state and resource variables is unchanged, i.e., it is a pair $\Phi = (\mathcal{F}, \mathcal{C})$, where $\mathcal{F}$ is a set of temporal assertions on state and resource variables and $\mathcal{C}$ is a set of object constraints and temporal constraints. However, the definition of a consistent chronicle (Definition 14.8) now has to be extended with specific requirements for the consistency of a set of temporal assertions about resource variables.

We are assuming that distinct resources are completely independent: drawing on a resource z does not affect another resource z'. Every assertion on a resource concerns a single resource variable.[7] Hence, two assertions on two distinct resource variables can never be mutually inconsistent. Consistency requirements are needed only for assertions about the same resource variable. Let $\Phi = (\mathcal{F}, \mathcal{C})$ be a chronicle; z is one of its resource variables, and $R_z = \{z@[t_1, t'_1):q_1, \ldots, z@[t_n, t'_n):q_n\}$ is the set of all temporal assertions in $\mathcal{F}$ on the resource variable z. A pair of assertions $z@[t_i, t'_i):q_i$ and $z@[t_j, t'_j):q_j$ in R_z is *possibly intersecting* iff the two intervals $[t_i, t'_i)$ and $[t_j, t'_j)$ are possibly intersecting.[8] This is the case iff there is no constraint in $\mathcal{C}$ or entailed from $\mathcal{C}$ that makes the two intervals disjoint, i.e., $\mathcal{C} \not\models (t'_i < t_j)$, and $\mathcal{C} \not\models (t'_j < t_i)$.

Similarly, a set of assertions $\{z@[t_i, t'_i):q_i \mid i \in I\} \subseteq R_z$ is possibly intersecting iff the corresponding set of intervals $\{[t_i, t'_i) \mid i \in I\}$ is possibly intersecting.

Definition 15.2 A set R_z of temporal assertions about the resource variable z is *conflicting* iff there is a possibly intersecting set of assertions $\{z@[t_i, t'_i):q_i \mid i \in I\} \subseteq R_z$ such that $\sum_{i \in I} q_i > Q$. ■

Intuitively there is a conflict if there exists a possible instantiation of Φ such that there is a time point at which some actions are attempting to use more of a resource than its total capacity. In other words, the set R_z is conflicting if there is a set of values for the temporal variables in R_z that are consistent with $\mathcal{C}$ such that at some point in $\bigcap_{i \in I}[t_i, t'_i)$, the total quantities of the resource z used according to R_z exceed the total capacity Q of z. It is interesting to characterize a conflicting set from the properties of *pairs* of assertions in this set, as in the following proposition.

---

7. An action that needs two resources z and z' leads to two distinct assertions.
8. See Definitions 13.1 and 13.2 and Propositions 13.4 and 13.5 for possibly intersecting intervals.

Proposition 15.1 *A set R_z of temporal assertions on the resource variable z is conflicting iff there is a subset $\{z@[t_i, t'_i):q_i \mid i \in I\} \subseteq R_z$ such that every pair $i, j \in I$ is possibly intersecting, and $\sum_{i \in I} q_i > Q$.*

Proof The proof for Proposition 15.1 follows directly from Proposition 13.5. ■

Definition 15.3 A chronicle $\Phi = (\mathcal{F}, \mathcal{C})$ is *consistent* iff all its temporal assertions on state variables are consistent (in the sense specified in Definition 14.8) and none of its sets of temporal assertions on resource variables is conflicting. ■

This definition of the consistency of chronicles extends Definition 14.8. We now can apply, unchanged, Definitions 14.9 through 14.11, to chronicles with resources supporting other chronicles. This is due to the fact that a temporal assertion on a resource variable does not need an enabler—it requires only a nonconflicting set of assertions. Hence, all our constructs about planning operators and plans as chronicles (Section 14.3.2) still hold with resource variables.

Example 15.4 Let us consider a DWR domain where the space available in each location for loading and unloading robots is described as a resource that gives the number of available loading/unloading spots in a location. Let us denote by space(l) the corresponding resource variable in location l, i.e., the number of loading/unloading spots available at location l. Each load/unload operation requires one such spot. If space(l) > 1, then there can be more than one robot in location l. The move operator for this domain (see Figure 15.5) is:

$$
\begin{aligned}
\text{move}(t_s, t_e, t_1, t_2, r, l, l') = \{&\text{robot-location}(r)@t_s : (l, \text{routes}),\\
&\text{robot-location}(r)@[t_s, t_e] : \text{routes},\\
&\text{robot-location}(r)@t_e : (\text{routes}, l'),\\
&\text{space}(l)@t_1 : +1,\\
&\text{space}(l')@t_2 : -1,\\
&t_s < t_1 < t_2 < t_e,\\
&\text{adjacent}(l, l')\ \}
\end{aligned}
$$

This operator says that when the robot leaves location l there is one more spot available in l at t_1 than the current value of space(l) before applying the move operator, and when the robot arrives at l' there is one position less in l' at t_2 than before t_2. ■

In Example 15.4, robot-location(r) is a state variable, and space(l) is a resource variable. It is important to note that the value of a state variable can be an object variable, e.g., the value of robot-location(r) is l or l'. However, we are restricting the relative values of increases, decreases, and uses of a resource variable to be integer constants.

An additional element needs to be specified in the example: the total capacity of each resource. One way to do this is to specify a fixed total capacity for the

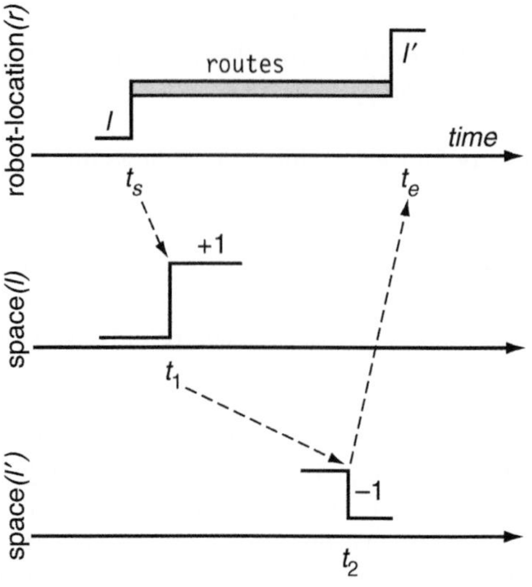

Figure 15.5 A move operator with resource variables.

set of resources {space(l) | l being a location}, e.g., $Q_{space} = 12$; i.e., there are at most 12 loading/unloading positions in each location. If a location, say loc1, has only 4 positions, then the initial chronicle will contain the temporal assertion space(loc1)@$[0, \infty)$:8. Another equivalent way to specify the total capacity of each resource is to allow this capacity to be given as a function of the object variable l for the resource space(l), i.e., Q_{space}(loc1) $= 4$, Q_{space}(loc2) $= 12$, etc.

A formal language for temporal planning domains with resources will have to integrate either form of these specifications as part of some initial declarations of object variables, state variables and their respective domains, and resource variables and their total capacities. Additional constraints such as rigid relations, initial resource profiles, etc., are specified as part of the initial chronicle.

Given these definitions, our previous specifications of planning domains and problems (Section 14.3.3) stand almost unchanged. A planning *domain* with time and resources is a pair $\mathcal{D} = (\Lambda_\Phi, \mathcal{O})$, where $\mathcal{O}$ is a set of temporal planning operators with resources (as in Example 15.4), and Λ_Φ is the set of all chronicles that can be defined with temporal assertions and constraints on the state and resource variables of X and Z, respectively, using the constants and the temporal and object variables of the representation.

A planning *problem* on $\mathcal{D}$ is a tuple $\mathcal{P} = (\mathcal{D}, \Phi_0, \Phi_g)$, where Φ_0 is a consistent chronicle that represents an initial scenario describing the initial state of the domain, the initial resource profiles, and the expected evolution that will take place independently of the actions to be planned, and Φ_g is a consistent chronicle that represents the goals of the problem. The *statement* of a problem $\mathcal{P}$ is given by $P = (\mathcal{O}, \Phi_0, \Phi_g)$.

A *solution plan* for the problem P is a set $\pi = \{a_1, \ldots, a_n\}$ of actions, each being an instance of an operator in $\mathcal{O}$, such that there is a chronicle in $\gamma(\Phi, \pi)$ that entails Φ_g.

Note that this formulation of a planning problem does not consider optimization criteria; it only seeks a feasible plan. Consequently, the approach of the chronicle planning procedure CP (Figure 14.7) is applicable here with an important extension: instead of dealing with only two types of flaws—open goals and threats—we also have to detect and manage *resource conflict flaws*.

15.4.2 Detecting Resource Conflicts

The chronicle planning procedure CP maintains a current chronicle $\Phi = (\mathcal{F}, \mathcal{C})$, which is refined successively for various types of flaws. Let us first focus on how to detect resource conflict flaws in Φ.

A resource conflict flaw is by definition a conflicting set of temporal assertions on a resource variable in the chronicle $\Phi = (\mathcal{F}, \mathcal{C})$. Let $R_z = \{z@[t_1, t_1'):q_1, \ldots, z@[t_n, t_n'):q_n\}$ be the set of all temporal assertions in $\mathcal{F}$ about the resource variable z. Let us associate with the variable z an undirected graph $H_z = (V, E)$ such that the following hold.

- A vertex $v_i \in V$ corresponds to an assertion $z@[t_i, t_i'):q_i$ of R_z.
- There is an edge $(v_i, v_j) \in E$ iff the two intervals $[t_i, t_i')$ and $[t_j, t_j')$ are possibly intersecting, given the constraints in $\mathcal{C}$.

H_z is called the graph of *Possibly Intersecting Assertions* (PIA) for z.

A set of vertices $U \subseteq V$ is *overconsuming* when $\sum_{i \in U} q_i \geq Q$, Q being the total capacity of the resource z. Consequently, the set R_z is conflicting iff H_z has an *overconsuming clique*. Recall that a clique in a graph is a subset of vertices that are pairwise adjacent. If U is a clique, then any subset of U is also a clique.

In order to solve resource conflicts, we are interested not in detecting all overconsuming cliques but in detecting only those that are minimal, in the set inclusion sense. This is will become clear in Section 15.4.3.

Definition 15.4 A *Minimal Critical Set* (MCS) for a resource z is a set of vertices $U \subseteq V$ such that U is an overconsuming clique and no proper subset $U' \subset U$ is overconsuming. ■

Example 15.5 Consider the following set of assertions for a resource z whose total capacity is $Q = 100$:

$$R_z = \{\, z@[t_1, t_1'):50, \quad z@[t_2, t_2'):60, \quad z@[t_3, t_3'):20, \quad z@[t_4, t_4'):50, \quad z@[t_5, t_5'):50, \quad z@[t_6, t_6'):70, \quad z@[t_7, t_7'):40\}$$

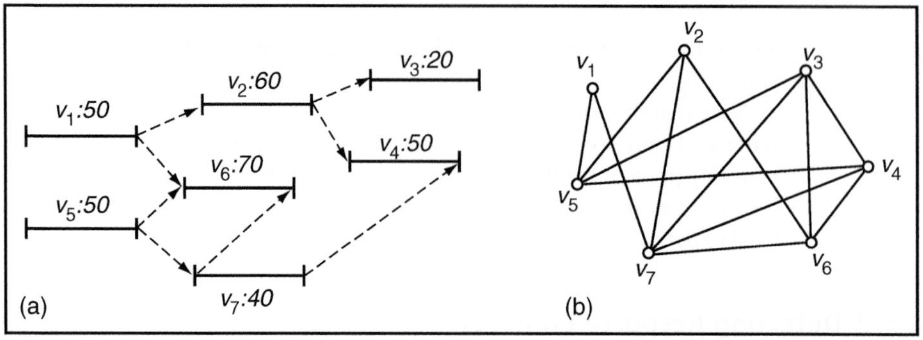

Figure 15.6 A possible intersection graph for a set of assertions for a resource whose total capacity is $Q = 100$. All the precedence constraints are represented as dotted lines in (a), i.e., v_7 ends before *or* after v_4 starts, but necessarily before the end of v_4.

Suppose that C contains the constraints $t'_1 < t_2$, $t'_1 < t_6$, $t'_2 < t_3$, $t'_2 < t_4$, $t'_5 < t_6$, $t'_5 < t_7$, $t_7 < t'_6$, and $t'_7 < t'_4$, in addition to the constraints on the end points of intervals, $\forall i, t_i < t'_i$. These assertions and constraints are depicted in Figure 15.6 (a). The corresponding PIA graph H_z is given in Figure 15.6 (b). In this figure an assertion $z@[t_i, t'_i):q_i$ is denoted as a temporal interval labeled $v_i:q_i$, for the corresponding vertex v_i of H_z. Note that $\{v_1, v_5\}$ is a clique, but it is not overconsuming; $\{v_3, v_4, v_6, v_7\}$ is an overconsuming clique, but it is not minimal because $\{v_6, v_7\}$, $\{v_4, v_6\}$ and $\{v_3, v_4, v_7\}$ are MCSs for the resource z.

■

The algorithm MCS-expand (Figure 15.7) performs a depth-first greedy search that detects all MCSs in a PIA graph, if any. Its main data structure is a pair (clique(p), pending(p)) for each node p of the search tree, where clique(p) is the

```
MCS-expand(p)
    for each v_i ∈ pending(p) do
        add a new node m_i successor of p
        pending(m_i) ← {v_j ∈ pending(p) | j < i and (v_i, v_j) ∈ E}
        clique(m_i) ← clique(p) ∪ {v_i}
        if clique(m_i) is overconsuming then MCS ← MCS ∪ clique(m_i)
        else if pending(m_i) ≠ ∅ then MCS-expand(m_i)
end
```

Figure 15.7 Searching for minimal critical sets.

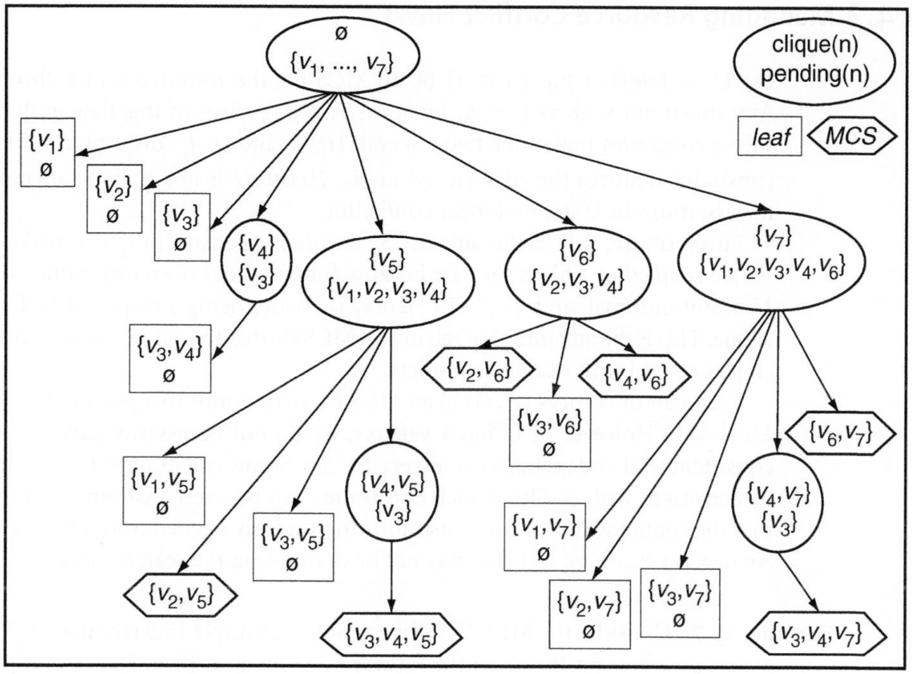

Figure 15.8 Search tree for detecting MCSs.

current clique being examined, and pending(p) is the set of candidate vertices of H_z that will be used in successor nodes to expand this current clique. The root node is associated with the pair $(\emptyset, V)$. For a leaf node n, either pending(n) is an empty set of vertices (in which case n is a dead end for the search) or clique(n) is an MCS. The global variable MCS is a set of MCSs. It is initially empty; when the algorithm stops, it contains all found MCSs. To simplify the notations, the set of vertices in H_z is supposed to be totally ordered in some arbitrary way, e.g., in the increasing order of the index i. This is used in the update of pending(m_i) in MCS-expand.

Example 15.6 The search tree of algorithm MCS-expand for the PIA graph of Example 15.5 is given in Figure 15.8. Each internal node p is labeled by the two sets clique(p) and pending(p). Leaves corresponding to MCSs are drawn in hexagons. The algorithm MCS-expand stops in this example with MCS $= \{\{v_2, v_5\}, \{v_3, v_4, v_5\}, \{v_2, v_6\}, \{v_4, v_6\}, \{v_3, v_4, v_7\}, \{v_6, v_7\}\}$. ■

Proposition 15.2 *Algorithm MCS-expand is sound and complete: it stops and returns all minimal critical sets in a PIA graph.*

15.4.3 Managing Resource Conflict Flaws

Let $U = \{z@[t_i, t'_i):q_i \mid i \in I\}$ be an MCS for the resource z in a chronicle Φ. Any constraint such as $t'_i < t_j$, for $i, j \in I$, is a resolver of this flaw in Φ. Indeed, such a constraint makes the two intervals $[t_i, t'_i)$ and $[t_j, t'_j)$ disjoint. Adding such a constraint removes the edge (v_i, v_j) in H_z. Hence U is not a clique anymore, and the assertions in U are no longer conflicting.

Furthermore, if U is the only MCS of z, then a constraint $t'_i < t_j$ makes the set R_z *nonconflicting*. This is the case because for any other overconsuming clique U': U' is not minimal, and $U \subset U'$. Hence, U' ceases being a clique when U is not a clique. This is the advantage of relying on MCSs instead of using any overconsuming cliques to deal with resource conflicts.

Each pair of vertices (v_i, v_j) in an MCS U corresponds to a potential resolver for U: $t'_i < t_j$. However, if U has k vertices, we do not necessarily have $k \times (k-1)$ consistent and independent resolvers for U. Some constraints $t'_i < t_j$ may not be consistent with C. Other such constraints can be overconstraining in the sense that they entail with C more constraints than strictly needed to resolve the flaw U. An overconstraining resolver may not be desirable in the search strategy.

Example 15.7 Consider the MCS $U = \{v_3, v_4, v_7\}$ in Example 15.5 (see page 367). There are six possible constraints of the form $t'_i < t_j$, for $i, j \in \{3, 4, 7\}, i \neq j$, as potential resolvers for U. But the constraint $t'_4 < t_7$ is inconsistent with C because C contains the constraints $t'_7 < t'_4$ and $t_i < t'_i, \forall i$. Furthermore, the constraint $t'_4 < t_3$ is overconstraining because it implies $t'_7 < t_3$ (through $t'_7 < t'_4$). A solution for the resource conflict U with the constraint $t'_4 < t_3$ is necessarily a particular case of a solution of U with the constraint $t'_7 < t_3$. Hence, we can remove $t'_4 < t_3$ from the set of resolvers of U. Finally, we end up with the following set of resolvers: $\{t'_3 < t_4, t'_3 < t_7, t'_7 < t_3, t'_7 < t_4\}$.

■

Let $U = \{z@[t_i, t'_i):q_i \mid i \in I\}$ be an MCS for the resource z in a chronicle Φ, and let $\rho = \{t'_i < t_j \mid i, j \in I, i \neq j \text{ and } t'_i < t_j \text{ consistent with } C\}$. Each constraint of ρ, when added to C in a refinement step, resolves the flaw U. However, the constraints in ρ are not all independent. As illustrated in Example 15.7, a constraint may entail another one with respect to C. A set of constraints ρ' is *equivalent* to ρ, given C, iff each constraint of ρ when added to C entails a constraint in ρ', and, symmetrically, each constraint in ρ' when added to C entails some constraint in ρ. It is possible to show that there exists a unique subset of ρ that is equivalent to ρ and is minimal under set inclusion. This minimal set of resolvers is desirable because it leads to a smaller branching factor for resolving the resource flaw characterized by U. It can be found in time $O(|U|^3)$ by a procedure that removes from the set ρ the overconstraining resolvers. Note, however, that any set of consistent resolvers is sufficient for resolving U, even if some of its elements are overconstraining.

We are now ready to extend the chronicle planning procedure CP of Chapter 14 into a procedure CPR that manages resources (Figure 15.9). Here CPR maintains

```
CPR(Φ, G, 𝒦, ℳ, π)
    if G = 𝒦 = ℳ = ∅ then return(π)
    perform the three following steps in any order
        if G ≠ ∅ then do
            select any α ∈ G
            if θ(α/Φ) ≠ ∅ then return(CPR(Φ, G − {α}, 𝒦 ∪ θ(α/Φ), ℳ, π))
            else do
                relevant ← {a | a applicable to Φ and has a provider for α}
                if relevant = ∅ then return(failure)
                nondeterministically choose a ∈ relevant
                ℳ' ← the update of ℳ with respect to Φ ∪ (ℱ(a), 𝒞(a))
                return(CPR(Φ∪(ℱ(a), 𝒞(a)), G∪ℱ(a), 𝒦∪{θ(a/Φ)}, ℳ', π∪{a}))
        if 𝒦 ≠ ∅ then do
            select any C ∈ 𝒦
            threat-resolvers ← {φ ∈ C | φ consistent with Φ}
            if threat-resolvers = ∅ then return(failure)
            nondeterministically choose φ ∈ threat-resolvers
            return(CPR(Φ ∪ φ, G, 𝒦 − C, ℳ, π))
        if ℳ ≠ ∅ then do
            select U ∈ ℳ
            resource-resolvers ← {φ resolver of U | φ is consistent with Φ}
            if resource-resolvers = ∅ then return(failure)
            nondeterministically choose φ ∈ resource-resolvers
            ℳ' ← the update of ℳ with respect to Φ ∪ φ
            return(CPR(Φ ∪ φ, G, 𝒦, ℳ', π))
end
```

Figure 15.9 CPR, a procedure for chronicle planning with resources.

a tuple $\Omega = (\Phi, G, \mathcal{K}, \mathcal{M}, \pi)$. As in the previous chapter, $\Phi = (\mathcal{F}, \mathcal{C})$ is the current chronicle, G is a set of assertions corresponding to the current open goals, $\mathcal{K} = \{C_1, \ldots, C_i\}$ is a set of pending sets of enablers, and π is the current plan.

The new component in Ω is $\mathcal{M}$, the current set of MCSs in Φ. Every update in Φ, such as adding new time points and constraints, may change $\mathcal{M}$. The set $\mathcal{M}$ can be maintained incrementally. If an update does not modify R_z and does not add a new constraint on a time point in R_z, then the MCSs of z in $\mathcal{M}$ are unchanged.

Each recursion of the procedure CPR on the current $\Omega = (\Phi, G, \mathcal{K}, \mathcal{M}, \pi)$ involves three main steps:

- Solving open goal flaws when $G \neq \emptyset$

- Solving threat flaws when $\mathcal{K} \neq \emptyset$
- Solving resource conflict flaws when $\mathcal{M} \neq \emptyset$

Note that the consistency test for threat resolvers is restricted to state variables, i.e., it is not concerned with resource conflicts.

As in Section 14.3.4, it is desirable to handle resource conflicts with a *resource constraints manager.* Its tasks will be to maintain incrementally $\mathcal{M}$ with respect to any update in Φ and to find a minimal set ρ_U of consistent resolvers for each MCS U. Here also a meta-CSP can be used to handle the set $\mathcal{M}$ of MCSs. A variable of that CSP corresponds to an MCS U; its domain is ρ_U. A backtracking in CPR occurs when that domain is empty. A constraint propagation and an update take place when that domain contains a single resolver. Otherwise, ρ_U is maintained according to the updates in the time-map manager and consequently in $\mathcal{M}$. Eventually ρ_U can be filtered out with other pending MCSs with an arc-consistency algorithm.

The discussion on the control issues of CP (Section 14.3.5) applies here as well. We can use heuristics similar to the variable ordering heuristics and the value selection heuristics (Section 8.4.1). These heuristics lead the algorithm to select as the next resource flaw the most constrained MCS, i.e., the one that has the smallest number of resolvers, and to choose as a resolver for the selected flaw a least constraining one.

Finally, the partial-order scheme, mentioned for state variables, can also be applied to state and resource variables. From the analysis of planning operators, it is possible to define a partial order on state and resource variables. Flaws are processed according to this order: no flaw is considered for a variable y, which can be either a state variable or a resource variable, until all flaws for all variables that precede y have been addressed. The partial order can guarantee that the resolution of flaws on y does not introduce new flaws for state variables that precede y.

15.5 Discussion and Historical Remarks

Scheduling is a broad research area. It has been a very active field within operation research for over 50 years. There is probably much more published material on the single topic of deterministic machine scheduling problems than published material on AI planning. Sections 15.2 and 15.3 are only a brief introduction to the field. Numerous books (e.g., [43, 200]) devote more space to the details and the techniques of scheduling than allowed here. Comprehensive surveys are also available (e.g., [21, 247, 355]).

The purpose of this chapter was only to give to the reader interested in extending automated planning to actions with resources the background and necessary entry points.

More and more planning systems rely on operation research tools and approaches such as linear programming [556], integer programming [539], and mixed ILP [155]. Many scheduling systems [60, 115, 177, 197, 492] deal with concerns close to those of planning and draw on AI techniques in order to handle more flexible activity models. But, as discussed in Smith *et al.* [484], the gap between planning and scheduling requires further research.

One of the first planners to offer resource-handling capabilities was probably FORBIN [143], an HTN planner. Other contributions involving scheduling techniques within HTNs have been pursued, notably within the O-Plan [162] and SIPE-2 planners [550, 552]. For example, in SIPE-2 the temporal and resource constraints are processed by plan critics during the critic phase. The OPIS system [491] is used, among others, as a scheduling critic. A critic can trigger a backtrack if constraints are unsatisfiable, or it can instantiate or further constrain variables. This is done together with the management of links in the task network.

The time-oriented view for temporal planning opened a promising avenue of development based on constraint satisfaction techniques. Systems such as HSTS and following developments for space applications [198, 199, 408] and the IxTeT system [346] rely on CSPs for handling resource and temporal constraints. The MCS approach for handling resource conflicts (Section 15.4.2) was developed in the context of IxTeT, drawing on maximal clique algorithms for particular graphs [212, 265]. This approach has been further extended for continuous resources or reservoirs and improved [344, 345].

It can be expected that this area of research will become essential in automated planning. The international planning conferences, AIPS and then ICAPS,[9] have been renamed to emphasize planning and scheduling. However, more work is needed to disseminate to the planning community benchmarks involving resources and action scheduling, as well as tools for handling them efficiently.

15.6 Exercises

15.1 In Exercise 14.11, suppose we modify the planning problem by assuming that the water flow is a resource with a maximum capacity of 2, and each fill operation uses 1 unit of this resource during the time it is executing.

(a) Draw the PIA graph. What minimal overconsuming cliques does it have?

(b) How many different ways are there to resolve the overconsumption? What does this tell us about the number of different possible solution plans?

(c) Draw a chronicle in which the overconsumption is resolved.

(d) Write the chronicle as a set of temporal assertions and a set of constraints.

15.2 Suppose we extend the DWR domain by assuming that for each container c there is a numeric value weight(c). For each robot r there is a resource variable called

9. The International Conference on Automated Planning and Scheduling; see http://www.icaps-conference.org/.

capacity(r), which represents the amount of weight that the robot can carry, with capacity(r) $= 10$ when the robot is completely unloaded. A robot may hold more than one container if the sum of the weights of the containers does not exceed its capacity.

(a) Extend the load and unload operators of Exercise 14.8 so they model this new situation.

(b) Write a chronicle that contains the following actions, starting with a robot r1 that is initially empty.

Load container c1 onto r1 at time t_1.
Unload container c1 from r1 at time t'_1.
Load container c2 onto r1 at time t_2.
Unload container c2 from r1 at time t'_2.
Load container c3 onto r1 at time t_3.
Unload container c3 from r1 at time v'_3.
Load container c4 onto r1 at time t_4.
Unload container c4 from r1 at time t'_4.

The weights of the containers are weight($c1$) $= 5$, weight($c2$) $= 3$, weight($c3$) $= 3$, and weight($c4$) $= 4$. There are the following time constraints: $t_i < t'_i \; \forall i$, and $t'_2 < t_3$.

(c) Draw the intersection graph for part (b) above, and find all maximal cliques.

(d) Describe each of the possible ways to resolve the overconsumption(s) in part (c).

(e) Draw a chronicle in which the overconsumption is resolved.

(f) Write the chronicle as a set of temporal assertions and a set of constraints.

Part V

Planning under Uncertainty

Classical planning relies on several restrictive assumptions (see the conceptual model described in Chapter 1), among which are the following.

1. *Determinism:* Actions have deterministic effects, i.e., each action, if applicable in a state, brings to a single new state.
2. *Full observability*: The controller has complete knowledge about the current state of the system, i.e., observations result in a single state, the current state of the system.
3. *Reachability goals*: Goals are sets of states, i.e., the objective is to build a plan that leads to one of the goal states.

As a consequence, plans in classical planning are sequences of actions, and feedback provided by observations is not necessary. In this part of the book, we relax these assumptions.

Nondeterminism. Determinism is a simplified view of the world that assumes it to evolve along a single fully predictable path. The world dynamic is supposed to be entirely "determined" and fixed along that path. In some cases, a model of a system as such a deterministic path can be a useful abstraction, e.g., to reason about nominal cases of behaviors. However, determinism claims that we just need to properly extend a model to predict all that may happen. With a perfect model, the throw of a die would be fully determined. This is, however, a rather unrealistic and impractical assumption because we know that it is impossible to predict everything.

Nondeterminism takes a more realistic stand. Perfect models are, in principle, unachievable. It is much more useful to model all six possible outcomes of the throw of the die and to reason about several possibilities, none of which are certain. It may be useful to model the fact that a component may stop or fail and to plan for "exception handling" or recovering mechanisms.

Even when the obvious model is nondeterministic, classical planning assumes that the nominal case accounted for by a deterministic model is highly frequent, positing that cases not taken into account are marginal and/or can be easily dealt with at the controller level. However, in several applications such an assumption does not hold.

- Nonnominal outcomes of actions are important and sometimes highly critical. They should be modeled at planning time as well as nominal outcomes. For instance, it is very important to model the possible failures of an action that moves a railway switch or that sets the signals of a railroad crossing.
- Sometimes nominal outcomes do not exist, e.g., when we throw dice or toss a coin. This is the case also of actions that ask the user for information, that query a database, or that model web services.

Planning with nondeterministic domains leads to the main difficulty that a plan may result in many different execution paths. Planning algorithms need efficient ways to analyze all possible action outcomes and generate plans that have conditional behaviors and encode trial-and-error strategies.

Nondeterminism can be modeled by associating probabilities to the outcomes of actions. This allows us to model the fact that some outcomes are more likely to happen than others. For instance, nonnominal outcomes may have a lower probability than nominal outcomes.

Partial Observability. In several applications, the state of the system is only partially visible at run-time, and as a consequence different states of the system are indistinguishable for the controller. Indeed, in many applications, we have the following situations.

- Some variables of the system may never be observable by the controller. This is the case in the "home sequencing" problem, i.e., the problem of how to reinitialize a microprocessor by executing some commands without having access to its internal registers.
- Some variables can be observable just in some states or only after some "sensing actions" have been executed. For instance, a mobile robot in a room may not know whether the door in another room is open until it moves to that room. A planner that composes web services for a travel agency cannot know whether there will be seats available until it queries the web services.

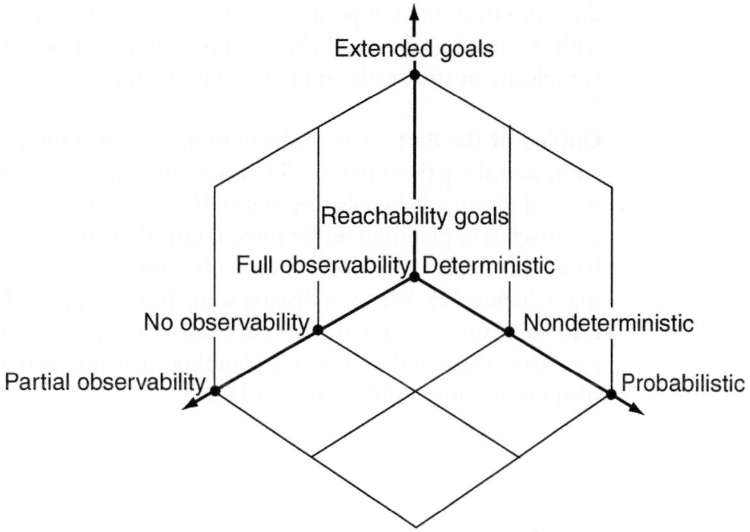

Figure V.1 Different dimensions of uncertainty.

Planning under partial observability has been shown to be a hard problem, both theoretically and experimentally. The main technical consequence of partial observability is that observations return sets of states rather than single states. This makes the search space no longer the set of states of the domain but its power set. Moreover, in the case of planning with probabilities, observations return probability distributions over sets of states. This makes the search space infinite.

Extended Goals. In nondeterministic domains, goals need to specify requirements of different strengths that take into account nondeterminism and possible failures. For instance, we might require that the system "tries" to reach a certain state, and if it does not manage to do so, it guarantees that some safe state is maintained. As an example, we can require that a mobile robot tries to reach a given location but guarantees to avoid dangerous rooms all along the path. Or we can require that the robot keeps moving back and forth between location A, and, if possible, location B. We thus specify that the robot must pass through location A at each round, while it should pass through location B just if possible: the strengths of the requirements for the two locations are different. This can be done with both simple goals like reachability goals and with more complex goals involving temporal conditions, e.g., conditions to be maintained rather than reached.

Extended goals of this kind can be represented in different ways. One approach is to represent extended goals with utility functions (e.g., costs and rewards). In this case, planning consists of searching for a plan that maximizes a utility function. An alternative approach is to represent extended goals with formulas in temporal logic. In this case, planning consists of generating a plan whose behaviors in the domain satisfy the temporal formula. In both cases, planning under uncertainty with extended goals is a challenging problem because extended goals add further complexity to an already complicated problem.

Outline of the Part. The problem of how to plan under uncertainty can thus be addressed along the different dimensions of nondeterminism, of partial observability, and of extended goals (see Figure V.1). In this part, we first describe two main approaches to planning under uncertainty along these three dimensions: planning based on Markov Decision Processes (Chapter 16) and planning by model checking (Chapter 17). We then discuss some further approaches originally devised for classical planning that have been extended to deal with some forms of uncertainty, e.g., state-space and plan-space planning, heuristic search, planning graphs, and planning as satisfiability (Chapter 18).

CHAPTER 16

Planning Based on Markov Decision Processes

16.1 Introduction

Planning based on Markov Decision Processes (MDPs) is designed to deal with nondeterminism, probabilities, partial observability, and extended goals. Its key idea is to represent the planning problem as an optimization problem. It is based on the following conventions.

- A planning domain is modeled as a *stochastic system*, i.e., a nondeterministic state-transition system that assigns probabilities to state transitions. Uncertainty about action outcomes is thus modeled with a probability distribution function.
- Goals are represented by means of *utility functions*, numeric functions that give preferences to states to be traversed and/or actions to be performed. Utility functions can express preferences on the entire execution path of a plan, rather than just desired final states.
- Plans are represented as *policies* that specify the action to execute in each state. The execution of a policy results in conditional and iterative behaviors.
- The planning problem is seen as an *optimization problem*, in which planning algorithms search for a plan that maximizes the utility function.
- Partial observability is modeled by observations that return a probability distribution over the state space, called *belief states*. The problem of planning under partial observability is reformulated as the problem of planning under full observability in the space of belief states, and the generated plans are policies that map belief states to actions.

This chapter describes MDP planning under the assumption of full observability (Section 16.2) and partial observability (Section 16.3). We also discuss planning for reachability and extended goals (Section 16.4). The chapter ends with discussion and exercises.

16.2 Planning in Fully Observable Domains

Under the hypothesis of full observability, we first introduce stochastic systems, policies, and utility functions and formalize planning as an optimization problem (Section 16.2.1). We then present and discuss some basic MDP planning algorithms: policy, value, and real-time iteration (Section 16.2.2).

16.2.1 Domains, Plans, and Planning Problems

Domains as Stochastic Systems. A stochastic system is a nondeterministic state-transition system with a probability distribution on each state transition. It is a tuple $\Sigma = (S, A, P)$, where:

- S is a finite set of states.
- A is a finite set of actions.
- $P_a(s'|s)$, where $a \in A$, s and $s' \in S$, and P is a probability distribution. That is, for each $s \in S$, if there exists $a \in A$ and $s' \in S$ such that $P_a(s'|s) \neq 0$, we have $\sum_{s' \in S} P(s, a, s') = 1$.

$P_a(s'|s)$ is the probability that if we execute an action a in a state s, then a will lead to state s'. We call $A(s) = \{a \in A \mid \exists s' \in S \,.\, P_a(s'|s) \neq 0\}$ the set of *executable actions* in s, i.e., the set of actions that have probability different than 0 to have a state transition. We do not restrict to the case in which we have at least one action that is executable in each state, i.e., we do not necessarily have that $\forall s \in S \; A(s) \neq \emptyset$. In a state s where a's preconditions are not satisfied, we have that $\forall s' \in S \; P_a(s, s') = 0$.

Example 16.1 Figure 16.1 shows a stochastic system that represents a DWR domain in which there is a single robot r1 that can move among five different locations (l1, l2, l3, l4, and l5). We have two sources of nondeterminism. First, when moving from location l2 to l3, there is a probability of 0.8 that the robot does it correctly and a probability of 0.2 that it gets confused and ends up in location l5. Second, when the robot tries to move from location l1 to l4, there is a probability of 0.5 that the way will be closed, in which case the robot will remain in l1. In the stochastic system, s1, s2, s3, s4, and s5 are the states in which the robot is at location l1, l2, l3, l4, and l5, respectively. We assume there is an action wait (not represented in the figure) that leaves each state of the domain unchanged. The set of states of the stochastic system is $S = \{\mathsf{s1}, \mathsf{s2}, \mathsf{s3}, \mathsf{s4}, \mathsf{s5}\}$. The actions are move(r1,li,lj) with $i, j = 1, 2, 3, 4, 5$ and $i \neq j$, and wait. We have probabilities $P_{\mathsf{move(r1,l1,l2)}}(\mathsf{s2}|\mathsf{s1}) = 1$, $P_{\mathsf{move(r1,l2,l3)}}(\mathsf{s3}|\mathsf{s2}) = 0.8$, and so on. ∎

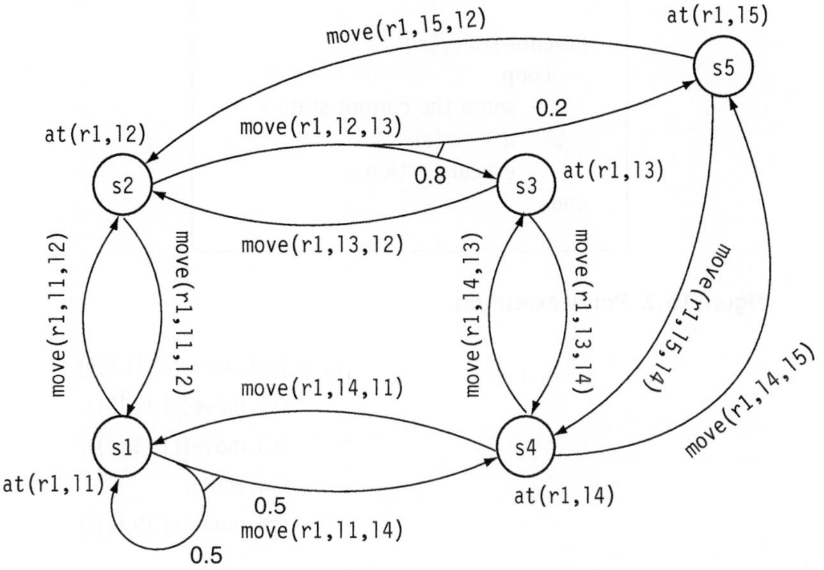

Figure 16.1 A stochastic system. There are five states (s1, s2, s3, s4, and s5), one for each location (l1, l2, l3, l4, and l5, respectively). In the figure, we label only arcs that have positive probability and the action wait such that, for each s, $P_{wait}(s|s) = 1$ is not represented. There are two nondeterministic actions: move(r1,l2,l3) and move(r1,l1,l4).

Plans as Policies. A plan specifies the actions that a controller should execute in a given state. A plan can thus be represented as a *policy* π, i.e., a total function mapping states into actions:

$$\pi : S \rightarrow A$$

This policy is generated by the planner and is given in input to a controller that executes actions one by one and observes into which state each action puts the system (see Figure 16.2).

Example 16.2 In the domain in Figure 16.1, consider the following policies.

$$\begin{aligned}\pi_1 = \{&(\text{s1}, \text{move(r1,l1,l2)}),\\ &(\text{s2}, \text{move(r1,l2,l3)}),\\ &(\text{s3}, \text{move(r1,l3,l4)}),\\ &(\text{s4}, \text{wait}),\\ &(\text{s5}, \text{wait})\}\end{aligned}$$

```
Execute-Policy(π)
    Loop
        sense the current state s
        a ← π(s)
        execute action a
end
```

Figure 16.2 Policy execution.

$$\pi_2 = \{(\texttt{s1}, \texttt{move(r1,l1,l2)}), (\texttt{s2}, \texttt{move(r1,l2,l3)}), (\texttt{s3}, \texttt{move(r1,l3,l4)}), (\texttt{s4}, \texttt{wait}), (\texttt{s5}, \texttt{move(r1,l5,l4)})\}$$

$$\pi_3 = \{(\texttt{s1}, \texttt{move(r1,l1,l4)}), (\texttt{s2}, \texttt{move(r1,l2,l1)}), (\texttt{s3}, \texttt{move(r1,l3,l4)}), (\texttt{s4}, \texttt{wait}), (\texttt{s5}, \texttt{move(r1,l5,l4)})\}$$

All three policies try to move the robot toward state s4. π_1 waits forever in s5 if execution gets to that point. π_2 is "safer": in the unlikely case that execution leads to state s5, it moves the robot to s4. π_3 tries to move the robot to s4 through state s1. π_2 takes a longer but "safer" route, and π_3 takes the shorter route that is "riskier" in the sense that the execution of π_3 may get stuck in s1 in the unlikely case that all the infinite attempts to move to l4 do not succeed. ■

Note that a policy does not allow sequencing, e.g., there is no policy equivalent to the sequential plan that executes move(r1,l1,l4) followed by move(r1,l1,l2). On the other hand, there are no sequential plans equivalent to the policy that executes move(r1,l1,l4) until state s4 is reached. Policy executions correspond to infinite sequences of states, called *histories*, which are Markov Chains, i.e., sequences of random values (in our case states) whose probabilities at a time interval (at each step) depend on the value of the number at the previous time (the previous step in the sequence).

Example 16.3 Some examples of histories for the stochastic system considered so far are the following.

$$h_0 = \langle \texttt{s1}, \texttt{s3}, \texttt{s1}, \texttt{s3}, \texttt{s1}, \ldots \rangle$$

$$
\begin{aligned}
h_1 &= \langle \mathtt{s1}, \mathtt{s2}, \mathtt{s3}, \mathtt{s4}, \mathtt{s4}, \ldots \rangle \\
h_2 &= \langle \mathtt{s1}, \mathtt{s2}, \mathtt{s5}, \mathtt{s5}, \ldots \rangle \\
h_3 &= \langle \mathtt{s1}, \mathtt{s2}, \mathtt{s5}, \mathtt{s4}, \mathtt{s4}, \ldots \rangle \\
h_4 &= \langle \mathtt{s1}, \mathtt{s4}, \mathtt{s4}, \ldots \rangle \\
h_5 &= \langle \mathtt{s1}, \mathtt{s1}, \mathtt{s4}, \mathtt{s4}, \ldots \rangle \\
h_6 &= \langle \mathtt{s1}, \mathtt{s1}, \mathtt{s1}, \mathtt{s4}, \mathtt{s4}, \ldots \rangle \\
h_7 &= \langle \mathtt{s1}, \mathtt{s1}, \ldots \rangle
\end{aligned}
$$

■

Given a policy, some histories are more likely to happen than others, i.e., they have greater probabilities than others. For instance, h_0 has zero probability for any policy, and it is rather intuitive that h_1 has a greater probability than h_3 if we execute policy π_2. Given a policy, we can compute the probability of a history. Let π be a policy and $h = \langle s_0, s_1, s_2, \ldots \rangle$ be a history. The probability of h induced by π is the product of all transition probabilities induced by the policy:

$$P(h|\pi) = \prod_{i \geq 0} P_{\pi(s_i)}(s_{i+1}|s_i) \tag{16.1}$$

Example 16.4 Some examples of computing probability with Formula 16.1 follow.

$$
\begin{aligned}
P(h_1|\pi_1) &= 0.8 \\
P(h_1|\pi_2) &= 0.8 \\
P(h_1|\pi_3) &= 0 \\
P(h_2|\pi_1) &= 0.2 \\
P(h_2|\pi_2) &= 0.2 \\
P(h_2|\pi_3) &= 0 \\
P(h_3|\pi_2) &= 0.2 \\
P(h_4|\pi_3) &= 0.5 \\
P(h_5|\pi_3) &= 0.5 \times 0.5 = 0.25 \\
P(h_6|\pi_3) &= 0.5 \times 0.5 \times 0.5 = 0.125 \\
P(h_7|\pi_3) &= 0.5 \times 0.5 \times 0.5 \ldots = 0
\end{aligned}
$$

■

Goals as Utility Functions. In planning based on MDPs, goals are utility functions. This is a major departure from classical planning, where goals are sets of states to be reached. Let us explore this choice with the following example.

Example 16.5 Using the scenario from Example 16.1 (see page 380), suppose that l1 is 100 miles from l2, that l3 and l5 are 100 miles from l4, that l1 is 1 mile from l4, and that l2 is 1 mile from l3 and l5. Suppose we want the robot to move to location l4 in as short a distance as possible. We can represent this by assigning "costs" to actions that are proportional to the distances, e.g., a cost of 100 to the action of moving the

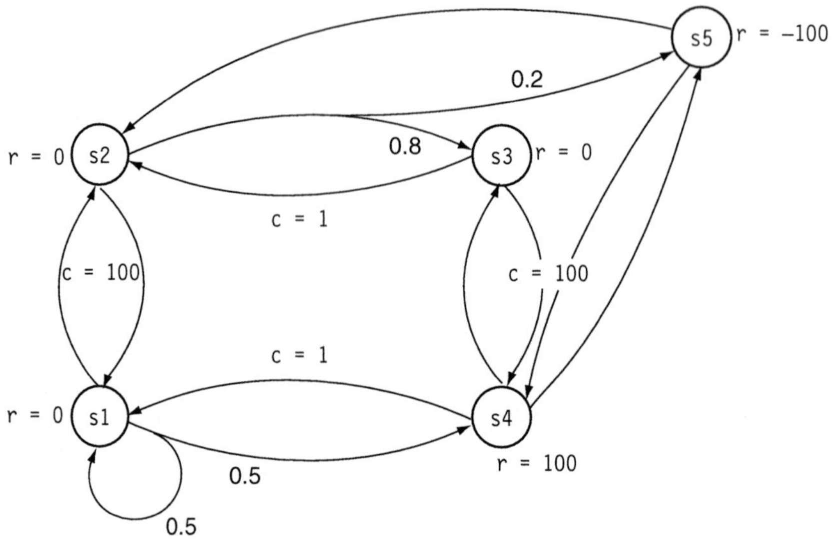

Figure 16.3 Costs and rewards.

robot from l1 to l2, and so on (see Figure 16.3). We assign a cost of 0 to the action of waiting in any state.

Suppose also that we want the robot to move to some states and to avoid other ones, e.g., l5 should be avoided as much as possible because it is a dangerous location. We can represent this by assigning different "rewards" to different states, e.g., a reward of −100 to state s5; a reward of 0 to states s1, s2, and s3; and a reward of 100 to state s4, as shown in the figure.

■

The costs and rewards introduced in Example 16.5 can represent more general conditions than goals as sets of desired final states because they provide a "quantitative" way to represent preferences along all the execution paths of a plan. For instance, in Figure 16.3, the numbers are a way to state that we want the robot to move to state s4 and avoid state s5. Note also that costs and rewards provide an easy way to express competing criteria. Consider, for instance, the criteria of shortest path versus location avoidance. They may be competing because the shortest path may go through locations that should be preferably avoided. We can assign a high cost to transitions that represent long distances for the robot and assign low rewards to states that represent locations that should be avoided by the robot.

The costs and rewards are criteria that can be used to define a *utility function*, i.e., a function that tells us how desirable the histories of a policy are. Let $C : S \times A \rightarrow \Re$ be a *cost function* and $R : S \rightarrow \Re$ be a *reward function* for a stochastic system Σ.

We can define the utility in a state s with an action a as $V(s, a) = R(s) - C(s, a)$, and the utility of a policy in a state as $V(s|\pi) = R(s) - C(s, \pi(s))$. This generalizes to histories. Let $h = \langle s_0, s_1, \ldots \rangle$ be a history. The *utility* of history h induced by a policy π is defined as

$$V(h|\pi) = \sum_{i \geq 0} (R(s_i) - C(s_i, \pi(s_i)))$$

One problem with this definition is that it usually will not converge to a finite value. In fact, it is important that the total accumulated utility is finite; otherwise, there is no way to compare histories. A common way to ensure a bounded measure of utilities for infinite histories is to introduce a *discount factor* γ, with $0 < \gamma < 1$, that makes rewards and costs accumulated at later stages count less than those accumulated at early stages. Let h be a history $\langle s_0, s_1, s_2, \ldots \rangle$. We then define the utility of h induced by a policy π as follows:

$$V(h|\pi) = \sum_{i \geq 0} \gamma^i (R(s_i) - C(s_i, \pi(s_i))) \tag{16.2}$$

The use of a discounting factor is often justified by another argument: to reduce the contribution of distant rewards and costs to the current state.[1] Given a utility function, we can compute the *expected utility of a policy* by taking into account the probability of histories induced by the policy. Let Σ be a stochastic system, H be the set of all the possible histories of Σ, and π be a policy for Σ. Then the expected utility of π is

$$E(\pi) = \sum_{h \in H} P(h|\pi) V(h|\pi) \tag{16.3}$$

Planning Problems as Optimization Problems. A policy π^* is an *optimal policy* for a stochastic system Σ if $E(\pi^*) \geq E(\pi)$, for any policy π for Σ, i.e., if π^* has maximal expected utility. We can now define a planning problem as an optimization problem: given a stochastic system Σ and a utility function, a *solution* to a planning problem is an *optimal policy*.

As a consequence, a policy that is not optimal is *not* a solution. Note that this is a significant departure from the notion of solution in other planning approaches, e.g., classical planning or even different approaches to planning under uncertainty (see Chapter 17), where the notion of optimal solution is distinct from that of solution (which, in general, may be nonoptimal).

1. In economics models (where a great deal of the basic MDP work originates), the rewards may be money earned following a transaction, that in MDP is represented by an action. A fixed amount of money that will be earned in two years has less value than the same amount of money that will be earned in two weeks because of inflation or because of the uncertainty in the future.

Example 16.6 In Figure 16.3, the expected utilities of the policies π_1, π_2, and π_3 are given by:

$$E(\pi_1) = V(h_1|\pi_1)P(h_1|\pi_1) + V(h_2|\pi_1)P(h_2|\pi_1)$$
$$E(\pi_2) = V(h_1|\pi_2)P(h_1|\pi_2) + V(h_3|\pi_2)P(h_3|\pi_2)$$
$$E(\pi_3) = V(h_4|\pi_3)P(h_4|\pi_3) + V(h_5|\pi_3)P(h_5|\pi_3) + \cdots$$

■

In the particular case when there are no rewards associated with the states, the optimal policy π^* minimizes the expected costs.[2]

$$E(\pi) = \sum_{h \in H} P(h|\pi)C(h|\pi) \tag{16.4}$$

where

$$C(h|\pi) = \sum_{i \geq 0} \gamma^i C(s_i, a_i) \tag{16.5}$$

Formula 16.5 can be obtained from Formula 16.2 by assuming $R(s_i) = 0$ for all $s_i \in h$ and by inverting the sign. Similarly, Formula 16.4 can be obtained from Formula 16.3 by replacing $V(h|\pi)$ with $C(h|\pi)$.

16.2.2 Planning Algorithms

In this section we focus on some basic planning algorithms for solving planning problems based on MDPs. For simplicity, we assume that utility functions are determined by cost functions. The discussion generalizes easily to the case of utility functions that include rewards.

Under this assumption, the planning problem is the problem of finding an optimal policy π^*, i.e., such that $E(\pi^*)$ given by Formula 16.4 is minimal. $E(\pi^*)$ is also called the *optimal cost*. Let $E(s)$ be the expected cost in a state s. We define $Q(s, a)$, the expected cost in a state s when we execute action a:

$$Q(s, a) = C(s, a) + \gamma \sum_{s' \in S} P_a(s'|s)\, E(s') \tag{16.6}$$

It can be shown that the optimal cost $E(\pi^*)$ satisfies the fixed-point equation

$$E(s) = \min_{a \in A} Q(s, a) \tag{16.7}$$

2. In the following text, we use the same symbol C for $C(s, a)$ and $C(h|\pi)$.

for all $s \in S$.[3] Formula 16.7 is called the *Bellman Equation*. We call $E_{\pi^*}(s)$ the optimal cost in state s. From the Bellman Equation we have that:

$$E_{\pi^*}(s) = \min_a \{C(s,a) + \gamma \sum_{s' \in S} P_a(s'|s)\, E_{\pi^*}(s')\} \tag{16.8}$$

Given the formulas above, two possible ways to compute π^* are the following two algorithms. The first algorithm, called *policy iteration*, given an initial arbitrary policy π, solves the system of equations:

$$E(s) = C(s,a) + \gamma \sum_{s' \in S} P_a(s'|s)\, E(s') \tag{16.9}$$

This is a system of $|S|$ equations in $|S|$ unknown variables $E(s)$, one for each $s \in S$. Note that because the policy is given, we know that the action a in Formula 16.9 is $\pi(s)$:

$$E_\pi(s) = C(s, \pi(s)) + \gamma \sum_{s' \in S} P_{\pi(s)}(s'|s)\, E_\pi(s') \tag{16.10}$$

Then policy iteration finds actions that decrease the value of $E_\pi(s)$ in state s and updates the policy with such actions until it converges to the optimal policy.

The second algorithm, called *value iteration*, given an initial arbitrary value for each $E(s)$, say $E_0(s)$, computes iteratively in a dynamic programming style the value

$$E_k(s) \leftarrow \min_{a \in A} \{(s,a) + \gamma \sum P_a(s'|s) E_{k-1}(s')\}$$

by increasing k at each step until $E_k(s)$ converges to the optimal cost and the corresponding policy to the optimal policy. In the following discussion we describe the two algorithms in more detail.

Policy Iteration. The Policy-Iteration algorithm is presented in Figure 16.4. Given a stochastic system Σ, a cost function C, and a discount factor γ, it returns an optimal policy π. The basic idea is to start with a randomly selected initial policy and to refine it repeatedly. The algorithm alternates between two main phases: (1) a *value determination phase*, in which the expected cost of the current policy is computed by solving the system of equations shown in Formula 16.9, and (2) a *policy improvement phase*, in which the current policy is refined to a new policy that has a smaller expected cost. For any state s, if an action a exists such that $C(s,a) + \gamma \sum_{s' \in S} P_a(s'|s)$, with $E_\pi(s')$ smaller than the current estimated cost $E_\pi(s)$, then $\pi(s)$ is replaced with a in the policy.

The algorithm terminates when no alternative actions exist that can improve the policy (condition $\pi = \pi'$ in the main loop).

3. This equation depends on π^* in the sense that $a = \pi^*(s)$.

```
Policy-Iteration(Σ,C,γ)
    π ← ∅
    select any π' ≠ ∅
    While π' ≠ π do
        π ← π'
        for each s ∈ S,
            E_π(s) ← the solution of the system of equations
                        E_π(s) = C(s, π(s)) + γ Σ_{s'∈S} P_{π(s)}(s'|s) E_π(s')
        for each s ∈ S do
            if ∃a ∈ A s.t. E_π(s) > C(s, a) + γ Σ_{s'∈S} P_a(s'|s) E_π(s')
                then π'(s) ← a
                else π'(s) ← π(s)
    return(π)
end
```

Figure 16.4 Policy iteration.

Example 16.7 Consider the situation shown in Figure 16.5. Suppose Policy-Iteration selects π_1 as the initial policy π'. We solve the system of equations and compute $E_{\pi_1}(s)$ for each $s \in \{\text{s1}, \text{s2}, \text{s3}, \text{s4}, \text{s5}\}$.

$$E_{\pi_1}(\text{s1}) = C(\text{s1}, \text{move(r1, l1, l2)}) + \gamma E_{\pi_1}(\text{s2})$$
$$E_{\pi_1}(\text{s2}) = C(\text{s2}, \text{move(r1, l2, l3)}) + \gamma(0.8\ E_{\pi_1}(\text{s3}) + 0.2\ E_{\pi_1}(\text{s5}))$$
$$E_{\pi_1}(\text{s3}) = C(\text{s4}, \text{move(r1, l3, l4)}) + \gamma E_{\pi_1}(\text{s4})$$
$$E_{\pi_1}(\text{s4}) = C(\text{s4}, \text{wait}) + \gamma E_{\pi_1}(\text{s4})$$
$$E_{\pi_1}(\text{s5}) = C(\text{s5}, \text{wait}) + \gamma E_{\pi_1}(\text{s5})$$

Suppose $\gamma = 0.9$. Then:

$$E_{\pi_1}(\text{s1}) = 100 + (0.9)\ E_{\pi_1}(\text{s2})$$
$$E_{\pi_1}(\text{s2}) = 1 + (0.9)(0.8\ E_{\pi_1}(\text{s3}) + 0.2\ E_{\pi_1}(\text{s5}))$$
$$E_{\pi_1}(\text{s3}) = 100 + (0.9)\ E_{\pi_1}(\text{s4})$$
$$E_{\pi_1}(\text{s4}) = 0 + (0.9)\ E_{\pi_1}(\text{s4})$$
$$E_{\pi_1}(\text{s5}) = 100 + (0.9)\ E_{\pi_1}(\text{s5})$$

and

$$E_{\pi_1}(\text{s1}) = 181.9$$
$$E_{\pi_1}(\text{s2}) = 91$$
$$E_{\pi_1}(\text{s3}) = 100$$
$$E_{\pi_1}(\text{s4}) = 0$$
$$E_{\pi_1}(\text{s5}) = 1000$$

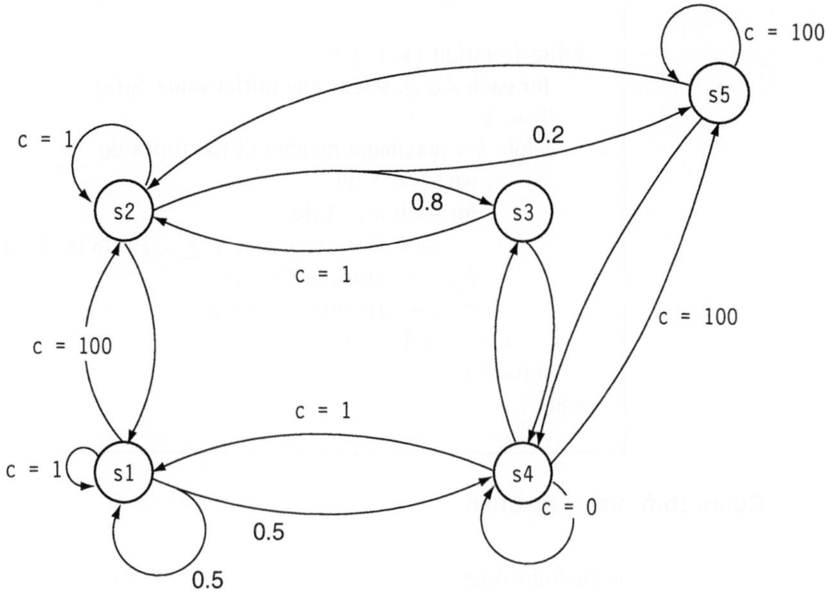

Figure 16.5 Utility function determined by costs.

We can improve the policy by choosing move(r1,l1,l4) in s1, move(r1,l2,l1) in s2, move(r1,l3,l4) in s3, and move(r1,l5,l4) in s5. Indeed, an optimal policy is:

$$\begin{aligned}\pi_4 \;=\; \{\, & (\text{s1}, \text{move}(\text{r1}, \text{l1}, \text{l4})) \\ & (\text{s2}, \text{move}(\text{r1}, \text{l2}, \text{l1})) \\ & (\text{s3}, \text{move}(\text{r1}, \text{l3}, \text{l4})) \\ & (\text{s4}, \text{wait}) \\ & (\text{s5}, \text{move}(\text{r1}, \text{l5}, \text{l4}))\,\}\end{aligned}$$

Policy π_4 tries to move the robot to location l4, where the cost of waiting is null, and avoids s5 as much as possible. ■

Value Iteration. The Value-Iteration algorithm is shown in Figure 16.6. It starts with a randomly selected estimated cost $E_0(s)$ for each $s \in S$. Then, it iteratively refines the value for each state by selecting an action that minimizes its expected cost. At each step k, the value of the expected cost E_k is computed for each state from the value E_{k-1} that was computed at the previous step. The algorithm finds an action a such that $E_k(s)$ is minimal and stores it in the policy. It can be shown that there exists a maximum number of iterations needed to guarantee that Value-Iteration returns an optimal policy. However, in practice, the condition used to stop iteration

```
Value-Iteration (Σ,C,γ)
    for each s ∈ S, select any initial value E_0(s)
    k ← 1
    while k < maximum number of iterations do
        for each s ∈ S do
            for each a ∈ A do
                Q(s,a) ← C(s,a) + γ Σ_{s'∈S} P_a(s'|s) E_{k−1}(s')
            E_k(s) ← min_{a∈A} Q(s,a)
            π(s) ← arg min_{a∈A} Q(s,a)
        k ← k + 1
    return(π)
end
```

Figure 16.6 Value iteration.

is the following:

$$\max_{s \in S} |E^n(s) - E^{n-1}(s)| < \epsilon \tag{16.11}$$

This stopping criterion guarantees that the returned policy is an ϵ-optimal policy, i.e., it has an expected cost that does not differ from the optimum by more than an arbitrarily small number ϵ.

Example 16.8 Consider again the situation shown in Figure 16.5. Suppose Value-Iteration initializes the expected cost value to zero: $E_0(s) = 0$ for any $s \in \{s1, s2, s3, s4, s5\}$. Suppose we require an ϵ-optimal policy, and we stop iteration according to Formula 16.11 with $\epsilon = 1$. We discuss the possible iterations for state s1. At the first step (with $n = 1$), in state s1:

1. If $a =$ move(r1, l1, l4), we have $E_1(s1) = 1$.
2. If $a =$ move(r1, l1, l2), we have $E_1(s1) = 100$.
3. If $a =$ wait, we have $E_1(s1) = 1$.

Then the algorithm can choose action $a =$ wait or $a =$ move(r1, l1, l4). ■

Policy versus Value Iteration. The essential difference between the policy and value iteration algorithms is the following. In policy iteration, we compute a sequence of policies $\pi_1, \pi_2, \pi_3, \ldots, \pi_i, \ldots$ and a sequence of sets of values $E_i(s)$ for each $s \in S$. For each state s:

$$E_i(s) = C(s, a_i) + \gamma \sum_{s' \in S} P_{a_i}(s'|s)\, E_i(s')$$

In value iteration, we also compute a sequence of policies $\pi_1, \pi_2, \pi_3, \ldots, \pi_i, \ldots$ and a sequence of sets of values $E_i(s)$ for each $s \in S$. For each state s:

$$E_i(s) = C(s, a_i) + \gamma \sum_{s' \in S} P_{a_i}(s'|s)\; E_{i-1}(s')$$

The essential difference is that, inside the summation, in the case of policy iteration we use E_i (and thus we need to solve n equations with n unknowns, with $n = |S|$), and in the case of value iteration we use E_{i-1}, i.e., we use the values computed during the previous iteration. Intuitively, each step of Policy-Iteration is computationally more expensive than each step of Value-Iteration. On the other hand, Policy-Iteration needs fewer iterations to converge than Value-Iteration. Both Value-Iteration and Policy-Iteration are polynomial in the number of states $|S|$, the number of actions $|A|$, and the maximum number of bits B required to represent any component of the probability distribution P or the cost function C. B represents the numerical precision of P and C (i.e., the number of significant digits). However, notice that the algorithms are polynomial *in the size of the state space.* In classical planning, the size of the state space is exponential in the size of the planning problem statement. Therefore, this does contradict the fact that the planning problem is NP-hard! In other words, the order of the polynomial is rather large. For realistic domains, the number of states $|S|$ is huge, and both Value-Iteration and Policy-Iteration can hardly be applied.

Real-Time Value Iteration. The simple algorithms we have presented in this chapter suffer clearly from the state explosion problem. Littman *et al.* [365, 366] have analyzed the complexity of MDP planning under the assumption that the states are produced by a set of nondeterministic actions. In the worst case, the complexity is EXPTIME-complete, although it can be made lower by imposing various restrictions. Recall that Value-Iteration updates the value $Q(s, a)$ in parallel for all the states $s \in S$. Since $|S|$ is usually huge, this is the major cause of inefficiency of the algorithm.

Several approaches exist to reduce the state explosion problem (see Section 16.5). One that has been applied successfully is *real-time value iteration* [82]. The name comes in part from the name used for "real-time search" algorithms, i.e., algorithms that search a state space by selecting at each step an action (or state transition) such that a heuristic function is maximized. Here the heuristic function consists of choosing the action such that $Q(s, a)$ is minimal. The idea underlying real-time value iteration is to perform a forward search from an initial set of states to a set of goal states and to update the value of $Q(s, a)$ only in the states visited by the search. The algorithm updates the value of $Q(s, a)$ in the states visited by a search guided by the value of the expected cost computed at each step.

In general, real-time value iteration is not guaranteed to return an optimal solution or even to not terminate. It can, however, be shown that if (1) the initial expected cost $E_0(s)$ is nonoverestimating, i.e., if $\forall s\; E_0(s) \leq E_{\pi^*}(s)$, and (2) there is a path with positive probability from every state to a state in the goal states, then the algorithm will eventually terminate and return a policy. If we add the condition that the search space is strongly connected, i.e., there is a path with positive probability from every state to every other state, then the algorithm will eventually return an optimal policy.

It has been shown experimentally that real-time value iteration can solve much larger problems than standard value and policy iteration [84]. The trade-off is that the solution is not optimal and the algorithm is not complete; in fact, it may even not terminate.

16.3 Planning under Partial Observability

Planning under Partial Observability in MDP (POMDP) relaxes the assumption that the controller has complete knowledge about the state of Σ. We introduce for the first time in the book *observations* that represent the part of Σ that is visible. In general, observations correspond to more than one state, and this is the cause of uncertainty. More precisely, in MDP, observations correspond to probability distributions over states of Σ. We formalize partial observable domains in Section 16.3.1 and briefly discuss possible algorithms in Section 16.3.2.

16.3.1 Domains, Plans, and Planning Problems

Partially Observable Domains. A partially observable stochastic system is:

- a stochastic system $\Sigma = (S, A, P)$, where S, A, and P are the same as defined in Section 16.2.1, and
- a finite set O of *observations* with probabilities $P_a(o|s)$, for any $a \in A$, $s \in S$, and $o \in O$. $P_a(o|s)$ represents the probability of observing o in state s after executing action a. We require that the probabilities are defined for each state $s \in S$ and action $a \in A$ and that, given a state s and an action a, their sum is 1, i.e., $\sum_{o \in O} P_a(o|s) = 1$.

The set of observations O is introduced to model partial observability. There is no way to get any information about the state other than through observation. Therefore, the controller may not distinguish among different states from the observations that are available. Indeed, different states of the system Σ may result from the same observation. Let s and s' be two distinguished states of Σ, i.e., $s, s' \in S$ and $s \neq s'$. We say that s and s' are *indistinguishable* if $\forall o \in O \; \forall a \in A \;\; P_a(o|s) = P_a(o|s')$.

The same state may correspond to different observations depending on the action that has been executed, i.e., we can have $P_a(o|s) \neq P_{a'}(o|s)$. The reason is that observations depend not only on the state in which the system is but also on the action that leads to that state. For instance, we can have some "sensing action" a that does not change the state, i.e., $P_a(s|s) = 1$, but that makes some observation

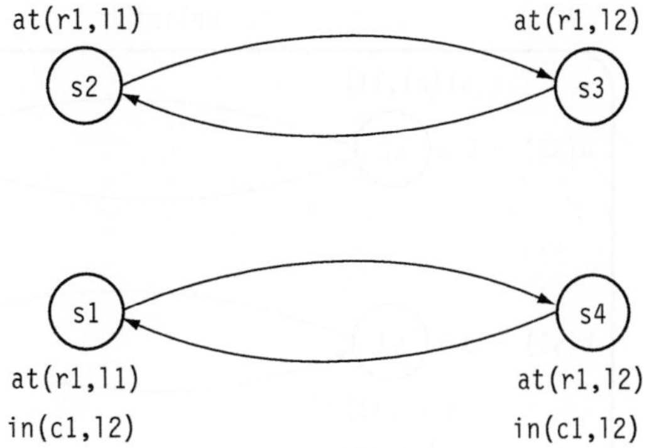

Figure 16.7 A partially observable stochastic system.

available, e.g., for some $o \in O$, $P_a(o|s) = 1$, while $P_{a'}(o|s) \neq 1$ for any $a' \neq a$. If an observation o in a state s does not depend on the action that has been executed, i.e., $\forall a \in A \, \forall a' \in A \;\; P_a(o|s) = P'_a(o|s)$, we write $P(o|s)$.

Example 16.9 Consider a simplified version of the DWR domain, in which there is one robot r1, which can move between two locations l1 and l2, and one container c1. Suppose that the container can be in location l2, written in(c1,l2), and that the robot can observe whether c1 is in l2 only if the robot is in l2. The stochastic system Σ is shown in Figure 16.7.

In states s1 and s2, the robot is in location l1, while in states s3 and s4, it is in location l2. In states s1 and s4 the container is in location l2, while there is no container at location l2 in the states s2 and s3 ($\neg$in(c1,l2) holds in states s2 and s3). Suppose we have two observations, $O = \{$f, e$\}$, with f for full, i.e., the container is in location l2, and e for empty, i.e., the container is not in location l2. We model the robot's ability to observe the container in location l2 by assigning the following probability distributions $P(o|s)$, for any $o \in \{$f, e$\}$ and any $s \in \{$s1, s2, s3, s4$\}$ (we suppose that observations do not depend on actions):

$$P(\text{f}|\text{s1}) = P(\text{e}|\text{s1}) = P(\text{f}|\text{s2}) = P(\text{e}|\text{s2}) = 0.5$$
$$P(\text{f}|\text{s4}) = P(\text{e}|\text{s3}) = 1$$
$$P(\text{f}|\text{s3}) = P(\text{e}|\text{s4}) = 0$$

Notice that states s1 and s2 are indistinguishable. ■

Belief States. In POMDPs, the controller can observe a probability distribution over states of the system, rather than exactly the state of the system. Probability distributions over states are called *belief states*. Let b be a belief state and B the set of belief states. Let $b(s)$ denote the probability assigned to state s by the

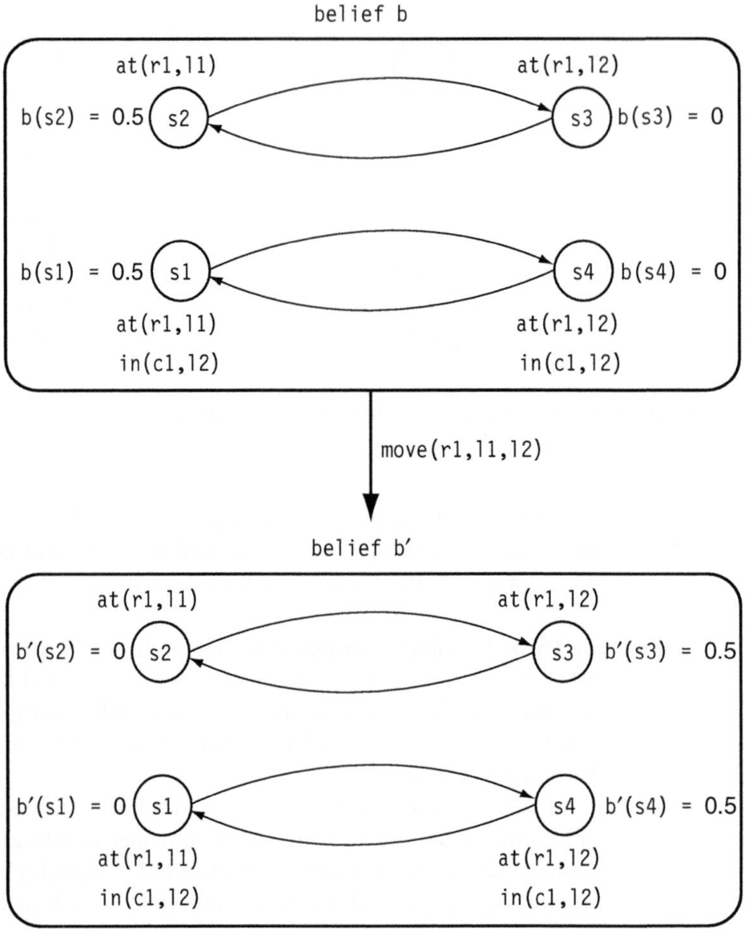

Figure 16.8 Belief states and transitions on belief states.

belief state b. Because $b(s)$ is a probability, we require $0 \leq b(s) \leq 1$ for all $s \in S$ and $\sum_{s \in S} b(s) = 1$.

Example 16.10 Consider the situation described in Example 16.9. Figure 16.8 (a) shows a belief state b such that $b(\mathtt{s1}) = b(\mathtt{s2}) = 0.5$ and $b(\mathtt{s3}) = b(\mathtt{s4}) = 0$. Belief state b models the fact that the controller knows that the system is either in state s1 or s2 with the same probability, 0.5. ■

Given a belief state b, the execution of an action a results in a new belief state b'. We call b_a the belief state that results from performing action a in belief state b.

For each $s \in S$, the probability $b_a(s)$ can be computed as the sum of the probability distribution determined by b weighted by the probability that action a leads from s' to s:

$$b_a(s) = \sum_{s' \in S} P_a(s|s')b(s') \tag{16.12}$$

Example 16.11 Figure 16.8 (b) shows a belief state $b' = b_a$ with $a = \mathsf{move(r1, l1, l2)}$. We have $b'(\mathsf{s1}) = b'(\mathsf{s2}) = 0$ and $b'(\mathsf{s3}) = b'(\mathsf{s4}) = 0.5$. The belief state b' models the ability of the controller to observe whether the system is in either state s2 or s3 with the same probability, 0.5. Indeed, moving the robot from location l1 to location l2, leads to a belief state where the robot is at l2, but the robot still cannot observe whether the location is full or empty.

■

We can compute the probability of observing $o \in O$ after executing action $a \in A$ as follows:

$$b_a(o) = \sum_{s \in S} P_a(o|s)b(s) \tag{16.13}$$

Example 16.12 Consider the situation shown in Figure 16.8. Let $a = \mathsf{move(r1, l1, l2)}$. Then $b'(e) = b_a(e) = b'(f) = b_a(f) = 0.5$. Because the system can be in either state s3 or s4 with the same probability, we can observe either e or f with the same probability. States s3 and s4 are indistinguishable.

■

We can now compute $b_a^o(s)$, i.e., the probability that the state is s after executing action a in belief state b and observing o:

$$b_a^o(s) = \frac{P_a(o|s)b_a(s)}{b_a(o)} \tag{16.14}$$

Example 16.13 In the same situation described previously, we have $b_a^f(\mathsf{s4}) = 1$ while $b_a^f(\mathsf{s1}) = b_a^f(\mathsf{s2}) = b_a^f(\mathsf{s3}) = 0$, and $b_a^e(\mathsf{s3}) = 1$ while $b_a^e(\mathsf{s1}) = b_a^e(\mathsf{s2}) = b_a^e(\mathsf{s4}) = 0$. This models the fact that we observe that the location l2 is full or empty in state s4 or in state s3. We can now distinguish between state s4 and s3 by observing that the former is full while the latter is empty.

■

Plans as Policies on Belief States. In POMDPs, a policy is a function that maps belief states to actions. Let B be the set of belief states. A policy is a function $\pi : B \rightarrow A$.

Notice that while the set of states S is finite, the set B of probability distributions over states is infinite and continuous because a belief is a probability distribution.

Example 16.14 Consider the POMPD domain used in Example 16.13. The policy that executes move(r1,l1,l2) in belief state $b = \{b(s1) = 0.5, b(s2) = 0.5, b(s3) = 0, b(s3) = 0\}$ determines whether there is a container in location l2. Suppose now that we have a further action available in the domain, **observe-container**, such that:

- $\forall o \, \forall s \, \forall a \neq \text{observe} - \text{container} P_a(o|s) = 0.5$
- $\forall o \forall s \in \{s1, s2\} P_{\text{observe-container}}(o|s) = 0.5$
- $P_{\text{observe-container}}(f|s4) = P_{\text{observe-container}}(e|s3) = 1$
- $P_{\text{observe-container}}(f|s3) = P_{\text{observe-container}}(e|s4) = 0$

The policy $\pi = \{(b0, \text{move}(r1, l1, l2)), (b1, \text{observe} - \text{container})$, where $b0 = b$ and $b1 = b'$, is the policy that determines whether there is a container in l2. ■

Planning Problems as Optimization Problems. Planning problems in POMDPs can be stated as optimization problems where an optimal policy $\pi : B \rightarrow A$ has to be generated. This can be done by seeing the POMDP planning problem as a fully observable MDP planning problem on the infinite set of belief states. The equation on belief states corresponding to the Bellman Equation (Formula 16.7) is the following:

$$E(b) = \min_{a \in A} C(b, a) + \gamma \sum_{o \in O} b_a(o) \; E(b_a^o) \tag{16.15}$$

where

$$C(b, a) = \sum_{s \in S} C(s, a) b(s) \tag{16.16}$$

16.3.2 Planning Algorithms

A way to solve POMDPs is to use the algorithms for completely observable MDPs over belief states. However, computationally the POMDP problem is very hard to solve because the resulting space of belief states, i.e., B, is infinite and continuous. The known POMDP algorithms that return optimal policies can in practice be applied only to problems of rather small size. Algorithms that return approximations of optimal policies can be more practical. A possible way to search for a plan is to perform a forward search on belief states. (Here we briefly give some hints.) At each step, the search procedure selects the action that minimizes the expected cost in the current belief state, computes the belief state that results from applying the action, and so on. One way to do this is to consider only actions that are "applicable" in the current belief state, i.e., actions such that for any state s of the belief state, there exists a s' such that $P_a(s'|s) \neq 0$. The search can be guided by different heuristics, i.e., by defining a heuristic function $h(b)$ for a belief state b, e.g., in terms of the expected cost. Typically these kinds of algorithms are not guaranteed to return an optimal policy; however, they can solve problems that cannot be solved in practice by algorithms returning optimal policies.

16.4 Reachability and Extended Goals

Given a stochastic system $\Sigma = (S, A, P)$, we could define goals in the classical way, i.e., as sets of states to be reached $S_g \subseteq S$, choose an initial state $s_o \in S$, and define the planning problem as the triple (Σ, s_0, S_g). However, the definition of a solution policy for the planning problem is not obvious as in classical planning. Indeed, while in classical planning a solution plan is a plan that results in a final state that is a goal state, the same policy may result, as we have seen, in different histories—some of them leading to a goal state, others not achieving the goal.

Example 16.15 Consider the stochastic system shown in Figure 16.1. Let s1 be the initial state and let {s4} be the set of goal states. All the history with positive probability for policy π_2 leads to the goal, while, if we consider policy π_1, history h_1 leads to the goal with probability 0. 8, while history h_2 does not lead to the goal with probability 0. 2. All the histories with positive probability lead to the goal state according to policy π_3. All the histories with positive probabilities of both π_2 and π_3 lead to the goal state. Notice indeed that h_7 has probability 0 both for π_1 and π_3. ∎

The MDP framework can be used to solve planning problems with classical reachability goals, i.e., goals that represent sets of desired final states. Given a stochastic system Σ and a planning problem $P = (\Sigma, s_0, S_g)$, and given the cost function C, we modify the stochastic system and the cost function such that the following hold.

- Actions in goal states produce no changes, i.e., $\forall s \in S_g \ \forall a \in A \ P(s|s) = 1$.
- Actions in goal states have no costs, i.e., $\forall s \in S_g \ \forall a \in A \ C(s, a) = 0$.

Given the stated assumptions, the planning problem can still be defined as the optimization problem defined in Section 16.2.

In Section 16.2 we showed how MDPs can represent goals that express preferences on the entire execution path. In the following examples we further explore how costs and rewards can be used to represent extended goals.

Example 16.16 Consider a DWR domain with two locations l1 and l2. Containers can dynamically and unpredictably be downloaded from a ship to a pile at location l1. We would like to express the condition that the robot should try to keep location l1 empty by continuing to deliver containers to location l2. We can represent this domain with the nondeterministic stochastic system shown in Figure 16.9. The fact that containers may nondeterministically arrive at location l1 is captured by

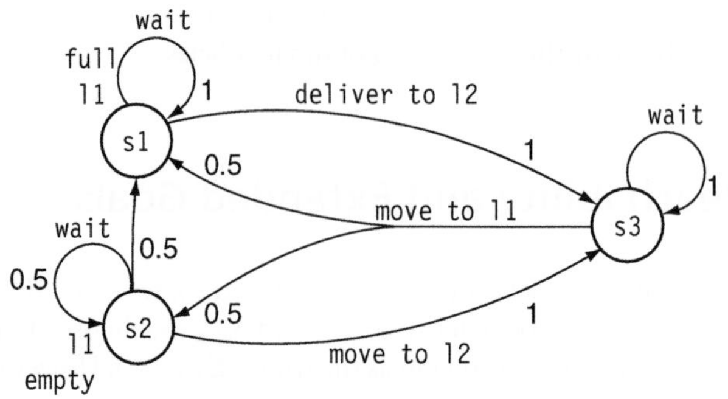

Figure 16.9 A stochastic system for continuous delivery.

the nondeterminism of actions move(r1,l2,l1) and wait that can lead to a state with or without containers (full or empty) with uniform probability distribution. We can express the goal described informally by assigning a high reward to state s2. Given this planning problem, the planning algorithms generate the obvious policy {(s1, deliver to l2), (s2, wait), (s3, move(r1, l2, l1)}. This policy continuously delivers containers to location l2 as soon as they are downloaded at location l1. ■

Example 16.17 Consider the stochastic system shown in Figure 16.1. Suppose the goal for the robot is to keep going around visiting all the locations but avoiding s5 (e.g., a dangerous zone). Assigning high rewards to all states but s5 is not enough because a policy that stays in a state other than s5 forever would have a high utility function. A possible way to express this goal is to give action wait a cost higher than the cost of the other actions, so that the robot is "pushed" to move to adjacent nodes.

It is possible to play with costs and rewards in order to specify different kinds of goals. An interesting problem is to express the condition that the robot has to visit infinitely often states s2 and s4 but never go through state s5. ■

16.5 Discussion and Historical Remarks

MDPs take a very different view from the approaches we have described in the previous chapters. The planning problem is seen as an optimization problem. The idea of maximizing a utility function has intrinsic advantages and disadvantages. A utility function can very easily express preferences on states and actions, and many applications require such preferences. Moreover, costs and rewards can very naturally express competing criteria for optimality. For example, it is usually easy to express two competing criteria such as shortest path and state avoidance by assigning proper costs to actions and penalties to states to be avoided. For instance, in Example 16.5 (see page 383), it is very easy to express competing criteria. On the other hand, sometimes it is not easy to formulate goals in terms of state rewards (or action costs). For instance, in the same example, one might wonder whether we would have the same optimal policy if we changed the reward for s5 from -100 to -1 or if we changed the reward for s4 from 100 to 0.

The idea of using transition probabilities also has its pros and cons. Probabilities allow a certain level of expressiveness. However, they are in most cases statistical estimates, and how they can affect solutions when those estimates deviate from the accurate values is a critical issue. This issue is even more critical in applications where statistical estimates are not available.

In this chapter, we described a rather basic class of MDP planning problems and rather simple planning algorithms. Some important works initially investigated the MDP approach to planning [108, 144, 294]. Here are some references to different problems and alternative solutions.

- We have considered the case of MDPs over infinite horizons, i.e., we assume histories to be infinite sequences of states and compute expected utilities over infinite histories. A discussion of the problem with a finite horizon can be found in Boutilier *et al.* [88].
- We have assumed the utility function to be a simple combination of rewards and costs. There are other possibilities, such as additive versus nonadditive, average versus discounted, etc. (see [88] for a review).
- We have assumed that policies are functions that map states to actions, i.e., they are memoryless and stationary. There exist more complex policies, e.g., those that take into account the whole history, such as nonmemoryless and/or nonstationary policies, decision trees, etc. (see again [88] for an overview).
- There are several different implementations of policy iteration and value iteration. Their complexity analysis can be found in two sources [108, 262].
- In the satisficing approach to MDPs [340], goals are sets of states, and the planning problem is defined by requiring that histories get to a goal state with probability over a given threshold.
- There exist different approaches to the POMPD planning problem (see, e.g., [80, 87, 446, 447]) and different approaches that address the problem of state explosion, such as factorized MDPs [89, 429], abstraction [147, 350], symbolic approaches to first-order MDPs [90], the use of decision diagrams, e.g., in the SPUDD planner [269], and heuristic search in AND/OR graphs [258].
- The problem of expressing goals in temporal logic in the MDP framework is addressed in several works [30, 31, 506].
- MDP planning can be seen as an extension to heuristic search in the unifying approach proposed by Bonet and Geffner [82, 84], where real-time value iteration algorithms are proposed and implemented in the GPT system [83], available at http://www.cs.ucla.edu/~bonet/.

- Markov games are an extension of MDPs where contingent events are taken into account [364]. In this framework, in addition to a set of controllable actions, we have a set of uncontrollable events, and the probability distribution is defined on the occurrence of an action and an event. Some common and general assumptions are that actions and events occur simultaneously at each step; the action is chosen by the planner; and the event is chosen by the environment, which is seen as an opponent. A utility function can then be defined as usual, and the problem is again to optimize the utility function.

16.6 Exercises

16.1 In Example 16.6 (see page 386), what are the utility values of π_1, π_2, and π_3?

16.2 Consider Example 16.5 (see page 383). Exchange the probabilities for nondeterministic actions (e.g., $P_{\text{move c2 to p2}}(2|1) = 0.2$ and $P_{\text{move c2 to p2}}(4|1) = 0.8$). Costs are uniform and unary. Assign reward 100 to state s3, and a reward 0 to all other states. What is the optimal policy?

16.3 In Example 16.5, if we change the reward for s5 from -100 to -1, do we have the same optimal policy? And what about changing the reward for s4 from 100 to 0? Describe how the optimal policy changes depending on different configurations of rewards and costs.

16.4 In Example 16.5, if we change the probability distribution of the two nondeterministic actions, how do they do impact the optimal policy? For instance, if $P_{\text{move(r1,l1,l4)}}(\text{s4}|\text{s1}) = 0.1$, which is the optimal policy?

16.5 Consider Example 16.5. How would you express a goal like "keep visiting s2 and s4"? Which policy would be returned by the planning algorithms? Do the same in the case where there are no arcs between s4 and s5.

16.6 Modify the policy and the value iteration algorithms so they can solve a classical planning problem with a fully deterministic stochastic system, an initial state, and a set of goal states.

16.7 Modify the policy and the value iteration algorithms so they can solve a planning problem with a nondeterministic stochastic system, a set of initial states, and a set of goal states.

16.8 Consider a simplified version of Exercise 5.7 in which there is no washing machine and no shower, and Dan only wants to wash the dishes. Suppose that start-fill and start-wash each have a 0.5 probability of working correctly and a 0.5 probability of doing nothing. Suppose that the other actions work correctly with probability 1. We can represent this as an MDP with the following states.

s_0 is the initial state.

s_1 is the result of executing start-fill(dw) successfully in s_0.

s_2 is the result of executing end-fill(dw) in s_1.

s_3 is the result of executing start-wash(dw) successfully in s_2.

s_4 is the result of executing end-wash(dw,dishes) in s_3.

Executing an inapplicable action leaves the state unchanged. Each state has a reward of 0, each action has a cost of 1, and the discount factor is $\gamma = 1/2$. If we ever reach s_4, the system terminates and there are no more costs and rewards.

(a) Consider this policy:

$$\pi = \{(s_0, \text{start-fill(dw)}), (s_1, \text{end-fill(dw)}), (s_2, \text{start-wash(dw)}), (s_3, \text{end-wash(dw)})\}$$

What is the cost of π?

(b) If we start with $E = 1$ at each node of the MDP and do one round of value iteration, what are the values of E at each node afterward?

(c) Let π' be any policy that produces the E values in part (b). If we start with π' and do one round of policy iteration, then what are the resulting policy and the resulting E values?

(d) Write all policies that have noninfinite cost.

(e) Professor Prune says, "To write the MDP representation of the washing problem takes at least as much work as it takes to solve the original classical planning version of the washing problem." Is he right? Why or why not?

16.9 Redo Exercise 16.8 with $\gamma = 1$.

16.10 Rewrite the Policy-Iteration algorithm (Figure 16.4) to incorporate rewards as shown in Formula 16.2.

16.11 Rewrite the Value-Iteration algorithm (Figure 16.6) to incorporate rewards as shown in Formula 16.2.

Chapter 17

Planning Based on Model Checking

17.1 Introduction

Planning by model checking is an approach to planning under uncertainty that deals with nondeterminism, partial observability, and extended goals. Its key idea is to solve planning problems model-theoretically. It is based on the following conventions.

- A planning domain is a nondeterministic state-transition system, where an action may lead from the same state to many different states. The planner does not know which of the outcomes will actually take place when the action will be executed.
- Formulas in temporal logic express reachability goals, i.e., a set of final desired states, as well as temporal goals with conditions on the entire plan execution paths. They can express requirements of different strengths that take into account nondeterminism.
- Plans result in conditional and iterative behaviors,[1] and in general they are strictly more expressive than plans that simply map states to actions to be executed.
- Given a state-transition system and a temporal formula, planning by model checking generates plans that "control" the evolution of the system so that all of the system's behaviors make the temporal formula true. Plan validation can be formulated as a model checking problem (see Appendix C).
- Planning algorithms can use symbolic model checking techniques (see Appendix C). In particular, sets of states are represented as propositional formulas, and searching through the state space is performed by doing logical transformations over propositional formulas. The algorithms can be

1. They are similar to programs with conditional statements and loops.

implemented by using symbolic techniques taking advantage of ordered binary decision diagrams (BDDs; see Appendix C), which allow for the compact representation and effective manipulation of propositional formulas.

The main advantage of planning by model checking is the ability to plan under uncertainty in a practical way. Nondeterminism leads to the need to deal with different action outcomes, i.e., different possible transitions. Partial observability leads to the need to deal with observations that correspond to more than a single state. Planning by model checking searches sets of states and sets of transitions at once, rather than single states. These sets are represented and manipulated symbolically: extremely large sets of states or huge sets of transitions are often represented very compactly, and in some cases they are manipulated at a low computational cost. Most often indeed, algorithms for planning by model checking do not degrade performances at increasing uncertainty; on the contrary, they are faster the more uncertain the domain is. Last but not least, the approach can be extended to deal with complex goals, expressing temporal conditions and requirements of different strengths. Even in this case, the idea of working on sets of states seems to be feasible and practical: symbolic algorithms for temporally extended goals do not degrade significantly with respect to those for reachability goals.

In conclusion, planning by model checking has great potential to deal with uncertainty in a general, well-founded, and practical way. As a consequence, the approach is in principle good for all applications where uncertainty is critical and nonnominal behaviors are relevant, such as safety-critical applications. The approach seems promising also in those cases where models cannot avoid uncertainty, for instance, the case of planning for web services.

This chapter describes planning by model checking under the assumption of full observability for reachability goals (Section 17.2) and for extended goals (Section 17.3), and planning under partial observability (Section 17.4). In Section 17.5 we discuss planning based on model checking versus MDPs. The chapter ends with discussion and exercises.

17.2 Planning for Reachability Goals

Reachability goals intuitively express conditions on the final state of the execution of a plan: we want a plan that, when executed, reaches a state that satisfies some condition, i.e., the final state is a goal state. The notion of solution for a reachability goal in classical planning, where domains are deterministic, is clear because the execution of a plan corresponds to a unique sequence of states: the final state must be a goal state. In the case of nondeterminism, the execution of a given plan may result, in general, in more than one sequence of states. Therefore, the solution to a reachability goal should be characterized with respect to the many possible executions of a plan, e.g., all the executions or just some of them can reach a goal state. In Section 17.2.1, we define precisely the three possible notions of solutions to a planning problem with a reachability goal, while in Section 17.2.2 we describe some planning algorithms that generate plans for these three different kinds of planning problems.

17.2.1 Domains, Plans, and Planning Problems

A *planning domain* is a nondeterministic state-transition system $\Sigma = (S, A, \gamma)$, where:

- S is a finite set of states.
- A is a finite set of actions.
- $\gamma : S \times A \rightarrow 2^S$ is the state-transition function.

Nondeterminism is modeled by γ: given a state s and an action a, $\gamma(s, a)$ is a set of states. We say that an action a is applicable in a state s if $\gamma(s, a)$ is not empty. The set of actions that are applicable in state s is $A(s) = \{a : \exists s' \in \gamma(s, a)\}$.

Example 17.1 Figure 17.1 shows a nondeterministic state-transition system for a simplified DWR domain. It is the same example as the one in Figure 16.1 but without probabilities. In this example, a robot can move among the five different locations

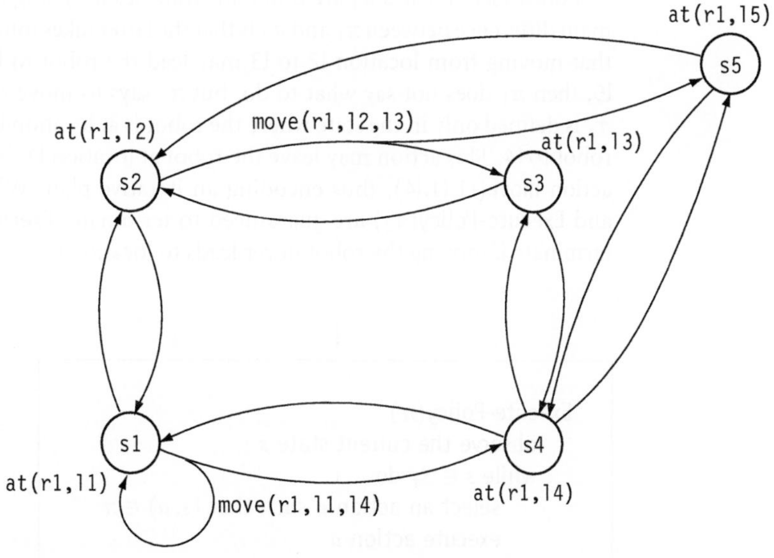

Figure 17.1 A nondeterministic state-transition system. There are five states (s1, s2, s3, s4,s5), one for each location (l1, l2, l3, l4,l5). An action, e.g., move(r1,l1,l2) labels the arc, e.g., s1 to s2. There are two nondeterministic actions, move(r1,l2,l3) and move(r1,l1,l4).

l1, l2, l3, l4, and l5, corresponding to the states s1, s2, s3, s4, and s5, respectively. There are two sources of nondeterminism: γ(s2, move(r1,l2,l3)) = {s3, s5} and γ(s1, move(r1,l1,l4)) = {s1, s4}. ■

As in MDP planning, we need to generate plans that encode conditional and iterative behaviors. Here plans are policies that are similar to MDP policies. A *policy* π for a planning domain $\Sigma = (S, A, \gamma)$ is a set of pairs (s, a) such that $s \in S$ and $a \in A(s)$. We require that for any state s there is at most one action a such that $(s, a) \in \pi$. The set of states of a policy is $S_\pi = \{s \mid (s, a) \in \pi\}$.

Similarly to MDPs, a controller uses a reactive loop to execute a policy (see Figure 17.2). The differences compared with MDP policies are that here policies are not necessarily defined over all S ($S_\pi \subseteq S$). In the following discussion, we use interchangeably the terms *policy* and *plan*.

Example 17.2 Consider the following policies for the domain in Figure 17.1.

$$\pi_1 = \{(\text{s1}, \text{move}(\text{r1}, \text{l1}, \text{l2})) \quad (\text{s2}, \text{move}(\text{r1}, \text{l2}, \text{l3})) \quad (\text{s3}, \text{move}(\text{r1}, \text{l3}, \text{l4}))\}$$

$$\pi_2 = \{(\text{s1}, \text{move}(\text{r1}, \text{l1}, \text{l2})) \quad (\text{s2}, \text{move}(\text{r1}, \text{l2}, \text{l3})) \quad (\text{s3}, \text{move}(\text{r1}, \text{l3}, \text{l4})) \quad (\text{s5}, \text{move}(\text{r1}, \text{l5}, \text{l4}))\}$$

$$\pi_3 = \{(\text{s1}, \text{move}(\text{r1}, \text{l1}, \text{l4}))\}$$

Policies π_1, π_2, and π_3 are different strategies for going from state s1 to s4. The main difference between π_1 and π_2 is that the latter takes into account the possibility that moving from location l2 to l3 may lead the robot to l5. If the robot goes to l5, then π_1 does not say what to do, but π_2 says to move the robot from l5 to l4. π_3 is defined only in the state where the robot is at location l1 and tries to move the robot to l4. This action may leave the robot at location l1, in which case π_3 repeats action move(r1,l1,l4), thus encoding an iterative plan. While Execute-Policy(π_1) and Execute-Policy(π_2) are guaranteed to terminate, Execute-Policy(π_3) may not terminate if moving the robot never leads to location l4. ■

```
Execute-Policy(π)
    observe the current state s
    while s ∈ Sπ do
        select an action a such that (s, a) ∈ π
        execute action a
        observe the current state s
end
```

Figure 17.2 Policy execution.

We represent the execution of a policy in a planning domain with an *execution structure*, i.e., a directed graph in which the nodes are all of the states of the domain that can be reached by executing actions in the policy, and the arcs represent possible state transitions caused by actions in the policy. Let π be a policy of a planning domain $\Sigma = (S, A, \gamma)$. The *execution structure* induced by π from the set of initial states $S_0 \subseteq S$ is a pair $\Sigma_\pi = (Q, T)$, with $Q \subseteq S$, $T \subseteq S \times S$, such that $S_0 \subseteq Q$, and for every $s \in Q$ if there exists an action a such that $(s, a) \in \pi$, then for all $s' \in \gamma(s, a)$, $s' \in Q$ and $T(s, s')$. A state $s \in Q$ is a *terminal state* of Σ_π if there is no $s' \in Q$ such that $T(s, s')$.

Let $\Sigma_\pi = (Q, T)$ be the execution structure induced by a policy π from S_0. An *execution path* of Σ_π from $s_0 \in S_0$ is a possibly infinite sequence $s_0, s_1, s_2, \ldots$ of states in Q such that, for every state s_i in the sequence, either s_i is the last state of the sequence (in which case s_i is a terminal state of Σ_π) or $T(s_i, s_{i+1})$ holds. We say that a state s' is *reachable from* a state s if there is a path from s to s'.

Example 17.3 Figure 17.3 shows the execution structures induced by π_1, π_2, and π_3 from $S_0 = \{\text{s1}\}$ in the planning domain of Figure 17.1. The execution paths of π_1 are $\langle \text{s1, s2, s3, s4} \rangle$ and $\langle \text{s1, s2, s5} \rangle$, and those of π_2 are $\langle \text{s1, s2, s3, s4} \rangle$ and $\langle \text{s1, s2, s5, s4} \rangle$. Some of the infinitely many execution paths of π_3 are $\langle \text{s1, s4} \rangle$, $\langle \text{s1, s1, s4} \rangle$, $\langle \text{s1, s1, s1, s4} \rangle$, and $\langle \text{s1, s1, s1}, \ldots \rangle$. ■

A reachability goal is similar to a goal in classical planning in that a plan succeeds if it reaches a state that satisfies the goal. However, because the execution of a plan may produce more than one possible path, the definition of a solution to a planning problem is more complicated than in classical planning. A *planning problem* is a triple (Σ, S_0, S_g), where $\Sigma = (S, A, \gamma)$ is a planning domain, $S_0 \subseteq S$ is a set of initial states, and $S_g \subseteq S$ is a set of goal states. Let π be a policy for Σ. Let $\Sigma_\pi = (Q, T)$ be the execution structure induced by π from S_0. Then we distinguish among three kinds of solutions.

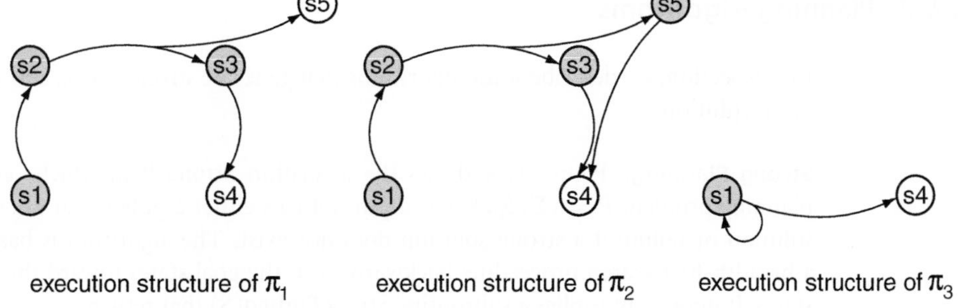

Figure 17.3 The execution structures of the policies listed in Example 17.2.

1. *Weak solutions* are plans that may achieve the goal but are not guaranteed to do so. A plan is a weak solution if there is at least one finite path that reaches the goal. Formally π is a weak solution to P if and only if for each state in S_0 there exists a state in S_g that is a terminal state of Σ_π.
2. *Strong solutions* are plans that are guaranteed to achieve the goal in spite of nondeterminism: all the paths are finite and reach the goal. Formally, π is a strong solution to P if and only if Σ_π has no infinite paths, i.e., it is acyclic, and all of the terminal states of Σ_π are in S_g.
3. *Strong cyclic solutions* are guaranteed to reach the goal under a "fairness" assumption, i.e., the assumption that execution will eventually exit the loop. These solutions are such that all their partial execution paths can be extended to a finite execution path whose terminal state is a goal state. Formally, π is a strong cyclic solution to P if and only if from each state in Q there exists a terminal state of Σ_π that is reachable and all the terminal states of Σ_π are in S_g.

Weak and strong solutions correspond to the two extreme requirements for satisfying reachability goals. Intuitively, weak solutions correspond to "optimistic plans." Strong solutions correspond to "safe plans." However, there might be cases in which weak solutions are not acceptable and strong solutions do not exist. In such cases, strong cyclic solutions may be a viable alternative.

The set of strong solutions to a planning problem is a subset of the set of strong cyclic solutions, which in turn is a subset of the set of weak solutions.

Example 17.4 In Figure 17.1, let the initial state and goal state be s1 and s4, respectively. π_1 is a weak solution, π_2 is a strong solution, and π_3 is a strong cyclic solution. π_3 can be described as the iterative trial-and-error strategy "move the robot to location l4 until it succeeds," which repeats the execution of the action. This solution is much stronger than a weak solution: if at least one of the executions of the action succeeds, then we reach the goal. The only execution that won't reach the goal is the "unfair" one in which the move action fails forever.

■

17.2.2 Planning Algorithms

In this section, we describe some algorithms that generate strong, weak, and strong cyclic solutions.

Strong Planning. Figure 17.4 shows the algorithm Strong-Plan which, given a planning problem $P = (\Sigma, S_0, S_g)$ as input, returns either a policy that is a strong solution or failure if a strong solution does not exist. The algorithm is based on a breadth-first search proceeding backward from the goal states toward the initial states. It iteratively applies a subroutine StrongPreImg(S) that returns:

$$\text{StrongPreImg}(S) = \{(s, a) \mid \gamma(s, a) \neq \emptyset \text{ and } \gamma(s, a) \subseteq S\}$$

```
Strong-Plan(P)
    π ← failure; π' ← ∅
    While π' ≠ π and S0 ⊈ (Sg ∪ Sπ') do
        PreImage ← StrongPreImg(Sg ∪ Sπ')
        π'' ← PruneStates(PreImage, Sg ∪ Sπ')
        π ← π'
        π' ← π' ∪ π''
    if S0 ⊆ (Sg ∪ Sπ') then return(MkDet(π'))
        else return(failure)
end
```

Figure 17.4 Strong planning algorithm.

PreImage is therefore the set of pairs (s, a) such that a is guaranteed to lead to states in S_g or to states in $S_{\pi'}$ for which a solution is already known,[2] where $S_{\pi'}$ is the set of states of π'. This set is then pruned by removing pairs (s, a) such that a solution is already known for s:

$$\text{PruneStates}(\pi, S) = \{(s, a) \in \pi \mid s \notin S\}$$

The algorithm terminates if the initial states are included in the set of accumulated states (i.e., $S_g \cup S_{\pi'}$) or if a fixed point has been reached from which no more states can be added to the policy π'. If there is no strong solution, then at some iteration StrongPreImg returns an empty set, and we get $\pi = \pi'$. In the first case, the returned policy is a solution to the planning problem. Notice, however, that π' may have more than one action for a given state. MkDet(π') returns a policy $\pi \subseteq \pi'$ such that $S_\pi = S_{\pi'}$, and π satisfies the requirement that one state has only one corresponding action. In the second case, no solution exists: indeed, there is some initial state from which the problem is not solvable.

Strong-Plan corresponds to the computation of a least fixed point where state–action pairs are incrementally added to the current policy until either the set of initial states is included or a fixed point is reached.

Example 17.5 We apply Strong-Plan to the planning domain in Figure 17.1 with $S_0 = \{s1\}$ and $S_g = \{s4\}$.

At the first iteration, *PreImage* is {(s3,move(r1,l3,l4)), (s5,move(r1,l5,l4))} while PruneStates has no effects. Therefore π' is the same as *PreImage*.

At the second iteration, *PreImage* becomes {(s3, move(r1,l3,l4)), (s5, move(r1,l5,l4)), (s2, move(r1,l2,l3)), (s4, move(r1,l4,l3)), (s4, move(r1,l4,l5))}. PruneStates eliminates (s3, move(r1,l3,l4)), (s5, move(r1,l5,l4)), (s4, move(r1,l4,l3)), and

2. Compare this with Γ and Γ^{-1} as defined in Chapter 2.

(s4, move(r1,l4,l5)). π' is therefore {(s3, move(r1,l3,l4)), (s5, move(r1,l5,l4)), (s2, move(r1,l2,l3))}.

At the next iteration, we get π' = {(s3, move(r1,l3,l4)), (s5, move(r1,l5,l4)), (s2, move(r1,l2,l3)), (s1, move(r1,l1,l2))}. At this point, the termination test $S_g \cup S_{\pi'}$ is satisfied, so Strong-Plan returns π_2. ■

Strong-Plan is guaranteed to terminate. It is sound, i.e., the returned policies are strong solutions, and it is complete, i.e., if it returns failure, then there exists no strong solution. Moreover, it returns policies that are optimal in the following sense. A policy results in a set of paths. Consider the longest path of the policy, and let us call it the *worst path*. Then the solution returned by Strong-Plan has a minimal worst path among all possible solutions. For the formal proofs, see Cimatti *et al.* [128].

Weak Planning. The algorithm Weak-Plan for weak planning is identical to the algorithm for strong planning, except that StrongPreImg is replaced by WeakPreImg:

$$\text{WeakPreImg}(S) = \{(s, a) : \gamma(s, a) \cap S \neq \emptyset\}$$

Example 17.6 In the planning problem described in Example 17.5, Weak-Plan stops at the first iteration and returns the policy π = {(s1, move(r1,l1,l4)), (s3, move(r1,l3,l4)), (s5, move(r1,l5,l4))}. Some remarks are in order. First, π is a strong cyclic solution, but this is fine because strong cyclic solutions also are weak solutions. Second, the pairs (s3, move(r1, l3, l4)) and (s5, move(r1, l5, l4)) are uneeded, and if we removed them from π, π still would be a weak solution. However, the presence of such pairs causes no harm, and it is very easy to build a procedure that removes them. Third, Weak-Plan returns not all the possible weak solutions but one that has the shortest path to the goal. ■

We can easily compare strong planning and weak planning in nondeterministic domains with classical planning in deterministic domains. Let $\mathcal{P} = (\Sigma, s_0, S_g)$ be a classical planning problem. Then $\mathcal{P}$ can be viewed as a nondeterministic planning problem in which every action happens to be deterministic. Because every action is deterministic, every solution policy for $\mathcal{P}$ is both a weak solution *and* a strong solution.

Suppose we invoke the strong planning algorithm (or the weak planning one) on such a planning problem. Then both algorithms will behave identically. In both cases, the algorithm will do a breadth-first search going backward from the goal states, ending when the algorithm has visited every node of Σ for which there is a path to a goal.

Let π be the solution policy returned by the planning algorithm. One way to visualize π is as a set of trees, where each tree is rooted at a different goal state. If S is the set of all states in Σ from which the goal is reachable, then the node sets of these trees are a partition of S.

```
Strong-Cyclic-Plan(S0,Sg)
   π ← ∅; π' ← UnivPol
   while π' ≠ π do
      π ← π'
      π' ← PruneUnconnected(PruneOutGoing(π',Sg),Sg)
   if S0 ⊆ (Sg ∪ Sπ')
      then return(MkDet(RemoveNonProgress(π',Sg)))
      else return(failure)
end
```

Figure 17.5 Strong cyclic planning algorithm: main routine. It repeatedly eliminates state–action pairs by calling the subroutines PruneOutgoing and PruneUnconnected till a greatest fixed point is reached. It then calls the subroutine RemoveNonProgress and checks whether a solution exists.

If s is any state from which it is possible to reach a goal state, then π gives us a path $\langle s, \pi(s), \pi(\pi(s)), \ldots \rangle$ to a goal state. For the case where $s = s_0$, this path is an irredundant solution plan for the classical planning problem.

Strong Cyclic Planning. The algorithm Strong-Cyclic-Plan is presented in Figure 17.5. It starts with the universal policy $UnivPol = \{(s, a) \mid a \in A(s)\}$ that contains all state–action pairs. It iteratively eliminates state–action pairs from the universal policy. This elimination phase, where state–action pairs leading to states out of the states of *UnivPol* are discarded,[3] corresponds to the while loop of Strong-Cyclic-Plan. It is based on the repeated application of PruneOutgoing and PruneUnconnected. (Figure 17.6 shows the three subroutines for Strong-Cyclic-Plan.) The role of PruneOutgoing is to remove every state–action pair that leads out of $S_g \cup S_\pi$. Because of the application of PruneOutgoing, from certain states it may become impossible to reach the set of goal states. The role of PruneUnconnected is to identify and remove such states. Due to this removal, the need may arise to eliminate further outgoing transitions, and so on. The elimination loop terminates when convergence is reached. Strong-Cyclic-Plan then checks whether the computed policy π tells what to do in every initial state, i.e., $S_0 \subseteq S_g \cup S_{\pi'}$. If this is not the case, then a failure is returned. The following example explains the need for the RemoveNonProgress subroutine.

Example 17.7 Figure 17.7 shows a variation of the domain in Figure 17.1. Consider the planning problem of going from location l1 (initial state s1) to location l6 (goal state s6). The action move(r1,l4,l1) in state s4 is "safe": if executed, it leads to

3. Note that *UnivPol* contains all the state–action pairs where the action is applicable to the state, and therefore there may be states that are not in the states of *UnivPol*.

```
PruneOutgoing(π,S_g) ;; removes outgoing state-action pairs
   π' ← π − ComputeOutgoing(π, S_g ∪ S_π)
   return(π')
end

PruneUnconnected(π,S_g) ;; removes unconnected state-action pairs
   π' ← ∅
   repeat
      π'' ← π'
      π' ← π ∩ WeakPreImg(S_g ∪ S_π')
   until π'' = π'
   return(π') end

RemoveNonProgress(π,S_g) ;; remove state-action pairs that
                         ;; do not lead toward the goal
   π* ← ∅
   repeat
      PreImage ← π ∩ WeakPreImg(S_g ∪ S_π*)
      π*_old ← π*
      π* ← π* ∪ PruneStates(PreImage, S_g ∪ S_π*)
   until π*_old = π*
   return(π*)
end
```

Figure 17.6 Strong cyclic planning algorithm: subroutines. PruneOutgoing removes every states–action pair that leads out of the current set of states $S_g \cup S_\pi$. PruneUnconnected removes every edges that are unconnected, i.e., do not lead to the goal. RemoveNonProgress removes pairs that do not lead toward the goal.

state s1, where the goal is still reachable. However, this action does not contribute to reaching the goal. On the contrary, it leads back to the initial state, from which it would be necessary to move again to state s4. Moreover, if the action move(r1,l4,l1) is performed whenever the execution is in state s4, then the goal will never be reached. ∎

After the elimination loop, we may have state–action pairs like (s4, move(r1, l4, l1)) that, while preserving the reachability of the goal, still do not make any progress toward it. RemoveNonProgress takes care of removing all those state–action pairs that cause this kind of problem. It is very similar to the weak planning algorithm: it iteratively extends the policy backward from the goal. In this case, however, the weak preimage computed at any iteration step is restricted to the

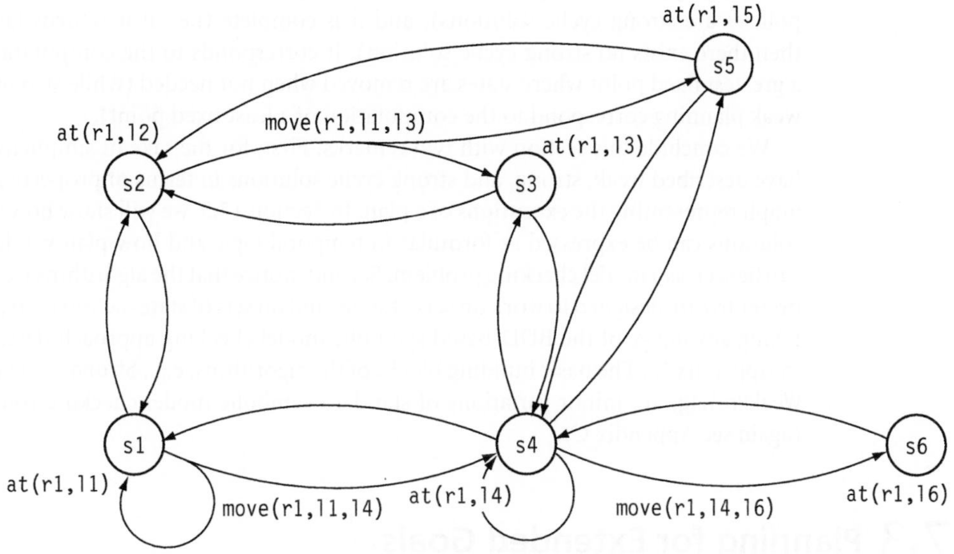

Figure 17.7 A nondeterministic state-transition system. It is a variation of the example in Figure 17.1. There is one additional state, state s6, and the two additional actions move(r1,l4,l6) and move(r1,l6,l4), which move the robot between locations l4 and l6.

state–action pairs that appear in the input policy and hence that are "safe" according to the elimination phase.

The subroutines PruneOutgoing, PruneUnconnected, and RemoveNonProgress, as shown in Figure 17.6, are based on the same routines WeakPreImg and PruneStates, which we already defined for the strong and weak planning algorithms (see Figure 17.4 and discussion), and on the primitive ComputeOutgoing, which takes as input a policy π and a set of states S and returns all state–action pairs that are not guaranteed to result in states in S:

$$\text{ComputeOutgoing}(\pi, S) = \{(s, a) \in \pi \mid \gamma(s, a) \not\subseteq S\}$$

Example 17.8 In Example 17.7, neither PruneOutgoing nor PruneUnconnected prune any pair from the universal policy, so the loop ends after the first iteration. RemoveNonProgress eliminates (s4, move(r1, l4, l1)), (s4, move(r1, l4, l3)), (s4, move(r1, l4, l5)), (s3, move(r1, l3, l2)), (s5, move(r1, l5, l2)), and (s2, move(r1, l2, l1)). MkDet returns either the policy that moves the robot from l1 to l6 through l4 or the policy that moves through l2 first and then to l3 or l5, and finally to l4, prior to reaching l6. ∎

Strong-Cyclic-Plan is guaranteed to terminate, it is sound (i.e., the returned policies are strong cyclic solutions), and it is complete (i.e., if it returns failure, then there exists no strong cyclic solution). It corresponds to the computation of a greatest fixed point where states are removed when not needed (while strong and weak planning correspond to the computation of a least fixed point).

We conclude this section with two remarks. First, for the sake of simplicity, we have described weak, strong, and strong cyclic solutions in terms of properties of a graph representing the executions of a plan. In Section 17.3, we will show how these solutions can be expressed as formulas in temporal logic and how plan validation can be seen as a model checking problem. Second, notice that the algorithms we have presented are designed to work on sets of states and on sets of state–action pairs, thus taking advantage of the BDD-based symbolic model checking approach described in Appendix C . The basic building blocks of the algorithms, e.g., StrongPreImg and WeakPreImg, are minor variations of standard symbolic model checking routines (again see Appendix C).

17.3 Planning for Extended Goals

In this section we relax the basic assumption that goals are sets of final desired states. We extend the framework in two directions.

1. We allow for temporal goals, i.e., goals that state conditions on the whole execution path, rather than on its final state. This extension allows for expressing goals such as "generate a plan such that the robot keeps surveilling some rooms."
2. We allow for goals that take into account the uncertainty of the domain and express conditions of different strengths, such as the requirement that a plan should *guarantee* that the robot keeps visiting some rooms versus a plan that *does its best* to make the robot keep visiting the rooms.

We first formalize the planning problem through the use of temporal logic (Sections 17.3.1 and 17.3.2), and then we discuss a different approach to the formalization of extended goals (Section 17.3.3).

17.3.1 Domains, Plans, and Planning Problems

A planning domain is a state-transition system $\Sigma = (S, A, \gamma)$, where S, A, and γ are the same as in previous sections, except for one minor difference. In order to simplify the definitions, we require γ to be total, i.e., $\forall s\ A(s) \neq \emptyset$.

Policies (see Section 17.2.1) map states to actions to be executed. In the case of extended goals, plans as policies are not enough. Different actions may need to be executed in the same state depending on the previous states of the execution path.

Example 17.9 Consider the situation shown in Figure 17.1. Suppose the robot is in state s4 and the goal is "move to s3 first, and then to s5." There exists no policy that satisfies this goal because in s4 we have to execute two different actions, depending on whether we have already visited s3. ■

A similar but more interesting example is the following: "starting from s4, keep moving back and forth between locations l3 and l5." Every time in s4, the robot has to take into account which state, s3 or s5, has just been visited and then move to the other one. In other words, plans have to take into account the *context of execution*, i.e., the internal state of the controller. A *plan* for a domain Σ is a tuple $(C, c_0, act, ctxt)$, where:

- C is a set of execution contexts.
- $c_0 \in C$ is the initial context.
- act: $S \times C \times A$ is the action function.
- $ctxt$: $S \times C \times S \times C$ is the context function.

If we are in state s and in execution context c, then $act(s, c)$ returns the action to be executed by the plan, while $ctxt(s, c, s')$ associates with each reached state s' the new execution context. Functions *act* and *ctxt* are partial because some state–context pairs are never reached in the execution of the plan.

In the following discussion, for the sake of readability, we write plans as tables whose columns describe the current state s, the current context c, the action to be performed in the current state and context (i.e., $act(s, c)$), the next state that may result from the execution of the action (i.e., $s' \in \gamma(s, act(s,c))$), and the next context $ctxt(s, c, s')$.

In Figure 17.1, suppose the goal is to move the robot from location l4 to l3 and then to l5. Table 17.1 shows a plan π_4 that satisfies the goal.

Now consider the goal "keep moving back and forth between locations l2 and l4, and never pass through l5." Notice that there is no plan that, at each round, can *guarantee* that the robot visits l2 and l4 without passing through l5. The requirement is too strong for the kind of uncertainty we have to deal with. However, in many cases, a weaker requirement is enough. For instance, we can require that at each round the robot *does* visit l2, *does not* pass through l5, and, *just if possible*, visits l4.

Table 17.1 An example of a plan for extended goals.

State	*Context*	*Action*	*Next state*	*Next context*
s4	c1	move(r1,l4,l3)	s3	c2
s3	c2	move(r1,l3,l4)	s4	c2
s4	c2	move(r1,l4,l5)	s5	c2

Table 17.2 A plan for goal "keep moving back and forth between two locations."

State	*Context*	*Action*	*Next state*	*Next context*
s1	c1	move(r1,l1,l2)	s2	c2
s1	c2	move(r1,l1,l4)	s1	c1
s1	c2	move(r1,l1,l4)	s4	c1
s2	c2	move(r1,l2,l1)	s1	c2
s4	c1	move(r1,l4,l1)	s1	c1

This goal expresses a different strength on the need to visit (or not visit) different locations. We can synthesize this goal with the following statement: "keep moving back and forth between locations l2 and, if possible, l4, and never pass through l5." A plan π_5 that satisfies this goal for the domain in Figure 17.1 is shown in Table 17.2.

We say that plan π is *executable* if, whenever $act(s, c) = a$ and $ctxt(s, c, s') = c'$, then $s' \in \gamma(s, a)$. We say that π is *complete* if, whenever $act(s, c) = a$ and $s' \in \gamma(s, a)$, then there is some context c' such that $ctxt(s, c, s') = c'$ and $act(s', c')$ is defined. Intuitively, a complete plan always specifies how to proceed for all the possible outcomes of any action in the plan. In the following discussion, we consider only plans that are *executable and complete.*

The execution of a plan results in a change in the current state and in the current context. It can therefore be described in terms of transitions from one state–context pair to another. Formally, given a domain Σ and a plan π, a transition of plan π in Σ is a tuple $(s, c) \xrightarrow{a} (s', c')$ such that $s' \in \gamma(s, a)$, $a = act(s, c)$, and $c' = ctxt(s, c, s')$. A *run* of plan π from state s_0 is an infinite sequence $(s_0, c_0) \xrightarrow{a_0} (s_1, c_1) \xrightarrow{a_1} (s_2, c_2) \xrightarrow{a_2} (s_3, c_3) \cdots$, where $(s_i, c_i) \xrightarrow{a_i} (s_{i+1}, c_{i+1})$ are transitions.

The *execution structure* of plan π in a domain Σ from state s_0 is the structure[4] $\Sigma_\pi = (Q, T, L)$, where:

- $Q = \{(s, c) \mid act(s, c) \text{ is defined}\}$
- $((s, c), (s', c')) \in T$ if $(s, c) \xrightarrow{a} (s', c')$ for some a

Example 17.10 Figure 17.8 (b) shows the execution structure of plan π_4, which moves the robot from location l4 to l3 and then to l5. ■

The goals we have considered so far can be expressed in computation tree logic (CTL) [171]. For instance, the goal "move the robot from location l4 to l3 and then to l5" is formalized as:

$$\text{at(r1, l4)} \rightarrow \text{AF}\,(\text{at(r1, l3)} \wedge \text{AF}\,\text{at(r1, l5)}) \tag{17.1}$$

4. Σ_π is a Kripke structure; see Appendix C.

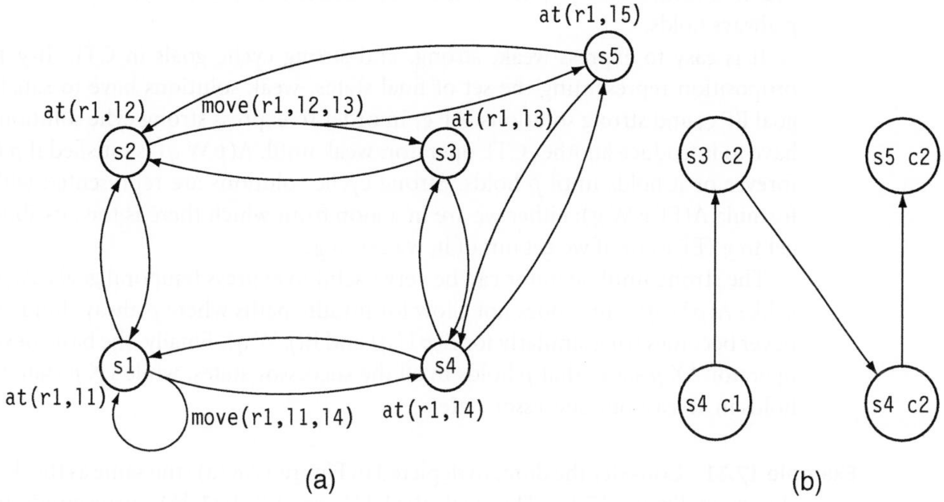

Figure 17.8 An example of a planning domain (a) and an execution structure (b).

AF is a CTL operator that is composed of two parts: a path quantifier A, which states that the formula should hold for all possible execution paths, a temporal operator F, which means "in the future" or "eventually." Therefore, AF at(r1, l5) means that for all possible execution paths, eventually there will be a state in the future where at(r1, l5) holds. The formula AF (at(r1, l3) $\wedge$ AF at(r1, l5)) means therefore that eventually in the future at(r1, l3) $\wedge$ AF at(r1, l5) will hold, i.e., there is a state in the future where at(r1, l3) holds, and from then on, at(r1, l5) holds. In general, AF ($p \wedge$ AF q) can be used to express the goal that p must become true and, after that p becomes true, then q becomes true.

Consider now the goal "keep moving back and forth between locations l2 and l4, and never pass through l5." It can be formalized in CTL with the formula:

$$\text{AG}\,(\text{AF}\,\mathsf{at(r1,l2)} \wedge \text{AF}\,\mathsf{at(r1,l4)}) \wedge \text{AG}\ \neg\mathsf{at(r1,l5)} \tag{17.2}$$

The CTL formula AGp states that p must hold "globally" or "always" in time, i.e., in all the future states. The formula AG (AF$p \wedge$ AF q) states that we should "keep to reach a state where p holds and keep moving to a state where q holds". As we know, the goal expressed in Formula 17.2 cannot be satisfied by any plan. The weaker goal "keep moving back and forth between locations l2 and, *if possible*, l4, and never pass through l5" is represented by:

$$\text{AG}\,(\text{AF}\,\mathsf{at(r1,l2)} \wedge \text{EF}\,\mathsf{at(r1,l4)}) \wedge \text{AG}\ \neg\mathsf{at(r1,l5)} \tag{17.3}$$

E is the CTL existential path quantifier, which means that there should exist a path such that a temporal property holds. EFp means that there exists a path such that in a future state p holds, while EG p means that there exists a path such that p always holds.

It is easy to express weak, strong, and strong cyclic goals in CTL. If g is the proposition representing the set of final states, weak solutions have to satisfy the goal EF g, and strong solutions, AF g. In order to express strong cylic solutions, we have to introduce another CTL operator: weak until. A(p W q) is satisfied if p holds forever or it holds until p holds. Strong cyclic solutions are represented with the formula A(EF g W g): either we are in a loop from which there is the possibility to get to g (EF g) or, if we get out of it, we get to g.

The strong until operator can be very useful to express temporal goals: A(p U q) is like A(p W q), but it does not allow for infinite paths where p always holds and q never becomes true; similarly for E(p U q) and E(p W q). Finally, the basic next step operator AX p states that p holds in all the successor states, while EX p state that p holds in at least one successor state.

Example 17.11 Consider the domain depicted in Figure 17.8 (a) (the same as the domain shown in Figure 17.1). The goal at(r1, l1) $\rightarrow$ EF at(r1, l4) corresponds to the requirement for a weak solution with initial state s1 and goal state s4. Similarly, at(r1, l1) $\rightarrow$ AF at(r1, l4) corresponds to the requirement of a strong solution. The requirement for the robot to try to reach location l4 from l1 by avoiding location l3 is expressed by the goal at(r1, l1) $\rightarrow$ (EF at(r1, l4) $\wedge$ AG $\neg$at(r1, l3)). The requirement for the robot "keep moving back and forth between locations l2 and, if possible, l4" can be expressed by the goal AG (AF at(r1, l2) $\wedge$ EF at(r1, l4)). ■

A *planning problem* is the tuple (Σ, S_0, g), where Σ is a nondeterministic state-transition system, $S_0 \subseteq S$ is a set of initial states, and g is a goal for Σ.

Let π be a plan for Σ and Σ_π be the corresponding execution structure. A plan π satisfies goal g from initial state $s_0 \in S$, written $\pi, s_0 \models g$, if $\Sigma_\pi, (s_0, c_0) \models g$. A plan π satisfies goal g from the set of initial states S_0 if $\pi, s_0 \models g$ for each $s_0 \in S_0$. The formal definition of $K, s_0 \models \phi$, where K is a Kripke structure and ϕ a CTL formula, can be found in Appendix C.

Σ_π is a Kripke structure. In model checking, Σ_π is the model of a system and g is a property to be verified. The plan validation problem, i.e., the problem of determining whether a plan satisfies a goal, is thus formulated as the model checking problem of determining whether the CTL formula g is true in the Kripke structure Σ_π, which represents the behaviors of the system Σ "controlled" by the plan π.

17.3.2 Planning Algorithms

Planning for CTL goals could in principle be done with a forward search and a progression of the CTL formula in a way similar to planning with LTL control rules (see Chapter 10). Thus, for instance, if the goal is A(p U q), we progress the goal to $q \vee$ AX ($p \wedge$ A(p U q)), we check whether q holds in the initial state, and if not,

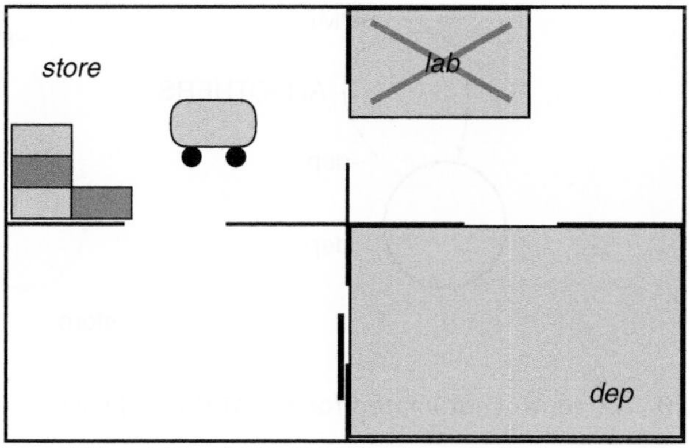

Figure 17.9 A domain example for planning for extended goals.

we select an action a applicable in the initial state. Then in all the states resulting from the application of a to the initial state, we check whether p holds and recursively call the procedure. The main difference from planning with LTL control rules is that particular attention must be paid to the universal and existential path quantifiers.

However, an explicit state forward search does not work in practice. Enumerating all the possible states is hopeless in the case of nondeterminism. An alternative approach is to use symbolic model checking techniques that work on sets of states rather than single states. In this section, we give some guidelines on how this can be done.

Consider a variation of Example 17.1 (see page 405) in which location l2 is a store, location l5 is a lab, and location l4 is a department ("dep" in Figure 17.9). Suppose the lab is a dangerous room, and if the robot gets into the lab, there is no way to come out. Suppose the goal is "keep moving back and forth between the store and, if possible, the department." Formally we have AG (AF store ∧ EF dep).

The idea underlying the planning algorithm is to construct a control automaton that controls the search in the state space. The control automaton can be constructed by progressing the CTL goal. Each state of the automaton corresponds to a subgoal to be solved, which then becomes a context in the resulting plan. Arcs between states in the control automaton determine when the search switches from one context to another. For instance, the control automaton extracted by progressing the goal AG (AF store ∧ EF dep) is shown in Figure 17.10. In the control automaton, we have two contexts: the one on the left, corresponding to the context where the next goal to satisfy is EF dep (and AF store afterward), and the one on the right, corresponding to the context where the next goal to satisfy is AF store (and EF dep afterward). The generated plan will have to keep satisfying both EF dep and AF store. When it is time to satisfy AF store (see the context on the right in the figure), the search has to find an action such that, if store holds, then we switch context (because the goal is

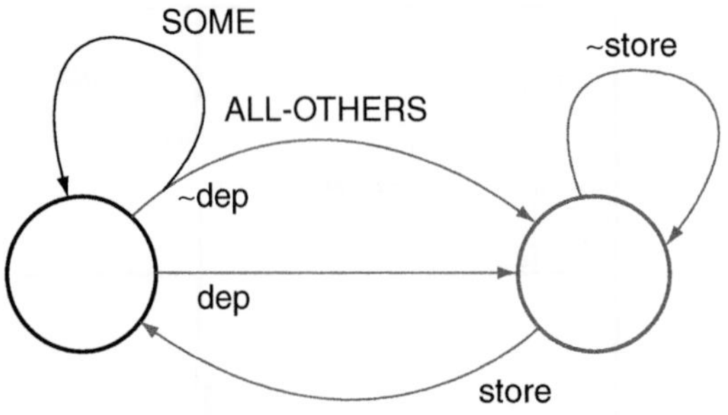

Figure 17.10 The control automaton for AG (AF store ∧ EF dep).

already satisfied) by searching for a plan that satisfies EF dep. If store does not hold, then we stay in the same context and search for a plan that satisfies AF store, i.e., that is guaranteed to reach the store. In order to satisfy EF dep (see the context on the left in the figure), the search has to find an action such that, if dep holds, then we switch context. If dep does not hold, then EF dep must be satisfied for *some* of the outcomes (the arc going back to the same context) and for *all the other* outcomes that do not satisfy EF dep. Indeed, if we generate a plan that satisfies EF dep, we have to take into account that the path that does not reach dep might invalidate the possibility to satisfy AF store at the next step. Consider, for instance, the case in which we generate a plan that moves from the store to the room north of the department, and the result is that the robot ends up in the lab. In this case, EF dep is satisfied, but this prevents achieving the goal of going back to the store because the robot is stuck in the lab forever. This is the reason why, in the control automaton, the arc that goes from the left context to the right context (in the case the robot is not in the department) is labeled ALL-OTHERS.

The control automaton is then used to guide the search for a plan. The idea is that the algorithm associates with each state of the control automaton (i.e., with each context that represents a subgoal) the plan that satisfies the subgoal. Initially, all plans are associated with each context. Then the association is iteratively refined: a context is chosen, and the search starts to get rid of the plans that do not satisfy the condition associated with the context. For instance, look at Figure 17.11. In step 1 we have chosen the context on the left, and we obtain the set of all the plans that satisfy EF dep. Notice that the plans specify when to change context. Notice also that, in this first step, the algorithm returns both the plan that goes through the door and the one that might end up in the lab. At this step, this is still a candidate plan because in the other context we have associated all the possible plans, and therefore for all the other plans that do not reach the department we can still reach the store.

The algorithm then considers the context on the right and generates the plans that satisfy AF store (step 2). The state in the lab is discarded because there is no plan that can reach the store from there. Control is back then to the context on the left (step 3). Because we have to guarantee that for all the cases where we do not

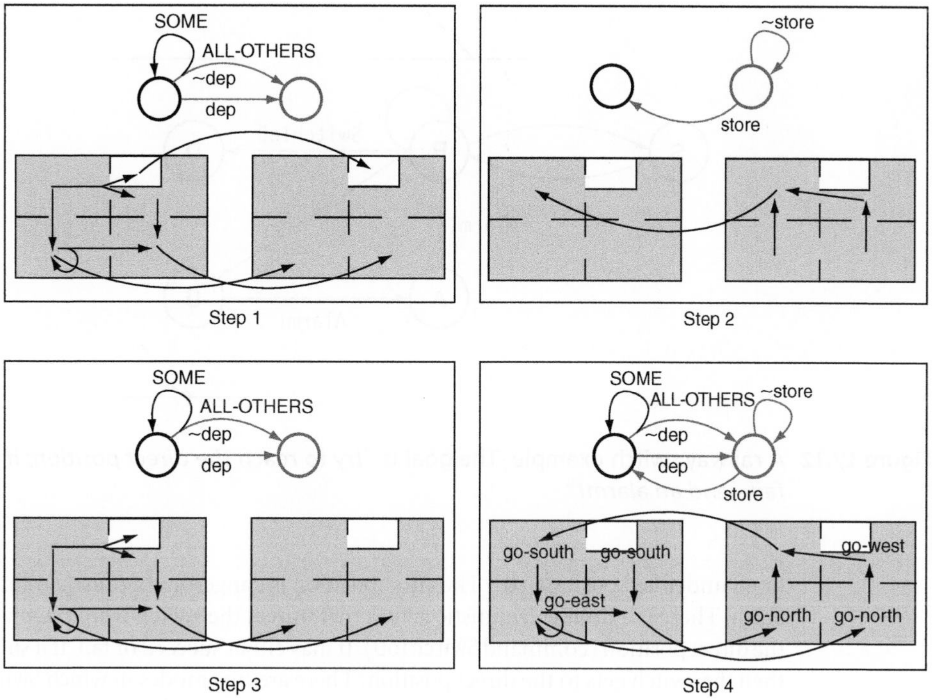

Figure 17.11 A simulation of the symbolic planning algorithm.

reach the department we thereafter reach the store, the plan that goes through the lab is discarded. We finally get to a fixed point and the final plan is returned (step 4).

Once the control automaton is constructed, the algorithm works on sets of states and sets of plans. It is then possible to implement it using BDDs effectively. It can be shown experimentally that, in the case of weak, strong, and strong cyclic reachability goals, beyond a small overhead for constructing the control automaton, the algorithm is comparable with the specialized algorithms for reachability defined in Section 17.2. It is easy to show that the algorithm outperforms by orders of magnitudes existing algorithms based on enumerative approaches.

17.3.3 Beyond Temporal Logic

In spite of the expressiveness of temporal logic, they cannot express some goals that seem to be important for, e.g., safety-critical applications. For instance, consider the model of a simplified controller of a railway switch in Figure 17.12. The switch can be in three main states: a reverse position (R) such that the train changes track, a direct position (D) such that the train keeps going on the same track,

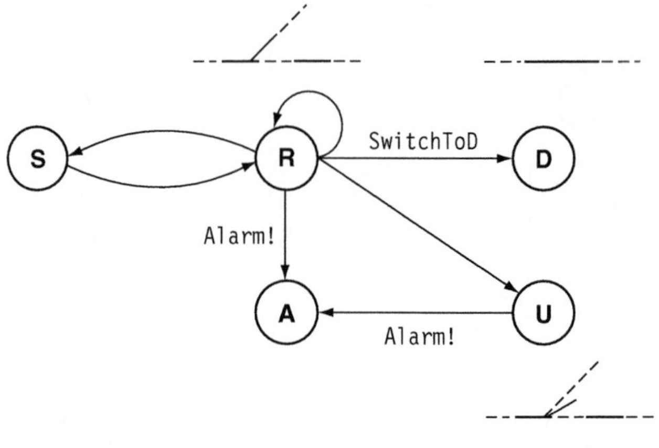

Figure 17.12 A railway switch example. The goal is *"try to reach the direct position; if you fail, send an alarm!"*

or an undefined position (U). The latter position is dangerous because a train might crash. There is a nondeterministic action that moves the switch from the reverse to the direct position (command SwitchToD). It may either succeed or fail. If it succeeds, then the switch gets to the direct position. There are two modes in which SwitchToD can fail. Either the switch does not move, or it ends up in the undefined position. We can send an alarm (command Alarm!) both from the reverse position and from the undefined position and get to the alarm state A. Consider the following goal:

Try to reach the direct position; if you fail, send an alarm!

There is no CTL formula (nor LTL formula) that can express this goal. There are indeed two problems here.

1. Consider the goal "try to reach the direct position." Its intended meaning is *do whatever is possible* to reach the direct position. Such a goal can be satisfied only by a plan that, in state R, always applies SwitchToD until it reaches either D or U. We cannot formalize this goal with the CTL formula EF D because then any plan that tries once, fails, and then keeps moving back and forth between R and S satisfies EF D without really trying its best to reach D. Notice also that a strong cyclic solution does not exist. Indeed, the *intentionality* of the goal is not captured in CTL.
2. In the goal, the intended meaning of "if you fail" is that you should first try to do whatever is possible to reach the direct position, and then, only in the case there is nothing else to do, you should send the alarm. In the example, this means we should send the alarm only in the case we get to U. Again, there is no way to express this in temporal logic. A formula that encodes the "if you fail" statement with a disjunction or with an implication cannot prevent the

planner from finding a plan that ignores the first part of the goal and satisfies the one that requires an alarm to be sent, e.g., by sending the alarm from R. In temporal logic, there is no way to express constructs for failure handling and, more generally for preferences. Indeed, the failure statement can be seen as a preference: the first preference is to try to move the switch to the right position; the second preference is to send an alarm.

We need a language with a different semantics that takes into account the points of failure. A first attempt toward this direction is the EaGle language [136]. EaGle has the following syntax.

- Reachability (basic) goals: DoReach p, TryReach p
- Maintenance (basic) goals: DoMaintain p, TryMaintain p
- Conjunction: g And g'
- Failure: g Fail g'
- Control operators: g Then g', Repeat g

Goal "DoReach p" requires a plan that guarantees to reach p despite nondeterminism. It fails if no such plan exists. Its semantics is similar to that of the CTL formula AF p, but DoReach keeps track of the points of failure and success. We explain this in the case of the goal "TryReach p." This goal requires a plan that does its best to reach p. It fails when there is no possibility to reach p. Figure 17.13 shows some examples that should help the reader understand its semantics. The trees in Figure 17.13 correspond to the unfolding of three different examples of domains. The semantics of TryReach p follows.

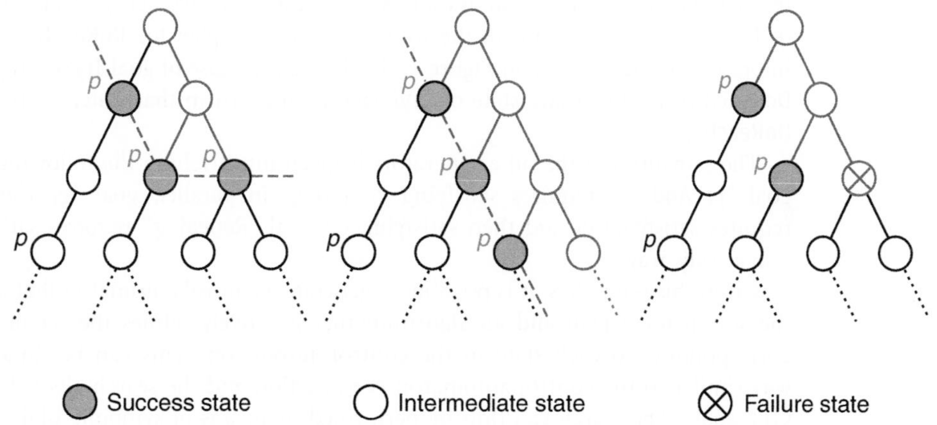

Figure 17.13 Semantics of TryReach p.

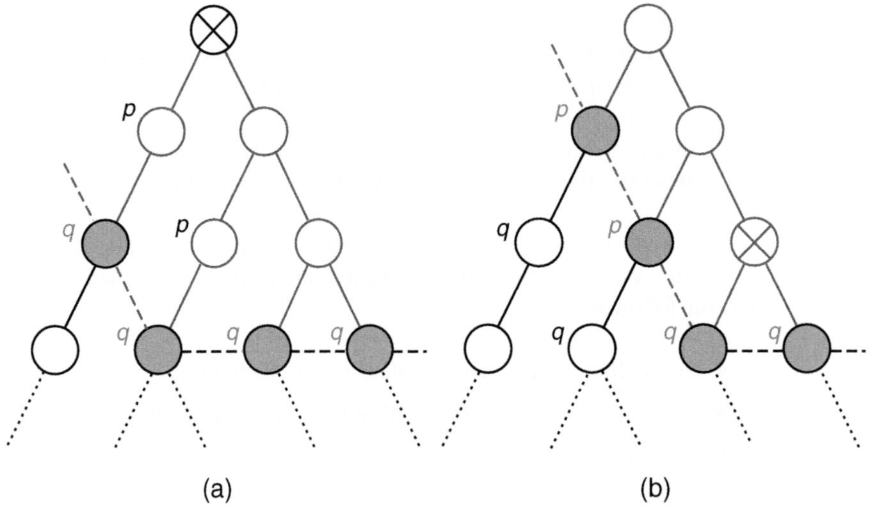

Figure 17.14 Semantics of g_1 Fail g_2: DoReach p Fail DoReach q (a); TryReach p Fail DoReach q (b).

- The states where p holds are *success states.*
- The states from which p can never be reached are *failure states.*
- The states where p does not hold but is reachable are marked as *intermediate states,* i.e., states that are neither success states nor failure states.

Goal "g_1 Fail g_2" deals with failure/recovery and with preferences among goals. The plan tries to satisfy goal g_1; whenever a failure occurs, goal g_2 is considered instead. Figure 17.14 (a), shows an example for goal DoReach p Fail DoReach q. Because DoReach p fails in the root state, then we plan for DoReach q. More interesting is the example in Figure 17.14 (b), i.e., the case of goal TryReach p Fail DoReach q. In the failure state of TryReach p, and just in that state, we plan for DoReach q.

The semantics of the other operators is given intuitively in the following way: goal "g_1 And g_2" requires satisfying g_1 and g_2 in parallel; goal "g_1 Then g_2" requires satisfying g_1 and then satisfying g_2; goal "Repeat g" requires satisfying g in a cyclic way.

Given this semantics, it is possible to generate a control automaton that guides the search for a plan and an algorithm that iteratively refines the set of plans corresponding to each state in the control automaton. This can be done in a way similar to the control automaton construction and the search algorithm for CTL goals. The search can thus be performed by means of symbolic BDD-based model checking techniques. See Dal Lago *et al.* [136] for a discussion of a possible algorithm.

17.4 Planning under Partial Observability

In this section we address the problem of planning under partial observability. We restrict the discussion to the case of reachability goals and in particular to strong solutions, i.e., solutions guaranteed to reach a given set of states (see Section 17.2), in spite of nondeterminism and in spite of partial observability.

17.4.1 Domains, Plans, and Planning Problems

We consider a nondeterministic state-transition system $\Sigma = (S, A, \gamma)$, where S is the set of states, A is the set of actions, and γ is the state-transition function (they are the same as in Section 17.2.1). Partial observability can be formalized with a set of *observations* that represent the part of the state-transition system that is visible and an *observation function* that defines what observations are associated with each state.

Definition 17.1 Let $\mathcal{S}$ be the set of states of a state-transition system, and let Ω be a finite set of observations. An *observation function* over $\mathcal{S}$ and Ω is a function $\mathcal{O} : \mathcal{S} \rightarrow 2^{\Omega}$, which associates with each state s the set of possible observations $\mathcal{O}(s) \subseteq \Omega$. We require that for each $s \in \mathcal{S}$, $\mathcal{O}(s) \neq \emptyset$. ■

The condition $\mathcal{O}(s) \neq \emptyset$ states the simple technical requirement that some observation is associated with each state. We allow for incomplete information in the case different states result in the same observation, i.e., $\mathcal{O}(s_1) = \mathcal{O}(s_2)$, with $s_1 \neq s_2$. Observation functions can model both full and null observability as special cases. *Null observability* is modeled with observation functions that map all the states to the same observation: $\Omega = \{o\}$ and $\mathcal{O}(s) = \{o\}$ for each $s \in \mathcal{S}$. In this case, observations carry no information because they are indistinguishable for all the states. *Full observability* is modeled with a one-to-one mapping between states and observations: $\Omega = \mathcal{S}$ and $\mathcal{O}(s) = \{s\}$. In this case, observations carry all the information contained in the state of the domain.

Definition 17.1 does not allow for a direct representation of *action-dependent* observations, i.e., observations that depend on the last executed action. However, these observations can be easily modeled by representing explicitly in the state of the domain the relevant information on the last executed action.

Example 17.12 Figure 17.15 shows a simple robot navigation domain. The robot can be in four positions corresponding to the states of the domain: $\mathcal{S} = \{\mathsf{NW}, \mathsf{NE}, \mathsf{SW}, \mathsf{SE}\}$. The robot can move in the four directions: $\mathcal{A} = \{\mathsf{GoNorth}, \mathsf{GoSouth}, \mathsf{GoEast}, \mathsf{GoWest}\}$. The actions are applicable if there is not a wall in the direction of motion. If the actions are deterministic, we have, e.g., $\gamma(\mathsf{NW}, \mathsf{GoEast}) = \{\mathsf{NE}\}$, while $\gamma(\mathsf{NW}, \mathsf{GoSouth}) = \emptyset$ because of the wall blocking movement there. We can

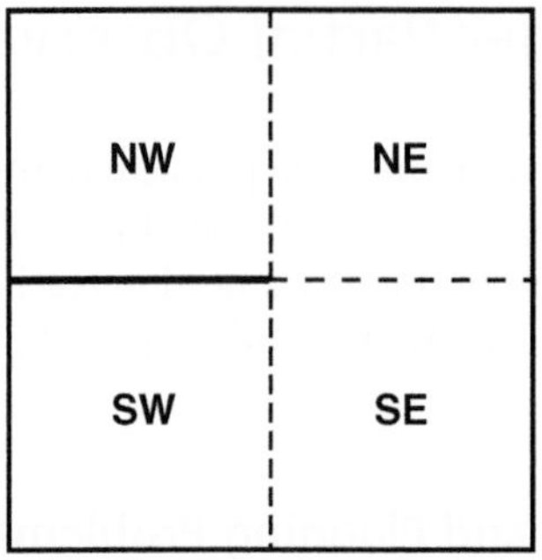

Figure 17.15 A simple partially observable domain.

define a set of propositions $\mathcal{P}$ = {north-west, north-east, south-west, south-east}, and $\mathcal{S}$ is defined to be the set of states where only one of the propositions in $\mathcal{P}$ holds.

If the robot can perform only local observations, it cannot distinguish between the two positions NW and SW. We model this partial observability with a set of observations Ω = {west, ne, se}, and the observation function $\mathcal{O}$ such that $\mathcal{O}$(NW) = $\mathcal{O}$(SW) = west, $\mathcal{O}$(NE) = ne, and $\mathcal{O}$(SE) = se. ■

An alternative way to represent partial observability is to define a set of *observation variables*, whose values can be observed at run-time, during the execution of a plan. We define the *evaluation of an observation variable* to be a relation that specifies what values can be assumed at run-time by the observation variables.

Definition 17.2 Let $\mathcal{S}$ be the set of states of a state-transition system, and let $\mathcal{V}$ be a finite set of observation variables. The *evaluation of an observation variable* $v \in \mathcal{V}$ is the relation $\mathcal{X}_v : \mathcal{S} \times \{\top, \bot\}$. ■

Without loss of generality, we assume that observation variables are Boolean. The symbols $\top$ and $\bot$ stand for true and false, respectively, and represent the evaluation of the Boolean variable v to true or false. In a state $s \in \mathcal{S}$, an observation variable $v \in \mathcal{V}$ may give no information: this is specified by stating that both $\mathcal{X}_v(s, \top)$ and $\mathcal{X}_v(s, \bot)$ hold, i.e., both the true and false values are possible. In this case, we say that the observation variable v is *undefined* in s. If $\mathcal{X}_v(s, \top)$ holds and $\mathcal{X}_v(s, \bot)$ does not hold, then the value of v in state s is true. The dual holds for the false value. In both cases, we say that v is *defined in* s. An observation variable is always associated with a value, i.e., for each $s \in \mathcal{S}$, at least one of $\mathcal{X}_v(s, \top)$ and $\mathcal{X}_v(s, \bot)$ holds. As the next example shows, the evaluation of observation variables can be easily related to observations by defining the set of observations as all the evaluations of observation variables.

Example 17.13 Consider the situation shown in Figure 17.15. Suppose that the sensors of the robot can detect walls in the current position. This can be formalized with the set of observation variables $\mathcal{V} = \{\mathsf{WallN}, \mathsf{WallS}, \mathsf{WallW}, \mathsf{WallE}\}$. The evaluation is such that $\mathcal{X}_{\mathsf{WallE}}(\mathsf{NW}, \bot)$ and $\mathcal{X}_{\mathsf{WallW}}(\mathsf{NW}, \top)$. In this case, every observation variable is defined in every state of the domain.

In a different formulation of the domain, a further observation variable could detect whether a wall is at distance 2 from the current position, e.g., 2WallS detects walls at south at distance 2. In this case, 2WallS is undefined in state NW, i.e., $\mathcal{X}_{\mathsf{2WallS}}(\mathsf{NW}, \bot)$ and $\mathcal{X}_{\mathsf{2WallS}}(\mathsf{NW}, \top)$.

There exists a relation between observations and observation variables. For instance, the observation west is equivalent to the following result of the evaluation: $\mathcal{X}_{\mathsf{WallN}}(\mathsf{NW}, \top)$, $\mathcal{X}_{\mathsf{WallW}}(\mathsf{NW}, \top)$, $\mathcal{X}_{\mathsf{WallS}}(\mathsf{NW}, \top)$, $\mathcal{X}_{\mathsf{WallE}}(\mathsf{NW}, \bot)$. ■

A partially observable planning domain is a state-transition system with partial observability. We represent partial observability with observation variables and their evaluations.

Definition 17.3 A *planning domain* $\mathcal{D}$ is a tuple $(\Sigma, \mathcal{V}, \mathcal{X})$, where:

- $\Sigma = (\mathcal{S}, \mathcal{A}, \gamma)$ is a state-transition system.
- $\mathcal{V}$ is a finite set of observation variables.
- $\mathcal{X}_v : \mathcal{S} \times \{\top, \bot\}$ is an evaluation of the observation variables.

■

In partially observable domains, plans need to branch on conditions on the value of observation variables.

Definition 17.4 The set of *conditional plans* Π for a domain $\mathcal{D} = (\Sigma, \mathcal{V}, \mathcal{X})$ is the minimal set such that:

- $\lambda \in \Pi$.
- If $a \in \mathcal{A}$, then $a \in \Pi$.
- If $\pi_1, \pi_2 \in \Pi$, then $\pi_1; \pi_2 \in \Pi$.
- If $v \in \mathcal{V}$, and $\pi_1, \pi_2 \in \Pi$, then **if** v **then** π_1 **else** $\pi_2 \in \Pi$.

■

Intuitively, λ is the empty plan, i.e., the plan that does nothing. The plan $\pi_1; \pi_2$ is the sequential composition of the plans π_1 and π_2. The plan **if** v **then** π_1 **else** π_2 is a conditional plan that branches on the value of the observation variable v.

Example 17.14 For the situation shown in Figure 17.15, a plan that moves the robot from the uncertain initial condition NW or SW to state SW is

GoEast ; (**if** WallN **then** GoSouth **else** λ) ; GoWest

Intuitively, action GoEast is executed first. Notice that in the initial condition, all the observation variables would have the same value for both NW and SW: therefore the states are indistinguishable, and it is pointless to observe. Action GoEast moves the robot either to state NE or to SE, depending on the initial position of the robot. If observation variable WallN is true, then the robot is in NE, and action GoSouth moves the robot to SE. If WallN is false, the conditional plan does nothing, i.e., λ is executed. Finally, GoWest moves the robot from state SE to SW. ∎

Let us formalize the execution of a plan. Given an observation variable $v \in \mathcal{V}$, we denote with $v_\top$ the set of states where v evaluates to true: $v_\top \doteq \{s \in \mathcal{S} : \mathcal{X}_v(s, \top)\}$. Similarly, $v_\bot \doteq \{s \in \mathcal{S} : \mathcal{X}_v(s, \bot)\}$ is the set of states where v is false. If v is undefined in a state s, then $s \in v_\top \cap v_\bot$. Under partial observability, plans have to work on sets of states whose elements cannot be distinguished, i.e., on belief states. We say that an *action a is applicable to a nonempty belief state Bs* iff a is applicable in all states of Bs. Plan execution is represented by the function $\Gamma(\pi, Bs)$, which, given a plan π and a belief state Bs, returns the belief state after execution.

Definition 17.5 Let Bs be a nonempty belief state, i.e., $\emptyset \neq Bs \subseteq \mathcal{S}$.

1. $\Gamma(\pi, \emptyset) \doteq \emptyset$.
2. $\Gamma(a, Bs) \doteq \{s' : s' \in \gamma(s, a), \text{ with } s \in Bs\}$, if $a \in \mathcal{A}$ is applicable in Bs.
3. $\Gamma(a, Bs) \doteq \emptyset$, if a is not applicable in Bs.
4. $\Gamma(\lambda, Bs) \doteq Bs$.
5. $\Gamma(\pi_1; \pi_2, Bs) \doteq \Gamma(\pi_2, \Gamma(\pi_1, Bs))$.
6. $\Gamma(\textbf{if } v \textbf{ then } \pi_1 \textbf{ else } \pi_2, Bs) \doteq \Gamma(\pi_1, Bs \cap v_\top) \cup \Gamma(\pi_2, Bs \cap v_\bot)$,
   if condition $app(v, \pi_1, \pi_2, Bs)$ holds, where:
$$\begin{aligned} app(v, \pi_1, \pi_2, Bs) = \quad & (Bs \cap v_\top \neq \emptyset \rightarrow \Gamma(\pi_1, Bs \cap v_\top) \neq \emptyset) \wedge \\ & (Bs \cap v_\bot \neq \emptyset \rightarrow \Gamma(\pi_2, Bs \cap v_\bot) \neq \emptyset). \end{aligned}$$
7. $\Gamma(\textbf{if } v \textbf{ then } \pi_1 \textbf{ else } \pi_2, Bs) \doteq \emptyset$, otherwise.

∎

We say that a plan π is applicable in $Bs \neq \emptyset$ if and only if $\Gamma(\pi, Bs) \neq \emptyset$. For conditional plans, we collapse into a single set the execution of the two branches (item 6). Condition $app(v, \pi_1, \pi_2, Bs)$ guarantees that both branches are executable: the then-branch π_1 must be applicable in all states of Bs where v is true, and the else-branch π_2 must be applicable in all states of Bs where v is false. This condition correctly allows for states where v is undefined, i.e., where v is both true and false.

Example 17.15 Figure 17.16 depicts the execution of the plan in Example 17.14. Γ(GoEast, {NW, SW}) = {NE, SE}, i.e., after the robot moves east, it is guaranteed to be either in NE or SE. The plan then branches on the value of WallN. This allows the planner to distinguish between state NE and SE: if the robot is in NE, then it moves south; otherwise, it does nothing. At this point the robot is guaranteed to be in SE and can finally move west. This plan is guaranteed to reach SW from any of the initial states, either with three actions (if the initial state is NW), or with two actions (if the initial state is SW). ∎

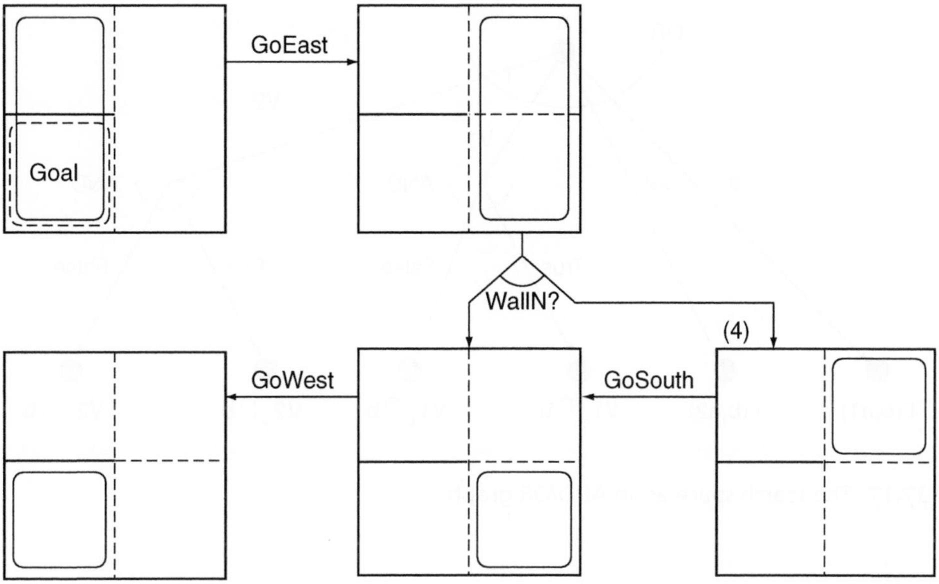

Figure 17.16 Execution of a conditional plan.

We formalize the notion of a planning problem under partial observability as follows.

Definition 17.6 A *planning problem* is a 3-tuple $(\mathcal{D}, S_0, S_g)$, where $\mathcal{D} = (\Sigma, \mathcal{V}, \mathcal{X})$ is a planning domain, $\emptyset \neq S_0 \subseteq \mathcal{S}$ is the initial belief state, and $\emptyset \neq S_g \subseteq \mathcal{S}$ is the goal belief state. The plan π is a strong solution to the problem $(\mathcal{D}, S_0, S_g)$ if and only if $\emptyset \neq \Gamma(\pi, S_0)) \subseteq S_g$. ■

Example 17.16 Consider the problem given by the domain shown in Figure 17.15, the initial belief state $S_0 = \{\mathsf{NW}, \mathsf{SW}\}$, and the goal belief state $S_g = \{\mathsf{SW}\}$. The plan in Example 17.14 is a strong solution to the planning problem. ■

17.4.2 Planning Algorithms

We do not describe any detailed algorithm in this section; rather, we give some hints on how different planning algorithms can be defined. The common underlying idea of the planning algorithms is that the search space can be seen as an AND/OR graph over belief states. The AND/OR graph can be recursively constructed from the initial belief state, expanding each encountered belief state by every possible combination of applicable actions and observations.

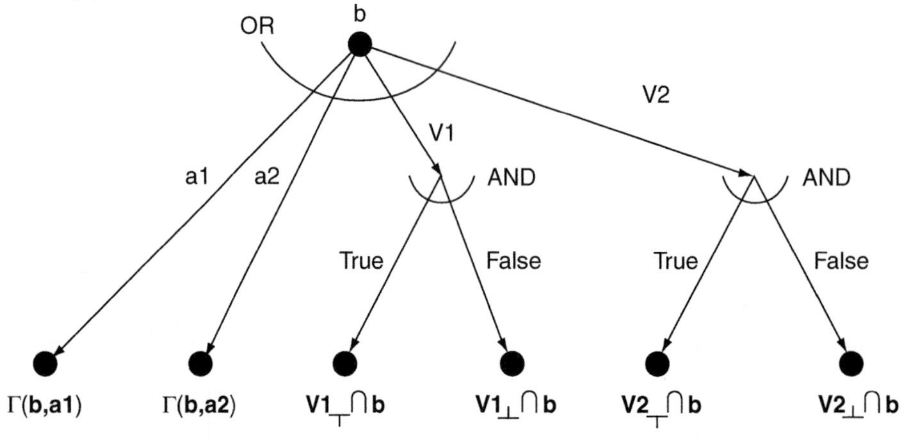

Figure 17.17 The search space as an AND/OR graph.

Figure 17.17 shows an example of an AND/OR graph on belief states. Each node in the graph is a belief state. A node b can be connected to OR-nodes or to AND-nodes. The OR-nodes connected to a node b are

- the belief states produced by the actions applicable to the belief state b (for each applicable action a, we have an OR-node $\Gamma(b, a)$ connected to node b), or
- the pairs of belief states produced by observations $v \in \mathcal{V}$ (each pair corresponds to two branches, one in which v is true and the other in which v is false).

The pair of belief states corresponding to the two branches over the observation variable v are AND-nodes in the AND/OR graph. For each $v \in \mathcal{V}$, a belief state b is connected to two AND-nodes: the subset of b in which the value of v is true (i.e., $v_\top \cap b$) and the subset of b in which the value of v is false (i.e., $v_\bot \cap b$).

A tentative solution plan can be incrementally constructed during the search. If π is the plan associated with node b, then the OR-node connected to b by an action a applicable in b will have an associated plan $\pi; a$. The OR-node connected to b by an observation variable $v \in \mathcal{V}$ will have an associated plan $\pi;$ **if** v **then** π_1 **else** π_2, where π_1 is the plan associated with the AND-node $v_\top \cap b$ and π_2 is the plan associated with the AND-node $v_\bot \cap b$.

The search terminates when it has constructed an acyclic subgraph of the AND/OR graph whose root is the initial belief state b_0 and all the leaf nodes are belief states that are subsets of the goal belief state b_g. Figure 17.18 shows a subgraph that corresponds to the plan a1; **if** v1 **then** π_1 **else** π_2, where $\pi_1 =$ a3; **if** v2 **then** π_3 **else** π_4, and $\pi_2 =$ a2; **if** v2 **then** π_5 **else** π_6, and so on.

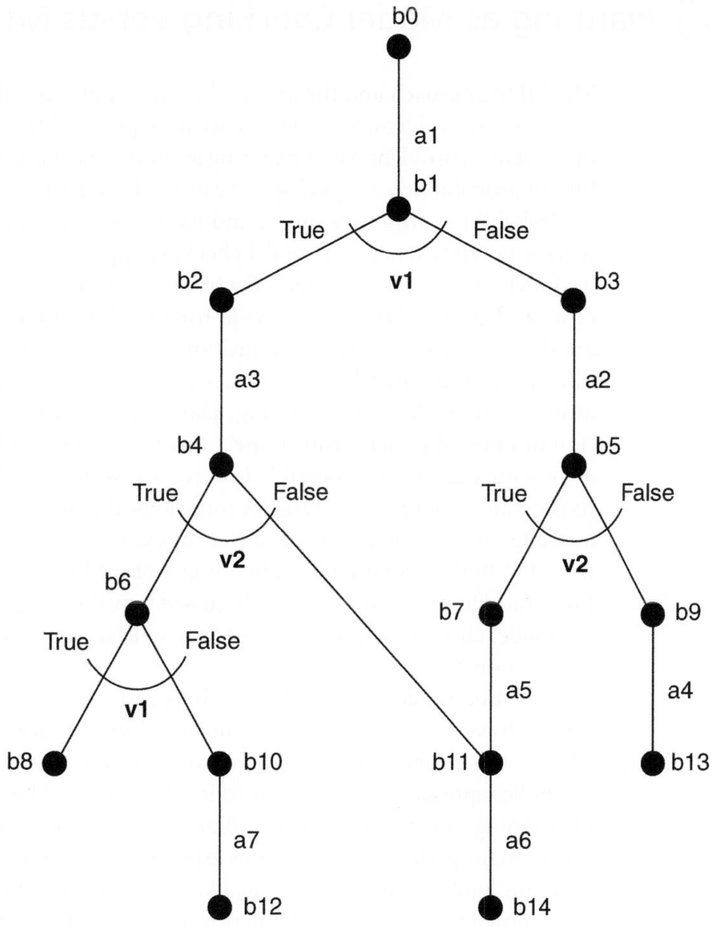

Figure 17.18 An AND/OR graph corresponding to a conditional plan.

A planning algorithm can search this AND/OR graph in different ways and with different strategies. For instance, a breadth-first forward search given a belief state *b* proceeds by exploring all the possible OR-nodes. The termination condition is reached when we have at least one AND/OR subgraph that meets the conditions described earlier. Breadth-first search can generate optimal plans, but this approach can be very expensive. A depth-first search selects one of the possible OR-nodes and needs to explore each branch of the selected AND-nodes. It can be much more convenient than a breadth-first search, but it does not guarantee to return optimal plans. Different heuristics can be applied in the depth-first search, e.g., select all the observations first, select the OR-nodes that produce smaller belief states, etc.

17.5 Planning as Model Checking versus MDPs

The MDP approach and the model checking approach take very different views of the planning problem. With MDPs, we have probabilities, a utility function, and an optimization problem. With planning as model checking, we have nondeterminism but no probabilities, a logical specification of the goal, and a satisfiability problem.

Probabilities are a very simple and natural way to express preferences, while the work on preferences in the model checking approach is still beginning [136]. Utility functions are a simple and effective way to express competing criteria. While costs and probabilities can provide useful information in some domains, there are domains where modeling transitions with costs and/or probabilities is rather difficult and unnatural in practice, e.g., because not enough statistical data are available. In MDP-based planning, planning is performed through the construction of optimal policies with respect to rewards and probability distributions. As a consequence, it is not possible to force a planner based on probabilistic models to generate a solution that satisfies some logical requirements. For instance, if both a strong and a strong cyclic solution do exist, an MDP-based planner cannot be forced to find a strong solution that is guaranteed to avoid possible loops at execution time. However, we have also discussed how the temporal logic currently used in the model checking approach is not fully satisfactory for expressing extended goals (see Section 17.3.3).

The basic version of MDP algorithms can rarely scale up to relevant applications. However, a significant amount of work on large state MDPs has tried to address this problem (see, e.g., the work on factorized MDPs, abstraction, and symbolic representations mentioned in Chapter 16). The model checking approach to planning can exploit the use of BDD-based symbolic techniques that have been shown to outperform in many cases explicit state enumerative techniques. Planners based on symbolic model checking, like the Model Based Planner (MBP) [65][5] have been shown to outperform planners based on MDPs (such as GPT [83]) in several experimental benchmarks [66, 128]. However, these results should be interpreted carefully because the two approaches and the two kinds of planners solve different problems.

17.6 Discussion and Historical Remarks

The idea of planning by using explicit state model checking techniques has been around since the work by Kabanza *et al.* [293] and the relative planner SimPlan. In SimPlan, temporal goals can be expressed in an extension of Linear Temporal Logic (LTL), and the associated plans are constructed under the hypothesis of full observability. SimPlan relies on the *explicit-state* model checking paradigm, where

5. MBP is available at http://sra.itc.it/tools/mbp.

individual states are manipulated (rather than sets of states as in the planning algorithms presented in this chapter). The enumerative nature of this approach can be a major drawback in large domains. For this reason, in SimPlan, LTL formulas are also used to describe user-defined control strategies, which can provide aggressive pruning of the search space. This is done in the same style of control strategies in TLPlan [33]. LTL allows for the specification of temporally extended goals. Because LTL and CTL have incomparable expressiveness, the classes of problems solved by SimPlan are incomparable with those discussed in this chapter. For instance, LTL can express strong goals but not strong cyclic goals, which require properties of branching computation structures. However, LTL can express fairness conditions, such as "always eventually *p*," that cannot be expressed in CTL.

The idea of using model checking techniques became popular with the proposal of the "planning via symbolic model checking" paradigm (the one described in this chapter), which has shown how the approach can deal in practice with planning under uncertainty. The idea of planning as model checking was first introduced in two works [127, 234]. Strong planning was first proposed by Cimatti *et al.* [130]. Strong cyclic planning was also first proposed by Cimatti *et al.* [129] and then revised by Daniele *et al.* [137]. A full formal account and an extensive experimental evaluation of weak, strong, and strong cyclic planning were presented by Cimatti *et al.* [128]. The framework has been extended to deal with partial observability [66] and with extended goals [136, 440, 441]. All the results described in the works cited here have been implemented in the MBP [65].

Along this line, there have been different proposals. The work by Jensen and Veloso [281] exploits the idea of planning via symbolic model checking as a starting point for the work on the UMOP.[6] Jensen *et al.* extended the framework to deal with contingent events in their proposal for adversarial weak, strong, and strong cyclic planning [283]. They also provided a novel algorithm for strong and strong cyclic planning that performs heuristic-based, guided, BDD-based search for nondeterministic domains [282].

BDDs have also been exploited in classical planners (see Traverso *et al.* [511] for a report about BDD-based planners for classical planning in deterministic domains). Among them, MIPS [169] showed remarkable results in the AIPS '00 planning competition for deterministic planning domains. BDD-based planners like MIPS are specialized to deal with deterministic domains and are therefore more efficient than planners like MBP on classical planning domains. One of the reasons for this is the use of advanced mechanisms to encode PDDL planning problems into BDDs (see, e.g., [168]). An interesting open research issue is whether these encoding techniques can be lifted to the case of nondeterministic domains.

Other approaches are related to model checking techniques. Bacchus and Kabanza [33] use explicit-state model checking to embed control strategies expressed in LTL in TLPlan (see Chapter 10). The work by Goldman *et al.* [238, 240, 241] presents a method where model checking with timed automata is used to verify that generated plans meet timing constraints.

6. UMOP is available at http://www-2.cs.cmu.edu/ runej/publications/umop.html.

Finally, the SPUDD planner [269] makes use of Algebraic Decision Diagrams, data structures similar to BDDs, to do MDP-based planning. In SPUDD, decision diagrams are used to represent much more detailed information (e.g., the probabilities associated with transitions) than in planning as model checking. This partly reduces the main practical advantages of decision diagrams as they are used in planning as model checking.

17.7 Exercises

17.1 Consider Example 17.1 (see page 405) with the goal to move the robot to state s4. Let the set of initial states be s1 and s2. Are π_1, π_2, and π_3 weak, strong, or strong cyclic solutions?

17.2 In Example 17.1, with the goal to move the robot to state s4, modify the action move(r1,l1,l4) such that its outcome can also be in state s3. Write a weak solution, a strong solution, and a strong cyclic solution (if they exist).

17.3 In Example 17.1, with the goal to move the robot to state s4, modify the action move(r1,l1,l4) such that its outcome can also be in a dead end state s6. Write a weak solution, a strong solution and a strong cyclic solution (if they exist).

17.4 Suppose we translate the MDP planning problem of Exercise 16.8 into a nondeterministic planning problem in which start-fill and start-wash may either succeed or fail, and end-fill and end-wash are guaranteed to succeed.

(a) Draw the state-transition system. How many weak policies are there? How many strong policies? How many strong cyclic policies?

(b) Suppose that Dan wants both to wash the dishes and wash his clothes (and that both start-fill(x) and start-wash(x) may either succeed or fail, regardless of whether x = dw or x = wm). Draw the state-transition system for this problem. (Hint: The diagram will be quite large. To make it easier to draw, do not give names to the states, and use abbreviated names for the actions.)

(c) In the state-transition system of part (b), are there any states that Strong-Plan will not visit? How about Weak-Plan?

17.5 Consider Example 17.11 (see page 418). Consider the plan π shown in Table 17.3. Let the initial state be s1 and the goal state s4. Is π a weak, strong, or strong cyclic solution? What about the plan shown in Table 17.4?

17.6 In the DWR domain, consider the possibility that containers are downloaded dynamically from boats at different locations. Write the CTL goal that makes the robot move all the containers as they appear to a given location.

17.7 In the DWR domain, the robot cannot know whether there is a container in a given location unless the robot is in the location. Consider the goal to have all containers in a given location. Write a conditional plan that is a strong solution.

Table 17.3 First Plan for Exercise 17.5.

State	*Context*	*Action*	*Next state*	*Next context*
s1	c0	move(r1,l1,l4)	s1	c1
s1	c0	move(r1,l1,l4)	s4	c4
s4	c0	wait	s4	c0
s1	c1	move(r1,l1,l2)	s2	c2
s2	c2	move(r1,l2,l1)	s1	c2
s1	c2	move(r1,l1,l2)	s2	c2

Table 17.4 Second Plan for Exercise 17.5.

State	*Context*	*Action*	*Next state*	*Next context*
s1	c0	move(r1,l1,l4)	s1	c1
s1	c0	move(r1,l1,l4)	s4	c4
s4	c0	wait	s4	c0
s1	c1	move(r1,l1,l2)	s2	c2
s2	c2	move(r1,l2,l1)	s1	c0

17.8 Run MBP on the scenarios described in Examples 17.1, 17.5, 17.7, and 17.11 (see pages 405, 409, 411, and 418, respectively).

17.9 Using the scenario from Example 17.1, find a policy that satisfies the EaGLe goal Try Reach at(r1,l4) Fail Try Reach at(r1,l5).

Chapter 18

Uncertainty with Neoclassical Techniques

18.1 Introduction

In Chapters 16 and 17, we discussed two approaches devised to solve the problem of planning under uncertainty: planning based on Markov Decision Processes and planning based on model checking. In addition, some approaches originally devised for classical planning problems have been extended to deal with some form of uncertainty. Some of them are based on plan-space planning, state-space planning, planning-graph techniques, and planning as satisfiability.

In this chapter, we focus on extensions to two neoclassical techniques, planning as satisfiability (Section 18.2) and planning-graph techniques (Section 18.3), while other approaches are mentioned in Section 18.4. We limit our discussion to the case of conformant planning, i.e., the case of planning in nondeterministic domains, for reachability goals, and with null observability, where the generated plans are sequences of actions. See Section 18.4 for a general discussion on the relevance and efficiency of the two neoclassical approaches.

18.2 Planning as Satisfiability

In this section, we first define the notion of weak and strong conformant solutions (Section 18.2.1). We show how planning problems can be encoded as propositional formulas: nondeterministic effects result in disjunctions of propositions (Section 18.2.2). Finally, we describe a planning algorithm based on satisfiability techniques (Section 18.2.3) and briefly discuss Quantified Boolean Formulas (Section 18.2.4).

18.2.1 Planning Problems

A nondeterministic action can be described with the following operator:

Action
  preconditions: P
  deterministic effects: E
  nondeterministic effects: $N_1, \ldots, N_n$

where P is the set of literals that represent the preconditions, E is the set of literals that represent *deterministic effects* (i.e., effects that hold deterministically after the action is executed), and $N_1, \ldots, N_n$ are n sets of literals that represent *nondeterministic effects*. The intended meaning is that some of the N_i will actually take place, but we do not know which ones.

Example 18.1 Here is a nondeterministic action $\mathsf{move}(r, l, l')$ that either succeeds and moves the robot from location l to destination l' or fails and leaves the robot in its original location l.

$\mathsf{move}(r, l, l')$
  preconditions: $\mathsf{at}(r, l)$
  deterministic effects: $\{\}$
  nondeterministic effects: $\{\mathsf{at}(r, l'), \neg\, \mathsf{at}(r, l)\}, \{\}$

■

In the rest of this section, we write $\mathsf{precond}(a)$, $\mathsf{deterministic\text{-}effects}(a)$, and $\mathsf{nondeterministic\text{-}effects}(a)$ to denote the sets $\{P\}$, $\{E\}$, and $\{N_1, \ldots, N_n\}$, respectively. We further assume that for any action a, any nondeterministic effect N_i is consistent with the deterministic effects E, and $N_i \cup E$ cannot contain both a literal and its negation.

A weak conformant solution is a sequence of actions that may achieve the goal but is not guaranteed to do so. A strong conformant solution is a sequence of action that is guaranteed to reach the goal.

Definition 18.1 Let $P = (\Sigma, S_0, S_g)$ be a planning problem, where $\Sigma = (S, A, \gamma)$ is a nondeterministic state-transition system, $S_0 \subseteq S$ is the set of initial states, and $S_g \subseteq S$ is the set of goal states. As in Chapter 7, let (P, n), where $n \in \mathcal{N}^+$, be a bounded planning problem of length n, i.e., the problem of finding a plan of length n that satisfies the original planning problem. Let π be a sequence of actions $a_1, \ldots a_n$.

1. π is a *weak conformant solution* to the bounded planning problem (P, n) iff there exists a sequence of states $\langle s_0, \ldots, s_n \rangle$ such that $s_0 \in S_0$, $s_{i+1} \in \gamma(s_i, a)$ for each $i = 0, \ldots, n-1$, and $s_n \in S_g$.
2. π is a *strong conformant solution* to the bounded planning problem (P, n) iff $s_n \in S_g$ for every sequence of states $\langle s_0, \ldots, s_n \rangle$ such that $s_0 \in S_0$ and $s_{i+1} \in \gamma(s_i, a)$.

■

Notice that the notion of a weak conformant solution given in this section is even weaker than the notion of a weak solution given for planning based on model checking (Chapter 17). Here we just require that there be *at least one state* in the set of initial states such that there exists a path to the goal. In planning based on model checking, we require that there be at *least one path for each initial state.*

18.2.2 Planning Problems as Propositional Formulas

A planning domain Σ of a planning problem $P = (\Sigma, S_0, S_g)$ can be encoded as a propositional formula $\Phi(\Sigma)$. $\Phi(\Sigma)$ is a conjunct of smaller formulas for each action and for each fluent. As in Chapter 7, a_i stands for an action at step i of the bounded planning problem, $0 \leq i \leq n-1$. For each a_i there is a formula to say that if action a takes place at step i, then its preconditions must hold at step i and its effects will hold at the next step $i+1$. This formula is the conjunct of two smaller formulas, one for the deterministic effects and one for the nondeterministic ones:

$$a_i \Rightarrow \left(\bigwedge_{p \in \text{precond}(a)} p_i \wedge \bigwedge_{e \in \text{deterministic-effects}(a)} e_{i+1} \right) \tag{18.1}$$

$$a_i \Rightarrow \bigvee_{N \in \text{nondeterministic-effects}(a)} \; \bigwedge_{e \in N} e_{i+1} \tag{18.2}$$

Formula 18.1 is the same as Formula 7.11. Formula 18.2 states that an action a executed at step i implies that *some* of its nondeterministic effects are true at step $i+1$.

Explanatory frame axioms have to take into account both deterministic and nondeterministic effects. In the case of deterministic effects, it is enough to require that one of the actions that causes the effect has been executed at step i, as in Chapter 7. In the case of a nondeterministic effect $e \in N$, where $N \in \text{nondeterministic-effects}(a)$, we must require that all the effects in N hold at step $i+1$. Formally, for each fluent f and for each $0 \leq i \leq n-1$:

$$\begin{aligned} \neg f_i \wedge f_{i+1} \Rightarrow & \left(\bigvee\nolimits_{a \in A | f_i \in \text{deterministic-effects}^+(a)} a_i\right) \vee \\ & \bigvee\nolimits_{a \in A} \bigvee\nolimits_{N | N \in \text{nondeterministic-effects}^+(a), e \in N} \left(a_i \wedge \bigwedge\nolimits_{e' | e' \in N} e'_{i+1}\right) \end{aligned} \tag{18.3}$$

We have a similar formula for negative effects.

The complete exclusion axioms are the same as in the case of deterministic domains, i.e., for each $0 \leq i \leq n-1$, and for each distinct $a_i, b_i \in A$:

$$\neg a_i \vee \neg b_i \tag{18.4}$$

Therefore we have propositional formulas that encode action effects (see Formula 18.2), explanatory frame axioms (Formula 18.3), and complete exclusion axioms (Formula 18.4). Let $\Phi_i(\Sigma)$ be the conjunction of Formulas 18.2, 18.3, and 18.4. $\Phi_i(\Sigma)$ encodes the planning domain at step i. Let $\Phi(\Sigma)$ be the conjunction of $\Phi_i(\Sigma)$ for any $0 \leq i \leq n-1$:

$$\bigwedge_{i=0}^{n-1} \Phi_i(\Sigma)$$

$\Phi(\Sigma)$ encodes the planning domain. Given the planning problem $P = (\Sigma, S_0, S_g)$, the encoding of the initial states S_0 and of the goal states S_g is the same as for deterministic domains (see Chapter 7). Let $\Phi(S_0)$ and $\Phi(S_g)$ be the encodings of S_0 and S_g, respectively. Finally, Let $\Phi(P)$, or simply Φ, be the encoding of the bounded planning problem (P, n):

$$\Phi(S_0) \wedge \Phi(\Sigma) \wedge \Phi(S_g)$$

Example 18.2 Consider the planning problem P of Example 7.1 in Chapter 7. Suppose we modify this example so that the move operator is the one in Example 18.1. Suppose the robot is at l1 in the initial state and at l2 in the goal state. Consider the bounded planning problem $(P, 1)$. The action is encoded as the following formulas:

$$\mathsf{move(r1, l1, l2, 0)} \Rightarrow \mathsf{at(r1, l1, 0)} \qquad (18.5)$$

$$\mathsf{move(r1, l1, l2, 0)} \Rightarrow (\mathsf{at(r1, l2, 1)} \wedge \neg\mathsf{at(r1, l1, 1)}) \vee \mathit{True} \qquad (18.6)$$

$$\mathsf{move(r1, l2, l1, 0)} \Rightarrow \mathsf{at(r1, l2, 0)} \qquad (18.7)$$

$$\mathsf{move(r1, l2, l1, 0)} \Rightarrow (\mathsf{at(r1, l1, 1)} \wedge \neg\mathsf{at(r1, l2, 1)}) \vee \mathit{True} \qquad (18.8)$$

Notice that Formulas 18.6 and 18.8 are tautologies. Indeed, we have two states in the planning domain, and each action may lead to any state in the domain.

The explanatory frame axioms are:

$$\neg\mathsf{at(r1, l1, 0)} \wedge \mathsf{at(r1, l1, 1)} \Rightarrow \mathsf{move(r1, l2, l1, 0)} \wedge \neg\mathsf{at(r1, l2, 1)} \qquad (18.9)$$

$$\neg\mathsf{at(r1, l2, 0)} \wedge \mathsf{at(r1, l2, 1)} \Rightarrow \mathsf{move(r1, l1, l2, 0)} \wedge \neg\mathsf{at(r1, l1, 1)} \qquad (18.10)$$

■

Given a bounded planning problem (P, n), we can automatically construct the formula Φ encoding (P, n). The formula Φ can be used to find weak conformant solutions. Recall that, if Φ is satisfiable, then it is possible to extract a plan from one of its models μ (see Chapter 7).

Proposition 18.1 *Let (P, n) be a bounded planning problem. Let Φ be the encoding of (P, n). Let μ be a model of Φ. Then a plan extracted from μ is a weak conformant solution to the bounded planning problem (P, n).*

Now consider the problem of finding a strong conformant solution. This can be done as follows.

1. Generate weak plans by finding a model μ of Φ.
2. Check whether the weak plan is a strong plan.

The second of these two steps is a plan validation problem, i.e., the problem of determining whether a given plan satisfies some condition. A plan π extracted from a model μ can be represented by a propositional formula $\psi(\mu)$. For instance, given an assignment $\mu = \{\mathsf{move(r1, l1, l2, 0)}, \mathsf{move(r1, l2, l1, 1)}, \ldots\}$, $\psi(\mu)$ is $\mathsf{move(r1, l1, l2, 0)} \wedge \mathsf{move(r1, l2, l1, 1)}$. We have to find a formula Φ' such that for any μ' that is a model of $\psi(\mu) \wedge \Phi'$, the plan extracted from μ' is a strong solution to (P, n). In order to construct Φ', we start from the observation that any model of $\psi(\mu) \wedge \Phi$ is a strong solution if each action in A is executable in any state. Given a bounded planning problem (P, n) whose planning domain is the state-transition system Σ, we therefore construct a planning domain Σ' such that actions that are not executable in Σ are instead executable in Σ', and all of them lead to failure states. For each state s in Σ, Σ' contains both s and a failure state s' in which a special fluent *Fail* holds. $\Sigma' = (S', A', \gamma')$ is constructed from $\Sigma = (S, A, \gamma)$ as follows.

1. $S' = S \cup \{s \cup \mathit{Fail} \mid s \in S\}$.
2. A' is the same as A.
3. Let s_1' and s_2' be states of S'. Let $s_1 = s_1' - \{\mathit{Fail}\}$ and $s_2 = s_2' - \{\mathit{Fail}\}$ be two states of S. $s_2' \in \gamma'(s_1', a)$ iff one of the following is true.
   (a) *Fail* holds neither in s_1' nor in s_2', and $s_2 \in \gamma(s_1, a)$.
   (b) *Fail* holds only in s_2', and a is not executable in s_1 (i.e., $\neg \exists s | s \in \gamma(s_1, a)$).
   (c) *Fail* holds both in s_1' and in s_2'.

Each action is executable in Σ', and given a sequence $s_0, \ldots, s_n$ in Σ, where each $s_{i+1} \in \gamma(s_i, a_i)$, we have a corresponding sequence $s_0', \ldots, s_n'$, where *Fail* does not hold in each s_0', and $s_{i+1}' \in \gamma'(s_i', a_i)$. Let $\mathsf{executable}_i$ be the conjunction of the formulas

$$a_i \rightarrow \bigwedge_{p \in \mathsf{precond}(a)} p_i$$

over all actions $a \in A$. $\mathsf{executable}_i$ represents the executable actions at step i. Then $\Phi_i(\Sigma')$ is:

$$(\Phi(\Sigma) \wedge \neg \mathit{Fail}_i \wedge \neg \mathit{Fail}_{i+1}) \vee (\mathit{Fail}_i \vee \neg \mathsf{executable}_i) \wedge \mathit{Fail}_{i+1})$$

Because each action is executable in Σ', then the plan extracted from the model μ of Φ is a strong conformant solution if:

$$\psi(\mu) \wedge \Phi(S_0) \wedge \bigwedge_{i=0}^{n-1} \Phi_i(\Sigma') \models \Phi(S_g) \wedge \neg \mathit{Fail}_n$$

We therefore define Φ' as:

$$\psi(\mu) \wedge \Phi(S_0) \wedge \bigwedge_{i=0}^{n-1} \Phi_i(\Sigma') \wedge \neg\Phi(S_g) \vee Fail_n \tag{18.11}$$

We call Φ' the *strong encoding* of the bounded planning problem (P, n).

Example 18.3 In Example 18.2, Σ has two states, s_1 and s_2. at(r1,l1) holds in s_1, while at(r1,l2) holds in s_2. Σ' has four states, s'_1, s'_2, s'_3, and s'_4. State s_1 corresponds to s'_1 and s'_3 (*Fail* holds in s'_3), while s_2 corresponds to s'_2 and s'_4 (*Fail* holds in s'_4).

executable$_i$ is the conjunction of:

(pre1) move(r1,l1,l2,i) $\Rightarrow$ at(r1,l1,i)
(pre2) move(r1,l2,l1,i) $\Rightarrow$ at(r1,l2,i)

From executable$_i$ it is easy to construct $\Phi(\Sigma')$. ■

The following proposition says that if Φ' is satisfiable, then the plan extracted from the model μ is a strong conformant solution.

Proposition 18.2 *Let (P, n) be a bounded planning problem, ϕ be the encoding of (P, n), μ be a model of ϕ, and ϕ' be the strong encoding (P, n). If ϕ' is unsatisfiable, then a plan extracted from μ is a strong conformant solution to the bounded planning problem (P, n).*

18.2.3 Planning by Satisfiability

Now that we have translated the problems of finding weak and strong conformant solutions into satisfiability problems, we can use standard satisfiability decision procedures, such as Davis-Putnam (see Chapter 7) to plan for strong conformant solutions. Figure 18.1 shows Strong-Conformant-Davis-Putnam, a planning algorithm based on the Davis-Putnam satisfiability decision procedure. Strong-Conformant-Davis-Putnam iteratively calls Generate-Weak, which generates weak conformant solutions, and then Test-if-Strong, which tests whether the weak solutions are strong. Generate-Weak is essentially a Davis-Putnam procedure that calls Test-if-Strong whenever the procedure finds a model. In Test-if-Strong, the first line takes into account that the assignments generated by Generate-Weak may be partial. It is possible to prove that Strong-Conformant-Davis-Putnam is a sound and complete planning algorithm for a bounded planning problem.

18.2.4 QBF Planning

Planning based on Quantified Boolean Formulas (QBFs) [456] is a generalization of the planning as satisfiability approach. A bounded planning problem is

```
Strong-Conformant-Davis-Putnam()
    return Generate-Weak(Φ,∅)
end

Generate-Weak(φ,μ)
    if φ = ∅ then return Test-if-Strong(μ)
    if ∅ ∈ φ then return False
    if a unit clause L occurs in φ then
        return Generate-Weak(assign(L,φ),μ ∪ {L})
    P ← an atom occurring in φ
    return Generate-Weak(assign(P,φ),μ ∪ {P}) or
        Generate-Weak(assign(¬P,φ),μ ∪ {¬P})
end

Test-if-Strong(μ)
    for each assignment μ' such that μ ⊆ μ' do
        if Φ' is not satisfiable then exit with μ'
    return False
end
```

Figure 18.1 Algorithm for generating and testing strong conformant solutions.

reformulated as a QBF rather than in propositional logic. QBF solvers are employed in place of SAT solvers. QBF logic is a definitional extension to propositional logic, where propositional variables can be universally and existentially quantified (see Appendix C).

This approach can tackle a wide variety of conditional planning problems. The user must provide the structure of the plan to be generated (e.g., the length in the case of conformant planning, the number of control points and observations in the plan in the case of conditional planning). This can provide a significant limitation of the search space. In QBF planning, the points of nondeterminism are explicitly codified in terms of environment variables, with a construction known as *determinization of the transition relation.* In general, in this approach, as in the planning as satisfiability approach, it is impossible to decide whether the given problem admits a solution because it works on bounded planning problems.

18.3 Planning Graphs

We now discuss how to extend planning-graph techniques to deal with conformant planning. In Chapter 6 we explained planning-graph techniques for classical planning. Given a planning problem with a single initial state, the planner constructs a planning graph where the nodes at level 0 are the propositions denoting the initial state. The preconditions of deterministic actions are connected through action nodes to the effects, keeping track of mutual exclusion relations. Then a plan is extracted by searching the planning graph backward.

Uncertainty in the initial condition means that there is a set of possible states rather than just a single state. Uncertainty in actions' effects means that an action can lead to a set of states rather than a single state. The basic idea is to model uncertainty by using several different planning graphs, one for each possible initial state and one for each possible nondeterministic action outcome.

Given this idea, we can write algorithms for weak conformant planning. It is sufficient to take one graph at a time and work on it in the same way as in the deterministic case. In order to generate strong conformant plans instead, we cannot work on the different graphs independently of the others. It is necessary to consider possible interactions among the effects of the same action in different graphs: an action that has some desired effects in one graph may have some undesired effects in another graph. Therefore, the planning algorithm works as follows.

1. It constructs a separate planning graph for each possible initial state and each possible nondeterministic evolution.
2. It checks mutual exclusion relations not only within one graph but also among different graphs.
3. It extracts a plan with a backward search by checking at each level the effects of an action in all the graphs.

We illustrate the algorithm through a simple example in the DWR domain. For simplicity, in the example we have uncertainty only in the initial state, while actions are deterministic. The generalization of the algorithm to the case of nondeterministic actions is not trivial. However, the simple example should give at least an idea of how a planning-graph algorithm can deal with uncertainty in general.

Example 18.4 Figure 18.2 shows a DWR domain, in which there are a robot r1, a container c1, n locations l1, ..., ln, and a location dock. Proposition at(r1,l1) is true if the robot is in l1, unloaded is true if the robot is not loaded, and in(c1,l1) is true if c1 is in l1. Action unload unloads the robot, and move moves the robot to the dock.

```
unload                  move
  preconditions :         preconditions :
  Effects : unloaded      effects :
                            ¬at(r1, l1) when at(r1, l1), unloaded;
                            ¬at(r1, l1), in(c1, dock)when at(r1, l1), ¬unloaded;
                            in(c1, dock) when ¬at(r1, l1), ¬unloaded
```

Initially, the robot is either loaded in l1 or it is unloaded somewhere else. The goal is to move the robot out of l1 without delivering c1 to the dock,

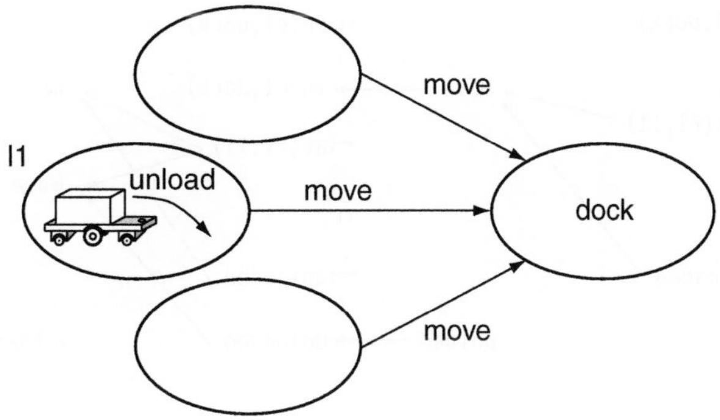

Figure 18.2 A simple DWR domain for conformant planning.

i.e., ¬at(r1,l1) ∧ ¬in(c1,dock). Notice that unload is applicable even if the robot is not loaded. The strong conformant plan is to unload the robot first, and then move it to the dock.

Figure 18.3 shows the two graphs corresponding to the two initial states expanded up to level 4.

■

We now illustrate how the strong conformant algorithm works on this example. The algorithm expands both graphs first, then it searches for a solution separately in each graph, and finally it checks whether a candidate solution for one graph is acceptable for the other ones. The first time, the algorithm expands both planning graphs up to to level 2 because, in both graphs, this level contains the two propositions of the goal ¬at(r1,l1) and ¬in(c1,dock).

The algorithm analyzes the two graphs separately. In G1, the two goal propositions are both initially true. In G2, ¬at(r1,l1) at level 2 is achieved by move, while ¬in(c1,dock) is initially true. There are no mutex relations between actions. A potential solution is therefore action move of the second graph, i.e., move applied to the robot in l1. An alternative potential solution extracted from the first graph is doing nothing.

The algorithm then checks the effects of the potential solution of a graph in all the other graphs. In the example, move in graph G1 has an undesired effect: in(c1,dock). This means that move is not a strong conformant solution. Similarly, doing nothing in G2 leads to at(r1,l1). No backtracking alternative remains; therefore, the algorithm has to further expand the graph. This expansion leads to level 4.

The two graphs are again analyzed separately. In G1, the two goal propositions are both already true at level 2, so no action is needed, while in G2, the algorithm selects the occurrence of move that has at(r1,l1) and unloaded as preconditions because it leads to the goal proposition ¬at(r1,l1).

The algorithm then checks the effects of move in the other graph, G1. This time we have two possibilities: we have one occurrence of move that has the undesired effect

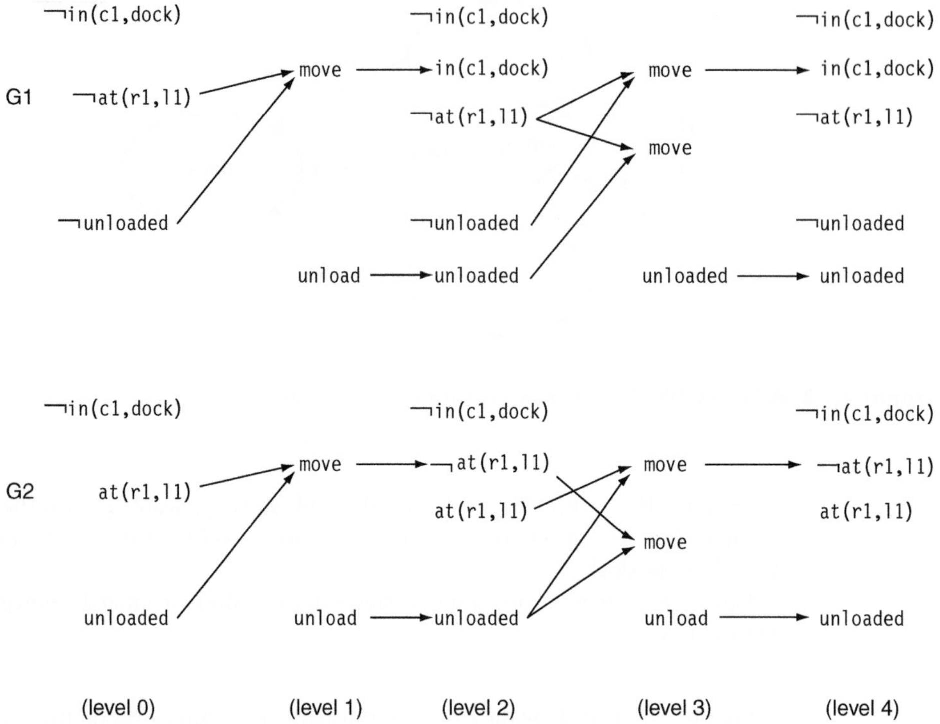

Figure 18.3 Examples of planning graphs for conformant planning.

in(c1,dock) and one occurrence that has no effects. The algorithm can therefore detect that the former should be avoided. The algorithm at this point checks the preconditions of the two occurrences of move: ¬at(r1,l1) is common to both, while ¬unloaded is a precondition of the dangerous occurrence. This precondition should be negated; unloaded is therefore chosen as a subgoal at level 2.

Extraction continues at level 2, where action unload is chosen and analyzed in both graphs. The final conformant plan is the sequence ⟨unload, move⟩.

18.4 Discussion and Historical Remarks

In this chapter, we focused on two neoclassical approaches, satisfiability and planning-graph techniques, as representative cases of approaches originally devised to deal with classical planning that were later extended to deal with uncertainty. So far they can deal with a rather limited portion of the problems in planning under uncertainty: planning as satisfiability can deal only with conformant planning

[109, 110, 188, 231], while planning-graph techniques can deal with conformant planning [490] and some limited form of partial observability [545]. Other than satisfiability and planning-graph techniques, different approaches have addressed the problem of conformant planning. Among them is extension to situation calculus (see Chapter 12), where hand-coded control strategies (in the style of those described in Chapter 10) have been used to significantly prune the search.

Conformant planning is a very particular case of planning under uncertainty. It does not seem to be of relevance to most planning problems, such as those in robotics, where the robot eventually has to do some sensing, otherwise it is lost. Claims that conformant planning can be applied to real-world applications are unsupported except for very peculiar cases, for instance, in the so-called "home sequencing" problem (i.e., the problem of executing a sequence of instructions that makes a microprocessor move to a desired set of states). In this case no observation is possible because memory variables are not readable.

A question is whether satisfiability and planning-graph techniques can scale up to problems of interesting size. While the question remains open for techniques based on satisfiability, planning-graph techniques have been significantly outperformed in several experimental evaluations by techniques based on model checking (Chapter 17), greedy search applied to the MDP framework, and satisfiability itself. On the other hand, we have to recall that planning-graph techniques outperformed earlier classical approaches to uncertainty, such as plan-space planning.

Indeed, the first attempts to deal with uncertainty were the pioneering extensions to plan-space planning [438, 448, 543]. This work has been referred to as *conditional planning*. The basic idea is to extend plan-space algorithms to take into account different alternatives and to generate strong solutions. In general, this approach has been considered a limited form of nondeterminism through the use of an extension of classical STRIPS operators called *conditional actions* (i.e., actions with different, mutually exclusive sets of outcomes). A major problem with this approach is the inability to deal in practice even with simple toy problems.

18.5 Exercises

18.1 Can a policy (as defined in Chapters 16 and 17) be translated into a conformant plan? Vice versa?

18.2 Does a weak or strong conformant solution exist for the planning problem in Example 17.1?

18.3 Describe the SAT encoding of Example 17.1.

18.4 Describe the CGP graph for the planning problem of Example 17.1.

18.5 How would the graphs in Figure 18.3 change in the case of partial observability?

Part VI

Case Studies and Applications

The variety of applications for automated planning is becoming quite significant. For example, the web repository of PLANET, the European network on automated planning, refers to about 20 applications in aeronautics and space, agricultural, industrial, commercial, and military domains,[1] and this list is doubtless incomplete. The Chapters in this part do not give a comprehensive survey of these planning applications. Rather, they provide case studies to illustrate some of the issues and approaches.

The application domains for our case studies include control of spacecraft (Chapter 19), robotics (Chapter 20), computer-aided design and manufacturing (Chapter 21), emergency rescue operations (Chapter 22), and the game of bridge (Chapter 23). In some cases (Chapters 19, 20, and 23), the systems have been successfully deployed, and some of them have made newspaper headlines. Other cases (Chapters 21 and 22) remain at the level of research prototypes. But in all cases, the focus is on how to address the issues that are important in the application domain at hand.

The planning paradigms that appear in our case studies include forward search, HTN planning, temporal and resource planning, MDP planning, plan merging, and case-based planning. HTN planning seems to be especially useful—various forms of it appear in all but one of our case studies—because it provides a flexible and efficient way to encode domain-specific knowledge about how to solve a problem. In several of the case studies, HTN planning is combined with other planning techniques: e.g., MDPs and HTNs in the robotics chapter, and HTNs and case-based planning in the chapter on emergency evacuation.

---

1. See http://www.planet-noe.org/ and http://scom.hud.ac.uk/planet/repository/.

Although the planning systems described in these chapters are based on general planning paradigms, most of the systems are *domain-specific*: they rely on representations and algorithms designed specifically for their respective application domains, and most of the systems were built by teams that included both planning researchers and domain experts. From a software engineering perspective, domain-independent planning is far behind areas such as database management, where it is comparatively easy to use off-the-shelf database server products.

In order to work effectively on practical applications, planning researchers must adjust how they think about planning problems. In research on automated planning, the typical approach has been to create an abstract class of problems that omit various details of a problem and then to look for general ways to solve problems in that class. In contrast, practical applications generally require a planning researcher to develop an understanding of the specific characteristics and requirements of the application domain at hand.

Some of the issues include the following.

- *How to acquire, validate, and verify information about the planning domain.* Some of the necessary information may be informal, anecdotal, proprietary, or otherwise hard to obtain and formalize.
- *What constitutes a planning problem, what constitutes a solution, and which simplifying assumptions might be appropriate.* What a planning researcher may consider to be an "unimportant detail" may, from the viewpoint of a domain expert, be a critical part of the problem. Assumptions that look appropriate to a planning researcher may not look credible to a domain expert, and vice versa.
- *How to represent the information and what planning paradigm(s) to use.* Often the approach will need to incorporate some domain-specific heuristics and algorithms, as well as *ad hoc* tweaks to handle special cases.
- *How best to interact with human users and/or how to integrate the planning system into the architecture of a larger system.* In some cases a fully automated planning system or subsystem may be the most appropriate approach, and in others it may be better to build a system that provides decision support while keeping the human user in charge of the planning process.

Developing an understanding of an application domain can be time-consuming, but the effort can be very worthwhile—not just to enable the development of useful planning tools but also to develop planning techniques that may be useful in other settings. In many of our case studies, research on specific applications has led to significant advances in planning theory, and advances in planning theory have led to better planning applications.

Chapter 19

Space Applications

19.1 Introduction

There are several applications of different planning technologies to space exploration. This chapter is mainly devoted to the description of NASA's Deep Space 1 (DS1) mission, a significant application of automated planning to spacecraft. We will described the Autonomous Remote Agent (RA) system, software based on planning and scheduling techniques, which ran on board a spacecraft for several days during the DS1 mission. Our description of DS1 is based largely on the NASA and JPL report [63].

19.2 Deep Space 1

Launched from Cape Canaveral on October 24, 1998, DS1 was the first mission of NASA's new millennium program chartered to test in space new technologies devised by NASA as strategic for future space science programs. The spacecraft was retired in December 18, 2001, after it completed the DS1 mission successfully by encountering Comet Borrelly and returning the best images and other science data ever returned from a comet (Figure 19.1). DS1 successfully tested 12 advanced technologies, including novel electronic, solar, and control devices and novel software components. The RA software system, which comprises automated planning techniques, was successfully tested during an experiment onboard DS1 between May 17 and May 21, 1999.

19.3 The Autonomous Remote Agent

The increased need for a high level of autonomy on board spacecrafts is the main original motivation for the use of automated planning technology in the DS1 mission [63, 410]. In the new millennium, NASA plans to build more and more

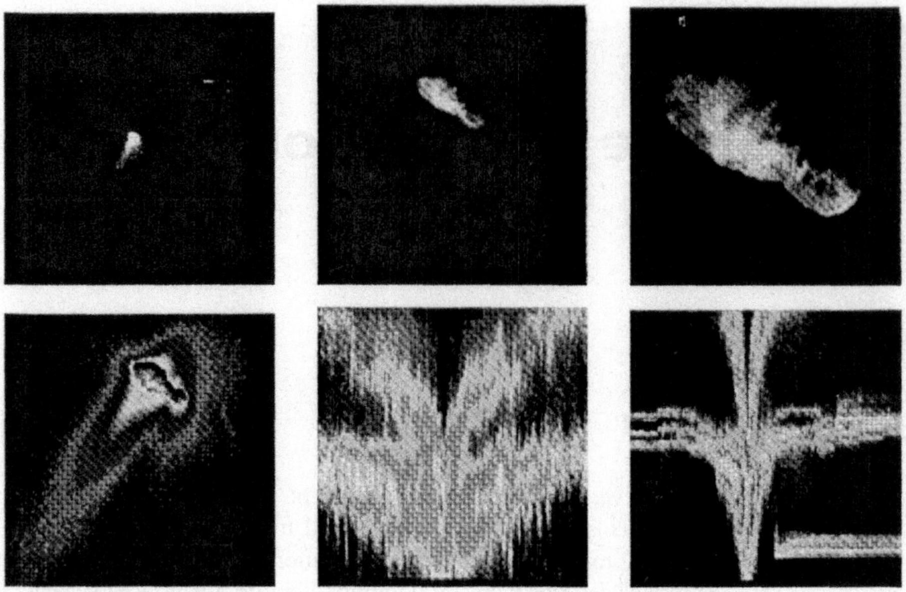

Figure 19.1 Some DS1 pictures of Comet Borrelly.

spacecrafts that must operate without human intervention on board or with limited intervention. Onboard autonomy can reduce the cost of ground control and increase functionality, robustness, flexibility, and adaptation to context.

RA is an onboard software system based on AI techniques. It is able to plan, execute, and monitor spacecraft activities. Its main novel characteristic is that it enables goal-based spacecraft commanding integrated with a robust fault recovery mechanism. A main difference with traditional spacecraft commanding is that ground operators can communicate with RA using goals, such as "during the next period, take pictures of the following asteroids," rather than with detailed sequences of timed commands to the flight software components, such as "at time T1, change the orientation of the spacecraft to D degrees; at time T2, turn on switch number X of camera Y with filter F and brightness level B" and so on.

Given a set of high-level goals, RA is able to generate automatically a plan of actions that achieves those goals and executes the plan by issuing commands to the spacecraft. Actions are represented with high-level tasks that, in order to be executed, need to be decomposed on-the-fly into more detailed tasks and, eventually, into commands to the underlying flight software. The RA component is integrated and can work in closed loop with the underlying real-time execution software that directly controls the spacecraft devices, e.g., the actuators that determine the orientation of the spacecraft and those that control the position of the cameras taking pictures of asteroids. When anomalies are detected (e.g., in the form of failures signaled by spacecraft components or discrepancies between the state expected by RA and the one monitored through spacecraft devices), RA is able to detect, interpret, and respond to failures and anomalies. This can be done either at the execution level or at the planning level, depending on the kind of failure or anomaly. In the case of anomalies that can be repaired at the execution level, RA responds to failures in real time, without any need to suspend the normal activities of the spacecraft. Failures that need to be addressed by replanning require longer response times because RA needs to generate new plans. During the replanning phase, the spacecraft is kept idle in a safe configuration.

RA allows the spacecraft to operate at different levels of increasing autonomy. Operators at the ground station can interact with the spacecraft with detailed sequences of real-time commands. RA executes and monitors the commands through the underlying flight software. This interaction mode allows the operators to interact with the onboard system in the traditional way. Ground operators can also send high-level tasks to the RA on board. RA decomposes the tasks on-the-fly into more detailed tasks and into commands to the underlying flight software. Similarly, ground operators can send goals to the RA on board. RA generates a plan and executes it by monitoring its execution. This is the fully automatic mode.

19.4 The Remote Agent Architecture

The RA architecture is shown in Figure 19.2. RA sends commands to the Real Time Flying Software (FSW), i.e., the software that controls the spacecraft devices (e.g., engines, cameras). It receives data about the actual status of the spacecraft through a set of monitors that filter and discretize sensor values. This communication can be done directly between RA and FSW, or it can be mediated by the Remote Agent Experiment Manager (RAXM), which provides an interface to run-time monitors in the FWS and to the real-time sequencer, which executes detailed sequences of commands. RAXM allows RA to be cleanly bundled on top of the existing flying software and thus makes it reusable in further experiments. Moreover, RA relies on specialized services provided by software modules external to RA, e.g., automated navigation facilities that provide information about asteroid positions.

The RA software is structured in three main components: the Planner and Scheduler (PS), the Smart Executive (EXEC), and the Mode Identification and Recovery (MIR) module. Indeed, RA's ability to provide goal-based spacecraft commanding with robust fault recovery is due to the tight integration of three AI technologies: automated planning and scheduling performed by the PS component, robust multithread execution provided by EXEC, and the model-based fault diagnosis and recovery mechanism of the MIR module. The Mission Manager (MM) is an additional component that stores the mission profile, which contains a set of goals received from the ground station (through the FWS) and selects and

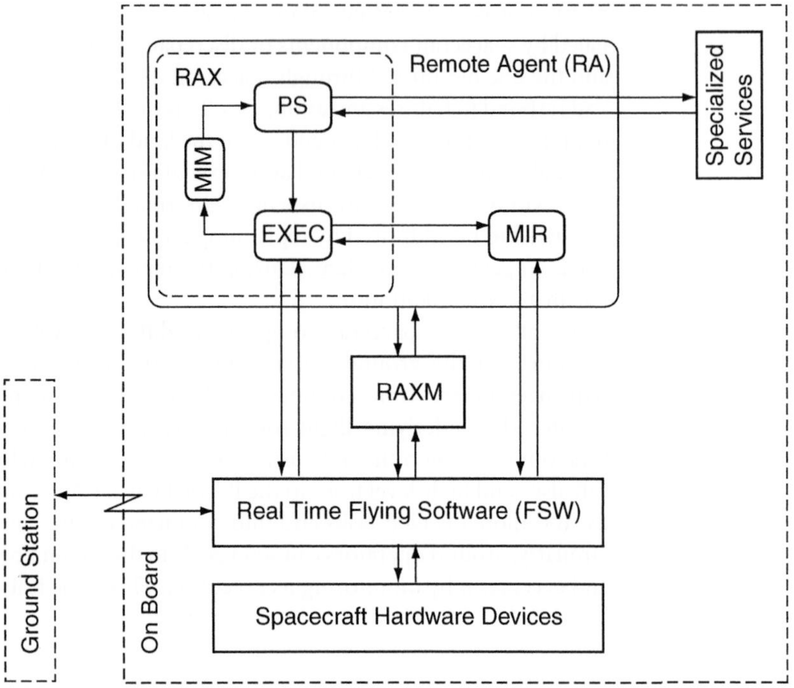

Figure 19.2 RA architecture.

sends to PS the goals related to the period when they need to be processed by PS component. The goals in the MM mission profile can be changed, e.g., on a week-by-week basis. The collection of the PS, EXEC, and MM modules is called the RAX module.

RA translates high-level goals into a stream of commands for FSW in two steps. First, MM selects goals for the next commanding horizon (e.g., two days) and sends them to PS. PS plans for and schedules the tasks that achieve the goals by using its model of the spacecraft. This activity may require that PS gets information from the specialized services. For example, a goal can be described as "perform orbit determination activities for 1 hour every day." PS determines that pictures of beacon asteroids need to be taken. In order to select these asteroids, PS interrogates the specialized service for autonomous navigation. Therefore, the task translates into taking a series of images of the asteroids with a particular camera. Moreover, PS knows that while images of an asteroid are being recorded, the orientation (called more specifically the *attitude*) of the spacecraft must be compatible with the target of the cameras pointing at it. If this is not the case, PS schedules an appropriate turn, changing the orientation so that it is compatible with the cameras pointing at the asteroid.

EXEC is responsible for sending the appropriate commands to the various flight systems it is managing. It is a multithreaded, reactive control system that is capable of asynchronously executing commands in parallel. It does much more than simply executing low-level commands. It is responsible for the following tasks.

- *Executing plans from PS by expanding tasks.* Because PS generates high-level tasks that are not directly executable by FWS, EXEC needs to expand these task at run-time. It provides a procedural language, called ESL [210], in which spacecraft software developers define how complex tasks are broken up into simple ones.
- *Controlling failure handling and recoveries at different levels.* In the event of a failure, EXEC attempts a recovery, either by executing a prespecified recovery sequence, by requesting a failure recovery to MIR, or by requesting a replanning activity to PS.
- *Reactively controlling the execution of commands.* EXEC exhibits its reactive behavior by performing event-driven and conditional commands that depend on conditions that occur at execution time.
- *Achieving and maintaining safe modes as necessary.* As a consequence of its reactive capability, EXEC is able to reach and maintain desired system states by monitoring the success of commands it issues and reactively reachieving states that are lost.
- *Managing time and resources flexibly.* EXEC is able to execute plans with soft time constraints [403], where time deadlines are specified as ranges rather than fixed time points. This decreases significantly the probability of execution failures due to time constraints. Moreover, EXEC manages resources whose constraints have not been resolved by the planner or by the ground operator. This is done by monitoring resource availability and usage, allocating resources to tasks when available, and suspending or aborting tasks if resources become unavailable due to failures [210, 211].

MIR is the component devoted to monitoring faults and diagnosing recovering actions. As each command is executed, MIR receives observations from spacecraft sensors, abstracted by monitors in lower-level device managers like those for cameras, bus controllers, and so on. MIR uses an inference engine called Livingstone to combine these commands and observations with declarative models of the spacecraft's components. Livingstone is composed of two main components: the Mode Identification (MI) and the Mode Recovery (MR) components (see Figure 19.3).

MI is responsible for identifying the current operating or failure mode of each component in the spacecraft, allowing EXEC to reason about the state of the spacecraft in terms of components' modes, rather than in terms of low-level sensor values. MI observes EXEC issuing commands, receives sensor observations from monitors, and uses model-based inference [553] to deduce the state of the spacecraft and to provide feedback to EXEC.

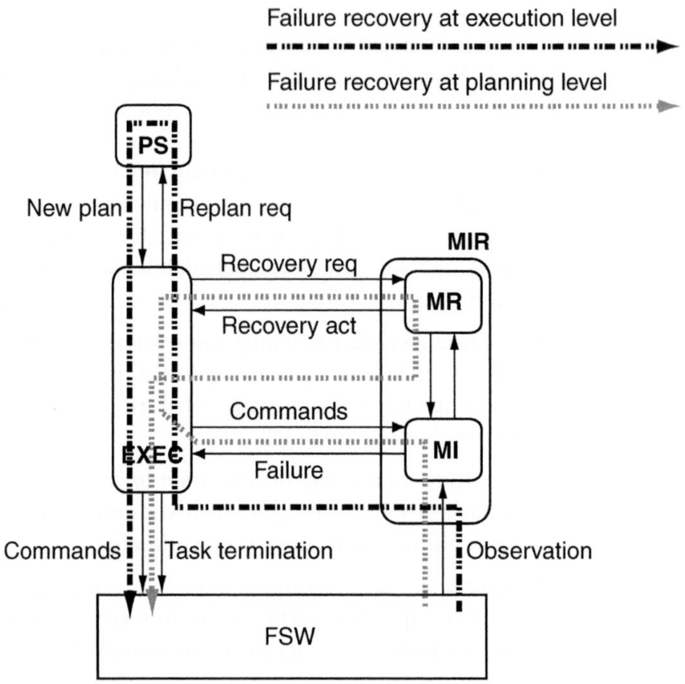

Figure 19.3 Failure recovery at the executing and planning levels.

MR is responsible for suggesting reconfiguration actions that move the spacecraft to a configuration that achieves all current goals as required by PS and EXEC. MR serves as a recovery expert, taking as input a set of EXEC constraints to be established or maintained, and recommends recovery actions to EXEC that will achieve those constraints.

MIR, EXEC, and possibly PS are involved in failure recovery, which can be performed either at the execution level or at the planning level (as depicted in Figure 19.3). The following subsections briefly discuss these two situations.

Failure Recovery at the Execution Level. This situation involves EXEC and MIR in the context of executing a single task generated by PS. Suppose that EXEC is commanding that a camera turn on in order to ensure that the camera is active during a task. EXEC does so by sending an appropriate command to the power driver. MI observes the command and, on the basis of its previous state estimate and its models, predicts the likely next state in which the system will be. Each component state or mode is captured using abstract, or qualitative, models [553], i.e., models that describe the spacecraft's structure or behavior without numerical details. These models cannot quantify how the spacecraft would perform with a failed component, but they can be used to infer which component failed. Livingstone uses algorithms adapted from model-based diagnosis [431, 547] to predict the likely next state and thus the possible failure. In model-based diagnosis, a combination of component modes is a description of the current state of the spacecraft only if the set of models associated with these modes is consistent with the observed sensor values. MI uses a conflict-directed, best-first search to find the most likely combination of component modes consistent with the observations.

The prediction of the likely next state has to be confirmed by MR reading the sensors of the spacecraft, e.g., the switch sensor and the current sensor should be consistent with the camera's power status. If the expected observations are not received, MI uses its model to hypothesize the most likely cause of the unexpected observations in terms of failures of the spacecraft's components. The information about the new state of the spacecraft hardware is sent to EXEC, which now asks MIR for an action to correct the problem. MIR activates MR, which, using the same model, determines the least-cost system state that satisfies EXEC's request and one that is reachable from the fault mode. MIR then gives to EXEC the first action in a possible sequence that will take the system to that state. Such a recovery may involve resetting a device, attempting a command again, or performing a complex reconfiguration of the spacecraft to enable a redundant system. EXEC executes the recovery action (always monitored by MIR) and receives further actions from MIR if needed. When the recovery is complete, EXEC continues to execute the recovery task in a nominal fashion.

Failure Recovery at the Planning Level. This is essentially a replanning activity triggered by MIR and then performed by EXEC and PS. This failure recovery mechanism is activated in the case the failure recovery at the execution level fails, i.e., all the recovery action sequences suggested by MIR fail. For example, if MIR does not manage to recover from the failure to turn on the camera, then it infers that the camera cannot be used. EXEC then knows there is no way to execute the command with success. Therefore EXEC terminates execution with a failure, discards the rest of the plan, and commands the spacecraft to enter an RA stand-by mode. EXEC then asks PS to replan (i.e., to generate a new plan) by passing PS the new initial state. PS receives the goals from MM, generates the new plan, and sends it to EXEC. EXEC exits the stand-by mode, resumes normal operations, and starts the execution of the new plan.

19.5 The Planner Architecture

The architecture of the PS module is shown in Figure 19.4. PS consists of a Search Engine (SE) operating over a constraint-based Temporal Database (TDB). SE begins with an incomplete plan and expands it into a complete plan by posting additional constraints in TDB. These constraints originate from (a) the goals that PS receives in input from MM, and (b) from the constraints stored in a Domain Model (DM) of the spacecraft. DM describes a set of actions, how goals decompose into actions,

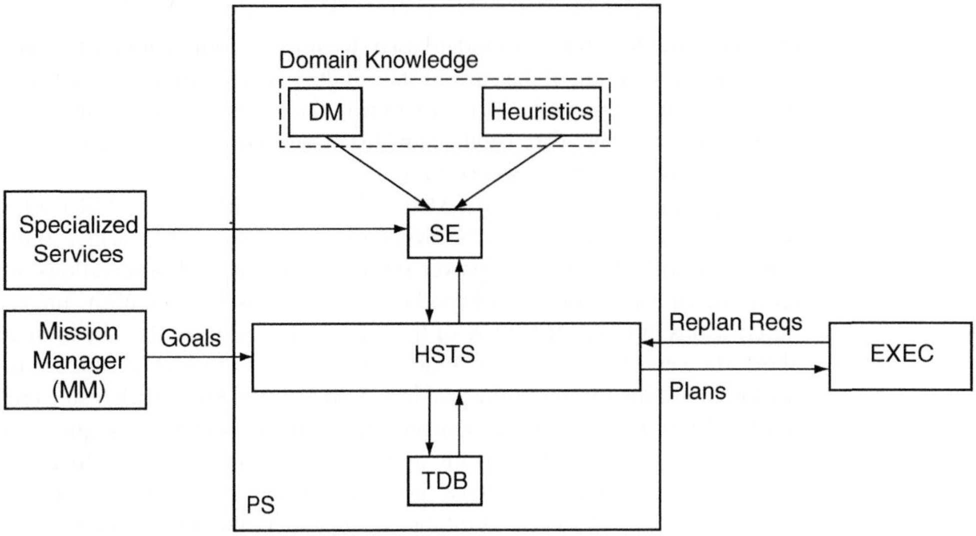

Figure 19.4 PS architecture.

the constraints among the actions, and resource utilization by the actions. For instance, DM encodes constraints such as "do not take images with the camera while thrusting." Access to TDB and DM is provided through the Heuristic Scheduling Testbed System (HSTS).

SE is domain-independent and implements a rather simple search mechanism with chronological backtracking. Because the search space is usually huge and the time allocated to the plan generation activity is limited, a domain-independent search would rarely generate a plan in the required time. Thus a very important component of PS is the module containing domain-dependent Heuristics, which guides the search depending on the domain.

PS tightly integrates planning and scheduling capabilities (see the discussion on this topic in Chapter 14). The planner needs to recursively select and schedule appropriate activities to achieve mission goals. It also needs to synchronize activities and allocate global resources over time (e.g., power and data storage capacity). Subgoals can be generated due to the limited availability of a resource. For example, it may be preferable to keep scientific instruments on as long as possible to gather as much information as possible. However, limited resource availability may schedule a temporary shutdown to allocate resources to mission-critical subsystems. In this case, the result of scheduling generates a subgoal, i.e., "turn scientific instruments off," which requires a planning activity. Therefore PS considers the consequences of action planning and resource scheduling simultaneously (see the general motivations for this choice in Chapter 14).

In the following subsections, we describe in more detail (with some examples) domain models, goals, constraints, plans, and the search algorithm used in the SE module. PS needs to take into account time and resources, where actions can occur concurrently and can have different durations, and goals can include time and different kinds of constraints, such as maintenance constraints. For instance, some control procedures of the spacecraft need to be executed either before, after, or in parallel with other procedures.

- The spacecraft orientation must be maintained so that it points at a direction d for all the time during which the engine is thrusting in a given direction d.
- A procedure that turns the orientation of the spacecraft from direction d_1 to direction d_2 can occur only after a procedure that has maintained the orientation at direction d_1, and it should precede a procedure that maintains the direction at d_2.

Examples of goals are the requirement to achieve the correct thrust vector of the spacecraft engine within a given deadline and the request to take a specified sequence of pictures in parallel with providing a certain level of thrust.

The Domain Model. DM is based on *state variables* and *timelines* (same as in Chapter 14), i.e., histories of states for a state variable over a period of time. Examples of state variables are *engine* and *orientation*. The former represents the status of the engine of the spacecraft, which can be either idle or thrusting in a direction d, i.e., thrust(d). The latter represents the orientation of the spacecraft, which can be turning from a direction d_1 to a direction d_2 (in which case its value is turn(d_1,d_2)) or can be pointing to a fixed direction d (with value point(d)). A further example is the variable *camera*, representing a camera that can take pictures of the surrounding space from the spacecraft. One of its values can be take-picture(b,f), representing the fact that the camera is taking a picture, where the parameter b is the brightness level of a target object and f is the camera filter. Notice that the values of state variables, such as thrust(d), turn(d_1,d_2), and take-picture(b,f), denote the control procedures of the spacecraft, and they contain parameters, e.g., the parameters d_1 and d_2 of the procedure turn(d_1,d_2).

In the following discussion, we call the value of a state variable over an interval a *token*. State variables are piecewise constant functions of time; each such piece is a token. Formally, a token is the tuple (x, p, t_0, t_1), where x is a state variable, and p is a procedure for the state variable x. The procedure p is active in the interval from the start time t_0 to the end time t_1. Thus, for instance, (*orientation*, turn(36, 38), 1,10) means that the spacecraft is changing orientation from 36 to 38 in the period from time 1 to time 10. Tokens can contain parameters, as in the case (*orientation*, turn(d_1, d_2), t_0, t_1), where d_1, d_2, t_0, and t_1 are variables. More generally, a token is $(x, p(y_1, \ldots, y_n), t_0, t_1)$, where $y_1, \ldots, y_n$ are the parameters that denote the variables of the procedure p.

```
(define Compatibility
    ;; compats on SEP-Thrusting
    (SEP-Thrusting ?heading ?level ?duration)
    :compatibility-spec
    (AND
        (equal (DELTA MULTIPLE (Power) (+2416 Used)))
        (contained-by (Constant-Pointing ?Heading))
        (met-by (SEP-Stand-by))
        (meets (SEP-Stand-by)))
)
```

Figure 19.5 Temporal constraints in DDL.

Goals. Goals are represented as constraints on tokens. Given two tokens $T_1 = (x_1, p_1(y_1, \ldots, y_n), s_1, e_1)$ and $T_2 = (x_2, p_2(z_1, \ldots, z_m), s_2, e_2)$, constraints can be of the following kinds.

- *Equality constraints* exist between parameters of procedures, e.g., $y_j = z_k$, with $1 \leq j \leq n$ and $1 \leq k \leq m$.
- *Temporal constraints* exist between the start and end time variables, e.g., s_1, e_1 of token T_1 and s_2, e_2 of token T_2. We allow for the temporal relations of interval algebra, described in Section 13.3.2, e.g., *before, after, during, meet,* and *is-met-by.*

For instance, the constraint that the thrusting procedure can be executed only while the orientation is maintained can be expressed by the constraint *during*$([s_1, e_1],[e_2, s_2])$, where $T_1 = (\mathit{engine}, \mathsf{thrust}(d), s_1, e_1)$ and $T_2 = (\mathit{orientation}, \mathsf{point}(d), s_2, e_2)$. More generally, goals are conjunctions and disjunctions of these kinds of constraints. Each atomic constraint of a goal is called a *subgoal.*

In DS1, constraints are called *compatibilities* and are encoded in a declarative form called Domain Description Language (DDL). Figure 19.5 shows an example of a DDL description of a temporal constraint. The master token (at the head of the compatibility) is SEP-Thrusting (when the Solar Electric Propulsion, or SEP, engine is producing thrust), which must be immediately preceded and followed by an SEP-Stand-by token (when the SEP engine is in a stand-by mode but has not been completely shut off). The master token must be temporally contained by a Constant-Pointing token. The complete thrusting activity requires 2,416 watts of power. The Constant-Pointing token implies that the spacecraft is in a steady state aiming its camera toward a fixed target in space.

Plans. In DS1, plans are special cases of chronicles, as described in Chapter 14. Candidate plans are refined incrementally by the planner until they are a solution for the given goal. A candidate plan contains the following elements.

- A horizon (h_s, h_e) represents the time window considered by the plan.
- A set of timelines, i.e., sequences of tokens $(T_1, \ldots, T_k)$, contains one token for each state variable x, with $T_i = (x, p(y_1, \ldots, y_m), s_i, e_i)$.
- Ordering constraints enforce that each token in the sequence is followed by the next token, i.e., $h_s \leq s_1 \leq e_1 \leq s_2 \leq \ldots \leq e_{n-1} \leq s_n \leq e_n \leq h_e$.
- A set of equality and temporal constraints enforces required conditions.

The Search Engine. SE starts from an initial candidate plan, which includes a finite horizon of interest (i.e., the time window we want to plan for), an initial timeline (i.e., an initialization token for each state variable), and a set of ordering, equality, and temporal constraints. This specifies the planning problem. It is a special case of temporal planning problems, as specified in Section 14.3.3. It specifies the initial condition with the initial timeline and the goal with the set of constraints. In general, a candidate plan contains *flaws*, i.e., elements that prevent the plan from being a solution plan. Flaws are uninstantiated variables, floating tokens (i.e., timelines with gaps between tokens), disjunctions of constraints, and unsatisfied constraints. The job of plan generation is to resolve the flaws and transform the initial candidate plan into a solution plan. Moreover, the constraints in a candidate plan give rise to a constraint network consisting of the variables in the tokens of the plan and the constraints that link token variables. Constraint propagation techniques (see Chapter 8) are therefore used to eliminate inconsistent values.

Different methods for controlling the search, selecting flaws to be resolved, and propagating constraints can be chosen. In its basic framework, the planning procedure is a recursive function that nondeterministically selects a resolution for a flaw in the current candidate plan. In practice, however, the version of the planner installed in DS1 makes use of a user-defined and domain-dependent search control mechanism that restricts significantly the amount of search needed. A first mechanism to control the search is a *flaw agenda*, which specifies a priority among the flaws to be resolved. The order of the flaws in the agenda defines a priority and a sorting strategy for the nondeterministic choices of the basic plan generation algorithm. A second mechanism is the introduction of new pruning mechanisms in the Heuristics module through a language for the specification of domain-dependent control strategies (see Part III). These pruning mechanisms are at the price of completeness, but they actually make it possible to generate plans that control the behaviors of a spacecraft.

19.6 The Deep Space 1 Experiment

The DS1 mission was designed to validate nonstandard technologies for space exploration, among which were the technologies applied in the RA component. In this section, we discuss the validation objectives, the scenarios, and the experiment results, as well as some lessons learned for the future.

19.6.1 Validation Objectives

The main objective was to demonstrate that RA could autonomously operate the DS1 spacecraft with communication from the ground limited to a few high-level goals for an extended period of time. This translated into specific objectives for RA's main components, i.e., PS, EXEC, and MIR.

- PS validation objectives:
  - Generate plans on board the spacecraft.
  - Reject low-priority unachievable goals.
  - Replan following a simulated failure.
  - Enable modification of mission goals from the ground.
- EXEC validation objectives:
  - Provide a low-level commanding interface.
  - Initiate onboard planning.
  - Execute plans generated on board and from the ground.
  - Recognize and respond to plan failures.
  - Maintain required properties in the face of failures.
- MIR validation objectives:
  - Confirm EXEC command execution.
  - Demonstrate failure detection, isolation, and recovery.
  - Demonstrate the ability to update MIR state via ground commands.

Beyond these main objectives, other validation objectives addressed the impact of the introduction of RA into "traditional" spacecraft software architecture. RA was designed to be integrated with the existing flying software (FSW), and a validation objective was to demonstrate that RA could safely cooperate with FSW and provide a flexibly definable level of autonomy. Even within the scope of the demonstration of the autonomy capabilities of RA, an important validation objective was to demonstrate that adopting RA was not an "all or nothing" proposition and could be commanded by the operator at different autonomous operation levels. Figure 19.6 shows different autonomy levels that were required, from having EXEC issuing low-level commands from a low-level script of commands (level 2, a very "low" level of autonomy), to preparing a plan on the ground station and uplinking

Level	Ground station	Onboard PS	Onboard EXEC
1	Real-time commands	None	None (FSW executes)
2	Command sequence	None	Execute sequence
3	Plan, upload to EXEC	None	Execute plan
4	Plan, upload to PS as goal	Confirm plan	Execute plan
5	Plan with unexpanded goals	Complete plan	Execute plan
6	Goals	Generate plan	Execute plan

Figure 19.6 Autonomy levels of RA. Reprinted from Bernard *et al.* [63] with permission.

it to the spacecraft for execution (autonomy level 3), to providing closed-loop planning and execution on the spacecraft (autonomy level 6). The experiment itself was designed to start working at level 3 and then to smoothly build confidence by migrating to level 6.

Finally, a further objective was to validate the feasibility of the development process of RA from the point of view of development costs, safety, integration with different technologies, reusability of the developed software for different missions, and achievement of high-level confidence by the DS1 team in the technology. Indeed, the RA technology is intended as a tool to support system engineering and operations for a mission—one that can be applied for future and different missions, at a reasonable cost, and with significant advantages—rather than a system that provides autonomous capabilities in a one-shot experiment.

19.6.2 Scenarios

The experiment is organized in three main scenarios: a 12-hour scenario that requires low-level autonomy capabilities, a 6-day scenario that requires high-level autonomy capabilities, and a 2-day scenario that represents a variation of the 6-day scenario.

Scenario 1: 12 Hours of Low-Level Autonomy. In the 12 hours scenario, there is no onboard planning by PS. The plan is generated at the ground station, uplinked to the spacecraft, and executed by EXEC and MIR. The scenario includes taking images of asteroids to support optical navigation and a simulated sensor failure. The planning of optical navigation imaging provides the planner the opportunity to reject low-priority, unachievable goals because, for instance, the optical navigation window had time only to take images of some asteroids.

Scenario 2: 6 Days of High-Level Autonomy. The 6-day scenario includes onboard planning by PS. We describe two parts of the scenario.

At the first horizon, PS generates a plan that includes camera imaging for optical navigation and engine thrusting. Execution of the first plan also includes a ground command that modifies the goals for the second horizon. At the end of the first horizon, PS plans to switch off the cameras. A simulated failure prevents RA from turning off the cameras. This failure is not recoverable at the execution level, i.e., by EXEC and MIR alone, and thus replanning is required. This *failure simulation* demonstrates how EXEC and MIR can make repeated attempts to recover a camera switch until it is deemed permanently stuck. A second plan is generated, and while the plan is executed, the *failure simulation* is undone: the ground station informs MIR that the failure is now fixed, and so the plan execution can succeed.

In the second horizon, another plan is generated and executed that includes engine thrusting, camera imaging, and two further simulated failures, one on a communication bus and another on the command that closes a valve involved in the thrusting process. These failures can be handled by the MIR and EXEC components at the execution level, thus demonstrating the failure recovery mechanisms at that level.

Scenario 3: 2 Days of High-Level Autonomy. This is the most important scenario because it relates to the encounter of DS1 with the comet. This scenario was designed during the experiment in March 1999 to ensure that DS1 could be on track for its Comet Borrelly asteroid encounter in July 1999. It is similar to scenario 2, except for the fact that RA should not switch the camera off after each use due to concerns about thermal effects. In addition, RA was required to produce at most 12 hours of thrusting of the spacecraft in order to assure that DS1 would be on track. A further difference is that the simulated camera switch-off failure was active for the duration of the scenario.

19.6.3 Experiment Results

The flight experiment was run safely on both scenarios 1 and 2. During the most significant scenario, scenario 3, three unexpected circumstances caused some unexpected behaviors by the RA system, which turned out to be the way RA managed to achieve even unexpected validation objectives.

A First Alarm. During scenario 3, PS started generating the first plan. It was generated correctly, but an unexpected circumstance occurred. The PS team monitored the behavior of SE by using a graphical tool, the PSGraph tool. This simple tool shows the search depth versus the number of search nodes visited for each successive step of the planner search. The purpose of the tool is to provide a quick summary of the PS planning process. For example, a trajectory that visits the same depth level several times while the search node number increases indicates that the planner is backtracking. The persistence of this situation for a large number of steps is an indication that PS may be thrashing and that it will be unlikely to return a solution within the allotted amount of time.

The PSGraph plot for the start of the scenario 3 experiment showed a discrepancy between the experiment run a few days before (with PS running on the ground under conditions identical to those of the flight test) and what happened during the flight. This deviation from the behavior of the experiment run on ground indicates that PS on board was backtracking much more! After the deviation, however, the behavior of the planner during the flight started going back to the behavior of the previous experiment. This assured that PS was finding the solution. However, the cause of this different behavior was unknown at the time of the experiment. Later it was discovered that the autonomous navigation system contained information different than expected, therefore generating a slightly different goal for PS. As a result, PS was solving a slightly different problem than the one it had solved on the ground. This unexpected circumstance demonstrated that PS was robust to last-minute changes to the planning goals.

A Second Alarm. The experiment went on smoothly, with RA dealing with the camera switch failures, the resulting replanning, long turns to point the camera at target asteroids, optical navigation imaging, and the start of the engine thrusting. However, at a certain point, it became apparent that RA did not commanded termination of engine thrusting as expected. The experiment was stopped (at this time, RA validation had achieved 70% of the objectives). The problem was then identified as a missing critical section in the plan execution code. This created a race condition between two EXEC threads. If the wrong thread won this race, a deadlock condition would occur in which each thread was waiting for an event from the other. This occurred in flight, even though it had not occurred in thousands of previous trials on the various ground platforms. The DS1 technical report stated that "the occurrence of this problem at the worst possible time provides strong impetus for research in formal verification of flight-critical systems." Indeed, formal methods like model checking have been shown to be effective techniques to discover subtle bugs, e.g., in the form of deadlocks, in concurrent processes.

A 6-hour scenario was then generated to demonstrate the remaining 30% of the validation objectives. This scenario was designed and implemented on the ground station overnight. Once the problem was identified, a patch was quickly generated for possible uplink, but it was not uploaded for lack of confidence in the patch and because the probability of another occurrence of the deadlock was judged to be very low. While it is not surprising that the patch was not uploaded, it was a real win that the DS1 team agreed to run the new scenario. This showed that the DS1 team had developed confidence in RA and its ability to deal with unexpected circumstances.

A Third Alarm. During the last part of the experiment, an unexpected and not yet identified problem occurring between FSW and RAXM caused a message loss. This caused RA to estimate a wrong status for the spacecraft. Fortunately, this discrepancy caused no effects. RA was able to continue running the experiment and to achieve 100% of the validation objectives. RA's vulnerability to message loss was deemed out of scope of the validation.

19.6.4 Lessons Learned

We briefly summarize some lessons learned from the successful experiments.

- The basic system must be thoroughly validated with a comprehensive test plan as well as with formal methods [63, 483]. It is very important to validate the basic system (SE, EXEC, etc.) prior to model validation.
- There is a need for model validation tools. Here there are two main directions. One is the use of automated test-running capabilities, including automated scenario generation and validation of test results. Preliminary work in the area of formal methods for model validation is a very promising attempt in this direction.
- The validation cost of model changes must be reduced as much as possible.
- Tools are needed that support the knowledge engineering process for the construction of the domain knowledge of PS. The effective and easy encoding of domain knowledge, in the form of both domain models and search heuristics, does seem to be the most critical success factor.
- There is also a need for a simple but expressive language to specify goals, including the use of graphical interfaces.

19.7 Discussion and Historical Remarks

We focused this chapter on a particular application, but many other successful space applications deserve to be discussed.

Some of the earliest planning and scheduling applications included automation for space shuttle refurbishment [141]. More recently, Chien and his co-workers [123, 124] present several applications, such as the SKICAT system for the analysis and cataloging of space images and the MVP system for the automatic software configuration of the image analysis. They have also developed two platforms, ASPEN and CASPER. ASPEN integrates various planning tools, ranging from search engines and temporal and resource reasoning to a domain modeling language and a user interface; it is used for spacecraft operations on the basis of spacecraft models, operability constraints, and flight rules. CASPER focuses on integrating planning with execution and plan repair; it has been applied to the space shuttle payload operations [125, 451]. Recent work in the area of planning for science data analysis [237] focuses on near real-time processing of earth weather and biomass data.

Some of the more recent high-profile ground applications include automated mission planning for the Modified Antarctic Mapping Mission [482] and the MER deployment by NASA [27]. It is also worth mentioning that an autonomous spacecraft flight is undergoing, the flight on EO-1 [126]. It is flying from August 2003 for approximately one year (with possibly an additional year). Finally, planning by model checking has recently been applied to the synthesis and verification of software on ground stations [6, 7].

The DS1 mission was one of the most famous applications of planning techniques. Its impact was significant. It was the first time that an automated planner ran on the flight processor of a spacecraft. The experiment, called the Remote Agent Experiment, achieved all the technology validation objectives. It demonstrated the potentialities of planning techniques in a mission that requires full autonomy on board. Among the main success factors, we recall the use of an expressive framework able to represent concurrent actions, action durations, and time deadlines and the use of domain-dependent heuristics to guide the search for a solution plan. Future research at NASA and JPL aims to extend this framework with a tighter integration between planning and execution, including a framework for continuous planning, model-based diagnosis, and reliable verification and validation techniques.

After the DS1 mission, the NASA and JPL teams that participated in the development of RA are now involved in a set of very ambitious programs, from autonomous rover navigation on Mars to the provision of an integrated planning and execution framework for missions in deep space like those for Jupiter's satellite, Europa.

CHAPTER 20
Planning in Robotics

20.1 Introduction

A robot is a machine capable of performing a collection of tasks with some level of autonomy and flexibility, in some type of environment. To achieve this capability, a robot integrates one or several sensory-motor functions together with communication and information processing capabilities. Examples of sensory-motor functions in a robot include locomotion on wheels, legs, or wings; manipulation with one or several mechanical arms, grippers, and hands; localization with odomoters, sonars, lasers, inertial sensors, and/or fixed devices such as the Global Positioning System (GPS); and scene analysis and environment modeling with a stereovision system on a pan-and-tilt platform.

Robots can be designed for specific tasks and environments such as:

- Manufacturing tasks: painting, welding, loading/unloading a power press or a machine tool, assembling parts.
- Servicing stores, warehouses, and factories: maintaining, surveying, cleaning the area, transporting objects.
- Exploring an unknown natural areas, e.g., in planetary exploration: building a map with characterized landmarks, extracting samples, setting various measurement devices.
- Assisting people in offices, public areas, and homes.
- Helping in tele-operated surgical operations, as in the so-called minimal invasive surgery.

Robotics is a reasonably mature technology when robots are restricted to operating within well-known and well-engineered environments, e.g., as in manufacturing robotics, or to performing single simple tasks, e.g., vacuum cleaning or lawn mowing. For more diverse tasks and open-ended environments, robotics remains a very active research field.

A robot may or may not integrate planning capabilities. For example, most of the one million robots deployed today in the manufacturing industry do not perform planning per se.[1] Using a robot without planning capabilities basically requires hand-coding the environment model and the robot's skills and strategies into a *reactive controller*. This is a perfectly feasible approach as long as this hand-coding is inexpensive and reliable enough for the application at hand. This will be the case if the environment is well structured and stable and if the robot's tasks are restricted in scope and diversity, with only a limited human-robot interaction.

Programming aids such as hardware tools (e.g., devices for memorizing the motion of a pantomime) and software systems (e.g., graphical programming interfaces) allow for an easy development of a robot's reactive controller. Learning capabilities, supervised or autonomous, significantly extend the scope of applicability of the approach by allowing a generic controller to adapt to the specifics of its environment. For example, this can be done by estimating and fine-tuning control parameters and rules or by acquiring a map of the environment.

However, if a robot has to face a diversity of tasks and/or a variety of environments, then planning will make it simpler to program a robot, and it will augment the robot's usefulness and robustness. Planning should not be seen as opposed to the reactive capabilities of a robot, whether hand-coded or learned; neither should it be seen as opposed to its learning capabilities. Planning should be closely integrated with these capabilities.

The specific requirements of planning in robotics, as compared with other application domains of planning, are mainly the need to handle:

- online input from sensors and communication channels;
- heterogeneous partial models of the environment and of the robot, as well as noisy and partial knowledge of the state from information acquired through sensors and communication channels; and
- direct integration of planning with acting, sensing, and learning.

These very demanding requirements advocate for addressing planning in robotics through domain-specific representations and techniques. Indeed, when planning is integrated within a robot, it usually takes several forms and is implemented throughout different systems. Among these various forms of robot planning, there is in particular *path and motion planning*, *perception planning*, *navigation planning*, *manipulation planning*, and *domain-independent planning*.

Today, the maturity of robot planning is mainly at the level of its domain-specific planners. Path and motion planning is a mature area that relies on computational geometry and efficiently uses probabilistic algorithms. It is already deployed in robotics and other application areas such as CAD and computer animation. Perception planning is a younger and much more open area, although some

1. Sophisticated path and manipulation planning may be deployed during the design stage.

focused problems are well advanced, e.g., the viewpoint selection problem with mathematical programming techniques.

Domain-independent planning is not widely deployed in robotics for various reasons, among which are the restrictive assumptions and expressiveness of the classical planning framework. In robotics, task planning should ideally handle time and resource allocation, dynamic environments uncertainty and partial knowledge, and incremental planning consistently integrated with acting and sensing. The mature planning techniques available today are mostly effective at the abstract level of *mission planning*. Primitives for these plans are tasks such as navigate to location5 and retrieve and pick up object2. However, these tasks are far from being *primitive* sensory-motor functions. Their design is very complex.

Several rule-based or procedure-based systems, such as PRS, RAP, Propice, and SRCs, enable manual programming of closed-loop controllers for these tasks that handle the uncertainty and the integration between acting and sensing. These high-level reactive controllers permit preprogrammed goal-directed and event-reactive modalities.

However, planning representations and techniques can also be very helpful for the design of high-level reactive controllers performing these tasks. They enable offline generation of several alternative complex plans for achieving the task with robustness. They are useful for finding a policy that chooses, in each state, the best such plan for pursuing the activity.

This chapter illustrates the usefulness of planning techniques, namely HTNs and MDPs (Chapters 11 and 16, respectively), for the design of a high-level navigation controller for a mobile robot (Section 20.3). The approach is by no means limited to navigation tasks. It can be pursued for a wide variety of robotics tasks, such as object manipulation and cleaning. However, to keep the presentation technically grounded with enough details about the sensory-motor functions controlled, it is necessary to illustrate a specific task. Several sensory-motor functions are presented and discussed in Section 20.3.1; an approach that exemplifies the use of planning techniques for synthesizing alternative plans and policies for a navigation task is described. Before that, the chapter introduces the reader to the important and mature area of path and motion planning (Section 20.2). The use of the techniques described here as well as in Chapters 14 and 15 is then briefly illustrated in Section 20.4. Finally, the relevant references for this chapter, such as Latombe [353], Siméon *et al.* [477], Beetz *et al.* [58], and others, are discussed in Section 20.5.

20.2 Path and Motion Planning

Path planning is the problem of finding a *feasible geometric path* in some environment for moving a mobile system from a starting position to a goal position. A geometric CAD model of the environment with the obstacles and the free space is supposed to be given. A path is feasible if it meets the kinematics constraints of the mobile system and if it avoids collision with obstacles.

Motion planning is the problem of finding a *feasible trajectory* in space and time, i.e., a feasible path and a control law along that path that meets the dynamics constraints (speed and acceleration) of the mobile system. If one is not requiring an optimal trajectory, it is always possible to *label* temporally a feasible path in order to get a feasible trajectory. Consequently, motion planning relies on path planning, the focus of the rest of this section.

If the mobile system of interest is a *free-flying rigid body*, i.e., if it can move freely in space in any direction without any kinematics constraints, then six *configuration parameters* are needed to characterize its position: x, y, z, and the three Euler angles. Path planning defines a path in this six-dimensional space. However, a robot is not a free-flying body. Its kinematics defines its possible motion. For example, a carlike robot has three configuration parameters, x, y, and θ. Usually these three parameters are not independent, e.g., the robot may or may not be able to turn on the spot (change θ while keeping x and y fixed) or be able to move sideways. A mechanical arm that has n rotational joins needs n configuration parameters to characterize its configuration in space, in addition to constraints such as the maximum and minimum values of each angular join. The carlike robot Hilare in Figure 20.1 (a) has a total of 10 configuration parameters: 6 for the arm and 4 for the mobile platform with the trailer [349]. The humanoid robot HRP in Figure 20.1 (b) has 52 configuration parameters: 2 for the head, 7 for each arm, 6 for each leg and 12 for each hand (four fingers, each with three configurations) [280, 308].[2]

Given a robot with n configuration parameters and some environment, let us define the following variables.

- q, the *configuration* of the robot, is an n-tuple of reals that specifies the n parameters needed to characterize the robot's position in space.
- CS, the *configuration space* of the robot, is the set of values that its configuration q may take.
- CS_{free}, the *free configuration space*, is the subset of CS of configurations that are not in collision with the obstacles of the environment.

Path planning is the problem of finding a path in the free configuration space CS_{free} between an initial configuration and a final configuration. If one could compute CS_{free} explicitly, then path planning would be a search for a path in this n-dimensional continuous space.[3] However, the explicit definition of CS_{free} is a computationally difficult problem, theoretically (it is exponential in the dimension of CS) and practically. For example, the configuration space corresponding to the

2. The *degrees of freedom* of a mobile system are its control variables. An arm or the humanoid robot have as many degrees of freedom as configuration parameters; a carlike robot has three configuration parameters but only two degrees of freedom.
3. Recall our remark in Section 1.5: *if we are given explicitly the graph Σ, then classical planning is a simple graph search problem.* However, the explicit definition of a continuous search space by a set of equations does not provide its connexity structure. The search in CS_{free} is not as easy as a graph search.

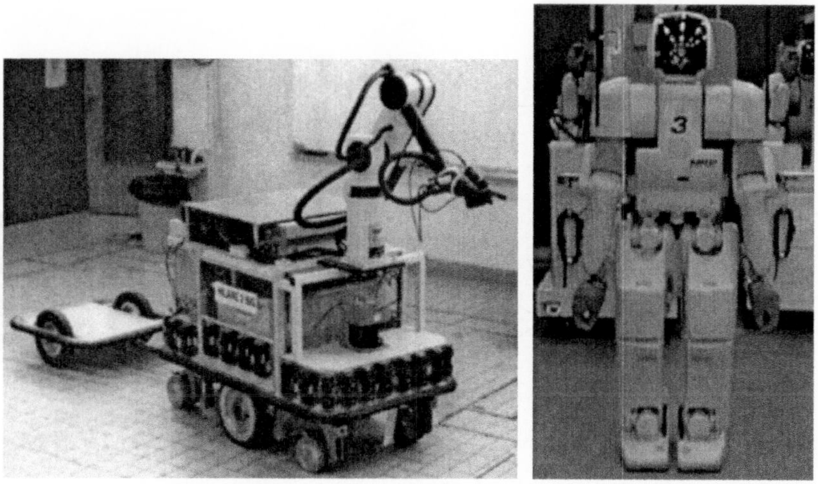

(a) (b)

Figure 20.1 Hilare, a carlike robot with an arm and a trailer (a); HRP, a humanoid robot (b).

simple carlike robot shown in Figure 20.2 (a) is the complex three-dimensional structure shown in Figure 20.2 (b). Fortunately, very efficient probabilistic techniques have been designed that solve path planning problems even for highly complex robots and environments. They rely on the two following operations.

1. *Collision checking* checks whether a configuration $q \in CS_{free}$ or whether a path between two configurations in CS is collision free, i.e., whether it lies entirely in CS_{free}.
2. *Kinematics steering* finds a path between two configurations q and q' in CS that meets the kinematic constraints, without taking into account obstacles.

Both operations can be performed efficiently. Collision checking relies on computational geometry algorithms and data structures [245]. Kinematic steering may use one of several algorithms, depending on the type of kinematics constraints the robot has. For example, *Manhattan paths* are applied to systems that are required to move only one configuration parameter at a time. Special curves (called *Reed&Shepp curves* [454]) are applied to carlike robots that cannot move sideways. If the robot has no kinematics constraints, then straight line segments in CS from q to q' are used. Several such algorithms can be combined. For example, to plan paths for the robot Hilare in Figure 20.1 (a), straight line segments for the arm are combined with dedicated curves for the mobile platform with a trailer [349].

Let $\mathcal{L}(q, q')$ be the path in CS computed by the kinematic steering algorithm for the constraints of the robot of interest; $\mathcal{L}$ is assumed to be symmetrical.

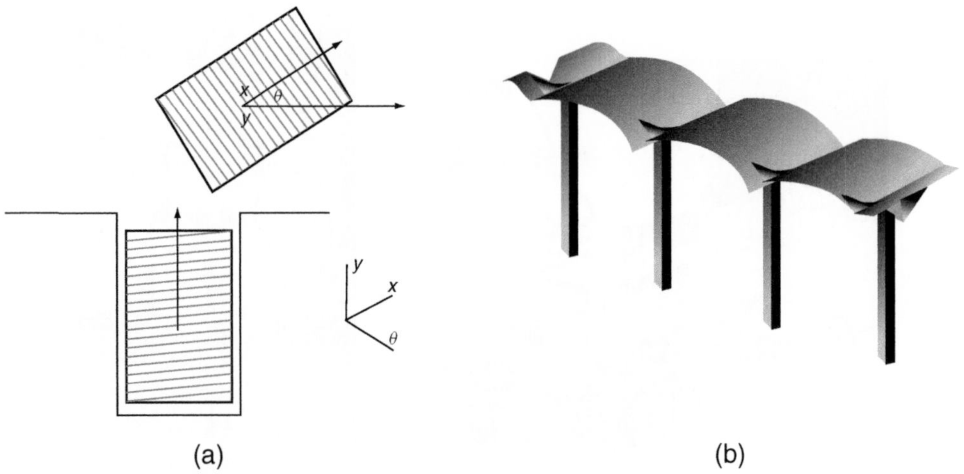

Figure 20.2 A simple carlike robot that is an $l \times l'$ rectangle with three configuration parameters, x, y, and θ, in a 2D environment (a) that looks like two-dimensional a pit of width L and depth h, and the corresponding configuration space (b).

Definition 20.1 A *roadmap* $\mathcal{R}$ for CS_{free} is a graph whose finite set of vertices are configurations in CS_{free}; two such vertices q and q' are adjacent in $\mathcal{R}$ only if $\mathcal{L}(q, q')$ is in CS_{free}. ■

Because $\mathcal{L}$ is symmetrical, $\mathcal{R}$ is an undirected graph. Note that every pair of adjacent vertices in $\mathcal{R}$ is connected by a path in CS_{free}, but the converse is not necessarily true. Given a roadmap for CS_{free} and two configurations q_i and q_g in CS_{free}, a feasible path from q_i to q_g can be found as follows.

1. Find a configuration $q'_i \in \mathcal{R}$ such that $\mathcal{L}(q_i, q'_i) \in CS_{free}$.
2. Find a configuration $q'_g \in \mathcal{R}$ such that $\mathcal{L}(q_g, q'_g) \in CS_{free}$.
3. Find in $\mathcal{R}$ a sequence of adjacent configurations from q'_i to q'_g.

If these three steps succeed, then the planned path is the finite sequence of subpaths $\mathcal{L}(q_i, q'_i), \ldots, \mathcal{L}(q'_g, q_g)$. In a postprocessing step, this sequence is easily optimized and smoothed locally by finding shortcuts in CS_{free} between successive legs.

Given a roadmap $\mathcal{R}$, path planning is reduced to a simple graph search problem, in addition to collision checking and kinematic steering operations. There remains the problem of finding a roadmap that *covers* CS_{free}, i.e., whenever there is a path in CS_{free} between two configurations, there is also a path through the roadmap. Finding such a roadmap using probabilistic techniques turns out to be easier than computing CS_{free} explicitly.

Let us define the *coverage domain* of a configuration q to be this set

$$\mathcal{D}(q) = \{q' \in CS_{free} | \mathcal{L}(q, q') \subset CS_{free}\}$$

```
Probabilistic-Roadmap(𝓡)
    iterate until(termination condition)
        draw a random configuration q in CS_free
        if ∀q' ∈ 𝓡: 𝓛(q, q') ⊄ CS_free then add q to 𝓡
        else if there are q1 and q2 unconnected in 𝓡 such that
                𝓛(q, q1) ⊂ CS_free and 𝓛(q, q2) ⊂ CS_free
            then add q and the edges (q, q1) and (q, q2) to 𝓡
    end iteration
    return(𝓡)
end
```

Figure 20.3 A probabilistic roadmap generation algorithm for path planning.

A set of configurations Q *covers* CS_{free} if:

$$\bigcup_{q \in Q} \mathcal{D}(q) = CS_{free}$$

The algorithm Probabilistic-Roadmap (Figure 20.3) starts initially with an empty roadmap. It generates randomly a configuration $q \in CS_{free}$; q is added to the current roadmap $\mathcal{R}$ iff either:

- q extends the coverage of $\mathcal{R}$, i.e., there is no other configuration in $\mathcal{R}$ whose coverage domain includes q, or
- q extends the connexity of $\mathcal{R}$, i.e., q enables the connection of two configurations in $\mathcal{R}$ that are not already connected in $\mathcal{R}$.

Let us assume that there is a finite set Q that covers CS_{free}.[4] Consider the roadmap $\mathcal{R}$ that contains all the configurations in Q, and, for every pair q_1 and q_2 in Q such that $\mathcal{D}(q_1)$ and $\mathcal{D}(q_2)$ intersect, $\mathcal{R}$ also contains a configuration $q \in \mathcal{D}(q_1) \cap \mathcal{D}(q_2)$ and the two edges (q, q_1) and (q, q_2). It is possible to show that $\mathcal{R}$ meets the following property: If there exists a feasible path between two configurations q_i and q_g in CS_{free}, then there are two configurations q'_i and q'_g in the roadmap $\mathcal{R}$ such that $q_i \in \mathcal{D}(q'_i)$, $q_g \in \mathcal{D}(q'_g)$, and q'_i and q'_g are in the same connected component of $\mathcal{R}$. Note that the roadmap may have several connected components that reflect those of CS_{free}.

The Probabilistic-Roadmap algorithm generates a roadmap that meets this property not *deterministically* but only up to some probability value, which is linked to

4. Depending on the shape of CS_{free} and the kinematics constraints handled in $\mathcal{L}$, there may or may not exist such a *finite* set of configurations that covers CS_{free} [320].

the termination condition. Let k be the number of random draws since the last draw of a configuration q that has been added to the roadmap because q extends the coverage of the current $\mathcal{R}$ (q meets the first if clause in Figure 20.3). The termination condition is to stop when k reaches a preset value k_{max}. It has been shown that $1/k_{max}$ is a probabilistic estimate of the ratio between the part of CS_{free} not covered by $\mathcal{R}$ to the total CS_{free}. In other words, for $k_{max} = 1000$, the algorithm generates a roadmap that covers CS_{free} with a probability of .999.

From a practical point of view, the probabilistic roadmap technique illustrated by the previous algorithm has led to some very efficient implementations and to marketed products used in robotics, computer animation, CAD, and manufacturing applications. Typically, for a complex robot and environment, and k_{max} in the order of a few hundreds, it takes about a minute to generate a roadmap on a normal desktop machine. The size of $\mathcal{R}$ is about a hundred configurations; path planning with the roadmap takes a few milliseconds. This is illustrated for the Hilare robot in Figure 20.4, where the task is to carry a long rod that constrains the path through the door: the roadmap in this nine-dimensional space has about 100 vertices and is generated in less than one minute. The same techniques have also been successfully applied to manipulation planning problems.

To summarize, the principle of the roadmap technique is to cover the search space at a preprocessing stage with a set of connected nodes and, during the planning stage, to connect the initial and goal states to the roadmap and to search through the roadmap. A natural question then is whether this technique can be applied to

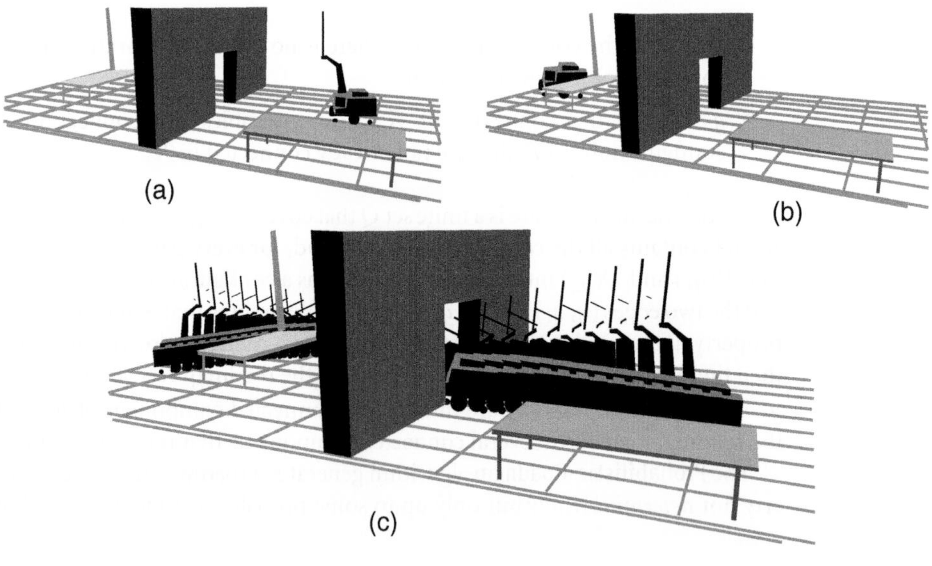

Figure 20.4 Initial (a) and goal (b) configurations of a path-planning problem and the generated path (c).

the state space Σ in domain-independent planning. Although Σ does not have the nice topological properties of CS that enable $\mathcal{L}(q, q')$ to be computed easily, it turns out that the roadmap principle can be successfully applied to classical planning, as shown by Guere and Alami [251].

20.3 Planning for the Design of a Robust Controller

Consider an autonomous mobile robot in a structured environment, such as the robot in Figure 20.1 (a), which is equipped with several sensors—sonar, laser, vision—and actuators, and with an arm. The robot also has several software modules for the same sensory-motor (*sm*) function, e.g., for localization, for map building and updating, and for motion planning and control. These redundant *sm* functions are needed because of possible sensor failures and because no single method or sensor has universal coverage. Each has its weak points and drawbacks. Robustness requires a diversity of means for achieving an *sm* function. Robustness also requires the capability to combine consistently several such *sm* functions into a plan appropriate for the current context.

The planning techniques described here illustrate this capability. They enable a designer to specify, offline, very robust ways to perform a task such as navigate to. The designer specifies a collection of HTNs (see Chapter 11), as illustrated later in this chapter in Figure 20.5, that are complex plans, called *modes of behavior*, or *modalities* for short,[5] whose primitives are *sm* functions. Each modality is a possible way to combine a few of these *sm* functions to achieve the desired task. A modality has a rich context-dependent control structure. It includes alternatives whose selection depends on the data provided by *sm* functions.

Several modalities are available for a given task. The choice of the right modality for pursuing a task is far from obvious. However, the relationship between control states and modalities can be expressed as a Markov Decision Process (see Chapter 16). This MDP characterizes the robot's abilities for that task. The probability and cost distributions of this MDP are estimated by moving the robot in the environment. The controller is driven by policies extracted online from this MDP.

To summarize, this approach involves three components.

1. Sensory-motor functions are the primitive actions.
2. Modalities are HTN plans. Alternate modalities offer different ways to combine the *sm* functions within a task.
3. MDP policies are used by the controller to achieve the task.

Let us describe these three levels successively.

5. Generally, *behavior* in robotics has a meaning different than our modalities.

20.3.1 Sensory-Motor Functions

The sensory-motor functions illustrated here and the control system itself rely on a model of the environment learned and maintained by the robot. The basic model is a two-dimensional map of obstacle edges acquired from the laser range data. The so-called Simultaneous Localization and Mapping (SLAM) technique is used to generate and maintain the map of the environment.

A labeled topological graph of the environment is associated with the two-dimensional map. Cells are polygons that partition the metric map. Each cell is characterized by its name and a color that corresponds to navigation features such as Corridor, Corridor with landmarks, Large Door, Narrow Door, Confined Area, Open Area, Open Area with fixed localization devices.[6] Edges of the topological graph are labeled by estimates of the transition length from one cell to the next and by heuristic estimates of how easy such a transition is.

An *sm* function returns to the controller a report either indicating the end of a normal execution or giving additional information about nonnominal execution. In order to give the reader an idea of the "low-level" primitives available on a robot, of their strong and weak points and how they can be used from a planning point of view, let us discuss some of these *sm* functions.

Segment-Based Localization. This function relies on the map maintained by the robot from laser range data. The SLAM technique uses a data estimation approach called Extended Kalman Filtering in order to match the local perception with the previously built model. It offers a continuous position-updating mode, used when a good probabilistic estimate of the robot position is available. This *sm* function estimates the inaccuracy of the robot localization. When the robot is lost, a relocalization mode can be performed. A constraint relaxation on the position inaccuracy extends the search space until a good matching with the map is found.

This *sm* function is generally reliable and robust to partial occlusions and much more precise than odometry. However, occlusion of the laser beam by obstacles gives unreliable data. This case occurs when dense unexpected obstacles are gathered in front of the robot. Moreover, in long corridors the laser obtains no data along the corridor axis. The inaccuracy increases along the corridor axis. Restarting the position-updating loop in a long corridor can prove to be difficult. Feedback from this *sm* function can be a report of bad localization, which warns that the inaccuracy of the robot position has exceeded an allowed threshold. The robot stops, turns on the spot, and reactivates the relocalization mode. This can be repeated in order to find a nonambiguous corner in the environment to restart the localization loop.

Localization on Visual Landmarks. This function relies on calibrated monocular vision to detect known landmarks such as doors and wall posters. It derives from

6. Some environment modeling techniques enable one to automatically acquire such a topological graph with the cells and their labels. They are discussed in Section 20.5. However, in the work referred to here, the topological graph is hand-programmed.

the perceptual data a very accurate estimation of the robot position. The setup is simple: a few wall posters and characteristic planar features on walls are learned in supervised mode. However, landmarks are generally available and visible only in a few areas of the environment. Hence this *sm* function is mainly used to update from time to time the last known robot position. Feedback from this *sm* function is a report of a potentially visible landmark, which indicates that the robot has entered an area of visibility of a landmark. The robot stops and turns toward the expected landmark; it searches using the pan-and-tilt mount. A failure report notifies that the landmark was not identified. Eventually, the robot retries from a second predefined position in the landmark visibility area.

Absolute Localization. The environment may have areas equipped with calibrated fixed devices, such as infrared reflectors, cameras, or even areas where a differential GPS signal is available. These devices permit a very accurate and robust localization. But the *sm* function works only when the robot is within a covered area.

Elastic Band for Plan Execution. This *sm* function updates and maintains dynamically a flexible trajectory as an *elastic band* or a sequence of configurations from the current robot position to the goal. Connectivity between configurations relies on a set of internal forces used to optimize the global shape of the path. External forces are associated with obstacles and are applied to all configurations in the band in order to dynamically modify the path to take the robot away from obstacles. This *sm* function takes into account the planned path, the map, and the online input from the laser data. It gives a robust method for long-range navigation. However, the band deformation is a local optimization between internal and external forces; the techniques may fail into local minima. This is the case when a mobile obstacle blocks the band against another obstacle. Furthermore, it is a costly process that may limit the reactivity in certain cluttered, dynamic environments. This also limits the band length.

Feedback may warn that the band execution is blocked by a temporary obstacle that cannot be avoided (e.g., a closed door, an obstacle in a corridor). This obstacle is perceived by the laser and is not represented in the map. If the band relies on a planned path, the new obstacle is added to the map. A new trajectory taking into account the unexpected obstacle is computed, and a new elastic band is executed. Another report may warn that the actual band is no longer adapted to the planned path. In this case, a new band has to be created.

Reactive Obstacle Avoidance. This *sm* function provides a reactive motion capability toward a goal without needing a planned path. It extracts from sensory data a description of free regions. It selects the closest region to the goal, taking into account the distance to the obstacles. It computes and tries to achieve a motion command to that region.

This *sm* function offers a reactive motion capability that remains efficient in a cluttered space. However, like all the reactive methods, it may fall into local minima.

It is not appropriate for long-range navigation. Its feedback is a failure report generated when the reactive execution is blocked.

Finally, let us mention that a path planner (as described in Section 20.2) may also be seen as an *sm* function from the viewpoint of a high-level navigation controller. Note that a planned path doesn't take into account environment changes and new obstacles. Furthermore, a path planner may not succeed in finding a path. This may happen when the initial or goal configurations are too close to obstacles: because of the inaccuracy of the robot position, these configurations are detected as being outside of CS_{free}. The robot has to move away from the obstacles by using a reactive motion *sm* function before a new path is queried.

20.3.2 Modalities

A navigation task such as (Goto x y θ) given by a mission planning step requires an integrated use of several *sm* functions among those presented earlier. Each consistent combination of these *sm* functions is a particular plan called a *modality*. A navigation modality is one way to perform the navigation task. A modality has specific characteristics that make it more appropriate for some contexts or environments and less for others. We will discuss in Section 20.3.3 how the controller chooses the appropriate modality. Let us exemplify some such modalities for the navigation task before giving the details of the HTN representation for modalities and the associated control system.

Modality M_1 uses three *sm* functions: the path planner, the elastic band for the dynamic motion execution, and laser-based localization. When M_1 is chosen to carry out a navigation, the laser-based localization is initialized. The robot position is maintained dynamically. A path is computed to reach the goal position. The path is carried out by the elastic band *sm* function. Stopping the modality interrupts the band execution and the localization loop; it restores the initial state of the map if temporary obstacles have been added. Suspending the modality stops the band execution. The path, the band, and the localization loop are maintained. A suspended modality can be resumed by restarting the execution of the current elastic band.

Modality M_2 uses three *sm* functions: the path planner, reactive obstacle avoidance, and laser-based localization. The path planner provides way points (vertices of the trajectory) to the reactive motion function. Despite these way points, the reactive motion can be trapped into local minima in cluttered environments. Its avoidance capability is higher than that of the elastic band *sm* function. However, the reactivity to obstacles and the attraction to way points may lead to oscillations and to a discontinuous motion that confuses the localization *sm* function. This is a clear drawback for M_2 in long corridors.

Modality M_3 is like M_2 but without path planning and with a reduced speed in obstacle avoidance. It starts with the reactive motion and the laser-based localization loop. It offers an efficient alternative in narrow environments like offices and in cluttered spaces where path planning may fail. It can be preferred to modality M_1 in order to avoid unreliable replanning steps if the elastic band is blocked by a cluttered environment. Navigation is only reactive, hence with a local minima problem. The weakness of the laser localization in long corridors is also a drawback for M_3.

Modality M_4 uses the reactive obstacle avoidance *sm* function with the odometer and the visual landmark localization *sm* functions. The odometer inaccuracy can be locally reset by the visual localization *sm* function when the robot goes by a known landmark. Reactive navigation between landmarks allows crossing a corridor without accurate knowledge of the robot position. Typically this M_4 modality can be used in long corridors. The growing inaccuracy can make it difficult to find the next landmark. The search method allows for some inaccuracy on the robot position by moving the cameras, but this inaccuracy cannot exceed one meter. For this reason, landmarks should not to be too far apart with respect to the required updating of the odometry estimate. Furthermore, the reactive navigation of M_4 may fall into a local minima.

Modality M_5 relies on the reactive obstacle avoidance *sm* function and the absolute localization *sm* function when the robot is within an area equipped with absolute localization devices.

Modalities are represented as HTNs. The HTN formalism is adapted to modalities because of its expressiveness and its flexible control structure. HTNs offer a middle ground between programming and automated planning, allowing the designer to express the control knowledge available here.

An internal node of the HTN AND/OR tree is a task or subtask that can be pursued in different context-dependent ways, which are the *OR-connectors*. Each such OR-connector is a possible decomposition of the task into a conjunction of subtasks. There are two types of *AND-connectors*: with sequential branches or with parallel branches. Branches linked by a sequential AND-connector are traversed sequentially in the usual depth-first manner. Branches linked by a parallel AND-connector are traversed in parallel. The leaves of the tree are primitive actions, each corresponding to a unique query to an *sm* function. Thus, a root task is dynamically decomposed, according to the context, into a set of primitive actions organized as concurrent or sequential subsets. Execution starts as soon as the decomposition process reaches a leaf, even if the entire decomposition process of the tree is not complete.

A primitive action can be *blocking* or *nonblocking*. In blocking mode, the control flow waits until the end of this action is reported before starting the next action in the sequence flow. In nonblocking mode, actions in a sequence are triggered sequentially without waiting for feedback. A blocking primitive action is considered ended after a report has been issued by the *sm* function and after that report has been processed by the control system. The report from a nonblocking primitive action may occur and be processed after an unpredictable delay.

The modality tree illustrated in Figure 20.5 starts with six OR-connectors labeled start, stop, suspend, resume, success, and fail. The start connector represents the nominal modality execution; the stop connector the way to stop the modality and to restore the neutral state, characterized by the lack of any *sm* function execution. Furthermore, the environment model modified by the modality execution recovers

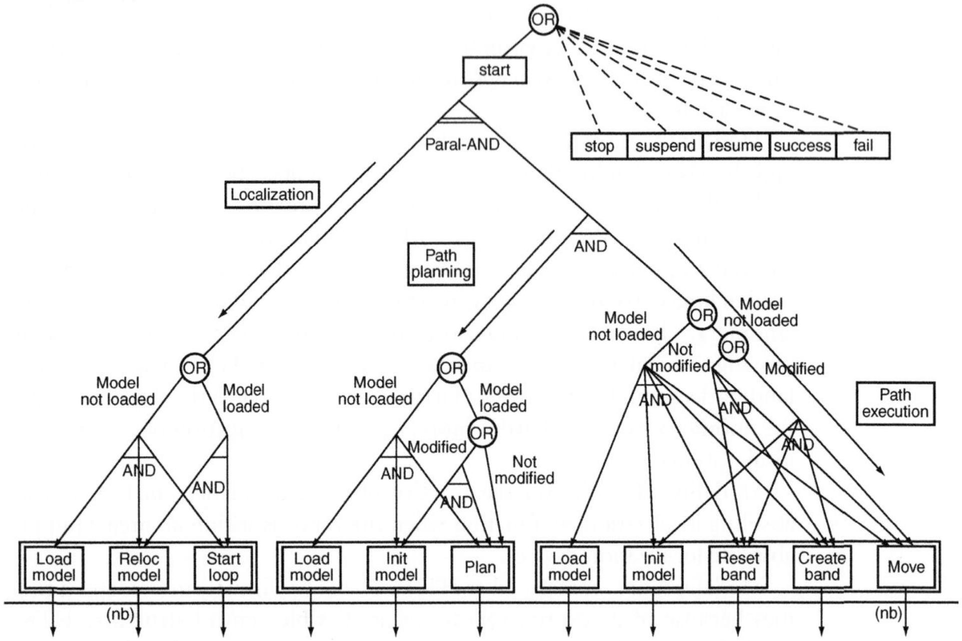

Figure 20.5 Part of modality M_1.

its previous form. The suspend and resume connectors are triggered by the control system described in the next paragraph. The suspend connector allows one to stop the execution by freezing the state of the active *sm* functions. The resume connector restarts the modality execution from such a frozen state. The fail and success connectors are followed when the modality execution reaches a failure or a success, respectively. These connectors are used to restore the neutral state and to allow certain executions required in these specific cases.

The feedback from *sm* functions to modalities has to be controlled as well as the resource sharing of parallel activities. The control system catches and reacts appropriately to reports emitted by *sm* functions. Reports from *sm* functions play the same role in the control system as tasks in modalities. A report of some type activates its own dedicated control HTN in a reactive way. A control tree represents a temporary modality and cannot be interrupted. A nominal report signals a normal execution. Otherwise, a nonnominal report signals a particular type of *sm* function execution. The aim of the corresponding control tree is to recover to a nominal modality execution. Some nonnominal reports can be nonrecoverable failures. In these cases, the corresponding control sends a fail message to the modality pursuing this *sm* function. Nominal reports may notify the success of the global task. In this case, the success alternative of the modality is activated.

Resources to be managed are either physical nonsharable resources (e.g., motors, cameras, pan-and-tilt mounts) or logical resources (the environment model that can be temporally modified). The execution of a set of concurrent nonblocking actions can imply the simultaneous execution of different *sm* functions. Because of that, several reports may appear at the same time and induce the simultaneous activation of several control activities. These concurrent executions may generate a resource conflict. To manage this conflict, a resource manager organizes the resource sharing with semaphores and priorities.

When a nonnominal report is issued, a control HTN starts its execution. It requests the resource it needs. If this resource is already in use by a start connector of a modality, the manager sends to this modality a suspend message and leaves a resume message for the modality in the spooler according to its priority. The suspend alternative is executed, freeing the resource and enabling the control HTN to be executed. If the control execution succeeds, waiting messages are removed and executed until the spooler becomes empty. If the control execution fails, the resume message is removed from the spooler and the fail alternative is executed for the modality.

20.3.3 The Controller

The Control Space. The controller has to choose a modality that is most appropriate to the current state for pursuing the task. In order to do this, a set of *control variables* has to reflect control information for the *sm* functions. The choice of these control variables is an important design issue. For example, in the navigation task, the control variables include the following.

- The *cluttering of the environment*, which is defined to be a weighted sum of the distances to the nearest obstacles perceived by the laser, with a dominant weight along the robot motion axis. This is an important piece of information for establishing the execution conditions of the motion and localization *sm* functions.
- The *angular variation of the profile of the laser range data*, which characterizes the robot area. Close to a wall, the cluttering value is high, but the angular variation remains low. In an open area the cluttering is low, while the angular variation may be high.
- The *inaccuracy of the position estimate*, as computed from the covariance matrix maintained by each localization *sm* function.
- The *confidence in the position estimate.* The inaccuracy is not sufficient to qualify the localization. Each localization *sm* function supplies a confidence estimate about the last processed position.
- The *navigation color of the current area.* When the robot position estimate falls within some labeled cell of the topological graph, the corresponding labels

are taken into account, e.g., Corridor, Corridor with landmarks, Large Door, Narrow Door, Confined Area, Open Area, Open Area with fixed localization devices.

- The *current modality*. This information is essential to assess the control state and possible transitions between modalities.

A control state is characterized by the values of these control variables. Continuous variables are discretized over a few significant intervals. In addition, there is a global failure state that is reached whenever the control of a modality reports a failure. We finally end up with a discrete control space, which enables us to define a *control automaton.*

The Control Automaton. The control automaton is nondeterministic: unpredictable external events may modify the environment, e.g., someone passing by may change the value of the cluttering variable or the localization inaccuracy variable. Therefore, the execution of the same modality in a given state may lead to different adjacent states. This nondeterministic control automaton is defined as the tuple $\Sigma = \{S, A, P, C\}$, where:

- S is a finite set of control states.
- A is a finite set of modalities.
- $P : S \times A \times S \rightarrow [0, 1]$ is a probability distribution on the state-transition *sm* function, $P_a(s'|s)$ is the probability that the execution of modality a in state s leads to state s'.
- $C : A \times S \times S \rightarrow \Re^+$ is a positive cost function, $c(a, s, s')$ corresponds to the average cost of performing the state transition from s to s' with the modality a.

A and S are given by design from the definition of the set of modalities and of the control variables. In the navigation system illustrated here, there are five modalities and about a few thousand states. P and C are obtained from observed statistics during a learning phase.

The control automaton Σ is an MDP. As such, Σ could be used reactively on the basis of a universal policy π that selects for a given state s the best modality $\pi(s)$ to be executed. However, a universal policy will not take into account the current navigation goal. A more precise approach explicitly takes into account the navigation goal, transposed into Σ as a set S_g of goal states in the control space. This set S_g is given by a look-ahead mechanism based on a search for a path in Σ that reflects a topological route to the navigation goal (see Figure 20.6).

Goal States in the Control Space. Given a navigation task, a search in the topological graph provides an optimal route r to the goal, taking into account the estimated costs of edges between topological cells. This route will help find in the

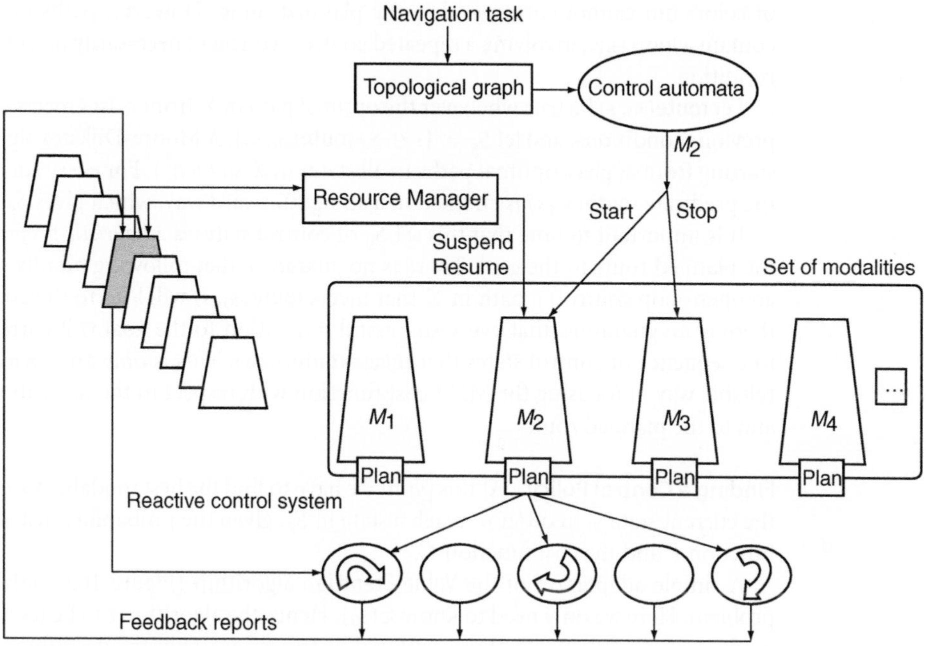

Figure 20.6 The ROBEL control system.

control automaton possible goal control states for planning a policy. The route r is characterized by the pair (σ_r, l_r), where $\sigma_r = \langle c_1 c_2 \ldots c_k \rangle$ is the sequence of colors of traversed cells, and l_r is the length of r.

Now, a path between two states in Σ defines also a sequence of colors σ_{path}, those of traversed states; it has a total cost, which is the sum $\sum_{path} C(a, s, s')$ over all traversed arcs. A path in Σ from the current control state s_0 to a state s corresponds to the planned route when the path *matches* the features of the route (σ_r, l_r) in the following way.

- $\sum_{path} C(a, s, s') \geq K l_r$, K being a constant ratio between the cost of a state transition in the control automaton and the corresponding route length.
- σ_{path} corresponds to the same sequence of colors as σ_r with possible repetition factors, i.e., there are factors $i_1 > 0, \ldots, i_k > 0$ such that $\sigma_{path} = \langle c_1^{i_1} c_2^{i_2} \ldots c_k^{i_k} \rangle$ when $\sigma_r = \langle c_1 c_2 \ldots c_k \rangle$.

This last condition requires that we will be traversing in Σ control states having the same color as the planned route. A repetition factor corresponds to the number of control states, at least one, required for traversing a topological cell. The first condition enables us to prune paths in Σ that meet the condition on the sequence of colors but cannot correspond to the planned route. However, paths in Σ that contain a loop (i.e., involving a repeated control sequence) necessarily meet the first condition.

Let route(s_0, s) be true whenever the optimal path in Σ from s_0 to s meets the two previous conditions, and let $S_g = \{s \in S \mid \text{route}(s_0, s)\}$. A Moore-Dijkstra algorithm starting from s_0 gives optimal paths to all states in Σ in $O(n^2)$. For every such path, the predicate route(s_0, s) is checked in a straightforward way, which gives S_g.

It is important to note that this set S_g of control states is a *heuristic projection* of the planned route to the goal. There is no guarantee that following blindly (i.e., in an open-loop control) a path in Σ that meets route(s_0, s) will lead to the goal; and there is no guarantee that every successful navigation to the goal will correspond to a sequence of control states that meets route(s_0, s). This is only an efficient and reliable way of focusing the MDP cost function with respect to the navigation goal and to the planned route.

Finding a Control Policy. At this point we have to find the best modality to apply to the current state s_0 in order to reach a state in S_g, given the probability distribution function P and the cost function C.

A simple adaptation of the Value-Iteration algorithm (Figure 16.6) solves this problem. Here we only need to know $\pi(s_0)$. Hence the algorithm can be focused on a subset of states, basically those explored by the Moore-Dijkstra algorithm.

The closed-loop controller uses this policy as follows. First, the computed modality $\pi(s_0)$ is executed. Then, the robot observes the new control state s, updates its route r and its set S_g of goal states with respect to s, and finds the new modality to apply to s. This is repeated until the control reports a success or a failure. Recovery from a failure state consists of trying from the parent state an untried modality. If none is available, a global failure of the task is reported.

Estimating the Parameters of the Control Automaton. A sequence of randomly generated navigation goals can be given to the robot. During its motion, new control states are met, and new transitions are recorded or updated. Each time a transition from s to s' with modality a is performed, the traversed distance and speed are recorded, and the average speed v of this transition is updated. The cost of the transition $C(a, s, s')$ can be defined as a weighted average of the traversal time for this transition, taking into account the eventual control steps required during the execution of the modality a in s together with the outcome of that control. The statistics on $a(s)$ are recorded to update the probability distribution function.

Several strategies can be defined to learn P and C in Σ. For example, a modality can be chosen randomly for a given task. This modality is pursued until either it succeeds or a fatal failure is notified. In this case, a new modality is chosen randomly and is executed according to the same principle. This strategy is used initially to expand Σ. Another option is to use Σ according to the normal control except in a state on which not enough data has been recorded. A modality is randomly applied to this state in order to augment known statistics, e.g., the random choice of an untried modality in that state.

20.3.4 Analysis of the Approach

The system described here was deployed on an indoor mobile platform and experimented with in navigation tasks within a wide laboratory environment. The approach is fairly generic and illustrates the use of planning techniques in robotics, not for the synthesis of mission plans but for achieving a robust execution of their high-level steps.

The HTN planning technique used for specifying detailed alternative plans to be followed by a controller for decomposing a complex task into primitive actions is fairly general and powerful. It can be widely applied in robotics because it enables one to take into account closed-loop feedback from sensors and primitive actions. It extends significantly and can rely on the capabilities of the rule-based or procedure-based languages for programming reactive controllers, as in the system described here.

The MDP planning technique relies on an abstract dedicated space, namely, the space of control states for the navigation task. The size of such a space is just a few thousand states. Consequently, the estimation of the parameter distributions in Σ is feasible in a reasonable time: the MDP algorithms can be used efficiently online, at each control step. The drawback of these advantages is the *ad hoc* definition of the control space, which requires a very good knowledge of the sensory-motor functions and the navigation task. While in principle the system described here can be extended by the addition of new modalities for the same task or for other tasks, it is not clear how easy it would be to update the control space or to define new spaces for other tasks.

20.4 Dock-Worker Robots

Up to here, the running example of the book has been the DWR domain, described as an abstract, highly simplified world. Now we can describe this application domain at a more concrete level.

A container is a large metallic cell of a standard size that can be conveniently piled on docks and loaded on ships, trains, and cargo planes. It is intended to allow safe transportation of some freight from a shipping point to a destination point. A significant part of the shipment cost lies in the transition phase between two transportation medias, e.g., when a container has to be moved between two ships, or from a ship to a train or a truck, usually via some storage area. The high cost of these *transshipment* operations explains the motivation of their automatization. Several sites, such as the Rotterdam Harbor (see Figure 20.7), already perform transshipment operations with Automated Ground Vehicles (AGVs). These AGVs are mostly teleoperated. They require fixed navigation equipment and a site specifically designed to suit their human-controlled operations. Ambitious projects aim at more flexible and autonomous operations.

One such project, the Martha project [10], has studied the use of autonomous robots evolving in already existing sites that are not designed specifically for AGVs

Figure 20.7 A crane loading containers on the *Ever Uranus* ship in the Rotterdam Harbor.

and that can be used by other vehicles. A container transportation robot is a trucklike robot, about 17 meters long, equipped with the type of range and localization sensors discussed in Section 20.3.1. A typical setting is that of a large harbour where a fleet of 50 to 100 such robots is in charge of loading and unloading containers from arriving vehicles to departing ones. In the Martha project, a map of the environment is provided to each robot (see Figure 20.8). This map is composed of metrical data and a topological graph labeled with a few types of attributes (routes, loading/unloading zones, docks, piles, etc.). The map is static, but the environment evolves. Because of other vehicles and nonmodeled obstacles, the current state of the environment may depart significantly from the map.

The planning and the execution control of a transshipment task are managed in the Martha project at several levels. At the highest level, the mission allocation is performed incrementally by a centralized planner that allocates to each robot the container transportation jobs it has to perform. This planner, detailed in Vidal *et al.* [535], relies on the scheduling techniques of Chapter 15. It views the robots as resources and container transportation tasks as jobs to be allocated to available robots. It can handle priorities and cost estimates of jobs, as well as a fairly flexible model of the uncertainty of the specified tasks, e.g., the uncertainty of the arrival time of the ships to be handled. The planner works incrementally, taking into account newly specified transportation tasks with respect to the running ones; it is able to modify part of the already allocated missions whose execution has not started yet.

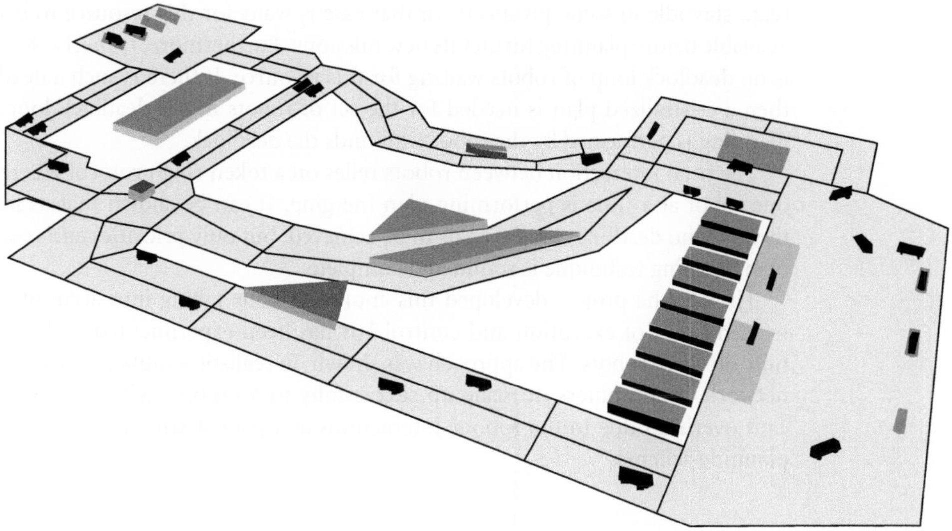

Figure 20.8 A dock work environment.

A robot plans and executes its allocated missions autonomously. Each job involves going to a loading position, taking a container, and moving it to an unloading position. However, a robot has to share many common resources of the site with the other robots of the fleet: routes, loading positions, and cranes. The Martha project developed an efficient distributed approach for coordinating without conflict a large set of plans: the *plan-merging technique.*

Let us assume that all plans currently being executed by the fleet of robots are conflict free. A robot r_i receives a new mission that allocates to it a sequence of jobs. While taking into account its current plan, robot r_i synthesizes a *provisional plan* for handling this mission. The provisional plan involves precise trajectories, generated with a planner similar to the one described in Section 20.2, and time-point variables. These temporal variables will be instantiated at the execution level by the actions of r_i as well as by external events, such as the actions of other robots. The provisional plan has temporal constraints between the time points of its actions and those of the external events.

Through an Ethernet radio link, the robot r_i advertises to the fleet of robots the resources it intends to use according to this provisional plan. Every robot that is going to use one or several of these resources returns to r_i its current plan. Robot r_i modifies its provisional plan in order to remove all resource conflicts. This is done by adding temporal constraints on the actions of the provisional plan of r_i, using the techniques of Chapter 14. This is the plan-merging step.

However, r_i may not succeed in finding a conflict-free plan because it cannot modify the plans of the other robots and because a robot may keep a resource (e.g., stay idle in some position). In that case r_i waits for this resource to become available before planning further its new mission.[7] Furthermore, r_i checks that there is no deadlock loop of robots waiting for this resource. If there is such a deadlock, then a centralized plan is needed for the set of robots in the deadlock loop. The planning is performed by the robot who finds the deadlock.

The total interaction between robots relies on a token ring protocol where only one robot at a time is performing plan merging. It can be shown that as long as there are no deadlines on the goals to be achieved, but only priorities and costs, the plan-merging technique is sound and complete.

The Martha project developed this approach while taking into account all the needed levels of execution and control.[8] It has been experimented with successfully on three robots. The approach was shown, in realistic simulations over a wide network of computers, to scale up successfully to 50 robots without any significant overhead due to the robots' interactions and plan sharing in the distributed planning schema.

20.5 Discussion and Historical Remarks

Robot motion planning is a very advanced research field [319, 354]. The early techniques in the 1980s were mostly dedicated to deterministic algorithms [353]. They led to a good understanding and formalization of the problem, as well as to several developments on related topics such as manipulation planning [11]. More recent approaches have built on this state of the art with probabilistic algorithms that permitted a significant scale-up [48]. The probabilistic roadmap techniques introduced by Kavraki *et al.* [321] gave rise to several successful developments [68, 85, 252, 273, 320, 338, 477], which today represent the most efficient approaches to path planning. Roadmap techniques are certainly not limited to navigation tasks; they have been deployed in other application areas within robotics, e.g., for manipulation, and in CAD and graphics animation. The illustrations and performance figures in Section 20.2 are borrowed from Move3D, a state-of-the-art system implementing roadmap techniques [476].

Sensory-motor functions are at the main core of robotics. They correspond to a very wide research area, ranging from signal processing, computer vision, and learning to biomechanics and neuroscience. Their detailed discussion is well beyond the scope of this section. However, several approaches are directly relevant to this chapter, such as the techniques used for localization and mapping, e.g., the SLAM methods [156, 404, 508, 509]; the methods for structuring the environment model into a topological map with areas labeled by different navigation colors [347, 507]; the visual localization techniques [264]; and the flexible control techniques [450, 462].

---

7. This waiting takes place at the planning level only, while the execution of already coordinated plans is being pursued.
8. Except for the operations of the cranes for loading the robots.

Several high-level reactive controllers are widely deployed in laboratory robots. They permit a preprogrammed goal-directed and event-reactive closed-loop control, integrating acting and sensing. They rely on rule-based or procedure-based systems, such as PRS, RAP, SRC, and others [93, 191, 214, 279]. More recent developments on these systems (e.g., [154]), aim at a closer integration to planning. The behavior-based controllers (e.g., [23]), which usually focus on a more reactive set of concurrent activities, have also led to more goal-directed developments (e.g., [268]). The *robot architecture* (i.e., the organization that enables proper integration of the sensory-motor functions, the reactive control system, and the deliberative capabilities [9, 479]) remains an important issue.

The planning and robotics literature reports on several plan-based robot controllers with objectives similar to those discussed in this chapter [55, 56, 57, 58, 337]. The approach of Beetz [56] has also been deployed for controlling an indoor robot carrying out the core tasks of an office courier. It relies on the SRC's reactive controllers. These are concurrent control routines that adapt to changing conditions by reasoning on and modifying plans. They rely on the XFRM system, which manipulates reactive plans and is able to acquire them through learning with XFRMLEARN [57]. The approach illustrated in Section 20.3 on navigation tasks was developed by Morisset and Ghallab [401, 402] and extensively experimented with on the Diligent robot, an indoor mobile platform. The approach is not limited to navigation; it can be deployed on other robot activities.

Chapter 21 Planning for Manufacturability Analysis

21.1 Introduction

Process planning is the task of preparing detailed operating instructions for transforming an engineering design into a final product. Most work on Computer-Aided Process Planning (CAPP) has focused on the development of process plans for mechanical parts.

Variant process planning, which is the basis for most commercial CAPP systems, is basically a case-based reasoning technique (see Section 24.1) in which the case adaptation is done manually by a human user. In generative process planning, the process plan is developed automatically by the computer. The development of generative systems has been a subject of much research, and there is a huge number of publications on that topic (for a comprehensive review, see [471]). However, due to the difficulty of the problem, few successful commercial systems exist.

Manufacturability analysis—the task of giving estimates of how easy it will be to manufacture a proposed design—is somewhat easier than process planning because it does not require generating all the details of the process plan. Manufacturability analysis is useful in order to help designers produce designs that are easier to manufacture.

IMACS (Interactive Manufacturability Analysis and Critiquing System) is a computer system for analyzing the manufacturability of designs for machined parts. As shown in Figure 21.1, IMACS evaluates the manufacturability of a proposed design by generating and evaluating manufacturing operation plans. Our description of IMACS is based largely on the one in Nau *et al.* [417].

21.2 Machined Parts

A machined *part*, P, is the final component created by executing a set of machining operations on a piece of *stock*, S. For example, Figure 21.2 shows a socket P_0 and the

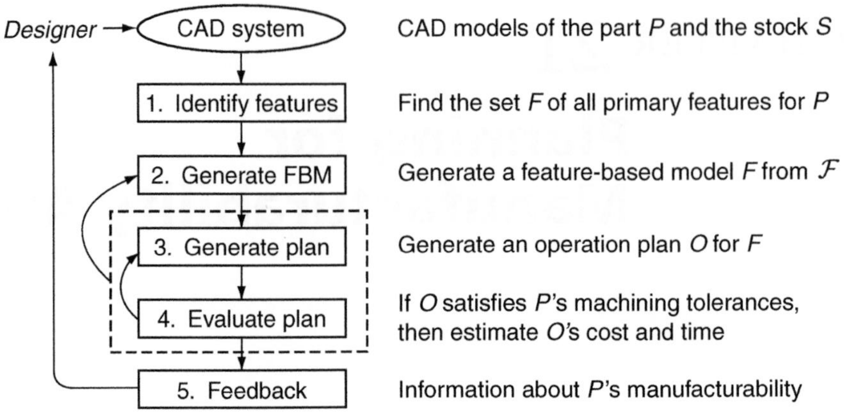
Designer
CAD system
1. Identify features
2. Generate FBM
3. Generate plan
4. Evaluate plan
5. Feedback
CAD models of the part P and the stock S
Find the set F of all primary features for P
Generate a feature-based model F from ℱ
Generate an operation plan O for F
If O satisfies P's machining tolerances, then estimate O's cost and time
Information about P's manufacturability

Figure 21.1 Basic approach used in IMACS.

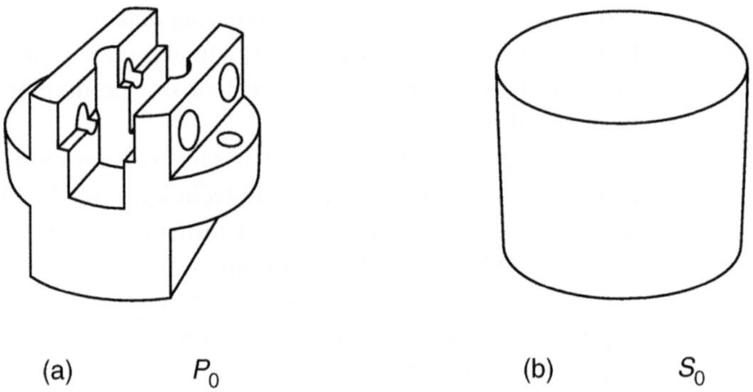
(a)
P_0
(b)
S_0

Figure 21.2 The socket P_0 (a) and the stock S_0 (b).

stock S_0 from which P_0 is to be produced. Note that the goal to be achieved (i.e., the part to be produced) is represented not as a set of atoms or state variables but instead as a CAD model (which IMACS represents using a commercial solid-modeling system).

An *operation plan* is a sequence of machining operations capable of creating the part P from the stock S. Because it would be physically impossible to produce P's *exact* geometry, designers give *design tolerance* specifications (see Figure 21.3) to specify how much variation from the nominal geometry is allowable in any physical realization of P. A plan is considered capable of achieving the goal if it can create an instance of P that satisfies the design tolerances.

A *workpiece* is the intermediate object produced by starting with S and performing zero or more machining operations. Currently, the machining operations

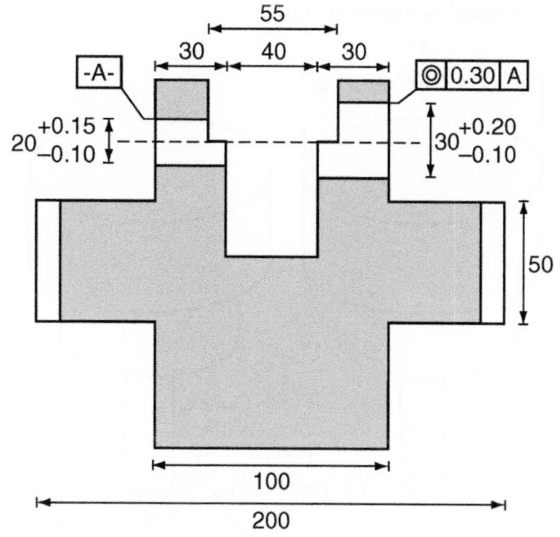

Figure 21.3 Dimensions and tolerances for the socket P_0.

considered in IMACS include end milling, side milling, face milling, and drilling operations on a three-axis vertical machining center. Each machining operation creates a *machining feature.* Different researchers use different definitions of machining features; as shown in Figure 21.4, IMACS considers a machining feature to include information about the type of machining operation, the material removal volume (the volume of space in which material can be removed), and the accessibility volume (the volume of space needed for access to the part).

21.3 Feature Extraction

IMACS incorporates algorithms to recognize portions of a CAD model that correspond to machining features [455]. One difficulty here is that depending on the geometry of P, there can be many—sometimes infinitely many—different machining features capable of creating various portions of P. In IMACS, this is addressed by defining a *primary* feature to be a feature that contains as much of the stock as possible without intersecting with P and as little space as possible outside the stock. Figure 21.5 shows examples of primary and nonprimary features; for more details, see Regli *et al.* [455].

In every operation plan that IMACS will ever want to consider, each machining operation will create either a primary feature or a truncation of a primary feature—and the number of primary features for a part is always finite (in fact, polynomial). Thus, IMACS's first step is to find the set $\mathcal{F}$ of all primary features for P and S. For example, for the socket P_0, the set $\mathcal{F}$ contains 22 primary features, a few of which are shown in Figure 21.6.

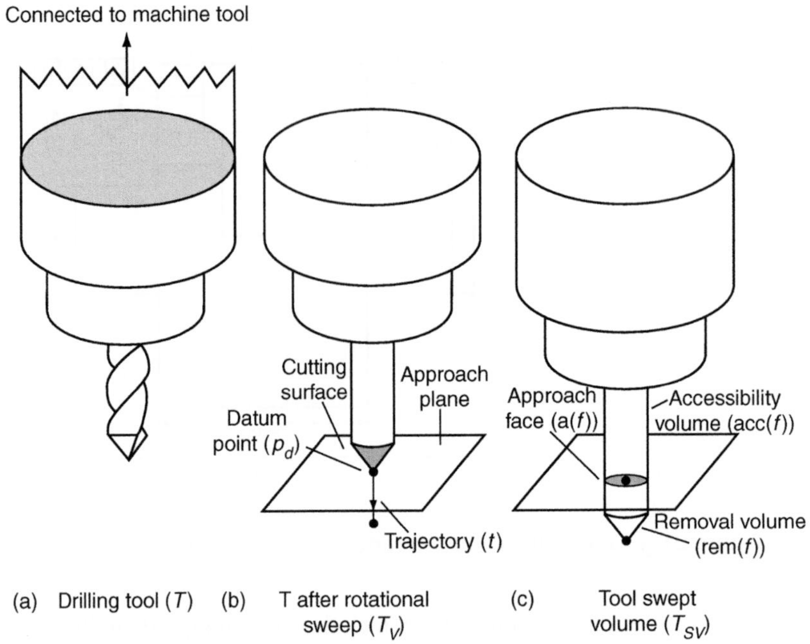

Figure 21.4 Example of a machining operation.

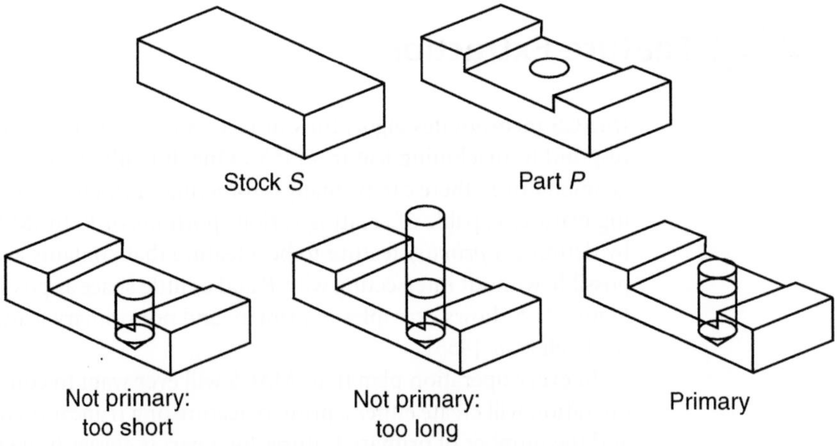

Figure 21.5 Nonprimary and primary drilling features.

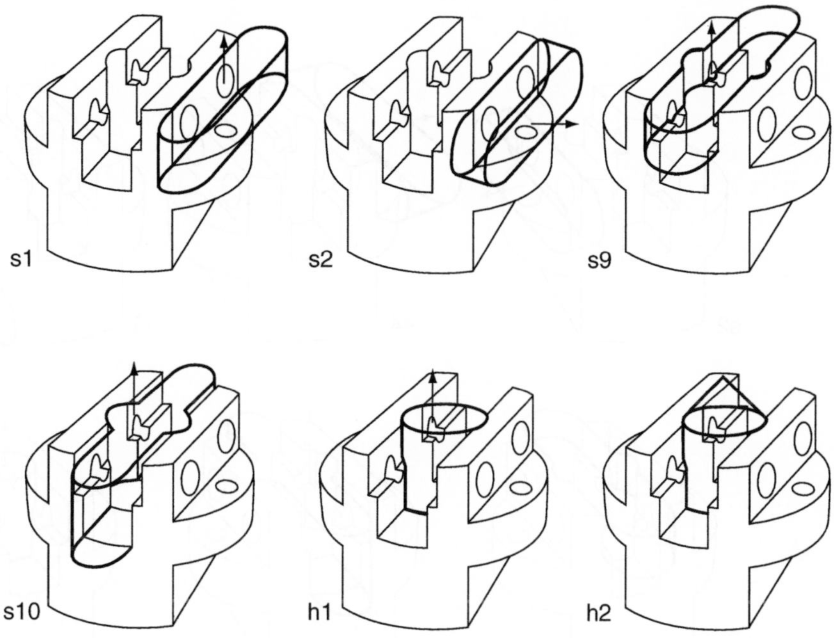

Figure 21.6 A few of the 22 primary features for the socket P_0. $s1, s2, s9$, *and* $s10$ are end-milling features; $h1$ and $h2$ are drilling features.

Machining operations correspond to elementary actions, and machining features correspond to tasks. $\mathcal{F}$ corresponds to the set of all tasks that might ever be relevant for achieving the goal.

21.4 Generating Abstract Plans

Figure 21.6 shows that the features in $\mathcal{F}$ may overlap in complicated ways, and some of them are redundant (e.g., it is not necessary to machine both s1 and s2). A *feature-based model* (FBM) is any nonredundant subset of features $F \subseteq \mathcal{F}$ such that subtracting those features from S produces P and none of the features are redundant. For example, Figure 21.7 shows an FBM, FBM1, for the socket P_0.

Each FBM corresponds to a set of tasks: if we can machine the features in the FBM, this will create the part. In general, the number of FBMs is exponential in the number of primary features. As an example, for the socket P_0, $\mathcal{F}$ contains 22 primary features from which one can form 512 FBMs. From a manufacturing point of view, some FBMs are better than others. We would like to find an optimal one—but obviously we do not want to examine every possible FBM in order to accomplish this.

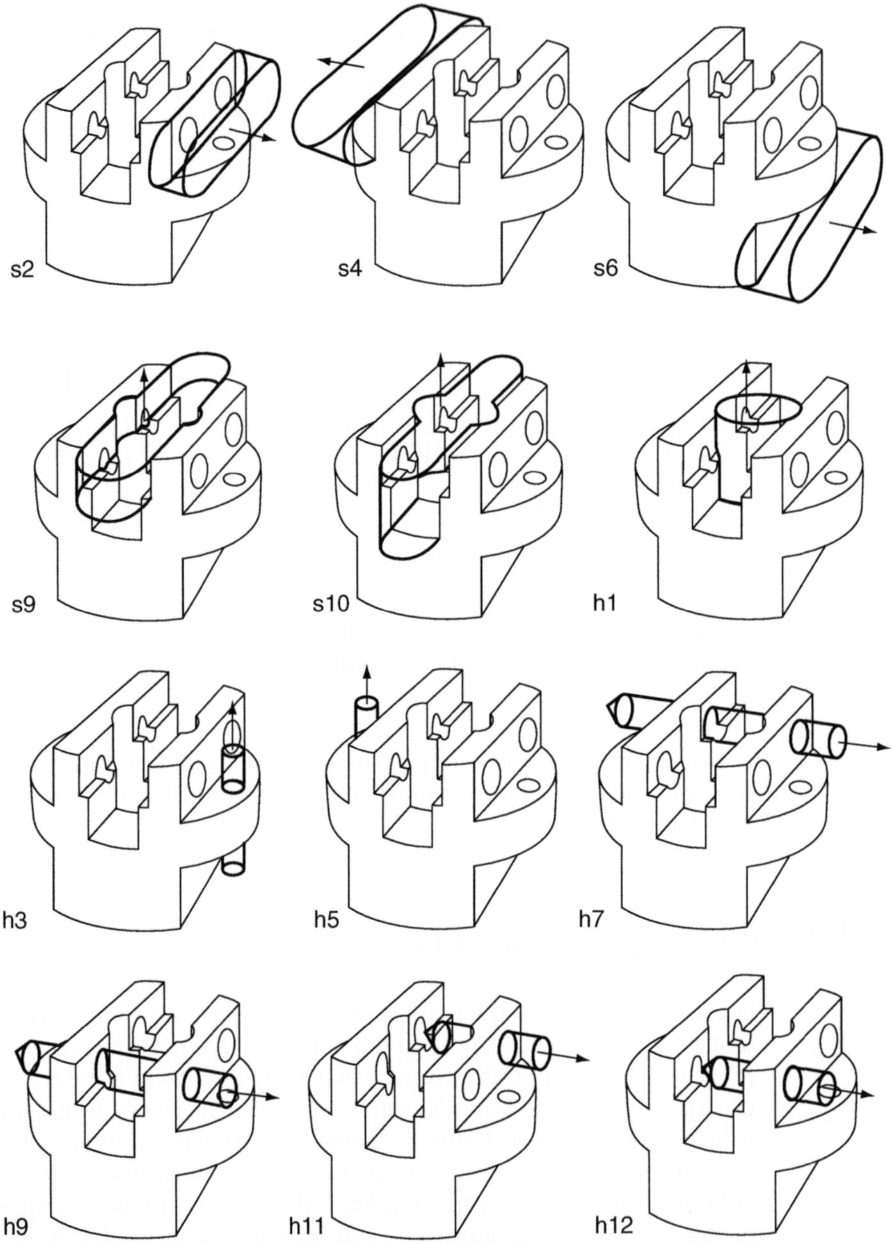

Figure 21.7 Feature-based model FBM1 for the socket P_0.

To avoid looking at every FBM, IMACS does a depth-first branch-and-bound search to generate and test FBMs one at a time, pruning unpromising FBMs as described in Section 21.8. To measure how good a plan is, IMACS uses an estimate of the plan's manufacturing time, as described in Section 21.7. A better measure would also incorporate estimates of production cost: this was not done in IMACS because IMACS is a prototype, but it would be straightforward to accomplish.

As an example of how much the branch-and-bound search reduces the size of the search space, IMACS generates only 16 of the 512 FBMs for the socket P_0.

21.5 Resolving Goal Interactions

An FBM corresponds to a set of tasks in which no ordering constraints have yet been imposed. To resolve goal interactions, IMACS adds ordering constraints as follows.

1. *Identify ordering constraints.* Due to complex geometric interactions (accessibility, etc.), some features must precede others. For example, in Figure 21.8, the hole h1 must be machined before the slot s9 in order to achieve reasonable machining tolerances and avoid tool breakage.
2. *Linearize.* Next IMACS generates all total orderings consistent with the precedences. If no such total ordering can be found, IMACS considers the FBM F to be unmachinable and discards it. Unlike the typical approaches used in AI planners, there would be no point in adding additional operators: they would just create redundant features, and if there is a feasible way to machine the part, it will be found among the other FBMs.
3. *Modify goals.* Suppose features f and g overlap, and f precedes g in some total ordering. Then when we machine f, we are also machining part of g. We don't want to machine that same portion of g again later in the sequence because we would merely be machining air. Thus, IMACS truncates g to remove the portion covered by f. As an example, several of the features shown in Figure 21.8 (a) were produced by truncating the corresponding features in FBM1.
4. *Unlinearize.* Once the truncated features have been produced, several of the resulting FBMs may have identical features but different precedence constraints. In such cases the precedence constraints that differ can be removed, translating the total orders into partial orders. For example, Figure 21.8 (b) shows the partial order for the FBM of Figure 21.8 (a).

21.6 Additional Steps

To obtain an operation plan from the partially ordered FBM, IMACS uses the following steps.

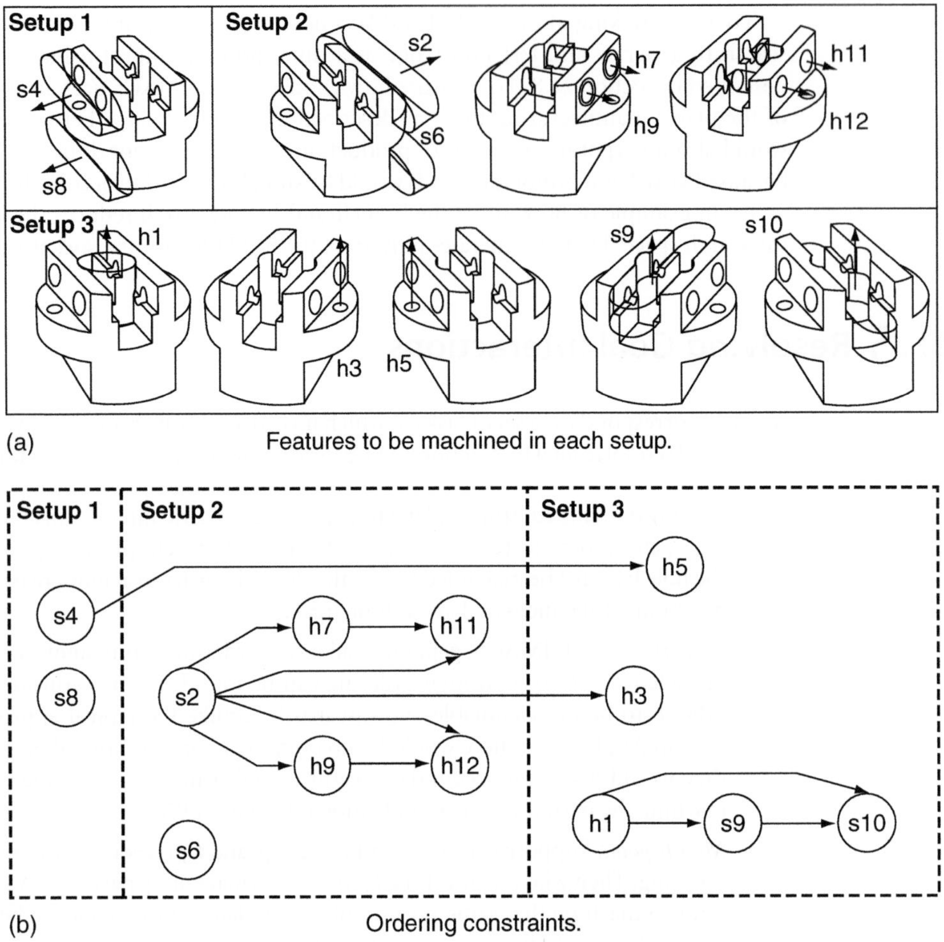

Figure 21.8 An operation plan derived form FBM1. This plan is the optimal one for making P_0. Note that each feature is either a primary feature from FBM1 or a truncation of a primary feature from FBM1. The details of the machining processes are shown in Table 21.1.

1. *Incorporate finishing operations.* For faces with tight surface finishes or tolerances, IMACS adds finishing operations, with precedence constraints to make them come after the corresponding roughing operations. Currently, one finishing operation per face is allowed.
2. *Determine setups.* On a three-axis vertical machining center, features cannot be machined in the same setup unless they have the same approach direction. This and the partial ordering constraints can be used to determine which features can be machined in the same setup, as shown in Figure 21.8 (b). This technique is a version case of plan merging (see Section 24.4).

Table 21.1 Cutting parameters for the operation plan.

Feature name	*Feature type*	*Tool diameter (mm)*	*Feed rate (mm/min)*	*Number of passes*	*Pass length (mm)*
s4	End-milling	50	166	2	225
s8	End-milling	50	166	2	225
s2	End-milling	50	166	2	225
s6	End-milling	50	166	2	225
h7	Drilling	20	244	1	106
h9	Drilling	20	244	1	106
h11	Drilling	30	203	1	39
h12	Drilling	30	203	1	39
h1	Drilling	75	108	1	172.5
h3	Drilling	20	244	1	56
h5	Drilling	20	244	1	56
s9	End-milling	50	166	1	250
s10	End-milling	40	207	3	240

3. *Determine process details.* To select cutting parameters such as those shown in Table 21.1, IMACS uses the recommendations in a standard handbook [113]. The maximum recommended cutting parameters are used, rather than attempting to select optimal cutting parameters; thus IMACS's estimates involve considerable approximation.

As shown in Figure 21.9, these steps correspond to a task decomposition like the ones in HTN planning (see Chapter 11).

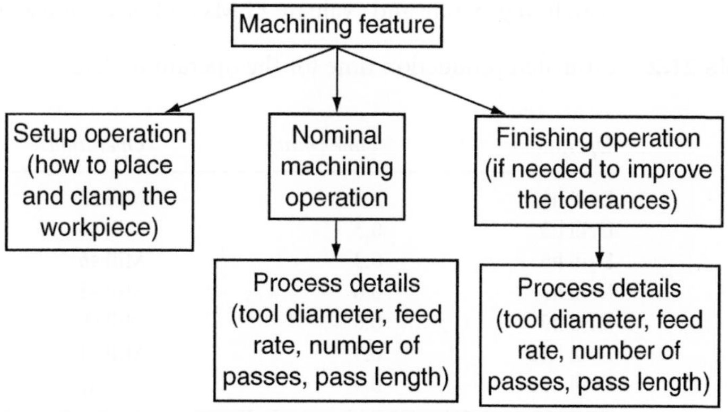

Figure 21.9 Task decomposition in IMACS.

Because each FBM can lead to several different operation plans, IMACS does the above steps inside a depth-first branch-and-bound search, evaluating the plans as described in Section 21.7 in order to find the optimal operation plan. For example, Figure 21.8 and Table 21.1 show the operation plan IMACS finds for the socket P_0.

21.7 Operation Plan Evaluation

Each time IMACS finds an operation plan, it tests whether the plan can achieve the design tolerances. IMACS does this by estimating what tolerances each operation can achieve. Typical approaches for computer-aided tolerance charting are computationally very intensive and consider only limited types of tolerances. Thus, IMACS simply evaluates the manufacturability aspects of a wide variety of tolerances without getting into optimization aspects [254]. As an example, the operation plan shown in Figure 21.8 and Table 21.1 satisfies the tolerances shown in Figure 21.3 and thus is an acceptable way to make P_0 from S_0.

If the plan can achieve the design tolerances, then IMACS estimates the plan's manufacturing time. The total time of a machining operation consists of the cutting time (when the tool is actually engaged in machining) plus the noncutting time (tool-change time, setup time, etc.). Methods have been developed for estimating the fixed and variable costs of machining operations; our formulas for estimating these costs are based on standard handbooks related to machining economics, such as Winchell [554]. As an example, Table 21.2 shows the estimated production time for the operation plan shown in Figure 21.8 and Table 21.1.

21.8 Efficiency Considerations

As described by Gupta and Nau [254], IMACS uses a depth-first branch-and-bound search to generate and evaluate FBMs and plans one at a time. By evaluating them

Table 21.2 Estimated production time for the operation plan.

Operation	*Time (min)*	*Operation*	*Time (min)*
Drill h1	2.3	Mill s2	5.0
Drill h3	0.3	Mill s4	5.0
Drill h5	0.3	Mill s6	5.0
Drill h7	0.6	Mill s8	5.0
Drill h9	0.6	Mill s9	4.0
Drill h11	0.3	Mill s10	4.2
Drill h12	0.3	3 setups	6.0
Total time: 39 minutes			

as they are being generated and keeping track of the best one it has seen so far, IMACS can discard FBMs and plans that look unpromising, even before they have been fully generated. For example, from the 22 primary features (some of which are shown in Figure 21.6), one can form 512 FBMs for the socket P_0, but IMACS generates only 16 of these FBMs. Here are some of IMACS's pruning criteria, which can be thought of as similar to critics in HTN planning.

- IMACS discards an FBM if it contains features whose dimensions and tolerances appear unreasonable. Examples include a hole-drilling operation that has too large a length-to-diameter ratio; a recess-boring operation that has too large a ratio of outer diameter to inner diameter; and two concentric hole-drilling operations with tight concentricity tolerance and opposite approach directions.
- IMACS discards an FBM if it appears that there will be problems with workholding during some of the machining operations. Currently, IMACS's workholding analysis is based on the assumption that a flat-jaw vise is the only available fixturing device [138]. A more sophisticated fixturability analysis would also need to consider the use of other kinds of fixtures, such as vise clamping and toe clamping.
- IMACS computes a quick lower bound on the machining time required for an FBM or plan and discards the FBM or plan if this lower bound is above the time required by the best plan seen so far.

21.9 Concluding Remarks

IMACS was written as a prototype for research purposes, and its operation plans do not contain all of the information that would be needed for a manufacturing process plan. In particular, IMACS does not determine what fixtures to use to hold the part in place during each manufacturing operation, and it does not determine the trajectory to be followed by the cutting tool during the manufacturing operation. However, even without this information, operation plans of the kind produced by IMACS may still provide useful feedback to the designer about the manufacturability of the design and suggest ways to change the design in order to improve its manufacturability while still fulfilling the designer's intent. A way to do this is discussed by Das *et al.* [138].

CHAPTER 22

Emergency Evacuation Planning

22.1 Introduction

Generative planners traditionally require a complete description of the planning domain. However, in practical planning applications, developing a complete description is not always feasible.

One example is the task of planning how to evacuate groups of people who may be in danger. In general, there will be an incomplete domain description, in the form of standard requirements and operating procedures. However, these cannot be used to derive detailed plans, which often require knowledge about previous experiences.

Formulating an evacuation plan can be quite complex: typically there will be hundreds of tasks to be carried out. These tasks will depend on a wide range of factors: sources of danger, available resources, geography, weather predictions, political issues, and so forth. Complete information about the current state will never be available; the planning must include dynamic information gathering, and plans must be formulated with an incomplete world state.

For such a problem, the planning must be done by a human expert or under the supervision of a human expert. It is unrealistic to expect that a planning system could produce good plans by itself, and flawed evacuation plans could yield dire consequences.

This chapter describes a plan formulation tool, Hierarchical Interactive Case-Based Architecture for Planning (HICAP), that was designed to assist human experts in planning emergency evacuations. Because the plans are strongly hierarchical in nature, HICAP represents plans using HTNs.

As shown in Figure 22.1, HICAP integrates a task decomposition editor, Hierarchical Task Editor (HTE), with a mixed-initiative planning system, SHOP integrated with NaCoDAE (SiN). HTE allows users to edit tasks, and SiN allows users to interactively refine HTN plans. Their integration in HICAP ensures that operational plans are framed within the standard requirements and operating procedures or within the changes made by human planners through interactive

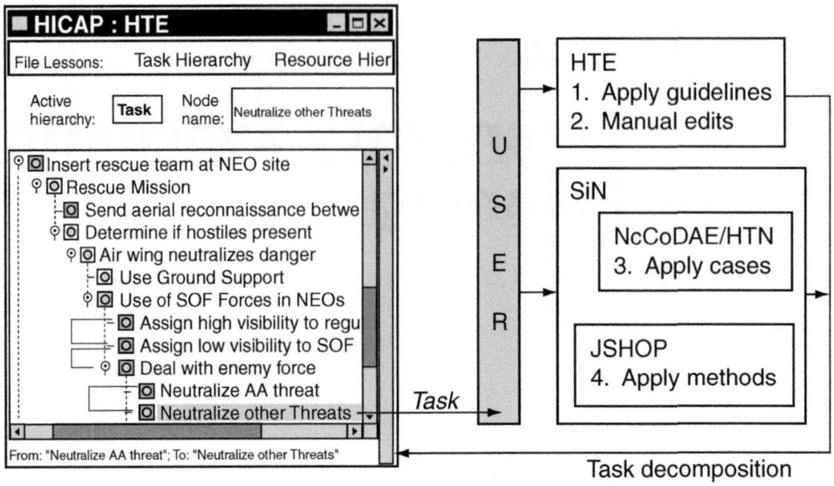

Figure 22.1 The HICAP plan-authoring system.

task editing and interactions with HICAP's case-based and generative planning modules.

Sections 22.4 and 22.5 describe HTE and SiN, and Section 22.6 gives an example of HICAP in operation. Section 22.7 gives a summary, and Section 22.8 discusses related work.

22.2 Evacuation Operations

The number of people involved in carrying out an evacuation operation can range into the hundreds, and they can be geographically distributed and often from several different countries. Depending on the situation, the number of evacuees can number into the thousands.

The official in charge of planning an evacuation operation will do so in the context of a set of standard procedures describing general aspects that must be considered. Figure 22.2 gives an example of the top-level tasks that may need to be performed. ISB denotes the *intermediate staging base*, the location where the evacuation team will be based prior to the evacuation. Arrows between tasks denote their execution order.

The standard procedures are limited: they are idealized and cannot account for characteristics of specific evacuation operations. Thus, whoever is in charge of planning the operation must always adapt these procedures to the needs of the specific operation by eliminating irrelevant planning tasks and adding others. This adaptation process depends partly on the operation's needs and resource availabilities. For example, the standard procedures may state that a small initial team should go into

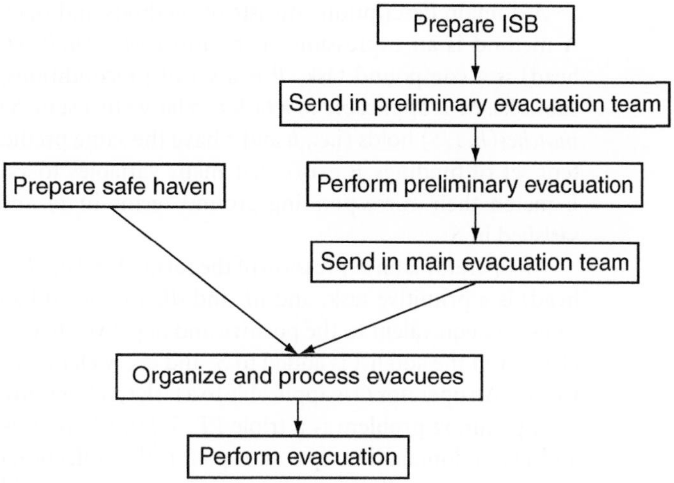

Figure 22.2 Top-level tasks.

the evacuation area prior to the main evacuation team, but in a specific evacuation operation, the time constraints may prevent this. It also depends on the planner's past experience, which may complement the standard procedures by suggesting refinements suitable for the current environment. For example, the planner could draw upon his or her own experience or the experience of others to identify whether it is appropriate to concentrate the evacuees in a single location or to plan multiple evacuation sites.

The following sections describe how HICAP can assist human planners by interactively developing evacuation plans.

22.3 Knowledge Representation

HICAP uses task networks similar to the ones discussed in Chapter 11. It also uses *cases*, portions of plans that were formulated during previous planning episodes (see Section 24.1). Both of these are described in the following subsections.

22.3.1 HTNs

In HICAP, an HTN is a set of tasks and their ordering relations, denoted as $N = (\{t_1, \ldots, t_m\}, \prec)$, where $m \geq 0$ and $\prec$ is a binary relation expressing temporal constraints between tasks. Decomposable tasks are called *compound*, while nondecomposable tasks are called *primitive*.

A domain description consists of methods and operators for generating plans. A method is an expression of the form $M = (h, P, ST)$, where h (the method's head) is a compound task, P is a set of preconditions, and ST is the set of M's subtasks. M is applicable to a task t, relative to a state S (a set of ground atoms), iff $matches(h, t, S)$ holds (i.e., h and t have the same predicate and arity, and a consistent set of bindings B exists that maps variables to values such that all terms in h match their corresponding ground terms in t) and the preconditions P are satisfied in S.

An operator is an expression of the form $O = (h, aL, dL)$, where h (the operator's head) is a primitive task, and aL and dL are the add and delete lists, respectively. These are equivalent to the positive and negative effects defined in Chapter 2: every element in the add list is added to S, and every element in the delete list is removed from S. An operator O is applicable to a task t, relative to a state S, iff $matches(h, t, S)$.

A planning problem is a triple (T, S, D), where T is a set of tasks, S is a state, and D is a domain description. A plan is the collection of primitive tasks obtained by decomposing all compound tasks in a planning problem (T, S, D).

22.3.2 Cases

In many domains it is impossible to assume that a complete domain description of the world is known. A partial domain description may exist, in the form of standard requirements and operating procedures—and these can be encoded into methods and operators.

For those parts of the domain for which no domain description is available, reasoning is done through cases. In HICAP, a case is a task decomposition that was created by the user while solving a previous planning problem. A case looks similar to an instance of a method, but usually it is not an instance of any method in the domain description.

Syntactically, a case is denoted by $C = (h, P, ST, Q)$, where h, P, and ST are defined as for methods and Q is a set of (*question*, *answer*) pairs. Q defines preferences for matching a case to the current state. Preferences are useful for ranking cases in the context of incomplete world states and/or domain theories because they focus users on providing relevant additional state information.

22.4 Hierarchical Task Editor

Because evacuation operations can be complex, it can be difficult to keep track of the completion status for each task to be performed and each element of the evacuation team. HTE was conceived to facilitate the planning process. A portion of the user interface to HTE is shown in the left-hand part of Figure 22.1. Given a domain-specific knowledge base for tactical planning, HTE can be used to browse and edit the knowledge base's components, select tasks for further decomposition, and investigate the status of tasks. HTE serves HICAP as a bookkeeping tool; it maintains the task agenda and helps planners formulate plans for decomposable tasks.

HTE's knowledge base consists of an HTN, a command hierarchy, and an assignment of tasks to commands. For applying it to plan formulation, an HTN (i.e., a task network decomposition hierarchy) was developed that captured critical planning knowledge corresponding to some standard requirements. This required a substantial manual knowledge acquisition effort; the HTN consists of more than 200 tasks and their ordering relations. The HTN also includes a tree structure to represent the command hierarchy among the team that will carry out the operation. In addition, HTE's knowledge base includes relations between tasks and the team elements responsible for them. This is represented by an assignment function from the team elements to the tasks because the mapping of tasks to team elements is many-to-one.

In addition to providing users with a visual description of the standard requirements and procedures, HTE can be used to edit the HTN, its ordering relations, the command hierarchy, and the mapping between tasks and command assignments. Thus, users can use HTE to tailor its knowledge base according to the particular circumstances of the current operation. Furthermore, users can modify the command hierarchy as needed to represent the resources available for the current planning scenario. Finally, they can reassign tasks and/or team elements.

22.5 SiN

HICAP incorporates a mixed-initiative planner, SiN. SiN is a synthesis of JSHOP, a generative planner, with NaCoDAE, a conversational case retriever [94]. SiN is a provably correct algorithm that does not require a complete domain description nor complete information about initial or intermediate world states.

Users can interact with HTE by selecting a task T to be decomposed. This invokes SiN to start decomposing the task under the supervision of the user. This decomposition can be recursive; subtasks of N can themselves be decomposed further. Eventually, nondecomposable tasks corresponding to operational actions will be reached. Task decompositions are immediately displayed by HTE.

The following subsections describe SiN, including theoretical results on its correctness with respect to incomplete domain descriptions, and describe an empirical analysis that demonstrates the impact of the preferences on plan quality.

22.5.1 How SiN Works

As mentioned, the SiN planning algorithm integrates the task decomposition algorithms of two planning systems: the JSHOP generative planner and the NaCoDAE case-based planner. A single (current) state S is maintained in SiN that is accessible to and updateable by both JSHOP and NaCoDAE. Answers given by the user during an interaction with NaCoDAE are added to S (i.e., each question has a translation into a ground atom). Changes to the state that occur by applying JSHOP's operators are also reflected in S.

JSHOP is a Java implementation of SHOP [414], a planning algorithm similar to the **TFD** procedure described in Chapter 11.[1]

NaCoDAE is a mixed-initiative case retriever. Users interact with NaCoDAE in *conversations*, which begin when the user selects a task t. NaCoDAE responds by displaying the top-ranked cases whose preconditions are satisfied and whose heads match t. Cases are ranked according to their similarity to the current state S, which is the state that exists at that time during the conversation. Similarity is computed for each case C by comparing the contents of S with Q, C's (q, a) preference pairs. (That is, each pair is represented as a monadic atom in S, and similarity for a given (q, a) preference pair becomes a membership test in S.) NaCoDAE also displays questions, whose answers are not known in S, ranked according to their frequency among the top-ranked cases. The user can select and answer (with a) any displayed question q, which inserts (q, a) into S. This state change subsequently modifies the case and question rankings. A conversation ends when the user selects a case C, at which time the task t is decomposed into ST (i.e., C's subtasks).

SiN receives as input a set of tasks T, a state S, and a knowledge base $I \cup B$ consisting of an incomplete domain description I and a collection of cases B. The output is a solution plan π consisting of a sequence of operators in I. Both JSHOP and NaCoDAE assist SiN with refining T into a plan. As does JSHOP, SiN maintains the set of tasks in T' that have not been decomposed and the partial solution plan π. At any point in time, either JSHOP or NaCoDAE is in control and is focusing on a compound task $t \in T'$ to decompose. SiN proceeds as follows.

- Rule 1: If JSHOP is in control and can decompose t, it does so and retains control. If JSHOP cannot decompose t but NaCoDAE has cases for decomposing t, then JSHOP will cede control to NaCoDAE.
- Rule 2: If NaCoDAE is in control, it has cases for decomposing t whose preconditions are satisfied. If the user applies one of them to decompose t, then NaCoDAE retains control. If NaCoDAE has no cases to decompose t or if the user decides not to apply any applicable case, then if t can be decomposed by JSHOP, NaCoDAE will cede control to JSHOP.

If neither of these rules applies, then SiN backtracks, if possible. If backtracking is impossible (e.g., because t is a task in T), this planning process is interrupted and a failure is returned.

By continuing in this way, assuming that the process is not interrupted with a failure, SiN will eventually yield a plan π.

1. JSHOP is available for downloading at http://www.cs.umd.edu/projects/shop.

22.5.2 Correctness of SiN

In this section we will assume that SiN performs ordered task decomposition. That is, we assume that all tasks are totally ordered and at each iteration, when refining a set of tasks T', SiN will start by decomposing the first task in T'.

If I is an incomplete domain description and B is a case base (i.e., a set of cases), then a domain description D is consistent with $I \cup B$ iff (1) every method and operator in I is an instance of a method or operator in D and (2) for every case $C = (h, P, ST, Q)$ in B, there is a method $M = (h', P', ST')$ in D such that h, P, and ST are instances of h', P' and ST', respectively. Although many different domain theories might be consistent with $I \cup B$, in general we will not know which of these is the one that produced I and B. However, SiN is correct in the sense that, if it succeeds in outputting a plan, then that plan could have been generated by JSHOP using any domain description consistent with $I \cup B$.

Proposition 22.1 *Let T be a collection of tasks, S be an initial state, I be an incomplete domain description, and B be a case base, and let SiN(T, S, I, B) represent the invocation of SiN with those items as inputs. Suppose that SiN performs ordered task decomposition. Then:*

- *If SiN(T, S, I, B) returns a plan π, then for every domain description D consistent with $I \cup B$, π is a solution plan for the planning problem (T, S, D).*
- *If SiN(T, S, I, B) cannot find a plan, then there is a domain description D consistent with $I \cup B$ such that no solution plan exists for (T, S, D).*

The proof is done by induction on the number of iterations of the SiN algorithm. The proof shows that each SiN task decomposition in $(T, S, I \cup B)$ corresponds to a JSHOP task decomposition in (T, S, D). This is sufficient to prove correctness because of the correctness of JSHOP's planning algorithm [414].

This proposition suggests that cases in SiN supply two kinds of knowledge. First, they provide control knowledge, similar to the knowledge encoded in cases using derivational replay when a complete domain description is available [275, 523]. Because cases are instances of methods, applying a case is comparable to a replay step in which the method selected to decompose a task is the one in the case's derivational trace. The main difference is that, while cases in replay systems correspond to a complete derivational trace, cases in SiN correspond to a single step in the derivational trace. Second, cases in SiN augment the domain description and thus provide domain knowledge as do cases in many case-based planners (e.g., [255]).

22.5.3 Imperfect World Information

SiN uses NaCoDAE to dynamically elicit the world state, which involves obtaining the user's preferences. Depending on the user's answers, cases will get reranked. When solving a task, the user can choose any of the cases, independent of their ranking, provided that all their preconditions are met. The preferences play a pivotal role in determining plan quality due to the absence of a complete domain description.

Consider the following two simplified cases.

Case 1:

```
Head: selectTransport(ISB,evacuation-site)
Preconditions: HelosAvailable(ISB)
Question-Answer pairs: Weather conditions? Fine
Subtasks: Transport(ISB,evacuation-site,HELOS)
```

Case 2:

```
Head: selectTransport(ISB,evacuation-site)
Preconditions: groundTransportAvailable(ISB)
Question-Answer pairs:
   Weather conditions? Rainy
   Imminent danger to evacuees? No
Subtasks: Transport(ISB,evacuation-site,GroundTransport)
```

These cases both concern the selection of transportation means between an ISB and the site to be evacuated. The first case suggests using helicopters provided that they are available at the ISB. The second one suggests using ground transportation provided that the corresponding transportation means are available at the ISB. If the two cases are applicable because both preconditions are met, the answers given by the user will determine a preference between them. For example, if the weather is rainy and there is no immediate danger for the evacuees, NaCoDAE would suggest the second case. The rationale behind this is that flying in rainy conditions is risky. Thus, selecting ground transportation would be a better choice.

22.6 Example

During a typical planning episode, the user views the top-level tasks first, revising them or their assignments if necessary. He or she may choose to decompose any of the tasks and view their decomposition. Figure 22.3 shows an intermediate stage during this process. The user has selected the task "Select assembly areas evacuation & ECC [Evacuation Control Center] sites." Thus, the left-hand pane highlights this task. The right-hand pane shows the hierarchical organization of the evacuation team, so that the user can assign the task to a particular part of the team.

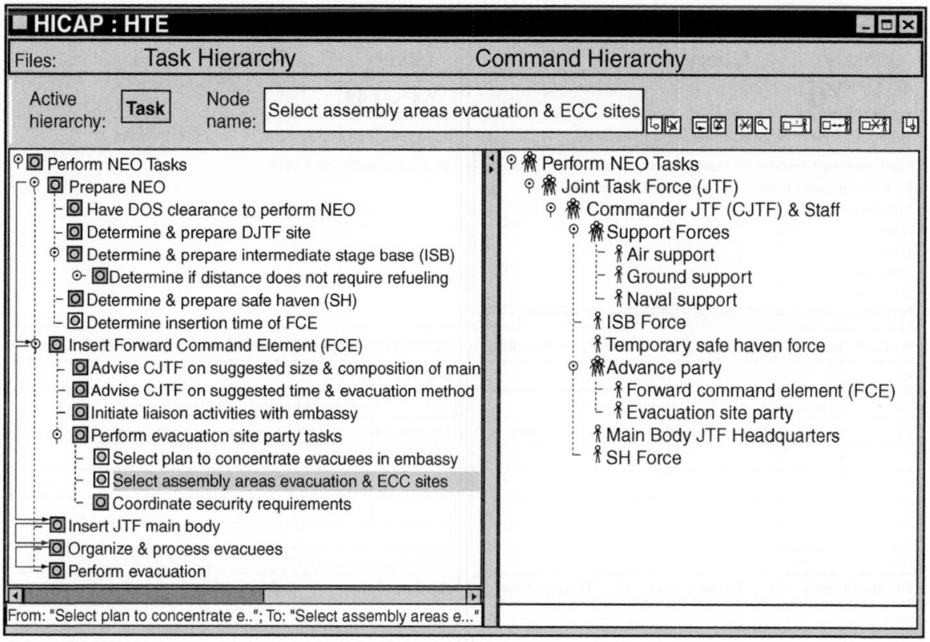

Figure 22.3 A snapshot of HTE's interface, displaying tasks (left) and the hierarchical organization of the evacuation team (right). Arrows denote ordering constraints.

Several alternative methods can be considered for decomposing the "Select assembly areas" task. When the planner selects this task, HICAP starts NaCoDAE, which displays the alternatives along with two questions to help distinguish which is the best match [see Figure 22.4 (a)].

In Figure 22.4 (b), the user has answered one of the questions, and this has yielded a perfect match to one of the cases for the "Select assembly areas" task. Suppose that the user selects this case to decompose this task. Figure 22.5 shows the result of this decomposition; two new subtasks are displayed that correspond to this case's decomposition network. Interaction can continue in a similar manner until all of the operational elements of the plan have been elaborated.

22.7 Summary

HICAP is an interactive planning tool that assists users in formulating an operational plan. As of the publication date of this book, HICAP had not been deployed but was still under development at the U.S. Naval Research Laboratory.

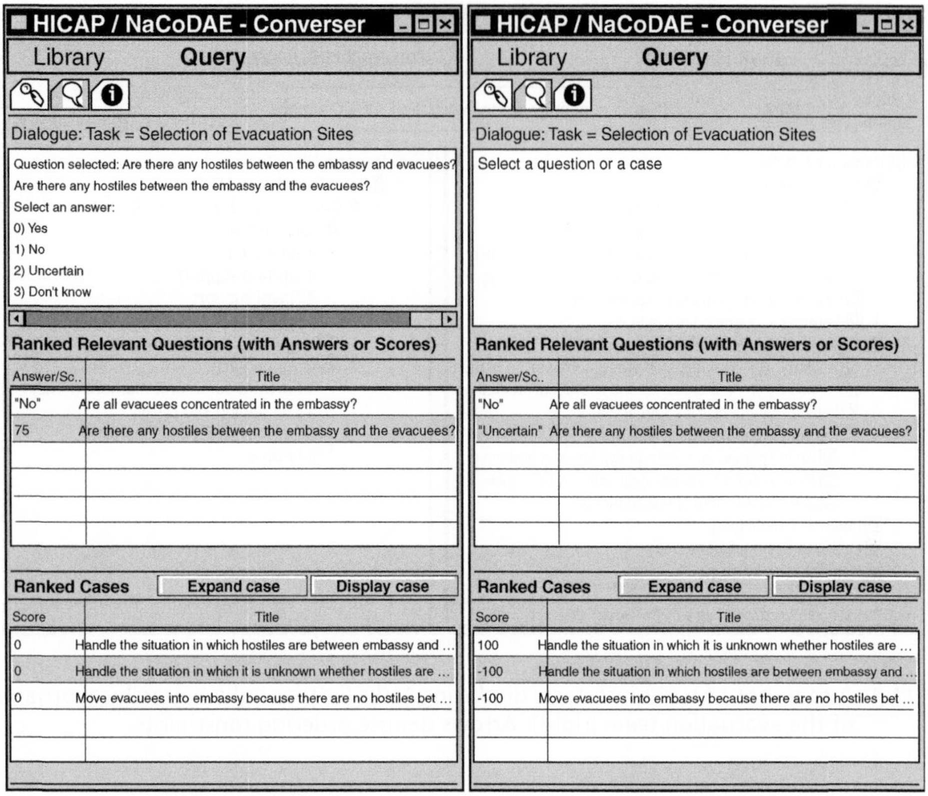

(a) Before a question has been answered (b) After a question has been answered

Figure 22.4 Two snapshots of NaCoDAE/HTE's interface. In each, the top window displays advice on what to do next and, when the user selects a question, lists the possible answers. The lower windows display the questions and cases, respectively.

HICAP is interactive; it supports task editing and triggers conversations for tasks that can be decomposed in more than one way. The planning process consists of HTN task decomposition, some of which is done by the user using the HTE editor and some of which is done by HICAP using the SiN planning algorithm. The HTE plan editor allows the user to visually check that all tasks are assigned the necessary resources.

HICAP's SiN procedure is a provably correct procedure for combined case-based and generative planning with incomplete domain descriptions. It tightly integrates NaCoDAE/HTE's case-based task decomposition and JSHOP's generative planning ability. Experimental results with SiN show that a user can dynamically guide SiN

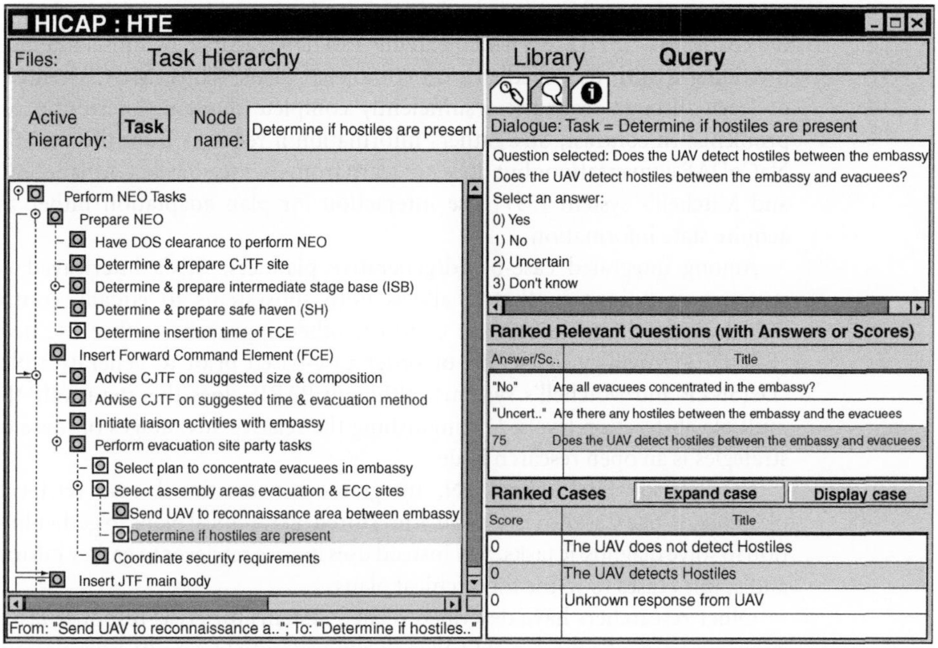

Figure 22.5 HICAP's interface after decomposing the "Select assembly areas" task.

by giving preferences to it as part of the user's normal interaction with SiN during the planning process.

SiN's ability to combine both experiential and generative knowledge sources can be beneficial in real-world domains where some processes are well known and others are obscure but recorded memories exist on how they were performed. Evacuation planning is an example of this type of domain.

22.8 Discussion and Historical Remarks

HICAP is being developed at the U.S. Naval Research Laboratory. Our descriptions of HICAP, SiN, and JSHOP are based on two sources [406, 414]. The following text summarizes other work related to HICAP.

CHEF [256] and DIAL [356] are case-based but do not have a generative component, and thus they need a large case base to perform well across a wide variety of problems. PRODIGY/Analogy [523], DerSNLP [275], and PARIS [61] integrate generative and case-based planning but require a complete domain theory and are not mixed-initiative.

At least three other integrated (case-based/generative), mixed-initiative planners exist. MI-CBP [526], which extends PRODIGY/Analogy, limits interaction to providing it with user feedback on completed plans. Thus, MI-CBP must input or learn through feedback a sufficiently complete domain description to solve problems. In contrast, SiN gathers information it requires from the user through NaCoDAE conversations but does not learn from user feedback. CAPlan/CbC [407] and Mitchell's system [397] use interaction for plan adaptation rather than to acquire state information.

Among integrated case-based/generative planners, SiN's interleaved control structure is unique in that it allows both subsystems to equally control the task decomposition process. In contrast, other approaches either use heuristics (PRODIGY/Analogy, MI-CBP) or order case-based prior to generative planning (DerSNLP and Mitchell's system), although PARIS does this iteratively through multiple abstraction levels. Distinguishing the relative advantages of these control strategies is an open research issue.

CaseAdvisor [107], like SiN, integrates conversational case retrieval with planning. While CaseAdvisor applies prestored hierarchical plans to gather information to solve diagnostic tasks, SiN instead uses its case retriever to gather information and applies cases to refine hierarchical plans.

Other researchers have described related systems for crisis response tasks. Tate *et al.* [505] describe the use of O-Plan as a mixed initiative multi-user planning and replanning aid generating multiple potential responses for a range of non-combatant evacuation and crisis response operations, Ferguson and Allen [186] describe an interactive planner for crisis response applications, and Wolverton and desJardins [557] describe a distributed planning tool, these systems are note case-based.

Gervasio *et al.* [221] describe an interactive hierarchical case-based scheduler for crisis response, but it does not perform interactive plan formulation. Avesani *et al.* [26] describe a case-based planning approach for fighting forest fires that supports interactive plan adaptation, but it does not use hierarchical guidelines to formulate plans as is done in HICAP. Finally, Leake *et al.* [357] describe a case-based planner applied to disaster response tasks that focuses on learning case adaptation knowledge, but it is not driven by standard requirements and operating procedures, and it focuses interactions on knowledge acquisition rather than problem elicitation.

Chapter 23

Planning in the Game of Bridge

23.1 Introduction

This chapter describes how an adaptation of HTN planning is used in Bridge Baron, a computer program for the game of bridge. The use of HTN planning in Bridge Baron contributed to Bridge Baron's winning the 1997 world championship of computer bridge.

23.2 Overview of Bridge

Bridge is a game played by four players, using a standard deck of 52 playing cards, divided into four suits (spades ♠, hearts ♡, diamonds ◇, and clubs ♣), each containing 13 cards. The players, who are normally referred to as North, South, East, and West, play as two opposing teams, with North and South playing as partners against East and West. A bridge deal consists of two phases, bidding and play.

1. *Bidding.* Whichever player was designated as dealer for the deal deals the cards, distributing them equally among the four players. Each player holds his or her cards so that no other player can see them.

   After the cards are dealt, the players make *bids* for the privilege of determining which suit (if any) is the *trump* suit (i.e., cards of this suit will win over cards not of this suit). Nominally, each bid consists of two things: a proposed trump suit or a bid of "notrump" to propose that no suit should be trump, and how many *tricks* (see below) the bidder promises to take. However, various bidding conventions have been developed in which these bids are also used to convey information to the bidder's partner about how strong the bidder's hand is.

   The bidding proceeds until no player is willing to make a higher bid. At that point, the highest bid becomes the contract for the hand. In the highest

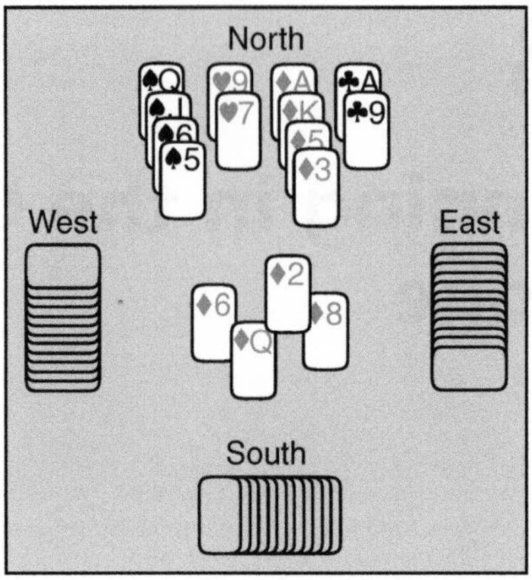

Figure 23.1 The basic unit of play is the trick, in which each player places a card face up in the middle of the table. In this example, West leads the 6 of diamonds, North (dummy) plays the 2 of diamonds, East plays the 8 of diamonds, and South (declarer) plays the queen of diamonds. The latter takes the trick.

bidder's team, the player who bid this suit first becomes the *declarer*, and the declarer's partner becomes the *dummy*. The other two players become the *defenders*.

2. *Play*. The first time that it is the dummy's turn to play a card (see below), the dummy lays her or his cards on the table, face up so that everyone can see them. During the card play, the declarer is responsible for playing both the declarer's cards and the dummy's cards.

   The basic unit of card play is the *trick*, in which each player in turn plays a card by placing it face up on the table as shown in Figure 23.1. Whenever possible, the players must *follow suit*: they must play cards of the same suit as the card that was *led*, i.e., played by the first player. The trick is taken by the highest card in the suit led, unless some player plays a card in the trump suit, in which case the highest trump card takes the trick. The first trick is led by the player to the left of the declarer, and the winner of each trick plays the lead card for the next trick.

   The card play proceeds, one trick at a time, until no player has any cards left. At that point, the bridge hand is scored according to how many tricks each team took and whether the declarer's team took as many tricks as promised during the bidding.

In most bridge hands, the declarer spends some time at the beginning of the game planning how to play his or her cards and the dummy's cards. Because the declarer cannot be certain of which cards are in each opponent's hand and how each opponent will choose to play those cards, the plan needs to contain contingencies for various possible card plays by the opponents. Thus, rather than being a single linear sequence of moves, the plan is more like a tree structure (see Section 23.3).

The plan is normally a combination of various stratagems for trying to win tricks. There are a number of well-known stratagems, which have names like ruffing, cross-ruffing, finessing, cashing out, discovery plays, and so forth (Section 23.4 gives an example). The ability of a bridge player depends partly on how skillfully he or she can plan and execute these stratagems. This is especially true for the declarer, who is responsible for playing both his or her cards and the dummy's cards.

23.3 Game-Tree Search in Bridge

Game-tree search is a technique for analyzing an adversarial game in order to try to determine who can win the game and what moves the players should make in order to win. Game-tree search is one of the oldest topics in AI. The original ideas were developed by Shannon [472] in 1950 and independently by Turing in 1951, in the context of the game of chess. Their ideas still form the basis for the techniques used today.

Computer programs based on game-tree search techniques are now as good as or better than humans in several popular games of strategy, such as chess [274] and checkers [465]. However, as described in this section, there are some difficulties in finding a good way to use game-tree search techniques in the game of bridge, and even the best bridge programs still play significantly more poorly than the best human bridge players.

A *game tree* is a tree whose nodes represent states of the game and whose branches represent the moves made by the agents who are playing the game. Game trees can be used to model any game that satisfies the following restrictions: The game is played by two players, whom we will call *Max* and *Min*, who make moves sequentially rather than simultaneously; at each turn a player can choose from only a finite number of possible moves; the game is guaranteed to end within some finite number of moves; the game is zero-sum (i.e., an outcome that is good for one player is equally bad for the other player); and at each point in the game, each player knows the entire state of the game and knows what moves the other player is able to make.

In a game tree, the leaf nodes represent the possible outcomes of the game and have numeric "payoff values" that represent the outcome for one of the players. (Because the game is a zero-sum game, the outcome for the other player is taken to be the negative of the payoff value.) Values are computed for the other nodes of the tree using the well-known *minimax formula*, which is defined recursively as follows:

$$m(u) = \begin{cases} \text{the payoff value for } u & \text{if } u \text{ is a leaf node} \\ \max\{m(v) \mid v \text{ is a child of } u\} & \text{if it is Max's move at } u \\ \min\{m(v) \mid v \text{ is a child of } u\} & \text{if it is Min's move at } u \end{cases}$$

The minimax computation is basically a brute-force search. If implemented as shown in the formula, it would examine every node in the game tree. In practical implementations of minimax game-tree searching, a number of techniques are used to improve the efficiency of this computation: putting a bound on the depth of the search, using alpha-beta pruning, doing transposition-table lookup, and so forth. However, even with enhancements such as these, minimax computations often involve examining huge numbers of nodes in the game tree. For example, in the match between Deep Blue and Kasparov in 1997, Deep Blue examined roughly 60 billion nodes per move [274]. In contrast, humans examine at most a few dozen board positions before deciding on their next moves [70].

In adapting the game-tree model for use in bridge, it is not too hard to accomodate four players rather than two because the players play as two opposing teams. However, it is more difficult to find a good way to accomodate the fact that bridge is a *partial-information* game. Since bridge players don't know what cards are in the other players' hands (except, after the opening lead, what cards are in the dummy's hand), each player has only partial knowledge of the state of the world, the possible actions, and their effects. If we were to construct a game tree that included all of the moves a player *might* be able to make, the size of this tree would vary from one deal of the cards to another—but it would include about 5.6×10^{44} leaf nodes in the worst case ([493], p. 226), and about 2.3×10^{24} leaf nodes in the average case ([369], p. 8). Because a bridge hand is normally played in just a few minutes, there is not enough time to search enough of this tree to make good decisions.

One way to make the game tree smaller is to generate many random hypotheses for how the cards might be distributed among the other players' hands, generate and search the game trees corresponding to each of the hypotheses, and average the results to determine the best move. This Monte Carlo approach removes the necessity of representing uncertainty about the players' cards within the game tree itself, thereby reducing the size of the game tree by as much as a multiplicative factor of 5.2×10^{6}. However, to reduce the number of nodes from 5.6×10^{44} down to about 10^{38} still leaves a prohibitively large game tree, unless other ways can be found to reduce the size of the tree even further.

Another way to reduce the size of the game tree is to take the value that was computed for one node of a game tree and use it as the value of other nodes that are sufficiently similar to the first one. For example, if a player could play the ♠6 or the ♠5, then these plays are basically equivalent, so the same value could be used for both of them. This scheme was originally developed for use in the game of Sprouts [22], but it is used in several computer bridge programs (e.g., [230]).

A third approach, which is the one described in this chapter, is based on the observation that bridge is a game of planning. The bridge literature describes a number of stratagems (finessing, ruffing, cross-ruffing, and so forth) that people combine into strategic plans for how to play their bridge hands. It is possible to take advantage of the planning nature of bridge, by adapting and extending some ideas from total-order HTN planning (see Chapter 11). For declarer play in bridge, a modified version of total-order HTN planning can be used to generate a game tree whose branching factor depends on the number of different stratagems that a

Table 23.1 Game-tree size produced in bridge by a full game-tree search and by the planning algorithm used for declarer play in Bridge Baron.

	Brute-force search	*Bridge Baron*
Worst case	About 5.6×10^{44} leaf nodes	About 305,000 leaf nodes
Average case	About 2.3×10^{24} leaf nodes	About 26,000 leaf nodes

player might pursue, rather than the number of different possible ways to play the cards [495]. Because the number of sensible stratagems is usually much less than the number of possible card plays, this approach generates game trees that are small enough to be searched completely, as shown in Table 23.1.

23.4 Adapting HTN Planning for Bridge

Tignum 2 is an algorithm for declarer play in bridge, based on a modified version of total-order HTN planning. To represent the various stratagems of card playing in bridge, Tignum 2 uses structures similar to totally ordered methods, but modified to represent uncertainty and multiple players.

- Although Tignum 2 cannot be certain about which cards have been dealt to each of the opponents, it can calculate the probabilities associated with the locations of those cards—and as part of the current state, Tignum 2 includes "belief functions" that represent those probabilities.
- Some methods refer to actions performed by the opponents. These methods make assumptions about the cards in the opponents' hands, and Tignum 2's authors wrote a large enough set of methods that most of the likely states of the world are each covered by at least one method.

To generate game trees, Tignum 2 uses a procedure similar to Forward-decomposition (see Chapter 11), but adapted to build up a game tree rather than a plan. The branches of the game tree represent moves generated by the methods. Tignum 2 applies all methods applicable to a given state of the world to produce new states of the world and continues recursively until there are no applicable methods that have not already been applied to the appropriate state of the world.

For example, Figure 23.2 shows a bridge hand and a portion of the task network that Tignum 2 would generate for this hand. (Note that it refers to actions performed by each of the players in the game.) This portion of the task network is generated by the HTN methods for *finessing*, a stratagem in which the declarer tries to win a trick with a high card by playing it after an opponent who has a higher card. West leads the ♠2. If North (a defender) has the ♠Q but does not play it, then East (dummy) will

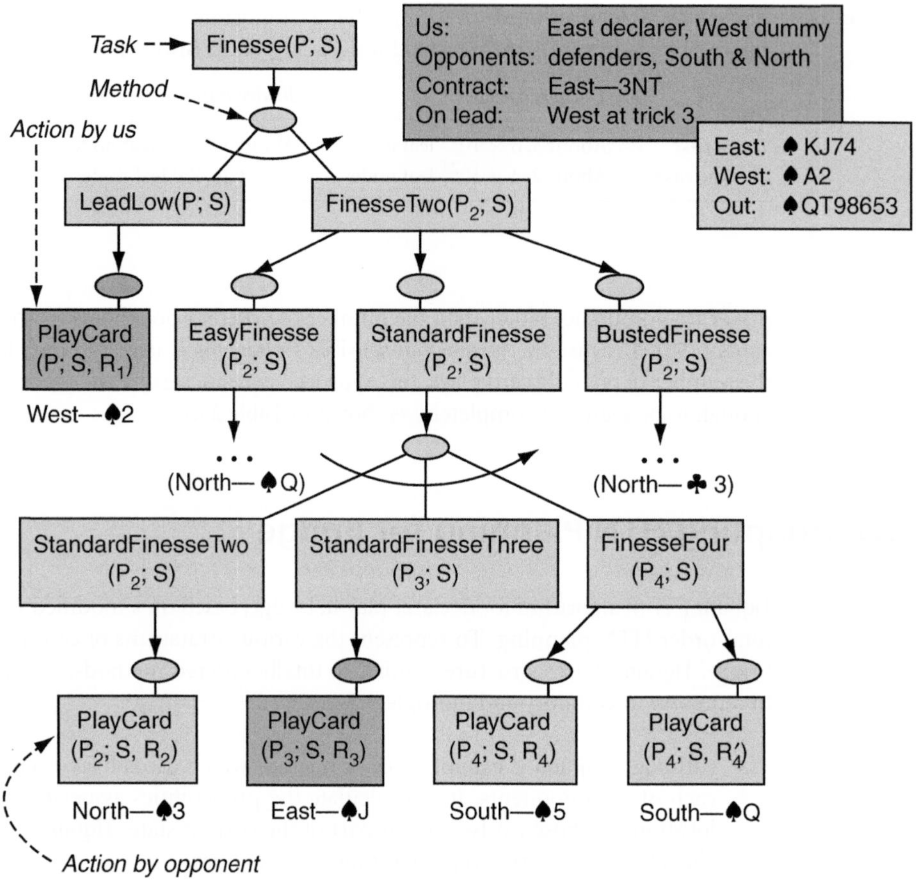

Figure 23.2 A bridge hand, and a portion of the task network that Tignum 2 would generate for finessing in this bridge hand.

be able to win a trick with the ♠J because East plays after North. (North wouldn't play the ♠Q if she or he had any alternative because then East would win the trick with the ♠K and would win a later trick with the ♠J.) However, if South (the other defender) has the ♠Q, South will play it after East plays the ♠J, and East will not win the trick.

In a task network generated by Tignum 2, the order in which the actions will occur is determined by the total-ordering constraints. By listing the actions in the order they will occur, the task network can be "serialized" into a game tree. As an example, Figure 23.3 shows the process of serializing the task network in Figure 23.2. Figure 23.4 shows a game tree that includes both the serialization produced in Figure 23.3 and the sequence of the actions generated by another stratagem called *cashing out*, in which the declarer simply plays all of the high cards that are guaranteed to win tricks.

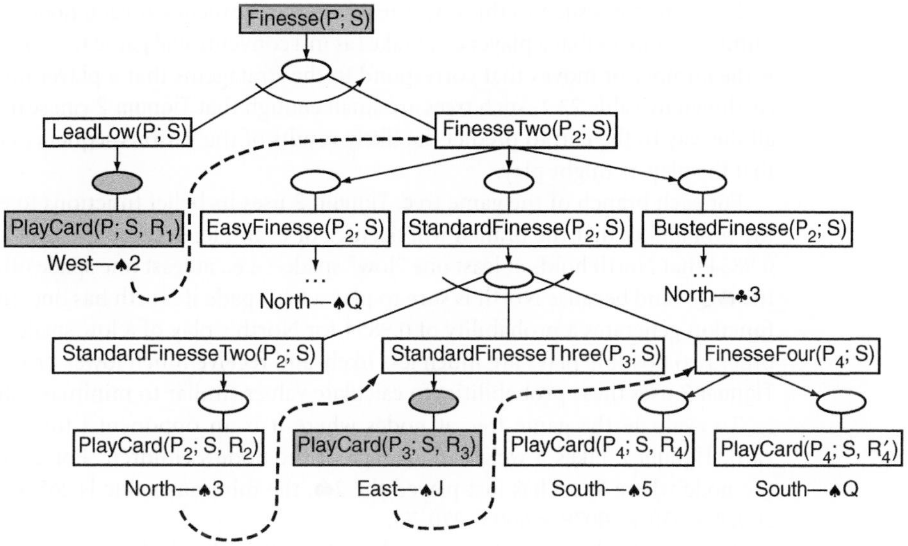

Figure 23.3 Serializing the task network for finessing.

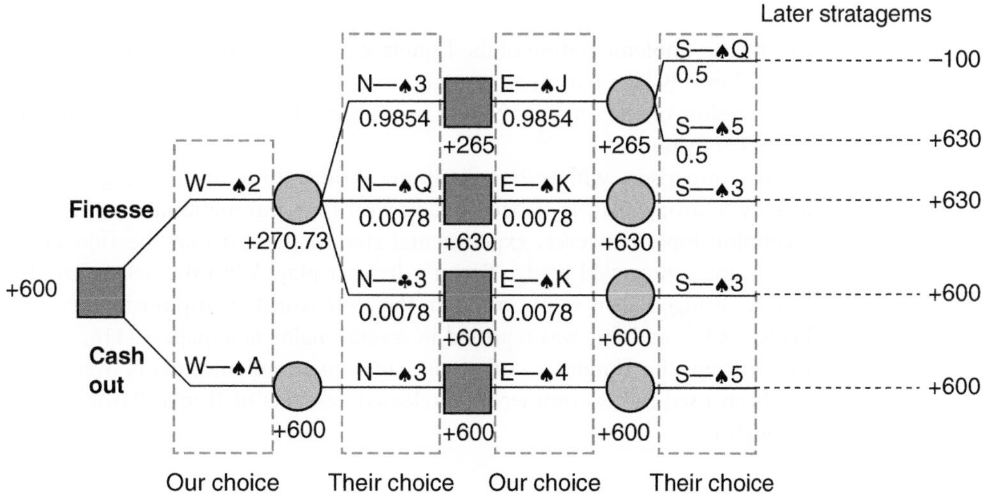

Figure 23.4 The game tree produced from the task network for finessing and a task network for cashing out.

For game trees such as this one, the number of branches at each node is not the number of moves that a player can make (as in a conventional game tree) but instead is the number of moves that correspond to the stratagems that a player might use. As shown in Table 23.1, such trees are small enough that Tignum 2 can search them all the way to the end to predict the likely results of the various sequences of cards that the players might play.

For each branch of the game tree, Tignum 2 uses its belief functions to estimate the probability that the branch will occur. For example, because the probability is 0.9854 that North holds at least one "low" spade—i.e., at least one spade other than the ♠Q—and because North is sure to play a low spade if North has one, the belief function generates a probability of 0.9854 for North's play of a low spade. North's other two possible plays are much less likely and receive much lower probabilities. Tignum 2 uses these probabilities to calculate values similar to minimax values.

To evaluate the game tree at nodes where it is an opponent's turn to play a card, Tignum 2 takes a weighted average of the node's children. For example, at the node where West has just played the 2♠, the minimax value is $265 \times .9854 + .0078 \times 630 + .0078 \times 600 = 270.73$.

To evaluate the game tree at nodes where it is the declarer's turn to play a card, Tignum 2 chooses the play that results in the highest score. For example, in Figure 23.4, West chooses to play the ♠A that resulted from the cashing out method, which results in a score of +600, rather than the ♠2 that resulted from the finesse method, which results in a score of +270.73.

23.5 Implementation and Results

In 1997, an implementation of the Tignum 2 procedure for declarer play was incorporated into Bridge Baron, an existing computer program for the game of bridge. This version of the Tignum 2 code contained 91 HTN task names and at least 400 HTN methods.

In comparison with other computer bridge programs, Bridge Baron was already a strong player: it had already won four international computer bridge championships. However, experimental studies showed that the Tignum 2 code significantly improved Bridge Baron's declarer play. With the help of the Tignum 2 code, Bridge Baron went on to win the 1997 world championship of computer bridge [495], and this was reported in several major newspapers [116, 513]. As of this writing, the Tignum 2 code (with subsequent enhancements over the years) has been used in six commercially released versions of Bridge Baron: versions 8 through 13.

Part VII
Conclusion

A simplified view of the evolution of automated planning consists of three overlapping phases and two primary orientations. Each of these had its merits and made essential contributions to the field, and each also had weak points.

The phases include the early work on classical planning, more recent work on neoclassical planning, and work on extended planning and scheduling representation and problems. The first and especially the second phase were characterized by a strong focus on search issues and by the evaluation and comparison of algorithms on simple "toy domains" and benchmarks. The third phase started as early as the first one but aimed at solving more ambitious problems; today it is becoming capable of addressing realistic applications.

The two primary orientations are toward theoretical work and application-oriented work. The former tended to remain quite narrow in scope, while publications of the latter type often tended to involve rather *ad hoc* programming efforts and search techniques. It is only recently that a significant amount of synergy between the theory and practice of automated planning has built up.

In this book, we deliberately chose not to focus solely on classical planning. Instead, we devoted large parts of the book to extended classes of automated planning that relaxed the various assumptions discussed in Chapter 1.

We also devoted a large part of the book to descriptions of application-oriented work. Unfortunately, however, these chapters remain only case studies. It is not yet possible to present a comprehensive mapping from the features of an application domain to the planning techniques that best address these features.

The published literature related to automated planning is quite large, and it is not feasible in a single book to give detailed discussions of it all. Chapter 24 gives brief summaries of several topics that we did not discuss in the previous chapters. These topics can be classified into other planning algorithms and approaches that were not covered earlier; techniques that help improve the performance of planners;

and problems that are related to planning or the use of planning representations and/or algorithms, although they do not directly aim at synthesizing plans.

Thus the following chapter discusses case-based planning, planning with linear and integer programming, multiagent planning, plan merging and plan rewriting, abstraction hierarchies, domain analysis, planning and learning, planning and acting, and plan recognition.

Several other issues—such as mixed-initiative and interactive planning [187, 412] and domain modeling and knowledge acquisition for planning [384, 385]—would certainly have deserved additional sections.

Chapter 24

Other Approaches to Planning

24.1 Case-Based Planning

In *case-based planning*, the planning system has a *case library* of solutions to previous problems and uses these cases to solve new planning problems. Here are some of the reasons why one might want to do this.

- One of the most difficult parts of developing robust planning systems for practical applications is compiling the domain-specific knowledge for each new planning domain. Generative planners traditionally require a complete domain description that provides a clear semantics for the planners' inferencing mechanisms. However, in many planning domains, it is not feasible to develop anything more than a partial description of the domain. One way to reason about parts of the domain for which no complete domain description is available is to reuse plans that worked in previous planning episodes.
- As we have seen, planning is a computationally difficult activity even in very restricted planning domains. If similar kinds of planning problems occur often enough in some planning domain, retrieving and adapting old planning information may yield a significant speedup in the planning process.

Example 24.1 In manufacturing industries, *process planning* is the task of planning which manufacturing operations to use to create a product. The most widely used technique for computer-aided process planning is *variant process planning* [118, 119], a case-based planning technique in which the case adaptation is done manually rather than by the computer. Given some information about a new product, a computer system will retrieve a process plan for a similar previous product, and a skilled human will modify this plan by hand to create a plan for the new product. One reason for the success of this technique is that when a company decides to produce a new product, the new product will usually be similar (in terms of its manufacturing requirements) to previous products that the company has produced. In such cases, adapting an old plan can be done much quicker than creating a new plan from scratch. ■

The typical problem-solving cycle of a case-based planner on a planning problem $\mathcal{P}$ consists of retrieval of one or more cases of solutions to planning problems similar to $\mathcal{P}$ according to some similarity metric, adaptation of the case or cases to solve $\mathcal{P}$, and possibly some revisions to the case base, retrieval mechanism, or adaptation mechanism based on feedback from the current planning episode.

Similarity Metrics. The purpose of a similarity metric is to enable the case-retrieval program to retrieve cases that can easily be adapted to solve the current problem. The basic assumption underlying most similarity metrics is that the more similar two planning problems are, the more likely it is that a solution to one of them can easily be adapted to produce a solution to the other one. Thus, the goal of a good similarity metric is to provide a good measure of how similar two problems are.

Several algorithms have been proposed for computing the similarity of two problems. A *static similarity measure* is one that will always return the same similarity value for a given pair of problems, regardless of when that value is computed. Examples are the similarity measures used in PRIAR [301], PRODIGY/Analogy [525], SPA [257], DerSNLP [275], and PARIS [61]. A *dynamic similarity measure* is one whose value may change after each problem-solving episode, in order to incorporate new information learned during that problem-solving episode. Examples include the similarity measures used in CaPER [322] and CAPlan/CbC [407].

Case Adaptation. Case-adaptation techniques can be classified into two primary approaches: transformational analogy [103] and derivational analogy [104]. In *transformational analogy*, the case or cases retrieved from the library will be modified to solve the new problem. The modifications may include reordering some of the actions in the plan, removing some of them, or changing some of the parameter bindings. A single case may be retrieved and transformed into a new solution, as in MOLGEN [203], PRIAR [301], SPA [257], and DIAL [356]. Alternatively, multiple cases, each corresponding to a small subproblem, may be combined and extended to solve a single larger problem [452, 453].

In *derivational analogy*, the case library contains *derivational traces* of the planning decisions, rather than the plans themselves, and the case adaptation consists of replaying the old decisions in the context of the new problem. Some examples of derivational case-based planners include PRODIGY/Analogy [525], PARIS [61], DerSNLP [275], CAPlan/CbC [407], and derUCP [25].

In many cases, the solution to $\mathcal{P}$ is obtained partly through case adaptation and partly through generative planning. Some case-based planners (e.g., CHEF [256] and DIAL [356]) do not have a generative component, and thus need a large case base to perform well across a wide variety of problems. PRODIGY/Analogy [523], DerSNLP [275], PARIS [61], and derUCP [25] integrate generative and case-based planning but require a complete domain description.

One way to do case-based planning without a complete domain description is through interactions with an expert human user. HICAP (see Chapter 22) gathers information it needs to determine the relevance of its cases through interaction with the user. CAPlan/CbC [407] and Mitchell's system [397] use interactions for plan adaptation.

Revisions. Several ways have been proposed for revising the planner's knowledge to incorporate information about the latest planning episode. Prominent among these are machine learning approaches, particularly explanation-based learning (EBL). PRODIGY [525] uses EBL to learn control rules to guide its search, PARIS [61] uses EBL to develop abstract cases that can later be refined after they have been retrieved, and DerSNLP+EBL [277] uses EBL to analyze cases where a retrieved plan was unhelpful, in order to improve the selection of retrieved cases in the future.

Performance. Nebel and Koehler's formal analysis of the complexity of plan adaptation [421] says that if certain conditions on the adaptation strategy are satisfied, plan adaptation can be exponentially harder than planning from scratch. At first glance, this result would seem to conflict with empirical studies, in which case-based planners based on derivational analogy have consistently outperformed the base-level generative planners on which the case-based planners were constructed [276, 405, 525].

However, a closer examination of the limitations of Nebel and Koehler's result resolves the conflict. In general, there may be several alternative ways to adapt a case to a new problem, and Nebel and Koehler's analysis requires the plan-adaptation strategy to find the adaptation that reuses as much of the case as possible. Au *et al.* [25] have shown (1) that derivational analogy does not satisfy this assumption, and hence the complexity result does not apply, and (2) that derivational analogy will never increase the size of the planner's search space and may potentially decrease it by an exponential amount.

24.2 Linear and Integer Programming

Linear programs (LPs) and *integer programs* (IPs) have a long history in the field of operations research and have been used to model a large number of problems in resource allocation, facility location, distribution, production, reliability, and design [422]. One potential advantage of using LP and IP techniques in planning is that they quite naturally allow the incorporation of numeric constraints and objectives into planning domains (e.g., [317]).

The general format for an LP or IP is

$$\text{minimize } CX \text{ subject to } AX \geq B,$$

where A is an $(m \times n)$ matrix, B is an m-dimensional column vector, C is an n-dimensional row vector, and X is an n-dimensional column vector. In an LP, X's elements $x_1, \ldots, x_n$ may be any real numbers; in an IP, they must be integers; and in a mixed IP, some but not all of them must be integers. If the integer variables of an IP (or mixed IP) are required to be in $\{0, 1\}$, then it is an 0-1 IP (or mixed 0-1 IP). A vector X which satisfies the constraints is called a *feasible solution.* If X also minimizes the objective function CX, then it is called an *optimal solution* and CX is called the *optimal value.*

Linear programming relies on the well-known Simplex technique and several recent algorithmic improvements that make it a polynomial and very efficiently solved problem, even for very large LP instances. LP is often used as a relaxation for an IP.

The standard technique for solving an IP involves a branch-and-bound search (see Appendix A) in which the bounding function is the LP relaxation of the IP. There are several solvers available for doing this; probably the best known of these is Cplex. The size of the problems that can be solved has increased by several orders of magnitude over the last few years. Current research on IPs generally involves exploring various ways to formulate other problem domains as IPs, to find formulations that increase the efficiency of problem solving.

Several recent works have explored ways to use LP and IP techniques for planning. Bylander [102] uses an LP formulation as a heuristic for classical plan-space planning, but it does not seem to perform well compared to planning-graph and satisfiability-based planners. Bockmayr and Dimopoulos [76, 77] describe domain-dependent IP models for specific classical planning domains, and Vossen *et al.* [539] compare two domain-independent ways to translate classical planning problems into IPs. Wolfman and Weld [556] use LP formulations for reasoning about resources in a satisfiability-based planner, and Kautz and Walser [317] use IP formulations for planning problems with resources, action costs, and complex objective functions.

One difficulty in developing IP formulations of planning problems is that the performance depends critically on *how* the planning problems are formulated as IPs. The easiest approach is to encode either the planning problem or a planning graph as a satisfiability problem (see Chapter 7) and then to express the satisfiability problem directly as an 0-1 IP. However, this approach does not compare well in efficiency with planning-graph or satisfiability-based planners. Better performance can be obtained by "compiling away" the original fluent variables and replacing them with "state-change" variables (not to be confused with state variables). In this way, Vossen *et al.* [539] obtained performance approaching that of Blackbox [316], a well-known classical planner that uses planning-graph and satisfiability techniques.

24.3 Multiagent Planning

Distributed and cooperative planning generalizes the problem of planning in domains where several agents plan and act together and have to share resources, activities, and goals. The problem, often called *multiagent planning* (MAP), is a major issue for the distributed AI and multiagents community. It arises in application areas such as multirobot environments, cooperating software (or softbots) distributed over the Internet, logistics, manufacturing, evacuation operations, and games.

Approaches to MAP vary depending on the type of planning problems and distribution processes. For example, one may consider a single planner that creates plans for several agents, and this planner may operate in either a single-agent [432] or multiagent [157] environment. Alternatively, there may be several coordinated planning processes local to each agent [167]. One may consider loosely coupled agents, each pursuing its own goal, while either competing for resources [495] or sharing them with others, or a team of agents pursuing a shared goal. The cooperation may rely on different assumptions about the agents' communication, perception, action, and computational capabilities and on their a priori knowledge. These capabilities can be either identical or distinct for the agents.

The plan-space paradigm offers a flexible framework for MAP. In this approach, planning evolves by modifying a current plan (considered to be a partial plan), aiming at completing it consistently by removing all its flaws. An agent may start planning from the plans of other agents, or it may modify its own plan with respect to the plans of others (e.g., repairing flaws due to conflicts). This scheme can be directly of use to MAP in the case where several agents share resources and a priori knowledge. A possible approach can use plan merging (see Section 24.4) and a coordination scheme where an agent generates a provisional plan and modifies it with respect to the set of plans whose coordination has already been achieved.

This coordination scheme has been instantiated into a fairly sophisticated multirobot system solving the DWR problem in a harbor [10]. It relies on a sound coordination protocol. It identifies coordination failures and the subset of robots concerned by failures by relying on global planning for these subsets, and it is complete as long as the robots' goals are not constrained in time. Other extensions to this system involve coordination with IxTeT, a planner handling time and resources [204], and coordination involving altruistic robots that have their own goals but may help each others [8, 86].

24.4 Plan Merging and Plan Rewriting

There are several cases in which it may be useful to decompose a planning problem into separate subproblems, plan for those subproblems separately, and merge the resulting plans. Here are some examples:

- In a multiagent planning situation, the agents may need to develop their plans separately.
- If a planning problem is decomposable into subproblems that are largely independent, then solving them separately may be more efficient than solving them together.

- If the subproblems are sufficiently different from each other, it may be best to solve them using separate domain-specific planning systems, such as a planner and a scheduler (see Chapter 15), or a manufacturing process planning system and a production planning system [117].

Plan merging often involves *operator merging*, i.e., merging some set of operators within a plan or set of plans into a single operator that achieves the same goals. The motivation for doing this is that if the operators can be merged, this may reduce the plan's cost, time, or resource requirements.

Domain-specific approaches for plan merging have been developed in some application domains, such as Hayes's Machinist system [263] for manufacturing process planning.

For domain-independent plan merging, the simplest situation in which plans for separate subproblems can be merged is if the subproblems are completely independent of each other. In this situation, Korf [336] has shown that solving each of the subgoals separately (and essentially concatenating the results) will divide both the base and the exponent of the complexity function by the number of subgoals.

Yang *et al.* [560] defined a set of allowable interactions among subproblems that are less severe than complete independence yet allow efficient plan merging to occur and developed a branch-and-bound algorithm for performing the merging. In addition, in Sacerdoti's NOAH system [461], some of the "critics" for improving plans can be viewed as operator-merging operations, as can phantomization of a goal in Wilkins's SIPE and Tate's NONLIN systems and in Kambhampati's plan-resuse framework.

Yang [560] describes a comprehensive theory for plan merging in classical planning and a dynamic-programming algorithm for plan merging based on their theory. This work was further elaborated and refined by Yang. Tsamardinos *et al.* [514] have extended this theory to use temporal networks similar to the ones described in Chapter 14.

Closely related to plan merging is *plan rewriting*, a hill-climbing approach in which a planner starts with a single solution to the planning problem and then repeatedly makes modifications to the solution in order to get better and better solutions. This idea was developed by Ambite and Knoblock [19]. In their experiments with this approach on a number of classical planning problems, it compared favorably with IPP [332], a well-known planning system based on planning graphs (Chapter 6).

24.5 Abstraction Hierarchies

In the AI planning literature, the phrase "planning with abstraction" has taken on a more specific meaning than a literal interpretation of the words might suggest. It refers to the following technique. Given a planning problem $\mathcal{P}_0$, first formulate a sequence of increasingly relaxed versions $\langle \mathcal{P}_1, \ldots, \mathcal{P}_k \rangle$ of $\mathcal{P}_0$. Next, find a solution π_k for $\mathcal{P}_k$, then modify π_k so that it is a solution π_{k-1} for $\mathcal{P}_{k-1}$, and so forth until a solution has been found for $\mathcal{P}_0$. The motivation for doing this is that if each solution can be used to help find the next one, then solving the sequence of relaxations can sometimes be much less work than solving $\mathcal{P}_0$ from scratch.

Because there are many different ways to generate relaxations of a planning problem, "planning with abstraction" has been used variously to refer to the skeletal plans used in some case-based planning systems [61], the task networks used in HTN planning [560], and the notion of partitioning a planning problem recursively into smaller and smaller planning problems [352]. However, the most commonly used notion of abstraction in planning, and the subject of this section, is *precondition-elimination abstraction.*

In precondition-elimination abstraction, the relaxations of a classical planning problem $\mathcal{P}_0$ are produced by omitting preconditions from the operators in $\mathcal{P}_0$. The following technique is generally used to decide which preconditions to omit. To each literal l that is a precondition of one or more planning operators in $\mathcal{P}_0$, assign a *criticality level* $c(l) \in \{1, \ldots, k\}$, where k is a fixed positive integer. Then, let $\mathcal{P}_{k-i}$ be the planning problem produced from $\mathcal{P}_0$ by omitting every precondition l such that $c(l) < k - i$.

Precondition-elimination abstraction can be implemented as a modification to any classical planning algorithm *Alg*, as follows. First, generate a sequence of relaxations $P_k = (O_k, s_0, g)$, $P_{k-1} = (O_{k-1}, s_0, g), \ldots, P_0 = (O_0, s_0, g)$ as described above. Next, try to solve $\mathcal{P}_k$ using *Alg*. If *Alg* finds a solution plan $\pi_k = \langle a_1, \ldots, a_n \rangle$, then let $\langle s_0, s_1, \ldots, s_n \rangle$ be the sequence of states produced by executing π_k in $\mathcal{P}_k$. To modify π_k to get a solution for $\mathcal{P}_{k-1} = (O_{k-1}, s_0, g)$, use *Alg* to find solutions for each of the planning problems (O_2, s_0, s_1), (O_2, s_1, s_2), $\ldots$, (O_2, s_{n-1}, s_n), and insert these solutions in between the actions of π_k to create a plan π_{k-1} that solves $\mathcal{P}_{k-1}$. In the same manner, modify π_{k-1} to get a solution π_{k-2} for $\mathcal{P}_{k-2}$, π_{k-2} to get a solution π_{k-3} for $\mathcal{P}_{k-3}$, and so forth.

Precondition-elimination abstraction was first developed and used by Sacerdoti [459] to modify STRIPS (see Section 4.4) in order to produce his ABSTRIPS planner. The same technique was subsequently used by Yang *et al.* [561] to modify Chapman's TWEAK plan-space planner [120], producing a planning procedure called ABTWEAK.

Precondition-elimination abstraction is guaranteed to be sound because it terminates only after $\mathcal{P}$ has been solved. However, it is not necessarily complete. Knoblock *et al.* [326] defined a property called *downward monotonicity* which, if satisfied, ensures that precondition-elimination abstraction is complete. Subsequently, Knoblock [325] used this property as the basis of an algorithm for generating abstraction hierarchies. Successively better algorithms for this task were devised by Bacchus and Yang [37] and by Bundy *et al.* [98], and Garcia and Laborie [205] generalized the approach for use in temporal planning using a state-variable representation.

There has been some debate about how much benefit precondition-elimination abstraction provides, and both positive and negative examples can be found in the literature [40, 98, 485, 561]. For a summary and discussion of these, see Giunchiglia [233].

24.6 Domain Analysis

Domain analysis is the technique of analyzing a planning domain to gather information that may help a planner find solutions more quickly for problems in that domain. We describe several in this section.

Typed Variables and State Invariants. Most of the research on domain analysis has focused on automatic discovery of typed variables and state invariants in classical planning domains. A *typed variable* (see Section 2.4) is one that can have only a limited range of possible values, namely, the ones in its type. A *state invariant* is a property that is true of every state. For example, in the DWR domain, one state invariant is that for each robot r, there is exactly one location l such that at(r, l) holds.

If it is known that some variable has only a limited range of values or that certain properties must be true in every state, this information can improve the efficiency of some planning systems. For example, in a planning-graph planner (Chapter 6) it can reduce the size of the planning graph, and in a satisfiability-based planner (Chapter 7) it can reduce the size of the search space.

Even if data types or state invariants are not explicitly specified for a planning domain, they sometimes can be discovered through domain analysis. For example, in the classical representation of the DWR domain, consider all atoms of the form at(r, l). In the initial state, suppose the only atoms of the form at(r, l) are at(r1,l1) and at(r2,l2). The only planning operator that ever asserts at$(r, \ldots)$ is the move operator, which requires at(r, l) as a precondition. Thus, in every state reachable from the initial state, at(r, l) will be true only for $r \in$ {r1,r2}. Thus, $r \in$ {r1,r2} constitutes a data type for the first argument r of at(r, l).

Several procedures have been developed for discovering types and/or state invariants, particularly TIM [192] and DISCOPLAN [218, 219]. TIM is used as the domain-analysis module in STAN, a planning-graph planner [367]. DISCOPLAN has been used to provide input to both SATPLAN [314], a satisfiablity-based planner, and MEDIC [172]. In all three cases, the domain analysis led to significant speedups.

TALplanner, a control-rule planner (Chapter 10) uses domain-analysis techniques to discover state invariants. If a state invariant is discovered that guarantees some of its control rules will always be satisfied, then TALplanner can avoid the overhead of using those control rules [341].

Other Kinds of Domain Analysis. Smith and Peot [486, 487] developed algorithms for constructing *operator graphs* for classical planning domains. In plan-space planners, these graphs can be used to decide which threats can be ignored during the planning process and to detect some cases in which a branch in the search space will be infinite—both of which can significantly improve the efficiency of plan-space planning.

In HTN planning (Chapter 11), an *external condition* is a condition that is needed in order to achieve a task but is not achieved in any possible decomposition of the task. Tsuneto *et al.* [516] wrote a domain-analysis algorithm to find external conditions and modified the UMCP planner to plan how to achieve each task's external conditions before planning how to achieve the task. This made UMCP significantly faster.

Finally, the automatic generation of abstraction hierarchies, discussed in Section 24.5, is a kind of domain analysis.

24.7 Planning and Learning

Two of the earliest systems to integrate machine learning and planning were SOAR [348], a general cognitive architecture for developing systems that exhibit intelligent behavior, and PRODIGY [396], an architecture that integrates planning and learning in its several modules [524].

Much of the work done on the integration of learning and planning is focused on classical planning. Usually, this work, as formulated by Minton [391], learns search-control rules to speed up the plan generation process or to increase quality of the generated plans. These rules give the planner knowledge to help it decide at choice points and include *selection rules* (i.e., rules that recommend using an operator in a specific situation), *rejection rules* (i.e., rules that recommend not using an operator in a specific situation or avoiding a world state), and *preference rules* (i.e., rules that indicate some operators are preferable in specific situations). As mentioned by Langley [351], the input for this kind of learning generally consists of partial given knowledge of a problem-solving domain and a set of experiences gained through search of the problem's search space.

Mitchell *et al.* [398] first suggested the use of *learning apprentices*, which acquire their knowledge by observing a domain expert solving a problem, as control rule learning algorithms. EBL has been used to induce control rules [390]. STATIC [182] uses a graph representation of problem spaces to elicit control rules based on analysis of the domain. Katukam and Kambhampati [309] discuss the induction of explanation-based control rules in partial-order planning. Leckie and Zukerman [358] use inductive methods to learn search-control rules. SCOPE [179] learns domain-specific control rules for a partial-order planner that improve both planning efficiency and plan quality [181] and uses both EBL and Inductive Logic Programming techniques.

There has been some recent work on applying various learning algorithms in order to induce task hierarchies. Garland *et al.* [207] use a technique called *programming by demonstration* to build a system in which a domain expert performs a task by executing actions and then reviews and annotates a log of the actions. This information is then used to learn hierarchical task models. KnoMic [522] is a learning-by-observation system that extracts knowledge from observations of an expert performing a task and generalizes this knowledge to a hierarchy of rules.

These rules are then used by an agent to perform the same task. CaMeL [278] learns preconditions for HTN methods using a modified version of candidate elimination.

Another aspect concerning the integration of planning and learning is *automatic domain knowledge acquisition.* In this framework, the planner does not have the full definition of the planning domain and tries to learn this definition by experimentation. Gil [227, 229] introduces a dynamic environment in which the preconditions or effects of operators change over time and discusses methods to derive these preconditions and effects dynamically. In another work by Gil [228], instead of revising existing operators, new operators are acquired by direct analogy with existing operators, decomposition of monolithic operators into meaningful suboperators, and experimentation with partially specified operators.

24.8 Planning and Acting, Situated Planning, and Dynamic Planning

In this book we focused mainly on the problem of plan generation. However, most real-world applications require systems with *situated planning* capabilities, i.e., systems that interleave planning with acting, execution monitoring, failure recovery, plan supervision, plan revision, and replanning mechanisms. Several situated planners have been proposed so far [4, 59, 190, 215, 411, 478] and have been successfully applied in particular application domains (like mobile robots and fault diagnosis for real-time systems). All these systems address the issue of integrating reactivity and reasoning capabilities, even if each of them uses quite different techniques.

Firby [191] introduced *reactive action packages* (RAP), which are programs that run until either the goal is reached or a failure occurs. The RAP interpreter refines tasks into more primitive commands and controls activation and conflict resolution. RAPs describe how to achieve a given task. Their semantics are strictly oriented toward task achievement and sequencing subtasks. The related system [190] implements a "partitioned architecture" where a strategic planner interacts with a completely reactive system (RAP Executor) through a shared world model and plan representation.

Going further toward the integration of planning and reacting, Lyons and Hendriks [372] developed a system called RS, where planning is seen as a permanent adaptation of a reactive process. The latter is a set of rules which is modified according to the context and goals. This has been tested for the design of an assembly robot [371]. Similarly, Bresina [93] proposes in the ERE system a planner that is able to synthesize new situated control rules when a failure situation is met.

3T [79] is a three-layer architecture. It comprises a set of skills and uses the RAP system in one of its layers to sequence them. One layer is a planning system that reasons on goal achievement, including timing constraints. XFRM [59], depending on the time constraints, executes either default plans or new plans obtained by transforming the default plans by means of heuristic rules.

The Task Control Architecture (TCA), developed by Simmons [478, 479], organizes processing modules around a central controller that coordinates their interactions. A goal is decomposed into a task tree with subgoals that are achieved by the decentralized modules. All communication is supported by the centralized control. TCA provides control mechanisms for task decomposition and takes into account temporal constraints in task scheduling. TCA is based on plans (called *task trees*) that provide a language for representing the various planning activities: plan formation, plan execution, information acquisition, and monitoring. The system can flexibly perform interleaving planning and execution, run-time changing of a plan, and coordinating multiple tasks. The TCA exception-handling facilities support context-dependent error recovery because different error handlers can be associated with different nodes in the task tree.

In Georgeff and Lansky's Procedural Reasoning System (PRS) [215], plans (called *KAs*) describe how certain sequences of actions and tests may be performed to achieve given goals or to react to particular situations. Metalevel KAs encode various methods for choosing among multiple applicable KAs. They provide a high amount of flexibility in forming plans. Despouys and Ingrand [154] integrate a planner on top of a PRS-like system.

Finally, several methods interleave planning and execution in order to deal with large state spaces, among which most notably is the method described by Koenig and Simmons [333], an approach based on Min-Max LRTA*. These methods open up the possibility of dealing with large state spaces. However, these methods cannot guarantee to find a solution, unless assumptions are made about the domain. For instance, Koenig and Simmons [333] assume "safely explorable domains" without cycles.

24.9 Plan Recognition

Plan recognition is the inverse problem of plan synthesis. The problem involves two characters: an *actor* and an *observer*. Given as input a sequence of actions executed by the actor, the observer has to map this observed sequence to the plan currently followed by the actor and ultimately to its goal. The problem arises in many application areas, such as natural-language processing and story understanding [548], psychological modeling and cognitive science [467], intelligent computer interfaces [140, 439], surveillance and supervision systems [91, 92, 266], plan execution monitoring [154], and multiagent cooperative planning.

Plan recognition arises in different settings. For example, the actor can cooperate with the observer and try to communicate his or her intentions clearly.

This problem is called the *intentional plan recognition problem.* It is of interest in particular for multiagent cooperative planning. In another setting, the actor is in an adverserial framework, trying to hide his or her intentions, e.g., in surveillance and military applications. Another setting has a neutral actor who ignores the observer. This *keyhole plan recognition problem* is the most widely studied case of plan recognition.

Approaches to plan recognition depend also on various assumptions, such as the following.

- *The a priori knowledge available to the observer.* Some possibilities include these.
  - The observer has complete knowledge of the actor's set of plans. It needs only to map the observed sequences to these plans.
  - The observer has complete knowledge of the actor's models of actions (its planning domain), and it may need to synthesize new plans that account for the observations.
  - The available knowledge is partial and/or uncertain.
- *The observations given as input.* These can be either the actor's actions or the effects of these actions on the world. In the latter case, these effects can be mixed with other unrelated events that are also observed. Moreover, observations may be reliable and complete or partial and erroneous.
- *The temporal assumptions about the actions models.* Examples of these assumptions include that time is explicit and the observations are time-stamped and/or the temporal assumptions about the plan recognition process itself (e.g., the observer is online with the actor and has real-time constraints).

In the simple case of keyhole plan recognition with complete knowledge of the actor's plans, and where the observations are directly the actor's actions, the popular approach of Kautz and Allen [311], well formalized in Kautz [310], relies on a hierarchical model of plans. This model is quite similar to the ordered task model of Chapter 11, where a task can be achieved by a disjunction of possible methods, and each method decomposes a task into a sequence of subtasks, down to primitive actions. The set of root tasks (tasks that are not subtasks of any other tasks) corresponds to the possible goals the actor may pursue.

From the observation of a sequence of primitive actions, one can find the set of possible goals of the actor that account for these actions: the decomposition of each goal in this set starts with the observed sequence. This set is called the *covering model* of the observed actions. Initially, when the observed sequence is empty, this set contains all known goals, then it decreases along with newly observed actions, and it may possibly become empty. A problem arises if the actor is pursuing more than one goal at a time. This problem is addressed with *minimal covering models* where each explanation is a minimal set of goals not subsumed by some other set.

Hence a single goal explanation, even if less likely, is preferred to several concurrent goals.[1]

Other approaches to plan recognition are more concerned with handling uncertainty in models and/or observations. They take a pattern recognition point of view, where one has to map some observations to an interpretation, with an explanation of why this interpretation accounts for the observations, and the likelihood of that interpretation. Among the proposed techniques are the Bayesian inference approach of Charniak and Goldman [121] and the abductive probabilist theory of Goldman *et al.* [239], which takes into account more properly negative evidence.

A third class of approaches to the plan recognition problem, called the *chronicle recognition problem*, emphasizes temporal models, low-level observations, and online recognition [161]. The given knowledge is a set of chronicle models. A chronicle, as defined in Chapter 14, is a set of temporal assertions, i.e., events and persistence conditions on values of state variables, together with domain and temporal constraints. The observer's input is a possibly infinite sequence of time-stamped, instantiated events, which can be the effects of the actor's actions or elements of the environment's dynamics. The chronicle models are supposed to describe the actor's plans *and* the environment's dynamics that are relevant to these plans. The observer does not need to account for all observed events but only for those that meet a possible instance of a chronicle model.

In the simplest case, the observations are assumed to be complete and reliable, i.e., any change in a state variable is supposed to be observed and all observations correspond to occurred changes. The chronicle recognition system has to detect online any subset of the sequence of observed events that meets a chronicle instance. The problem can be addressed as a formal language-recognition problem with temporal constraints [222]. An observed event may trigger a hypothesis of a chronicle instance. This hypothesis corresponds to a set of predicted events and their temporal windows of possible occurrence and associated deadline.

The hypothesis may progress in two ways: (1) a new event may be detected that can either be integrated into the instance and make the remaining predictions more precise or may violate a constraint for an assertion and make the corresponding hypothesis invalid; or (2) time passes without anything happening and, perhaps, may make some deadline violated or some assertion constraints obsolete. For each chronicle model, one needs to manage a tree of hypotheses of current instances. When a hypothesis of a chronicle instance is completed or killed (because of a violated constraint), it is removed from this tree. Because of the temporal constraint, the size of the hypothesis tree is bounded.

The chronicle recognition techniques have been extended to take into account uncertainty and partial observation (e.g., [246]). They proved to be quite effective in addressing supervision problems in various application areas, ranging from gas

---

1. In Kautz's example [310], going hunting *and* cashing a check at a bank can be more likely than robbing the bank, two possible explanations for the same set of observations "about a person in a bank with a gun."

turbines and blast furnaces to power networks and telecommunication networks. They have also been used in surveillance applications [266] and in the execution monitoring of plans, where the observer is also the actor [154].

24.10 Suggestions for Future Work

Clearly, more effort is needed on the development of planning from an engineering perspective. More effort is also needed to integrate various approaches to automated planning, especially the integration of planning and scheduling and the integration of planning and acting. These integration efforts should be not merely from an engineering perspective but also at the levels of knowledge representation and domain modeling and should involve consistent integration of several problem-solving techniques. We hope that future planning books will describe the results of such work, and we encourage the reader to contribute to their development.

Part VIII

Appendices

Appendix A

Search Procedures and Computational Complexity

A.1 Nondeterministic Problem Solving

A problem-solving procedure is a computational procedure whose input is some problem P that has some (possibly empty) set of solutions. The procedure may *succeed*, in which case it returns some value v that purports to be a solution for P; or it may *fail*, in which case it either does not terminate or else returns some special value such as failure to indicate that it cannot solve the problem.

Most of the problem-solving procedures in this book are *nondeterministic*, i.e., they involve nondeterministic choices, which we will write in the pseudocode for our procedures as

$$\text{nondeterministically choose } v \in V$$

where V is some finite set.[1]

If a procedure does not involve such a nondeterministic choice, then it is *deterministic*. There are several theoretical models of nondeterminism [133, 206, 428]. Probably the easiest one to understand intuitively is based on an analogy to parallel computing, with an unlimited supply of CPUs. If b is the number of elements in V, then we start b CPUs running in parallel, one for each value of V. Each CPU will have a different execution trace. If one or more solution traces succeed, then the nondeterministic procedure may immediately terminate and return a solution found by any successful execution trace. Otherwise, the nondeterministic procedure fails.

In nondeterministic search procedures, the nondeterministic choice will be embedded in a loop or a recursive call, so that the procedure makes a sequence

1. Note that these nondeterministic choices are different from the nondeterministic actions that are introduced briefly in Chapter 1 and are the focus of Chapter 17. The multiple meanings for "nondeterministic" are unavoidable because the terminology was developed independently in two different fields.

of nondeterministic choices. Because each nondeterministic choice corresponds to spawning a set of parallel CPUs, the set of execution traces can be represented as an *execution tree* in which each node represents one of the iterations or recursive invocations of the procedure, the children of each node represent the subprocesses spawned by the procedure at this point of its iteration or recursion, and each path in the tree represents an execution trace. This tree is called the procedure's *search tree* or *search space.*

Here are some of the properties that a problem-solving procedure may have.

- *Soundness.* A deterministic procedure is sound if, whenever it is invoked on some problem P and returns a value $v \neq$ failure, v is guaranteed to be a solution for P. A nondeterministic procedure is sound if every successful execution trace returns a value that is guaranteed to be a solution to P.
- *Completeness.* A deterministic procedure is complete if, whenever it is invoked on a solvable problem P, it is guaranteed to return a value $v \neq$ failure. A nondeterministic procedure is complete if, whenever it is invoked on a solvable problem P, at least one of its execution traces will return a value $v \neq$ failure whenever P is solvable.
- *Admissibility.* If there is some measure of optimality for solutions to a problem P, then a deterministic procedure is admissible if it is guaranteed to return an optimal solution whenever P is solvable. Note that if a procedure is admissible, then it is also sound and complete.

A.2 State-Space Search

A well-known class of search problems are *state-space search problems.* The *state space* is a set of nodes called *states,* and the objective is to find a state s that satisfies some *goal condition* g. The set of all states is not given at the outset. Instead, an initial state s_0 is given, and the other states are generated as needed, by applying *state-space operators* to existing states. The problem specification is a triple (s_0, g, O), where s_0 is the *initial state,* O is the set of *operators,* and g is the *goal condition.* The set S of all possible states in the state space is defined recursively as follows: $s_0 \in S$; and if s is a state and o is an operator such that $o(s)$ is defined, then $o(s)$ is also a state. Each state $o(s)$ is called a *child* of s. Figure A.1 shows a nondeterministic state-space search procedure.

Any practical implementation of a nondeterministic search procedure must be deterministic rather than nondeterministic; thus it must have a control strategy for visiting the nodes in the execution tree. In the following subsections we discuss several well-known control strategies.

Breadth-First Search. The primary advantage of breadth-first search is that if a nondeterministic procedure p is complete, then the breadth-first version of p will

```
State-space-search(s, g, O)
    if g(s) then return s
    applicable ← {all operators applicable to t}
    if applicable = ∅ then return failure
    nondeterministically choose o ∈ applicable
    s' ← o(s)
    return State-space-search(s', g, O)
```

Figure A.1 Nondeterministic state-space search procedure.

also be complete. However, in most cases the breadth-first search procedure will have a huge space requirement. For example, suppose that every node of the search space has b children, the terminal nodes are at depth d, the time needed to visit each node is $\Theta(1)$, and the space needed to store each node is also $\Theta(1)$. Then the running time for a breadth-first search will be $\Theta(b^d)$, and because a breadth-first search must keep a record of each node visited, then the memory requirement will also be $\Theta(b^d)$.

Depth-First Search. If a nondeterministic search procedure is complete, then the corresponding depth-first search will be complete if the search space contains no infinite paths or if the procedure can reliably detect and prune every infinite path. If there are infinitely many possible different nodes, then there is usually no good way to accomplish this. However, if there are only finitely many possible different nodes, then it can be accomplished by keeping track of the nodes on the current path and backtracking whenever the search procedure generates a node that is already in that path.

In the worst case, a depth-first search may need to examine the entire search space before finding a solution; then its running time may be worse than that of a breadth-first search. However, if the search procedure has a good heuristic for selecting which of a node's children to visit first, it may be able to find a good solution very quickly. In this case, its running time will usually be much better than that of a breadth-first search.

Because a depth-first search keeps track of only the nodes on the current path (plus possibly the siblings of those nodes), its space requirement is $\Theta(d)$, where d is the depth of the deepest node it visits.

Best-First Search. In some cases, the objective is to find a goal state s that minimizes some objective function $f(s)$. In this case, a nondeterministic search will not work properly: instead of returning the solution found in a single execution trace, we must look at *all* of the execution traces to see which one leads to the best solution.

One way to do this deterministically is to use a best-first search. This is like a breadth-first search in the sense that it maintains an *active list* of nodes that have been generated but not yet visited. However, instead of using this list as a queue the way a breadth-first search does a best-first search instead uses the list as a priority queue: the next node chosen from the active list will be the one whose f value is smallest. Best-first search is sound. If f is monotonically nondecreasing, i.e., if $f(s) \leq f(s')$ whenever s' is a child of s, then a best-first search will never return a nonoptimal solution and is admissible in finite search spaces. If there is a number $\delta > 0$ such that if $f(s) + \delta \leq f(s')$ whenever s' is a child of s, then a best-first search is admissible even in infinite search spaces.

The well-known A* search procedure is a special case of best-first state-space search, with some modifications to handle situations where there are multiple paths to the same state.

Depth-First Branch-and-Bound Search. Another search procedure for minimizing an objective function is branch-and-bound. The most general form of branch-and-bound is general enough to include nearly all top-down search procedures as special cases [415]. The best-known version of branch-and-bound is a simple depth-first version similar to the procedure shown in Figure A.2. In this procedure, s^* is a global variable that holds the best solution seen so far, with s^* equal to some dummy value and $f(s^*) = \infty$ when the procedure is initially invoked. If the state space is finite and acyclic and if f is monotonically nondecreasing, then Depth-first-BB is admissible. If f is nonmonotonic, then Depth-first-BB may not be admissible, and if the state space is infinite, then Depth-first-BB may fail to terminate.

Greedy Search. A greedy search is a depth-first search procedure with no backtracking. It works as follows. If s is a solution, then return it; otherwise, repeat the search at the child $o(s)$ whose f value is smallest. There are no guarantees of whether this procedure will find an optimal solution, but it can sometimes save

```
Depth-first-BB(s, g, f, O)
    if g(s) = true and f(s) < f(s*) then
        s* ← s
        return s
    applicable ← {all operators applicable to s}
    if applicable = ∅ then return failure
    for every o ∈ applicable
        Depth-first-BB(o(s), g, f, O)
    return s*
```

Figure A.2 A branch-and-bound version of state-space search.

a huge amount of time over what would be needed to find a guaranteed optimal solution.

Hill-Climbing Search. This is similar to greedy search, except that in a hill-climbing problem, every node is a solution, and a hill-climbing procedure will only go from s to $o(s)$ if $f(o(s)) < f(s)$.

Most of the above search procedures can be modified using a variety of heuristic techniques. These can be divided roughly into two classes.

1. *Pruning techniques.* These are ways to determine that some nodes will not lead to a solution (or to a desirable solution), so that the procedure can prune these nodes (i.e., remove them from the search space).
2. *Node-selection techniques.* These are ways to guess which nodes will lead to desirable solutions (e.g., solutions that are optimal or near-optimal, or solutions that can be found quickly), so that the procedure can visit these nodes first.

In general, pruning and node-selection heuristics will not necessarily preserve completeness or admissibility. However, there are a number of special cases in which these properties can be preserved.

Iterative deepening is a technique that can be used in conjunction with a depth-first search procedure to make it complete. It can be done in two ways: breadth-first or best-first.

Breadth-first iterative deepening does a depth-first search that backtracks whenever it reaches depth i and repeats this search for $i = 1, 2, \ldots$ until a solution is found. Like ordinary breadth-first search, breadth-first iterative deepening is complete but not admissible.

Best-first iterative deepening does a depth-first search that backtracks during its ith iteration whenever it reaches a node s such that $f(s) \geq f_i$, where $f_0 = f(s_0)$, and for $i > 0$,

$$f_i = \min\{f(s) \mid \text{the search backtracked at } s \text{ during iteration } i - 1\}$$

As before, it repeats this search for $i = 1, 2, \ldots$ until a solution is found. The well-known IDA* procedure uses best-first iterative deepening.

The admissibility properties of best-first iterative deepening are the same as for breadth-first search. If f is monotonically nondecreasing, then best-first iterative deepening will never return a nonoptimal solution and is admissible in finite search spaces. If there is a number $\delta > 0$ such that if $f(s) + \delta \leq f(s')$ whenever s' is a child of s, then best-first iterative deepening is admissible even in infinite search spaces.

For either kind of iterative deepening, if the time taken by the depth-first search grows exponentially at each iteration, then the total time taken by the iterative-deepening procedure is proportional to the time needed by the last depth-first search. Mathematically, if the ith depth-first search takes time $T(i) = \Omega(2^i)$ for each i, then the iterative-deepening procedure takes time $\Theta(T(n))$, where n is the total number of iterations.

A.3 Problem-Reduction Search

Another kind of search space is a *problem-reduction space*, in which each state s represents a problem to be solved, and each operator $o(s)$ produces not just a single child state s' but an entire set of children $\{s_1, \ldots, s_k\}$ (the number of children may vary from one state to another). The children are called *subproblems* of s, and a solution for one of them represents a portion of the solution to s. Thus, to solve s it is not sufficient just to find a solution below some descendant of s. Instead, the search space is an AND/OR graph, and a solution for s consists of a set of solutions $\{v_1, \ldots, v_k\}$ that are the leaf nodes of a *solution graph* rooted at s.

Figure A.3 gives an example of a solution graph in an AND/OR graph. Each AND-branch is indicated by drawing an arc to connect the edges in the branch. In some cases, the order in which the subproblems are solved may matter, so the

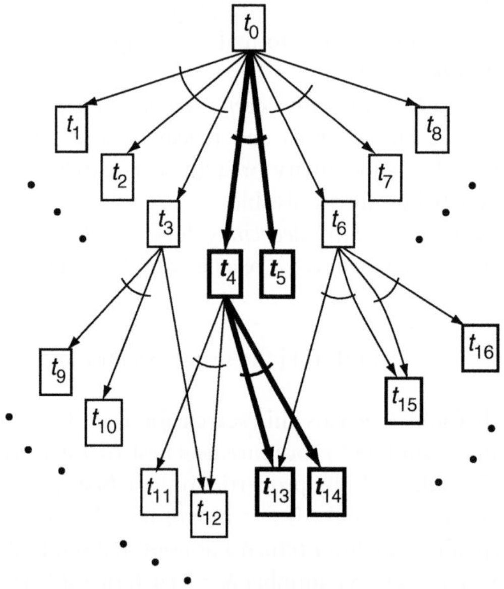

Figure A.3 A portion of an AND/OR graph. The AND-branches include $(t_0, \{t_1, t_2, t_3\})$, $(t_0, \{t_4, t_5\})$, $(t_0, \{t_6, t_7\})$, $(t_0, \{t_8\})$, $(t_3, \{t_9, t_{10}\})$, and so forth. If t_5, t_{13}, and t_{14} satisfy the goal condition, then the portion of the graph shown in boldface is a solution graph.

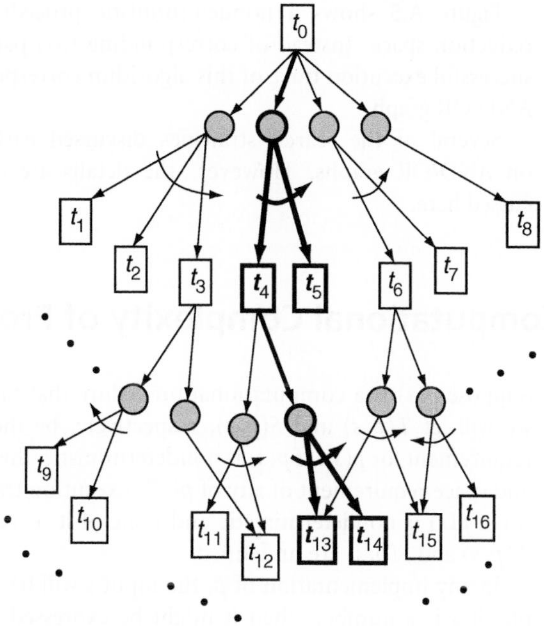

Figure A.4 An AND/OR graph similar to Figure A.3, but this time the OR-branches are shown explicitly, and orderings are imposed as indicated with arrows for each of the AND-branches.

ordering may be indicated by putting arrows on the arcs, as shown in Figure A.3. OR-branches may be indicated either implicitly by having more than one AND-branch coming out of a node, as shown in Figure A.3, or explicitly by introducing additional nodes and edges into the graph, as shown in Figure A.4.

```
Problem-reduction-search(s, g, O)
    if g(s) then return s
    applicable ← {all operators applicable to t}
    if applicable = ∅ then return failure
    nondeterministically choose o ∈ applicable
    {s1, ..., sk} ← o(s)
    for every si ∈ {s1, ..., sk}
        vi ← Problem-reduction-search(si, g, O)
        if vi = failure then return failure
    return {v1, ..., vk}
```

Figure A.5 Nondeterministic problem-reduction search procedure.

Figure A.5 shows a nondeterministic procedure for searching a problem-reduction space. Instead of corresponding to a path through a state space, each successful execution trace of this algorithm corresponds to a solution graph of the AND/OR graph.

Several of the search strategies discussed earlier can be adapted to work on AND/OR graphs. However, the details are complicated and are not discussed here.

A.4 Computational Complexity of Procedures

Suppose $p(s)$ is a computational procedure that takes a single argument s. Then we will let $T(p, s)$ and $S(p, s)$, respectively, be the running time and the space requirement for $p(s)$. If $p(s)$ is nondeterministic, this is the minimum running time and space requirement of any of $p(s)$'s execution traces. If $p(s)$ does not terminate (or if $p(s)$ is nondeterministic and none of its execution traces terminates), then $T(p, s)$ and $S(p, s)$ are undefined.

In any implementation of p, the input s will be a string of symbols. For example, if s is a number, then it might be expressed as a sequence of binary digits or as an ASCII character string, or if s is a classical planning problem, it might be expressed as a string of symbols that define the initial state, the goal, and the planning operators. Let $|s|$ be the length of such a string. Then the procedure p's worst-case running time and space requirement are defined, respectively, as follows:

$$T_{\max}(p, n) = \max\{T(p, s) \mid |s| = n\}$$

$$S_{\max}(p, n) = \max\{S(p, s) \mid |s| = n\}$$

Complexity analyses of $T_{\max}(p, n)$ and $S_{\max}(p, n)$ normally focus not on the exact values of $T_{\max}(p, n)$ and $S_{\max}(p, n)$ but instead on their "big O" values. Intuitively, $O(f(n))$ is the set of all functions that grow no faster than proportional to $f(n)$. Mathematically, a function $f(n)$ is in the set $O(g(n))$ if there are numbers c and n_0 such that:

$$\forall n > n_0, 0 \leq f(n) \leq cg(n)$$

It is standard usage to write $f(n) = O(g(n))$ to mean $f(n) \in O(g(n))$.

A function $f(n)$ is said to be *logarithmically bounded* if $f(n) = O(\log n)$; *polynomially bounded* if there is a constant c such that $f(n) = O(n^c)$; and *exponentially bounded* if there is a constant c such that $f(n) = O(c^n)$.

Example A.1 Suppose that by analyzing p's behavior, we can show that $T_{\max}(p, n)$ is a polynomial of the form $a_k n^k + a_{k-1} n^{k-1} + \ldots + a_0$. Then from the previous definition, it follows that $T_{\max}(p, n) = O(n^k)$.

Thus in this case $T_{max}(p, n)$ is polynomially bounded. ■

A.5 Computational Complexity of Problems

Traditional analyses of the complexity of computational problems (e.g., [206, 428]) have focused on *language-recognition problems.* Mathematically, a *language* is a set $\mathcal{L}$ of character strings over some finite alphabet; i.e., if L is a finite set of characters and L^* is the set of all strings of characters of L, then $\mathcal{L}$ may be any subset of L^*. The language-recognition problem for $\mathcal{L}$ is the following problem:

Given a character string s, is $s \in \mathcal{L}$?

A computational procedure p is a *recognition procedure* for $\mathcal{L}$ if for every string $s \in L^*$, $p(s)$ returns yes if $s \in \mathcal{L}$, and $p(s)$ does not return yes if $s \notin \mathcal{L}$. In the latter case, $p(s)$ either may return another value such as no or may fail to terminate.

For a language-recognition procedure, the worst-case running time and space requirement are defined slightly differently than before:

$$T_{max}(p, n, \mathcal{L}) = \max\{T(p, s) \mid s \in \mathcal{L} \text{ and } |s| = n\}$$
$$S_{max}(p, n, \mathcal{L}) = \max\{S(p, s) \mid s \in \mathcal{L} \text{ and } |s| = n\}$$

In other words, if p is a procedure for recognizing a language $\mathcal{L}$, then we do not care how much time or space $p(s)$ takes if $s \notin \mathcal{L}$. To readers who have never seen it before, this may seem counterintuitive, but it has some theoretical advantages. For example, if p is a procedure that is not guaranteed to terminate when $s \notin \mathcal{L}$, then $T_{max}(p, n)$ and $S_{max}(p, n)$ will not always be defined.

If $\mathcal{L}_1$ is a language over some alphabet L_1 and $\mathcal{L}_2$ is a language over some alphabet L_2, then a *reduction* of $\mathcal{L}_1$ to $\mathcal{L}_2$ is a deterministic procedure $r : L_1^* \to L_2^*$ such that $s \in \mathcal{L}_1$ iff $r(s) \in \mathcal{L}_2$. This definition is useful because if r is a reduction of $\mathcal{L}_1$ to $\mathcal{L}_2$ and p is a procedure for recognizing $\mathcal{L}_2$, then the composite procedure $p(r(s))$ recognizes $\mathcal{L}_1$ because it returns yes iff $r(s)$ is in $\mathcal{L}_2$, which happens iff $s \in \mathcal{L}_1$.

If r's worst-case running time is polynomially bounded, then we say that $\mathcal{L}_1$ is *polynomially reducible* to $\mathcal{L}_2$. In this case, the worst-case running time and space requirement of $p(r(s))$ are at most polynomially worse than those of $p(s)$. This means that we can recognize strings of $\mathcal{L}_1$ with only a polynomial amount of overhead beyond what is needed to recognize strings of $\mathcal{L}_2$.

Here are some complexity classes dealing with time.

- P is the set of all languages $\mathcal{L}$ such that $\mathcal{L}$ has a deterministic recognition procedure whose worst-case running time is polynomially bounded.

- NP is the set of all languages $\mathcal{L}$ such that $\mathcal{L}$ has a nondeterministic recognition procedure whose worst-case running time is polynomially bounded.
- EXPTIME is the set of all languages $\mathcal{L}$ such that $\mathcal{L}$ has a deterministic recognition procedure whose worst-case running time is exponentially bounded.
- NEXPTIME is the set of all languages $\mathcal{L}$ such that $\mathcal{L}$ has a nondeterministic recognition procedure whose worst-case running time is exponentially bounded.

Here are some complexity classes dealing with space.

- NLOGSPACE is the set of all languages $\mathcal{L}$ such that $\mathcal{L}$ has a nondeterministic recognition procedure whose worst-case space requirement is logarithmically bounded.
- PSPACE is the set of all languages $\mathcal{L}$ such that $\mathcal{L}$ has a recognition procedure whose worst-case space requirement is polynomially bounded. It makes no difference whether the procedure is deterministic or nondeterministic; in either case we will get the same set of languages.
- EXPSPACE is the set of all languages $\mathcal{L}$ such that $\mathcal{L}$ has a recognition procedure whose worst-case space requirement is exponentially bounded. It makes no difference whether the procedure is deterministic or nondeterministic; in either case we will get the same set of languages.

It can be shown [428] that

$$\text{NLOGSPACE} \subseteq \text{P} \subseteq \text{NP} \subseteq \text{PSPACE} \subseteq \text{EXPTIME} \subseteq \text{NEXPTIME} \subseteq \text{EXPSPACE}$$

Some of these sets are known to be unequal (e.g., P $\neq$ EXPTIME), but it is unknown whether all of them are unequal (e.g., the question of whether or not P $=$ NP is the most famous unsolved problem in the entire theory of computing).

If C is one of the complexity classes and $\mathcal{L}$ is a language, then $\mathcal{L}$ is *C-hard* if every language in C is reducible to $\mathcal{L}$ in polynomial time. $\mathcal{L}$ is *C-complete* if C is $\mathcal{L}$-hard and $\mathcal{L} \in C$. Intuitively, if $\mathcal{L}$ is C-complete, then $\mathcal{L}$ is one of the hardest languages in C: if we can recognize $\mathcal{L}$, then we can also recognize any other language in C with at most a polynomial amount of additional overhead.

A.6 Planning Domains as Language-Recognition Problems

In order to discuss the computational complexity of planning problems, the problems must be reformulated as language-recognition problems. There are several standard ways to do this. Given an alphabet L in which to write statements of planning problems, we can define the following languages.

- PLAN-EXISTENCE is the set of all strings $s \in L^*$ such that s is the statement of a solvable planning problem.
- PLAN-LENGTH is the set of all strings of the form (s, k) such that s is the statement of a solvable planning problem, k is a nonnegative integer, and s has a solution plan that contains no more than k actions.

The definition of PLAN-LENGTH follows the standard procedure for converting optimization problems into language-recognition problems (cf. [206, pp. 115–117]). What really interests us, of course, is not the problem of determining whether there is a plan of length k or less but the problem of finding the shortest plan. If the length of the shortest plan is polynomially bounded, then it can be shown that the two problems are polynomially reducible to each other. However, if the length of the shortest plan is not polynomially bounded, then finding the shortest plan can be much harder than determining whether there is a plan of length k or less. For example, in the well-known Towers of Hanoi problem [5] and certain generalizations of it [248], the length of the shortest plan can be found in low-order polynomial time—but actually producing a plan of that length requires exponential time and space because the plan has exponential length.

A.7 Discussion and Historical Remarks

Some of the best-known heuristic-search algorithms include the A* algorithm [426] for searching state-space graphs, the HS [380] and AO* [426] algorithms for searching AND/OR graphs, the alpha-beta algorithm [328, 426] for searching game trees, and a variety of branch-and-bound algorithms [44, 415]. All of these algorithms can be viewed as special cases of a general branch-and-bound formulation [415]. Breadth-first iterative deepening was first used in game-tree search [468]. Best-first iterative deepening was first used in Korf's IDA* procedure [335]. For further reading on heuristic search, see Pearl [430] and Kanal and Kumar [307].

For further reading on algorithms and complexity, see Cormen *et al.* [133] and Papadimitriou [428]. Also, Garey and Johnson [206] is a compendium of a large number of NP-complete problems.

Appendix B
First-Order Logic

B.1 Introduction

First-order logic is a formal system with three fundamental constituents.

1. A *language* $\mathcal{L}$ defines the set of possible statements, usually called (well-formed) *formulas*, e.g., $p \rightarrow q$ (read p implies q).
2. The *semantics* is a way to assign a meaning to each statement in $\mathcal{L}$ and to determine whether a formula is true. For instance, if both p and q are true, then the statement $p \rightarrow q$ is true.
3. A *proof theory* provides rules to transform statements of $\mathcal{L}$ and derive new statements, e.g., the modus ponens rule that from p and $p \rightarrow q$ derives q. We write $p, p \rightarrow q \vdash q$.

In this appendix, we first introduce propositional logic and then extend its expressiveness to first-order logic.

B.2 Propositional Logic

The language $\mathcal{L}$ of propositional logic is the set P of propositions. P is defined inductively starting from an enumerable set of atomic propositions P_0.

1. If $p \in P_0$, then $p \in P$.
2. If $p \in P$, then $\neg p \in P$.
3. If $p \in P$ and $q \in P$, then $p \wedge q \in P$.
4. Nothing else is a propositional formula.

We define $p \vee q$ as $\neg(\neg p \wedge \neg q)$, and $p \rightarrow q$ as $\neg p \vee q$. The symbols $\wedge$ (and), $\vee$ (or), and $\rightarrow$ (if ... then, or implies) are called *connectives*. Given a propositional formula, its atomic propositions are called *propositional variables*.

Example B.1 Let p, q, and r be atomic propositions. Examples of propositional formulas are p, $\neg p$, $p \wedge q$, and $(p \rightarrow q) \vee \neg r$. The propositional variables of $(p \rightarrow q) \vee \neg r$ are p, q, and r. ■

If $\mathcal{L}$ is a propositional language, then the usual way to assign a meaning to each formula in $\mathcal{L}$ is to assign a truth value (either true or false) to the propositional variables and to take into account the connectives. Thus $\neg p$ evaluates to true if and only if p is false and $p \wedge q$ evaluates to true if and only if both p and r are true. We call an assignment of truth values to the propositional variables of a proposition an *interpretation*. A *model* of a proposition is an interpretation for which the formula evaluates to true. A *satisfiability problem* is the problem of determining whether a formula has a model. We say that a formula is *satisfiable* if there exists a model of the formula. A formula is *valid* if and only if any possible interpretation is a model. In other words, a formula is valid if and only if it evaluates to true for any interpretation. If a formula p is valid, then we write $\models p$. Valid propositional formulas are called *tautologies*.

Example B.2 We have the following models of $(p \rightarrow q) \vee \neg r$: all the interpretations that assign *false* to r, all the interpretations that assign *false* to p, and all the interpretations that assign *true* to q. Examples of tautologies are $p \vee \neg p$, $p \rightarrow p$, and $(p \rightarrow (q \rightarrow p))$. ■

A widely used proof theory is *resolution*. It is based on two main ideas. The first idea is to work on formulas with a standard syntactic structure (called *normal form*). The second idea is to apply just a unique and powerful inference rule (called *resolution*). A propositional formula is in *Conjunctive Normal Form* (CNF) if and only if it is a conjunction of clauses, where a *clause* is a disjunction of literals. A *literal* is a propositional variable (*positive literal*) or its negation (*negative literal*). Intuitively, two literals are complementary if and only if one is the negation of the other. For instance, p and $\neg p$ are two complementary literals. A *unit clause* is a clause with one literal. A CNF formula can thus be represented as a set of clauses, where each clause is represented as a set of literals. The *resolution inference rule* is the following.

> *For any two clauses C_1 and C_2, if there is a literal L_1 in C_1 that is complementary to a literal L_2 in C_2, then delete L_1 and L_2 from C_1 and C_2, respectively, and construct the disjunction of the remaining clauses. The constructed clause is called a* resolvent *of C_1 and C_2.*

The reasoning underlying the resolution principle is that, if we have A in C_1 and $\neg A$ in C_2, then we can have two cases.

1. A is true, and therefore C_1 is true and can be eliminated, while $\neg A$ can be eliminated from C_2.

2. A is false, and therefore C_2 is true and can be eliminated, while A can be eliminated from C_1.

In the limiting case, in which C_1 and C_2 are unit clauses and the two literals are complementary, the resolution principle generates the *empty clause* $\emptyset$.

If C is a resolvent of C_1 and C_2, we say that C *logically follows* from C_1 and C_2. We can now define the notion of deduction based on resolution. Given a set of clauses S, a *deduction* of the clause C from S is a finite sequence $C_1, \ldots, C_n$ of clauses such that each C_i either is a clause in S or is a resolvent of clauses preceeding C_i, and $C_n = C$. A deduction of the empty clause $\emptyset$ from S is called a *refutation* of S.

Example B.3 Let us build a deduction of $p \rightarrow r$ from $p \rightarrow q$ and $q \rightarrow r$, i.e., let us show that $p \rightarrow r$ logically follows from $p \rightarrow q$ and $q \rightarrow r$. First, we transform in CNF. We have $S = \{\neg p \vee q, \neg q \vee r\}$ and $C = \neg p \vee r$. We have a one-step deduction: $C_1 = \{\neg p \vee r\}$. Now let us suppose we want to prove $p \rightarrow p$. The CNF version of $p \rightarrow p$ is $\{\neg p \vee p\}$. We take its negation: $S = \{p \wedge \neg p\}$, which resolves in one step to the empty clause. ■

It can be shown that resolution is correct and complete, i.e., if a clause C logically follows from a set of clauses S, then C is valid if any clause in S is valid, and vice versa.

B.3 First-Order Logic

The nice thing about propositional logic is its simplicity. Its weakness is its lack of expressivity. Many ideas cannot be treated in this simple way, such as the fact that any object that has a given property also has another property, or the fact that there exists an object that satisfies some property. A first-order language $\mathcal{L}$ is based on four types of symbols: constant, variable, function, and predicate symbols. A *term* is defined recursively as follows.

1. A constant is a term.
2. A variable is a term.
3. If $t_1, \ldots t_n$ are terms and f is an n-place function symbol, then $f(t_1, \ldots, t_n)$ is a term.
4. Nothing else is a term.

We define *atoms* (or atomic formulas) as the basic building blocks for constructing formulas in first-order logic. If $t_1, \ldots, t_n$ are terms and P is an n-place predicate, then $P(t_1, \ldots, t_n)$ is an atom. We can now define *formulas* in first-order logic.

1. An atom is a formula.
2. If ϕ and ψ are formulas, then $\neg\phi$ and $\phi \wedge \psi$ are formulas.
3. If ϕ is a formula and x is a variable, then $\forall x\phi$ is a formula.
4. Nothing else is a formula.

We define $\exists x\, \phi$ as $\neg\forall x\, \neg\phi$. An occurrence of a variable in a formula is *bound* if and only if the occurrence is within the scope of a quantifier employng the variable or is the occurrence in that quantifier. An occurrence of a variable is *free* if and only if this occurrence of the variable is not bound. A variable is free in a formula if at least one occurrence of it is free in the formula, and similarly for bound variables. Formulas without free variables are called *closed formulas.*

If $\mathcal{L}$ is a first-order language, then the usual way to assign a meaning to each statement in $\mathcal{L}$ is to define an *interpretation* that maps each constant symbol, function symbol, and predicate symbol of $\mathcal{L}$ into an object, a function, or a relation in some world W, where a *world* is a set of objects.[1]

A very common interpretation is the *Herbrand interpretation,* in which the objects of W are the constant symbols of $\mathcal{L}$, and the interpretation maps each constant symbol into itself. If $\mathcal{L}$ is function-free, then a state s can be viewed as a Herbrand interpretation that assigns *true* to all ground atoms in s, and *false* to all ground atoms not in s. From this, a truth value can be computed for every closed formula of $\mathcal{L}$ (i.e., every formula of $\mathcal{L}$ that contains no free variables) using the usual rules for logical composition. For example, a conjunction $\phi_1 \wedge \phi_2$ is true in s (written $s \models \phi_1 \wedge \phi_2$) if and only if both ϕ_1 and ϕ_2 are true in s. Similarly, a quantified formula $\forall x\, \phi$ is true in s if and only if for every substitution θ that substitutes a constant symbol for x, $\theta(\phi)$ is true in s. We will use the notation $s \models \phi$ to mean that ϕ is true in s. Also, if $\theta = \{x \leftarrow c\}$ is a substitution and ϕ is a formula, then we will use the notation $\phi[x \leftarrow c]$ to refer to $\theta(\phi)$. Thus, we have that $s \models \forall x\, \phi$ if and only if $s \models \phi[x \leftarrow c]$ for every constant symbol c of $\mathcal{L}$.

The notion of literal, clause, and CNF is easily extended to first-order logic. The resolution principle is then extended to first-order logic. Recall the resolution principle for propositional logic: a resolvent is obtained by eliminating two complementary literals. The notion of complementary literals in propositional logic is very simple. For clauses that contain variables, this operation is more complicated. For example, consider these clauses:

$$C_1 : P(x) \vee Q(x)$$
$$C_2 : \neg P(f(x)) \vee R(x)$$

There are no complementary literals in C_1 and C_2. However, if we substitute $f(c)$ (where f is a function symbol and c is a constant) for x in C_1 and c for x in C_2,

1. The world of an interpretation is often called the *domain* of the interpretation.

we obtain:

$$C_1' : P(f(c)) \vee Q(f(c))$$
$$C_2' : \neg P(f(c)) \vee R(c)$$

Now we have two complementary literals, and we can obtain the resolvent:

$$C_3' : Q(f(c)) \vee R(c)$$

More generally, if we substitute $f(x)$ for x in C_1, we obtain a resolvent for C_1 and C_2:

$$C_3 : Q(f(x)) \vee R(x)$$

By substituting appropriate terms for the variables in C_1 and C_2 as shown here, we can resolve them. Furthermore, clause C_3 is the "most general clause" in the sense that all the other clauses that can be generated by this process are instances of C_3. In general, a substitution θ is a finite set of the form $\theta = \{t_1 \leftarrow x_1, \ldots, t_n \leftarrow x_n\}$, where every x_i is a variable, every t_i is a term different from x_i, and $x_i \neq x_j$ for any $i \neq j$. When $t_1, \ldots, t_n$ are ground terms (i.e., terms containing no variables), then the substitution is called *ground substitution.* Let θ be a substitution and e be an expression of first-order logic, i.e., a term or a formula. Then $\theta(e)$ is an expression obtained from e by replacing simultaneously each occurrence of the variable x_i with the term t_i. $\theta(e)$ is called an *instance* of e.

If we want to apply the resolution principle to a set of clauses, then in order to identify a pair of complementary literals, we have to match or *unify* two or more expressions. That is, we have to find a substitution that can make several expressions identical. A substitution θ is called a *unifier* for a set of expressions $\{e_1, \ldots, e_k\}$ if and only if $\theta(e_1) = \theta(e_2) = \ldots = \theta(e_k)$. The set $\{e_1, \ldots, e_k\}$ is said to be *unifiable* if and only if there exists a unifier for it.

A unifier σ for a set $\{e_1, \ldots, e_k\}$ of expressions is a *most general unifier* if and only if for each unifier θ for the set there is a substitution ρ such that $\theta = \sigma \circ \rho$, where $\circ$ is the usual composition of substitutions.

It is possible to define an algorithm for finding a most general unifier for a finite unifiable set of nonempty expressions. When the set is not unifiable, the algorithm returns failure.

We can now define the resolution principle for first-order logic. We start with some definitions. If two literals of a clause C have a most general unifier σ, then $\sigma(C)$ is a *factor* of C. Let C_1 and C_2 be two clauses with no variables in common. Let L_1 and L_2 be two literals in C_1 and C_2, respectively. If L_1 and $\neg L_2$ have a most general unifier σ, then the clause

$$(\sigma(C_1) - \sigma(L_1)) \cup (\sigma(C_2) - \sigma(L_2))$$

is a *binary resolvent* of C_1 and C_2.

We can finally define the notion of a resolvent. A *resolvent* of the clauses C_1 and C_2 is one of the following binary resolvents:

1. A binary resolvent of C_1 and C_2
2. A binary resolvent of C_1 and a factor of C_2
3. A binary resolvent of a factor of C_1 and C_2
4. A binary resolvent of a factor of C_1 and a factor of C_2

It is possible to show that the resolution principle is *complete*, i.e., it is guaranteed to generate the empty clause ∅ from an unsatisfiable set of clauses.

APPENDIX C

Model Checking

C.1 Introduction

Model checking is becoming a popular technique that has been successfully applied to the verification of industrial hardware and software systems. It is a formal verification technique based on the exhaustive exploration of the states of a system. Actually, the term *model checking* refers to several different problems, theories, and techniques, e.g., from finite-state to infinite-state model checking, from liner-time to branching-time model checking, from model checking based on automata theory to model checking based on Kripke structures, from explicit-state to symbolic model checking, from symbolic model checking based on BDDs to symbolic model checking based on satisfiability decision procedures.

This appendix focuses on finite-state systems. It describes a formal framework based on Kripke Structures and branching-time temporal logic. We discuss symbolic model checking and its implementation through BDDs because these techniques are of interest for practical applications where model checking has to deal with large state spaces. Indeed, symbolic model checking is routinely applied in industrial hardware design and is beginning to be used in other application domains (see [131] for a survey).

C.2 Intuitions

Intuitively, the model checking problem is the problem of determining whether a property holds in a model of a system. As an example, consider an interlocking system, i.e., a system that controls the equipment in a railway station: the signals to the trains, the position of the switches, the signals at railroad crossings, etc. A desired property is that the interlocking system never allows trains to crash, e.g., by letting a train enter a route crossed by a railroad crossing that is open to cars. The interlocking system can be modeled by a finite-state machine. The property that a train should never crash can be represented in temporal logic. A *model checker* (see Figure C.1) is a software system that takes as input a model of a system and

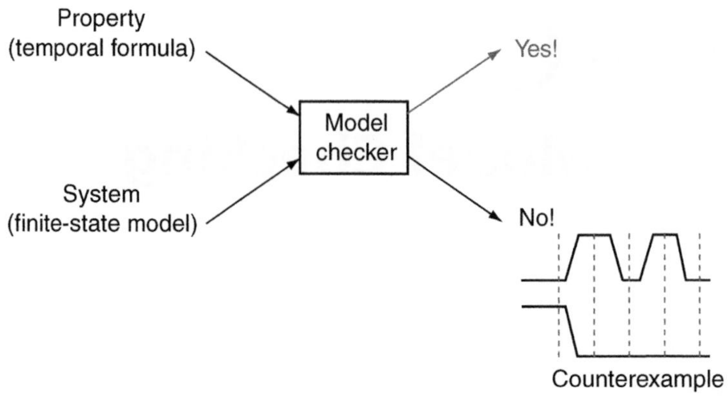

Figure C.1 Model checker.

a description of a property to be checked, and returns "yes" if the property is true in the model. If the property does not hold, the model checker returns a counterexample, i.e., a description of a behavior of the system that does not satisfy the property.

Example C.1 Figure C.2 shows a very simple example of a model of an interlocking system and of some properties that should be checked. The interlocking system can be in three states: (1) the signal to the train is red and the crossing road is closed, (2) the signal is green and the road is closed, and (3) the signal is red and the road

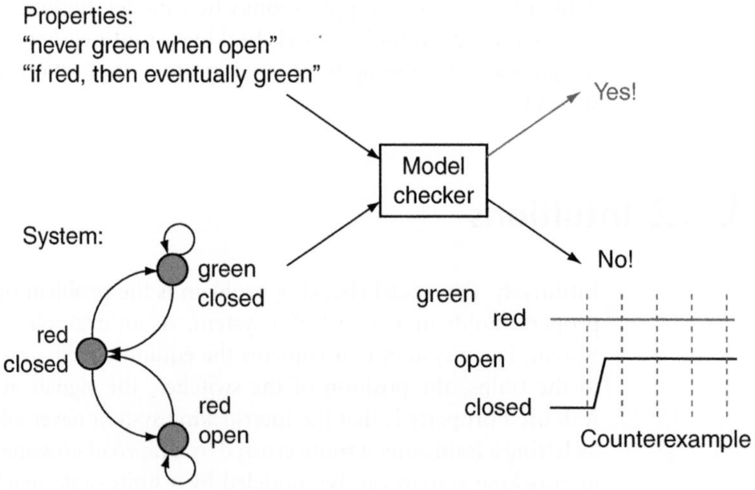

Figure C.2 Examples of model checking.

is open. A safety requirement is that "the signal is never green when the road is open." Given this property as input, the model checker should return "yes." Indeed, there is no state of the system where the road is open and the signal is green.

We are also interested in the *liveness requirements*, i.e., properties that assure that the system "works," such as the fact that "if the signal is red, then eventually in the future it will be green." This corresponds to the fact that we want to allow some train to proceed sooner or later. In this case the model checker finds a counterexample. It is represented by the infinite sequences of states that start with red and closed, and then have red and open forever.

■

Some remarks are in order. When we say that a finite-state model of a system is given as input to the model checker, we do not mean that the data structure is provided explicitly as input to the model checker. In the DWR domain, there are cases with 10^{277} states. In practice, it is not feasible to give the finite-state model explicitly. Instead, different languages are used to describe finite-state models. In this appendix, we will describe the model checking performed on state-transition systems, without discussing the languages used to describe them.

C.3 The Model Checking Problem

In model checking, models of systems can be formalized as Kripke structures. A *Kripke Structure* K is a 4-tuple (S, S_0, R, L), where:

- S is a finite set of *states*.
- $S_0 \subseteq S$ is a set of initial states.
- $R \subseteq S \times S$ is a binary relation on S, the *transition relation*, which gives the possible transitions between states. We require R to be total, i.e., for each state $s \in S$ there exists a state $s' \in S$ such that $(s, s') \in R$.
- $L : S \mapsto 2^{\mathcal{P}}$ is a *labeling function*, where $\mathcal{P}$ is a set of proposition symbols. L assigns to each state the set of atomic propositions true in that state.

A Kripke structure encodes each possible evolution of the domain (or behavior) as a *path*, i.e., an infinite sequence $s_0, s_1, s_2, \ldots$ of states in S such that $s_0 \in S_0$ and for each i, $(s_i, s_{i+1}) \in R$.

Example C.2 Figure C.3 shows a simple example of a Kripke structure.

$S = \{s_0, s_1, s_2\}$
$S_0 = \{s_0\}$
$R = \{(s_0, s_1), (s_0, s_2), (s_1, s_1), (s_1, s_0), (s_2, s_2), (s_2, s_0)\}$
$L(s_0) = \emptyset$, $L(s_1) = \mathsf{green}$, $L(s_2) = \mathsf{open}$

■

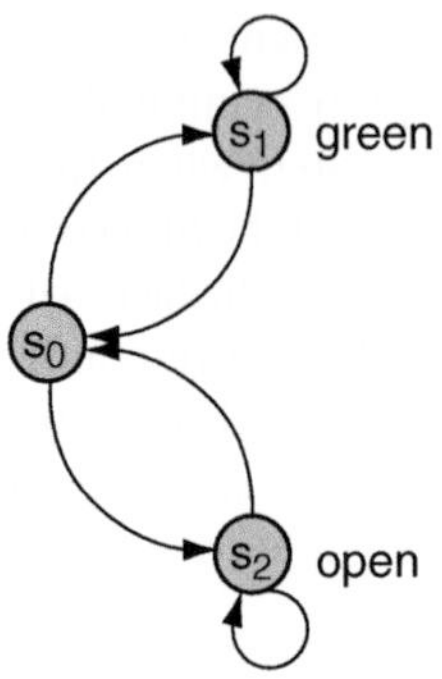

Figure C.3 Example of a Kripke structure.

Properties to be checked can be formalized in a temporal logic called Computation Tree Logic (CTL) [171]. Given a finite set $\mathcal{P}$ of atomic propositions, CTL formulas are inductively defined as follows.

1. Every atomic proposition $p \in \mathcal{P}$ is a CTL formula.
2. If p and q are CTL formulas, then so are the following formulas.
   (a) $\neg p, p \vee q$
   (b) $\mathbf{AX}p, \mathbf{EX}p$
   (c) $\mathbf{A}(p\mathbf{U}q)$, and $\mathbf{E}(p\mathbf{U}q)$

X is the "next time" temporal operator and **A** and **E** are path quantifiers; the formula $\mathbf{AX}p$ or $\mathbf{EX}p$ means that p holds in every or in some immediate successor of the current state. **U** is the "until" temporal operator; the formula $\mathbf{A}(p\mathbf{U}q)$ or $\mathbf{E}(p\mathbf{U}q)$ means that for every path or for some path there exists an initial prefix of the path such that q holds at the last state of the prefix and p holds at all the other states along the prefix.[1] Formulas $\mathbf{AF}p$ and $\mathbf{EF}p$ (where the temporal operator **F** stands for "future" or "eventually") are abbreviations of $\mathbf{A}(\top\mathbf{U}p)$ and $\mathbf{E}(\top\mathbf{U}p)$ (where $\top$ stands for truth), respectively. $\mathbf{EG}p$ and $\mathbf{AG}p$ (where **G** stands for "globally" or "always") are abbreviations of $\neg\mathbf{AF}\neg p$ and $\neg\mathbf{EF}\neg p$, respectively.

Example C.3 Consider the example of the Kripke structure in Figure C.3. Recall the safety and the liveness requirements expressed in Example C.1 and Figure C.2. To represent the safety requirement "the signal is never green when the road is open," let us use the formula $\mathbf{AG}(\mathsf{open} \rightarrow \neg\mathsf{green})$. Consider the liveness requirement "if the signal is red, then eventually it will be green." If we want to say that the signal eventually will be green for *all* of the system's evolutions, then we write the formula $\mathbf{AG}(\neg\mathsf{green} \rightarrow \mathbf{AF}\mathsf{green})$. If we want the weaker requirement that *there exists*

1. Given a path $s_0, s_1, \ldots$, a prefix of the path is any sequence $s_0, \ldots, s_i$, with $i \geq 0$.

a system's evolution such that the signal will eventually be green, then the formula is **AG**(¬green → **EF**green). Consider the formulas ¬green → **AF**green and ¬green → **EF**green. They state that we must start in one of the two states s_0 and s_2 (where the signal is red), and then we will eventually reach a state where the signal is green.

■

We give semantics to CTL formulas in terms of Kripke Structures. Let p be a CTL formula. $K, s \models p$ is defined inductively as follows.

If $p \in \mathcal{P}$, then $K, s \models p$ iff $p \in L(s)$

$K, s \models \neg p$ iff $K, s \not\models p$

$K, s \models p \vee q$ iff $K, s \models p$ or $K, s \models q$

$K, s \models \mathbf{AX}p$ iff for all paths $\pi = s_0, s_1, s_2, \ldots$ such that $s = s_0$, we have $K, s_1 \models p$

$K, s \models \mathbf{EX}p$ iff there exists a path $\pi = s_0, s_1, s_2, \ldots$ such that $s = s_0$, such that $K, s_1 \models p$

$K, s \models \mathbf{A}(p\mathbf{U}q)$ iff for all paths $\pi = s_0, s_1, s_2, \ldots$ such that $s = s_0$, there exists $i \geq 0$ such that $K, s_i \models q$ and for all $0 \leq j < i$, $K, s_j \models p$

$K, s \models \mathbf{E}(p\mathbf{U}q)$ iff there exists a path $\pi = s_0, s_1, s_2, \ldots$ such that $s = s_0$, and a number $i \geq 0$ such that $K, s_i \models q$ and for all $0 \leq j < i$, $K, s_j \models p$

We say that p is true in a state s of the Kripke structure K if $K, s \models p$. We say that p is true in K ($K \models p$) if $K, s \models p$ for each $s \in S_0$.

The *model checking problem* for a CTL formula p and a Kripke structure K is the problem of determining whether p is true in K.

Example C.4 In the example in Figure C.3, it follows that $K \models$ **AG**(open → ¬green), $K \not\models$ **AG**(¬green → **AF**green), and $K \models$ **AG**(¬green → **EF**green).

■

C.4 Model Checking Algorithms

Algorithms for model checking exploit the structure of CTL formulas. For instance, an atomic formula p is model checked by verifying that $p \in L(s)$ for all $s \in S_0$. As another example, model checking $\mathbf{AX}p$ or $\mathbf{EX}p$ is performed by model checking p in all states or in some state s' such that $(s, s') \in R$, for each $s \in S_0$. As a further example, $\mathbf{A}(p\mathbf{U}q)$ or $\mathbf{E}(p\mathbf{U}q)$ can be model checked by exploiting the fact that:

$$\begin{aligned} p\mathbf{U}q = q \vee & \\ & (p \wedge \mathbf{X}q) \vee \\ & (p \wedge \mathbf{X}p \wedge \mathbf{XX}q) \vee \\ & \ldots \end{aligned}$$

```
1. MCheckEF(p,K)
2.    CurrentStates← ∅;
3.    NextStates ← States(p,K);
4.    while NextStates ≠ CurrentStates do
5.      if (S0 ⊆ NextStates)
6.        then return(True);
7.      CurrentStates ← NextStates;
8.      NextStates ← NextStates ∪ pre-img-ef(NextStates,K);
9.    return(False);
```

Figure C.4 Model checking EFp.

As a simple example, we show in Figure C.4 a possible algorithm for model checking the CTL formula **EF**p, with $p \in \mathcal{P}$. Given a Kripke Structure $K = (S, S_0, R, L)$ and a propositional formula p, the algorithm starts by computing the set of states where p holds (line 3):

$$\textsc{States}(p, K) = \{s \in S : p \in L(s)\} \qquad \text{(C.1)}$$

Next, MCheckEF explores the state space of K. It accumulates in *NextStates* the states returned by pre-img-ef (line 8). Given a set of states $\mathit{States} \subseteq S$, pre-img-ef returns the set of states that have at least one immediate successor state in *States*:

$$\textsc{pre-img-ef}(\mathit{States}, K) = \{s \in S : \exists s'. (s' \in \mathit{States} \wedge R(s, s'))\} \qquad \text{(C.2)}$$

Notice that **EF**p always holds in each state in *NextStates*. The loop terminates successfully if *NextStates* contains all the initial states (termination condition at line 5). MCheckEF returns *False* if *NextStates* does not contain all the initial states and there are no new states to explore, i.e., $\mathit{NextStates} = \mathit{CurrentStates}$. Indeed, if this happens, then $K \not\models p$ because there exists $s \in S_0$ such that $K, s \not\models p$ and we have no further states to explore. It can be shown that there exists a least fixed point and that the algorithm is guaranteed to terminate.

A possible algorithm for model checking the CTL formula **AF**p can be obtained from MCheckEF simply by replacing pre-img-ef with pre-img-af, where:

$$\textsc{pre-img-af}(\mathit{States}, K) = \{s \in S : \forall s'. (R(s, s') \rightarrow s' \in \mathit{States})\} \qquad \text{(C.3)}$$

Compare this algorithm with the Strong-Plan algorithm in Chapter 17.

Example C.5 Let us model check the formula **EF**green in the Kripke Structure in Figure C.3. MCheckEF assigns state s_1 to the variable *NextStates*. After the first iteration, *NextStates* is $\{s_0, s_1\}$, and then the algorithm stops returning *True*.

As another example let us check the formula **AF**green. Initially s_1 is assigned to the variable *NextStates*, but at the first iteration PRE-IMG-AF returns the empty set, then the loop terminates and the algorithm returns *False*. ■

C.5 Symbolic Model Checking

Most often, realistic models of systems need huge numbers of states. For example, an interlocking system may have something like 10^{200} states. Symbolic model checking [99] has been devised to deal with large state spaces. It is a form of model checking in which propositional formulas are used for the compact representation of finite-state models, and transformations over propositional formulas provide a basis for efficient exploration of the state space. Most often, the use of symbolic techniques allows for the analysis of large systems, even systems with 10^{200} states [99]. The fundamental ideas of symbolic model checking are the following.

1. Model checking is performed by exploring sets of states, rather than single states.
2. The model checking problem is represented symbolically: the sets of states and the transitions over sets of states are represented by logical formulas.

In order to represent a model checking problem symbolically, we need to represent symbolically the sets of states of a Kripke Structure, its transition relation, and the model checking algorithms.

Symbolic Representation of Sets of States. A vector of distinct propositional variables $\boldsymbol{x}$, called *state variables*, is devoted to the representation of the states of a Kripke structure. Each of these variables has a direct association with a proposition symbol of $\mathcal{P}$. Therefore, in the rest of this section we will not distinguish between a proposition and the corresponding propositional variable. For instance, in the Kripke structure in Example C.2 (see page 563), $\boldsymbol{x}$ is the vector $\langle$green, open$\rangle$. A state is the set of propositions of $\mathcal{P}$ that hold in the state. For each state s, there is a corresponding assignment of truth values to the state variables in $\boldsymbol{x}$: each variable in s is *True*, and all other variables are *False*. We represent s with a propositional formula $\xi(s)$, whose unique satisfying assignment of truth values corresponds to s. For instance, the formula representing state s_1 in Example C.2 is green $\wedge$ $\neg$open. This representation naturally extends to any set of states $Q \subseteq S$ as follows:

$$\xi(Q) = \bigvee_{s \in Q} \xi(s)$$

That is, we associate a set of states with the disjunction of the formulas representing each of the states. The satisfying assignments of $\xi(Q)$ are exactly the assignments representing the states of Q.

A remark is in order. We are using a propositional formula to represent the set of assignments that satisfy it (and hence to represent the corresponding set of states), but we do not care about the actual syntax of the formula used, and thus in the following discussion we will not distinguish among equivalent formulas that represent the same sets of assignments. Although the actual syntax of the formula may have a computational impact, in the next section we will show that the use of formulas for representing sets of states is indeed practical.

The main efficiency of the symbolic representation is that the cardinality of the represented set is not directly related to the size of the formula. For instance, $\xi(2^{\mathcal{P}})$ and $\xi(\emptyset)$ are the formulas *True* and *False*, respectively, independent of the cardinality of $\mathcal{P}$.

As a further advantage, the symbolic representation can provide an easy way to ignore irrelevant information. For instance, notice that the variable open does not appear in the formula $\xi(\{s_0, s_2\}) = \neg\text{green}$. For this reason, a symbolic representation can have a dramatic improvement over an explicit state representation that enumerates the states of the Kripke Structure. This is what allows symbolic model checkers to handle finite-state models that have very large numbers of states (see, e.g., [99]).

Another advantage of the symbolic representation is the natural encoding of set-theoretic transformations (e.g., union, intersection, complementation) into propositional operations, as follows:

$$\xi(Q_1 \cup Q_2) = \xi(Q_1) \vee \xi(Q_2)$$
$$\xi(Q_1 \cap Q_2) = \xi(Q_1) \wedge \xi(Q_2)$$
$$\xi(S - Q) = \xi(S) \wedge \neg\xi(Q)$$

Symbolic Representation of Transition Relations. We represent transition relations through the vector of state variables $\boldsymbol{x} = \langle x_1, \ldots, x_n \rangle$ and a further vector $\boldsymbol{x}' = \langle x'_1, \ldots, x'_n \rangle$ of propositional variables, called *next-state variables*. We write $\xi'(s)$ for the representation of the state s in the next-state variables. $\xi'(Q)$ is the formula corresponding to the set of states Q. In the following, $\Phi[\boldsymbol{x} \leftarrow \boldsymbol{y}]$ is the parallel substitution in formula Φ of the variables in vector $\boldsymbol{x}$ with the corresponding variables in $\boldsymbol{y}$. We define the representation of a set of states in the next variables as follows:

$$\xi'(s) = \xi(s)[\boldsymbol{x} \leftarrow \boldsymbol{x}'].$$

We call the operation $\Phi[\boldsymbol{x} \leftarrow \boldsymbol{x}']$ *forward shifting* because it transforms the representation of a set of current states in the representation of a set of next states. The dual operation $\Phi[\boldsymbol{x}' \leftarrow \boldsymbol{x}]$ is called *backward shifting*. In the following, we call the variables in $\boldsymbol{x}$ the *current-state variables* to distinguish them from the next-state variables.

For the interlocking example in Figure C.3, the single transition from state s_0 to state s_1 is represented by the formula

$$\xi(\langle s_0, s_1\rangle) = \xi(s_0) \wedge \xi'(s_1),$$

that is,

$$\xi(\langle s_0, s_1\rangle) = (\neg\mathsf{green} \wedge \neg\mathsf{open}) \wedge (\mathsf{green}' \wedge \neg\mathsf{open}')$$

The transition relation R of a Kripke Structure is a set of transitions and is thus represented by the formula in the variables of $\boldsymbol{x}$ and of $\boldsymbol{x}'$,

$$\xi(R) = \bigvee_{r \in R} \xi(r),$$

in which each satisfying assignment represents a possible transition.

Symbolic Representation of Model Checking Algorithms. In order to make explicit that the formula $\xi(Q)$ contains the variables $x_1, \ldots, x_n$ of $\boldsymbol{x}$, in the following we will use the expression $Q(\boldsymbol{x})$ to mean $\xi(Q)$. Similarly, we will use the expression $Q(\boldsymbol{x}')$ to mean $\xi'(Q)$. Let $S(\boldsymbol{x})$, $R(\boldsymbol{x}, \boldsymbol{x}')$, and $S_0(\boldsymbol{x})$ be the formulas representing the states, the transition relation, and the initial states of a Kripke structure, respectively.

In the following, we will use quantification in the style of the logic of Quantified Boolean Formulas (QBFs). QBFs are a definitional extension to propositional logic, in which propositional variables can be universally and existentially quantified. If Φ is a formula and v_i is one of its variables, then the existential quantification of v_i in Φ, written $\exists v_i. \Phi(v_1, \ldots, v_n)$, is equivalent to $\Phi(v_1, \ldots, v_n)[v_i \leftarrow \mathit{False}] \vee \Phi(v_1, \ldots, v_n)[v_i \leftarrow \mathit{True}]$. Analogously, the universal quantification $\forall v_i. \Phi(v_1, \ldots, v_n)$ is equivalent to $\Phi(v_1, \ldots, v_n)[v_i \leftarrow \mathit{False}] \wedge \Phi(v_1, \ldots, v_n)[v_i \leftarrow \mathit{True}]$. QBFs allow for an exponentially more compact representation than propositional formulas.

The symbolic representation of the *image* of a set of states Q, i.e., the set of states reachable from any state in Q with one state transition, is the result of applying the substitution $[\boldsymbol{x}' \leftarrow \boldsymbol{x}]$ to the formula $\exists \boldsymbol{x}. (R(\boldsymbol{x}, \boldsymbol{x}') \wedge Q(\boldsymbol{x}))$:

$$(\exists \boldsymbol{x}. (R(\boldsymbol{x}, \boldsymbol{x}') \ \wedge \ Q(\boldsymbol{x})))[\boldsymbol{x}' \leftarrow \boldsymbol{x}]$$

Notice that, with this single operation, we symbolically simulate the transition from any of the states in Q. The dual backward image is the following:

$$(\exists \boldsymbol{x}'. (R(\boldsymbol{x}, \boldsymbol{x}') \ \wedge \ Q(\boldsymbol{x}')))$$

From the definition of PRE-IMG-EF(Q) (see Equation C.2), we have therefore that ξ(PRE-IMG-EF(Q)) is:

$$\exists \boldsymbol{x}'.\,(R(\boldsymbol{x},\boldsymbol{x}') \wedge Q(\boldsymbol{x}'))$$

while ξ(PRE-IMG-AF(Q)) (see Equation C.3) is:

$$\forall \boldsymbol{x}'.\,(R(\boldsymbol{x},\boldsymbol{x}') \rightarrow Q(\boldsymbol{x}'))$$

In both cases, the resulting formula is obtained as a one-step computation and can often describe compactly a large set of states.

Given the basic building blocks just defined, the algorithms presented in the previous section can be symbolically implemented by replacing, within the same control structure, each function call with the symbolic counterpart and by casting the operations on sets into the corresponding operations on propositional formulas.

C.6 BDD-Based Symbolic Model Checking

BDDs provide a way to implement the symbolic representation mechanisms presented in the previous section (e.g., tautology checking, quantification, shifting).

A BDD is a directed acyclic graph (DAG). The terminal nodes are either *True* or *False* (alternatively indicated with 0 and 1, respectively). Each nonterminal node is associated with a Boolean variable and with two BDDs that are called the *left* and *right branches.* Figure C.5 shows some simple BDDs for the interlocking example. At each nonterminal node, the right or left branch is depicted as a solid or dashed line and represents the assignment of the value *True* or *False* to the corresponding variable.

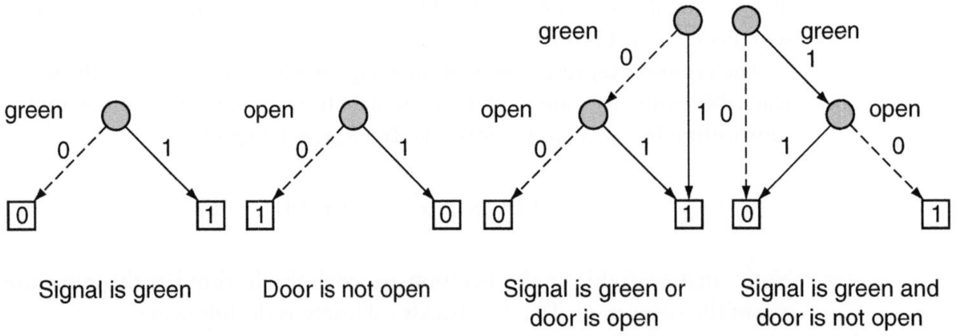

Figure C.5 BDDs for the Boolean formulas green, ¬open, green ∨ open, and green ∧ ¬open.

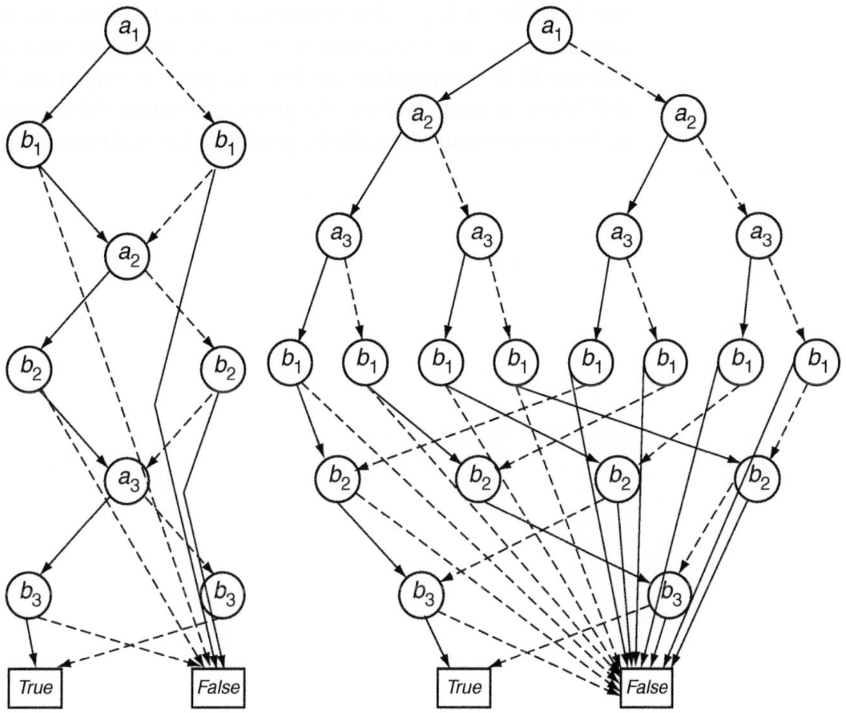

Figure C.6 Two BDDs for the formula $(a_1 \leftrightarrow b_1) \wedge (a_2 \leftrightarrow b_2) \wedge (a_3 \leftrightarrow b_3)$.

Given a BDD, the value corresponding to a given truth assignment to the variables is determined by traversing the graph from the root to the leaves, following each branch indicated by the value assigned to the variables. A path from the root to a leaf can visit nodes associated with a subset of all the variables of the BDD. The reached leaf node is labeled with the resulting truth value. If v is a BDD, its size $|v|$ is the number of its nodes. If n is a node, we use $var(n)$ to denote the variable indexing node n. BDDs are a canonical representation of Boolean formulas if (1) there is a total order $<$ over the set of variables used to label nodes, such that for any node n and respective nonterminal child m, their variables must be ordered, i.e., $var(n) < var(m)$; and (2) the BDD contains no subgraphs that are isomorphic to the BDD itself.

The choice of variable ordering may have a dramatic impact on the dimension of a BDD. For example, Figure C.6 depicts two BDDs for the same formula $(a_1 \leftrightarrow b_1) \wedge (a_2 \leftrightarrow b_2) \wedge (a_3 \leftrightarrow b_3)$ obtained with different variable orderings.

BDDs can be used to compute the results of applying the usual Boolean operators. Given a BDD that represents a formula, it is possible to transform it to obtain the BDD representing the negation of the formula. Given two BDDs representing two formulas, it is possible to combine them to obtain the BDD representing the conjunction or the disjunction of the two formulas. For instance, Figure C.5 shows how the BDD representing the formula green $\wedge$ $\neg$open can be obtained from the BDDs representing the formulas green and $\neg$open. Substitution and quantification on Boolean formulas can also be performed as BDD transformations.

Bibliography

[1] M. Aarup, M. M. Arentoft, Y. Parrod, I. Stokes, H. Vadon, and J. Stader. Optimum-AIV: A knowledge-based planning and scheduling system for spacecraft AIV. In *Intelligent Scheduling*, pp. 451–469. M. Zweben and M. S. Fox, eds., Morgan Kaufmann, 1994.

[2] S. Adali, L. Console, M. L. Sapino, M. Schenone, and P. Terenziani. Representing and reasoning with temporal constraints in multimedia presentations. In *TIME*, pp. 3–12. IEEE 2000.

[3] J. M. Agosta. Formulation and implementation of an equipment configuration problem with the SIPE-2 generative planner. In *Proc. AAAI-95 Spring Symposium on Integrated Planning Applications*, pp. 1–10. 1995.

[4] P. Agree and D. Chapman. Pengi: An implementation of a theory of activity. In *Proc. of the 6th National Conference on Artificial Intelligence*, pp. 268–272. Seattle: AAAI, 1987.

[5] A. V. Aho, J. E. Hopcroft, and J. D. Ullman. *The Design and Analysis of Computer Algorithms.* Addison-Wesley, 1976.

[6] L. C. Aiello, A. Cesta, E. Giunchiglia, M. Pistore, and P. Traverso. Planning and verification techniques for the high level programming and monitoring of autonomous robotic devices. In *Proceedings of the European Space Agency Workshop on On Board Autonoy* (Noordwijk, The Netherlands, ESTEC October 2001).

[7] L. C. Aiello, A. Cesta, E. Giunchiglia, and P. Traverso. Merging planning and verification techniques for "safe planning" in space robotics. In *6th International Symposium on Artificial Intelligence, Robotics and Automation in Space: A New Space Odyssey (ISAIRAS01)* (Montreal, Canada, June 2001).

[8] R. Alami and S. Botelho. Plan-based multi-robot cooperation. In Beetz *et al.* [58], pp. 1–20, 2002.

[9] R. Alami, R. Chatila, S. Fleury, M. Ghallab, and F. Ingrand. An architecture for autonomy. *International Journal of Robotics Research*, 17(4), pp. 315–337, 1998.

[10] R. Alami, S. Fleury, M. Herrb, F. Ingrand, and F. Robert. Multi-robot cooperation in the Martha project. *IEEE Robotics and Automation Magazine*, 5(1):36–47, 1998.

[11] R. Alami, J. P. Laumond, and T. Siméon. Two manipulation planning algorithms. In Goldberg *et al.* [235], pp. 109–125, 1995.

[12] J. F. Allen. Towards a general theory of action and time. *Artificial Intelligence*, 23:123–154, 1984.

[13] J. F. Allen. Temporal reasoning and planning. In Allen *et al.* [15], pp. 1–68, 1991.

[14] J. F. Allen, J. Hendler, and A. Tate, *Readings in Planning*. Morgan Kaufmann, 1990.

[15] J. F. Allen, H. Kautz, R. Pelavin, and J. Tenenberg, *Reasoning about Plans*. Morgan Kaufmann, 1991.

[16] J. F. Allen. Maintaining knowledge about temporal intervals. *Communications of the ACM*, 21(11):832–843, 1983.

[17] J. F. Allen. Planning as temporal reasoning. In *Proceedings of the International Conference on Knowledge Representation and Reasoning (KR)*, Morgan Kaufmann, 1991.

[18] J. F. Allen and J. A. Koomen. Planning using a temporal world model. In *Proceedings of the International Joint Conference on Artificial Intelligence (IJCAI)*, 1983.

[19] J. Ambite and C. Knoblock. Planning by rewriting. *Journal of Artificial Intelligence Research*, 15:207–261, 2001.

[20] C. Anderson, D. Smith, and D. Weld. Conditional effects in Graphplan. In *Proceedings of the International Conference on AI Planning Systems (AIPS)*, pp. 44–53, 1998.

[21] E. Anderson, C. Glass, and C. Potts. Machine scheduling. In E. Aarts and J. Lenstra, eds., *Local Search in Combinatorial Optimization*, pp. 361–414, Wiley, 1997.

[22] D. Applegate, G. Jacobson, and D. Sleator. *Computer Analysis of Sprouts*. Technical report, Carnegie Mellon University, 1991.

[23] R. Arkin. *Behavior-Based Robotics*. MIT Press, 1998.

[24] E. Asarin, O. Maler, and A. Pnueli. Symbolic controller synthesis for discrete and timed systems. In *Hybrid Systems II, LNCS 999*, pp. 1–20, Springer-Verlag, 1995.

[25] T.-C. Au, H. Muñoz-Avila, and D. S. Nau. On the complexity of plan adaptation by derivational analogy in a universal classical planning framework. In *Proceedings of the European Conference on Case-Based Reasoning (ECCBR)*, (Aberdeen, Scotland, September 4–7, 2002), pp. 13–27.

[26] P. Avesani, A. Perini, and F. Ricci. The twofold integration of CBR in decision support systems. In D. Aha and J. Daniels, eds., *Case-Based Reasoning Integrations: Papers from the 1998 Workshop* (Technical Report WS-98-15). AAAI Press, 1998.

[27] A. Baba, J. Bresina, L. Charest, W. Edgington, A. Jonsson, A. Ko, B. Kanefsky, P. Maldague, P. Morris, N. Muscettola, and K. Rajan. MAPGEN: Mixed Initiative Planning and Scheduling for the Mars'03 MER Mission. In *Proceedings of the International Symposium on Artificial Intelligence, Robotics, and Automation in Space (i-SAIRAS)* (Nara, Japan, May 2003).

[28] F. Bacchus. The AIPS '00 planning competition. *AI Magazine*, 22(1):47–56, 2001.

[29] F. Bacchus and M. Ady. Planning with resources and concurrency: A forward chaining approach. In *Proceedings of the International Joint Conference on Artificial Intelligence (IJCAI)*, pp. 417–424, 2001.

[30] F. Bacchus, C. Boutilier, and A. Grove. Rewarding behaviors. In *AAAI/IAAI Proceedings*, pp. 1160–1167, 1996.

[31] F. Bacchus, C. Boutilier, and A. Grove. Structured solution methods for non-Markovian decision processes. In *AAAI/IAAI Proceedings*, 1997.

[32] F. Bacchus and F. Kabanza. Planning for temporally extended goals. *Annals of Mathematics and Artificial Intelligence*, 22:5–27, 1998.

[33] F. Bacchus and F. Kabanza. Using temporal logics to express search control knowledge for planning. *Artificial Intelligence*, 116:123–191, 2000.

[34] F. Bacchus and P. van Beek. On the conversion between non-binary and binary constraint satisfaction problems. In *AAAI/IAAI Proceedings*, pp. 311–318, 1998.

[35] F. Bacchus and P. van Run. Dynamic variable ordering in CSPs. In *Proceedings of the International Conference on Knowledge Representation and Reasoning (KR)*, pp. 258–275, 1995.

[36] F. Bacchus and Q. Yang. The downward refinement property. In *Proceedings of the International Joint Conference on Artificial Intelligence (IJCAI)*, pp. 286–292, 1991.

[37] F. Bacchus and Q. Yang. Downward refinement and the efficiency of hierarchical problem solving. *Artificial Intelligence*, 71:43–100, 1994.

[38] C. Bäckström. Planning in polynomial time: The SAS-PUB class. *Computational Intelligence*, 7:181–197, 1991.

[39] C. Bäckström. Equivalence and tractability results for SAS^+ planning. In *Proceedings of the International Conference on Knowledge Representation and Reasoning (KR)*, 1992.

[40] C. Bäckström and B. Nebel. Complexity results for SAS^+ planning. *Computational Intelligence*, 11(4):1–34, 1995.

[41] M. Baioletti, S. Marcugini, and A. Milani. C-SATPlan: A SATPlan-based tool for planning with constraints. In *Proceedings of the International Conference on AI Planning Systems (AIPS)*, 1998.

[42] M. Baioletti, S. Marcugini, and A. Milani. DPPlan: An algorithm for fast solutions extraction from a planning graph. In *Proceedings of the International Conference on AI Planning Systems (AIPS)*, pp. 13–21, 2000.

[43] K. Baker. *Introduction to Sequencing and Scheduling*. Wiley, 1974.

[44] E. Balas. A note on the branch-and-bound principle. *Operations Research*, 16:442–444, 1968.

[45] P. Baptiste, C. LePape, and W. Nuijten. *Constraint-Based Scheduling*. Kluwer Academic Publishers, 2001.

[46] C. Baral and V. S. Subrahmanian. Dualities between alternative semantics for logic programming and non-monotonic reasoning. *Journal of Automated Reasoning*, 10:399–420, 1993.

[47] F. Barber. Reasoning on interval and point-based disjunctive metric constraints in temporal contexts. *Journal of Artificial Intelligence Research*, 12:35–86, 2000.

[48] J. Barraquand and J. C. Latombe. Robot motion planning: A distributed representation approach. *International Journal of Robotics Research*, 10(6): 628–649, 1991.

[49] A. Barrett. *Frugal Hierarchical Task-Network Planning*. Ph.D. thesis, University of Washington, 1997.

[50] A. Barrett, K. Golden, J. S. Penberthy, and D. S. Weld. *UCPOP User's Manual (Version 2.0)*. Technical Report TR-93-09-06. Department of Computer Science and Engineering, University of Washington, 1993. ftp://ftp.cs.washington.edu/tr/1993/09/UW-CSE-93-09-06.PS.Z.

[51] A. Barrett and D. S. Weld. Characterizing subgoal interactions for planning. In *Proceedings of the International Joint Conference on Artificial Intelligence (IJCAI)*, pp. 1388–1393, 1993.

[52] A. Barrett and D. S. Weld. Partial order planning: Evaluating possible efficiency gains. *Artificial Intelligence*, 67(1):71–112, 1994.

[53] A. Barrett and D. S. Weld. Task-decomposition via plan parsing. In *Proceedings of the National Conference on Artificial Intelligence (AAAI)*, Volume 2, pp. 1117–1122. AAAI Press/MIT Press, 1994.

[54] M. Bauer, S. Biundo, D. Dengler, J. Koehler, and G. Paul. A logic-based tool for intelligent help systems. In *Proceedings of the International Joint Conference on Artificial Intelligence (IJCAI)*, pp. 460–466. Morgan Kaufmann, 1997.

[55] M. Beetz. Structured reactive controllers—a computational model of everyday activity. In *3rd Int. Conf. on Autonomous Agents*, pp. 228–235, 1999.

[56] M. Beetz. *Plan-Based Control of Robotics Agents*. Volume 2554 of *Lecture Notes in Artificial Intelligence (LNAI)*. Springer-Verlag, 2002.

[57] M. Beetz and T. Belker. Environment and task adaptation for robotics agents. In *Proceedings of the European Conference on Artificial Intelligence (ECAI)*, pp. 648–657, IOS Press 2000.

[58] M. Beetz, J. Hertzberg, M. Ghallab, and M. Pollack, eds. *Advances in Plan-Based Control of Robotics Agents. LNAI* 2466. Springer-Verlag, 2002.

[59] M. Beetz and D. McDermott. Declarative goals in reactive plans. In J. Hendler, eds., *Proceedings of the International Conference on AI Planning Systems (AIPS)*, pp. 3–12. CA: Morgan Kaufmann, 1992.

[60] E. Bensana, G. Bel, and D. Dubois. OPAL: A multi-knowledge-based system for industrial job-shop scheduling. *International Journal of Production Research*, 5(26):795–819, 1988.

[61] R. Bergmann and W. Wilke. Building and refining abstract planning cases by change of representation language. *Journal of Artificial Intelligence Research*, 3:53–118, 1995.

[62] A. Beringer, G. Aschemann, H. Hoos, M. Metzger, and A. Weiss. GSAT versus simulated annealing. In *Proceedings of the European Conference on Artificial Intelligence (ECAI)*, pp. 130–134. Wiley, 1994.

[63] D. Bernard, E. Gamble, N. Rouquette, B. Smith, Y. Tung, N. Muscettola, G. Dorias, B. Kanefsky, J. Kurien, W. Millar, P. Nayak, and K. Rajan. *Remote Agent Experiment. DS1 Technology Validation Report.* NASA Ames and JPL report, 1998.

[64] A. Berthoz. *The Brain's Sense of Movement (Perspectives in Cognitive Neuroscience).* Harvard University Press, 2000.

[65] P. Bertoli, A. Cimatti, M. Pistore, M. Roveri, and P. Traverso. MBP: A Model Based Planner. In *Proceedings of ICAI-2001 Workshop on Planning under Uncertainty and Incomplete Information,* (Seattle, WA, August 2001), pp. 93–97.

[66] P. Bertoli, A. Cimatti, M. Roveri, and P. Traverso. Planning in nondeterministic domains under partial observability via symbolic model checking. In *Proceedings of the International Joint Conference on Artificial Intelligence (IJCAI)*: Morgan Kaufmann, (Seattle, WA, August 2001), pp. 473–478.

[67] C. Bessiere and M. Cordier. Arc-consistency and arc-consistency again. In *Proceedings of the National Conference on Artificial Intelligence (AAAI),* pp. 108–113, 1993.

[68] P. Bessiere, J. Ahuactzin, E. Talbi, and E. Mazer. The Ariadne's clew algorithm: Global planning with local methods. In Goldberg *et al.* [235], pp. 39–47, 1995.

[69] W. Bibel, L. Farinas del Cerro, B. Fronhöfer, and A. Herzig. Plan generation by linear proofs: On semantics. In *German Workshop on Artificial Intelligence—GWAI'89,* Volume 216 of *Informatik-Fachberichte.* Springer-Verlag, 1989.

[70] A. W. Biermann. Theoretical issues related to computer game playing programs. *Personal Computing,* pp. 86–88, September 1978.

[71] S. Biundo, D. Dengler, and J. Koehler. Deductive planning and plan reuse in a command language environment. In *Proceedings of the European Conference on Artificial Intelligence (ECAI),* pp. 632–638, 1992.

[72] S. Biundo and B. Schattenberg. From abstract crisis to concrete relief—a preliminary report on combining state abstraction and HTN planning. In *Proceedings of the European Conference on Planning (ECP),* pp. 157–168, 2001.

[73] A. L. Blum and J. Langford. Probabilistic planning in the Graphplan framework. In *Proceedings of the European Conference on Planning (ECP),* pp. 319–332, 1999.

[74] A. L. Blum and M. L. Furst. Fast planning through planning graph analysis. *Proceedings of the International Joint Conference on Artificial Intelligence (IJCAI),* pp. 1636–1642, 1995.

[75] A. L. Blum and M. L. Furst. Fast planning through planning graph analysis. *Artificial Intelligence,* 90:281–300, 1997.

[76] A. Bockmayr and Y. Dimopoulos. Mixed integer programming models for planning problems. In *Working Notes of the CP-98 Constraint Problem Reformulation Workshop,* 1998.

[77] A. Bockmayr and Dimopoulos. Integer programs and valid inequalities for planning problems. In *Proceedings of the European Conference on Planning (ECP),* pp. 239–251, LNAi 1809, Springer-Verlag, 1999.

[78] M. Boddy and T. Dean. Solving time-dependent planning problems. In *Proceedings of the International Joint Conference on Artificial Intelligence (IJCAI)*, pp. 979–984, 1989.

[79] R. P. Bonasso, D. Kortenkamp, D. Miller, and M. Slack. *Experiences with an Architecture for Intelligent reactive agents*, pp. 187–202. Wooldridge, Mueller, and Tambe, eds., ATAL, LNCS 1037, Springer-Verlag, 1995.

[80] B. Bonet and H. Geffner. Learning sorting and decision trees with POMDPs. In *Proceedings of the International Conference on Machine Learning (ICML)*, 1998.

[81] B. Bonet and H. Geffner. Planning as heuristic search: New results. In *Proceedings of the European Conference on Planning (ECP)*, pp. 360–372, LNAi 1809, Springer-Verlag, 1999.

[82] B. Bonet and H. Geffner. Planning with incomplete information as heuristic search in belief space. In S. Chien, S. Kambhampati, and C. Knoblock, eds., *Proceedings of the International Conference on AI Planning Systems (AIPS)*, pp. 52–61. AAAI Press, 2000.

[83] B. Bonet and H. Geffner. GPT: A tool for planning with uncertainty and partial information. In *Proceedings of the International Joint Conference on Artificial Intelligence (IJCAI)*, pp. 82–87, 2001.

[84] B. Bonet and H. Geffner. Planning and control in artificial intelligence: A unifying perspective. *Applied Intelligence*, 14(3):237–252, 2001.

[85] V. Boor, M. H. Overmars, and A. F. van der Stappen. The Gaussian sampling strategy for probabilistic roadmap planners. In *IEEE International Conference on Robotics and Automation (ICRA)*, pp. 1018–1023, 1999.

[86] S. Botelho and R. Alami. Cooperative plan enhancement in multi-robot context. In *Intelligent Autonomous Systems 6*, pp. 131–138. IOS Press, 2000.

[87] C. Boutilier. A POMDP formulation of preference elicitation problems. In *AAAI/IAAI Proceedings*, pp. 239–246, 2002.

[88] C. Boutilier, T. Dean, and S. Hanks. Decision-theoretic planning: Structural assumptions and computational leverage. *Journal of Artificial Intelligence Research*, 11:1–93, 1999.

[89] C. Boutilier, R. Dearden, and M. Goldszmidt. Stochastic dynamic programming with factored representations. *Artificial Intelligence*, 121(1–2):49–107, 2000.

[90] C. Boutilier, R. Reiter, and B. Price. Symbolic dynamic programming for first-order MDPs. In *Proceedings of the International Joint Conference on Artificial Intelligence (IJCAI)*, pp. 690–697, 2001.

[91] F. Brémond and M. Thonnat. Recognition of scenarios describing human activities. In *International Workshop on Dynamic Scene Recognition from Sensor Data*, 1997.

[92] F. Brémond and M. Thonnat. Issues of representing context illustrated by video-surveillance applications. *International Journal of Human-Computer Studies*, 48:375–391, 1998.

[93] J. L. Bresina. Design of a reactive system based on classical planning. In *Foundations of Automatic Planning: The Classical Approach and Beyond: Papers from the 1993 AAAI Spring Symposium*, pp. 5–9. AAAI Press, 1993.

[94] L. A. Breslow and D. W. Aha. *NACODAE: Navy Conversational Decision Aids Environment.* Technical Report AIC-97-018. *Naval Research Laboratory, Navy Center for Applied Research in Artificial Intelligence*, 1997.

[95] V. Brusoni, L. Console, and P. Terenziani. On the computational complexity of querying bounds on differences constraints. *Artificial Intelligence*, 74(2):367–379, 1995.

[96] V. Brusoni, L. Console, P. Terenziani, and D. T. Dupr. A spectrum of definitions for temporal model-based diagnosis. *Artificial Intelligence*, 102(1):39–79, 1998.

[97] V. Brusoni, L. Console, P. Terenziani, and B. Pernici. Qualitative and quantitative temporal constraints and relational databases: Theory, architecture, and applications. *IEEE Transactions on Knowledge and Data Engineering*, 11(6):948–968, 1999.

[98] A. Bundy, F. Giunchiglia, R. Sebastiani, and T. Walsh. Computing abstraction hierarchies by numerical simulation. In *AAAI/IAAI Proceedings*, 1996.

[99] J. R. Burch, E. M. Clarke, K. L. McMillan, D. L. Dill, and L. J. Hwang. Symbolic model checking: 10^{20} states and beyond. *Information and Computation*, 98(2):142–170, 1992.

[100] T. Bylander. Complexity results for planning. In *Proceedings of the International Joint Conference on Artificial Intelligence (IJCAI)*, 1991.

[101] T. Bylander. Complexity results for extended planning. In *Proceedings of the National Conference on Artificial Intelligence (AAAI)*, 1992.

[102] T. Bylander. A linear programming heuristic for optimal planning. In *AAAI/IAAI Proceedings.* (Providence, RI, 1997): AAAI Press/MIT Press, pp. 694–699.

[103] J. Carbonell. Learning by analogy: Formulating and generalizing plans from past experience. In R. Michalsky, J. Carbonell, and T. Mitchell, eds., *Machine Learning: An Artificial Intelligence Approach*, pp. 137–162. Tioga Publishing, 1983.

[104] J. Carbonell. Derivational analogy: A theory of reconstructive problem solving and expertise acquisition. In R. S. Michalski, J. G. Carbonell, and T. M. Mitchell, eds., *Machine Learning: An Artificial Intelligence Approach: Volume II*, pp. 371–392. Los Altos, CA: Morgan Kaufmann, 1986.

[105] J. Carbonell, C. Knoblock, and S. Minton. PRODIGY : An integrated architecture for planning and learning. In van Lehn [521], 1990.

[106] J. Carlier. The one-machine sequencing problem. *European Journal of Operational Research*, 11:42–47, 1982.

[107] C. Carrick, Q. Yang, I. Abi-Zeid, and L. Lamontagne. Activating CBR systems through autonomous information gathering. In *Proceedings of the International Conference on Case-Based Reasoning (ICCBR)*, pp. 74–88. Springer-Verlag, 1999.

[108] A. Cassandra, L. Kaelbling, and M. Littman. Acting optimally in partially observable stochastic domains. In *Proceedings of the National Conference on Artificial Intelligence (AAAI)*, AAAI Press, 1994.

[109] C. Castellini, E. Giunchiglia, and A. Tacchella. Improvements to SAT-based conformant planning. In A. Cesta and D. Borrajo, eds., *Proceedings of the European Conference on Planning (ECP)*, pp. 241–252, 2001.

[110] C. Castellini, E. Giunchiglia, and A. Tacchella. SAT-based planning in complex domains: Concurrency, constraints and nondeterminism. *Artificial Intelligence*, 147:85–118, 2003.

[111] M. Cayrol, P. Régnier, and V. Vidal. New results about LCGP, a least committed Graphplan. In *Proceedings of the International Conference on AI Planning Systems (AIPS)*, pp. 273–282, 2000.

[112] M. Cayrol, P. Régnier, and V. Vidal. Least commitment in Graphplan. *Artificial Intelligence*, 130:85–118, 2001.

[113] M. D. Center. *Machining Data Handbook*, Cincinnati, OH: Metcut Research Associates, 3 ed., 1980.

[114] A. Cesta and A. Odi. Gaining efficiency and flexibility in the simple temporal problem. In *Proc. 3rd Int. Workshop on Temporal Representation and Reasoning*, IEEE-CS Press, 1996.

[115] A. Cesta and C. Stella. A time and resource problem for planning architectures. In S. Steel and R. Alami, eds., *Proceedings of the European Conference on Planning (ECP)*, pp. 117–129. *LNAI* 1348. Springer-Verlag, 1997.

[116] R. Chandrasekaran. Program for a better bridge game: A college partnership aids industry research. *The Washington Post*, pp. 1, 15, 19, 1997.

[117] T. C. Chang. *Expert Process Planning for Manufacturing*. Reading, MA: Addison-Wesley, 1990.

[118] T. C. Chang. *Expert Process Planning Systems*. Reading, MA: Addison-Wesley, 1989.

[119] T. C. Chang and R. A. Wysk. *An Introduction to Automated Process Planning Systems*. Englewood Cliffs, NJ: Prentice-Hall, 1985.

[120] D. Chapman. Planning for conjunctive goals. *Artificial Intelligence*, 32:333–379, 1987.

[121] E. Charniak and R. Goldman. A probabilistic model of plan recognition. In *Proceedings of the National Conference on Artificial Intelligence (AAAI)*, pp. 160–165, 1991.

[122] Y. Cheng, B. Selman, and H. Kautz. Control knowledge in planning: Benefits and tradeoffs. In *AAAI/IAAI Proceedings*, 1999.

[123] S. Chien, D. DeCoste, R. Doyle, and P. Stolorz. Making an impact: Artificial intelligence at the Jet Propulsion Laboratory. *AI Magazine*, 18(1):103–122, 1997.

[124] S. Chien, F. Fisher, E. Lo, H. Mortensen, and R. Greeley. Using artificial intelligence planning to automate science data analysis for large image databases. In *Knowledge Discovery and Data Mining*, pp. 1997.

[125] S. Chien, P. Zetocha, R. Wainwright, P. Klupar, J. V. Gaasbeck, P. Cappelaere, D. Oswald, R. Sherwood, G. Rabideau, R. Castano, A. Davies, M. Burl, R. Knight, T. Stough, and J. Roden. The Techsat-21 autonomous science agent. In *Int. Conf. on Autonomous Agents*, 2002.

[126] S. Chien, R. Sherwood, D. Tran, *et al.* Autonomous science on the EO-1 mission. In *Proceedings of the International Symposium on Artificial Intelligence, Robotics, and Automation in Space (i-SAIRAS)*, May 2003.

[127] A. Cimatti, E. Giunchiglia, F. Giunchiglia, and P. Traverso. Planning via model checking: A decision procedure for $\mathcal{AR}$. In *Proceedings of the European Conference on Planning (ECP)*, pp. 130–142. *LNAI* 1348. Springer-Verlag, 1997.

[128] A. Cimatti, M. Pistore, M. Roveri, and P. Traverso. Weak, strong, and strong cyclic planning via symbolic model checking. *Artificial Intelligence*, 147(1–2): 35–84, 2003.

[129] A. Cimatti, M. Roveri, and P. Traverso. Automatic OBDD-based generation of universal plans in non-deterministic domains. In *AAAI/IAAI Proceedings*, pp. 875–881, 1998.

[130] A. Cimatti, M. Roveri, and P. Traverso. Strong planning in non-deterministic domains via model checking. In *Proceedings of the International Conference on AI Planning Systems (AIPS)*, (June 1998), AAAI Press, pp. 36–43.

[131] E. M. Clarke and J. M. Wing. Formal methods: State of the art and future directions. *ACM Computing Surveys*, 28(4):626–643, 1996.

[132] S. A. Cook and D. G. Mitchell. Finding hard instances of the satisfiability problem: A survey. In Du, Gu, and Pardalos, eds. *Satisfiability Problem: Theory and Applications*, Volume 35, pp. 1–17. American Mathematical Society, 1997.

[133] T. H. Cormen, C. E. Leiserson, and R. L. Rivest. *Introduction to Algorithms.* MIT Press, 1990.

[134] S. Cresswell and A. Smaill. Recursive plans in linear logic. In *Proceedings of the European Conference on Planning (ECP)*, pp. 252–264, 1999.

[135] K. Currie and A. Tate. O-PLAN: The open planning architecture. *Artificial Intelligence*, 52(1):49–86, 1991.

[136] U. Dal Lago, M. Pistore, and P. Traverso. Planning with a language for extended goals. In *AAAI/IAAI Proceedings*, (Edmonton, Canada, August 2002): AAAI Press/The MIT Press, pp. 447–454.

[137] M. Daniele, P. Traverso, and M. Vardi. Strong cyclic planning revisited. In *Proceedings of the European Conference on Planning (ECP)*, pp. 35–48, 1999.

[138] D. Das, S. K. Gupta, and D. S. Nau. Generating redesign suggestions to reduce setup cost: A step towards automated redesign. *Computer Aided Design*, 28(10):763–782, 1996.

[139] A. J. Davenport, C. Gefflot, and J. C. Beck. Slack-based techniques for robust scheduling. In A. Cesta and D. Borrajo, eds. *Proceedings of the European Conference on Planning (ECP)*, pp. 181–192, 2001.

[140] J. Davis and A. Bobick. The representation and recognition of action using temporal templates. In *IEEE Conference on Computer Vision and Pattern Recognition*, pp. 928–934, 1997.

[141] M. Deale, M. Yvanovich, D. Schnitzius, D. Kautz, M. Carpenter, M. Zweben, G. Davis, and B. Daun. The space shuttle ground processing scheduling system. In M. Zweben and M. Fox, eds. *Intelligent Scheduling*, Volume 35, pp. 423–449. Morgan Kaufmann, 1994.

[142] T. Dean and M. Boddy. Reasoning about partially ordered events. *Artificial Intelligence*, 36:375–399, 1988.

[143] T. Dean, R. Firby, and D. Miller. Hierarchical planning involving deadlines, travel time and resources. *Computational Intelligence*, 6(1):381–398, 1988.

[144] T. Dean, L. Kaelbling, J. Kirman, and A. Nicholson. Planning with deadlines in stochastic domains. In *Proceedings of the National Conference on Artificial Intelligence (AAAI)*, pp. 574–579, 1993.

[145] T. Dean and D. McDermott. Temporal data base management. *Artificial Intelligence*, 32(1):1–55, 1987.

[146] T. Dean and M. Wellman. *Planning and Control*. Morgan Kaufmann, 1991.

[147] R. Dearden and C. Boutilier. Abstraction and approximate decision-theoretic planning. *Artificial Intelligence*, 89(1–2):219–283, 1997.

[148] R. Dechter. Enhancement schemes for constraint processing: Backjumping, learning and cutset decomposition. *Artificial Intelligence*, 41(3):273–312, 1990.

[149] R. Dechter. On the expressiveness of networks with hidden variables. In *Proceedings of the National Conference on Artificial Intelligence (AAAI)*, pp. 379–385, 1990.

[150] R. Dechter. From local to global consistency. *Artificial Intelligence*, 55:87–107, 1992.

[151] R. Dechter, and F. Rossi. Constraint satisfaction. In *MIT Encyclopedia of the Cognitive Sciences*, (MITECS), 1998.

[152] R. Dechter, I. Meiri, and J. Pearl. Temporal constraint networks. *Artificial Intelligence*, 49:61–95, 1991.

[153] R. Dechter and J. Pearl. Network-based heuristics for constraint satisfaction problems. *Artificial Intelligence*, 34(1):1–38, 1987.

[154] O. Despouys and F. Ingrand. PropicePlan: Toward a unified framework for planning and execution. In *Proceedings of the European Conference on Planning (ECP)*, pp. 280–292, 1999.

[155] Y. Dimopoulos and A. Gerevini. Temporal planning through mixed integer programming. In *AIPS Workshop on Planning for Temporal Domains*, pp. 2–8, 2002.

[156] M.W.M. Dissanayake, P. Newman, S. Clark, H. Durrant-Whyte, and M. Csorba. A solution to the simultaneous localization and map building (SLAM) problem. *IEEE Transactions on Robotics and Automation*, 17(3):229–241, 2001.

[157] J. Dix, H. Munoz-Avila, D. S. Nau, and L. Zhang. IMPACTing SHOP: Putting an AI planner into a multi-agent environment. *Annals of Mathematics and AI*, 37(4):381–407, 2003.

[158] M. B. Do and S. Kambhampati. Solving planning graph by compiling it into CSP. In *Proceedings of the International Conference on AI Planning Systems (AIPS)*, pp. 82–91, 2000.

[159] M. B. Do and S. Kambhampati. SAPA: A domain independent heuristic metric temporal planner. In *Proceedings of the European Conference on Planning (ECP)*, pp. 109–121, 2001.

[160] P. Doherty and J. Kvarnström. TALplanner: A temporal logic based planner. *AI Magazine*, 22(3):95–102, 2001.

[161] C. Dousson, P. Gaborit, and M. Ghallab. Situation recognition: Representation and algorithms. In *Proceedings of the International Joint Conference on Artificial Intelligence (IJCAI)*, pp. 166–172, 1993.

[162] B. Drabble and A. Tate. The use of optimistic and pessimistic resource profiles to inform search in an activity based planner. In *Proceedings of the International Conference on AI Planning Systems (AIPS)*, pp. 243–248, 1994.

[163] T. Drakengren and P. Jonsson. Eight maximal tractable subclasses of Allen's algebra with metric time. *Journal of Artificial Intelligence Research*, 7:25–45, 1997.

[164] M. E. Drummond and K. Currie. Goal Ordering in Partially Ordered Plans. In *Proceedings of the International Joint Conference on Artificial Intelligence (IJCAI)*, pp. 960–965, 1989.

[165] D. Dubois and H. Prade. Processing fuzzy temporal knowledge. *IEEE Trans. SMC*, 19(4):729–744, 1989.

[166] D. Dubois, H. Prade, and J. Lang. Time possibilistic logic. *Fundamenta Informaticae*, 15:211–234, 1991.

[167] E. Durfee. Scaling up agent coordination strategies. *IEEE Computer*, 34(7):39–46, 2001.

[168] S. Edelkamp and M. Helmert. Exhibiting knowledge in planning problems to minimize state encoding length. In S. Biundo and M. Fox, eds., *Proceedings of the European Conference on Planning (ECP), LNAI*, 1809, pp. 135–147. Springer-Verlag, 1999.

[169] S. Edelkamp and M. Helmert. On the implementation of MIPS. In *AIPS Workshop on Model-Theoretic Approaches to Planning*, pp. 18–25, 2000.

[170] A. El-Kholy and B. Richard. Temporal and resource reasoning in planning: The ParcPlan approach. In *Proceedings of the European Conference on Artificial Intelligence (ECAI)*, pp. 614–618. Wiley, 1996.

[171] E. A. Emerson. Temporal and modal logic. In J. van Leeuwen, eds., *Handbook of Theoretical Computer Science, Volume B: Formal Models and Semantics*, pp. 995–1072. Elsevier, 1990.

[172] M. Ernst, T. Millstein, and D. S. Weld. Automatic SAT-compilation of planning problems. In *Proceedings of the International Joint Conference on Artificial Intelligence (IJCAI)*, pp. 1169–1176, 1997.

[173] K. Erol, J. Hendler, and D. S. Nau. *Semantics for Hierarchical Task-Network Planning*. Technical Report CS TR-3239, UMIACS TR-94-31, ISR-TR-95-9. University of Maryland, March 1994. http://www.cs.umd.edu/~nau/Papers/htn-tr.ps.

[174] K. Erol, J. Hendler, and D. S. Nau. UMCP: A sound and complete procedure for hierarchical task-network planning. In *Proceedings of the International Conference on AI Planning Systems (AIPS)*, pp. 249–254, 1994.

[175] K. Erol, J. Hendler, and D. S. Nau. Complexity results for hierarchical task-network planning. *Annals of Mathematics and Artificial Intelligence*, 18:69–93, 1996.

[176] K. Erol, D. S. Nau, and V. S. Subrahmanian. Complexity, decidability and undecidability results for domain-independent planning. *Artificial Intelligence*, 76(1–2):75–88, 1995.

[177] J. Erschler, P. Lopez, and C. Thuriot. Temporal reasoning under resource constraints: Application to task scheduling. In G. Lasker and R. Hough, eds., *Advances in Support Systems Research*, pp. 189–194, 1990.

[178] P. Esquirol, P. Lopez, H. Fargier, and T. Schiex. Constraint programming. *Belgian Journal of Operations Research*, 35(2):5–36, 1995.

[179] T. A. Estlin. *Using Multi-Strategy Learning to Improve Planning Efficiency and Quality*. Ph.D. thesis, Department of Computer Sciences, University of Texas at Austin, 1998.

[180] T. A. Estlin, S. A. Chien, and X. Wang. An argument for hybrid HTN/operator-based approach to planning. In *Proceedings of the European Conference on Planning (ECP)*, pp. 184–196, 1997.

[181] T. A. Estlin and R. J. Mooney. Learning to improve both efficiency and quality of planning. In *Proceedings of the International Joint Conference on Artificial Intelligence (IJCAI)*, pp. 1227–1232.

[182] O. Etzioni. A structural theory of explanation-based learning. *Artificial Intelligence*, 60:93–139, 1993.

[183] O. Etzioni, S. Hanks, D. S. Weld, D. Draper, N. Lesh, and M. Williamson. An approach to planning with incomplete information. In *Proceedings of the International Conference on Knowledge Representation and Reasoning (KR)*, pp. 115–125, 1992.

[184] H. Fargier, M. Jourdan, N. Layada, and T. Vidal. Using temporal constraint networks to manage temporal scenario of multimedia documents. In *ECAI Workshop on Spatial and Temporal Reasoning*, pp. 51–56, 1998.

[185] H. Fargier, J. Lang, and T. Schiex. Mixed constraint satisfaction: A framework for decision problems under incomplete knowledge. In *Proceedings of the National Conference on Artificial Intelligence (AAAI)*, pp. 175–180, 1996.

[186] G. Ferguson and J. Allen. TRIPS: An integrated intelligent problem-solving assistant. In *AAAI/IAAI Proceedings*, pp. 567–572, 1998.

[187] G. Ferguson, J. Allen, and B. Miller. TRAINS-95: Towards a mixed-initiative planning assistant. In *Proceedings of the International Conference on AI Planning Systems (AIPS)*, pp. 70–77, 1996.

[188] P. Ferraris and E. Giunchiglia. Planning as satisfiability in nondeterministic domains. In *AAAI/IAAI Proceedings*, 2000.

[189] R. Fikes and N. Nilsson. STRIPS: A new approach to the application of theorem proving to problem solving. *Artificial Intelligence*, 2(3–4):189–208, 1971.

[190] R. J. Firby. Building symbolic primitives with continuous control routines. In J. Hendler, eds., *Proceedings of the International Conference on AI Planning Systems (AIPS)*, pp. 62–69, Morgan Kaufmann, 1992.

[191] R. J. Firby. Task networks for controlling continuous processes. In *Proceedings of the International Conference on AI Planning Systems (AIPS)*, pp. 49–54, 1994.

[192] M. Fox and D. Long. The automatic inference of state invariants in TIM. *Journal of Artificial Intelligence Research*, 9:367–421, 1998.

[193] M. Fox and D. Long. Utilizing automatically inferred invariants in graph construction and search. In *Proceedings of the International Conference on AI Planning Systems (AIPS)*, pp. 102–111, 2000.

[194] M. Fox and D. Long. PDDL+ Level5: An extension to PDDL2.1 for modeling domains with continuous time-dependent effects. Technical note, University of Durham, September 2001.

[195] M. Fox and D. Long. International planning competition. http://www.dur.ac.uk/d.p.long/competition.html, 2002.

[196] M. Fox and D. Long. PDDL2.1: An extension to PDDL for expressing temporal planning domains. In http://www.dur.ac.uk/d.p.long/competition.html, 2002.

[197] M. Fox and S. Smith. ISIS: A knowledge-based system for factory scheduling. *Expert Systems*, 1(1):25–49, 1984.

[198] J. Frank and A. Jonsson. Constraint-based attribute and interval planning. *Constraints*, 8(4): 339–364, October 2003.

[199] J. Frank, A. Jonsson, R. Morris, and D. Smith. Planning and scheduling for fleets of earth observing satellites. In *International Symposium on Artificial Intelligence, Robotics, Automation and Space*, 2001.

[200] S. French. *Sequencing and Scheduling: An Introduction to the Mathematics of the Job Shop*. Horwood, 1982.

[201] E. C. Freuder. A sufficient condition for backtrack-free search. *Communications of the ACM*, 29(1):24–32, 1982.

[202] E. C. Freuder. Synthesizing constraint expressions. *Communications of the ACM*, 21(11):958–966, 1978.

[203] P. Friedland and Y. Iwasaki. The concept and implementation of skeletal plans. *Journal of Automated Reasoning*, 1(2):161–208, 1985.

[204] P. Gaborit. Planification distribuée pour la coopération multi-agents. Ph.D. thesis 96494, LAAS-CNRS, 1996.

[205] F. Garcia and P. Laborie. Hierarchisation of the search space in temporal planning. In *Proceedings of the European Workshop on Planning (EWSP)*, pp. 235–249, 1995.

[206] M. R. Garey and D. S. Johnson. *Computers and Intractability: A Guide to the Theory of NP-Completeness*. W. H. Freeman, 1979.

[207] A. Garland, K. Ryall, and C. Rich. Learning hierarchical task models by defining and refining examples. In *First International Conference on Knowledge Capture*, pp. 44–51, 2001.

[208] A. Garrido. A temporal plannnig system for level 3 durative actions of PDDL2.1. In *AIPS Workshop on Planning for Temporal Domains*, pp. 56–66, 2002.

[209] S. I. Gass. *Linear Programming*, 5th ed., Thomson International Publishing, 1985.

[210] E. Gat. ESL: A language for supporting robust plan execution in embedded autonomous agents. In *Proceedings of the 1997 Aerospace Conference*, pp. 319–324, 1997.

[211] E. Gat and B. Pell. Abstract resource management in an unconstrained plan execution system. In *Proceedings of the 1998 Aerospace Conference*, 1998.

[212] F. Gavril. Algorithms for maximum coloring, maximum clique, minimum covering by cliques and maximum independant set of a chordal graph. *SIAM, Journal on Computing*, 1:180–187, 1972.

[213] B. Gazen and C. Knoblock. Combining the expressivity of UCPOP with the efficiency of Graphplan. In *Proceedings of the European Conference on Planning (ECP)*, pp. 221–233, 1997.

[214] M. Georgeff and F. Ingrand. Decision-making in an embedded reasoning system. In *Proceedings of the International Joint Conference on Artificial Intelligence (IJCAI)*, 1989.

[215] M. Georgeff and A. L. Lansky. Procedural knowledge. *Proceedings of IEEE*, 74(10):1383–1398, 1986.

[216] A. Gerevini and L. Schubert. Efficient algorithms for handling qualitative reasoning about time. *Artificial Intelligence*, 74(1):207–248, 1995.

[217] A. Gerevini and L. Schubert. Accelerating partial-order planners: Some techniques for effective search control and pruning. *Journal of Artificial Intelligence Research*, 5:95–137, 1996.

[218] A. Gerevini and L. Schubert. Inferring state constraints for domain-independent planning. In *AAAI/IAAI Proceedings*, 1998.

[219] A. Gerevini and L. Schubert. Discovering state constraints in DISCOPLAN: Some new results. In *AAAI/IAAI Proceedings*, 2000.

[220] A. Gerevini and I. Serina. LPG: A planner based on local search for planning graphs. In *Proceedings of the International Conference on AI Planning Systems (AIPS)*, pp. 968–973, 2002.

[221] M. Gervasio, W. Iba, and P. Langley. Case-based seeding for an interactive crisis response assistant. In D. Aha and J. Daniels, eds. *Case-Based Reasoning Integrations: Papers from the 1998 Workshop* (Technical Report WS-98-15). AAAI Press, 1998.

[222] M. Ghallab. On chronicles: Representation, on-line recognition and learning. In *Proceedings of the International Conference on Knowledge Representation and Reasoning (KR)*, pp. 597–606, 1996.

[223] M. Ghallab, R. Alamai, and R. Chatila. Dealing with time in planning and execution monitoring. In R. Bolles and B. Roth, eds. *Robotics Research 4*, pp. 431–443. MIT Press, 1987.

[224] M. Ghallab and H. Laruelle. Representation and control in IxTeT, a temporal planner. In *Proceedings of the International Conference on AI Planning Systems (AIPS)*, pp. 61–67, 1994.

[225] M. Ghallab and A. Mounir-Alaoui. Managing efficiently temporal relations through indexed spanning trees. In *Proceedings of the International Joint Conference on Artificial Intelligence (IJCAI)*, pp. 1297–1303, 1989.

[226] M. Ghallab and T. Vidal. Focusing on a sub-graph for managing efficiently numerical temporal constraints. In *Proceedings of Florida AI Research Symposium (FLAIRS)*, 1995.

[227] Y. Gil. *Acquiring Domain Knowledge for Planning by Experimentation.* Ph.D. thesis, School of Computer Science, Carnegie Mellon University, Pittsburgh, PA, 1992.

[228] Y. Gil. Learning new planning operators by exploration and experimentation. In *Proceedings of the AAAI Workshop on Learning Action Models* (Washington, DC) 1993.

[229] Y. Gil. Learning by experimentation: Incremental refinement of incomplete planning domains. In *Proceedings of the International Conference on Machine Learning (ICML)*, 1994.

[230] M. Ginsberg. Partition search. In *Proceedings of the National Conference on Artificial Intelligence (AAAI)*, pp. 228–233, 1996.

[231] E. Giunchiglia. Planning as satisfiability with expressive action languages: Concurrency, constraints and nondeterminism. In *Proceedings of the Seventh International Conference on Principles of Knowledge Representation and Reasoning (KR'00)*, 2000.

[232] E. Giunchiglia, A. Massarotto, and R. Sebastiani. Act, and the rest will follow: Exploiting determinism in planning as satisfiability. In *AAAI/IAAI Proceedings*, 1998.

[233] F. Giunchiglia. Using ABSTRIPS abstractions—where do we stand? *Artificial Intelligence Review*, 13(3):201–213, 1999.

[234] F. Giunchiglia and P. Traverso. Planning as model checking. In *Proceedings of the European Conference on Planning (ECP)*, pp. 1–20, 1999.

[235] K. Goldberg, D. Halperin, J. C. Latombe, and R. Wilson, eds. *Algorithmic Foundations of Robotics.* A K Peters, 1995.

[236] K. Golden, O. Etzioni, and D. S. Weld. Omnipotence without omniscience: Sensor management in planning. In *Proceedings of the National Conference on Artificial Intelligence (AAAI)*, pp. 1048–1054, 1994.

[237] K. Golden, W. Pang, R. Nemani, and P. Votava. Automating the processing of earth observation data. In *Proceedings of the International Symposium on Artificial Intelligence, Robotics, and Automation in Space (i-SAIRAS)*, 2003.

[238] R. P. Goldman, M. Pelican, and D. Musliner. Hard real-time mode logic synthesis for hybrid control: A CIRCA-based approach. Working notes of the 1999 AAAI Spring Symposium on Hybrid Control, March 1999.

[239] R. P. Goldman, C. W. Geib, and C. A. Miller. A new model of plan recognition. In *Uncertainy in AI*, 1999.

[240] R. P. Goldman, D. J. Musliner, K. D. Krebsbach, and M. S. Boddy. Dynamic abstraction planning. In *AAAI/IAAI Proceedings*, pp. 680–686. AAAI Press, 1997.

[241] R. P. Goldman, D. J. Musliner, and M. J. Pelican. Using model checking to plan hard real-time controllers. In *AIPS Workshop on Model-Theoretic Approaches to Planning* (Breckeridge, CO, April 2000).

[242] M. Golumbic and R. Shamir. Complexity and algorithms for reasoning about time. In *Proceedings of the National Conference on Artificial Intelligence (AAAI)*, pp. 741–747, 1992.

[243] M. Golumbic and R. Shamir. Complexity and algorithms for reasoning about time: A graph-theoretic approach. *Journal of the ACM*, 40(5):1108–1133, 1993.

[244] C. Gomes, B. Selman, and H. Kautz. Boosting combinatorial search through randomization. In *AAAI/IAAI Proceedings*, 1998.

[245] J. Goodman and J. O'Rourke. *Handbook of Discrete and Computational Geometry.* CRC Press, 1997.

[246] M. Grabish. Temporal scenario modeling and recognition based on possibilistic logic. *Artificial Intelligence*, 148:261–289, 2003.

[247] R. L. Graham, E. Lawler, J. Lenstra, and A. R. Kan. Optimization and approximation in deterministic sequencing and scheduling: A survey. *Annals of Discrete Mathematics*, 5:287–326, 1979.

[248] R. L. Graham, D. E. Knuth, and O. Patashnik. *Concrete Mathematics: A Foundation for Computer Science.* Addison-Wesley, 1989.

[249] C. Green. Application of theorem proving to problem solving. In *Proceedings of the International Joint Conference on Artificial Intelligence (IJCAI)*, 1969.

[250] G. A. Grün. An efficient algorithm for the maximum distance problem. *Discrete Mathematics and Theoretical Computer Science*, 4:323–350, 2001.

[251] E. Guere and R. Alami. One action is enough to plan. In *Proceedings of the International Joint Conference on Artificial Intelligence (IJCAI)*, 2001.

[252] K. Gupta and A. del Pobil, eds. *Practical Motion Planning in Robotics.* Wiley, 1998.

[253] N. Gupta and D. S. Nau. On the complexity of blocks-world planning. *Artificial Intelligence*, 56(2–3):323–342, 1992.

[254] S. K. Gupta and D. S. Nau. A systematic approach for analyzing the manufacturability of machined parts. *Computer Aided Design*, 27(5):342–343, 1995.

[255] K. J. Hammond. Learning to anticipate and avoid planning problems through the explanation of failures. In *Proceedings of the National Conference on Artificial Intelligence (AAAI)*, 1986.

[256] K. J. Hammond. *Case-Based Planning: Viewing Learning as a Memory Task.* New York: Academic Press, 1989.

[257] S. Hanks and D. S. Weld. A domain-independent algorithm for plan adaptation. *Journal of Artificial Intelligence Research*, 2:319–360, 1995.

[258] E. A. Hansen and S. Zilberstein. Heuristic search in cyclic AND-OR graphs. In *AAAI/IAAI Proceedings*, 1998.

[259] D. Harel. Dynamic logic. In D. Gabbay and F. Guenthner, eds. *Handbook of Philosophical Logic*, Volume 2, pp. 497–604. D. Reidel Publishing, 1984.

[260] P. Haslum and H. Geffner. Admissible heuristics for optimal planning. In *Proceedings of the International Conference on AI Planning Systems (AIPS)*, pp. 140–149, 2000.

[261] P. Haslum and H. Geffner. Heuristic planning with time and resources. In *Proceedings of the European Conference on Planning (ECP)*, pp. 121–132, 2001.

[262] P. Haslum and P. Jonsson. Some results on the complexity of planning with incomplete information. In S. Biundo, ed., *Proceedings of the European Conference on Planning (ECP)*, 1999.

[263] C. Hayes. A model of planning for plan efficiency: Taking advantage of operator overlap. In *Proceedings of the International Joint Conference on Artificial Intelligence (IJCAI)*, (Detroit, MI) pp. 949–953, 1989.

[264] J. Hayet, F. Lerasle, and M. Devy. Planar landmarks to localize a mobile robot. In *SIRS'2000*, pp. 163–169, 2000.

[265] R. Hayward, C. Hoang, and F. Maffray. Optimizing weakly triangulated graphs. *Graphs and Combinatorics*, 5(4):339–350, 1989.

[266] F. Heintz. Chronicle recognition in the WITAS UAV project. In *The Swedish AI Society's Annual Conference* (Skövde, Sweden, 2001), 2001.

[267] J. Hertzberg and A. Hortz. Towards a theory of conflict detection and resolution in nonlinear plans. In *Proceedings of the International Joint Conference on Artificial Intelligence (IJCAI)*, pp. 937–942, 1989.

[268] J. Hertzberg, H. Jaeger, U. Zimmer, and P. Morignot. A framework for plan execution in behavior-based robots. In *Proceedings of the 1998 IEEE International Symposium on Intelligent Control*, pp. 8–13, 1998.

[269] J. Hoey, R. St-Aubin, A. Hu, and C. Boutilier. SPUDD: Stochastic Planning Using Decision Diagrams. In *Proceedings of the Conference on Uncertainty in Artificial Intelligence (UAI)*, 1999.

[270] J. Hoffmann. A heuristic for domain independent planning and its use in an enforced hill-climbing algorithm. In *Proceedings of the 12th International Symposium on Methodologies for Intelligent Systems* (Charlotte, NC, October 2000).

[271] J. Hoffmann. FF: The Fast-Forward planning system. *AI Magazine*, 22(3): 57–62, 2001.

[272] J. Hoffmann and B. Nebel. The FF planning system: Fast plan generation through heuristic search. *Journal of Artificial Intelligence Research*, 14:253–302, 2001.

[273] D. Hsu, L. Kavraki, J. Latombe, R. Motwani, and S. Sorkin. On finding narrow passages with probabilistic roadmap planners. In P. A. *et al.*, eds., *Robotics: The Algorithmic Perspective (WAFR98)*, 1998.

[274] IBM. How Deep Blue works, 1997. http://www.chess.ibm.com/meet/html/d.3.2.html.

[275] L. Ihrig and S. Kambhampati. Derivational replay for partial order planning. In *Proceedings of the National Conference on Artificial Intelligence (AAAI)*, pp. 992–997. AAAI Press, 1994.

[276] L. Ihrig and S. Kambhampati. *Plan-Space vs. State-Space Planning in Reuse and Replay*. Technical report. Arizona State University, 1996.

[277] L. Ihrig and S. Kambhampati. Storing and indexing plan derivations through explanation-based analysis of retrieval failures. *Journal of Artificial Intelligence Research*, 7:161–198, 1997.

[278] O. Ilghami, D. S. Nau, H. Muñoz-Avila, and D. Aha. CaMeL: Learning methods for HTN planning. In *AIPS-2002* (Toulouse, France, 2002).

[279] F. Ingrand and M. Georgeff. An architecture for real-time reasoning and system control. *IEEE Expert*, 6:33–44, 1992.

[280] H. Inoue, S. Tachi, Y. Nakamura, K. Hirai, N. Ohyu, S. Hirai, K. Tanie, K. Yokoi, and H. Hirukawa. Overview of humanoid robotics project of METI. In *32nd International Symposium on Robotics*, 2001.

[281] R. Jensen and M. Veloso. OBDD-based universal planning for synchronized agents in non-deterministic domains. *Journal of Artificial Intelligence Research*, 13:189–226, 2000.

[282] R. Jensen, M. Veloso, and R. Bryant. Guided symbolic universal planning. In *International Conference on Automated Planning and Scheduling (ICAPS)* (Trento, June, 2003), AAAI Press.

[283] R. M. Jensen, M. M. Veloso, and M. H. Bowling. OBDD-based optimistic and strong cyclic adversarial planning. In *Proceedings of the European Conference on Planning (ECP)*, 2001.

[284] D. Johnson, C. Aragon, L. McGeoch, and C. Schevon. Optimization by simulated annealing: An experimental evaluation, part ii. *Journal of Operations Research*, 39(3):378–406, 1991.

[285] A. K. Jonson, P. Morris, N. Muscettola, and K. Rajan. Planning in interplanetary space: theory and practice. In *Proceedings of the International Conference on AI Planning Systems (AIPS)*, 2000.

[286] P. Jonsson and C. Bäckström. State-variable planning under structural restrictions: Algorithms and complexity. *Artificial Intelligence*, 100(1–2):125–176, 1998.

[287] P. Jonsson, T. Drakengren, and C. Bäckström. Computational complexity of relating time points and intervals. *Artificial Intelligence*, 109:273–295, 1999.

[288] D. Joslin and M. Pollack. Least-cost flaw repair: A plan refinement strategy for partial-order planning. In *Proceedings of the National Conference on Artificial Intelligence (AAAI)*, 1994.

[289] D. Joslin and M. Pollack. Passive and active decision postponement in plan generation. In *Proceedings of the European Conference on Planning (ECP)*, 1995.

[290] D. Joslin and M. Pollack. Is "early commitment" in plan generation ever a good idea? In *AAAI/IAAI Proceedings*, pp. 1188–1193, 1996.

[291] D. Joslin and J. Roach. A theoretical analysis of conjunctive-goal problems. *Artificial Intelligence*, 41, 1990.

[292] N. Jussien and O. Lhomme. Local search with constraint propagation and conflict-based heuristics. *Artificial Intelligence*, 139(1):21–45, 2002.

[293] F. Kabanza, M. Barbeau, and R. St-Denis. Planning control rules for reactive agents. *Artificial Intelligence*, 95(1):67–113, 1997.

[294] L. P. Kaelbling, M. L. Littman, and A. R. Cassandra. Partially observable Markov decision processes for artificial intelligence. In *Proceedings of Reasoning with Uncertainty in Robotics*, 1995.

[295] S. Kambhampati. On the utility of systematicity: Understanding the trade-offs between redundancy and commitment in partial-order planning. In *Proceedings of the International Joint Conference on Artificial Intelligence (IJCAI)*, pp. 1380–1385, 1993.

[296] S. Kambhampati. Multi-contributor causal structures for planning: A formalization and evaluation. *Artificial Intelligence*, 69(1–2):235–278, 1994.

[297] S. Kambhampati. A comparative analysis of partial order planning and task reduction planning. *SIGART Bulletin*, 6(1), 1995.

[298] S. Kambhampati. On the relations between intelligent backtracking and failure-driven explanation-based learning in constraint satisfaction and planning. *Artificial Intelligence*, 105(1–2):161–208, 1998.

[299] S. Kambhampati. Improving Graphplan search with EBL and DDB techniques. In *Proceedings of the International Joint Conference on Artificial Intelligence (IJCAI)*, pp. 982–987, 1999.

[300] S. Kambhampati. Planning graph as (dynamic) CSP: Exploiting EBL, DDB and other CSP techniques in Graphplan. *Journal of Artificial Intelligence Research*, 12:1–34, 2000.

[301] S. Kambhampati and J. A. Hendler. A validation structure based theory of plan modification and reuse. *Artificial Intelligence*, 55:193–258, 1992.

[302] S. Kambhampati, C. Knoblock, and Q. Yang. Planning as refinement search: A unified framework for evaluating design tradeoffs in partial-order planning. *Artificial Intelligence*, 76(1–2):167–238, 1995.

[303] S. Kambhampati and D. S. Nau. On the nature and role of modal truth criteria in planning. *Artificial Intelligence*, 82(2), 1996.

[304] S. Kambhampati and R. S. Nigenda. Distance based goal ordering heuristics for Graphplan. In *Proceedings of the International Joint Conference on Artificial Intelligence (IJCAI)*, pp. 315–322, 2000.

[305] S. Kambhampati, E. Parker, and E. Lambrecht. Understanding and extending Graphplan. In *Proceedings of the European Conference on Planning (ECP)*, pp. 260–272, 1997.

[306] S. Kambhampati and X. Yang. On the role of disjunctive representations and constraint propagation in refinement planning. In *Proceedings of the International Conference on Knowledge Representation and Reasoning (KR)*, 1996.

[307] L. N. Kanal and V. Kumar, eds. *Search in Artificial Intelligence.* New York: Springer-Verlag, 1988.

[308] F. Kanehiro, M. Inaba, H. Inoue, H. Hirukawa, and S. Hirai. Developmental software environment that is applicable to small-size humanoids and life-size humanoids. In *IEEE International Conference on Robotics and Automation (ICRA)*, 2001.

[309] S. Katukam and S. Kambhampati. Learning explanation-based search control rules for partial-order planning. In *Proceedings of the National Conference on Artificial Intelligence (AAAI)*, pp. 582–587, 1994.

[310] H. Kautz. A formal theory of plan recognition and its implementation. In Allen *et al.* [15], pp. 69–125, 1991.

[311] H. Kautz and J. Allen. Generalized plan recognition. In *Proceedings of the National Conference on Artificial Intelligence (AAAI)*, pp. 32–37, 1986.

[312] H. Kautz, D. McAllester, and B. Selman. Encoding plans in propositional logic. In *Proceedings of the International Conference on Knowledge Representation and Reasoning (KR)*, 1996.

[313] H. Kautz and B. Selman. Planning as satisfiability. In *Proceedings of the European Conference on Artificial Intelligence (ECAI)*, 1992.

[314] H. Kautz and B. Selman. Pushing the envelope: Planning, propositional logic and stochastic search. In *AAAI/IAAI Proceedings*, 1996.

[315] H. Kautz and B. Selman. The role of domain-specific knowledge in the planning as satisfiability framework. In *Proceedings of the International Conference on AI Planning Systems (AIPS)*, 1998.

[316] H. Kautz and B. Selman. Unifying SAT-based and graph-based planning. In *Proceedings of the International Joint Conference on Artificial Intelligence (IJCAI)*, pp. 318–325, 1999.

[317] H. Kautz and J. P. Walser. State-space planning by integer optimization. In *AAAI/IAAI Proceedings*, pp. 526–533, 1999.

[318] H. Kautz. Planning with first order dynamic logic. In *Proceedings of the CSCSI/SCEIO*, pp. 19–26, 1982.

[319] L. Kavraki. Algorithms in robotics: The motion planning perspective. In *Frontiers of Engineering Publication*, pp. 90–93. *National Academy of Engineering*, 1999.

[320] L. Kavraki, M. Kolountzakis, and J. Latombe. Analysis of probabilistic roadmaps for path planning. *IEEE Transactions on Robotics and Automation*, 14(1):166–171, 1998.

[321] L. Kavraki, P. Svestka, J. Latombe, and M. Overmars. Probabilistic roadmaps for path planning in high-dimensional configuration spaces. *IEEE Transactions on Robotics and Automation*, 12(4):566–580, 1996.

[322] B. P. Kettler, J. A. Hendler, W. A. Andersen, and M. P. Evett. Massively parallel support for case-based planning. *IEEE Expert*, 2:8–14, 1994.

[323] L. Khatib, P. Morris, R. Morris, and F. Rossi. Temporal constraint reasoning with preferences. In *Proceedings of the International Joint Conference on Artificial Intelligence (IJCAI)*, Morgan Kaufmann, 2001.

[324] S. Kirkpatrick, C. D. Gelatt, and M. P. Vecchi. Optimization by simulated annealing. *Science*, 220:671–681, 1983.

[325] C. A. Knoblock. Automatically generating abstractions for planning. *Artificial Intelligence*, 68(2):243–302, 1994.

[326] C. A. Knoblock, J. D. Tenenberg, and Q. Yang. Characterizing abstraction hierarchies for planning. In *Proceedings of the National Conference on Artificial Intelligence (AAAI)*, pp. 692–698, 1991.

[327] C. A. Knoblock and Q. Yang. Relating the performance of partial-order planning algorithms to domain features. *SIGART Bulletin*, 6(1), 1995.

[328] D. E. Knuth and R. W. Moore. An analysis of alpha-beta pruning. *Artificial Intelligence*, 6:293–326, 1975.

[329] J. Koehler. Flexible plan reuse in a formal framework. In *Proceedings of the European Conference on Planning (ECP)*, IOS Press, 1993.

[330] J. Koehler. Planning under resource constraints. In *Proceedings of the European Conference on Artificial Intelligence (ECAI)*, pp. 489–493, 1998.

[331] J. Koehler. Handling of conditional effects and negative goals in IPP. Technical note 128. Freiburg University, 1999.

[332] J. Koehler, B. Nebel, J. Hoffmann, and Y. Dimopoulos. Extending planning graphs to an ADL subset. In *Proceedings of the European Conference on Planning (ECP)*, pp. 275–287, 1997.

[333] S. Koenig and R. Simmons. Solving robot navigation problems with initial pose uncertainty using real-time heuristic search. In *Proceedings of the International Conference on AI Planning Systems (AIPS)*, 1998.

[334] G. Kondrack and P. van Beek. A theoretical evaluation of selected backtracking algorithms. *Artificial Intelligence*, 98:365–387, 1997.

[335] R. Korf. Depth-first iterative-deepening: An optimal admissible tree search. *Artificial Intelligence*, 27:97–109, 1985.

[336] R. Korf. Planning as search: A quantitative approach. *Artificial Intelligence*, 33:65–88, 1987.

[337] D. Kortenkamp, R. Bonasso, and R. Murphy, eds. *AI-Based Mobile Robots: Case Studies of Successful Robot Systems.* MIT Press, 1997.

[338] J. Kuffner and S. Lavalle. RRT-connect: An efficient approach to single-query path planning. In *IEEE International Conference on Robotics and Automation (ICRA)*, 2000.

[339] V. Kumar. Algorithms for constraint satisfaction problems: A survey. *AI Magazine*, 13(1):32–44, 1992.

[340] N. Kushmerick, S. Hanks, and D. S. Weld. An algorithm for probabilistic planning. *Artificial Intelligence*, 76(1–2):239–286, 1994.

[341] J. Kvarnström. Applying domain analysis techniques for domain-dependent control in TALplanner. In *Proceedings of the International Conference on AI Planning Systems (AIPS)*, pp. 101–110. AAAI Press, 2002.

[342] J. Kvarnström and P. Doherty. TALplanner: A temporal logic based forward chaining planner. *Annals of Mathematics and Artificial Intelligence*, 30:119–169, 2001.

[343] J. Kvarnström, P. Doherty, and P. Haslum. Extending TALplanner with concurrency and resources. In *Proceedings of the European Conference on Planning (ECP)*, 2000.

[344] P. Laborie. Algorithm for propagating resource constraints in AI planning and scheduling existing approaches and new results. In A. Cesta and D. Borrajo, eds., *Proceedings of the European Conference on Planning (ECP)*, pp. 205–216, 2001.

[345] P. Laborie. Algorithms for propagating resource constraints in AI planning and scheduling: Existing approaches and new results. *Artificial Intelligence*, 143(2):151–188, 2003.

[346] P. Laborie and M. Ghallab. Planning with sharable resource constraints. In *Proceedings of the International Joint Conference on Artificial Intelligence (IJCAI)*, pp. 1643–1649, 1995.

[347] S. Lacroix and R. Chatila. Motion and perception strategies for outdoor mobile robot navigation in unknown environments. In O. Khatib and J. K. Salisbury, eds., *International Symposium on Experimental Robotics*, pp. 538–547. LNCIS 223. Springer-Verlag, 1997.

[348] J. E. Laird, P. S. Rosenbloom, and A. Newell. Chunking in SOAR: The anatomy of a general learning mechanism. *Machine Learning*, 1:11–46, 1986.

[349] F. Lamiraux, S. Sekhavat, and J. Laumond. Motion planning and control for Hilare pulling a trailer. *IEEE Transactions on Robotics and Automation*, 15(4), 1999.

[350] T. Lane and L. Kaelbling. Nearly deterministic abstractions of Markov decision processes. In *AAAI/IAAI Proceedings*, 2002.

[351] P. Langley. *Elements of Machine Learning*. San Francisco, CA: Morgan Kaufmann, 1996.

[352] A. L. Lansky and L. C. Getoor. Scope and abstraction: Two criteria for localized planning. In *Proceedings of the International Joint Conference on Artificial Intelligence (IJCAI)*, pp. 1612–1618. 1995.

[353] J. C. Latombe. *Robot Motion Planning*. Kluwer Academic Publishers, 1991.

[354] J. C. Latombe. Motion planning: A journey of robots, molecules, digital actors, and other artifacts. *International Journal of Robotics Research*, 18(11):1119–1128, 1999.

[355] E. Lawler, J. Lenstra, A. R. Kan, and D. Shmoys. Sequencing and scheduling: Algorithms and complexity. In S. Graves, A. R. Kan, and P. Zipkin, eds., Logistics of Production and Inventory, Handbooks in Operations Research and Management Science, Volume 4, pp. 445–552, 1993.

[356] D. Leake, A. Kinley, and D. Wilson. A case study of case-based CBR. In *Proceedings of the International Conference on Case-Based Reasoning (ICCBR)*, pp. 371–382. Springer-Verlag, 1997.

[357] D. Leake, A. Kinley, and D. Wilson. Acquiring case adaptation knowledge: A hybrid approach. In *AAAI/IAAI Proceedings*, pp. 684–689. AAAI Press, 1996.

[358] C. Leckie and I. Zukerman. Inductive learning of search control rules for planning. *Artificial Intelligence*, 101:63–98, 1998.

[359] Y. Lesperance, H. Levesque, L. F. Lin, D. Marcus, R. Reiter, and R. Scherl. A logical approach to high-level robot programming—a progress report. In *Control of the Physical World by Intelligent Systems: AAAI Fall Symposium*, 1994.

[360] H. Levesque, R. Reiter, Y. Lesperance, F. Lin, and R. Scherl. GOLOG: A logic programming language for dynamic domains. *Journal of Logic Programming*, 31:59–83, 1997.

[361] V. Liatsos and B. Richard. Scalability in planning. In S. Biundo and M. Fox, eds., *Proceedings of the European Conference on Planning (ECP)*, volume 1809 of *Lecture Notes in Artificial Intelligence (LNAI)*, pp. 49–61. Springer-Verlag, 1999.

[362] V. Lifschitz. On the semantics of STRIPS. In M. P. Georgeff and A. L. Lansky, eds., *Reasoning about Actions and Plans*, pp. 1–9. Los Altos, CA: Morgan Kaufmann, 1987. Reprinted in Allen *et al.* [14], pp. 523–530, 1990.

[363] G. Ligozat. On generalized interval calculi. In *Proceedings of the National Conference on Artificial Intelligence (AAAI)*, pp. 234–240, 1991.

[364] M. L. Littman. Markov games as a framework for multi-agent reinforcement learning. In *Proceedings of ICML 94*, pp. 157–163, 1994.

[365] M. L. Littman. Probabilistic propositional planning: Representations and complexity. In *AAAI/IAAI Proceedings*, pp. 748–761. Providence, RI, AAAI Press/MIT Press, 1997.

[366] M. L. Littman, J. Goldsmith, and M. Mundhenk. The computational complexity of probabilistic planning. *Journal of Artificial Intelligence Research*, 9:1–36, 1998.

[367] D. Long and M. Fox. Efficient implementation of the plan graph in STAN. *Journal of Artificial Intelligence Research*, 10(1–2):87–115, 1999.

[368] D. Long and M. Fox. Encoding temporal planning domains and validating temporal plans. In *UK Planning and Scheduling SIG*, 2001.

[369] A. Lopatin. Two combinatorial problems in programming bridge game. Computer Olympiad, 1992.

[370] A. Lotem and D. S. Nau. New advances in GraphHTN: Identifying independent subproblems in large HTN domains. In *Proceedings of the International Conference on AI Planning Systems (AIPS)* (Breckenridge, CO, April 14–17, 2000), pp. 206–215.

[371] D. M. Lyons. Representing and analysing action plans as networks of concurrent processes. *IEEE Transactions on Robotics and Automation*, 9(3):241–256, 1993.

[372] D. M. Lyons and A. J. Hendriks. Testing incremental adaptation. In *Proceedings of the International Conference on AI Planning Systems (AIPS)*, pp. 116–121, 1994.

[373] A. Mackworth. Consistency in networks of relations. *Artificial Intelligence*, 8(1):99–118, 1977.

[374] O. Maler, A. Pnueli, and J. Sifakis. On the synthesis of discrete controllers for timed systems. In *STACS, LNCS 900*, pp. 229–242. Springer-Verlag, 1995.

[375] J. Malik and T. Binford. Reasoning in time and space. In *Proceedings of the International Joint Conference on Artificial Intelligence (IJCAI)*, pp. 343–345, 1983.

[376] O. Maller. Timed automata as an underlying model for planning and scheduling. In *AIPS Workshop on Planning in Temporal Domains*, pp. 67–70, 2002.

[377] Z. Manna and R. Waldinger. How to clear a block: Plan formation in situation logic. *Journal of Automated Reasoning*, 3:343–377, 1997.

[378] Z. Manna, R. Waldinger, A. Apostolico, and Z. Galil. Fundamentals of deductive program synthesis. In *Combinatorial Algorithms on Words, NATO ISI Series*. Springer-Verlag, 1992.

[379] K. Mariott and P. Stuckey. *Programming with Constraints: An Introduction*. MIT Press, 1998.

[380] A. Martelli and U. Montanari. Additive AND/OR graphs. In *Proceedings of the International Joint Conference on Artificial Intelligence (IJCAI)*, pp. 1–11, 1973.

[381] D. McAllester and D. Rosenblitt. Systematic nonlinear planning. In *Proceedings of the National Conference on Artificial Intelligence (AAAI)*, pp. 634–639, 1991.

[382] J. McCarthy. *Formalizing Common Sense: Papers by John McCarthy*. Ablex Publishing, 1990.

[383] J. McCarthy and P. J. Hayes. Some philosophical problems from the standpoint of artificial intelligence. In B. Meltzer and D. Michie, eds., *Machine Intelligence 4*, pp. 463–502. Edinburgh University Press, 1969. Reprinted in McCarthy [382], 1990.

[384] T. McCluskey, M. Fox, and R. Aylett. Planform: An open environment for building planners. *PLANET Newsletter*, 5:38–45, 2002.

[385] T. McCluskey, D. Liu, and R. Simpson. Gipo ii: HTN planning in a tool-supported knowledge engineering environment. In E. Guinchiglia, N. Muscettola, and D. Nau, eds., *International Conference on Automated Planning and Scheduling (ICAPS)*, pp. 92–101, 2003.

[386] D. McDermott. A temporal logic for reasoning about processes and plans. *Cognitive Science*, 6:101–155, 1982.

[387] D. McDermott. PDDL, the Planning Domain Definition Language. Technical report. Yale Center for Computational Vision and Control, 1998. ftp://ftp.cs.yale.edu/pub/mcdermott/software/pddl.tar.gz.

[388] I. Meiri. Faster Constraint Satisfaction Algorithms for Temporal Reasoning. R-151, Los Angeles: UCLA, 1990.

[389] I. Meiri. Combining qualitative and quantitative constraints in temporal reasoning. *Artificial Intelligence*, 87:343–385, 1996.

[390] S. Minton. Learning Effective Search Control Knowledge: An Explanation-Based Approach. Technical Report TR CMU-CS-88-133. School of Computer Science, Carnegie Mellon University, 1988.

[391] S. Minton. Quantitative results concerning the utility of explanation-based learning. *Artificial Intelligence*, 42:363–391, 1990.

[392] S. Minton, J. Bresina, and M. Drummond. Commitment strategies in planning: A comparative analysis. In *Proceedings of the International Joint Conference on Artificial Intelligence (IJCAI)*, pp. 259–265, 1991.

[393] S. Minton, J. Carbonell, C. Knoblock, C. Kuokka, O. Etioni, and Y. Gil. Explanation-based learning: A problem solving perspective. *Artificial Intelligence*, 40:63–118, 1989.

[394] S. Minton, M. Drummond, J. Bresina, and A. Philips. Total order vs. partial order planning: Factors influencing Performance. In *Proceedings of the International Conference on Knowledge Representation and Reasoning (KR)*, pp. 83–92, 1992.

[395] S. Minton, M. Johnson, and P. Laird. Minimizing conflicts: A heuristic repair method for constraint satisfaction and scheduling algorithms. *Artificial Intelligence*, 58(1):161–206, 1992.

[396] S. Minton, C. Knoblock, D. R. Kuokka, Y. Gil, R. L. Joseph, and J. G. Carbonell. *PRODIGY 2.0: The Manual and Tutorial.* Technical Report CMU-CS-89-146. Carnegie Mellon University, 1989.

[397] S. Mitchell. A hybrid architecture for real-time mixed-initiative planning and control. In *Proceedings of the Innovative Applications of Artificial Intelligence Conference (IAAI)*, pp. 1032–1037, 1997.

[398] T. M. Mitchell, S. Mahadevan, and L. Steinberg. LEAP: A learning apprentice for VLSI design. In *Proceedings of the International Joint Conference on Artificial Intelligence (IJCAI)*, (Los Angeles, CA) pp. 573–580, Morgan Kaufmann, 1985.

[399] R. Mohr and T. Henderson. Arc and path consistency revisited. *Artificial Intelligence*, 28(2):225–233, 1986.

[400] U. Montanari. Network of constraints: Fundamental properties and applications to picture processing. *Information Science*, 7:97–132, 1974.

[401] B. Morisset and M. Ghallab. Learning how to combine sensory-motor modalities for a robust behavior. In Beetz *et al.* [58], pp. 157–178, 2002.

[402] B. Morisset and M. Ghallab. Synthesis of supervision policies for robust sensory-motor behaviors. In *7th International Conference on Intelligent Autonomous Systems*, pp. 236–243, 2002.

[403] P. Morris, N. Muscettola, and T. Vidal. Dynamic control of plans with temporal uncertainty. In *Proceedings of the International Joint Conference on Artificial Intelligence (IJCAI)*, pp. 494–502, 2001.

[404] P. Moutarlier and R. G. Chatila. Stochastic multisensory data fusion for mobile robot location and environment modelling. In *Proceedings of the International Symposium on Robotics Research*, 1989.

[405] H. Muñoz-Avila. Case-base maintenance by integrating case index revision and case retention policies in a derivational replay framework. *Computational Intelligence*, 17(2):280–294, 2001.

[406] H. Muñoz-Avila, D. W. Aha, D. S. Nau, R. Weber, L. Breslow, and F. Yaman. SiN: Integrating case-based reasoning with task decomposition. In *Proceedings of the International Joint Conference on Artificial Intelligence (IJCAI)*, 2001.

[407] H. Muñoz-Avila and F. Weberskirch. Planning for manufacturing workpieces by storing, indexing and replaying planning decisions. In *Proceedings of the International Conference on AI Planning Systems (AIPS)*, 1996.

[408] N. Muscettola. HSTS: Integrating planning and scheduling. In M. Zweben and M. Fox, eds., *Intelligent Scheduling*, pp. 169–212. Morgan Kaufmann, 1994.

[409] N. Muscettola, G. Dorais, C. Fry, R. Levinson, and C. Plaunt. IDEA: Planning at the core of autonomous reactive agents. In *International NASA Workshop on Planning and Scheduling for Space*, 2002.

[410] N. Muscettola, P. Nayak, B. Pell, and B. Williams. Remote Agent: To boldly go where no AI system has gone before. *Artificial Intelligence*, 103(1–2):5–47, 1998.

[411] K. L. Myers. A continuous planning and execution framework. *AI Magazine*, 20(4): 63–69, 1999.

[412] K. L. Myers, P. A. Jarvis, W. M. Tyson, and M. J. Wolverton. A mixed-initiative framework for robust plan sketching. In *Thirteenth International Conference on Automated Planning and Scheduling (ICAPS-03)*, 2003.

[413] D. S. Nau, T.-C. Au, O. Ilghami, U. Kuter, W. Murdock, D. Wu, and F. Yaman. SHOP2: An HTN planning system. *Journal of Artificial Intelligence Research*, 20:379–404, 2003.

[414] D. S. Nau, Y. Cao, A. Lotem, and H. Muñoz-Avila. SHOP: Simple Hierarchical Ordered Planner. In *Proceedings of the International Joint Conference on Artificial Intelligence (IJCAI)*, pp. 968–973, 1999.

[415] D. S. Nau, V. Kumar, and L. N. Kanal. General branch and bound, and its relation to A* and AO*. *Artificial Intelligence*, 23(1):29–58, 1984.

[416] D. S. Nau, H. Muñoz-Avila, Y. Cao, A. Lotem, and S. Mitchell. Total-order planning with partially ordered subtasks. In *Proceedings of the International Joint Conference on Artificial Intelligence (IJCAI)* (Seattle, WA, August 2001).

[417] D. S. Nau, W. C. Regli, and S. K. Gupta. AI planning versus manufacturing-operation planning: A case study. In *Proceedings of the International Joint Conference on Artificial Intelligence (IJCAI)*, 1995.

[418] B. Nebel. On the compilability and expressive power of propositional planning formalisms. *Journal of Artificial Intelligence Research*, 12:271–315, 2000.

[419] B. Nebel and H. Burckert. Reasoning about temporal relations: A maximal tractable subclass of Allen's interval algebra. *Journal of the ACM*, 42(1):43–66, 1995.

[420] B. Nebel, Y. Dimopoulos, and J. Koehler. Ignoring irrelevant facts and operators in plan generation. In *Proceedings of the European Conference on Planning (ECP)*, pp. 340–352, 1997.

[421] B. Nebel and J. Koehler. Plan reuse versus plan generation: A theoretical and empirical analysis. *Artificial Intelligence*, 76:427–454, 1995.

[422] G. Nemhauser and L. Wolsey. *Integer and Combinatorial Optimization.* Wiley, 1988.

[423] N. Nguyen and S. Kambhampati. Extracting effective and admissible state space heuristics from the planning graph. In *AAAI/IAAI Proceedings*, 2000.

[424] N. Nguyen and S. Kambhampati. Reviving partial order planning. *Proceedings of the International Joint Conference on Artificial Intelligence (IJCAI)*, 2001.

[425] N. Nguyen, S. Kambhampati, and R. Nigenda. Planning graph as the basis for deriving heuristics for plan synthesis by state space and CSP search. *Artificial Intelligence*, 135(1–2):73–123, 2002.

[426] N. J. Nilsson. *Principles of Artificial Intelligence.* Tioga Publishing, 1980.

[427] H. Palacios and H. Geffner. Planning as branch and bound: A constraint programming implementation. In *XVIII Latin-American Conference on Informatics (CLEI-2002)*, 2002.

[428] C. Papadimitriou. *Computational Complexity.* Addison-Wesley, 1994.

[429] R. Patrascu, P. Poupart, D. Schuurmans, C. Boutilier, and C. Guestrin. Greedy linear value-approximation for factored Markov decision processes. In *AAAI/IAAI Proceedings*, 2002.

[430] J. Pearl. *Heuristics: Intelligent Search Strategies for Computer Problem Solving.* Addison-Wesley, 1985.

[431] C. Pecheur and R. Simmons. From Livingstone to SMV. In *FAABS*, pp. 103–113, 2000.

[432] F. Pecora and A. Cesta. Planning and scheduling ingredients for a multi-agent system. In *ICMAS*, 2002.

[433] E. Pednault. Synthetizing plans that contain actions with context-dependent effects. *Computational Intelligence*, 4(4):356–372, 1988.

[434] E. P. Pednault. ADL: Exploring the middle ground between STRIPS and the situation calculus. In *Proceedings of the International Conference on Knowledge Representation and Reasoning (KR)*, pp. 324–332, 1989.

[435] E. P. Pednault. ADL and the state-transition model of action. *Journal of Logic and Computation*, 4(5):467–512, 1994.

[436] J. Penberthy and D. S. Weld. UCPOP: A sound, complete, partial order planner for ADL. In *Proceedings of the International Conference on Knowledge Representation and Reasoning (KR)*, pp. 103–114, 1992.

[437] J. Penberthy and D. S. Weld. Temporal planning with continuous change. In *Proceedings of the National Conference on Artificial Intelligence (AAAI)*, pp. 1010–1015, 1994.

[438] M. Peot and D. Smith. Conditional nonlinear planning. In *Proceedings of the International Conference on AI Planning Systems (AIPS)*, pp. 189–197, 1992.

[439] C. Pinhanez and A. Bobick. Human action detection using PNF propagation of temporal constraints. In *IEEE Conference on Computer Vision and Pattern Recognition*, 1998.

[440] M. Pistore, R. Bettin, and P. Traverso. Symbolic techniques for planning with extended goals in non-deterministic domains. In *Proceedings of the European Conference on Planning (ECP)*, Springer-Verlag, 2001.

[441] M. Pistore and P. Traverso. Planning as model checking for extended goals in non-deterministic domains. In *Proceedings of the International Joint Conference on Artificial Intelligence (IJCAI)*, pp. 479–484. Morgan Kaufmann, 2001.

[442] D. A. Plaisted. Mechanical theorem proving. In R. B. Banerji, ed., *Formal Techniques in Artificial Intelligence.* Elsevier, 1990.

[443] M. E. Pollack, L. Brown, D. Colbry, C. E. McCarthy, C. Orosz, B. Peintner, S. Ramakrishnan, and I. Tsamardinos. Autominder: An intelligent cognitive orthotic system for people with memory impairment. *Robotics and Autonomous Systems*, 44(3–4):273–282, 2003.

[444] M. E. Pollack, D. Joslin, and M. Paolucci. Flaw selection strategies for partial-order planning. *Journal of Artificial Intelligence Research*, 6:223–262, 1997.

[445] M. E. Pollack, C. E. McCarthy, S. Ramakrishnan, I. Tsamardinos, L. Brown, S. Carrion, D. Colbry, C. Orosz, and B. Peintner. Autominder: A planning, monitoring,

and reminding assistive agent. In *International Conference on Intelligent Autonomous Systems*, 2002.

[446] P. Poupart and C. Boutilier. Value-directed belief state approximation for POMDPs. In *Proceedings of the Conference on Uncertainty in Artificial Intelligence (UAI)*, 2000.

[447] P. Poupart and C. Boutilier. Vector-space analysis of belief-state approximation for POMDPs. In *Proceedings of the Conference on Uncertainty in Artificial Intelligence (UAI)*, 2001.

[448] L. Pryor and G. Collins. Planning for contingency: A decision based approach. *Journal of Artificial Intelligence Research*, 4:81–120, 1996.

[449] A. Pujari and A. Sattar. A new framework for reasoning about points, intervals and durations. In *Proceedings of the International Joint Conference on Artificial Intelligence (IJCAI)*, 1999.

[450] S. Quinlan and O. Khatib. Towards real-time execution of motion tasks. In R. G. Chatila and G. Hirzinger, eds., *Experimental Robotics 2*. Springer-Verlag, 1992.

[451] G. Rabideau, S. Chien, J. Willis, and T. Mann. Interactive, repair-based planning and scheduling for shuttle payload operations. *Artificial Intelligence*, 2004. To appear.

[452] S. Ram and A. Francis. Multi-plan retrieval and adaptation in an experience-based agent. In D. B. Leake, ed., *Case-Based Reasoning: Experiences, Lessons, and Future Directions*. AAAI Press/MIT Press, 1996.

[453] M. Redmond. Distributed cases for case-based reasoning: Facilitating use of multiple cases. In *Proceedings of the National Conference on Artificial Intelligence (AAAI)*, 1990.

[454] J. A. Reed and R. A. Shepp. Optimal paths for a car that goes both forward and backwards. *Pacific Journal of Mathematics*, 145(2):367–393, 1990.

[455] W. C. Regli, S. K. Gupta, and D. S. Nau. Extracting alternative machining features: An algorithmic approach. *Research in Engineering Design*, 7(3):173–192, 1995.

[456] J. Rintanen. Constructing conditional plans by a theorem-prover. *Journal of Artificial Intellegence Research*, 10:323–352, 1999.

[457] S. Rosenschein. Plan synthesis: A logical perspective. In *Proceedings of the International Joint Conference on Artificial Intelligence (IJCAI)*, 1981.

[458] S. Russel, and P. Norvig. *Artificial Intelligence: A Modern Approach*. Prentice Hall, 2003.

[459] E. Sacerdoti. Planning in a hierarchy of abstraction spaces. *Artificial Intelligence*, 5:115–135, 1974.

[460] E. Sacerdoti. The nonlinear nature of plans. In *Proceedings of the International Joint Conference on Artificial Intelligence (IJCAI)*, pp. 206–214, 1975. Reprinted in Allen *et al.* [14], pp. 162–170, 1990.

[461] E. Sacerdoti. *A Structure for Plans and Behavior*. Elsevier, 1977.

[462] A. Saffiotti. Handling uncertainty in control of autonomous robots. In M. J. Wooldridge and M. Veloso, eds., *Artificial Intelligence Today*, pp. 381–408. Springer-Verlag, 1999.

[463] E. Sandewall. *Features and Fluents.* Oxford University Press, 1995.

[464] E. Sandewall and R. Rönnquist. A representation of action structures. In *Proceedings of the National Conference on Artificial Intelligence (AAAI)*, pp. 89–97, 1986.

[465] J. Schaeffer. *One Jump Ahead: Challenging Human Supremacy in Checkers.* Springer-Verlag, 1997.

[466] T. Schiex and G. Verfaillie. Nogood recording for static and dynamic constraint satisfaction problems. *International Journal on Artificial Intelligence Tools*, 3(2):187–207, 1994.

[467] C. F. Schmidt, N. S. Sridharan, and J. L. Goodson. The plan recognition problem, an intersection of psychology and AI. *Artificial Intelligence*, 11(1):45–83, 1978.

[468] J. Scott. A chess-playing program. In B. Meltzer and D. Michie, eds., *Machine Intelligence*, Volume 4, pp. 255–265. Edinburgh University Press, 1969.

[469] B. Selman, H. Kautz, and B. Cohen. Noise strategies for local search. In *AAAI/IAAI Proceedings*, 1998.

[470] A. Shaerf. Combining local search and look-ahead for scheduling and constraint satisfaction problems. In *Proceedings of the International Joint Conference on Artificial Intelligence (IJCAI)*, pp. 1254–1259, 1997.

[471] J. Shah, M. Mantyla, and D. S. Nau, eds., *Advances in Feature Based Manufacturing.* Elsevier/North Holland, 1994.

[472] C. Shannon. Programming a computer for playing chess. *Philosophical Magazine (Series 7)*, 41:256–275, 1950.

[473] Y. Shoham and D. McDermott. Problems in formal temporal reasoning. *Artificial Intelligence*, 36:49–61, 1988.

[474] Y. Shoham. Temporal logic in AI: Semantical and ontological considerations. *Artificial Intelligence*, 33:89–104, 1987.

[475] Y. Shoham. *Reasoning about Change.* MIT Press, 1988.

[476] T. Siméon, J. Laumond, and F. Lamiraux. Move3d: A generic platform for path planning. In *4th International Symposium on Assembly and Task Planning*, 2001.

[477] T. Siméon, J. Laumond, and C. Nissoux. Visibility based probabilistic roadmaps for motion planning. *Advanced Robotics Journal*, 14(6):445–550, 2000.

[478] R. Simmons. An architecture for coordinating planning, sensing and action. In *Proceedings of the Workshop on Innovative Approaches to Planning, Scheduling and Control*, pp. 292–297, 1990.

[479] R. Simmons. Structured control for autonomous robots. *IEEE Transactions on Robotics and Automation*, 10(1):34–43, 1994.

[480] H. Simon. *The Sciences of the Artificial.* MIT Press, 1996.

[481] J. Slaney and S. Thiébaux. Blocks world revisited. *Artificial Intelligence*, 125(1–2): 119–153, 2001.

[482] B. D. Smith, B. E. Engelhardt, and D. H. Mutz. The RADARSAT-MAMM Automated Mission Planner. *AI Magazine*, 23(2):25–36, 2002.

[483] B. D. Smith, M. S. Feather, and N. Muscettola. Challenges and methods in testing the Remote Agent planner. In *Proceedings of AIPS00*, pp. 254–263, 2000.

[484] D. Smith, J. Frank, and A. Jonsson. Bridging the gap between planning and scheduling. *Knowledge Engineering Review*, 15(1):47–83, 2000.

[485] D. Smith and M. Peot. A critical look at Knoblock's hierarchy mechanism. In *Proceedings of the International Conference on AI Planning Systems (AIPS)*, 1992.

[486] D. Smith and M. Peot. Postponing threats in partial-order planning. In *Proceedings of the National Conference on Artificial Intelligence (AAAI)*, pp. 500–506, 1993.

[487] D. Smith and M. Peot. Suspending recursion causal-link planning. In *Proceedings of the International Conference on AI Planning Systems (AIPS)*, 1996.

[488] D. Smith and D. Weld. Conformant Graphplan. In *AAAI/IAAI Proceedings*, pp. 889–896, 1998.

[489] D. Smith and D. Weld. Temporal planning with mutual exclusion reasoning. In *Proceedings of the International Joint Conference on Artificial Intelligence (IJCAI)*, 1999.

[490] D. Smith and D. Weld. Conformant Graphplan. In *AAAI/IAAI Proceedings* (Menlo Park, July 26–30, 1998), pp. 889–896, AAAI Press, 1998.

[491] S. Smith. OPIS: A methodology and architecture for reactive scheduling. In M. Zweben and M. Fox, eds., *Intelligent Scheduling*, pp. 29–65. Morgan Kaufmann, 1994.

[492] S. Smith, M. Fox, and P. Ow. Constructing and maintaining detailed production plans: Investigations into the development of knowledge-based factory scheduling systems. *AI Magazine*, 7(4):45–61, 1986.

[493] S.J.J. Smith. *Task-Network Planning Using Total-Order Forward Search, and Applications to Bridge and to Microwave Module Manufacture*. Ph.D. thesis, University of Maryland, 1997.

[494] S.J.J. Smith, K. Hebbar, D. S. Nau, and I. Minis. Integrating electrical and mechanical design and process planning. In M. Mantyla, S. Finger, and T. Tomiyama, eds., *Knowledge Intensive CAD*, Volume 2, pp. 269–288. Chapman and Hall, 1997.

[495] S.J.J. Smith, D. S. Nau, and T. Throop. Computer bridge: A big win for AI planning. *AI Magazine*, 19(2):93–105, 1998.

[496] L. Spalazzi and P. Traverso. A dynamic logic for acting, sensing, and planning. *Journal of Logic and Computation*, 10(6):787–821, 2000.

[497] R. M. Stallman and G. J. Sussman. Forward reasoning and dependency directed backtracking in a system for computer-aided circuit analysis. *Artificial Intelligence*, 9(2):135–196, 1977.

[498] M. Stefik. Planning with constraints. *Artificial Intelligence*, 16:111–140, 1981.

[499] W. Stephan and S. Biundo. A new logical framework for deductive planning. In *Proceedings of the International Joint Conference on Artificial Intelligence (IJCAI)*, pp. 32–38. Morgan Kaufmann, 1993.

[500] V. S. Subrahmanian. Nonmonotonic logic programming. *IEEE Transactions on Knowledge and Data Engineering*, 11(1):14–152, 1999.

[501] G. Sussman. *A Computational Model of Skill Acquisition*. New York: Elsevier, 1975.

[502] A. Tate. Interacting goals and their use. In *Proceedings of the International Joint Conference on Artificial Intelligence (IJCAI)*, pp. 215–218, 1975.

[503] A. Tate. Generating project networks. In *Proceedings of the International Joint Conference on Artificial Intelligence (IJCAI)*, pp. 888–893, 1977.

[504] A. Tate, B. Drabble, and R. Kirby. *O-Plan2: An Architecture for Command, Planning and Control*. Morgan Kaufmann, 1994.

[505] A. Tate, J. Dalton, and J. Levine. O-Plan: a web-based AI planning agent. In *Proceedings of the National Conference on Artificial Intelligence (AAAI)*, pp. 1131–1132, August 2000.

[506] S. Thiebaux, F. Kabanza, and J. Slaney. Anytime state-based solution methods for decision processes with non-Markovian rewards. In *Proceedings of the Conference on Uncertainty in Artificial Intelligence (UAI)*, 2002.

[507] S. Thrun. Learning metric-topological maps for indoor mobile robot navigation. *Artificial Intelligence*, 99(1):21–71, 1998.

[508] S. Thrun, A. Bücken, W. Burgard, D. Fox, T. Frölinghaus, D. Hennig, T. Hofmann, M. Krell, and T. Schmidt. Map learning and high-speed navigation in RHINO. In Kortenkamp et al. [337], 1997.

[509] S. Thrun, W. Burgard, and D. Fox. A probabilistic approach to concurrent mapping and localization for mobile robots. *Machine Learning*, 31:29–53, 1998.

[510] P. Traverso and L. Spalazzi. A logic for acting, sensing and planning. In *Proceedings of the International Joint Conference on Artificial Intelligence (IJCAI)*, 1995.

[511] P. Traverso, M. Veloso, and F. Giunchiglia, eds. *AIPS Workshop on Model-Theoretic Approaches to Planning* (Breckeridge, CO, April 2000).

[512] R. Trinquart and M. Ghallab. An extended functional representation in temporal planning: Towards continuous change. In A. Cesta and D.Borrajo, eds., *Proceedings of the European Conference on Planning (ECP)*, pp. 217–228, 2001.

[513] A. Truscott. Bridge: Bridge software is improving and already beats humans in one respect: It never blames partner. *The New York Times*, page A19, August 16, 1997.

[514] I. Tsamardinos, M. E. Pollack, and J. F. Horty. Merging plans with quantitative temporal constraints, temporally extended actions, and conditional branches. In *Proceedings of the International Conference on AI Planning Systems (AIPS)*, pp. 264–272, 2000.

[515] E. Tsang. *Foundations of Constraint Satisfaction*. Academic Press, 1993.

[516] R. Tsuneto, J. Hendler, and D. S. Nau. Analyzing external conditions to improve the efficiency of HTN planning. In *AAAI/IAAI Proceedings*, pp. 913–920, 1998.

[517] R. Tsuneto, D. S. Nau, and J. Hendler. Plan-refinement strategies and search-space size. In *Proceedings of the European Conference on Planning (ECP)*, 1997.

[518] P. van Beek. CSPLIB: A library for CSP routines. 1994. http://ai.uwaterloo.ca/vanbeek/software/software.html.

[519] P. van Beek and X. Chen. Cplan: A constraint programming approach to planning. In *AAAI/IAAI Proceedings*, 1999.

[520] J. van Benthem. *The Logic of Time.* Dordrecht, 1983.

[521] K. van Lehn, ed. *Architectures for Intelligence.* Lawrence Erlbaum, 1990.

[522] M. van Lent and J. Laird. Learning hierarchical performance knowledge by observation. In *Proceedings of the International Conference on Machine Learning (ICML)*, pp. 229–238. San Francisco, CA: Morgan Kaufmann, 1999.

[523] M. Veloso. *Planning and Learning by Analogical Reasoning.* Springer-Verlag, 1994.

[524] M. Veloso, J. Carbonell, A. Pérez, D. Borrajo, E. Fink, and J. Blythe. Integrating planning and learning: The PRODIGY architecture. *Journal of Experimental and Theoretical Artificial Intelligence*, 7(1):81–120, 1995.

[525] M. Veloso and J. G. Carbonell. Derivational analogy in PRODIGY: Automating case acquisition, storage and utilization. *Machine Learning*, 10:249–278, 1993.

[526] M. Veloso, A. Mulvehill, and M. Cox. Rationale-supported mixed-initiative case-based planning. In *Proceedings of the Innovative Applications of Artificial Intelligence Conference (IAAI)*, pp. 1072–1077, 1997.

[527] M. Veloso and P. Stone. FLECS: Planning with a flexible commitment strategy. *Journal of Artificial Intelligence Research*, 3:25–52, 1995.

[528] S. Vere. Planning in time: Windows and duration for activities and goals. *IEEE Transaction on Pattern Analysis and Machine Intelligence*, 5(3):246–264, 1983.

[529] G. Verfaillie and T. Schiex. Solution reuse in dynamic constraint satisfaction problems. In *Proceedings of the National Conference on Artificial Intelligence (AAAI)*, pp. 307–312, 1994.

[530] T. Vidal. Controllability characterization and checking in contingent temporal constraint networks. In *Proceedings of the International Conference on Knowledge Representation and Reasoning (KR)*, pp. 559–570, 2000.

[531] T. Vidal. A unified dynamic approach for dealing with temporal uncertainty and conditional planning. In *Proceedings of the International Conference on AI Planning Systems (AIPS)*, pp. 395–402, 2000.

[532] T. Vidal and H. Fargier. Handling contingency in temporal constraint networks: From consistency to controllabilities. *Journal of Experimental and Theoretical Artificial Intelligence*, 11(1):23–45, 1999.

[533] T. Vidal and M. Ghallab. Temporal constraints in planning: Free or not free? In *CONSTRAINT*, 1995.

[534] T. Vidal and M. Ghallab. Dealing with uncertain durations in temporal constraint networks dedicated to planning. In *Proceedings of the European Conference on Artificial Intelligence (ECAI)*, 1996.

[535] T. Vidal, M. Ghallab, and R. Alami. Incremental mission allocation to a large team of robots. In *Proceedings of the IEEE International Conference on Robotics and Automation (IEEE-ICRA)*, 1996.

[536] L. Vila. A survey on temporal reasoning in artificial intelligence. *AI Communications*, 7(1):4–28, 1994.

[537] M. Vilain and H. Kautz. Constraint propagation algorithms for temporal reasoning. In *Proceedings of the National Conference on Artificial Intelligence (AAAI)*, pp. 377–382, 1986.

[538] M. Vilain, H. Kautz, and P. van Beek. Constraint propagation algorithms for temporal reasoning: A revised report. In J. de Kleer and D. S. Weld, eds., *Reading in Qualitative Reasoning about Physical Systems*. Morgan Kaufmann, 1989.

[539] T. Vossen, M. Ball, A. Lotem, and D. S. Nau. On the use of integer programming models in AI planning. In *Proceedings of the International Joint Conference on Artificial Intelligence (IJCAI)*, pp. 304–309, 1999.

[540] R. Waldinger. Achieving several goals simultaneously. In *Machine Intelligence 8*, pp. 94–138. Halstead and Wiley, 1977. Reprinted in Allen *et al.* [14], 1990.

[541] T. Walsh. Stochastic constraint programming. In *Proceedings of the European Conference on Artificial Intelligence (ECAI)*, 2002.

[542] D. Waltz. Understanding line drawings of scenes with shadows. In Winston, ed., *The Psychology of Computer Vision*. McGraw-Hill, 1975.

[543] D.H.D. Warren. Generating conditional plans and programs. In *Proceedings of the Summer Conference on Artificial Intelligence and Simulation of Behaviour (AISB-76)*, 1976.

[544] D. S. Weld. An introduction to least commitment planning. *AI Magazine*, 15(4):27–61, 1994.

[545] D. S. Weld, C. R. Anderson, and D. E. Smith. Extending Graphplan to handle uncertainty and sensing actions. In *AAAI/IAAI Proceedings*, pp. 897–904. AAAI Press, 1998.

[546] D. S. Weld and O. Etzioni. The first law of robotics (a call to arms). In *Proceedings of the National Conference on Artificial Intelligence (AAAI)*, pp. 1042–1047, 1994.

[547] D. S. Weld and J. D. Kleer, eds., *Readings in Qualitative Reasoning about Physical Systems*. Morgan Kaufmann, 1990.

[548] R. Wilensky. *Planning and Understanding*. Addison-Wesley, 1983.

[549] D. Wilkins. *Practical Planning: Extending the Classical AI Planning Paradigm*. San Mateo, CA: Morgan Kaufmann, 1988.

[550] D. Wilkins. Can AI planners solve practical problems? *Computational Intelligence*, 6(4):232–246, 1990.

[551] D. Wilkins and M. desJardins. A call for knowledge-based planning. *AI Magazine*, 22(1):99–115, 2001.

[552] D. Wilkins, K. L. Myers, J. D. Lowrance, and L. P. Wesley. Planning and Reacting in Uncertain and Dynamic Environments. *Journal of Experimental and Theoretical AI*, 7(1):197–227, 1995.

[553] B. Williams and P. P. Nayak. A model based approach to reactive self-reconfiguring systems. In *AAAI/IAAI Proceedings*, pp. 971–978, 1996.

[554] W. Winchell. *Realistic Cost Estimating for Manufacturing.* Society of Manufacturing Engineers, 1989.

[555] T. Winograd. *Understanding Natural Language.* Academic Press, 1972.

[556] S. A. Wolfman and D. S. Weld. The LPSAT engine and its application to resource planning. In *Proceedings of the International Joint Conference on Artificial Intelligence (IJCAI)*, pp. 310–317, 1999.

[557] M. Wolverton and M. desJardins. Controlling communication in distributed planning using irrelevance reasoning. In *AAAI/IAAI Proceedings*, pp. 868–874, 1998.

[558] Q. Yang. Formalizing planning knowledge for hierarchical planning. *Computational Intelligence*, 6(1):12–24, 1990.

[559] Q. Yang. A theory of conflict resolution in planning. *Artificial Intelligence*, 58:361–392, 1992.

[560] Q. Yang. *Intelligent Planning: A Decomposition and Abstraction Based Approach.* Springer-Verlag, 1997.

[561] Q. Yang, J. Tenenberg, and S. Woods. On the implementation and evaluation of ABTWEAK. *Computational Intelligence*, 12(2):295–318, 1996.

[562] J. Yolkowski. Large numbers in the universe, January 26, 2002. http://www.stormloader.com/ajy/reallife.html.

[563] H. Younes and R. Simmons. *On the role of ground actions in refinement planning*, In *proceedings of the International Conference on AI Planning Systems (AIPS)*. pp. 54–61. AAAI Press, 2002.

[564] R. M. Young, M. E. Pollack, and J. D. Moore. Decomposition and causality in partial-order planning. In *Proceedings of the International Conference on AI Planning Systems (AIPS)*, 1994.

[565] T. Zimmerman and S. Kambhampati. Exploiting symmetry in the planning graph via explanation guided search. In *AAAI/IAAI Proceedings*, pp. 605–611, 1999.

Index

Printed and bound by CPI Group (UK) Ltd, Croydon, CR0 4YY

03/10/2024

01040344-0004